P9-CJH-885

Some Instructor comments about Lancom Technologies courses . . .

"I have been teaching technology courses for seven years and this is the best lab manual that I have encountered to teach an operating system course. The exercises all work extremely well and are practical to what is seen in business and industry."

Joe McLaughlin, Instructor, Computer Technology
Northern Maine Technical College, Presque Isle, Maine

"The Lancom Technologies course has been added to two of our curriculums. It is a valuable reference for students to take on the job and use after the class has finished."

Nicole Hanaburgh, Associate Professor
Rockland Community College, Suffern, New York

"This course material details the technical information that our students need! The Instructor support materials provide everything required to deliver the course and evaluate our students."

Alex Kuskis, Chair, Continuing Education
DeVry College of Technology, Toronto, Ontario

"The Lancom Technologies course is of excellent quality. It presents concepts gradually and has practical hands-on exercises that are easy for students to follow."

Nathan McMinn, Assistant Professor
University of Montevallo, Montevallo, Alabama

"This course material provides thorough tutorials, hands-on exercises and reference in a single manual. It gives real-world examples and our students are able to successfully complete the course and obtain employment in their field of study."

Rick Burgess, Coordinator, Computer Hardware/Software Technology
Lewis & Clark Community College, Godfrey, Illinois

"This course is excellent! It can be used for both instructor-led and self-paced learning. It has very clear descriptions of concepts and exercises. I found this course not only a great tool for students, but also a very useful reference for myself."

Chris McBride, Coordinator for Communications and Computer Services
Mid Michigan Community College, Harrison, Michigan

Hello Linux! A Comprehensive Hands-On Course

Copyright © 2003 Lancom Technologies
ISBN: 1-896814-22-0

Lancom Technologies

150 South Eighth Street
P.O. Box 1438
Lewiston, NY
14092-8438

Phone: (800) 718-7318
Fax: (716) 754-4714

Outside of North America, phone: +1-416-410-7816.
Our email address is: info@lancom-tech.com.

September 2003. Developed by Lancom Technologies.

Author: Clyde Boom
Desktop Publisher: Shirley Kryklywy
Technical Consultants:
        Ronald Douglas - rond@ronald-douglas.com
                http://www.ronald-douglas.com
        Harold Tomlinson - Crea.Com Inc. - haroldt.craecom@rogers.com
                http://members.rogers.com/haroldt.creacom
Technical Editor and Indexer: Lee Romberg
Book Design: Connor Boegel
Additional Book Design: Cindy Massoiin

TRADEMARK ACKNOWLEDGEMENTS

Linux is a registered trademark of Linus Torvalds. Red Hat and RPM are registered trademarks of Red Hat, Inc. XFree86 is a trademark of The XFree86 Project, Inc, and is pending registration. The X logo, X11, and The X Window System are Registered Trademarks of The Open Group. KDE and K Desktop Environment are trademarks of KDE e.V. CUPS, the Common UNIX Printing System and the CUPS logo are registered trademarks of Easy Software Products. Apache is a trademark of The Apache Software Foundation. UNIX is a registered trademark in the United States and other countries, licensed exclusively through X/Open Company, Ltd. IBM is a registered trademarks of International Business Machines Corporation. Intel, 486 and Pentium are trademarks of Intel Corp. EtherNet is a trademark of 3Com Corporation. Microsoft and Windows are registered trademarks of Microsoft Corporation. Sun Microsystems and NFS are registered trademarks of Sun Microsystems, Inc. PostScript is a registered trademark of Adobe Systems. Macintosh and FireWire are registered trademarks of Apple Computer, Inc. All other trademarks are the property of their respective owners.

SPECIAL ACKNOWLEDGEMENTS

Thanks to Ronald Douglas and Harold Tomlinson for their technical support and assistance throughout the creation of this book.

Many thanks to all those who have contributed to the Linux kernel, GNU software components and Open Source Software components. Thanks as well to Andrew Clausen and other members of the GNU Parted project at www.gnu.org for technical assistance regarding the usage of the GNU Parted disk patitioning utility.

Table of Contents

Chapter 1: The Linux Operating System

This chapter of the course includes three sections. During this chapter you will learn about the following:

Hello Linux! Course Overview

This section provides you with an overview of each chapter in the course. You will also learn about the Course Objectives, Hands-On Exercises, Section Review Questions and the icons that are used at the side of the text to highlight important points.

UNIX, Linus and Linux

In this section, we will discuss the similarities between the Unix and Linux operating systems and describe the process used by Linus Torvalds for the development of Linux.

This section also describes the GNU Project, the GNU General Public License (GPL) and the benefits of GPL software. We will also discuss why people develop software for free and the reasons for the popularity of Linux.

You will get an overview of the market demand for Linux professionals and an understanding of the expected future of Linux. This section also details the main Linux operating system components.

Understanding the Linux Distributions

This section explains the concept of a Linux distribution and describes the key components of a distribution. These components are required in addition to the Linux kernel and the GPL software that has been created for it.

This section also introduces several of the popular Linux distributions and provides an overview of the similarities and differences between them.

Hello Linux! Course Overview

Topics Covered in this Section

Provide an overview of each chapter in the course
Describe the format of the section review questions
Discuss the hands-on exercises used throughout the course
Show the icons that are used to highlight important points

An overview of the topics covered in each chapter are presented below.

Chapter 1: The Linux Operating System

The first section of this chapter is an overview of the entire course.

The second section discusses the similarities between the Unix and Linux operating systems and describes the development of Linux. It describes the GNU Project, the GNU General Public License (GPL) and the benefits of GPL software. You will get an overview of the market demand for Linux professionals and an understanding of the expected future of Linux.

The last section in this chapter is used to explain the concept of a Linux distribution and describe the key components of a distribution. These components are required in addition to the Linux kernel and the GPL software that has been created for it.

Chapter 2: Understanding x86 Hardware Components, Partitions, Filesystems and Device Names

The first section of this chapter provides you with a description of Linux hardware requirements and general information regarding the installation of Linux. You will do the steps to locate the specifications for your hardware and document the settings of the hardware components that need to be specified during the Linux installation.

In the second section, you will learn about different interface card types, how they communicate with a system and the settings that they require. Some hardware devices attach to a system via interface cards and some can be attached via other methods. You will also learn about these other methods.

The last section of this chapter is used to explain partitions, filesystems, device names and the naming convention that is used to refer to partitions on storage devices.

Chapter 3: Installing Linux On An x86 System

In the first section, you will learn about the different methods that can be used to install Linux and the boot disks that are created for these different methods.

In the second section, you will learn about boot loaders, the Master Boot Record (MBR), and how to boot a system into Rescue Mode to repair a damaged or overwritten MBR.

The third section describes the Linux OS software components and installation routines. During the Hands-On Exercises of this section you will run the Anaconda installation routine and do all of the steps to install Linux!

In the last section, you will learn about the various text-based and GUI utilities that are used to configure a system after the installation of Linux.

Chapter 4: Working with Desktops and Terminals

In this chapter, you will learn about the components of the GNOME and KDE desktops. You will also learn how to create a terminal emulation window icon that provides access to the shell prompt so that you can run commands and programs.

During this chapter, you will also learn about terminal emulation windows and how to: log in and work in these terminals, move from one terminal to another, and to move from a virtual terminal to a desktop.

You will also learn the various methods of mounting a CD or floppy disk to make the filesystem of it accessible, and all of the methods of logging out, shutting down and rebooting a Linux system. This chapter also covers the differences between logging in as the root user and using the su command to log in as the root user.

During the Hands-On Exercises of this section you will log in to each of the two desktops and use the icons and menus on them, access virtual terminals from a desktop, and use different methods of accessing the filesystem of a CD.

Chapter 5: The Linux Filesystem and the Shell Environment

During this chapter you will learn about the specifications provided in the Filesystem Hierarchy Standard (FHS), including the default Linux directories that are located off of the root directory. You will also find out about file names, file suffixes, hidden directories and files, and the difference between the full path to a directory or file and the relative path.

The Linux OS relies heavily on symbolic links, which are small files that point to other directories and files. You will see why these links exist and learn about the benefits provided by these links.

The shell "environment" is accessed by opening a terminal emulation window when running in GUI desktop mode or by booting to a virtual terminal in text mode. This chapter explains how to work effectively at the shell prompt, in the shell environment. It details the key features and benefits of the shell environment and the shell environments that are available.

During the Hands-On Exercises, you will work at the shell prompt and learn how to move around the directory structure. You will view the contents of all of the main directories that are located off of the root directory to see the files that are typically located in these directories. You will also view many different types of files, including binary, script, configuration, hidden, compressed, and symbolic links.

Chapter 6: Using Linux Commands

This chapter provides an overview of using fourteen "general purpose" Linux commands. It describes the components of a command, syntax of a command and using options and patterns. Several examples of each command are provided so that you can get a good idea of how each one works.

You will also learn about various methods of I/O (Input/Output) redirection to output commands to files, other commands and other locations.

During the Hands-On Exercises, you will use several commands to: list files, output the contents of files, restrict the output of files and commands, search directories and files for text, and find directories and files.

Chapter 7: Getting Help with Linux

Linux documentation is available in many locations, such as manuals, files, web sites and by running commands. This chapter describes how to get help from documentation in these locations and by using commands.

In this chapter, you will also learn about the Linux Documentation Project, which provides access to many sources of Linux information, including hundreds of HOWTOs, FAQs and man pages.

During the Hands-On Exercises you will use many commands that provide information on Linux software components.

Chapter 8: The VIM (Vi IMproved) Editor

During this chapter, you will learn about Linux text files, text editors and the use of the very popular vi editor. This editor works in two "modes" and you will see how to change between these modes and the tasks that can be done in each mode.

The vi editor also has several command-line commands. These commands are detailed along with the methods of using them.

You can run Linux commands and scripts from within the vi editor without having to exit out of it. This allows you to run commands to see information, such as get a directory listing, and it also allows you to test the changes that you have made to a file, such as a configuration file or script file.

During the Hands-On Exercises you will create a text file, use various keys to move around in the text, delete text and "put" text. You will also run commands from within the vi editor.

Chapter 9: Understanding the PATH and Shell Configuration Files

During this chapter, you will see the purpose of the PATH environment variable, and view the directory paths in it so that you can understand the reasons for them. All of the directory paths in the default PATH for the root user and non-root users are described in detail.

You will learn how to run binary and script files that are not in a directory that is in the PATH. You will also learn the difference between executables and builtin commands and how these relate to the PATH.

You will get an overview of all of the shell configuration files and the way in which they are processed. This includes the hidden bash configuration files and other bash configuration files.

During the Hands-On Exercises, you will remove all directory paths in the PATH and then see what is required to execute programs that are not in the PATH. You will also view all of the shell configuration files, modify some shell configuration files, view alias settings, create temporary aliases, remove aliases and create permanent aliases in two locations.

Chapter 10: Adding a Disk and Partition to a Linux System

In this chapter, you are provided with an overview of all of the steps to add a hard disk and partition to a Linux system so that the partition is automatically mounted when the system boots.

You will use commands to determine if a hard disk that you have added to a system is "seen" by the system when the system boots and learn how to use the fdisk utility to add a new partition and remove a partition. You will also use a command to assign a filesystem to a partition and another command to assign a label to a partition.

This chapter also details the columns of settings in the /etc/fstab file. You will edit this file to add settings for the partition that you create with fdisk.

During the Hands-On Exercises you will create a partition, assign it a filesystem, assign it a label, add a statement for it to fstab, and reboot to test that it is automatically mounted during the boot process.

Chapter 11: Using Filesystem Commands

During this chapter, you will learn that an X GUI or text-based GUI file manager will not always be available to use for file management tasks, and the benefits of using commands to perform these tasks.

You will also find out about several filesystem commands and the options that are commonly used with them.

A Case Study scenario is introduced in this section regarding a fictitious company named RMG Inc. This company requires data directory structures to be created for its Production and Sales Departments.

During the Hands-On Exercises you will use filesystem commands to create the data directory structures for this company and copy and move data files into the directories that you create.

Chapter 12: Users, Groups, Permissions and Attributes

In this chapter, you will learn how users access Linux servers and the process that is used to allow users at RMG Inc. to access an NFS file server. You will also learn how users can be added to a group so that they acquire the permissions of the group on the server.

All of the permissions that can be assigned to users and groups are detailed in this chapter, including the methods of creating users and groups and assigning them permissions. The attributes that can be assigned to files and the method of assigning them are also described.

Important text files that contain user, group and password information are also detailed.

During the Hands-On Exercises, you will create users and groups and add users to groups. You will also assign permissions, users and groups to the directory structures of the Production and Sales Departments of RMG Inc.

Chapter 13: Backing Up Your System

During this chapter, you will learn the importance of doing system backups and gain information regarding backup hardware, software, strategies and procedures.

The main focus of this chapter is the on tar command and how it can be used to combine files into a single tar file (backup file) and how options of this command can be used to compress and decompress a backup tar file.

During the Hands-On Exercises, you will use various options of the tar command to combine and compress files into a single file and also view the contents of a tar file.

Chapter 14: The X Window System

In this chapter, you will learn about the operations of the X Window System, its main software components and recent versions. You will also learn about important X directories, X files, man pages and documentation files.

The XF86Config file is the main configuration file for the X Server. Settings that configure X are made in several "sections" of this file and the purpose of each of these sections is described.

The XF86Config file can be configured manually with a text editor or it can be modified by using several utilities. An overview of the utilities that can be used to configure the XF86Config file is provided here.

During the Hands-On Exercises, you will look at the main X directories and X files, configure X using a GUI utility and configure X by manually editing the XF86Config file.

Chapter 15: Creating and Running Linux Scripts

During this chapter, you will learn how to use a text editor to create a script, make it executable, and run it like any other Linux command. You will get an overview of shell script syntax, the benefits of using comments in scripts, and the types of shell variables.

Conditional expressions are used in scripts to compare items and test for conditions. Many different types of conditional expressions are described, including those used for directory and file comparison, numerical comparison, string comparison, and logical operators. Several examples of all of these conditional expressions are also presented.

Control structures are used with conditional expressions to control the processing of the statements in scripts. The syntax of all of the control structures that can be used in scripts are discussed, with examples that illustrate their use.

During the Hands-On Exercises you will create a directory for scripts that is in the PATH. You will then use the vi editor to create several scripts, use the chmod command to make them executable, and then run these scripts to test them.

Chapter 16: Runlevels, the Boot Process, Services and Processes

In this chapter, you will learn about the runlevels or "modes" in which a Linux system can operate and how these can be configured to run the services that are required for each runlevel.

We will discuss the boot process of a Linux system, from selecting the OS on a boot loader menu through to the login prompt. During this process, the kernel is loaded, the init binary is executed, and several script files are processed to initialize the system. You will learn the purpose of each of these scripts and the system components and services that they set up in the memory of a system.

Several system services are described, and then the initialization process and directory structure that is used to start these services is detailed.

Linux allows incredible control over the processes that are running in memory. You can use commands to monitor the memory of a system and view a large amount of information on each process that is running. This allows you to locate processes that are not working properly, so that you can remove them from memory and then start them again if necessary. This can be done without having to reboot a system.

During the Hands-On Exercises, you will view the scripts that are used during the boot process and use commands to: configure the default settings for a service, immediately start and stop services, change the current runlevel, view the current runlevel setting, view the status of processes, stop processes and view memory statistics.

Chapter 17: Scheduling Tasks and Working with Log Files

During this chapter, you will learn how to schedule unattended tasks with at, cron and anacron. You will see how these programs work, the differences between them, and the benefits of using each of them. The fields used in the configuration files for cron, anacron and user crontab files are also covered. This will show you how to set up these programs to run unattended tasks.

Linux uses many log files that contain messages which are written to these files by programs that are running on the system. We will cover the locations and uses of several common log files, and how this information can be used to get support via a mailing list, newsgroup or search engine.

The Linux email system is used by various programs to send messages regarding "system events" to one or more users. You will learn how to use the mail system to view email messages.

During the Hands-On Exercises you will schedule tasks with at, cron and anacron and find out about the "inner workings" of these programs. You will also see how log files are affected by the operation of various programs.

Chapter 18: Linux Networking and Setting Up an NFS Server

Linux is extremely popular as a server operating system and is used for many different types of servers. These servers, and the hosts that access them, can all communicate via the TCP/IP protocol and use IP addresses. This chapter describes the components of TCP/IP and the IP address numbering scheme used for the different classes of networks.

IP addresses consists of a network address, host address and subnet mask. You will learn to differentiate between the network address portion of an IP address and the host address portion of an IP address. You will also see several methods of specifying an IP address in a configuration file, such as a configuration file used by some type of server.

This chapter will also provide you with an overview of: the purpose of a DNS server, accessing hosts with domain names, the benefits of using DHCP, and the commonly used network interface devices.

This chapter also details each of the files used to configure networking on a system.

During the Hands-On Exercises you will look at several network configuration files and also do the steps to required to set up, configure and test an NFS file server.

Chapter 19: Printing and Setting Up a Print Server

During this chapter, you will learn about general printing terms and concepts, and the benefits and differences between the two common Linux printing systems named LPRng and CUPS.

The utilities and commands for each printing system are described in detail as well as the main directories, configuration files and log files that are used by each printing system.

During the Hands-On Exercises you will use the commands for each printing system to create printers (print queues), send print jobs to print queues, view jobs in queues, remove jobs from queues, and move jobs up in queues.

You will also do the steps to switch from the LPRng Printing System to the CUPS Printing System and configure a CUPS Print Server system and a Client system. You will then use the web-browser-based CUPS Printer Configuration utility to create printers and test the Print Server system.

Chapter 20: Installing Software On A Linux System

In the first section of this chapter you will learn to differentiate between "installation format files" and tarballs and how to search the Internet for software packages.

You will also get an overview of the benefits of RPM package management software and learn to use many options of the rpm command to install, erase and query .rpm package files.

During the Hands-On Exercises of this section you will use many options of the rpm command, erase some software packages, and then install the SSH software components that will allow you to "ssh into a server".

In the second section, we will provide an overview of http, html and the Apache Web server. You will also learn about some of the directives (settings) in the main Apache configuration file.

In the Hands-On Exercises you will install the software packages for the Apache Web server and view the main software components and directory structure used by the Apache Web server.

The last section describes downloading binary and source code packages that exist as tarballs. It provides an overview of installing binaries that have been extracted from a tarball. It also details the steps required to install source code that has been extracted from a tarball.

While doing the Hands-On Exercises, you will do the steps to untar, compile and install the source code in a tarball for a package named Anjuta. You will then use the Anjuta program to modify the source code of a small program, compile the program, tar it, untar it and then install it.

Chapter 21: Configuring, Compiling and Installing a New Kernel

The Linux kernel kernel is highly configurable. It consists of hundreds of software components that exist as source code. When configuring the kernel for a system, you can specify what to do with the source code components of it. Some components, such as commonly used hardware components, are compiled into the kernel. Other components can either be compiled into the kernel, compiled as modules, or excluded altogether.

In this chapter, you will learn about the kernel source code, the methods of configuring the kernel components, the benefits of compiling your own kernel, and the documentation provided with the source code.

During the Hands-On Exercises, you will do all of the steps to configure and compile your own kernel and the modules for the kernel. You will also modify the Grub boot loader configuration file so that you can select your new kernel when the system boots and test these components.

Chapter 22: Working with Modules and the Kudzu Utility

During this chapter, you will get an overview of how modules are configured, compiled and loaded into memory to provide software support for system components. You will also learn about module dependencies and how to unload modules that are in memory and are no longer needed.

You will see the contents of the configuration files that specify the hardware components in a system and that specify the alias names of modules. Some of the commonly used modules will also be discussed.

Over time, a driver for a hardware component may need to be updated and installed on a system. You will learn how to compile the source code for a driver and install it.

This chapter also covers the Kudzu utility, which checks for hardware that has been added to a system and also for hardware that has been removed from a system. This utility allows you to easily add the software configuration required for a new hardware component or remove the software configuration of a component that has been removed.

During the Hands-On Exercises, you will view the module configuration file, do the steps to compile and install a hardware driver, and use various commands to work with modules. You will also see the steps used by the Kudzu utility to determine the module required for a hardware component and add the module to the system.

Course Objectives

Our goal is to assist you in becoming technically knowledgeable regarding the administration of systems that are running the Linux operating system. To provide you with the greatest assistance, we have included over 300 pages of detailed Hands-On Exercises throughtout this course. By the end of this course you will feel very comfortable with the concepts and tasks that have been described!

Section Review Questions

In each section there are several questions that help you to review the key concepts covered in the section.

 The Section Review Questions icon appears at the beginning of these questions.

Most questions are multiple choice. The answers to these questions appear with either a circle or square at the left of each answer. If a circle appears at the left of each possible answer, there is only one answer that should be selected. If there is a square at the left of each answer, there is more than one correct answer to the question. Other questions are True or False questions.

Hands-On Exercises

At the end of each section there are also extensive Hands-On Exercises that provide you with the practical experience you need to work with the Linux operating system.

 The Hands-On Exercises icon appears at the beginning of these exercises.

In addition to the Hands-On Exercises at the end of each section, there are also Optional Exercises that you may work through if time permits.

Other Icons used in this Course

Below are other icons that appear throughout the text of this course.

 The Caution icon is used to warn you and to help you avoid potential problems.

 The FYI icon is used to provide additional clarification of some of the information provided, and to provide background information that you will find useful in the workplace.

 The Terms icon is used to explain any unfamiliar computer terms that are introduced. A new term is described in the text immediately after it is used.

The Use of "a.k.a." to Provide Alternate Words and Terms

The letters "a.k.a." are an abbreviation for "also known as". These letters are used in this course to present you with alternate words or acronyms for various terms. For example, Linux uses the X Window System (a.k.a. X, X11, X Windows).

Lancom Technologies Web Site

To get the latest information about our courses, you are invited to visit our web site at:

> http://www.lancom-tech.com

Our Internet email address is:

> info@lancom-tech.com.

Instructor Support Materials

If this book is used in a classroom setting, supplemental materials are available to Instructors by calling 1-800-718-7318.

Copyright

This book is protected by international copyright law. No portion of this book may be reproduced in any form without the express written permission of the publisher.

Hello Linux! Course CDs

CD 1 and CD 2 - Red Hat® Linux® 8.0 Publisher's Edition

This book includes a copy of the Publisher's Edition of Red Hat® Linux® from Red Hat, Inc., which you may use in accordance with the license agreement found at www.redhat.com/licenses. Official Red Hat® Linux®, which you may purchase from Red Hat, includes the complete Red Hat Linux distribution, Red Hat's documentation, and may include technical support for Red Hat® Linux®. You may also purchase technical support from Red Hat. You may purchase Red Hat® Linux® and technical support from Red Hat through the company's web site (www.redhat.com) or its toll-free number 1-888-REDHAT1.

CD 3 - Lab Data and Source Code Files

The third CD includes student lab data files and source code files that are used during the Hands-On Exercises.

UNIX, Linus and Linux

Topics Covered in this Section

Discuss the similarities between UNIX and Linux

Describe the development of the Linux operating system

Introduce the GNU General Public License and the benefits of GPL software

Discuss why people develop free software and the reasons for the popularity of Linux

Describe the market demand for Linux professionals and the future of Linux

Detail the main Linux operating system components

This section is designed to provide you with an overview of the Linux operating system (OS) and definitions of several key terms that are used throughout this course.

The UNIX Operating System

UNIX is a very popular and relatively expensive computer operating system that first became available for large mainframe computers and minicomputers. It was created about thirty years ago by Ken Thompson and Dennis Richie at AT&T Bell labs. Over time, it has been developed by many people at various different organizations and has evolved into several different, but similar, "variants" (a.k.a. dialects, versions). The UNIX variants have been sold by numerous major organizations, including IBM, Sun Microsystems and Hewlett-Packard.

From the beginning, UNIX was designed as a system that could run more than one program at once (a multitasking OS). UNIX is also a network operating system that can be accessed by many users at once (a multiuser OS). The architecture of the Internet was created with UNIX and it still plays a major part in the workings of the Internet.

Linux is rightly considered to be "UNIX-like" and "a free version of UNIX". The Linux OS was developed to follow the **POSIX** (**P**ortable **O**perating **S**ystem **I**nterface for uni**X**) standard and is therefore POSIX-like. All major versions of UNIX are POSIX-like and so is Linux. Therefore, whenever anything in this courseware describes Linux, the same applies to UNIX, unless otherwise specified.

For example, Linux is a multitasking, multiuser operating system. This statement is also true for UNIX.

Linus Torvalds and the Linux Operating System

Linux is an operating system that was started in Helsinki, Finland in 1991 by a computer science student named Linus Torvalds. He wanted an operating system that was like the UNIX operating system, but he didn't have the money to buy it. So he decided to use UNIX as a model for developing a new operating system - Linux!

Using UNIX as a model for his operating system proved to be an excellent idea. UNIX is a well-designed and thoroughly tested operating system that is used by millions of people around the world. Linus had the opportunity to use this example of an existing OS, to build his own OS from the ground up.

Linus designed the Linux kernel so that it would work on his IBM PC compatible computer. The kernel is the "core" or main component of the operating system. His intention was to create an operating system with the same functionality as the UNIX operating system (to be POSIX-like), and it worked! Linux is named after Linus, by using a combination of the words Linus and UNIX. It is pronounced something like "lynn-ux".

The "ux" in Linux leads to the word "tux". Penguins appear (to some) to be wearing tuxedos. Therefore, Linus selected a penguin named Tux to become the official "mascot" of the Linux operating system. Apparently Linus is quite fond of penguins. I wonder if he knows Opus (the penguin) from Bloom County?

The Development of Linux

As fortune would have it, Finland had excellent Internet access in 1991 and Linus was able to use the Internet to enlist the assistance of other programmers from all over the world to help him with his project. Linus let these software developers know that he was working on Linux and the ones that were interested in the project joined in! The first complete version of Linux became available in 1994.

Linus continues to work with developers to improve the Linux OS. Developers that have expertise in certain areas work on those areas of the project. Once the kernel reaches a point where the developers believe that it should be released again, it becomes available for download over the Internet. Thousands of people have downloaded the source code (text version of the program). Once downloaded, they use a program called a compiler to "compile" (convert) the source code text into executable form, so that the OS will run on their systems.

Many of the people that download the OS report back to Linus and the developers. They describe how well the software works, what they would like to see added, and they also identify any bugs that they have encountered. The developers are continuously revising the source code of the OS to fix bugs and create enhancements for it.

 The source code for the Linux kernel is available via "ftp" (file transfer protocol) at ftp://ftp.funet.fi. The .fi at the end of this address stands for Finland.

The License Selected by Linus for the Linux OS

Copyright is used to protect the author of a creative work, such as a software program, from the illegal reproduction of the work. This stops anyone from stealing the work from the author and allows the author to control the sale and use of the work. The author of a software program can be one or more individuals, a company or an organization. The person(s), company or organization that holds the copyright, controls who has the "right" to "copy" the work that is protected under copyright.

For computer software, copyright is protected by licenses. A software license is used to describe who can use a software program and how it can be used. Most "commercial software" is licensed to the user, for use (not ownership) of the software. The author is protected from unauthorized reproduction of their program by copyright law.

The Free Software Foundation and the GNU Project

The Free Software Foundation (FSF) is dedicated to eliminating the restrictions on copying, redistribution, understanding, and modification of computer programs. It was founded at the Massachusetts Institute of Technology by Richard Stallman in 1983. He and other members of the FSF presented the concept that companies could charge for software services and software customization, but that the software itself should not be restricted by a standard "commercial software" license.

The FSF is the governing body of the GNU Project, under which hundreds of software utilities for UNIX (and therefore Linux) have been created and distributed for free around the world.

GNU (pronounced "guh-new") stands for GNU's Not UNIX. This name emphatically states that GNU is not the UNIX operating system. The mission of the GNU Project was to create a free operating system that is functionally the same as UNIX. Near the end of the project, Linus Torvalds joined up and delivered the Linux kernel, the key component of the Linux OS.

 Due to the many GNU project software components that are included with the Linux kernel (in a Linux distribution), Linux is sometimes referred to as GNU/Linux. But most people just call it "Linux".

You can find out more about the FSF, the GNU Project and its relationship with Linux at: http://www.fsf.org.

The GNU General Public License

Linus Torvalds chose to use the General Public License (a.k.a. GPL, GPL agreement) for the distribution of Linux. The Linux kernel and most of the free software components in a Linux "distribution" were created as part of the GNU project. They are made available to everyone under the GNU General Public License, often referred to as the GPL. The GPL is different from most other software licenses and radically different from standard "commercial software" licenses.

The important principles for software that is licensed under the GPL are:

♦ Anyone can distribute GPL software for free or charge for it. They may not restrict the redistribution of it and the software does not have any warranty.

♦ A complete copy of the source code must be freely available for the software and must include clear copyright documentation. Most "commercial software" is only provided in binary (compiled, non-source code) form and therefore cannot be changed as needed. Since the source code of a GPL program is freely available, any programmer can modify the program.

♦ If program code is added to an existing GPL program, the modified version may also be redistributed. As always though, the source code and copyright information must be available for all programs derived from GPL software. This is the feature that allows all kinds of programmers to contribute to the Linux project. At the same time, it prevents someone from altering part of a GPL package and then claiming the software as their own.

The complete GNU/GPL license can be seen at:

http://www.gnu.org/licenses/gpl.txt.

Copyright and Copyleft

When software is distributed under the GPL, the author of the program still legally holds the copyright to the program (its source code and binaries) and the author's name is still associated with it. The GPL is quite different from the typical copyright used for many software programs. As such, the GPL is sometimes referred to as "copyleft software", which is a play on the word "copyright". The Linux community has an interesting sense of humor. Later, you will learn how "less" is "more".

 Linus Torvalds is the computer scientist most responsible for the development of the Linux kernel. Although the kernel is distributed under the terms of the GPL, Linus holds the trademark and copyright on Linux. Even so, if Linus Torvalds were to stop working on Linux, another member of the core team of Linux developers would take his place.

Benefits of GPL Software

GPL software is developed by hundreds of programmers in many different occupations. Some of these people are: computer instructors, university professors, tech support staff, college students, scientists, researchers and system administrators in small and large organizations.

With hundreds of programmers in many different walks of life working on GPL programs, these programs are produced more co-operatively and thus have fewer bugs and more enhancements than commercial software. In addition to these benefits, new program code can be created quickly using existing code as a stepping stone. Many people contribute suggestions for improvements and others test the code and provide critical analysis of it.

All of the above benefits are reflected in the Linux kernel and the other GPL software components that are distributed with it!

Open Source Software

The Linux kernel and the GNU software components fall under the broader category of "open source software". The word "source" in "open source software" represents the source code of the software. Saying that the source code is "open", means that the programming instructions used to generate the software are made available to the users of the program. This in turn means that users can modify the software to better suit their purposes. As well, as anyone can obtain the code to generate the software, no-one can make the program proprietary and prevent others from using it.

The Open Source Initiative (OSI) is an organization that defines the license for open source software. This license is similar to the GPL license and can be used in other software products. The creators of software that is "closed source" do not make the source code of their software available to the public.

The Open Source Software license is similar to the GPL, but it is not the same. You can find out more about Open Source Software and the Open Source Initiative at: http://www.opensource.org.

 There are differences between the licenses of GPL software and Open Source Software. The Free Software Foundation does not consider that the two are the same. However, the two licenses are often referred to interchangeably by people in the Linux community.

Why Do People Develop Free Software?

The GPL and the Internet enable a programmer to create a program and make it, and its source code, available to millions of others. However, you may be wondering why so many people work on developing Linux software components for free. There are actually several possible reasons. People that are a part of the free software culture are not just motivated by money. Often, a person or organization has a need for a software component that does not exist, or the existing software is simply not good enough.

For example, a NASA engineer (a rocket scientist) needs a fast and efficient driver for the Ethernet cards on his network. Therefore, he writes a very fast driver (software interface for the Ethernet cards) and then decides to share the development with others! This is a way of thanking others for developing the free software that he has used. It is also a way of making a contribution to the free software community, of which Linux is a part.

As another example, a programmer writes a utility that she needs to manage user passwords. She creates the utility and then makes it available under the GPL. She releases the source code over the Internet and other programmers make enhancements to the utility, add them to the source code, and then make the code available to her (and everyone). This has been described as loaning your tools out to someone and getting them back sharpened!

Being recognized in the free software community for having developed quality programs is a great feeling! People that like your work will respect you and thank you for your contribution. Having your software accepted by the community is good for your self esteem, your career, and your resume!

The Reasons for the Popularity of Linux

Linux is a fast and free OS that can be used as a workstation OS (a.k.a. desktop OS) and as a server OS. It is an excellent server OS because it is based on the multiuser UNIX operating system. Linux is most often used as some type of server.

Linux is extremely popular as the foundation OS for many types of servers, including: Web server, Anonymous FTP server, NFS file server, Windows file (a.k.a. Samba, smb) server, Database (SQL) server, News server and Domain Name (DNS) server. The Apache web server is most commonly found running on Linux and it is the most popular web server in the world!

Linux does not have demanding hardware requirements. Therefore, it can be installed on older hardware to provide "utility" services. It can be used as a print server or **router**.

 A **router** is a device that physically connects two or more networks.

Linux can be installed on a system that contains two or more network cards. Each network card connects to a different segment of the network. Router software is then run in the system to provide the software connection between the segments and to efficiently "route" packets of data to their destination.

The Purpose of an Operating System

A computer system consists of several hardware components, such as processor, memory, circuit boards, hard disk, monitor and keyboard. It is the job of the operating system to allow you to interact with these components and use the applications installed on the system.

A software component of the OS is used to prepare the hard disk(s) of the system so that the OS can be installed. The OS is then installed on the hard disk(s) and loads into the memory of the system when it boots. Once the OS has booted, it provides access to your hardware components and gives you the capability of running programs.

Application software programs depend on an operating system and take advantage of the services provided by the operating system. These services include the capabilities of creating, saving and printing data files.

Linux is a multitasking OS. It can run and keep track of multiple programs at once. For example, while working on a Linux system you can view a web page, recalculate the formulas in a large spreadsheet, copy a file and print a document, all at the same time! Linux is also a very robust operating system. It will continue to run the rest of its applications even when a program has "crashed" (a.ka. "hung").

Linux is also a multiuser OS. More than one person (each at a different computer) can access the same system. A very common example of this occurs when Linux has been installed as a web server and has hundreds of people accessing it at once.

The Main Components of the Linux Operating System

Several main components are combined to make up the Linux operating system. These components are: the kernel, utility programs, library files, device drivers and a graphical user interface. All of these items are derived from source code and are described below.

Technically speaking, the Linux operating system is just the kernel. However, all of the Linux software components described below are commonly referred to as the Linux operating system.

When we refer to the Linux operating system (OS) in this course, we are referring to all of the software components described below.

Source Code

Software programs and operating systems are written in source code (a.k.a. code). This is the text version of the program that actually looks a little bit like a human language (e.g. English). The code is understood by a program called a compiler. The compiler processes the text of the code and "compiles" it so that your computer can understand what to do with it (if the program works!).

The compiled source code becomes an "executable" program file that your system can run. This program file is referred to as a "binary" and only consists of the binary numbers of 0 and 1 - thousands of them.

Theoretically, it would be possible to actually write programs in binary and skip the step of compiling them. However, humans simply don't think well in 0s and 1s, so writing binary programming would be very time consuming and frustrating indeed. The purpose of source code is to provide a kind of middle ground. It allows humans to use a programming language, which is relatively easy for them to understand, yet the resulting code can be efficiently translated into the binary version that computers need.

To provide an example of source code, a portion of the code of the Linux kernel is shown below. The lines of text that begin with "/*" or "*", and end with "*/" are comments in the file. The name of the file, "time.c", is shown at the top. Also notice the copyright and the modification-history information at the top. Linus holds the copyright and the names of the people that contributed to the code are also shown in the comments.

The following is an excerpt (a.k.a. snippet) of the source code for a program called time.c:

```
/*
 *  linux/kernel/time.c
 *
 *  Copyright (C) 1991, 1992  Linus Torvalds
 *
 *  This file contains the interface functions for the various
 *  time related system calls: time, stime, gettimeofday, settimeofday,
 *                              adjtime
 */
/*
 * Modification history kernel/time.c
 *
 * 1993-09-02    Philip Gladstone
 *     Created file with time related functions from sched.c and adjtimex()
 * 1993-10-08    Torsten Duwe
 *     adjtime interface update and CMOS clock write code
 * 1995-08-13    Torsten Duwe
 *     kernel PLL updated to 1994-12-13 specs (rfc-1589)
 * 1999-01-16    Ulrich Windl
 *     Introduced error checking for many cases in adjtimex().
 *     Updated NTP code according to technical memorandum Jan '96
 *     "A Kernel Model for Precision Timekeeping" by Dave Mills
 *     Allow time_constant larger than MAXTC(6) for NTP v4 (MAXTC == 10)
 *     (Even though the technical memorandum forbids it)
 */

#include <linux/mm.h>
#include <linux/timex.h>
#include <linux/smp_lock.h>

#include <asm/uaccess.h>

/*
 * sys_time() can be implemented in user-level using
 * sys_gettimeofday().  Is this for backwards compatibility?  If so,
 * why not move it into the appropriate arch directory (for those
 * architectures that need it).
 *
 * XXX This function is NOT 64-bit clean!
 */
asmlinkage long sys_time(int * tloc)
{
    int i;

    /* SMP: This is fairly trivial. We grab CURRENT_TIME and
       stuff it to user space. No side effects */
    i = CURRENT_TIME;
    if (tloc) {
            if (put_user(i,tloc))
                    i = -EFAULT;
            }
    return i;
}
```

The text of the source code is created in a "text editor", which is a program that is similar to a word processor. However, most text editors do not provide the formatting capabilities of word processors, such as bold, underline and left and right margins. The most basic text editors allow you to enter text, edit it, copy, paste and save it.

The Linux Kernel

The "core" or main component of the Linux OS is the kernel (not to be confused with Elvis' manager or the founder of a fast-food chicken chain). This is the compiled version of the source code that was created by Linus Torvalds and hundreds of other programmers working together over the Internet.

The source code (text version) of the Linux kernel is provided to you on CD 2 as a file named kernel-source-x.x.x-x.i386.rpm in /RedHat/RPMS. The x.x.x-x in the kernel source code file name represents the version number of the kernel, such as 2.4.18-14. The source code for the Linux kernel and its components is now over *four million* lines of text!

The Linux kernel source code is compiled to create the kernel of the Linux OS. The compiled kernel and its supporting program files are installed on your hard disk when Linux is installed. The kernel is the "core" (main component) of the operating system and provides many basic operating system services, such as access to the file system, accepting input, providing output, managing memory and tracking other system resources.

The kernel manages all application and utility programs as "processes", in order to provide them with basic operating-system services. Being a multitasking operating system, the kernel can run many processes at the same time. It keeps track of all processes and assigns resources, such as processor time and memory, to these processes as needed.

When your system boots, the kernel loads into memory and starts the processes that it requires, in order to provide the user or application programs with services. If you request a service from the operating system for which a process is not currently running, the kernel will start a new process in order to supply it to you. When some processes are no longer required, they are stopped. Therefore, Linux can dynamically (instantly and automatically) start and stop processes as required. This produces an excellent savings in memory and processor utilization, which in turn makes the system more efficient and faster!

By default, the processes that are running to provide basic system services do not appear on the screen when they are running. These processes are called "background processes" or "daemons".

For example, when you send something to print, the "printer daemon" named "lpd" is run in the background to provide you with the service of printing. However, you do not see any indication on the screen that the lpd daemon has been used to provide you with the printing service.

Many services are not actually supplied by the kernel, but are provided by utility programs (binary files) and library files. When the OS needs a service that is not part of the kernel, it makes a "call" (request) to a utility program or a library asking it to deliver the service.

Utility Programs

Utility programs are another one of the main Linux OS components. These are independent binary files that reside on the hard disk and are used to perform specific functions. Utility programs are "called" (run) by the kernel to deliver a service. They are not application software programs, such as a word processor or spreadsheet.

Library Files

Linux uses library files (a.k.a. libraries) that contain program code in binary form (binaries). These files are accessed by the OS and other programs and supply them with a collection of commonly used software routines (parts of programs). These routines are "code" that is required on a regular basis. This is an efficient method of providing commonly used routines to multiple programs. As a block of code is stored in a central location (a library file), it does not have to be repeated in numerous programs. This saves on disk space. As well, libraries are accessed only when needed, thus reducing memory utilization. Libraries supply routines that are needed for many functions, whereas a utility program is typically used for one specific function.

Device Driver Software

Device driver software provides the "interface" that is used by the OS to communicate with various hardware devices in the system.

For example, there are many different video circuit boards (a.k.a. video cards, graphics cards) that can be used in your system. A device driver interprets communications from the OS to your graphics card so that the card can display information on your screen. When you install Linux, you specify the manufacturer and model of your graphics card and then the installation routine selects and installs the device driver that is required.

Graphical User Interface (a.k.a. GUI, gooey)

The Linux OS can be installed with a GUI interface that includes a "graphical desktop environment". This "environment" is supplied by a collection of software components called the X Window System, and other software components called a GUI desktop and window manager.

The software components of the X Window System deliver a foundation for a "GUI desktop", such as the GNOME or KDE desktop environments. The GUI desktop works with a window manager, such as Sawfish, to present the "look and feel" of the desktop environment.

The "GUI desktop" causes the screen of your system to look like a desktop. This allows you to work in a "point-and-click", mouse-driven environment, with a graphical interface to the services of the operating system. You use this graphical interface to interact with the operating system to do many different tasks, such as viewing the file system, providing input, accepting output and running software programs.

The Market Demand for Linux Professionals

In today's economic climate, many organizations have limited or tight IT (Information Technology) budgets. Since Linux is free, it is becoming more and more attractive to these organizations. This provides an excellent problem. It causes a high demand in the marketplace for qualified people that know how to make Linux work!

System Administrators are needed in the thousands of organizations that are running Linux on both workstations and servers. Software developers are needed to create custom software programs to run on the Linux platform. There is a demand for technical trainers that can explain how to use the OS and the application software programs (a.k.a. applications) that are being run on it. Technical writers are also required to describe Linux and its applications in courses, magazines, books and other publications.

After about 10 years, Linux is finally entering the mainstream. IBM spent over a billion dollars on Linux in 2001 and within a year had recovered most of that investment. Almost all of the mainframe computers sold by IBM in the last quarter of 2001 used Linux as the OS!

And it keeps getting better. The OS is constantly being enhanced by Linus and the developers that work with him. More software components are being created for it all the time. The companies that create distributions of Linux continue to provide enhancements for it and more and more applications are becoming available.

All of this increases the demand for Linux *and the demand for people that know how to make it tick*!

You can visit the following web sites to get information on careers that are specific to Linux and also careers that are related to having knowledge of Linux. At these sites, do a search on "Linux".

www.hotlinuxjobs.com
www.jobpenguin.com
www.mojolin.com
www.brassring.com
www.dice.com
www.linux.ittoolbox.com
www.careerbuilder.com
www.careerjournal.com
www.itmoonlighter.com
www.linuxnow.com
www.linuxdevices.com

Section Review

1. Select three benefits of General Public License (GPL) software.

   ☐ A. it has more enhancements because many talented programmers contribute suggestions

   ☐ B. it is basically error-free because it is created by one main company and tested by several others

   ☐ C. it is produced with fewer errors because many people test it

   ☐ D. new code can be created quickly using existing code as a stepping stone

2. Select three of the main Linux operating system components.

   ☐ A. library files

   ☐ B. device drivers

   ☐ C. the kernel

   ☐ D. text emulators

3. Library files provide the "interface" that is used by the OS to communicate with various hardware devices in the system. T F

4. What are three of the components that make up the Linux graphical desktop environment?

   ☐ A. a GUI desktop

   ☐ B. a screen merger

   ☐ C. the X Window System

   ☐ D. a window manager

5. Which of the following are characteristics of the Linux operating system (choose two)?

   ☐ A. it consists of the kernel and several other software components

   ☐ B. it does not require device drivers

   ☐ C. it was created by one non-profit organization

   ☐ D. it is a multitasking operating system

6. Linus Torvalds holds the copyright on Linux, but only the FSF holds the trademark. T F

7. Select two statements that are requirements of the GPL agreement.

    ☐ A. a fee must be charged for the software
    ☐ B. the software does not have any warranty
    ☐ C. a contract that specifies hourly or yearly charges for technical service must accompany the software
    ☐ D. if code is added to GPL software and it interacts with the original program, then both components must be distributed together

8. The licenses of GPL software and Open Source software are so similar that the Free Software Foundation considers them to be the same. T F

9. Which of the following items describe library files (choose three)?

    ☐ A. they are an efficient method of providing software routines to multiple programs
    ☐ B. they contain program code in binary form
    ☐ C. they supply the OS and other programs with a collection of commonly used code
    ☐ D. they are independent binary files that are only used to load the kernel when it boots

10. Select three characteristics of GNU/Linux.

    ☐ A. it is POSIX-like
    ☐ B. it consists of the Linux kernel and GNU utilities
    ☐ C. it mostly consists of a "closed source" software components
    ☐ D. it is a multitasking, multiuser operating system

11. Which statements are true regarding Linux software components (choose two).

    ☐ A. utility programs are the same as application programs
    ☐ B. all processes that are running appear on the screen
    ☐ C. the kernel manages all application and utility programs as processes
    ☐ D. a GUI desktop provides a graphical, point-and-click, mouse-driven environment

12. Linux is sometimes referred to as GNU/Linux, due to the many GNU project software components that are included with the Linux kernel in a distribution. T F

13. Which of the following are correct statements regarding source code (choose three).

    ☐ A. it is compiled to create binary program files
    ☐ B. an excerpt of source code is also called a snippet
    ☐ C. it is the text version of a software program
    ☐ D. it can be compiled with a standard text editor

14. Which software license is used for the Linux kernel.

    ☐ A. OSS
    ☐ B. FSF
    ☐ C. GPL
    ☐ D. ATT

Understanding the Linux Distributions

Topics Covered in this Section

Describe the concept of a Linux distribution
Discuss the software components of the Linux operating system
Detail the key components that are required in a distribution
Introduce several of the popular Linux distributions and provide
an overview of the similarities and differences between them

This section explains the concept of a Linux distribution and describes the key components of a distribution. This section also introduces several of the popular Linux distributions and provides an overview of their main characteristics.

Linux Distributions

The Linux OS components were developed by Linus Torvalds, the developers that work with him, and hundreds of other developers. However, these components do not provide everything that is required for a "complete" version of the operating system, known as a Linux "distribution".

A Linux distribution is a "version" of Linux that is put together by an organization, given a name and then "distributed" to the marketplace. A number of organizations are involved in the distribution of Linux. These range from for-profit companies that sell Linux packages, to web-based organizations that provide Linux for free as a service to the community. Notice that both ends of the spectrum are provided for by the GPL license. There are currently over 150 Linux distributions. A distribution consists of several software components including the kernel, the GNU software utilities, libraries and device drivers.

In addition to the above software components, an organization that puts together a distribution typically provides their own installation routine, software manuals and technical support. Some of these organizations also provide other services, such as professional installation and custom programming.

The following are the key components that are required to make a distribution commercially successful.

A Comprehensive and Effective Installation Routine

An installation routine is a software program that is run to request information regarding the hardware components of your system and your software needs. After requesting this information, the installation routine automatically installs the OS on the hard disk of your system, as per your specifications.

The installation routine allows you to specify: the method to be used to boot the OS, settings for hard disk space usage, the hardware components attached to your system and the software components (utilities and applications) that should be installed.

Without the installation routine, specifying hard disk space usage and manually installing and configuring all of the many individual OS components would be unreasonably difficult and time consuming for most people. In this situation, many people would not even consider installing and using the operating system. If the majority of technically-oriented people can't easily install Linux, they won't use it. Virtually all Linux distributions have installation routines, although some work much better than others. The intuitiveness of its installation routine is one of the key "selling points" of a distribution.

Graphical Interface

A way of controlling the computer using a mouse and buttons or icons is also required to make an OS commercially viable. This should include programs used to administer the operating system, monitor its performance, configure hardware components and configure the network environment. Most distributions of Linux come with many GUI utilities and these are increasing in quality and sophistication.

Application Software Programs

An operating system cannot be successful without plenty of high quality, commonly-used application software programs, such as word processor, spreadsheet, database, email, accounting and other productivity programs. Linux currently has applications to meet all of these needs and more are being added constantly.

Other Hardware Drivers

In addition to the "basic" hardware drivers, such as those required to access a commonly-used graphics card, other hardware drivers are also required. These drivers provide "support" (access) for a variety of devices attached to your system. This might include such things as different brands of network card as well as more exotic hardware such as the graphics drawing tablets and plotters used by engineering companies, scanners, audio and video components, and other "weird hardware".

Documentation

Although there is plenty of documentation available for the Linux kernel and its support components, a Linux distribution requires documentation that is specific to itself. This documentation must provide specifics for the use of the distribution's installation routine, its software utilities and its GUI desktop environment(s).

Technical Support

Technical support for Linux is available free of charge on the Internet. There are *many* technical documents and user groups that can provide useful assistance. Often, however this free support is slow to arrive. This is not sufficient when you have a problem with your network and need help immediately because a few hundred people are unable to do their work!

Some organizations have highly trained, technical support staff that understand the inner workings of Linux well enough to handle most technical difficulties. Others do not. Even organizations that have well-trained staff may still get into problems and need help. Bottom line - organizations must be able to contact the vendor of the distribution they are using when technical problems arise. They must be able to get fast, complete and accurate assistance for whatever problem they are having.

When you purchase a Linux distribution, you usually get some type of "basic" technical support. This may be provided by email, phone or a newsgroup. In addition to this "basic" technical support, most companies that sell a distribution also sell comprehensive technical support on an hourly basis, or by a yearly subscription. There are also many other companies that provide technical support and other related services, such as consulting, custom programming and training.

Popular Linux Distributions

Linux distributions are created by many different organizations. Currently, there are over 150 different distributions of Linux. Many distributions are created for specialized functions, such as distributions that specialize in providing specific types of servers. Under the terms of the GPL (General Public License), these companies can charge as much as they want for their distribution, or charge nothing at all!

Some Linux distributions are bundled with technical books, such as this one, and most can be downloaded free of charge from the organizations that create them. However, in these situations the OS is provided without technical support. In addition to this, downloading the OS is time-consuming and tedious over a slow internet connection. Therefore, we recommend that you purchase a distribution. Most distributions charge a very reasonable sum for the "shrink-wrapped" version of the OS (CDs and manuals) and the support that is included.

Here are some of the popular Linux distributions and their characteristics:

Red Hat Linux (www.redhat.com) This is one of the most popular Linux distribution available today. It has an excellent installation routine that makes installing the operating system a relatively easy process.

In the "olden days" (just a few years ago) it was a very tricky process to install *any* distribution of Linux. Many detailed hardware specifics were required and relatively few device drivers were available even for common components, such as graphics cards.

In addition to the graphical interface provided under the GNU license agreement, Red Hat also includes their own graphical utilities for system administration. They also offer fast, high quality technical support.

Red Hat has also created and released RPM (Red Hat Package Manager) software. Programs that use this software, use files with the RPM "format". This format is used to deliver software in a compressed "package" file. RPM files have the suffix (file name ending) of .rpm. Over 1,200 .rpm files (the Linux OS, utilities and applications) are on the CDs that come with this book!

The RPM software makes installing software much easier than previous methods. The RPM format is great because it allows you to run an easy-to-use GUI utility, or a command to automatically put the files in the .rpm file into the various directories where they are required. The RPM format is also used to easily remove old software and update existing software. It is a key benefit to the evolution of Linux.

Red Hat released the RPM software components under the GNU license agreement and as a result, many other Linux distributions can and are using it.

MandrakeLinux (www.mandrakesoft.com) Mandrake is based in France and is "built on" the Red Hat distribution (it is a "derivative" of Red Hat). It has a simple (but good) installation routine, uses the RPM format, and provides several utilities in addition to the Red Hat utilities.

SCO Linux (www.sco.com) SCO Linux is derived from a product called OpenLinux. It has a very easy-to-use GUI installation and also several configuration utilities. Although not directly derived from Red Hat, it uses the RPM format.

SuSE Linux (www.suse.com) This is a very popular distribution in Germany and has become popular in other European countries. It provides both German and English language versions. SuSE is now available in North America and is a serious commercial distribution that comes with a large number of applications. The Professional Edition has been described as one of the most inclusive distributions of Linux applications available. It is not derived from Red Hat, but uses the RPM format. It has GUI installation and configuration utilities.

Debian GNU/Linux (www.debian.org) Debian is a non-profit organization (note the .org, rather than .com, at the end of the web address). It was created and is maintained by developers of free software. It is a non-commercial distribution that abstains from the use of GUI utilities and it appeals to open source software enthusiasts. It uses its own package format called DEB. This format uses a .deb filename suffix and is similar in concept to the RPM format.

Xandros Linux (www.xandros..com) This distribution is based on the Debian distribution. It has a relatively easy-to-use installation routine and is typically used as a workstation OS to replace Windows. Xandros Corporation has an exclusive licensing agreement with Corel Corporation, which provides them with Corel's Linux desktop OS and related technologies.

Slackware (www.slackware.com) This is one of the first distributions of Linux and primarily uses text-based installation and administration utilities rather than GUI utilities. Slackware uses **tarballs** as well as the RPM format to deliver software.

The tar (**tape ar**chive) command is a standard Linux command. It is used to combine one or more files into a single file.

A **tarball** is a single file that contains one or more files that are used to provide Linux software components. Tarballs are also compressed using a software compression utility, in order to make them faster to download over the Internet. The old "standard" for delivering Linux software was through the use of tarballs.

Although tar stands for tape archive, which implies the use of a tape backup device, this command can be used to combine and compress files, and then put them on any storage medium that can be accessed by the system.

Turbolinux (www.turbolinux.com) This distribution is the leading distribution of Linux in Japan and China. It is typically used by System Administrators in large organizations to automatically deliver and add applications to many workstations at once.

UnitedLinux (www.unitedlinux.com) The SCO Group, Conectiva, SuSE and Turbolinux have partnered to create a global, uniform distribution of Linux that is designed for business. This distribution is intended to provide a "standard" Linux distribution that is certified to work across hardware and software platforms.

These four companies have collaborated on the development of one common core Linux operating environment. Each company will bundle value added products and services with UnitedLinux and each will market and sell the product under their own brands.

General Linux Information

General Information on the Linux operating system and all distributions of Linux can be found at http://www.linux.com. This site has links to many other Linux sites and is a good "jumping point" for getting more information on Linux. You can also subscribe to various Linux email newsletters at this site!

Section Review

1. Select the correct description of a tarball.

   - ○ A. a file that contains one or more other files and may also be compressed
   - ○ B. an installation routine used to install Linux
   - ○ C. something that the cat dragged in
   - ○ D. a binary source code file that is used to provide a compiler driver for a specialized user group

2. Which of the following are characteristics that are most likely to be used when selecting a Linux distribution (choose three)?

   - ☐ A. the availability of technical documentation
   - ☐ B. availability of fast, high quality technical support
   - ☐ C. the number of hard disks in the system that will be used
   - ☐ D. the method used to install, uninstall, upgrade and remove programs

3. All distributions of Linux use the same standard GUI installation routine. T F

4. Which of the following statements regarding distributions are correct (choose three)?

   - ☐ A. Debian Linux is a non-profit organization created and maintained by developers of free software
   - ☐ B. MandrakeLinux is based in France and is a derivative of Red Hat Linux
   - ☐ C. SCO Linux is derived from a product called OpenLinux
   - ☐ D. Xandros Linux is based on the Red Hat distribution

5. The Free Software Foundation has released the RPM format under the GNU license agreement. T F

6. A Linux distribution requires the following software components to become commercially viable (choose three):

   ☐   A.   device drivers for non-standard hardware
   ☐   B.   inexpensive hardware components
   ☐   C.   documentation that is specific to the distribution
   ☐   D.   a comprehensive and effective installation routine

7. The Linux kernel, and many of the other software components that are provided with a distribution, are available free of charge from the developers that created them.   T   F

8. Which distribution is currently very popular in Germany and also in other European countries?

   ○   A.   Debain
   ○   B.   SuSE
   ○   C.   Mandrake
   ○   D.   LinuxPPC

Chapter 2: Understanding x86 Hardware Components, Partitions, Filesystems and Device Names

This chapter of the course includes three sections. During this chapter you will learn about and work with the following:

Linux Hardware Requirements and Documenting Your Hardware Setup

This section provides you with a description of Linux hardware requirements and general information regarding the installation of Linux.

During this section, you will do the steps to locate the specifications for your hardware and document the settings of the hardware components that need to be specified during the Linux installation. You will also learn methods of determining the compatibility of non-standard hardware and the steps that are taken to get drivers for non-standard hardware.

Interface Card Types and Methods of Hardware Communication

In this section, you will learn about different interface card types, how they communicate with a system and the settings that they require. Some hardware devices attach to a system via interface cards and some can be attached via other methods. You will also learn about these other methods.

Partitions, Filesystems and Device Names

This section is used to explain partitions, filesystems, storage device names and the naming convention that is used to refer to partitions on these devices. You will also learn about the main partitions used by Linux, the default filesystems used by Linux and the use of non-Linux filesystems on Linux Partitions.

Linux Hardware Requirements and Documenting Your Hardware Setup

Topics Covered in this Section

Provide the minimum Linux hardware requirements and general information regarding the installation of Linux

List and describe the hardware components that need to be specified during the Linux installation

Do the steps to locate hardware specifications and document system hardware components

Describe methods of determining the compatibility of non-standard hardware

Discuss the steps that can be taken to get drivers for non-standard hardware

In this section, you will learn the minimum Linux hardware requirements; do the steps to locate the specifications for your hardware; and document the settings of the hardware components that need to be specified during the Linux installation.

Minimum Linux Hardware Requirements

The following are the recommended processor, memory and storage requirements for the Red Hat version of Linux that is included with this book. While documenting your hardware setup below, make sure that your system meets these requirements.

 In this section you will learn the minimum requirements for the Red Hat distribution of Linux. In addition to this distribution, there are many other distributions of Linux that can be installed for various purposes and some have very "low" hardware requirements. Many other distributions can work on older (legacy) hardware (with earlier versions of processors that are relatively slow, small hard disks and interface cards that were created before the "Plug-and-Play" era).

Minimum Central Processor Unit (CPU)

A minimum of a Pentium PC and a minimum of a 200 MHz processor.

Minimum Memory

A minimum of 64 MB of RAM if you are only using text (non-GUI) mode.

A minimum of 128 MB of RAM if you are using GUI (desktop) mode and 192 MB is recommended.

During this course you will install the GNOME and KDE desktops and you will be working in GUI (desktop) mode. Therefore, you will need a minimum of 128 MB of RAM and 192 MB is recommended.

When you install and use Linux with a desktop environment (such as GNOME or KDE), then you are working in GUI mode. When you do not install a desktop, or boot a system and do not start a desktop, you are working in text mode. When you are using Linux as a server, you do not usually require a desktop and the server is only used in text mode.

You can use Linux in text (non-GUI) mode to do various tasks on a system, other than using the system as a server. This type of system may be used to create the source code of programs, compile programs and do other tasks that do not require a GUI desktop environment.

In the past, the amount of memory and storage required by a GUI desktop environment was relatively large (in comparison to the memory and storage resources of an "older" system) and so the GUI desktop software components were not typically installed when they were not needed. The memory and storage requirements of these software components on current systems is now relatively small and they can easily be installed. For simplicity of discussion, we will consider that systems that are being used in text mode (only) are server systems.

Minimum Hard Disk Space

Red Hat Linux has the following hard disk space requirements: 650 MB minimum, 2.5 GB recommended and 4.5 GB for a full installation (all software components). These disk space amounts do not include the space required for additional program files, such as application software programs that you may need and the space required for the data files that will be used on the system.

During the Linux installation section of this course you will install the GNOME and KDE desktops and several other Linux OS components.

In the next chapter, you will spend a bit of time working in the GNOME and KDE desktop environments and working at virtual terminals. After this, you will spend quite a bit of time using Linux commands by opening a "terminal emulation window" (from the desktop) and working at the command line (a.k.a. shell prompt). *The large majority of the practical exercises in this course are done by using commands at the command line.*

The Linux software components that you will install during the installation section of this course and then later in other sections of the course require a minimum of 3.25 GB of hard disk space. This disk space also allows for data files used during the course.

Protecting Yourself and Your Hardware while Working with It

While working through this course, you may need to open your computer system to work with the components installed in it.

For example, if you have an older system, you may need open it to look the settings of an interface card that is installed in it. If you have a system that was put together in the last few years, then you will not likely need to open it.

Be sure to unplug your computer system before opening it. When working with internal computer components, such as memory modules and interface cards, always handle them by the edges.

Computer components contain various chips and circuitry that are very sensitive to electrostatic discharge (static electricity). Simply touching a chip or a part of computer circuitry can damage or destroy it. To prevent this, we recommend that you use an antistatic wristband. This is a simple device that you attach to your wrist and also to a source of "ground". It "grounds" you and removes static electricity from your body. Instructions for the use of an antistatic wristband come with it. You can purchase one for about five dollars from many stores that supply computer components.

Backing Up Your System

If you already have an operating system installed on your computer and also want to install Linux, you will be doing steps during this course that could cause the loss of your operating system, program files and data files.

If you already have an OS on your system, we highly recommend that you back up your hard disk(s) before doing any of the tasks described in this book.

You are responsible for the OS, programs and data files on your hard disk. If you do any steps that cause your system (hardware, OS or programs) to malfunction, or do any steps that cause the loss of data files, please do not contact Lancom Technologies. Use the backups that you have made of your system to restore your system.

If Windows is the OS installed on your system, you can do a backup with the backup utility that comes with Windows, or use another backup utility. See Help in Windows for information on doing a backup and on how to use the backup utility that is provided with Windows.

We recommend that you make two backups of your entire system (OS, program files and data files) to some type of removable media, such as CD or tape. After this, test that the data that you have backed up can be read and restored from the media that you used.

When backing up your data, be sure to back up all of your hard disks. Also, be sure to back up all of your data, including email data and any settings associated with any programs, such as settings used to access your Internet Service Provider (**ISP**).

Make sure that you still have all of the software for your system (OS and programs) before making any changes to your system.

After backing up your hard disk you may want to do a bit of "house cleaning" and remove programs and data files that you no longer require.

Abbreviations that are Used for Hands-On Exercises Tasks

The following methods are used to abbreviate the steps that are required to do the Hands-On Exercises in this course.

If you need to click on an item and then click on another item, the name of the item appears, then a ";" (semicolon) and then the next item. A ; (semicolon) is used as a separator between items.

For example, the following indicates that you should click on the Menu and then click on the Run... menu heading:

    Menu ; Run...

If you need to double-click on an item, then the name of the item and "x 2" will be shown.

For example, the following indicates that you should double-click on the Start Here icon:

    Start Here icon x 2.

If you need to right-click on an item, then the name of the item and "x r" will be shown.

For example, the following indicates that you should right-click on the CD-ROM icon and then select the Unmount Volume menu heading:

CD-ROM icon x r ; Unmount Volume.

A "dialog box" is a graphical box that appears so that you can respond to it (have a dialog with it). Sometimes you will need to type information into a "field" (blank area) of a dialog box. When you need to type information into a "dialog box", the name of the field will appear and then the text that you need to type in will be shown in italics.

Also, there will be times when you need to press a key on your keyboard that is not a letter or any other single character, such as the Enter key. You will see "press *keyname*" and *keyname* will be replaced by the name of the key to be pressed, such as "press Enter".

For example, when you boot a workstation a GUI dialog box appears with a "Login:" field. The following indicates that you need to type the word *cwest* in the Login: field and press the Enter key:

Login: *cwest* ; press Enter.

Doing the Hands-On Exercises for this Chapter

There are many tasks that are described in this chapter and you will need to do some of them, but not all of them. Most chapters in this course have Hands-On Exercises at the end. However, this chapter has Hands-On Exercises throughout. If you need to do a task for your system, such as look at the CMOS settings, then do the task when it appears.

Technical Support for the CDs Included with this Book

The Linux operating system and other software included on CDs with this courseware is provided under the GNU General Public License agreement, and any other license agreements that appear with the software on the CD. *This software is provided free of charge and is without any warranty or technical support.* **Please do *not* contact Lancom Technologies for technical support.**

Linux technical support is available free of charge on the Internet as described earlier. Technical support is also available for a fee from several locations that were also described earlier.

If you already have an OS installed on your system and you do some of the steps described in this book incorrectly, your system could stop functioning. If this happens, all programs and data files may no longer be accessible.

Before doing any steps described in this book, be sure to back up your system (twice) and test that you can restore the backup.

General Information Regarding Installing Linux

The first four Sections of this chapter provide details regarding the information that you need to know about your system prior to starting the Linux installation. The fourth Section covers steps to create space for Linux on your system. The fifth Section covers running the Linux installation routine.

If you have a current **x86** system that can boot from its CD-ROM drive, and is set up to boot from its CD-ROM drive, and does not have an operating system on it, you can usually install Linux in about an hour (after working through the first four sections). If this is not the current setup of your system, then you need to do some extra steps before installing Linux.

An **x86** PC is a computer that originated from the Intel 8086 CPU (Central Processing Unit) chip. The CPU is the main processor in the system. x86 represents the family of CPUs that includes 8086, 8088, 80186, 80286, 386 and 486. This chip family also includes the first Pentium chip, simply called Pentium, and the Pentium models II, III, 4, MMX and Pro.

Prior to the Pentium series of processors, all of the chips in this family end with the numbers "86", except the 8088 chip. The name of "x86" for this chip family was given (prior to the release of the Pentium chip) because the "x" in "x86" represents any of the numbers prior to the last two last two digits (86), such as the "801" in "80186" and the "3" in "386". This provides an easy method of referring to a whole series computers by using the term "x86".

The last chip in the x86 family to end in "86" was the 486 and Intel did not use the name 586 for the next chip, but used the name Pentium instead. However, systems with Pentium chips are still considered to be x86 PCs and x86 computers have the largest installed base in the world!

You can install Linux on a system that does not already have an operating system on it, or install it on one that has. If you install it on a system that already has an OS, you may be able to keep the existing OS and add Linux. In this case, you can create a "dual-boot" system.

The Windows OS comes installed on most x86 "desktop" (non-server) PCs that are currently being sold. You may be able to keep Windows on your system and install Linux as an additional operating system. However, unless you purchase some additional specialized software, you can only run one OS at a time.

Determining Your Hardware Specifications

Prior to running the Linux installation routine you must know the specifications of several of the hardware components of your system. You need to document these specs so that you can provide them to the installation routine. Therefore, you will "fill in the blanks" below with all of the hardware specifications that are requested by the installation routine.

If Windows is installed on your system, you can use it to find out many of the specs that you need to fill in below.

If Windows is not installed on your system, you will need to get these specs from: the hardware manuals, the invoice, or by contacting your hardware manufacturer (by web site, email or phone).

Installing Linux on Older Systems

If you have a current system with standard hardware and enough hard disk space and memory for Linux, and the system is set up to boot from its CD-ROM drive, then installing Linux is relatively easy. Installing it on older or non-standard hardware can be more of a challenge.

Keep in mind that Linux does not have the demanding hardware requirements of other popular operating systems and so legacy hardware is often used by companies to provide some basic network services, such as being used as a router to connect two parts of a network. In addition to this, you may be working in a classroom environment that has current systems, *but want to install Linux on an older system at home*.

To get as much practical experience with Linux as possible, you may want to install it at home and then work through the Hands-On Exercises that are provided in this course.

Because you will likely need to install Linux on older hardware at some point, this chapter includes the steps to determine older hardware specifications and the steps to install Linux on older hardware.

Viewing Your CMOS Settings

CMOS (pronounced "see-moss") is an area of system memory that holds important settings that are used by your system. When your system boots, it looks at the settings in the CMOS to get information about some of the devices attached to it. The CMOS uses a setup utility that displays your current settings and allows you to change and save the settings.

The **BIOS** of a system provides access to the settings in the CMOS through the CMOS setup utility. To access the CMOS setup utility and view and change settings in your PC, you must press one or more keys during the startup of your PC. The keys used to access the CMOS, the menus of the setup utility, and the names used for the settings, differ from BIOS to BIOS (system to system). The following example demonstrates accessing the CMOS on a system that has an Award BIOS and CMOS Setup Utility.

BIOS (**B**asic **I**nput **O**utput **S**ystem) is a program burned into a chip in your system that is used to get your system up and running. This program exists even when the system is disconnected from a power source and the battery in your system has run out. However, the *settings* in the CMOS are lost if the battery in your system runs out and your system is turned off.

Some interface cards also have BIOSes. For example, most SCSI host adapters (interface cards to which SCSI devices attach, such as hard disks and CD-ROMs) have a BIOS. If a SCSI host adapter has a BIOS, you can boot from a hard disk attached to it.

When your system starts, the BIOS program checks the settings in your CMOS to see what devices are attached to it and that they are all accounted for. It also checks to see if there are BIOSes on other cards installed in your system, such as a BIOS on a SCSI host adapter. If it finds a BIOS on a card, it uses it to provide support for the devices attached to the card, such as SCSI hard drives attached to a SCSI host adapter card. After doing these steps, your system boots.

There are many manufacturers of BIOSes. Three commonly used BIOSes are from: Award Software, Phoenix Software and American Megatrends.

Unless you know the settings in your CMOS and that your system is currently set up to boot from your CD-ROM drive, you need to do the following steps now.

Turn on your PC and watch carefully for a message that describes the key(s) to press to access the CMOS settings (such as Del, F1 or F2) and press these key(s).

In our example (Award BIOS), "Press Del to enter Setup" appears when the system boots, so the Del key is pressed and the CMOS SETUP UTILITY screen appears. You may need to hold down (rather than just press) the required key(s) when your system boots, to get to the CMOS SETUP UTILITY.

The opening screen of the CMOS SETUP UTILITY provides many different menu headings. There will be an indication somewhere on this screen of the keys to use to navigate from item to item and to exit and save your settings. Be very careful not to change any of the existing settings unless you need to. If you accidentally make a typo, then do the steps to exit out of the CMOS SETUP UTILITY without saving your changes.

In the steps below, you may need to change the boot sequence setting in your CMOS. Do not change any other system settings unless you need to. Remember that you can easily exit without saving your changes if you make a mistake.

Determining Your Memory from the CMOS

Select STANDARD CMOS SETUP (or equivalent). This screen shows the amount of memory in your system.

Look for the Total Memory setting. In our example, the Total Memory setting is 262,144K. This figure is in K (kilobytes). One kilobyte is 1,024 bytes and one megabyte is 1,048,576 bytes. To convert the figure shown (262,144K) to megabytes, first convert it from kilobytes to bytes (multiply by 1,024) and then convert it to megabytes (divide by 1,048,576).

For example, 262,144 (total memory in kilobytes) x 1,024 (bytes per kilobyte) = 268,435,456 (total bytes) / 1,048,576 (bytes per megabyte) = 256 MB.

Fill in the amount of memory in the space below.

Memory: _____ MB

IDE Drives for Hard Disk and CD-ROM Storage

The STANDARD CMOS SETUP screen shows the drives installed in your system.

Most current systems use one or more internal **IDE** hard drives and one IDE CD-ROM drive.

 IDE ("**I**ntegrated" **D**rive **E**lectronics) means that the drive has the *circuitry* of the drive controller integrated as part of the drive. This circuitry is attached to the outside of the drive, or is inside the drive, rather than being located on a controller inside of the system. These drives use the AT-API (a.k.a. AT Attachment Packet Interface, ATA) specification.

Most current systems have two IDE controllers to which IDE drives (hard disks or CD-ROM drives) can be attached. These two controllers are referred to as the Primary and Secondary controllers. Each controller can support two IDE drives.

The first drive on the Primary controller is called the "Master" (Primary Master) and the second drive is called the "Slave" (Primary Slave). The first drive on the Secondary controller is the Secondary Master and the second drive is the Secondary Slave.

In most x86 systems, the first hard disk is installed as the Primary Master (first device on the first controller) and the CD-ROM drive is installed as the Secondary Master (first device on the second controller). The CD-ROM drive is not usually installed as the Primary Slave (second device on the first controller).

The Size of hard disks that appears in the CMOS is usually in MB. For example, if the size is 62,750 MB, then the drive is 62.75 GB. If one of your drive types appears as "Auto", it is probably your CD-ROM drive.

For each of your IDE drives, specify the Type (User, Auto or None), Size, Cylinders, Heads, and Sectors below.

Primary Master: _____

Primary Slave: _____

Secondary Master: _____

Secondary Slave: _____

The above specifications include the size of your IDE drives, but they do not provide the size of any **partitions** that may be on them. You will do steps to view partition information later.

A **partition** is a "**part**" of a hard disk. One partition can take up a part of a hard disk or it can take up all of a hard disk. If a partition is just a part of a hard disk, then the partition operates as though it is a complete physical hard disk.

For example, if a hard disk has two partitions, then each partition operates as though it is a complete physical hard disk. The disk can operate as though it is two disks.

A partition is space on a hard disk that is created by a software utility or the installation routine of an operating system. After being created, it can be assigned a filesystem type (which specifies the type of files that can be put on it) and then it can be formatted. Once formatted, it can hold an operating system, program files and data files.

When a hard disk is partitioned into more than one partition, you can install more than one filesystem (including operating system) on it. A partition can contain a filesystem and an operating system that uses the filesystem, but it does not contain more than one filesystem or more than one operating system (unless some specialized software is used).

Floppy Disk Storage

The STANDARD CMOS SETUP screen also shows the number of floppy drives installed in your system, the drive letter used by the floppy and its capacity.

Most current PCs have one floppy drive named A: (in Windows) and this is a 1.44 MB drive that accepts 3.5" floppy disks. Beside the drive letter below, fill in the size of the drive in MB and in inches.

Drive A: _____

The STANDARD CMOS SETUP screen also shows the type of video (graphics) card installed in your system. In our example it shows "Video: EGA/VGA". This provides a bit of information regarding the card, but more information is needed.

Press Esc (or equivalent) to go back to the opening screen (main menu) of your CMOS SETUP UTILITY, but do not exit out of this utility yet.

Checking the Boot Sequence Setting in your CMOS

To boot from a CD in your CD-ROM drive or from a floppy disk in your floppy drive, you must have a "bootable" CD or floppy in the drive. A "bootable" CD or floppy is one that has been created so that your system can start (boot) with it.

The easiest way to start the Linux installation routine is by booting from the first Linux CD (CD 1).

If you cannot boot from CD 1, then you need to create a boot disk (floppy) and start the Linux installation routine by booting with this floppy. The floppy disk is used to boot the system and it automatically accesses CD 1 so that the opening screen of the installation routine appears. CD 1 must be in the CD-ROM drive when you boot with this floppy.

Once the opening screen of the installation routine appears, you can (usually) simply press Enter to run the installation routine and install Linux. To see if it is possible for your system to boot from a CD in your CD-ROM drive, you will now check the boot sequence in your CMOS.

The boot sequence specifies the order in which the devices in your system are checked, to see if the system can boot from them. If the boot sequence has not been set up to boot from your CD-ROM drive first, and if your system can be set up this way, you will change the boot sequence.

The most desirable boot sequence for our purposes is in the following order: CD-ROM drive, then drive A: and then drive C:. When your system is set up like this, it will try to boot from your CD-ROM drive first. If there is nothing in your CD-ROM drive, it will then try to boot from drive A:. If there is nothing in drive A:, it will then try to boot from your hard disk.

The boot sequence in the CMOS of your system will likely refer to the drive letters A: and C:. These are actually the names used by the Windows operating system to refer to the first floppy drive and the first partition on the first hard disk, respectively.

Remember that the first partition on the first hard disk may be the only partition on the disk and that it may include all of the hard disk. A Windows desktop system is typically installed so that all of the space on the first hard disk is one partition and this partition is referred to as drive C:.

Linux does not use drive letters to refer to floppy disks, hard disks, or partitions on hard disks; it uses device names.

For example, Linux refers to the first IDE hard disk as /dev/hda and the first partition on the first hard disk as /dev/hda1.

At the opening screen of the CMOS SETUP UTILITY select BIOS FEATURES SETUP (or equivalent heading) and then highlight the settings for "Boot Sequence" (or equivalent, such as "Boot Order" or "Boot Options"). Basically, you need to find the spot where you specify the boot sequence of your system.

If the settings for the Boot Sequence (or equivalent) heading are "CDROM, A, C" (or equivalent), then your system is set up to boot from CD-ROM, then drive A:, and then drive C:.

If you have a "bootable" CD in the CD-ROM drive, and if your CD-ROM *drive* is capable of booting from a CD, then when you start your system, it will boot from the CD.

However, on some systems, even if you can set up the CMOS to boot from the CD-ROM drive first, your CD-ROM *drive* may not be capable of booting from a CD! Some legacy CD-ROM drives cannot be used to boot a system from a bootable CD (even if you can set up the BIOS to boot from the CD-ROMdrive first.).

If the settings for Boot Sequence are "CDROM, A, C", and you have not made any changes to the settings in CMOS, then do the steps to exit out of the CMOS setup utility without saving your changes. After exiting, your system will likely reboot. If Windows is installed on your system, let this OS load. If not, turn the power off for now. Skip the next few paragraphs and go to the "CD-ROM Drive" heading.

If the Boot Sequence is not "CDROM, A, C", then change it to "CDROM, A, C". For example, to change a setting when using the Award BIOS, you press the Page Up and Page Down keys.

If your system is not using an Award BIOS, look for the keys that are used to modify the existing settings. Use these keys to set up your system so that it boots from your CD-ROM drive first. A setting of "CDROM, A, C" or "CDROM, C, A" will work, but the setting of "CDROM, A, C" is preferable because the system will try to boot from drive A: if it cannot boot from the CD-ROM drive.

If you cannot specify that your system boots from its CD-ROM drive, or if you cannot boot from your CD-ROM *drive*, then you must create a Linux boot floppy and boot with it to start the Linux installation routine.

Most SCSI host adapter cards have a BIOS and a system can be booted from a SCSI hard disk that is attached to one of these adapters. To do this, "SCSI" is specified at the start of the boot sequence in the CMOS of the system that contains the SCSI adapter.

For example, rather than having the boot sequence of "CDROM, A, C" as shown above, the system will have SCSI at the start of the boot sequence, as in "SCSI, A, C". This will allow a system to boot from a SCSI hard disk attached to a SCSI host adapter. Many servers only use SCSI hard disks and this boot sequence is used to boot them.

On a system that is only using SCSI hard disks, you may not be able to specify a boot sequence of "CDROM, SCSI, A" (to boot from CD before booting from a SCSI hard disk). In this situation, the system may be using a default boot sequence of "SCSI, A, C". In this case, you need to change the boot sequence in the CMOS to be "CDROM, A, C" and then boot from CD 1 to run the Linux installation routine. After the installation, you need to change the boot sequence back to "SCSI, A, C" so that the system can boot from a SCSI hard disk.

Do the steps to exit out of the CMOS SETUP UTILITY and save your changes. After exiting, your system will reboot. If Windows is installed on your system, let this OS load. If not, turn the power off for now.

CD-ROM Drive

Most x86 systems have a CD-ROM drive that is an IDE device. If your CD-ROM drive is IDE, then write "standard" beside the "CD-ROM Interface and Settings:" heading below.

If your CD-ROM drive is not an IDE drive, it will either be a SCSI CD-ROM drive or a proprietary CD-ROM drive (that uses a non-standard interface card that was designed by the CD-ROM manufacturer). Most current systems use a CD-ROM drive that is either an IDE or SCSI device.

If your CD-ROM is a SCSI device, write "SCSI" and the settings for it beside the heading below. See your CD-ROM drive manual for its settings and the steps to have it "seen" (accessed) by the Linux installation routine.

If your CD-ROM drive not IDE or SCSI, write "Other" and the settings for it below. See your CD-ROM drive manual for its settings and the steps to have it "seen" by Linux.

 If your CD-ROM drive is not connected via IDE or SCSI, it is a likely a legacy CD-ROM drive. See if Linux supports this drive by doing the steps described in the "Determining Hardware Compatibility and Getting the Drivers You Need" heading near the end of this Section. Then contact the manufacturer of the drive to find out how to have it "seen" by Linux.

CD-ROM Interface and Settings: _____

Video Graphics Card

Your graphics card is a circuit board in your computer that provides video output to your monitor.

If you have Windows installed on your system, boot to it now. Some of the hardware specifications that you need to fill in below can be seen from within Windows. If your hardware is working correctly, then the information seen in Windows should be correct.

If you do not have Windows installed on your system, you will need to get this information (from the manuals, invoice or manufacturer).

Even if you have Windows installed, you may need to get more information.

For example, let's say that you can find out the make and model of your monitor in Windows, but this make and model is not available in the Linux installation routine. In this situation, you will need to provide the installation routine with the name of a similar (compatible) monitor and also provide the horizontal and vertical scanning frequencies of your monitor.

The best and easiest place to get hardware specs is in the manual for the hardware component (if you can find it!). The invoice for a system (or a component of it), may provide the details that you require, but it may not be specific enough in many cases. If you can't get the info that you need from a manual or invoice, we recommend that you contact the manufacturer.

As another example, if you are not able to find the manual or invoice for a graphics card, you won't know who to call for its specs. Therefore, you will need to open your system and get the make and model off of the card. If this is necessary, write down the make and model of the card and also write down the information on the largest chip on your graphics card. Be sure to take the precautions mentioned earlier when handling hardware.

The largest chip on your graphics card may only state the model of the graphics card, but it may also specify a "chipset" name. Many graphics cards do not have or require a chipset.

A chipset is a set of chips that work together to provide some kind of additional functionality to your system. In the case of a graphics card, the chipset may provide accelerated speed or 3D capabilities. If there is a chipset specification on the largest chip on your graphics card, write it in the space provided beside "Graphics Card Chipset:" below.

Your graphics card probably has some amount of memory installed on it. The amount of memory is not always obvious when looking at the card. Use one of the methods described (i.e. manual, invoice, or manufacturer) to get the amount of memory on your graphics card.

There are many different versions of Windows, but they are all similar. When we are describing the steps to do tasks with Windows, you will be provided with a "generic" set of steps. These steps will work with most versions of Windows. If these steps do not work for your version, use the Help system in Windows to determine how to do a task.

If you have Windows installed, do the following steps to get to the Device Manager and see some of the settings that are required below.

> My Computer icon x r (right-click on My Computer) ; Properties ;
>
> > for Windows 95 or 98: Device Manager tab.
> >
> > for other Windows versions: Hardware tab ; Device Manager button.

To see your graphics card make and model:

> click on the "+" (plus sign) beside Display adapters to "expand" this item ;
>
> your display adapter name (graphics card name) will now appear ;
>
> adapter name x r ; Properties.

Write the make and model below. If a chipset name appears, also write it down below. If a chipset name does not appear, simply do not specify a chipset during the Linux installation.

If the amount of memory on the card appears, write this down as well. If the amount of memory does not appear, find out the amount from one of the sources (i.e. manual, invoice, manufacturer). You need to specify the correct amount of graphics card memory to the installation routine.

> Graphics Card Make and Model: _____
>
> Graphics Card Chipset: _____
>
> Graphics Card Memory: _____ MB

Click on Cancel to close the dialog box for your adapter.

To find out the settings of your graphics card, you did several steps above to view the properties of your graphics card in the Device Manager (in Windows).

When filling in the blanks below, you may need to look at the settings of other items in the Device Manager. When you need to repeat the above steps for another device, we will simply say: "Use the Device Manager to view the properties of your (device name)."

Video Monitor

You can usually get the make and model of a monitor from the outside of it. However, if you cannot, do the steps below.

Use the Device Manager to view the properties of your monitor. The setting here may simply show "**Plug and Play** Monitor". If not, write the settings for your monitor below.

An interface card requires certain settings. such as interrupt, I/O port and DMA channel, so that it can be "seen" by a system. These settings allow the system to access the card and use it. *These settings are described in the next section.*

Current "**P**lug-a**n**d-**P**lay" (a.k.a. **PnP**) interface cards are automatically configured (have the settings made for them) when a system boots and are therefore automatically "seen" by a system.

Non-PnP (legacy) cards need to be configured manually so that a system can "see" the card and use it. They are configured with switches, jumpers or via software (by running a small program and specifying the settings for the card).

Current PnP cards do not need to have any settings specified via switches, jumpers or software in order for them to be "seen".

Plug-and-Play (PnP) technology came into existence in 1993, but it took time for this technology to evolve and become reliable. Therefore, some early PnP cards could still be configured manually via switches, jumpers or software, in case the card was not automatically "seen" by a system. PnP did not become fully adopted and reliable until around 1996.

In summary, non-PnP cards need to be configured manually; some early PnP cards (up to about 1996) could be configured manually; and current PnP cards do not need to be configured manually.

Remember that if the make and model number of your monitor does not appear (on a list) in the Linux installation routine, you will need to accept a generic monitor or specify the make and model of a similar (compatible) monitor. In addition to this, you will need to specify the horizontal and vertical scanning frequencies of your monitor. If you have these two frequencies, write them down below.

Even if you know the make and model of a monitor that is *similar* in specs to yours, you must be sure that you do not select a monitor that has "higher" (scanning frequency) specs than yours. If you do, **you may damage or destroy your monitor.**

Monitor Make and Model: _____

Horizontal Scanning Frequency: _____

Vertical Scanning Frequency: _____

Mouse

When you run the Linux installation routine later in this chapter, it will "autoprobe" your system to try to determine your mouse port and type. It can usually detect the correct make and model of a "standard" mouse. If you are using a common two button mouse, simply write "Standard" beside make and model below. If you have a "non-standard" mouse, write the make and model below.

Mouse Make and Model: _____

Your mouse "type" can also be determined by the "port" (connector) at the back of the system to which it is attached. To determine your mouse "type", look at where it is connected to your computer. Most laptop computers use a setting of "PS/2 compatible".

An AT mouse port (legacy) is round and connects with five pins.

A PS/2 mouse port (current and common) is round and connects with six pins.

A Serial mouse port is not round and connects with nine pins.

A USB mouse port is rectangular and does not connect with pins.

If necessary, use the Device Manager to view the properties of your mouse. In addition to the make and model, the General tab shows you the "Location:". This will indicate the method of communication being used by the mouse. If COM1, COM2, COM3 or COM4 appears beside "Location:", then your "Mouse Port Type" (as requested below) is "Serial".

Mouse Port Type (AT, PS/2, Serial or USB): _____

If you are using a serial mouse, underline the port name and number below that the mouse is using. The port name and number is often shown beside the port (at the back of the system).

Serial Port: COM1, COM2, COM3 or COM4

Keyboard

The Linux installation routine will also "autoprobe" your system to try to determine your keyboard and can usually detect the correct settings for it. If you are using a "standard" keyboard, simply write "Standard" beside make and model below. If you have a "non-standard" keyboard, write the make and model below.

Keyboard Make and Model: _____

Modem

If your system has a modem, write the make and model of it below and then select the serial port that it is using.

If necessary, use the Device Manager to view the properties of your modem. In addition to the modem make and model, one of the "tabs" in the Device Manager, such as the Modem tab, will show you the serial port being used by your modem.

Modem Make and Model: _____

Serial Port: COM1, COM2, COM3 or COM4

Network Interface Card

Most current x86 systems that have network interface cards (NICs) are using PnP cards. If you are using a PnP network card, then simply write "PnP" beside the "NIC Make and Model:" heading below. The installation routine will automatically detect the card and install the required software support for it.

If you are using a non-PnP (legacy) network card, you will need to fill in the settings for it below. If you do not have the settings, you may need to run some software that came with the card to get its settings or look at the settings on the card. You may also need to look at the manual for the card to interpret the jumper or switch settings that you see on the card.

If necessary, use the Device Manager to view the properties of your network card. Select the Resources tab to view the I/O Range, Memory Range, IRQ (a.k.a. interrupt) and any other settings.

NIC Make and Model: _____

I/O Range: _____

Memory Range: _____

IRQ: _____

Other Settings: _____

SCSI Devices and SCSI Hard Disk Storage

SCSI (Small Computer System Interface, pronounced "scuzzy") devices are internal and external devices that are attached to an internal or external SCSI port in a system. Most SCSI devices are hard disks, but they can also be other devices, such as a CD-ROM drive or scanner.

Most workstation (desktop) PCs that are being used to run business applications use IDE hard disks and do not use SCSI hard disks. *However, many Linux servers use SCSI hard drives to provide them with fast, reliable and huge storage capabilities*. Therefore, SCSI devices, including SCSI hard disks are described in (quite a bit of) detail below. ***Keep in mind that the description below is a general description of SCSI devices***. See the manufacturer's manuals for specifics on installing and configuring SCSI devices.

 SCSI technology has been around for many years. There are countless different "types" and "standards" (combinations and permutations) of SCSI cards and SCSI devices that have been created by a variety of different manufacturers. Some examples of these "types" or "standards" are: SCSI-1, SCSI-2, Wide SCSI, Ultra SCSI and Wide Ultra SCSI. The discussion below gives you a general overview of SCSI components.

The specifics for installing a SCSI host adapter (a.k.a. card, interface, controller) and for installing internal and external SCSI devices are provided in the documentation that is supplied with this hardware.

There are internal and external SCSI devices. Internal SCSI devices, such as internal hard disks, are installed inside of a system and attach via a single cable to a port inside the system. External SCSI devices, such as hard disks and scanners attach via a series of cables to a port at the back of a system.

A SCSI host adapter (card) is a hard disk controller that has its own BIOS and typically has one port for internal devices (an internal port) at the side of it and one port for external devices (an external port) at the end of it (allowing a cable to be attached to it at the back of the system).

If a SCSI hard disk controller is built into a system, then the system typically also has one internal port and one external port (but may have more than one of each).

SCSI internal and external devices such as hard disks, CD-ROM drives and scanners, are connected to one another in a "series" or "daisy chain". Internal devices are connected in series by a *single* flat cable and external devices are connected in series by *multiple* round cables.

The Internal SCSI Port and Internal SCSI Devices

One or two *internal* SCSI devices can be attached to an internal SCSI port. Internal SCSI devices have one location for a cable to connect and external devices have two locations for a cable to connect.

A "ribbon" (flat) cable connects to the internal SCSI port (on a card or built into the system) and runs to the single location at the back of the first device and then runs to the single location at the back of the second device (if there is one). This is a series or "daisy chain" of devices. The second device does not attach directly to the internal SCSI port; it attaches via cable to the first device and the first device attaches via the same cable to the internal SCSI port.

The External SCSI Port and External SCSI Devices

All external SCSI devices connect in series to an external SCSI port at the back of a system. Unlike internal devices, multiple external devices connect via multiple cables, rather than with a single cable that runs from one device to another. For external devices, a cable runs from an external SCSI port (on a card or built into the system) to the first device and another cable runs from the first device to the second device and so on.

Each external SCSI device has two locations at the back to which cables can be attached. The "first" location is for the cable that is coming from the external SCSI port (or from another device). The "second" location is for a cable that goes to the next device.

For example, a cable is connected to an external SCSI port (on a card or built into the system) and is then connected to the "first" location at the back of the first SCSI device in the series. To connect the next device, another cable is connected to the "second" location at the back of the first device. This cable is then run to the "first" location at the back of the second device. Each additional SCSI device is connected in series this way (in a "daisy chain").

Terminating an Internal or External Series of Devices

When using SCSI devices, the last device in an internal or external series of devices must be "terminated" so that the system knows where the series ends.

For internal devices, a switch or jumper on the last device is used to specify the end (terminate) the series.

For external devices, a terminator can be a physical device that you attach to the "second" location on the last device in the series. However, most external SCSI devices have a simple jumper or switch marked "Terminator" or "Term" and show the settings of Off and On. To terminate the last device, simply move the Term jumper or switch to On.

When installing SCSI devices, always check that only the last device in an internal or external series is terminated. The other devices should not be terminated.

Let's say, for example, that you have two external SCSI devices that you need to connect. The first one is a large external hard disk and the second is a CD-ROM burner.

Your system does not have a SCSI controller built into it, so you install a SCSI card in your system. You then connect one end of a SCSI cable to the end of the card (at the back of the system) and connect the other end of the cable to the "first" location on the external hard disk. After this, you connect one end of *another* cable to the "second" location of the external hard disk and connect the other end to the "first" location on the CD-ROM burner. The CD-ROM burner is the last device in the series.

If the CD-ROM burner has a "Terminator" or "Term" jumper or switch, you move it to the On position. If it does not, then you attach a terminator to the "second" location on the CD-ROM burner. The hard disk does not get terminated.

To Terminate or Not to Terminate (the SCSI Card)

If you are using a SCSI card (rather than a SCSI controller that is built into the system) then you need to either terminate the card or not terminate the card, as described below.

If you only have an internal series of SCSI devices, or if you only have an external series of SCSI devices, then the SCSI card needs to be terminated. The termination on the card indicates the end of either the internal or external series of devices.

If you have both internal and external SCSI devices, then the SCSI card does not need to be terminated and should not be terminated. The terminator at the end of the series of internal devices and the one at the end of the series of external devices indicates the ends of the entire series of devices.

If you are using a SCSI controller that is built into a system (rather than a SCSI card) then you may also need to specify a terminator setting inside of your system. See your system manual for more information.

General SCSI Device Specifications

If you are using a SCSI card (rather than internal SCSI controller) for your series of SCSI devices, it can be an 8-bit (regular SCSI) or 16-bit device (wide SCSI). If you have an 8-bit host adapter (card), your SCSI devices are 8-bit and are called "regular" SCSI. If you have a 16-bit host adapter, then your SCSI devices are called "wide" SCSI devices. An 8-bit SCSI card can support eight devices and a 16-bit SCSI card can support sixteen devices.

A SCSI host adapter uses an IRQ (interrupt) setting and an I/O address setting, but the devices attached to it do not. Each SCSI device, such as a hard disk or CD-ROM burner, is assigned a number that is used by the system to access the device. Regular SCSI devices use the numbers 0 through 7 and wide SCSI devices use the numbers 0 through 15.

You specify the number of the SCSI device *right on the device itself* or use SCAM software.

To specify the number on a SCSI device (when not using SCAM), jumpers or switches are used to indicate the number of the device.

SCAM stands for **SCSI Configured Automatically** and is a part of the "Plug-and-Play" (PnP) specification. It allows the device numbers of SCSI devices to be specified by software, rather than by using jumpers or switches on the device itself. All SCSI components that are a part of a system (the SCSI card and all internal and external SCSI devices) must support SCAM in order for it to be used.

As described above, an 8-bit SCSI card can support eight devices and a 16-bit SCSI card can support sixteen devices. However, when counting the number of SCSI devices that you can have, the SCSI card is counted as one of the devices. Therefore, you can have an additional seven devices attached to an 8-bit SCSI card and an additional fifteen attached to a 16-bit SCSI card. There are also SCSI cards that have two controllers and can support up to thirty (2x15) devices.

When using 8-bit SCSI and a 16-bit SCSI cards (that have only one controller), and assigning numbers to SCSI devices, the number seven has the highest priority of all numbers and is reserved for use by the SCSI card. The device numbers for SCSI devices go from highest priority to lowest, in the following order: 7, 6, 5, 4, 3, 2, 1, 0 and then 15, 14, 13, 12, 11, 10, 9, 8 (think of this as 7 down to 0 and then 15 down to 8).

If you are using Windows and have a "legacy" SCSI host adapter (non-PnP), you may be able to see some settings for it in files named AUTOEXEC.BAT and CONFIG.SYS in the root of drive C:. To look for these settings, run Windows and then run Notepad. Open AUTOEXEC.BAT and CONFIG.SYS and look for a line for the settings of your SCSI host adapter that shows PORT=, IRQ= and DMA=. The number beside PORT= is the number of the I/O Address, the number beside IRQ= is the interrupt and the number beside DMA= is the DMA channel.

 If you have a legacy SCSI host adapter, see if Linux supports it by doing the steps described in the "Determining Hardware Compatibility and Getting the Drivers You Need" heading near the end of this section. Then contact the manufacturer to find out how to have it "seen" by Linux.

If you have a legacy SCSI host adapter, write the settings for it below:

SCSI Host Adapter Settings: _____

Current SCSI host adapters have their own BIOS and the settings in it are read at the "hardware level" when the system boots. The devices attached to the host adapter are numbered as described above and are automatically detected by the system so that they can be used. Access to the SCSI BIOS is provided by pressing one or more keys, in the same way as pressing the Del key provides access to the CMOS SETUP UTILITY when you are using an Award BIOS.

If you have specified "SCSI" at the start of the boot sequence in the BIOS of a system, then the system can boot from a hard disk attached to the SCSI card.

As described above, many servers use SCSI hard disks. Some of these servers have SCSI cards installed in them and some have SCSI controllers built into them. Many systems that have been specifically designed to be servers have SCSI controllers (or RAID controllers, described below) built into them and do not require a SCSI card. A system with a built-in SCSI controller is configured to boot from a SCSI hard disk attached to it.

Although SCSI devices are typically found in server systems, some high-end workstations, such as those used in video production, also have built-in SCSI controllers.

RAID Hard Disk Storage

RAID (Redundant Array of Independent Disks) is a technology that is commonly used in systems that are working as Linux servers.

A system that is using RAID contains two or more regular IDE or SCSI hard disks. These disks may be attached to a standard IDE or SCSI controller or they may be attached to a specialized hard disk controller (RAID controller) that implements one or more of the features of RAID technology.

RAID technology exists in RAID hard disk controllers (hardware), but can also be achieved by using software (when standard IDE or SCSI controllers are used). The software method does not provide the same level of performance as the hardware method.

The features of RAID technology are: increased performance due to disk striping, fault tolerance due to disk mirroring, and the capability of using of these two features (through several methods) in various combinations and permutations (referred to as "levels").

Disk striping dramatically increases system performance by reading from, and writing to, multiple hard disks in the same system at the same time.

Fault tolerance is the capability of a system to be able to withstand errors (to be tolerant of faults). In this case, we are talking about hard disk errors or hard disk failures. Fault tolerance is achieved through disk "mirroring", which is having data on one disk "mirrored" (saved to) another disk.

The benefit of fault tolerance is that if a hard disk error or hard disk failure occurs on one disk and data cannot be read from it, or written to it, then it can be read from, or written to, another disk. Disk mirroring requires one or more addition drives in a system and therefore increases the cost of the system.

RAID has several "levels" that are represented by the numbers 0, 1, 2, 3, 4, 5, 6 and 10. Each level represents one or more of the features being used and also the method by which the features are being implemented.

For example, level 0 uses disk striping, but does not use disk mirroring and level 1 uses disk mirroring, but not disk striping. The RAID level that is used for a system is dependent on what the system will be used for and the expense that can be justified (the depth of the pockets).

In some configurations (levels), RAID controllers allow you to "hot swap" (change while the system is running) a defective drive with a new one.

A RAID (hard disk) controller can either be installed as a card in a system or be built into a system. High-end servers have RAID controllers built into them and often use SCSI hard disks.

 RAID technology was originally created in the late 1980s. At that time, the relatively inexpensive PC hard disks that were being used in RAID systems were being compared to the very expensive hard disks being used by mini and mainframe computers. So, **RAID** originally stood for **R**edundant **A**rray of **I**nexpensive **D**isks. Since that time, the acronym has been changed to mean **R**edundant **A**rray of **I**ndependent **D**isks.

For more information on RAID, go to the web site of the RAID Advisory Board at: http://www.raid-advisory.com

Sound Card

If you have a PnP sound card, simply write PnP beside the "Sound Card Settings:" heading below.

If you are using a non-PnP (legacy) sound card, write the settings below. If you do not have the settings, you may need to run some software that came with the card to get its settings or look at the settings on the card. You may also need to look at the manual for the card to interpret the jumper or switch settings that you see on the card.

If necessary, use the Device Manager and look at "Sound, video and game controllers" or look at the contents of AUTOEXEC.BAT and CONFIG.SYS and look for a line for your sound card that shows PORT=, IRQ= and DMA=. The number beside PORT= is the number of the I/O Address, the number beside IRQ= is the interrupt and the number beside DMA= is the DMA channel.

Write the settings for your sound card below.

Sound Card Settings: _____

Support for a sound card is installed the first time a system is booted after the Linux OS installation. If you are using a "standard" PnP sound card, it will automatically be detected and your system will be able to access it.

If your PnP sound card cannot be detected, or if you are using a legacy sound card, then you must supply the settings of your sound card (I/O address, IRQ and DMA channel).

Determining Hardware Compatibility and Getting the Drivers You Need

If you have "standard" and current x86 components, then they will likely be detected and selected by the Linux installation routine, or you can select them from a list during the installation routine, and they will work just fine.

Many x86 hardware components are supported by the software drivers that are included with a Linux distribution. Unless you have legacy or unusual hardware components and know that your hardware is *not* supported as part of your Linux distribution, we recommend that you run the installation routine of your distribution and try to install support for all of your devices.

If you have a legacy or unusual hardware component that is not detected correctly and the make and model of it (or a compatible equivalent) cannot be selected from a list, then go to the web site below to see if the hardware is compatible with Linux.

A Linux Hardware Compatibility List (HCL) is available at:

http://en.tldp.org/HOWTO/Hardware-HOWTO/index.html

The end of this HCL shows hardware that is specifically not compatible with Linux.

If the hardware component in question is compatible, then get information on installing it from the web site of your distribution or the web site of the manufacturer.

If your hardware does not appear on the HCL (as compatible or incompatible), then check for it at the web site of your distribution or the web site of the manufacturer.

Section Review

1. Which of the following statements are correct regarding RAID technology (choose two).

   ☐ A. it has increased security due to parity extraction
   ☐ B. it has increased performance due to disk striping
   ☐ C. it has fault tolerance due to disk mirroring
   ☐ D. it has decreased rotational errors due to load balancing

2. By default, Linux allows you to have more than one filesystem in the same partition and to run two operating systems at the same time. T F

3. The most desirable boot sequence in the CMOS for installing Linux is:

   ○ A. A, C, CDROM
   ○ B. CDROM, A, C
   ○ C. C, A, CDROM
   ○ D. SCSI, A, C

4. Plug and Play (PnP) interface cards are automatically "seen" by a system and are automatically configured when a system boots. However, the PnP technology does not always work properly for some legacy PnP cards and they still have to be configured manually. T F

5. The term "x86" is used to refer to:

   ○ A. the model number of a BIOS
   ○ B. a family of CPUs
   ○ C. the year that PnP technology was invented
   ○ D. a standard hard disk rotation speed

6. A partition that is only using a part of a hard disk operates as though it is a complete physical hard disk. T F

7. Select two correct statements regarding SCSI devices.

   ☐ A. they can be hard disks, CD-ROM drives and scanners
   ☐ B. they are uniquely identified by double drive letters, starting with CC
   ☐ C. both ends of a series of devices must be terminated
   ☐ D. they all conform to a single standard that is specified by the SCSI Controller Board

8. If a Windows partition exists on a system, it is automatically removed when you install Linux. T F

9. Which of the following statements are true regarding IDE drives (choose two)?

   ☐ A. they connect to the hard disk controller with multiple terminators
   ☐ B. the first drive on the Primary controller is called the Primary Master
   ☐ C. they can be connected to a RAID controller
   ☐ D. an IDE CD-ROM drive is typically attached to the Master Slave

10. In some configurations (levels), RAID controllers allow you to "hot swap" a defective drive with a new one. T F

11. If a system on which you need to install Linux cannot boot from a CD, then it needs to boot from:

   ○ A. drive A:
   ○ B. drive D:
   ○ C. a SCSI scandisk device
   ○ D. a RAID partition merger

12. If the make and model of your monitor does not appear in the Linux installation routine, then you can select a similar model, even if it has "higher" (scanning frequency) specs than yours. The installation routine will automatically install software that will prevent any damage that could be caused to your monitor. T F

Interface Card Types and Methods of Hardware Communication

Topics Covered in this Section

Learn the specifications of different types of interface cards
Discuss the methods of connecting devices to an x86 system
Detail the methods of hardware communication including interrupts,
I/O addressing and DMA Channels
Provide the device names and settings for serial and parallel ports
Describe the system information text files in the /proc directory

In this section, you will learn about different interface card types, how they communicate with a system and the settings that they require. Some hardware devices attach to a system via interface cards and some can be attached via other methods. You will also learn about these other methods.

Interface Card Types

There are many different types of interface cards that can be installed in an x86 system. Some of these are used for video display, modem, network and sound. These cards connect to your system by being installed in slots in the **bus** of the system.

 The **bus** is a data transfer channel inside of your computer. It is used to provide communication between the devices in it. Interface cards are installed in slots in the system and this connects them to the bus and allows them to communicate with the system.

General Interface Card Information

As mentioned earlier, Linux does not have demanding hardware requirements and so you may end up installing and maintaining it on "older" (legacy) systems. Even though some of the cards described below are rare, you may encounter them when installing Linux on a legacy system.

Several different interface cards are described below. Of these, the EISA, MCA and VL-Bus are now considered legacy hardware and are rarely found in use. ISA cards are still used in lots of existing systems, but current x86 systems are typically only using PCI and AGP cards. These systems use PCI cards for many different functions, such as modems and network cards, and typically use an AGP card for video display. All PCI and AGP cards are PnP (Plug-and-Play) cards.

Interface cards can generally be described as being PnP or non-PnP (legacy) cards. Both of these types of interface cards use interrupts (a.k.a. IRQs), DMA channels and I/O addresses as the three methods of communicating with the system in which they are installed. These methods are described below.

As described earlier, PnP cards are automatically "seen" by a system, and the settings for them (IRQ, DMA and I/O) are automatically configured by a system when it boots.

Non-PnP cards must be manually configured via dip switches, jumpers or software. The dip switches and jumpers used to specify the settings are located on the card. Settings that can be made via software are made using software provided by the manufacturer of the card. To make these settings you run a small program and specify the settings (IRQ, DMA and I/O) for the card.

Installing Interface Cards

Documentation for an interface card should be provided to you by its manufacturer. This is usually a small manual or sheet of paper that provides specific information regarding how the card should be physically installed in your system. For non-PnP cards, the documentation will also specify the settings that the card requires and how to make the settings (via switches, jumpers or software). If you do not have any documentation for a card, contact the manufacturer.

In addition to documentation, an interface card often includes software drivers from the manufacturer that provide support for various OSes. These drivers provide the software interface between an OS and the card, so that the OS can use the card.

For example, a graphics card may include a diskette or CD that contains drivers for Linux (and also for various versions of other OSes).

The Linux OS (files supplied with a distribution) includes drivers for many common makes and models of interface cards and other hardware components. If a card (or other hardware component, such as a monitor) conforms to the specifications of a common make and model of component, such as a popular graphics card, then the driver software that is supplied with the card may not be required. You may be able to install support for the component by selecting an existing similar (compatible) make and model.

If you can select the make and model of a hardware component during the Linux installation process, then the driver file(s) that you require are included with your distribution and will be installed by the installation routine.

If you are using a non-standard component, then you may need to supply Linux with the driver software for it.

The information below gives an overview of interface card types and shows a graphic for each card so that you can identify each type.

 Interface cards are most easily distinguished from one another by the "edge connector". This is the part at the bottom of the card that fits into a slot to connect the card to the bus. In the graphics below, notice the difference in length, depth and the number of edge connectors in the box marked "Edge Connector Area".

Inside an x86 system, the ISA slots (in the bus) are typically black, PCI slots are white and AGP slots are brown.

ISA Cards

ISA (Industry Standard Architecture, pronounced "eye-suh") cards are 8-bit or 16-bit cards that were introduced early in the IBM PC era. They operate at 8-10 MHz.

There are still lots of older systems that are currently using 16-bit ISA cards. Many newer systems do not have slots in the bus for ISA cards and these cards are no longer sold in new systems. Some ISA cards, manufactured at the end of the ISA "era", had PnP (Plug-and-Play) capabilities. PnP did not always work for these cards and so their settings sometimes had to be made manually (via switches, jumpers or software).

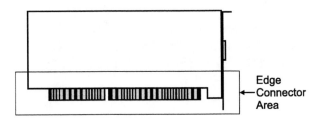

Figure 2-1: ISA Card

Edge
← Connector
Area

MCA Cards

MCA (Microchannel Architecture) cards were used in the IBM PS/2 model of computer and some other models. MCA cards were a part of IBM's proprietary Microchannel Architecture and were discontinued in 1996. These are legacy 32-bit cards that operate at 5-20 MHz.

Figure 2-2: MCA Card

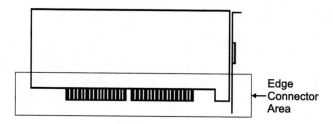

EISA Cards

EISA (Extended Industry Standard Architecture, pronounced "ee-suh") cards were introduced in 1988 by a group of nine large computer manufacturers to compete with the proprietary Microchannel architecture (MCA) of the IBM PS/2 computer. ISA cards can also be inserted into an EISA slot. These are legacy 32-bit cards that operate at 8-10 MHz.

Figure 2-3: EISA Card

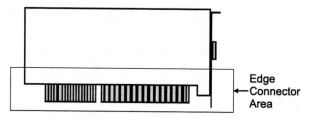

VESA Local-Bus

VESA (Video Electronics Standards Association) Local-Bus (a.k.a. VL-Bus) cards were mostly used in 486 systems. They were introduced to provide greater speed than ISA cards. These are legacy 32-bit cards that operate at up to 50 MHz.

Figure 2-4: VESA Local-Bus

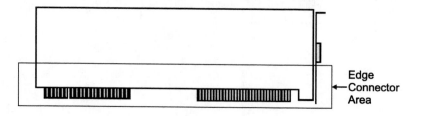

PCI Cards

PCI (Peripheral Component Interconnect) cards came into common use around 1996 when 486 computers were being produced. PCI cards are 32-bit and 64-bit PnP cards.

PCI cards use PnP and are easy to install because their settings are automatically configured when a system boots. These cards allow interrupts to be shared with other PCI cards. PCI cards are the "standard" card in use today, along with an AGP card for video display.

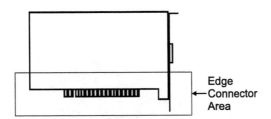

Figure 2-5: PCI Card

AGP Cards

AGP (Accelerated Graphics Port) cards are a standard type of PnP graphics card. They allow for direct communication between the memory of the system and the card. Current computers often have a slot specifically for an AGP (graphics) card, which leaves an additional slot for a PCI card. These are 32-bit PnP cards.

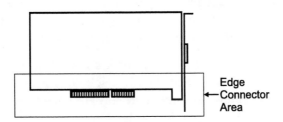

Figure 2-6: AGP Card

PCMCIA Card

PCMCIA (Personal Computer Memory Card International Association) cards (a.k.a. PC Card) are "plug-and-play" (via Card and Socket Services software) peripheral devices that are about the size of a credit card. They were introduced in 1989 to provide the capability of easily adding peripherals to portable computers, such as laptop and notebook computers.

PCMCIA Cards are available as many types of devices, including solid state hard disks, modems and network interface cards. These are 16-bit and 32-bit cards and most are "**hot swappable**".

 "Hot swappable" means that you can attach or detach ("swap") a device while your system is running (while it is "hot").

When you insert a PCMCIA card into a Linux system that is running (and has had the software components required to support the card installed), then the OS (kernel) will detect it and automatically load the driver for it (theoretically). If the card is not detected, then you will need to reboot your system to have the device "seen".

Figure 2-7: PCMCIA Card

Other Methods of Connecting Devices to an x86 System

An interface card is inserted into the bus of a system and includes some type of functionality on the card, or it allows one or more devices to attach to a system.

For example, an internal modem is a device on a card that is inserted into a slot in the bus. It is a card to which a phone line is attached, but other devices do not attach to it. In contrast, a graphics card is not a device, but it allows a device (a monitor) to be attached to a system.

USB and IEEE 1394 are bus types that provide a port at the back of a system to which multiple additional devices can be attached. Devices, such as scanners, digital cameras and video equipment are not attached to these bus types via slots, they are attached via a cable that is plugged into the USB or IEEE 1394 port. Devices that attach to these ports are "hot swappable" (theoretically).

To connect more than one device to a USB or IEEE 1394 port, you can attach a hub (that is like a "splitter box") to the port. You run a cable between the port and the hub and then the hub provides several ports to which devices can attach. Some monitors have hubs built in to them. By attaching a device to this type of monitor, you are actually attaching the device to the hub that is built in to the monitor.

USB Port

USB (Universal Serial Bus) was introduced in 1997 as a method of connecting up to 127 low-speed devices to an x86 system. On current systems, the keyboard and mouse use the Universal Serial Bus and attach via their own ports (which are connected to the USB bus). Other devices are attached via two USB ports at the back of a system.

Current x86 systems have two small rectangular USB ports at the back to which external devices can be attached. If you need to connect more than two USB devices, you can use a USB hub. You can attach a printer, digital camera, scanner and other devices to this type of bus via this port. The port can be identified by a small graphic beside it, as shown in Figure 2-8. This graphic also appears on the ends of cables that attach to USB ports. This is not the logo of the artist that was formerly nameless.

Figure 2-8: USB Port graphic

IEEE 1394 Port

IEEE 1394 is a standard that defines a type of bus, similar to USB, to which several different types of devices, including scanners, digital cameras and video equipment can attach. It supports up to 63 devices.

 IEEE (**I**nstitute of **E**lectrical and **E**lectronics **E**ngineers) is a standards organization. It develops specifications for computer hardware and communications systems. Each standard that is created is assigned a number, such as the number "1394" in "IEEE 1394".

Apple Computer, Inc. owns the trademark for the name FireWire, which conforms to the IEEE 1394 standard. Until early in 2002, Apple required a fee for the use of the word "FireWire". Therefore, FireWire is usually referred to as an IEEE 1394 port (rather than FireWire), when referring to this type of bus on an x86 (non-Apple) system.

Sony refers to IEEE 1394 with the name i.Link and it is also referred to as **HPSB** (**H**igh **P**erformance **S**erial **B**us) by other companies.

In summary, IEEE 1394 is known as FireWire, i.link and HPSB.

Some models of Apple computers support FireWire and have this type of port built into them. An IEEE 1394 bus (port) can be added to an x86 system by installing an interface card for it.

Avoiding Conflicts Between Interface Cards

x86 systems communicate with interface cards through the use of interrupts, Input/Output addresses and DMA channels .

When you install a PnP card in a system, the system should recognize the card and automatically configure the settings for it so that it will be "seen" by the system.

When you install a *non-PnP* (legacy) interface card in a system, it is important to configure its settings to avoid conflicts with existing components. A conflict occurs when two components are using the same number for an interrupt, I/O address or DMA channel.

Interrupt Assignments

Interrupt Request Line (**a.k.a. IRQ**). is one of the methods of communication between your system and an interface card, or between your system and a device that is built into your system. It is a number that represents a "request line" (as in: line of communication) that is used to request the use of a device.

Sixteen IRQs are available in current x86 systems. The table below shows the use of IRQ numbers and the items that are usually accessed by each number.

Table 2-1 "Standard" IRQ Assignments

IRQ	Device Name
0	System Timer
1	Keyboard
2	Redirected to IRQ 9
3	COM2 or COM4 Serial Ports
4	COM1 or COM3 Serial Ports
5	LPT2 (second printer port) and some sound cards
6	Floppy Disk Controller
7	LPT1 (first printer port)
8	Realtime clock
9	Redirected from IRQ 2
10	Available
11	Available
12	PS/2 Mouse
13	Math Coprocessor
14	Primary AT-API Hard Disk Controller
15	Secondary AT-API Hard Disk Controller

COM1, COM2, COM3 and COM4 are the DOS/Windows names for serial ports. These names appear in the above Table beside interrupts 3 and 4. LPT1 and LPT2 also appear in the above Table and these are the DOS/Windows names for parallel printer ports.

In the Table above, the devices shown for the IRQs of 0, 1, 8, 13, 14 and 15 are usually the same in all systems. The USB bus typically uses IRQ 9 or 11.

If an IRQ is not being used by a device, it may be used for an interface card that you are installing.

For example, most systems only use one printer and only need one printer port. Current systems also usually have a sound card. Therefore, IRQ 5 is typically used for a sound card, rather than a second printer port (rather than for LPT2, see IRQ 5 in Table 2-1).

However, if you are setting up a server, which does not typically require a sound card, but may require an additional printer, then this interrupt may be used for a second parallel port (to which a printer is attached) or for a different device.

 IRQs are sometimes shown as hexadecimal numbers, such as when being viewed in the CMOS of a system or in a software utility. These are numbers that are based on a 16 digit numbering system (represented by the decimal numbers 0 through 15) rather than the standard 10 digit system (using 0 through 9).

When hex (hexadecimal) numbers are used, the numbers above 9 appear as letters. In hex, the decimal number 10 is represented by the letter A, 11 is B, 12 is C, 13 is D, 14 is E and 15 is F. Hex numbers above 9 are also represented by the lower case letters a through f.

For example, if you are looking at the setting for a device in CMOS, or in a software utility, and see that it is using an IRQ of E (or e), then it is using interrupt 14.

Two legacy (non-PnP) interface cards cannot usually use the same interrupt request line. If two legacy cards are set up to use the same interrupt, then this usually causes a "conflict" and neither device can be accessed. To avoid the conflict (when using a non-PnP card), change the interrupt of one of the devices.

For example, you have a serial mouse attached to the COM1 serial port (IRQ 4) and the COM2 serial port (IRQ 3) is not being used. You install an internal (non-PnP) modem that is set up to use the *manufacturer's default* setting of COM1 (IRQ 4), which is already in use by your mouse. You boot your system and try to use the modem to dial out. It does not work because there is a conflict between the two devices. They are both trying to use the same interrupt (IRQ 4). To remedy this problem, simply change the setting of the modem (using switches, jumpers or software) so that it uses COM2 (IRQ 3), which is not being used.

Viewing Interrupts from within Linux

Once you have installed Linux, you can see the IRQ settings of your system in the text file named interrupts, in the directory named /proc (/proc/interrupts). If you need to add a non-PnP device that requires an interrupt, this file shows you the interrupts that have been used so that you can select one that is available. An example of the contents of /proc/interrupts is shown below.

```
        CPU0
  0:  2886567    XT-PIC    timer
  1:    10635    XT-PIC    keyboard
  2:        0    XT-PIC    cascade
  5:        0    XT-PIC    EMU10K1
  8:        1    XT-PIC    rtc
 10:    10437    XT-PIC    usb-uhci, eth0
 12:    19933    XT-PIC    PS/2 Mouse
 14:    19532    XT-PIC    ide0
 15:   444018    XT-PIC    ide1
NMI:        0
ERR:        0
```

Most of the output of /proc/interrupts above is described in Table 2-1. In addition to this, IRQ 5 shows "EMU10K1". This interrupt is being used by a Creative Labs SoundBlaster Live sound card and this card uses a emu10k1.o driver file. Driver file names have a .o ending (a.k.a. file suffix, filename extension).

Interrupt 10 shows the device name of eth0, which is the name of the first Ethernet network interface card in a system. IRQs 14 and 15 show the device names of ide0 and ide1 respectively. ide0 represents the Primary AT-API Hard Disk Controller and ide1 represents the Secondary AT-API Hard Disk Controller.

The numbers used to represent Linux device names start at 0 (zero) rather than 1, such as eth0 (the first Ethernet card), ide0 (the primary hard disk controller), ttys0 (serial port 1) and lp0 (parallel port 1).

Also, all Linux devices are represented by files (with the same name as the device) in the /dev directory. Therefore, the /dev directory contains the files named eth0, ide0, ttys0 and lp0 (for the items described in the paragraph above).

Linux treats everything as a file. All hardware components, ports and even directories are files.

The text in the text file named interrupts in the /proc directory is shown above. There are several text files in the /proc directory that can be viewed to see the settings of your system. These files are detailed below, in Table 2-5.

I/O Addressing

I/O (Input/Output) addressing is another method of communication between your x86 system and an interface card or a device that is built into your system. In addition to an IRQ, some cards use a few bytes of RAM (an I/O address) to communicate with the system. Table 2-2 below shows a listing of serial ports and their associated COM number, IRQ and I/O address.

For example, Serial Port 1 is referred to as COM1 (in DOS/Windows) and ttyS0 (in Linux) and is communicated with using IRQ 4 and I/O address 03f8. I/O addresses usually appear as hex numbers. The number 03f8 is a hex number representing a memory address. It is a location in memory that is used to access the COM1 serial port.

Serial Ports

A serial port is used to communicate with a serial device, such as mouse, modem and some models of printers. Serial ports are also referred to as "COM" ports. DOS and Windows refer to serial ports with COM1, COM2, COM3 and COM4 and Linux uses ttyS0, ttyS1, ttyS2 and ttyS3, respectively.

A standard called **R**ecommended **S**tandard**-232 (RS-232)** was used to define serial communications and serial ports are commonly referred to as RS-232 ports.

The RS-232 standard was renamed to TIA/EIA-232-E in 1984, but virtually everyone still refers to these ports as "serial ports", "com ports" or "RS-232 ports".

Table 2-2 Serial Port Assignments

Serial Interface	DOS/Windows Port Name	Linux Port Name	Linux Device Name	IRQ	I/O Address
Serial Port 1	COM1	ttyS0	/dev/ttyS0	4	03f8
Serial Port 2	COM2	ttyS1	/dev/ttyS1	3	02f8
Serial Port 1	COM3	ttyS2	/dev/ttyS2	4	03e8
Serial Port 2	COM4	ttyS3	/dev/ttyS3	3	02e8

In Table 2-2 each Linux Device name, such as /dev/ttyS0, begins with /dev. The device names are shown this way because each Linux device has a corresponding file, that is the same name as the device, and each file is located in the /dev directory.

For example, the ttyS0 device has a corresponding file named ttyS0 in the /dev directory.

After installing Linux, you can see the I/O address settings of your system in the text file named ioports, in the directory named /proc. An example of the contents of /proc/ioports is shown below.

```
0000-001f : dma1
0020-003f : pic1
0040-005f : timer
0060-006f : keyboard
0070-007f : rtc
0080-008f : dma page reg
00a0-00bf : pic2
00c0-00df : dma2
00f0-00ff : fpu
0170-0177 : ide1
01f0-01f7 : ide0
02f8-02ff : serial(auto)
0376-0376 : ide1
0378-037a : parport0
037b-037f : parport0
03c0-03df : vga+
03f6-03f6 : ide0
03f8-03ff : serial(auto)
0778-077a : parport0
0cf8-0cff : PCI conf1
4000-403f : Intel Corporation 82371AB PIIX4 ACPI
5000-501f : Intel Corporation 82371AB PIIX4 ACPI
6400-641f : Intel Corporation 82371AB PIIX4 USB
6400-641f : usb-uhci
6800-687f : VIA Technologies, Inc. VT86C100A [Rhine 10/100]
6800-687f : via-rhine
6c00-6c1f : Creative Labs SB Live! EMU10000
6c00-6c1f : EMU10K1
7000-7007 : Creative Labs SB Live!
e000-efff : PCI Bus #01
e000-e0ff : ATI Technologies Inc 3D Rage Pro AGP 1X/2X
f000-f00f : Intel Corporation 82371AB PIIX4 IDE
f000-f007 : ide0
f008-f00f : ide1
```

In the above output, the I/O ports (range of numbers) at the left of "serial(auto)" are for serial ports and the ranges at the left of "parport0" are for parallel ports.

The ranges at the left of "VIA Technologies, Inc. VT86C100A [Rhine 10/100]" and "via-rhine" are the ranges being used by the Ethernet network interface card. The card in this system is a D-Link (brand) DFE-530TX (model) PCI (card type) Fast Ethernet Adapter (name). Although this card is sold under the D-Link brand name, it has been detected and "seen" by Linux (by the Linux Kudzu utility created by Red Hat) as a "VIA Technologies, Inc. VT86C100A [Rhine 10/100]" card and uses the via-rhine.o driver file.

The ranges at the left of "Creative Labs SB Live! EMU10000", "EMU10K1" and "Creative Labs SB Live!" are the ranges being used by the Creative Labs SoundBlaster Live sound card.

The range at the left of "ATI Technologies Inc 3D Rage Pro AGP 1X/2X" is being used by the ATI Technologies graphics card model 3D Rage Pro AGP 1X/2X.

Parallel Ports

Parallel ports are primarily used to communicate with printers and are also referred to as "**LPT**" (Line Print Terminal) ports. An interrupt and an I/O address are used to communicate with these ports.

DOS and Windows refer to parallel ports with LPT1, LPT2 and LPT3 and Linux uses lp0, lp1 and lp2, respectively. Table 2-3 below shows a listing of parallel ports and their associated LPT number, lp number, IRQ and I/O address.

Table 2-3 Parallel Port Assignments

Parallel Interface	DOS/Windows Port Name	Linux Port Name	Linux Device Name	IRQ	I/O Address
Parallel Port 1	LPT1	lp0	/dev/lp0	7	0378
Parallel Port 2	LPT2	lp1	/dev/lp1	5	0278
Parallel Port 3	LPT3	lp2	/dev/lp2	5	03bc

Floppy Disk Drive Names

The table below shows the DOS/Windows and Linux device names for floppy drives. Linux uses fd0 to represent the first floppy and fd1 to represent the second.

Table 2-4 Floppy Drive Names

DOS/Windows Device Name	Linux Device Name
A:	/dev/fd0
B:	/dev/fd1

DMA Channels

DMA (Direct Memory Address) channels are used as a method of communication by floppy disk controllers, sound cards, tape backup units and other devices. There are eight DMA channels.

Once Linux has been installed, you can see the dma port settings in the text file named dma, in the directory named /proc. If a system is not using DMA to communicate with an interface card, then the contents of one of these files appears as shown below.

    4: cascade

The System Information Text Files in the /proc Directory

The /proc directory contains several text files that can be viewed so that you can see the settings being used on your system. Table 2-5 below shows the names of *some* of the text files in /proc and a description of the contents.

Table 2-5 System Information Text Files in the /proc Directory

Text File Name	System Information Provided
interrupts	interrupts being used
ioports	I/O addresses being used
dma	DMA channels being used
pci	PCI devices being used
cpuinfo	CPU information, such as vendor, model and speed
meminfo	system memory and swap memory size and usage
filesystems	filesystems installed
version	version number of the Linux kernel

Information on installed IDE devices is in the ide directory below /proc. Information on installed SCSI devices is in the scsi directory below /proc.

Information on the network configuration of a system is in the net directory below /proc.

Section Review

1. Select two correct statements regarding interface cards.

   ☐ A. current computers often have a slot specifically for an AGP (graphics) card
   ☐ B. all ISA cards have PnP capabilities
   ☐ C. EISA cards were introduced in 1988 by IBM
   ☐ D. PCI and AGP cards are the "standard" cards in use today

2. Which directory holds files that can be viewed to see the settings used by various hardware components?

   ○ A. /
   ○ B. /interrupts
   ○ C. /proc
   ○ D. /system

3. Settings for interface cards that are non-PnP (legacy) cards are automatically configured by a system when it boots. T F

4. The manufacturer of an interface card will typically provide you with (choose two):

   ☐ A. free chip upgrades for memory components, but not graphics components
   ☐ B. various CMOS tools that are used to optimize floppy disk seek times
   ☐ C. a diskette or CD that contains software drivers for various OS versions
   ☐ D. documentation that provides information regarding how the card should be installed

5. Select two correct statements regarding USB and IEEE 1394 ports.

   ☐ A. Apple uses the name FireWire for IEEE 1394
   ☐ B. Sony uses the name i.Link for IEEE 1394
   ☐ C. USB ports can be used for up to 250 high speed devices
   ☐ D. IEEE 1394 ports can support up to 27 devices

6. In general, interface cards can use IRQs, DMA channels and I/O addresses as the three methods of communicating with the system in which they are installed. T F

---

7. Of the following statements regarding Linux device names, which two are correct?

   ☐ A. the first floppy drive is fd0
   ☐ B. the first floppy drive is fd1
   ☐ C. the first parallel port is lp1
   ☐ D. the second parallel port is lp1

8. Which of the following are bus types to which multiple "hot swappable" devices, such as printers, digital cameras and scanners can be attached (choose two)?

   ☐ A. USB
   ☐ B. AGP
   ☐ C. IEEE 1394
   ☐ D. Fireware

9. Non-PnP interface cards do not typically use the same interrupt as other non-PnP cards in the same system and PCI cards allow interrupts to be shared with other PCI cards in the same system. T F

10. You are installing an ISA card in an existing Linux server. You need to manually set some switches on the card to specify an IRQ number for it. Which directory and file combination can be used to see the interrupts that are being used and those that are available?

    ○ A. /irqs
    ○ B. /proc/ioports
    ○ C. /interrupts
    ○ D. /proc/interrupts

11. Which two statements regarding interface card communication are correct?

    ☐ A. most legacy interface cards can share an IRQ with another interface card or devices
    ☐ B. there are eight DMA channels
    ☐ C. interface card settings are sometimes shown with hexadecimal numbers
    ☐ D. I/O addressing uses a few bytes of hard disk storage for communication

12. Which of the following statements are correct regarding interface cards (choose two)?

    ☐ A. current x86 systems are typically only using PCI and AGP cards
    ☐ B. MGI cards are a standard type of "mega-graphics" card
    ☐ C. EISA, MCA and VL-Bus cards are now considered legacy hardware
    ☐ D. PCI and AGP cards are non-PnP cards

Partitions, Filesystems and Device Names

Topics Covered in this Section

Learn the various types of partitions and how they are numbered

Discuss the different types of hard disk and CD-ROM device names

Detail the naming convention used to refer to partitions on storage devices

Describe the default filesystems and the use of non-Linux filesystems on Linux Partitions

Discover the main partitions used by Linux and how partitions are used to restrict disk space

In this section, you will learn about partitions, filesystems, storage device names and the naming convention that is used to refer to partitions on these devices.

Partitions and Filesystems

Prior to installing an operating system on a hard disk, a partition is created on the disk, the partition is assigned a **filesystem** type, and then the partition is formatted (assigned a filesystem). After the hard disk has been formatted, an operating system can be installed on it. You can have the installation routines of most operating systems do all of these steps (create partition, assign filesystem type and format) for you.

A hard disk is partitioned and then the partition is assigned a filesystem *type* and then partition is formatted (assigned a *filesystem*). Assigning a filesystem type to a partition specifies the *type* of the partition. Assigning a *filesystem* to a partition prepares (formats) the partition so that it can accept files. Do not confuse assigning a filesystem *type* with assigning a *filesystem* (formatting).

Most Linux documentation and utilities refer to a file system as **filesystem** (one word). A filesystem type is assigned to (specified for) a partition to provide the partition with support for the file structure of itself (for its directories and subdirectories) and for all of the files that will be used on it, such as program files and data files.

For example, the current default filesystem type for Red Hat Linux files is **ext3** (**ext**ended filesystem **3**). Prior to ext3, the default filesystem was **ext2** (**ext**ended filesystem **2**). Some other distributions have a different default filesystem, but ext3 is on the way to becoming the de facto standard for Linux.

As described earlier, a partition is all or part of a hard disk. If you have two hard disks in a system, then one disk can have one partition, filesystem type and operating system on it that uses the entire disk and the other disk can have a different partition, filesystem type and operating system that uses the entire disk. Both disks can also have more than partition, filesystem type and operating system. If you only have one disk in a system, then you can create two or more partitions on the disk, assign each partition a different filesystem type and install a different operating system on each.

A partition cannot contain more than one filesystem type and does not typically contain more than one operating system. However, you can have a single OS on a system that uses multiple filesystem types on multiple partitions (one filesystem type per partition). The "standard" Windows and Linux operating systems require at least one partition each (see the FYI icon below). If a system requires both of these operating systems, then you need at least one partition for each of them.

"Standard" versions of Linux and Windows require at least one partition each. However, you can purchase additional software and install it on a Linux partition so that you can run Windows from "within" Linux and vise versa. You can also purchase "non-standard" versions of Linux that will run from "within" Windows or use a Windows emulator program to run Windows programs from "within" Linux.

All further descriptions in this course are for "standard" versions of Linux and Windows, and do not involve further discussion of this type of specialized software, or "non-standard" versions of Linux, or "Windows" emulator programs (as described in the paragraph above).

Overview of Partitions

There are three types of partitions that can exist on a hard disk: Primary, Extended and Logical.

The main Linux partitioning utility is fdisk. Virtually every Linux distribution includes fdisk and some also include a utility called parted (GNU **Parted - partition editor**). Some distributions also use other partitioning utilities, particularly during their (own) installation routines.

For example, the installation routine of Red Hat Linux allows you to use a partitioning tool called Disk Druid to partition your hard disk(s). Disk Druid is actually a GUI interface (front end) for the parted utility. When you do a task with Disk Druid, such as create a partition, the parted utility is actually used "in the background" to accomplish the partitioning task.

The options available on the "Disk Setup" screen (of Disk Druid) do not currently utilize all of the capabilities of the parted utility. For example, the parted utility can be used at the command line to resize (increase or decrease) the size of a partition and you cannot do this with Disk Druid (from withing the installation routine).

As the fdisk utility is the main Linux partitioning utility and is used by all distributions, we will discuss Primary and Extended partitions and partition numbering in terms of the tasks that can be done with fdisk. The Primary and Extended partition, and the partition numbering information below, is the same for parted and Disk Druid as it is for fdisk. When you see "fdisk" below, consider this to read: "fdisk, parted, Disk Druid (and some other Linux partitioning utilities)".

Primary Partitions

fdisk can create a maximum of four Primary partitions per drive. Linux does not use drive letters to refer to partitions. It refers to hard disks and partitions with a naming system that is described in detail further below.

Extended Partitions

If a hard disk has a Primary partition, then it can also have one Extended partition. fdisk cannot create more than one Extended partition per drive. To be able to use the disk space in an Extended partition, it must have at least one Logical partition (within the Extended partition).

Logical Partitions

Extended partitions contain one or more Logical partitions. An Extended partition is not accessed directly. It is accessed via one or more Logical partitions within the Extended partition. If a hard disk has an Extended partition, then it has at least one Logical partition in that Extended partition.

Linux refers to Logical partitions in an Extended partition with a naming system that is described in detail further below.

The information in this chapter regarding Windows is mainly provided in case you need to create space for Linux on an existing Windows system. The steps to do this are provided in the next section.

Windows refers to Primary partitions and Logical partitions (that are in an Extended partition) with drive letters. Windows refers to Logical partitions as Logical drives or Logical DOS drives.

If a hard disk in a Windows system has one Primary partition, one Extended partition and only one Logical drive (partition) in the Extended partition, then the Primary partition is C: and the Logical drive in the Extended partition is D:. This single hard disk is then referred to as though it is two disks, C: and D:. The Extended partition (not the Logical drive in the Extended partition) does not have a drive letter and does not need a drive letter. Think of an Extended partition as a "container" for one or more Logical partitions.

To continue the example, if the Extended partition has two Logical drives, then they are called D: and E:. In this situation, the disk is referred to with three drive letters: C:, D: and E:.

Partition Numbering

The maximum number of Primary partitions that fdisk can create is four and the maximum number of Extended partitions that it can create is one.

 Some "commercial" (purchased) and "non-commercial" partition managers can be used to create more Primary and Extended partitions than the Linux fdisk utility.

The following discussion only relates to the use of fdisk and not other "commercial" or "non-commercial" partition managers. This discussion is mainly used to illustrate the reason that the Logical drives in an Extended partition start with the number five. This discussion is necessary because you must use numbers (rather than drive letters) to refer to all Linux partitions and you must understand how the numbering system works.

Partitions that Can Be Created with Linux fdisk

Many Linux systems, particularly servers, often use five or more partitions on one hard disk. Therefore, you often need more than four partitions on a disk.

When using fdisk, the maximum number Primary partitions is four. Also, the maximum number of *the combination of* Primary and Extended partitions on one hard disk is four. If you want to have more than four partitions on a disk, then one of the partitions must be an Extended partition, in which Logical partitions are created.

For example, if you need five partitions, you can create three Primary partitions and one Extended partition and then create two Logical partitions in the Extended partition. You cannot create four primary partitions and then an Extended partition because you cannot have a combined total of more than four (Primary and Extended) partitions. You cannot create three Primary partitions and two Extended partitions because you cannot have more than one Extended partition.

The numbers 1 through 4 are used for Primary partitions. You start your Linux partitioning setup with a Primary partition and number your additional Primary partitions sequentially. Therefore, the first partition is always a Primary partition and it always has the number 1.

The remaining numbers, 2 through 4 are used for other Primary partitions or a single Extended partition. Only one of the numbers (2, 3 or 4) is used for an Extended partition because you can only have one Extended partition. The number that is used for an Extended partition is the first number after the number of the last Primary partition.

If a system has four Primary partitions, they are simply numbered 1 through 4. If a system has three Primary partitions and an Extended partition, then the first three partitions are numbered 1 through 3 and the Extended partition becomes number 4. *The first Logical partition in an Extended partition, regardless of the number of Primary partitions, always has the number 5.* The second Logical partition is 6 and so on.

For example, you have a disk with one Primary partition (with the number 1) and one Extended partition (with the number 2). To access the disk space in the Extended partition, it must have at least one Logical partition and even though the Extended partition has the number 2, the first Logical partition has the number 5, rather than the number 3.

Any partition with the number 5 or above is a Logical drive in the Extended partition of the disk.

In summary, the numbers 1 through 4 are only used for Primary partitions or a single Extended partition and Logical partitions start at 5.

IDE Hard Disk Drive and Controller Names

IDE (hard disk and CD-ROM) drives and controller types were described in the first section of this chapter. These drives use the AT-API specification.

Table 2-6 shows the controller type, position and Linux device names for IDE (hard disk and CD-ROM) drives.

Table 2-6 Linux Names for IDE (AT-API) Drives

Controller Type	Position	Linux Device Name
Primary	Master	hda
Primary	Slave	hdb
Secondary	Master	hdc
Secondary	Slave	hdd

The first IDE hard disk in a system is usually attached to the Primary Master and is referred to by Linux as **hda** (**hard disk a**). If the system has a second IDE hard disk, it is usually attached to the Primary Slave and if so, it is referred to as hdb.

The "Linux Device Name" column in Table 2-6 shows the letters that are used for IDE (hard disk and CD-ROM) drives. These letters represent an entire drive and do not indicate the partitions on the drive. The numbers that are used for partitions on a hard disk are described further below.

IBM XT and ESDI Hard Disk Drive Names

In the highly unlikely event that you come across an old IBM model XT (sort of like a "Model T" car), Linux uses the prefix of **xd** for **XT d**isks. Therefore, the first XT hard disk is xda, the second is xdb, and so on.

ESDI stands for Enhanced Small Device Interface. Like IDE, this is another type of hard disk interface. ESDI hard disks were popular on some computer systems for a time and are now rare. Linux uses the prefix of **ed** (**E**SDI **d**isk) for this type of hard disk. Therefore, the first ESDI hard disk is eda, the second is edb, and so on.

Most hard disks in x86 systems are now either IDE (for desktop systems) or SCSI (typically used for servers).

CD-ROM Drive Names

Current x86 systems have at least one CD-ROM drive. Unless the system is a server, this CD-ROM drive is almost always an IDE (as opposed to SCSI) CD-ROM drive, but may be a SCSI CD-ROM drive.

If it is an IDE CD-ROM drive, then it is usually installed on the Secondary Master. Linux uses the name of hdc for an IDE CD-ROM drive in this (third) position. See the name shown for the Secondary Master in Table 2-6 above.

SCSI Drive and Device Names

The first section of this chapter described SCSI hard drives, controllers and the numbering system used for a "series" of SCSI devices.

Linux uses **sd** for **s**csi **d**rive and then a letter and a number to identify a partition on a SCSI hard disk. The letter that follows sd indicates the position of the SCSI device in the series of devices. The first device in the series of devices is a, the second is b and so on.

To refer to a SCSI CD-ROM drive, Linux still uses sd and then a letter to identify the drive, *but does not use a number* because the drive does not have partitions. A CD-ROM drive that is installed as the second SCSI device in the series of SCSI devices is referred to as sdb. If it were the third SCSI device, then it would be sdc.

The Partition Naming Convention

Linux uses a naming convention (a.k.a. naming scheme) of xxyn to refer to partitions on hard disks. This naming convention provides much more information than simply using a drive letter. It indicates the drive type, drive position and partition number.

The xx part of the xxyn naming convention is used to specify the hard disk type. In place of xx, the letters hd are used for an IDE hard disk or CD-ROM drive, sd for SCSI, ed for ESDI and xd for an XT hard disk.

For the y part of xxyn, a letter is used for the "position" of the drive. The letter a is for the first drive, b for the second and so on.

For the n part of xxyn, a number is used to represent the partition on the drive.

As described above, the numbers 1 through 4 are used for Primary and Extended partitions. Logical partitions can only be created in an Extended partition and a hard disk can only have one Extended partition. The first Logical drive (partition) that is located in an Extended partition is always 5, even if the Extended partition in which it is created does not have the number 4.

The first Primary partition on the first IDE hard disk is referred to as hda1. If Windows is installed on the first partition of the first hard disk, then Linux still refers to this partition as hda1 (rather than drive C:).

If there is a second Primary partition on the first IDE hard disk, it is referred to as hda2, the third is hda3 and the fourth is hda4.

There can be no more than four Primary partitions on a hard disk; there can be no more than four Primary and Extended partitions (combined); and there can be no more than one Extended partition on a hard disk. Therefore, if you have an Extended partition on a hard disk, you can only have a maximum of three Primary partitions on it. To have more than four partitions (of any kind), you must create an Extended partition and then create Logical partitions within it.

If there is an Extended partition on the first hard disk, the first Logical partition in it is hda5, the second is hda6 and so on.

If there is a second IDE hard disk, the first Primary partition on it is hd**b**1 and the second Primary partition on it is hdb2. If the disk has an Extended partition, then the first Logical partition in it is hdb5.

If there is a CD-ROM drive on the Secondary Master, it is hdc (without a number).

On a SCSI hard disk, the first Primary partition on the first drive is sda1. The first Logical partition (in an Extended partition) on this hard disk is sda5.

If the second device in the SCSI series is a CD-ROM drive, then it is sdb (without a number).

The Default Filesystems

The default filesystems that are recognized by Linux are specified in the text file named filesystems in the /proc directory. An example of the contents of this file are shown below. The four filesystems that are recognized appear in bold and do not have the word "nodev" at the left of them. In addition to these four filesystems many other filesystems can be added to a Linux system if needed.

nodev	rootfs
nodev	bdev
nodev	proc
nodev	sockfs
nodev	tmpfs
nodev	shm
nodev	pipefs
	ext2
nodev	ramfs
	iso9660
nodev	devpts
	ext3
nodev	usbdevfs
	vfat
nodev	autofs

In addition to the above four filesystems, by default Linux can also recognize a partition that is a "swap" partition. Depending on the documentation that you are reading and the command or utility that you are using, "swap" is not typically considered to be a filesystem type. It is a type of partition that is treated by the OS as virtual memory.

The following is a description of these five filesystems.

ext2 (second **ext**ended filesystem) supports UNIX/Linux files and directories and allows for long file names (up to 255 characters).

ext3 (third **ext**ended filesystem) is the current default Red Hat Linux filesystem. Some other distributions use this as the default filesystem and some use a different default filesystem. ext3 is on the way to becoming the de facto standard for Linux.

ext3 is based on the previous ext2 filesystem. It is basically the same as ext2, with the main difference being that ext3 supports a feature called "journalling". The greatest benefit of this feature is that it provides a quicker recovery when a filesystem crash occurs.

If files are corrupted on a partition using ext2, then the **fsck** (file**s**ystem **c**hec**k**) utility is run to check the filesystem and repair it. This can take a very long time.

When the files on an ext3 filesystem become corrupted, then the fsck utility is still run to check and repair the filesystem, but this takes much less time due to the journalling feature of ext3.

If a system is not working properly and it "hangs" or if it loses power (due to a power failure or some other reason), then the system has not been shut down "cleanly" (a.k.a. "properly"). If a system was not shut down cleanly, watch its screen as it starts again. Important information appears on the screen when a system starts. This can help you to diagnose and fix a problem.

When you are finished working at a system and need to turn the power off, you should do the steps to shut the system down cleanly (via software) prior to turning the power off.

To do this from a GUI desktop, you select: Menu ; Log Out ; Shut Down ; OK (or equivalent).

If you are working at the shell prompt in "text mode" you run a command, such as: shutdown -h now.

The above steps shut the OS down "cleanly" via software, prior to shutting the system down manually by turning the power off. On most current systems, doing the steps to shut the OS down via software will also automatically turn off the power (you will not need to turn the power off manually).

If the power to a Linux system (that is using any one of several filesystems, including ext2 and ext3, on any of its partitions) has gone off before the system was properly shut down via software, then watch the screen as it boots. You will likely see a message that states that the system was not shut down "cleanly" and requests that you press "Y" (for Yes) to force a filesystem integrity check (i.e. run the fsck utility).

The system may only give you a few seconds to respond to the message before automatically continuing to boot. If you press "Y", then the system will run a filesystem check. Unless you are certain that a filesystem check is not required, always press "Y" when asked if you want to run a filesystem check.

A filesystem check that is run on a partition that is using ext3 is much faster than one that is run on a partition that is using ext2.

vfat is the Linux filesystem that is compatible with DOS file names and Windows long file names. In some Linux utilities, "vfat" appears as "fat" or "fat32".

iso9660 is the filesystem used on a CD-ROM.

swap (a.k.a. swap partition, swap drive, swap space) is a disk partition that is used by the Linux OS as "virtual memory". Linux uses the disk space that you have specified for the swap drive as though it were RAM (memory chips in your system).

The swap partition should be at least 32 MB (of disk space) and should be twice the size as the amount of RAM in your system, but not exceed 2,048 MB (2 GB).

Using Non-Linux filesystems on Linux Partitions

A Linux system can have more than one partition and each partition can have a different filesystem. A filesystem provides support for the file structure of itself and the files in it. Linux supports the use of filesystems of other operating systems on its partitions, such as Windows. Depending on the use of your Linux system, you may need to install additional filesystems.

For example, you may need a Linux file server on a network to be able to hold files for a "non-Linux" operating system. This would allow users at "non-Linux" workstations to access the shared data files of the "non-Linux" OS.

To continue the example, you could install support for one of the Windows filesystems on one or more partitions on a Linux server. This would allow Windows workstations attached to the network to access shared data files on the Linux server as though it were a Windows server.

Viewing Partition Information from within the Linux fdisk Utility

As described earlier, the Linux fdisk utility can be used to create and delete partitions and assign them filesystem types. Figure 2-9 shows the partitions on an IDE hard disk as seen in the Linux fdisk utility.

Figure 2-9: The partitions on an IDE hard disk as seen in the Linux fdisk utility

```
Disk /dev/hda: 255 heads, 63 sectors, 1550 cylinders
Units = cylinders of 16065 * 512 bytes

    Device Boot    Start      End    Blocks   Id  System
/dev/hda1    *         1      510   4096543+   b  Win95 FAT32
/dev/hda2            511      516     48195   83  Linux
/dev/hda3            517     1518   8048565   83  Linux
/dev/hda4           1519     1550    257040    f  Win95 Ext'd (LBA)
/dev/hda5           1519     1550    257008+  82  Linux swap
```

In Figure 2-9, the device names of each partition appear below the "Device" heading. The device names are prefixed with /dev/. The /dev (or /dev/) directory is a Linux directory that contains files that have the same names as the devices that they represent.

The first partition is hda1 and contains all of Windows XP (OS, programs and data files). For this device, "Win95 FAT32" appears below the "System" heading. The "Win95" part of "Win95 FAT32" is inaccurate, as this partition actually contains Windows XP. The "FAT32" part of "Win95 FAT32" is accurate and this appears as "fat" or "vfat" in some other Linux utilities. Below the "Boot" heading there is an asterisk to indicate that the hda1 partition is used to boot the system.

The starting cylinder for hda1 is shown below the "Start" heading. This partition starts at 1 and ends at the 510th cylinder. The size of the partition is below the "Blocks" heading and is 4,094,452. This partition is approximately 4 GB.

The hda2 and hda3 partitions are Linux partitions, as can be seen below the "System" heading. The hda2 partition is actually the /boot partition, although the /boot (mount point - directory assigned to a partition) is not shown by fdisk. This partition is approximately 48 MB.

The hda3 partition is the / (root) partition and is approximately 8 GB.

The hda4 partition is an Extended partition that contains one Logical partition, named hda5. The hda5 partition takes up (almost) all of the space in the Extended partition.

The hda5 partition is a Linux swap partition that is approximately 256 MB. This system has 128 MB of RAM and the swap partition is about twice the size of the amount of RAM in the system.

Notice that "83" appears below "Id" for hda2 and hda3. This is the "code" (hex number) used by fdisk for a Linux partition. Notice that "82" appears below "Id" for hda5. This is the "code" used by fdisk for a Linux "swap" partition.

Partitions Used by Linux

On a hard disk in a Linux system, Linux directories, such as the / (root) directory, are assigned to partitions. The / directory is always assigned to a partition and this is sometimes referred to as the "root partition". Directories "below" (or "off of") the root can also be assigned to partitions.

For example, the boot directory, which is below the / directory (/boot) is assigned to a partition by default. This is directory can be referred to as the "boot partition".

During the installation of Linux, you assign directories to partitions. Each Linux partition has a directory assigned to it, except for the swap partition (which does not represent a directory).

In general, the Linux OS only *requires* one partition and this is the partition for the / (root) directory. This partition is also referred to as the "root partition".

However, some distributions of Linux *require* at least two partitions, one partition for the / (root) directory and one that is a swap partition. Other distributions require a /boot partition in addition to the / and swap partitions.

A hard disk requires a /boot partition below the 1,024th cylinder if the disk has over 1,024 cylinders. Most hard disks currently in use have more than 1,024 cylinders and therefore, the installation routines of many distributions will create a /boot partition below the 1,024th cylinder, if this is the case.

Linux uses the /boot directory to hold files that are used to boot the OS. Linux cannot boot if the files in the /boot partition are above the 1,024th cylinder. Therefore, the installation routines of some Linux distributions automatically create a /boot partition below the 1,024th cylinder when a disk has more than 1,024 cylinders.

You can create partitions and specify the sizes of Linux partitions with a partitioning utility prior to installing Linux, or during the Linux installation (with the fdisk utility or with the Disk Druid component of the installation routine).

Restricting Directory Sizes with Partitions

Each partition that is created on a disk has a fixed size. Other than the swap partition, all partitions are assigned a directory. Once a directory has been assigned to a partition, files can only be created in the directory (and use up the space in it), up to the size of the partition. This restricts the amount of space that is available in a directory.

To restrict the amount of disk space that a particular directory can take up, a partition is created for the directory and then the directory is assigned to the partition.

For example, on a Linux Web server, the **/var** directory is used to contain **var**iable length "log" files. These log files keep track of the activity on the server, such as access requests that people have made of the server. These log files increase in size as time passes and more requests are made. The more the server is accessed, the greater the size of the log files.

If log files are left unchecked, they can become hundreds of megabytes and even use up all of the space on a disk. These files are sometimes referred to as "runaway" log files. The system should be set up to automatically stop log files from becoming too large, but this does not always happen.

To restrict the space that can be taken up by "runaway" log files, you can create a partition that is large enough to hold the log files and assign the /var directory to it.

For example, if you know that the maximum amount of space that you need for log files (and other files) in the /var directory is 200 MB, you can create a 200 MB partition and assign the /var directory to it. This will stop "runaway" log files from taking up more than 200 MB of disk space.

As another example, you can restrict the size of the "home" (/home) directory by setting it up as a mount point and specifying a size for it.

The / (root) directory contains the home directory and is the "parent" of the home directory. When users are created in Linux, they are assigned a "home" directory below /home. The name of the home directory is the same as the user name.

In our examples, the Chris West user is created and assigned the user name of cwest and a password. When this user is created, a "home" directory named cwest is automatically created for this user, below /home. The "path" (series of directories) to the home directory of the Chris West user is /home/cwest.

By default, Chris West logs in to the system as cwest and has the permissions (a.k.a. access rights, capabilities) of creating files in the cwest directory (in the path of /home/cwest). Also by default, this user cannot create files in the parent directory of cwest, which is /home, or create any files in any other directories on any hard disks, except the /tmp directory (which is used to hold temporary files).

A "home" directory, such as the cwest directory below /home, is the place in which a user creates his or her data files. If the / (root) directory (which contains the /home directory) is assigned to a 120 GB partition and the /home directory is not assigned to a specific partition, then cwest will be able to create files in the /home/cwest directory and fill the entire 120 GB partition!

However, if the /home directory is assigned to a partition that is only 2 GB, then cwest will only be able to create a maximum of 2 GB of data (in /home/cwest). By assigning /home to a 2 GB partition, you restrict the space of the directory (including subdirectories and files in the directory) to 2 GB.

Other benefits of assigning directories to partitions (as mount points) are described later in this course.

Linux Mount Points

When a directory is assigned to a partition, the directory becomes the "mount point" for the partition. A directory must be "mounted" so that it can be used (accessed).

For example, when /home is assigned to a partition, such as hda6, the /home directory becomes the mount point of the hda6 partition. The /home directory is the point in the directory structure that is used to "mount" the partition (hda6) so that it is available for use.

To continue the example, you can use a Linux utility (such as a GUI file manager utility) to view a directory and the subdirectories and files in it. When the /home directory is assigned to a partition (such as hda6) and you view the contents of it (including the subdirectories in it and the files in those subdirectories), you are actually viewing the entire contents of the hda6 partition and you are only viewing the contents of that partition.

By default, the installation routine creates a / directory and this directory "points" to a partition, such as hda3. The / directory is the mount point of the partition to which it points (hda3).

When specifying a mount point, a single directory is assigned to a single partition. The directory can be the / directory, a subdirectory of the /, such as /home, or a subdirectory even further down the file structure, such as /home/common/wordpro-data.

Section Review

1. Select two correct statements regarding partitions that can be created with fdisk.

    ☐ A. a hard disk can have a maximum of two Primary and two Extended partitions
    ☐ B. a hard disk can have a maximum of four Primary partitions
    ☐ C. a hard disk can only have one Extended partition
    ☐ D. a hard disk can only have one Primary partition

2. Select the item that is a disk partition that is used by Linux as "virtual memory".

    ○ A. /
    ○ B. /boot
    ○ C. /home
    ○ D. swap

3. Select two filesystems that allow for long file names and support UNIX/Linux files and directories.

    ☐ A. ext2
    ☐ B. ext3
    ☐ C. swapram
    ☐ D. vfat3

4. What is the name of the first Logical partition on the second IDE hard disk?

    ○ A. hdb2
    ○ B. hdb6
    ○ C. hdb5
    ○ D. ide2

5. A device has the name of hdc. Select the item that this device could be.

    ○ A. an AT-API CD-ROM drive
    ○ B. a SCSI CD-ROM drive
    ○ C. the third partition on an IDE hard disk drive
    ○ D. the third partition on an ESDC hard disk drive

6. Which statement regarding partitions that can be created with fdisk is correct?

    ○ A. the maximum number of Logical partitions is one
    ○ B. the maximum number of Primary and Logical partitions is four
    ○ C. the maximum number of the combination of Primary and Extended partitions on one hard disk is four
    ○ D. the maximum number of the combination of Primary and Logical partitions on one hard disk is four

7. Which two statements regarding Linux partitions are correct?

   ☐ A. a / (root) partition is always required
   ☐ B. the swap partition is only used to hold device driver files
   ☐ C. a /boot partition is always required
   ☐ D. a /boot partition is required on a disk that has over 1,024 cylinders

8. Which of the following two comments regarding Linux are correct?

   ☐ A. when a hard disk is assigned to a filesystem, the size of the disk is restricted by the number of users attached to the server
   ☐ B. when a directory is assigned to a partition, the size of the directory is restricted to the size of the partition
   ☐ C. when a directory is assigned to a partition, the directory becomes the "mount point" for the partition
   ☐ D. when a server is installed on a network, the cabling system becomes the "mount point" for all of its cable devices

9. What is the name of the third Logical partition on the fourth SCSI device (hard disk)?

   ○ A. scd3
   ○ B. sdc6
   ○ C. sdd7
   ○ D. sdc7

10. Which of the following statements regarding "standard" Linux partitions (created without the use of additional specialized software) are correct (choose two)?

   ☐ A. a partition can contain more than one filesystem
   ☐ B. a partition cannot contain more than one filesystem
   ☐ C. Linux can only access the same (single) filesystem type on all of the partitions on any hard disk in a system
   ☐ D. Linux can access multiple filesystem types on multiple partitions (one filesystem per partition) on any hard disk in a system

11. Select the description of the drive that has the device name of sdb.

   ○ A. it is the Primary Master AT-API drive
   ○ B. it is the second Primary partition on an ESDD hard disk drive
   ○ C. it is the Secondary Slave IDE hard disk drive
   ○ D. it is the second SCSI drive

12. Which of the following statements are correct (choose two)?

   ☐ A. vfat9660 is a journalling filesystem
   ☐ B. the journalling feature of ext3 provides a quicker recovery (than ext2) when a filesystem crash occurs
   ☐ C. ext2 and ext3 are similar, but ext2 does not include journalling
   ☐ D. both ext2 and ext3 include journalling

Chapter 3: Installing Linux On An x86 System

This chapter of the course includes four sections. During this chapter you will learn about and work with the following:

Linux Installation Methods and Boot Disks

In this section, you will learn about the different methods that can be used to install Linux and the boot disks that are created for these different methods.

Creating Space for Linux

During this section, you will learn about boot loaders, the Master Boot Record, the order in which Linux and Windows should be installed on a system that does not have an OS, and how to create space for Linux on an existing Windows system.

Installing Linux

This section describes the Linux OS software components and installation routines. You will learn about running various options available through the Installation Options Screen and the types of installation that can be performed on a system.

During the Hands-On Exercises of this section you will run the Anaconda installation routine, configure all of your hardware components, manually partition your hard disk, select the packages required for your system and do all of the steps to install Linux!

Post-Installation Configuration of Linux

In this section, you will learn about the various text-based and GUI utilities that are used to configure a system after the installation of Linux and the difference between running utilities at the command line and from a menu. You will also learn about hardware modems, winmodems, boot loader problems and how to re-install boot loaders.

Linux Installation Methods and Boot Disks

Topics Covered in this Section

Learn the various methods that can be used to install Linux on a system
Discuss the different .img files that are used to create Linux boot disks
Detail the steps used to create boot disks from within Linux and Windows
Do the steps necessary to create boot disks for various types of installations
In this section, you will learn about several methods of installing Linux, including how to install "over a LAN" and all of the steps to create boot disks for these installation methods.

In this section, you will learn about various boot disks, installing from CD, doing an automated installation and upgrading an existing system.

Methods of Installing Red Hat Linux

Installation from a CD to a Hard Disk in a System

A common method of installing Red Hat Linux is by running the installation routine from CD 1. In the first section of this chapter you did the steps to see if you could set up your system to boot from a CD in its CD-ROM drive. If possible, you set up your system to boot from its CD-ROM drive prior to booting from drive A: or drive C:.

If your system can boot from a bootable CD in its CD-ROM drive, then this is the easiest method of starting the installation routine. Simply put CD 1 in the CD-ROM drive and restart your system.

If your system cannot boot from a bootable CD in its CD-ROM drive, then you will need to create a Linux CD/Hard Disk Installation Boot Disk (floppy) and boot from this floppy (*with CD 1 in the CD-ROM drive*) to start the installation routine.

Remember that if you cannot boot from a CD and need to run the installation routine from CD (rather than from a hard disk, as described further below), then you must have CD 1 in the CD-ROM drive when you boot from the Linux CD/Hard Disk Installation Boot Disk.

The same as above is true when you need to boot from a CD to use any options on the "Installation Options Screen" (the opening Red Hat Linux 8.0 splash screen), such as to go into "Rescue Mode" to do system repair and maintenance tasks.

If you need to run the installation routine from hard disk (rather than CD), then boot with the Linux CD/Hard Disk Installation Boot Disk *without* CD 1 in the CD-ROM drive.

Other Installation Methods

You can boot from CD and type: linux askmethod and press Enter at the "Installation Options Screen" (the opening splash screen). When you do this, you can select the following installation methods: Local CDROM, NFS Image, FTP, HTTP and Hard Drive.

You can also create a boot disk (floppy) to start a CD/hard disk installation and a different boot disk to start a LAN installation. The steps to create a boot disk are detailed in the Hands-On Exercises below.

Installing from a Hard Disk in a System to a Partition in the Same System

A hard disk is much faster than a CD-ROM drive and so a system can read files from a hard disk faster than from a CD (in a CD-ROM drive). Therefore, running the Red Hat Linux installation routine from hard disk is faster than running it from a CD.

If you need to repeatedly run the installation routine on one system, such as a test system in your lab, you can copy the Linux OS (CDs) to a hard disk and run the installation routine from hard disk. The boot disk that you create for this type of installation allows you to access the CD files on the hard disk.

To be able to do a hard disk installation, you copy the **ISO image** of the CDs to a partition on a hard disk and then use this to install the OS onto one or more (other) partitions on a hard disk *in the same system*. This provides a faster method of running the installation routine.

CDs have the filesystem type of iso9660. The entire contents of a CD is called an **ISO "image"**. The ISO image of a CD is a single file that contains all of the directories and files that are on the CD.

ISO stands for **I**nternational **S**tandards **A**ssociation. This organization defined the ISO 9660 specification, which specifies the standard for CDs and CD-ROM drives.

Installing from a Server on a LAN to a Workstation Attached to the LAN

Red Hat Linux can also be installed "over a LAN". This means that you can create a boot disk that starts a workstation (connected to the LAN) and the files on this disk allow you to connect to a server on which the files used by the installation routine are located. This method allows you to run the installation routine at any workstation that is connected to the LAN.

Installing "over a LAN" is a fast, convenient and common method of installing Linux on a new system, or upgrading an existing system. Also, you may need to do this type of installation by booting from floppy if a workstation attached to the network does not have a CD-ROM drive from which to run the installation routine.

This type of installation can be done from an **NFS** server, **FTP** server or **HTTP** server. To use one of these servers, the server must be accessed via the network cabling system (using the TCP/IP protocol) and cannot be done by using a direct dial-up connection (accessing a server via modem).

NFS stands for **N**etwork **F**ile **S**ystem. It is a protocol that is used to allow "shares", which are shared directories (and the files in them) on a network. An NFS server is one that is running the UNIX or Linux OS and it can be accessed by another UNIX or Linux system. A person at a UNIX or Linux workstation can access the directories and files on the NFS server as though they are "local" files (the files appear as though they are on the hard disk of the workstation).

FTP stands for **F**ile **T**ransfer **P**rotocol. This is an Internet protocol used to transfer files via TCP/IP. An FTP server is used to provide people with access to files and it allows them to download them quickly. An FTP server is also called an FTP "site".

The letters **HTTP** represent the words **H**yper**T**ext **T**ransfer **P**rotocol. An HTTP server is one that is using "hypertext". This is text on the server that is marked with "tags" (text markers) to indicate that the text is to be used to provide a "hyperlink" to other text on the same server or on another server. An HTTP server is commonly referred to as a web server. When you specify a web site address of **http**://www.lancom-tech.com, the **http** part of the address stands for **h**yper**t**ext **t**ransfer **p**rotocol.

Doing a Kickstart Installation

During a "standard" (manual) Linux installation (from CD, hard disk, or server) you have to watch the screen and wait to respond to several prompts that request the settings that are required by the installation routine. An alternative to this is another installation method called a "kickstart" installation.

A kickstart installation is a method of automating the installation process so that it can be run from start to finish without any intervention. You do not have to wait and then respond to prompts that appear. This installation method can be used to quickly and automatically install many systems at once.

A text file is used to provide all of the settings that are required by the installation routine. After you do a Linux installation, the installation routine automatically creates a text file named **anaconda-ks.cfg** in the /root directory. This file contains the settings that you made during the installation.

The file named **anaconda-ks.cfg** is the **anaconda k**ickstart **c**onfiguration (text) file. This file is created by the Red Hat Linux installation routine, which is named Anaconda.

You can either edit (if necessary) the anaconda-ks.cfg file, or edit a sample kickstart (text) file (included with the OS), to provide the settings required for a kickstart installation. After specifying the settings you require, you can start the installation and have it run non-stop from beginning to end using the settings in the kickstart file.

Upgrading an Existing Red Hat Linux Installation

To upgrade an existing Red Hat Linux system you select "Upgrade Existing System" while running the installation routine. The upgrade will attempt to maintain your existing configuration settings and existing data files. We recommend that you do a complete back up (twice) prior to doing an upgrade.

Linux Boot Disks

As described above, if you need to run the Linux installation routine from CD, but cannot boot from CD, you will need to boot from a Linux boot disk (floppy) to get access to your CD-ROM drive.

In addition to this, you may need to create a boot disk to do an installation "over a LAN". The steps used to put a .img file on a floppy are detailed in the Hands-On Exercises below.

The .img files discussed in this section are 1.44 MB in size, which is exactly the same size as the floppy disk onto which an image file is copied. The .img file is the "image" that was taken of a boot floppy, that was created for a specific task. It was created by taking a "snapshot" of an existing boot floppy and putting the image in a single .img file.

A boot disk is created by using a command (small program) to copy a .img file to a formatted 1.44 MB floppy disk. A .img file is a "raw" disk image file. When a raw disk image file (a single file) is copied to a floppy, the floppy acquires the filesystem of the .img file and also the files included in the .img file. These files provide the functionality required by the boot disk (i.e. if the disk will be used to do a LAN installation, it will get the files required for that task). When the .img file of a boot disk is copied to a floppy, the floppy becomes bootable.

You can create a Linux boot disk at a system that has been booted with Linux or on one that has been booted with Windows. If you boot a system with Linux, then the **dd** (**d**isk to **d**isk) command is used to create a boot disk. If you boot with Windows, then the **rawrite** (as in: **raw** disk image **write**) command is used to create a boot disk.

Boot disk image files that are used for various tasks can be obtained from several locations on the internet. The boot.img and bootnet.img files that are described below are located in the images directory on CD 3.

boot.img - Used for a CD/Hard Disk Installation

If you cannot boot from CD to start installing Linux or if you want to do a hard disk installation, then create a boot disk with the boot.img file and use it to boot the system.

Starting a CD Installation with a Boot Disk

To install from CD (using CD 1 and then CD 2), you put CD 1 in the CD-ROM drive and then boot with a floppy that has been created with boot.img. Once you have booted, the "Installation Options Screen" appears so that you can run the installation routine and do some other tasks. This screen provides several methods of running the installation routine, but easiest way is to simply press Enter.

 When you boot with CD 1, or boot from the boot.img floppy and access CD 1, you see a Red Hat Linux 8.0 "splash" screen that allows you to install the OS and do some other tasks. We will refer to this screen as the "Installation Options Screen".

Starting a Hard Disk Installation with a Boot Disk

A hard disk installation is used to install Linux from ISO images of CD 1 and CD 2 in a directory on one partition, to other partitions in the same system.

Prior to starting a hard disk installation, copy the ISO images of CD 1 and CD 2 into a directory on the system.

To do a hard disk installation, you boot with the floppy that has been created with boot.img, but *without* CD 1 in the CD-ROM drive.

When the "Installation Options Screen" appears, press Enter. CD 1 is not in the CD-ROM drive and therefore the installation routine prompts you to choose a language and then choose a keyboard type.

At the next dialog box, select "Hard Drive" (rather than "Local CDROM").

At the "Select Partition" dialog box, specify the partition and directory in which the ISO images of CD 1 and CD 2 are located and then select OK to start the installation routine.

bootnet.img - Used for Network Installations

An installation can be done "over a LAN" from files on an NFS, FTP or HTTP server to a workstation that has been booted with bootnet.img.

Prior to booting a system with the disk created with bootnet.img, put the files required for the installation in a directory on the server. Copy the directories and files on CD 1 and CD 2 into a directory on the server. This creates an "Installation Tree" on the server, which is a directory "tree" structure from which the OS can be installed.

 For more information on copying the files from CD 1 and CD 2 onto a server, see the README file in /mnt/cdrom on CD 1.

Once the files are on the server, boot the workstation (onto which you are installing Linux) with bootnet.img (*without CD 1 in the CD-ROM drive*) and press Enter. You will be prompted for your language and keyboard type and then the "Installation Method" dialog box will appear. This dialog box presents you with the options of: NFS Image, FTP and HTTP. Select the desired method and then you will be prompted for network information, such as TCP/IP settings, the name of the server and the directory on the server that contains the files.

Hands-On Exercises

Part of the Hands-On Exercises below describe creating a boot disk at a Linux system. If you are working through this book chronologically, then you have not installed Linux yet and may not have access to a Linux system.

We recommend that you **read all of the information below** (so that you can answer the Section Review questions). If you have access to a Windows system, then do the steps at the "Creating Boot Disks at a Windows Workstation" below. Once you have installed Linux, then return to these exercises and do steps described at the "Creating Boot Disks at a Linux Workstation" heading below.

 Testing to See if You Can Boot from CD

In an earlier section, you did the steps to see if you could set up your CMOS so that your system can boot from its CD-ROM drive.

If you know that your system cannot be set up to boot from its CD-ROM drive, then you will need to create a boot disk for your system, as described below.

In addition to this, even if you can set up your CMOS so that your system can boot from its CD-ROM drive, your CD-ROM drive may still not be able to boot from a CD. This situation is rare and typically occurs with legacy CD-ROM drives. The steps below will test to see if you can boot from CD 1.

Start your system with CD 1 (included with this book) in your CD-ROM drive.

If you see the "Installation Options Screen" (the Red Hat Linux 8.0 splash screen with some installation options on it), then your system booted from CD 1 and you will not need to create a boot disk for your system.

 Creating Boot Disks at a Linux Workstation

The following steps describe creating a boot disk at a workstation that has been booted with Linux.

Go to a system that has had Linux installed on it ;

boot the system and log in as a non-root user (such as the cwest user).

At this point, you will either be in text mode at a shell prompt, or at a GUI desktop (GUI mode).

If you are in GUI mode, either click on the Terminal Emulation Window icon (if one exists) to go to the shell prompt, or do the following steps to go to the shell prompt:

at the GNOME or KDE desktop, select Menu ; System Tools ; Terminal.

Label a blank formatted 3.5 inch, 1.44 MB floppy with "Linux CD/Hard Disk Installation Boot Disk" (if you are creating a boot disk with boot.img), or "Linux Network Installation Boot Disk" (if you are creating a boot disk with bootnet.img).

Put the floppy disk in your floppy drive.

The example below shows you how to create a boot disk with the boot.img file (for a CD or hard disk installation). By following this example and specifying a different .img file name, you can create a different boot disk.

Put CD 3 in the CD-ROM drive.

If you booted to a desktop, then a CD is (likely) automatically mounted when you put it in your CD-ROM drive and you do not need to run the following command. If a GUI file manager window opens, close it. If you are prompted to run anything from the CD, select No.

When you logged in (to a desktop or in text mode), you did so as a non-root user. You need to run the su command and log in as the root user to be able to run some of the commands in the steps below.

All of the commands used below are described in more detail in upcoming sections.

The indented "]#" (prompt) below is used to represent the shell prompt. Type the commands below that appear at the right of the shell prompt and press Enter.

For the steps below, type in: su and then a - (dash) and press Enter and then type in the password of the root user and press Enter.

]# su -

Password: *password*

If you booted to into text mode, you need to run the following command to make your CD-ROM drive accessible.

]# mount /dev/cdrom /mnt/cdrom

Run the following commands at the command line regardless of the mode or desktop that you booted to.

]# cd /mnt/cdrom/images

Now use the **ls** (list) command with the **-l** (long listing) option to view the files in the images directory. The image files (ending in .img), such as boot.img, should appear.

    ]# ls -l

Notice that the .img files are 1,474,560 bytes (1.44 MB) in size. This is the maximum capacity of a 3-1/2" floppy.

With the next command, you will run the Linux dd command to copy the boot.img file (for a CD or hard disk installation) to your floppy disk.

Do not use the mount command to mount the floppy prior to using the dd command below. Make sure the "slider" on the floppy disk is not moved to the position that "write protects" the floppy.

If you are creating a boot disk for a network ("over a LAN") installation, replace: boot.img in the command below with: bootnet.img.

When using the dd command, **if=** is used to specify the input file (boot.img) and **of=** is used to specify the output file (/dev/fd0, the floppy in the fd0 device). The **bs=** option of the command is used to specify the **b**lock **s**ize (of the input and output bit streams) of 1440k (1,440 kilobytes, which is 1.44 MB). This causes the command to read (input) and write (output) 1,440 k at a time.

    ]# dd if=boot.img of=/dev/fd0 bs=1440k

Look at the light on your floppy drive. The dd command is now putting the .img file onto the floppy.

At the "Testing Your Linux CD/Hard Disk Installation Boot Disk" heading below, you will do the steps to test your new boot disk.

You don't have to look at the contents of a boot disk after creating it, but we will do this now so that you can see that when the .img file was put on a floppy, it actually included several files.

You don't need to mount a floppy prior to running the dd command, but you do need to mount it to look at the files on it.

Use the following command to mount your floppy and make it accessible.

    ]# mount /dev/fd0 /mnt/floppy

Now run the following command to look at the files on your boot disk. The .img file made your floppy bootable and also provided the files that you see in the list.

```
]# ls -l /mnt/floppy
```

Your "current" (a.k.a. active working) directory is the images directory on the CD. The command: cd / changes directory to the root directory so that you are not "in" (accessing) the images directory on the CD. You cannot unmount a device if you are accessing the filesystem of it (you will see a message stating that the device is "busy").

Trying to unmount a device and getting a "busy" message is a common problem. This problem occurs when you are "in" a directory on the media (such as a CD or floppy disk) that is in the device. If you are at the shell prompt and are "in" a directory on the media, or if you are using a GUI utility, such as the Nautilus file manager and are accessing a directory on the media, then you must change to a directory that is not "on" the media.

In other words, when you need to unmount a device that is busy, such as a CD in the CD-ROM drive or a floppy disk in the floppy drive, you need to move "off" ("out") of a directory on the CD or floppy. If you are at the shell prompt, use the **cd** (**c**hange **d**irectory) command to move "off" of the CD. If you are in a GUI file manager, click to move "off" of the directory so that it is not being accessed.

The next two commands below unmount the CD-ROM drive and floppy drive with the **umount** (**un**mount device) command. Always unmount drives that contain removable media before removing the media.

Another common problem occurs when you have done something to put files on a removable disk, such as copy files to a disk or save files to a disk, and then remove the disk prior to "unmounting" it with the umount command.

Files are not always written to a disk (such as a floppy disk or zip disk) immediately. The system may do other tasks prior to writing files to disk. However, when the umount command is run, it forces the system to write files to the disk prior to unmounting it. Therefore, if you have done something to put files on a disk and remove the disk without running the umount command, then the files may not be on the disk! Therefore, always unmount drives that contain removable media before removing the media. This forces the system to write files to the disk.

```
]# umount /dev/fd0
```

If you booted to a GUI desktop and see a message (after running the above command) that states that the device is busy, close all applications (programs), including file management utilities and try again.

You should still be "in" the images directory on the CD. Therefore, the output of the following command should show that the device is busy.

    ]# umount /dev/cdrom

Now change to a directory that is not "on" the media (in the device) and run the umount command again.

    ]# cd /

    ]# umount /dev/cdrom

The following command is used to exit from the su command that was used to log in as the root user.

    ]# exit

Now remove your CD and boot disk and and do the steps below to "properly" shut down your system.

If you booted to a GUI desktoop, selecct Menu ; Log Out ; Shut Down ; OK.

If you booted to text mode, use the command: shutdown -h now

Congratulations, you just used Linux to create a boot disk and learned a lot in the process!

 ## ③ Creating Boot Disks at a Windows Workstation

If you do not have access to a system that has had Linux installed on it, you can create boot disks at a Windows system. The following steps describe creating a boot disk at a workstation that has been booted with Windows.

In the steps below, you will use the rawrite command at the DOS prompt to create a boot disk using the boot.img file in the images directory on CD 3.

 The rawrite command has the restriction of DOS filenames. It does not work with files that have more than eight characters prior to the . (period) in the file name, or more than three characters after the period in the file name. This is referred to as an 8.3 file name. Therefore, if you have downloaded a .img file from the Internet so that you can create some type of boot disk and the .img file has too many characters, rename it to have an 8.3 file name prior to using the rawrite command "on it".

For example, if you have downloaded a file with the name bootimage-082603.img, rename the file to something like boot0826.img (an 8.3 file name) and put it in a directory on your Windows system. In the steps below, specify the path to this directory in place of the path to the images directory.

Boot your Windows system and put CD 3 in your CD-ROM drive. If a window opens showing the contents of your CD, close it.

Label a blank formatted 3.5 inch, 1.44 MB floppy with the name of the boot disk that you are creating and put it in drive A:.

Do the following steps (or equivalent) to open a "DOS window", so that you can run commands at the DOS prompt (a.k.a. DOS command line):

Start ; Run ... ;

Open: *command.com* (for Windows 9x, XP) ; OK.

Open: *cmd.exe* ; OK (for Windows 2000, XP) ; OK.

The DOS prompt shows a drive letter, a path and a > (greater than) symbol at the right of the drive letter and path. The DOS prompt is shown in bold below. For the commands below, type in the text at the right of the (bold) DOS prompt (i.e. at the right of the > symbol) and then press Enter.

Change to the drive letter of your CD-ROM drive and run the following commands. If your CD-ROM drive letter is not "d:", replace the "d" below with the drive letter of your CD-ROM drive.

C:*path*> d:

D:\\> cd\images

D:\images> dir

Notice the files that end in ".img" and that they are the same size. You are using DOS/Windows to put a .img file onto a floppy and create a Linux boot disk.

The dosutils directory contains the rawrite command (program) that is used to "write" the raw disk image file to a floppy disk. Now change into the dosutils directory so that you can run the rawrite command in the dosutils directory.

D:\images> cd\dosutils

D:\dosutils> rawrite

At the right of the prompt (in bold) below, replace the "d" with the letter of your CD-ROM drive. If necessary, replace boot.img with the name of the file that you require for the boot disk that you need to create (such as bootnet.img for the boot disk for a network installation).

Enter disk image source file name: d:\images\boot.img

Enter target diskette drive: a:

Please insert a formatted diskette into drive A: and press -Enter- :

Look at the light on your floppy drive. The rawrite program is now putting the .img file on the floppy.

After the file has been written, look at the contents of the floppy to see that it contains files, and then close the "DOS window".

D:\dosutils> dir a:

D:\dosutils> exit

Remove the CD and floppy disk from their drives and shut down Windows.

Congratulations, you used Windows to create a boot disk and learned a lot in the process!

 When you do a Linux installation you have the opportunity to create a boot disk (Installation Routine Boot Disk). This boot disk is not the same the as one that you create when you follow any of the steps above to create a boot disk. The one that you create during the installation contains information that is specific to the system on which the installation was done. Among other differences, the one created during installation contains a statement similar to the following in a file named syslinux.cfg:

append initrd=initrd.img hdc=ide-scsi root=/dev/hda3

The above statement specifies the name of the partition (hda3) that is used for the / (root=) directory, in the system on which the boot disk was created. The partition used for the / directory on another system could be different from hda3.

We recommend that you always create the Installation Routine Boot Disk during the installation and have it available to boot the system on which it was created. This may not be absolutely necessary, but it can make things easier if there are problems with a system.

④ Testing Your Linux CD/Hard Disk Installation Boot Disk

The steps below test booting from the "Linux CD/Hard Disk Installation Boot Disk" and accessing CD 1 in the CD-ROM drive. They are only required if you cannot boot your system from CD.

If your system is set up to boot from CD before booting from drive A:, then the following steps will not work correctly if CD 1 is in the CD-ROM drive when the system boots because the system will simply boot from CD 1.

If you are doing an installation from CD and cannot boot from CD, boot your system with CD 1 in the CD-ROM drive and the "Linux CD/Hard Disk Installation Boot Disk" in the floppy drive. The "Installation Options Screen" will appear. However, this screen is provided by files on the floppy and does not indicate that you have accessed CD 1.

Press Enter at the "Installation Options Screen" to start the installation routine. This is done to test to see if you can access CD 1. After loading some files from the boot disk, the system should automatically access CD 1 in the CD-ROM drive and the GUI-based "Welcome" screen should appear.

If you are able to get to the GUI-based "Welcome" screen (a screen with "Welcome" at the top middle), congratulations, you are now ready to install Linux!

Now that you have tested that you can run the installation from CD, you can turn your system off (you do not need to exit out of the installation routine).

A few sections from now, you will see instructions to boot to the "Installation Options Screen". When you see these instructions, do the steps necessary to boot your system (from CD 1 or from the "Linux CD/Hard Disk Installation Boot Disk" with CD 1 in the CD-ROM drive) so that you can run the installation routine from CD.

Testing CD 1 and CD 2

When you boot from CD 1 (or boot with the boot disk to access CD 1), you are presented with the "Installation Options Screen". At this screen, you can test a CD by typing in: linux mediacheck and pressing Enter.

If you have not tested CD 1 and CD 2 (supplied with this book), then boot to the "Installation Options Screen" and do the steps above to test them. After tesing CD 1, do the steps to test CD 2.

If a CD appears to be defective, do the same steps as above to test it in a different (current) CD-ROM drive (in case your CD-ROM drive is defective). If a CD works properly in a different CD-ROM drive, then you may need to replace your CD-ROM drive.

If CD 1 or CD 2 are defective, please contact us immediately at 1-800-718-7318 for instructions on returning a defective CD so that you can get a replacement.

The above steps only apply to the testing of CD 1 and CD 2. Do not do these steps to test CD 3. These steps are not required for CD 3.

Section Review

1. Select two correct statements regarding boot disks.

    ☐ A. a boot disk created with netboot.img is used to do an installation from a server to a workstation

    ☐ B. a boot disk created with boot.img is used to boot a system and do a CD installation or a hard disk installation

    ☐ C. a boot disk created with bootcd.img is used to boot a system and do a CD installation

    ☐ D. a boot disk created with bootnet.img is used to do an installation from a server to a workstation

2. Select the two commands that can be used to create boot disks.

    ☐ A. rawrite
    ☐ B. dd
    ☐ C. diskcp
    ☐ D. isocp

3. Which file is created by Anaconda and can be used to provide settings that are used during a kickstart installation?

    ○ A. a binary file named kickstart.img
    ○ B. a text file named kickstart.cfg
    ○ C. a binary file named anaconda-ks.cfg
    ○ D. a text file named anaconda-ks.cfg

4. Which of the following items is a server type that is also referred to as a web server?

    ○ A. FTP
    ○ B. HTTP
    ○ C. TCP/IP
    ○ D. NFS

5. Which of the following statements regarding the installation of Linux are correct (choose two)?

☐ A. a network installation is used to install Linux (OS files) from the hard disk in a server to the same partition in the same server

☐ B. a kickstart installation is a method of automating the installation process so that it can be run without any intervention

☐ C. an installation "over a LAN" can be done from an NFS, FTP or HTTP server

☐ D. a hard disk installation is run by booting from CD 1 and then running: linux hdinstall

6. Which of the following statements can be used to unmount a floppy disk in a floppy drive?

○ A. umount /dev/fd0
○ B. umount /mnt/fd0
○ C. unmount /dev/fd0
○ D. umount /dev/cd0

7. Select the Internet protocol used to transfer files via TCP/IP.

○ A. NFS
○ B. STP
○ C. FTP
○ D. UTP

8. After booting from CD 1, what command can you run at the Installation Options Screen that allows you to select the following methods of installation: Local CDROM, NFS Image, FTP, HTTP and Hard Drive.

○ A. linux rescue
○ B. linux askmethod
○ C. linux netinstall
○ D. linux wherever

Creating Space for Linux

Topics Covered in this Section

Discuss the Linux boot loaders and the purpose of the Master Boot Record
Describe installing Windows and Linux on the same system
Discuss the steps used to create space for Linux on an existing Windows system
Detail the steps to use the GNU Parted utility to reduce the size of a Windows partition
Do the steps to create space for Linux on an existing Windows system

---

In this section, you will learn the order in which Linux and Windows should be installed on a system that does not have an OS and how to create space for Linux on an existing Windows system.

Minimum Disk Space Required by Linux

As described earlier in this chapter, a system requires a minimum of 3 GB of hard disk storage for the installation of the Linux software components that are covered in this book.

You will be using GUI (a.k.a. desktop, X Windows) mode, which requires a minimum of 128 MB of RAM and swap space must be twice the amount of RAM (256 MB).

For this course, a system requires 3 GB of disk space for Linux non-swap partitions, plus sufficient space for the swap partition (256 MB if you have 128 MB of RAM and twice the size of RAM if you have more than 128 MB of RAM).

When creating disk space for Linux, allow for 3 GB, plus the amount of disk space that is required for swap space.

Boot Loaders

Linux and other OSes require a boot loader to boot the system on which they are installed. A boot loader is a software component that is used to boot an OS and it can also be used to provide a menu from which you can select the OS to be booted on a multi-boot system (one that has had more than one OS installed on it).

When you run the Red Hat Linux installation routine (named Anaconda), you have the choice of installing either the **GRUB** (Grand Unified Boot Loader) or **LILO** (LInux LOader) boot loaders. By default, the Red Hat Linux installation routine will install the GRUB boot loader in the **MBR** (Master Boot Record). The MBR is an area on a hard disk that contains a boot loader. It is located on the first sector of the hard disk that is used to boot a system.

If you have installed more than one OS on a system (such as a dual-boot or multi-boot) system that contains Linux and Windows), then the GRUB or LILO boot loader can be set up to present you with the names of the OSes that can be booted when the system starts. At this point, you select the OS to boot with.

When you use the Red Hat Linux installation routine (a.k.a. Anaconda) to install Linux on a system (after installing Windows), then you are automatically presented with a (GRUB or LILO) screen at which you can select which of the two OSes to boot.

Installing Windows and Linux on the Same System

If you have not installed an OS on an x86 system and will be installing both Windows and Linux on the same system, you should install Windows first. When most versions of Windows are installed, they automatically replace the contents of the Master Boot Record (MBR) with a Windows boot loader and this boot loader only allows access to Windows.

If you install Linux and then Windows, Windows will likely replace the existing boot loader (GRUB or LILO in the MBR) with a Windows boot loader and after this, you will not be able to boot Linux. The Linux OS will still be on the hard disk of the system, but there will no longer be a boot loader to give you access to it. If the Linux boot loader is removed from the MBR, you will need to do some extra steps to restore it so that you can boot to Linux as well as Windows. To avoid this problem, simply install Windows before Linux.

When you run the installation routine of almost all versions Windows (see the FYI Icon below), you can specify the size of your Windows partition and set a limit (maximum size) on the amount of disk space that will be used by Windows. Therefore, when installing Windows, specify a size for the Windows partition (the OS, program files and data files) that allows enough space for Windows and still leaves enough unpartitioned space for Linux (3 GB plus the disk space required for the swap space).

Windows 95 and early versions of Windows 98 do not allow you to specify the size of a Windows partition during the installation process. The installation routines of these versions use all of the available disk space for Windows.

Later versions of Windows 98 and all other later versions of Windows (such as NT 4.x, 2000, Me and XP) allow you to specify the size of the Windows partition during the installation process. This allows you to specify a maximum size for Windows and leave disk space free for Linux.

If you are installing a version of Windows that uses all available disk space (Windows 95 or an early version of Windows 98), do the installation and then use the GNU Parted utility (run with the parted command) to reduce the size of the Windows partition to create space for Linux. This utility is included on CD 1 and is described in detail below.

Creating Space for Linux on a System that Already has Windows

Most "desktop" (non-server) x86 systems that are currently being sold have Windows "pre-installed" on them. These systems typically have one hard disk with one partition and Windows takes up all of the space on the partition. This type of system is very common and we will refer to it as a "standard Windows desktop system".

If you have a standard Windows desktop system (where Windows takes up all of the hard disk space), then one simple solution to create space for Linux is to install another hard disk in the system. New and used hard disks are much cheaper than they used to be.

However, most of the hard disks that have been sold in the last few years have plenty of room for both Windows and Linux. If this is the case for your system, you can use a disk partitioning program (a.k.a. partition management utility) to reduce the size of the Windows partition to create space for Linux. This is much easier than creating space by: backing up the data on the Windows partition, removing the partition, reinstalling Windows with a smaller partition size (and then installing your programs and restoring your data). When you use a disk partitioning program to reduce the size of the Windows partition, make sure that you leave enough space for Windows program files and data files that will be added in the near future.

A standard Windows desktop system uses the filesystem types of FAT16, FAT32 and NTFS on its partitions. You can reduce the size of a Windows partition that is using the filesystem type of FAT16 or FAT32 with the Parted utility (included on CD 1). In this case, you will not need to purchase a disk partitioning program. However, the Parted utility does not currently work with the NTFS filesystem. If your Windows partition is using NTFS, then you will need to either find a reliable free disk partitioning program on the Internet that works with NTFS (very difficult to find) or purchase one (recommended).

 The Windows FDISK and Linux fdisk utilities do not allow you to resize (reduce or enlarge) the size of a partition, regardless of filesystem type and the Parted utility does not currently work with NTFS.

If you need to reduce the size of an NTFS partition, there are a few good reliable "third party" disk partitioning programs that will allow you to reduce the size of a Windows partition that is using NTFS. Since you are working with a Windows filesystem (NTFS), these programs are typically GUI utilities that work from within Windows.

To locate a good reliable "third party" disk partitioning program, do a search on the Internet for "partition management utilities", evaluate the programs that are available, and then select the one that will best suit your needs. Make sure the program that you select can work *reliably* with NTFS and that it can **reduce** the size of an NTFS partition *on which Windows is installed*. A utility like this can also be used to create space on partitions that are using FAT16 or FAT32.

The filesystem type of a Windows partition cannot be determined by the version of Windows that you are working with because some versions of Windows can be installed with more than one type of filesystem and also because a Windows system may have kept its "older" filesystem type when it was upgraded. The filesystem type of a Windows partition (represented by a drive letter) can be seen by simply viewing the "properties" of the drive letter from within Windows. These steps are detailed in the Hands-On Exercises.

After you have created space for Linux and installed it on an existing Windows (desktop or server) system, the system can also be used to learn Linux (as a desktop system and/or a server system). This type of installation is commonly done on a Windows system that is in a classroom or home environment, so that the users of the system can learn Linux, but still boot to Windows.

A system that has been set up to run both Windows and Linux is called a "dual-boot" system. When the system starts up, you are presented with a menu (from GRUB or LILO) that allows you to either boot to Windows or boot to Linux. By default, you cannot run both operating systems on the same system at the same time.

When you boot to Windows on a "dual-boot" system, Windows refers to the first partition (on which it is installed) as drive C:. By default, the Linux partition(s) (on one or more disks in the same system) are not "seen" from within Windows (as a drive letter or anything else) and the Windows partitions are not "seen" from within Linux.

The GNU Parted Utility

The Parted utility is a GNU program and is included on CD 1. This utility can be used to reduce the size of a Windows FAT16 or FAT32 partition to make space for Linux. It does not currently work with NTFS partitions, but it will likely do so in the future. The **parted** (**part**ition **ed**itor) command is used to run the Parted utility.

Anaconda (the Red Hat Linux installation routine) allows you to automatically or manually partition a disk for Linux. Anaconda uses the Parted utility "in the background" (behind its text-based or GUI interface) to do all of its partitioning tasks. The partitioning tasks that can be done from within Anaconda are not as extensive as those that can be done when you run the Parted utility from the command line.

For example, you cannot resize (increase or decrease) a partition or copy a partition from within Anaconda, but you can do these tasks when you run the parted command at the command line.

Among other partitioning tasks, the Parted utility can create, remove, check and resize (increase or decrease the size of) partitions. It can also be used to assign filesystems to partitions and copy partitions (and their filesystems).

For more information on GNU Parted, including its extensive documentation, go to:

http://www.gnu.org/software/parted/

The documentation for Parted states that you do not need to defragment your hard disk prior to using this utility. This documentation also states that if you use its resize command to reduce the size of a partition on which Windows is installed, Parted treats your Windows swap file as any other file and will move it, and any other files that need to be moved, to within the new size of the partition that you have specified (if possible).

If you use the resize command (from within the Parted utility) and specify a partition size that is too small (one that cannot hold the existing files on the Windows partition, including the Windows swap file), then the utility will resize the partition to as small a size as it can.

Using Parted to Reduce the Size of a FAT16 or FAT32 Partition

The following steps describe booting a system with Linux, going into rescue mode, and using the Parted utility to reduce the size of a FAT16 or FAT32 partition. Rescue mode is also referred to as "the rescue environment".

Do not do the steps below until you get to the Hands-On Exercises of this section. Read the text below to get an overview of using Parted prior to running this utility.

As described earlier, do not do any Hands-On Exercises in this course until you have backed up your system twice and you are sure that you can retrieve files properly from your backups.

Boot Linux from CD 1 or boot with the Linux CD/Hard Disk Installation Boot Disk (with CD 1 in the CD-ROM drive) so that the "Installation Options Screen" appears.

If you do not type at the boot: prompt or press a function key when the "Installation Options Screen" appears, then Anaconda will automatically start running after a few seconds, as though you pressed the Enter key.

Press F5 and read the information on the Rescue Mode Help screen.

Now you will do the steps to go into rescue mode using the "Skip" option on the Rescue dialog box (rather than the "Continue" or "Read-Only" options). After doing this, the system will have been booted with Linux and you will have access to many (but not all) Linux commands, including the parted command (used to run the Parted utility).

The commands (programs and utilities) that are available in rescue mode are the ones that are commonly needed to "rescue" a system that is not working properly. This includes commands that are used to work with and repair the filesystem, disk partitioning utilities, such as Parted and fdisk, and text editors.

Some Linux distributions (and some *general* Linux documentation) suggest that you boot a system with "the rescue disk" (usually meaning a floppy disk) to go into rescue mode. Older versions of Linux and some current distributions can boot from a floppy and go into rescue mode without CD 1 being in the drive. They do not require a CD to go into rescue mode.

Type in the text shown at the right of the "boot:" prompt below and press Enter.

> boot: *linux rescue*

At the "Choose a Language" dialog box, select your language and press Enter.

At the "Keyboard Type" dialog box, select your keyboard and press Enter.

In upcoming exercises, if the "Choose a Language" and "Keyboard Type" dialog boxes appear, select the desired items and press Enter. These dialog boxes will not be mentioned again in upcoming exercises.

The "Rescue" dialog box appears with the three options of: "Continue" and "Read-Only" and "Skip".

Read the text of the "Rescue" dialog box. The "Continue" and "Read-Only" options are only used when Linux has been installed on a system. When you select "Skip" below, you will be using rescue mode to get to the command shell (a.k.a. command line, shell prompt, shell) so that you can run the Parted utility.

Press Tab twice to highlight "Skip" and press Enter.

The "#" prompt appears and commands can now be run at this prompt. In the steps below, type in the commands that appear at the right of the "#" prompt and press Enter.

When running the parted command in the step shown below, replace the "x" in "hdx" with the letter for your hard disk. For example, if you are modifying a partition on the first EDI hard disk, replace the "x" in "hdx" with "a". In this case, the command to use is: parted /dev/hda.

If you are not using an EDI hard disk, replace "hdx" with the device name of your hard disk. For example, if you are using a SCSI hard disk that is referred to with the letter "b", then replace "hdx" with "scb".

```
# parted  /dev/hdx
```

After running the Parted utility, the "(parted)" prompt appears. Type in the commands shown at the right of the "(parted)" prompt and press Enter.

Press Enter at the following prompt to see a list of commands for this utility.

```
(parted)
```

Read the description of the print, quit and resize commands. The "print" command can be abbreviated by simply typing "p" and the "quit" command can be abbreviated with "q".

The "print" or "p" command causes the utility to "print" to the default output device, which is the screen (not a printer). Many Linux utilities use the word "print" to refer to "printing to the default output device", which is the screen, rather than using the word "print" to refer to sending output to a printer.

```
(parted)  p
```

The utility "prints" (to the screen) a list of partitions that are on the disk.

The first line, "Disk geometry ... ", shows the start and end of the disk in megabytes. The partition number(s) appear below the "Minor" heading; the start of each partition (in megabytes) appears below the "Start" heading; and the end of each partition (in megabytes) appears below the "End" heading.

The "Start" may not appear exactly at "0". It may show a number similar to "0.031". Use this number when specifying the amount for "START" when you are using the resize command below.

Notice the number of the partition that you want to resize and the start and end of it.

The resize command has the following syntax (format):

```
resize MINOR  START  END
```

This command uses the three settings of: MINOR, START and END. MINOR is used to specify the partition number; START is used to specify the start of the partition in megabytes; and END is used to specify the end of the partition in megabytes.

Example of Reducing the Size of a Primary Partition

Here is the first scenario: Windows has been installed on one of your systems. The system has one 12 GB EDI hard disk and Windows is using all of the space on it. Windows refers to this disk as drive C:. You need to reduce the size of the Windows partition to create space for Linux. You have estimated that the Windows partition on this system (with the OS, program files, data files and some room for growth) only requires 3 GB (3,000 MB). Therefore, there will be about 9 GB available for Linux. Lots!

You have run the Parted utility (with the command: parted /dev/hda) and used: p   to print the partition table of the hard disk (to the screen). It shows that Primary partition number 1 starts at 0.031 and ends at 12158.569. The disk is approximately 12 GB.

To reduce the size of this Windows partition to 3 GB, run the following command, which resizes partition 1 (MINOR) with a starting point at 0.031 MB (START) and an ending point at 3000 MB (END).

```
(parted) resize 1 0.031 3000
```

After a brief period of time (usually less than a minute), the "(parted)" prompt appears again and the partition has been resized! The disk space between 3 GB (3000 MB) and 12 GB (12158.569 MB) is now empty and is available for you to install Linux on it!

Now use the "p" (print) command and look at the partition(s) again to see that the resizing worked the way that you expected.

```
(parted) p
```

If you run the resize command and specify an ending megabyte size that is too small to hold the existing Windows files (OS, programs, data and swap file), then you will see the ending megabyte size at a setting that is higher than the amount that you specified. This amount is the minimum size that can be used.

 If you are really tight for space and the resize command does not reduce the size of the partition enough, you may be able to: run Windows; reduce the size of your Windows swap file and then do the steps to resize the partition again.

Some versions of Windows allow you to reduce the swap file size fairly easily and others do not. To see the steps to reduce the size of the Windows swap file, search for "virtual memory" or "swap file" in Help in Windows.

You do not need to save the partition change to the disk prior to exiting out of the Parted utility. Now quit out of the utility.

> (parted) q

The "#" prompt appears again. Run the following command to exit out of your rescue mode command line "session".

>]# exit

Remove the CD from the drive and allow your system to boot to Windows.

Select Yes if you are prompted (from within Windows) to reboot Windows. This prompt may appear because Windows has detected a change in your system (the reduced partition size), has made a modification to its settings, and needs to be rebooted to accommodate the change.

Reboot Windows. Select Yes again if you are prompted (from within Windows) to reboot Windows.

After rebooting, run a few programs and retrieve a few data files to check that Windows still works as expected.

Example of Reducing the Size of a Logical Partition

Here is the second scenario: Windows has been installed on another one of your systems. The system has one 8 GB EDI hard disk and Windows is using all of the space on it. There are two Windows partitions on the disk, one 3 GB Primary and one 5 GB Logical (in an Extended partition). Windows refers to the partitions on this disk as drives C: and D:.

You have estimated that Windows requires all of the space on the Primary partition (3 GB on drive C:) and 500 MB of space (out of the 5 GB of space) on the Logical partition (drive D:). The Logical partition has the number 5. You need to reduce the size of the Logical partition so that it only provides the 500 MB that Windows requires.

Even though Windows considers that the system has two drive letters, C: and D:, and you are reducing the size of drive D:, you still run the parted command with /dev/hda, rather than /dev/hdb, because the partition that you need to resize is on the first (and only) hard disk in the system.

You have gone into rescue mode with the Skip option, run the parted command and printed the partition table. It shows that the Primary partition starts at 0.031 and ends at 3000.312 and that the Logical partition (in the Extended partition) starts at 3000.312 and ends at 8135.695.

To reduce the size of the Logical partition so that it only takes up 500 MB, the following command is used. It resizes partition 5 (MINOR) so that it has a starting point at 3000.312 MB (START) and an ending point at 3500 MB (END).

 (parted) resize 5 3000.312 3500

Now the 4.5 GB of disk space on the Logical partition between 3500 MB and 8000 MB is available for Linux.

After using the print command to see that the resize command worked as expected, you quit out of the Parted utility, exit out of rescue mode and reboot Windows. If Windows requests a reboot, you select Yes, reboot Windows and run a few programs and retrieve a few data files to check that Windows still works as expected.

The fips Utility

Some Linux documentation suggests using the fips utility to create space for Linux. Therefore, we are briefly describing this utility here. However, the Parted utility is much more powerful than fips and is easier to use.

The sole purpose of the fips utility is to split a Windows partition into two (not necessarily equal) partitions so that you can create space for Linux. After splitting a Windows partition, you must run another partitioning utility, such as fdisk or parted and delete the "second" partition. The space that was being used by the "second" partition is the space that is then used for Linux.

The fips utility can only split a FAT16 or FAT32 partition. It cannot split an NTFS partition. *It also cannot split an Extended partition* (any Logical partitions in an Extended partition) regardless of the filesystem type of the Logical partitions in the Extended partition. This utility does not do any other partitioning tasks, such as create or delete partitions.

For more information on fips, go to: www.igd.fhg.de/~aschaefe/fips/

 As described earlier in this chapter, we recommend that you take certain precautions, such as using an antistatic wristband, and backing up your system, prior to doing any of the tasks described in this book.

Hands-On Exercises

The minimum hard disk space required for all of the Linux software components that will be used in this course is 3 GB, plus the disk space required for the swap space.

Do the steps described below if you:

- have a Windows system that meets the minimum hardware requirements
- your system has does not have enough unpartitioned free hard disk space for Linux
- one of your Windows partitions may have enough space for Linux

 ### Checking a Windows System for Free Disk Space and the Filesystem Types on Its Partitions

If you are installing Linux on an existing Windows system, then boot to Windows and do the following steps to check for free disk space and the filesystem type of your first Windows partition (drive C:).

> My Computer x 2 ; C: x r ; Properties.

If drive C: does not provide you with enough free space, check any other hard disk drive letters in My Computer.

Fill in the following settings of the drive that provides you with the space that you require:

> Drive letter: _____
>
> Total space (capacity): _____
>
> Free Space: _____
>
> Filesystem type: _____

If you will be using the Parted utility below to reduce the size of a FAT16 or FAT32 filesystem on a Windows partition, you need to specify the Linux device name of the hard disk that you want to resize.

In Windows, any drive letter above C: does not necessarily indicate the Linux device name. For example, a Windows drive C: is usually a Linux drive /dev/hda, but drive D: is not necessarily /dev/hdb. If a Windows system with a single drive has two partitions, then Windows refers to these as drives C: and D:. But if they are both on the same drive, then D: is the second partition on the first drive, and Linux refers to the first drive as /dev/hda (not /dev/hdb).

For information on the hard disks in your system, see the notes that you made on the hard disks in your system, while documenting your hardware setup earlier.

Be sure to specify the correct hard disk device name, such as /dev/hda or /dev/hdb, when running the parted utility to reduce the size of your Windows partition.

After running the Parted utility (and specifying the device name of your hard disk), you will type "p" (for "print" to the screen) and press Enter to see a listing of the partitions on the drive.

Use the settings in the partition listing to make sure that you reduce the size of the correct partition. In other words, make sure that you reduce the size of the partition that corresponds to the Windows drive letter that you wrote down above (the one on which you will be reducing the partition size).

For example, check that the filesystem type of the partition that you are about to resize, as seen under the "Filesystem" heading, is "FAT". This indicates that the partition is using a filesystem type of FAT16 or FAT32. As described earlier, the Parted utility does not currently work with partitions that are using the NTFS filesystem.

Also, use the "Start" and "End" settings (shown in MB) of the partition to calculate the size of the partition and compare this to the "Total space" setting that you wrote down above.

Make sure that you specify the correct drive (device name) when you run the parted command and that you specify the correct partition on the drive when you run the resize command!

 ## Creating Space for Linux with the Parted Utility

If you have a partition that is using a filesystem of FAT16 or FAT32, then follow the steps described earlier in this section and use the Parted utility to reduce the size of one of your Windows partitions to create at least 3.5 GB of space for Linux. See the "Using Parted to Reduce the Size of a FAT16 or FAT32 Partition" heading above.

③ Creating Space for Linux with a Reliable "Third Party" Partition Management Utility

If the Windows partition on which you need to create space is using the NTFS filesystem, then use a reliable "third party" partition management utility to create the space you need.

The steps to search the Internet for this type of utility are described at the FYI Icon below the "Creating Space for Linux on a System that Already has Windows" heading.

Section Review

1. Select the location in which a boot loader is installed.

   ○ A. LILO
   ○ B. MBR
   ○ C. GRUB
   ○ D. RAM

2. The Parted utility can be used to resize partitions that are using the FAT16 and FAT32 filesystems. T F

3. Which of the following can be used to reduce the size of a Windows partition (choose two)?

   ☐ A. the fdisk utility
   ☐ B. the FDISK (Windows) utility
   ☐ C. the Parted utility
   ☐ D. some "third party" partition management utilities

4. If Windows is installed after Linux on the same system, the Windows installation routine will usually wipe out all Linux partitions. T F

5. Select two boot loaders that can be used with Linux.

   ☐ A. MBR
   ☐ B. LILO
   ☐ C. FDISK
   ☐ D. GRUB

6. Windows has been installed on a 10 GB EDI hard disk in one of your systems and is taking up all of the space on the disk. The disk has a 4 GB Primary partition and a 6 GB Logical partition. You have estimated that Windows only requires 5 GB. The Logical partition starts at 4000.482 MB.

Select the command that will reduce the size of the Logical partition so that Windows only has access to the space that it requires.

- ○ A. resize 2 4000.482 5000
- ○ B. parted 2 4000.482 1000
- ○ C. resize 5 4000.482 5000
- ○ D. reduce 5 4000.482 5000

7. What is a benefit of installing (most versions of) Windows prior to installing Linux on the same system?

- ○ A. Windows will use less space if it is installed first
- ○ B. Linux will run faster if it is installed second
- ○ C. the Windows installation routine will not replace the boot loader installed by Linux with its own boot loader and therefore will not stop the Linux boot loader from providing access to Linux
- ○ D. the Windows installation routine will "strap-load" itself to the ram disk partition of the Linux kernel so that both operating systems can be run simultaneously

8. By default, when you use the "p" (print) command in the Parted utility, you are sending a listing of the partitions on the disk to the default printer. T F

9. You are working on a system that has not had an operating system installed on it yet. Select the "mode" that can be used to get to the shell prompt so that you can access and run some of the Linux commands and utilities.

- ○ A. binary
- ○ B. GUI
- ○ C. login
- ○ D. rescue

Installing Linux

Topics Covered in this Section

Discuss the Linux OS software components and installation routines
Describe running various options available through the Installation Options Screen
Learn the types of installation that can be performed on a system
Run the Anaconda installation routine and do all of the steps to install a server system
Learn the various directories that are typically used as mount points
Manually partition the hard disk and assign directories as mount points to partitions
Do the steps to configure: the boot loader, various network settings, the
X Window System and all of your hardware components
Select and install packages (software components) and discuss package dependencies
Log in to your new system and work with icons on the desktop and the panel

In this section, you will run the Anaconda installation routine, configure all of your hardware components, manually partition your hard disk, select the packages required for your system and do all of the steps to install Linux!

Linux Software Components and Installation Routines

GNU/Linux consists of a thousands of software components (in source code and binary form) that are available free of charge via the Internet from all over the world. These components include the Linux kernel and several types of GNU software components, such as programs that provide commands and utilities, software libraries and programming languages.

Some of the GNU/Linux software components are selected by a company that creates a distribution and are included in a distribution. A company that creates a distribution decides which of the GNU software components (and other software components) are put together with the Linux kernel and included with the distribution. A company that creates a distribution may also include software components that they have created specifically for their distribution.

For example, the Red Hat distribution includes the Anaconda, Kudzu and RPM software components. These three components were created by Red Hat and are all available under the GNU General Public License. Any distribution can use the source code of these three components. However, some do and some do not.

Anaconda provides the Red Hat distribution with its installation routine. Kudzu is used for hardware detection and configuration. RPM allows for easy software program (a.k.a. package) installation, upgrade and uninstallation.

The set of packages provided in one distribution may be similar to those provided in other distributions, but they will not be exactly the same.

Some of the packages included in one version of a distribution will likely not be included in the next version (of the same distribution) and some new packages will likely be added. Binaries (supplied in packages) that are used for commands do not change as frequently as binaries (supplied in packages) that are used for GUI utilities or applications.

For example, a GUI media player utility or GUI network monitoring tool included in the current version of a distribution may be removed from the next version, but a commonly used command, such as the ls (list) command, will not likely be removed.

Virtually all Red Hat software components are provided as packages in .rpm files. The CDs included with this book contain over 1,200 .rpm files. When you purchase the Red Hat Linux distribution you get even more .rpm files on CD. You can also locate and download thousands of .rpm files at http://www.rpmfind.net.

When you run Anaconda (the Red Hat Linux installation routine) during this section to install Red Hat Linux, you will be using a GUI interface to select the software components required for this course. You will select category (package group) headings, such as "Development Tools", that will cause the packages that exist in the category (as .rpm files on CD 1 and CD 2) to be installed. After selecting a heading, you can select "Details ..." to see the names of the packages that are installed for the category. In addition to this, you can select individual packages that you need by name so that you can install the .rpm files that provide those packages.

The Anaconda Installation Routine

One of the main components that is usually created (modified and maintained) by a company that creates a distribution is the installation routine of the distribution, such as Anaconda.

When you run the Anaconda installation routine, you can install some or all of the software components that have been selected by Red Hat to be included in their distribution. A different distribution may use a different installation routine (which may be a modified version of source code that was created by someone else) and this will allow you to install a similar, but different selection of software components.

From a Linux system administration perspective, the main software components that are similar from one distribution to another are the commands that are run at the command line. After working with the GNOME and KDE desktops in the next chapter, the main focus of the remainder of this book is on working at the command line to learn how to use the commands that are common to most Linux distributions.

While learning commands, you will learn when and why you need to run a command, how to run it with the commonly used options, and what the benefits are of using it. You will also learn about many different Linux OS features and concepts, and then use the commands required to work with these features.

Starting the Linux Installation

 As described in the first section of this chapter, we recommend that you back up your system (twice) and make sure that you can restore from your backup, prior to doing any of the tasks described in this book.

If you need more information on your system while working through the installation process below, look at the notes that you made earlier, in the section named Linux Hardware Requirements and Documenting Your Hardware Setup.

Hands-On Exercises

Boot your system from CD 1 (or from floppy with CD 1 in the CD-ROM drive) so that the "Installation Options Screen" appears ;

immediately press the F2 function key and then the F1 key to return to the "Installation Options Screen".

If you boot to this screen and do nothing for a few seconds, then the installation will automatically start as though you had pressed Enter.

Read the options that appear on the opening "Installation Options Screen".

You can simply press Enter to begin the installation or type in options at the "boot:" prompt and press Enter.

Notice the "function key menu" at the bottom of the screen.

Press the F2 function key to see the Installer Boot Options screen and read this screen.

The "Installation Options Screen" allows you to use function keys to see how to run other options, such as typing: linux rescue at the boot: prompt to go into Rescue Mode or typing: linux askmethod to install from: Local CDROM, NFS Image, FTP, HTTP or Hard Drive.

Press F3 and read the General Boot Help screen.

Press F4 and read the Kernel Parameter Help screen.

Press F5 for Rescue Mode Help and read this screen.

To go into rescue mode, you must either boot from CD 1, or boot with the "Linux CD/Hard Disk Installation Boot Disk" and have the Linux Installation CD 1 in the CD-ROM drive when you start. You can *not* go into rescue mode by simply booting from floppy (without the Linux Installation CD 1 in the CD-ROM drive).

Press F1 to go back to the opening "Installation Options Screen".

The most commonly used option is shown at the top and you simply press Enter to start Anaconda. This runs the routine in GUI mode and most systems can be installed in this mode.

Press Enter to start the installation routine.

A lot of lines of text will appear on the screen, then it will turn solid blue, and then some more text will appear at the bottom of the blue screen. If the routine can properly access your graphics card and monitor, then you will see the GUI-based "Welcome" (near the top middle) screen. If this screen appears, then go to the "Responding to the Screens in the Installation Routine" heading below.

 Running Other Options of the Installation Routine

If the installation routine starts and then your screen flickers and continues to flicker, then your graphics card and monitor may not be accessible to the routine. Restart your system and try running the installation routine by using a different option (other than just pressing Enter).

If the routine starts and nothing happens for over a minute (it hangs), you may have a defective CD or a defective CD-ROM drive.

If you have not already tested your CDs, then use the "linux mediacheck" option (seen by pressing F2) to test your CDs. If a CD appears to be defective, do the same steps as above to test it in a different (current) CD-ROM drive (in case your CD-ROM drive is defective). If a CD works properly in a different CD-ROM drive, then you may need to replace your CD-ROM drive.

If CD 1 or CD 2 are defective, please contact us immediately at 1-800-718-7318 for instructions on returning a defective CD so that you can get a replacement.

The above steps apply to the testing of CD 1 and CD 2. Do not do these steps to test CD 3. These steps are not required for CD 3.

 Responding to the Screens in the Installation Routine

The installation routine presents several screens in which you select items and specify settings. The headings that appear below are the same as the screens that appear, and the text below the headings describes how to respond to them.

By default, Online Help appears on the left side of the screen. This provides you with lots of useful information. Don't forget to read this information!

 Welcome

This screen greets you to start the installation. Read the Online Help information at the left. You can read or download the Red Hat manuals at http://www.redhat.com.

All of the Red Hat Linux manuals are available at http://www.redhat.com as HTML (hypertext) files and as PDF (.pdf) files. When you do the default installation below, you will install a utility called xpdf. This program is the equivalent of the Acrobat Reader program and is used to read .pdf files.

You may want to download the Red Hat Linux manuals (in .pdf form) and put them on your system so that you can search them for additional information. Clicking on a .pdf file from within a file manager (also installed by default as part of the GNOME and KDE desktops) automatically runs the xpdf utility so that you can view the Red Hat Linux manuals.

Click on Next at the bottom right.

④ Language Selection

Select your language ; Next.

⑤ Keyboard

Select your keyboard ; Next.

⑥ Mouse Configuration

If you have a fancy mouse (one that likes to go to parties), look for and select your specific mouse brand, and model. Otherwise, select Generic and then select the 2 or 3 button mouse that matches your mouse port type. The correct mouse type and port may be highlighted by default.

If you are using a PS/2 mouse, you do not need to specify a setting (serial port) below Device ;

if you are not using a PS/2 mouse, select the correct COM number for your mouse below Device (if it is not already selected) ;

If you have a 2 button mouse, the Emulate 3 Buttons option at the bottom of the screen is selected by default ; if this item is selected, leave it selected.

The Linux GUI environment uses a three button mouse. When you choose to emulate a three button mouse, pressing the left and right mouse buttons together is the equivalent of pressing the middle (third) mouse button.

Select Next.

Installation Type

Read the text below Online Help.

In a minute, you will select "Manually partition with Disk Druid" and select the partitions on which to install the OS. If you select a partition that contains data (OS, programs and data files) and do an installation, then the contents of the partition will be deleted. However, if you select a partition that does not contain data, then the data on other partitions is *not* deleted.

At the top, "Install on System" is selected, as opposed to the "Upgrade Existing System" option at the bottom of the screen.

Select Server ; Next.

When you install a server, you can also install the X Window System and the GNOME and KDE desktops. This allows the system to also work as a desktop system.

 Disk Partitioning Setup

The option of "Automatically partition" is selected. This causes the installation routine to automatically set up and create the partitions that you require. However, if you accept the default setup provided after selecting this option, then you may end up with a directory assigned as a mount point to a very large Primary partition and this can waste space. This default setup can be modified, but rather than modifying the "automatic" partition settings, we will manually partition the disk with the Disk Druid component of Anaconda (which uses the Parted utility "in the background").

 If you ever select "Automatically partition" (not recommended), then be sure that you never select "Remove all partitions on this system" unless you want to have all of the data on your system removed.

Select Manually partition with Disk Druid ; Next.

 Partitioning

This screen of the installation routine is the Disk Druid (manual) partitioning tool. It is a powerful and flexible GUI utility that can be used to add, modify and delete partitions.

Read the Online Help at the side and then select Hide Help at the bottom of the screen if you can not see all of the Partitioning screen information.

At the top of the screen, information regarding the drive(s) that you selected on the previous screen appears.

Below this, buttons which are used to specify settings appear, such as New, Edit and Delete.

Below the "Device" heading, the device name of a drive appears, such as /dev/hda. This is used to represent the entire drive. Below this, you may see partitions that already exist.

Below "Start" and "End" are the starting and ending cylinders of each partition. At the left of this, the "Size (MB)" of each partition appears.

Below "Type", the filesystem type of the partition appears and below "Mount Point", the Linux directory (if any) to which the partition will be assigned appears.

As you specify new partitions, a "check mark" will appear below the "Format" heading to indicate that they will be formatted by the installation routine.

If you have Windows installed this hard disk, the partition(s) used by Windows will show "vfat" below "Type" and a "check mark" will not appear below "Format".

Earlier, we described using partitions to restrict the space available to a directory, such as the /home directory or the /var directory. You will specify directory sizes for various mount points in the steps below and this will restrict the sizes of these directories.

Your Instructor may suggest partition settings that are different from the settings below.

Below the "Type" heading, only select "Free space" while doing the steps below. Do not select any partitions that show vfat or any other partition type.

At this point in the course you either have an empty hard disk, or free space on a hard disk, on which to install the OS. If you do not see "Free space" below the "Type" heading, go back to the section named Creating Space for Linux and create the free disk space that you require.

Now you will specify the settings for the mount points, filesystem types and directory sizes for your Linux installation.

⑩ Creating the /boot Partition

Below the "Type" heading, select "Free space" on the disk on which you want to install Linux ;

New (button at the middle of the screen) ;

A dialog box appears that allows you to specify settings for a new partition (mount point).

A "down arrow" at the right of "Mount Point:" can be used to provide access to a "drop-down menu".

Click on the "down arrow" at the right of "Mount Point:" to see the default names that can be used for directories that can become mount points.

The following directories are commonly set up as mount points (on *various* types of Linux systems) and can be selected in Anaconda so that they can become mount points:

/, /boot, /home, /tmp, /usr, /var, /usr/local, /opt

In addition to the swap partition, the following directories are typically created as mount points and assigned to a partition on a Linux *server* system: /, /boot, /home, /usr and /var. The size of the partitions to which these directories points is dependent on the usage of the system. You will learn more about the commonly used Linux directories in an upcoming section.

The Linux OS uses many directories that are common to all distributions. Of these directories, the following directories are not commonly used as mount points and cannot be set up as mount points from within the Disk Druid component of Anaconda:

/bin, /dev, /etc, /lib, /mnt, /proc, /root and /sbin

The above directories must exist off of the / directory and be in the partition to which the / directory points.

Beside Mount Point:, select /boot ;

beside File System Type:, ext3 is selected by default ;

click on the "down arrow" at the right of "File System Type:" to see filesystem types that can be selected.

The following filesystems can be selected from within Disk Druid:

ext2, ext3, physical volume (LVM), software RAID, swap, vfat

beside File System Type:, select ext3 (if it is not already selected) ;

beside Size:, specify 100 MB ;

below Additional Size Options, select Fixed size (if it is not already selected) ; OK.

You may see a Warning dialog box with a message that suggests that you create a boot disk.

if you see the Warning dialog box, select Continue.

Your partition settings for the "boot partition" (/boot) appear. Your partition size may be up or down a few megabytes from the size that you specified.

⑪ Creating the / (root) Partition

Now you will create a partition for the / (root) directory.

Below the "Type", select "Free space" (on the correct hard disk) ; New (button) ;

beside Mount Point:, select / ; beside File System Type:, select ext3 ;

beside Size:, specify 300 MB ; below Additional Size Options, select Fixed size ; OK.

Your partition settings for the / (root) partition appear.

⑫ Creating Additional Partitions

Repeat the above steps to create the partitions described below.

Always select "Free space" (below "Type") prior to selecting "New" during the steps below.

After creating a few mount points, they may appear on the bottom half of the "Partitioning" screen in a different order than the order in which they were created.

While creating the partitions below, make sure that you have at least 50 MB of free (unpartitioned) hard disk space for an exercise that will be done later in the course. If you are really tight on disk space, only create a 400 MB partition (rather than 450 MB) for the /var directory (mount point) below.

Create an ext3 partition that is 200 MB for the /home directory (mount point).

Create an ext3 partition that is 2000 MB (2 GB) for the /usr directory (mount point).

Create an ext3 partition that is 450 MB for the /var directory (mount point).

(13) Creating the swap Partition

You need at least 128 MB of RAM for GUI mode (used in this course) and swap space should be twice the amount of RAM, up to 2,048 MB (2 GB).

Do the steps below and specify the swap size (2 x RAM) that you require.

Below the "Type", select "Free space" ; New (button) ;

do not select a directory path beside Mount Point: ;

beside File System Type:, select swap ;

beside Size:, specify the swap size that you require ;

below Additional Size Options, select Fixed size ; OK ;

check that your partitions are the correct size ; select Next.

(14) Boot Loader Configuration

As described earlier, a boot loader is a utility program that is used to boot your operating system. There are two types of boot loader that can be selected here. GRUB is the default boot loader used with this version of Linux. LILO was used in earlier versions of Linux as the default boot loader.

GRUB is a graphical boot loader that appears when your system boots. It presents you with the names of the operating systems that can be booted.

If you install Windows on a system after installing Linux, Windows will usually overwrite the boot loader in the MBR. If this happens, you need to boot Linux into Rescue Mode and reinstall the GRUB (or LILO) boot loader.

As described earlier, the MBR is located on the first hard disk in your system and is the first area read by the system when the hard disk boots. It is used to contain the information required to boot your OS(es).

By default, the "Label" for a DOS/Windows partition is "DOS". Leave this as is. Also by default, the "Label" for Red Hat Linux is simply "Red Hat Linux". Also leave this as is.

Below "Default", a "check mark" appears at the left of "Red Hat Linux" and at the right of "Red Hat Linux" is the partition device name of the partition to which the / directory points, such as /dev/hda7. This is the default OS that will be booted (this is the OS to be booted, not the boot partition). Notice the path to the device name of the / partition, such as /dev/hda7.

Select Back.

Below Mount Point, look for the / (root) partition and notice that the device name path at the left matches the device name path on the next screen.

When this system boots, the GRUB screen will appear and "Red Hat Linux" (the boot loader label) will appear highlighted at the top. The Windows operating system, shown as "DOS" (same as the boot label), will appear below Linux and can easily be selected by pressing the down arrow key and pressing Enter. The selected OS is then loaded. This provides an easy method of selecting the OS to load on a dual-boot system.

Select Next.

 Boot Loader Password Configuration

Read the Help at the left and the text above "Use a boot loader password".

Select "Use a boot loader password".

When creating passwords, we recommend that you use at least six characters, use some non-alpha characters, such as numbers and also use a mixture of upper and lower case letters.

Linux is "case sensitive". If you type a letter of a password in upper case when you create a password, then you must also type it in upper case when using the password.

This also applies to commands and files. When specifying the name of a command or file, you must type in the letters of the command or file in the correct "case" (upper or lower).

When creating passwords, we also recommend that you use a password that you can remember, but also that you do not use a word that would easily be associated with you, such as the name of your favorite pet.

Passwords do not "echo" (display) on the screen as they are typed in. All passwords that you type in must be confirmed by typing them in again. This ensures that you actually typed in what you thought you typed in!

Type in a password beside "Password:" and then type in the same password beside "Confirm:". Write the password down in a secure place and don't forget where you put it!

Select OK ; Next.

 Network Configuration

If a network card is not installed in your system, you will not see this screen. This screen is used to specify settings for a local area network.

Your system is likely using an Ethernet network card. The first Ethernet card in a system is eth0 and by default, "Active on Boot" is selected so that the card (and therefore your system) can access the network.

Also by default, IP/Netmask is set to DHCP.

Settings for this screen are provided below.

Network Configuration - IP/Netmask set to DHCP

If you are using DHCP, leave this item selected.

 On a network, your system needs an IP (Internet Protocol) address to uniquely identify your system. An IP address can either be provided using DHCP (see below) or you can type in a "static" address. Organizations with a fixed number of IP addresses and users that do not continually need them, can use DHCP to deliver IP addresses as needed.

DHCP stands for **D**ynamic **H**ost **C**onfiguration **P**rotocol. This is a method of dynamically (automatically) providing an IP address to a system. If your network is using DHCP, the DHCP software is set up on a host (server) and is provided with a "pool" of IP addresses. When a system needs an IP address, DHCP delivers it to the system. The system has the capability of using the address for a period of time and when that time is up, the address is returned to the "pool" so that it can be delivered to a different system (or the same system).

The other method of specifying an IP address is to use a "static" address. In this case, an address is typed in for a workstation and does not change until it is manually changed or removed.

If you are in a classroom environment, your Instructor may need to provide you with settings that are different from the settings below.

If you are not using DHCP, select Edit and deselect "Configure using DHCP" ;

leave "Activate on boot" selected ; this causes your network card to "start" (have software access it) when you boot.

Network Configuration - IP Address

If you are in a classroom environment, add your student number to the last number in the following IP address: 192.168.100.50.

For example, if you are student 1, use 192.168.100.51, if you are student 7, use 192.168.100.57 and if you are student 14, use 192.168.100.64.

Beside IP Address, type in this number ; press Tab.

Network Configuration - Netmask

This setting specifies which part of the IP address is used to represent the network and which part is used to represent the host computer.

For Netmask, type in 255.255.255.0 ; OK.

 Network Configuration - Hostname

This name is used to identify your system within the Internet domain.

Beside "manually", type in your Hostname:, using the following format: lancomx.lancom.com. Use all lower case letters. If you are in a classroom environment, replace the **x** in lancomx with your student number, plus 50.

For example, if you are student 7, replace the **x** with 57 (50 plus 7) and type in:

lancom57.lancom.com.

If you are not in a classroom environment, use: lancom51.lancom.com for the Hostname:.

 Network Configuration - Gateway

The number specified here is the number that is used by a computer that is acting as a gateway to connect your LAN to one or more networks outside of your LAN. Unless you are provided with a number for this item, leave it blank.

 Network Configuration - Primary DNS

A number is entered here to specify the IP address of the Primary DNS server. Unless you are provided with a number for this item, leave it blank.

 Domain names, such as lancom-tech.com have a corresponding IP address, such as 199.202.234.101. People use names because they are much easier to remember than IP addresses, but your system needs to use the address (number).

DNS stands for **D**omain **N**ame **S**ervice (a.k.a. **D**omain **N**ame **S**ystem). This is software that is installed on a host (server) that converts a domain name into an IP address, so that the address can be contacted. The DNS software contains a database of domain names and the IP addresses that are associated with the names.

When you type a domain name into a program, such as at the top of your web browser, your system accesses the IP address (specified by the Primary DNS setting) of the Primary DNS server. The DNS server then converts the domain name (that you typed in) into an IP address and provides it to your system so that you can contact the address.

For example, you have specified a Primary DNS address of 192.168.0.1 on the Network Configuration screen. You start your web browser and type in the address of www.lancom-tech.com. Your system goes to the address of the Primary DNS server (192.168.0.1). The DNS software looks in its database for www.lancom-tech.com, finds the IP address of 199.202.234.101, returns it to your system and then your web browser goes to the web site!

 ## Network Configuration - Secondary DNS and Tertiary DNS

Unless you have been provided with numbers for these settings, they are not required. Secondary and Tertiary DNS numbers are alternate addresses that the system can use if the Primary DNS address can not be contacted.

Select Next ;

if you have not specified a Gateway IP address or a Primary DNS address, you may see an error message ;

if you do not require these addresses, select Continue.

 ## Firewall Configuration

To find out more about this screen, read the Help information at the left.

For some of the upcoming Hands-On Exercises, we do *not* want or require a firewall.

By default, the security level is set to Medium.

Change this by selecting **No firewall** ; Next.

 ## Additional Language Support

This screen allows you to add other languages to your system. The default of English (USA) appears at the top (right) of the screen and is also selected further below.

Select your language ; Next.

Time Zone Selection

Notice that there is a red "x" on the map that appears. This is the "you are here" part of the installation. You can click on the map to indicate your time zone or select it from the list at the bottom of the screen.

Select your time zone ; Next.

 Account Configuration

An "account" is a user name and the permissions (a.k.a. access capabilities) that the user has to the system. The system always has a user named "root" (a.k.a. superuser, su) that has access to all areas of the system.

 Assigning the root User a Password

Type in a password for this user beside Root Password: ;

type in the same password beside Confirm:.

 The root user requires a password and it must be a minimum of six characters. Remember our suggestions above for creating passwords.

It is not a good idea to access the system as the root user when you are not doing system administration tasks, such as installing software and doing system maintenance. It is also not a good idea to use the root user when doing relatively short system administration tasks. It is easy to make a mistake when logged in as root that could damage a system or erase all of the files on a system.

Therefore, you will now create another user (account) so that you can log in as this user and do "day-to-day" tasks, and also to "see" the system from the perspective of a "regular" (non-root) user. This will be used to demonstrate the access (rights) of a "regular" user.

When you are logged in as a non-root user, you can use the command: su - at the command line and then provide a password so that you can temporarily work as the root user.

Some people believe that you should never log in as the root user and only use the above su command (or a variation of it) to do system administration tasks.

 Creating a User Account

Start to create another user by clicking on the Add button.

When doing the Hands-On Exercises for this course, we will refer to the user name of cwest rather than referring to "your username". Whenever you see cwest, replace this with the user name that you create now.

So, if you see instructions to "log in as cwest", then log in with the user name that you create here. If you see a reference to "your the home directory" or a directory path that includes the directory named cwest, replace cwest with the username that you create here.

In some of the examples and exercises throughout this course, we will be using a user name of cwest for a person named Chris West. Either create a user named cwest now or use your own name for your own account.

Beside User Name:, use all lower case letters and type in: *cwest* or use the first letter of your first name and all of your last name ; press Tab ;

type in a password ; make this password slightly different from the password that you used for the root user ; press Tab ;

type in the password again ; press Tab ;

beside Full Name:, type in: *Chris West* or type in your first name, a space and your last name ; capitalize the first letters of your first and last name ;

click OK.

If you made a mistake while creating a user, you can use the Edit button to modify settings of the user or the Delete button to remove the user.

select Next.

Remember that a user named root has been created and that you also created another user. Both of these users have passwords and they are slightly different.

Package Group Selection

"Packages" are Linux software components and include programs, such as a applications, utilities and programming languages. This screen is used to choose the programs that the system will install. There are over 1,200 "packages" on the CDs that accompany this book!

Notice the Total install size: setting at the bottom right of the screen. This will increase as you select items in the steps below.

When you select a package group, "Details . . ." appears at the right of the screen. This can be selected to see the items (packages) in the package group and allows you to select additional items.

To ensure that all of the Hands-On Exercises in this course work smoothly, please **select only** the packages listed below and also **deselect** the packages listed below.

Select the following package groups:

X Window System, GNOME Desktop Environment, KDE Desktop Environment

Editors, Graphical Internet, leave Text-based Internet selected,

Office/Productivity, Sound and Video, Graphics

leave Server Configuration Tools selected ;

deselect Web Server and Windows File Server ;

select Development Tools, Kernel Development ;

leave Administration Tools and Printing Support selected ;

beside Printing Support, select Details ;

below Optional Packages, select Cups ; OK.

Be sure to click on "Select individual packages" (at the bottom of the screen) in the step below. This will allow you to individually select some packages that are required for the Hands-On Exercises to work smoothly.

click on Select individual packages ; select Next.

 Individual Package Selection

By default, Tree View is selected so that you can select individual packages by category. Do not deselect any packages in the steps below.

You need to select Flat View so that you can easily locate packages alphabetically and select them. When you select a package, a description of it appears at the bottom of the screen.

Select Flat View ; there will be a short wait before the Flat View (alphabetical listing) appears.

Scroll down and select the following packages:

freetype-devel, GConf-devel, gdk-pixbuf-devel,

gnome-print-devel, gnome-vfs-devel, oaf-devel ;

select Next.

Unresolved Dependencies

Sometimes a package requires one or more other packages in order to function. When a packages requires one or more other packages, this is called a dependency. One package is dependent on another (or more than one other).

Two columns appear below "Unresolved Dependencies". The left column shows the name of a package and the right column is the package that is required by the package on the left.

At the bottom, "Install packages to satisfy dependencies" is selected and this needs to be selected.

Select Next.

 About to Install

This is it! When you click Next (after reading the paragraph below), the installation will begin.

Read the text on this screen. Notice that a log of the installation (a text file named install.log) will be put in the /root directory after the installation and that a kickstart text file named anaconda-ks.cfg will also be put in /root.

Select Next.

 Installing Packages

Watch the screen as the installation progresses. The mount points that you specified earlier are formatted and then the packages that you selected are installed. At the top of the screen you will see the names of the packages, their size and a brief description of each one.

The Installing Packages screen also shows the total number of packages to be installed, the number completed, the number remaining and the estimated time for each of these items.

Boot Disk Creation

After all of the packages have been installed, you can create a Boot Disk. We will refer to this disk as the "Installation Routine Boot Disk" (as opposed to calling it a "Rescue Boot Disk", which may imply booting into "rescue mode" rather than booting to "rescue" a system with an overwritten or corrupted boot loader in the MBR).

The "Installation Routine Boot Disk" can be used to boot a system if you have chosen not to install a boot loader or if your third-party boot loader does not work with Linux.

In addition to this, the "Installation Routine Boot Disk" is also commonly used to boot a system if the Linux boot loader (configuration - set up during the installation process) does not work. The boot loader (configuration) will not work if the boot loader in the MBR of a system has been overwritten by another boot loader, or if the boot loader has been corrupted in some way. This boot disk allows you to boot from floppy *and bypass the (incorrect or corrupted) boot loader in the MBR* and boot directly to Linux (from the hard disk) as though you had booted with a (correct and functional) boot loader (in the MBR) and then had selected "Red Hat Linux" to boot to Linux.

As described earlier, on a dual-boot or multi-boot system that will have both Windows and Linux installed on it, install Windows and then Linux. This will prevent the installation routine of Windows from overwriting the Linux boot loader in the MBR. However, you may need to install Windows after installing Linux if the installed version of Windows fails to function properly or if you need to upgrade your version of Windows. Therefore, it is quite common to need to install Windows again (after installing Windows and then Linux).

If you install Windows on a system after installing Linux, then the Linux boot loader (GRUB or LILO) is usually overwritten (in the MBR) by the Windows boot loader. At this point, you can no longer boot with the Linux boot loader (and then select "Red Hat Linux" to boot to Linux). After installing Windows on a system that already has Linux, the system will simply boot to Windows and the Linux boot loader screen will not appear. All of the Linux OS, program and data files will still be on the hard disk (unless you wiped out the Linux partitions during the Windows installation), but you will not be able to boot to Linux because the Linux boot loader no longer exists in the MBR.

It is possible (and relatively easy) to restore an overwritten or corrupted Linux boot loader (GRUB or LILO) by booting into "rescue mode" and re-installing the boot loader. The steps to do this for both GRUB and LILO are described in the next section. The "Installation Routine Boot Disk" allows you to boot Linux until the (overwritten or corrupted) boot loader is re-installed.

If you have installed Windows (and it has overwritten the Linux boot loader in the MBR) and then boot with the "Installation Routine Boot Disk", then you boot directly from floppy to Linux (on the hard disk). If you boot without the "Installation Routine Boot Disk", then you boot directly to Windows (and cannot access Linux).

The Installation Routine Boot Disk has the following statement in a file named syslinux.cfg:

append initrd=initrd.img hdc=ide-scsi root=/dev/hda7

The above statement specifies the location of the Linux / (root) partition for the system on which it was created. The text: root=/dev/hda7 specifies that the / (root) partition (root=) is on the hda7 partition. If the Installation Routine Boot Disk was created on a system that had the / (root) directory on the hdb2 partition, then the above statement would show: root=/dev/hdb2 rather than: root=/dev/hda7.

The above statement in syslinux.cfg allows the Installation Routine Boot Disk to boot directly to the Linux OS installed on the hard disk.

If you are in a classroom environment, you may want to skip the following step.

Select "Yes, I would like to create a boot disk" ; select Next ; Make boot disk.

(37) Graphic Interface (X) Configuration

The X in the above screen name refers to the X Window System. This "system" provides a graphic foundation for any GUI desktop that you will be using.

Read the Help information at the left and the description at the top of the screen.

If your graphics card does not match the one automatically selected, then select your card from the list, or select "Other" (at the top) and select a "generic" card that is compatible with your graphics card, or select "Unsupported VGA compatible" (if your card is a VGA compatible card).

Beside Video card RAM, specify the amount of memory on your video card, if the correct amount does not already appear.

Do *not* select "Skip X Configuration" at the bottom.

Select Next.

(38) Monitor Configuration

Do not confuse the "Monitor Configuration" screen with the "Graphic Interface (X) Configuration" screen that you used above to specify your graphics card.

Read the text at the top of the screen and the Help information at the left.

If the installation routine cannot automatically detect the make and model of your monitor, it will select "Unprobed Monitor", below "Unprobed Monitor".

Look for the make of your monitor on the list and click on the triangle beside it to see the models that are available. If you cannot find your make of monitor, use "Unprobed Monitor", below "Unprobed Monitor".

If you can find the make, but not the model of your monitor, you *may* want to select a model that is similar to your monitor, *but this is risky*, unless you are absolutely certain that the similar model does not *exceed* the capabilities of your monitor.

If you select a monitor that is similar to your monitor, be absolutely certain that it does not "overclock" your monitor (run it at a higher specification than it can handle) and damage it or destroy it!

To find out the model of a monitor that is similar (compatible) to yours, but does not exceed its capabilities, contact the manufacturer of your monitor.

If you are uncertain whether or not a "similar" monitor will overclock your monitor, leave "Unprobed Monitor", below "Unprobed Monitor" selected and specify the correct range of values for Horizontal Sync: and Vertical Sync: at the bottom of the screen. These values can be found in the manual for your monitor or by contacting the manufacturer.

The "probe" of your monitor (by the installation routine) may have determined correct values for the Horizontal Sync: and Vertical Sync: settings, but it is best to check the manual or contact the manufacturer (rather than damage or destroy your monitor). If you have changed these values, but want the original values back, you can select the "Restore original values" button at the bottom right.

Select Next.

 Customize Graphics Configuration

Almost done! This is the second last screen of the installation. At this point, the operating system has been completely installed. If your system "hangs" while doing the steps below, then the X Window System is not configured correctly or your graphics card is defective.

The Customize Graphics Configuration screen is used to specify the default settings for the Color Depth and Screen Resolution of your graphics card and monitor. See the manuals for these components to determine the settings that they can handle.

Only select settings that you know your hardware can use. If you do not know the settings that your hardware can handle, select the lowest settings for Color Depth and Screen Resolution. Most of the current hardware can handle a Color Depth of: True Color (24 Bit) and a Screen Resolution of: 800x600.

 If you are unsure of the settings for your hardware, select the lowest setting for Color Depth and Screen Resolution and then select the "Test Setting" button.

When you select the "Test Setting" button (below), your system may hang. If this happens, press the Ctrl+Alt+Backspace key combination to return to the Customize Graphics Configuration screen. This key combination may not always work. **Do not test settings that your hardware is not capable of displaying. You could damage or destroy your hardware!**

If your system can handle the settings of a Color Depth of: True Color (24 Bit) and a Screen Resolution of: 800x600, select them as the default Color Depth and Screen Resolution.

Select the "Test Setting" button to test your settings.

You will either see a desktop and a dialog box at which you select Yes (to indicate that you can see the desktop) or you will not see a desktop. If the desktop does not appear, press Ctrl+Alt+Backspace to go back to the Customize Graphics Configuration screen.

Leave Graphical selected for the default login type ;

select Next.

 ## Congratulations

This screen congratulates you on finishing the installation process. Read this screen. It describes booting from floppy, if you created a boot disk during the installation. However, you installed the GRUB boot loader during the installation and do not need to boot from a floppy.

Remove your CD and floppy ; select Exit.

You may see some messages that look like error messages that end in the word "failed" before your system reboots. These messages are usually erroneous and your system should boot properly to the (blue) GRUB boot loader screen.

Watch the screen as your system boots to see if any error messages appear.

When the GRUB boot loader appears, "Red Hat Linux" should be highlighted at the top.

Press Enter to boot Linux.

If you do not do anything for several seconds, the highlighted operating system will boot anyway!

Watch your screen as the system boots to see if any error messages appear.

 The Red Hat Setup Agent

When your system boots for the first time after an installation, a "Welcome to Red Hat Linux!" screen appears. An arrow is pointing to the word Welcome at the top left. Read the text on this screen.

Select Forward ;

the Date and Time Configuration screen appears ; set the time and date ; Forward ;

the Sound Card Configuration screen appears ; Play test sound ; Forward ;

the Red Hat Update Agent screen appears ; select your desired option ; Forward ;

the Install Additional Software screen appears ; Forward ;

the Finished Setup! screen appears ; Forward.

 Logging In to Your New System

At the GUI login prompt for Username, type in: *cwest* and press Enter.

At the prompt for Password, type in the password and press Enter.

Now you should see the GNOME desktop with some icons on it and a "panel" across the bottom with some icons on it.

Congratulations again! You have successfully installed the Linux operating system. No small feat!

Try running some programs and "looking around" the desktop. In the next chapter you will learn how to work with the GNOME and KDE desktops and all of the components on them.

 Shutting Down Your System

Do the following steps to "properly" shut down your system from the desktop.

Menu (at the bottom left) ; Log Out ; Shut Down ; OK.

Section Review

1. Which Linux filesystems can be assigned to partitions during the installation process (choose two)?

    ☐ A. ld2
    ☐ B. ext3
    ☐ C. physical volume (LVM)
    ☐ D. exp2

2. Which item can be run at the boot: prompt of the "Installation Options Screen" to test a CD?

    ○ A. checkcd
    ○ B. linux mediacheck
    ○ C. linux cdtest
    ○ D. testcd

3. When a 2 button mouse is set up to emulate a 3 button mouse, what steps do you do that are the equivalent of pressing the third mouse button?

    ○ A. press the right mouse button and drag the mouse from right to left
    ○ B. press the left mouse button and drag the mouse from left to right
    ○ C. press the right mouse button and push upwards
    ○ D. press the left and right mouse buttons at the same time

4. Which two items are boot loaders that can be used with Linux?

    ☐ A. GRUB
    ☐ B. LILO
    ☐ C. MBR
    ☐ D. LINLOAD

5. When you install a server, you cannot also install the X Window System and a GUI desktop. T F

6. Which directories are commonly used as mount points (choose two)?

    ☐ A. /
    ☐ B. /etc
    ☐ C. /boot
    ☐ D. /dev

7. Select the correct statements regarding Linux utilities (choose two).

   ☐ A. RPM is used for CD-ROM drive calibration
   ☐ B. Anaconda is an installation routine
   ☐ C. Kudzu is used for hardware detection and configuration
   ☐ D. Disk Druid is used for archaeological site mapping

8. Which of the following statements is true of the boot disk that is created during the Linux installation?

   ○ A. it is used to boot a system to do an installation via FTP
   ○ B. it is used to boot a Linux system if the Linux boot loader has become overwritten (removed) or corrupted
   ○ C. it is used to boot a system from CD 1 in the CD-ROM drive
   ○ D. it is used to boot a system to do a network installation

9. What do you type at the boot: prompt of the "Installation Options Screen" to go into Rescue Mode.

   ○ A. rescue
   ○ B. linux rescue
   ○ C. linux rescuemode
   ○ D. rescue mode

10. All distributions contain the same software components and use the same installation routine. T F

11. Select three items that are good pointers to use when creating passwords.

   ☐ A. use at least six characters
   ☐ B. use a password that would easily be associated with you
   ☐ C. use a mixture of upper and lower case letters
   ☐ D. use some non-alpha characters

12. What is the most common way of running the installation routine?

   ○ A. type: linux anaconda at the boot: prompt and press Enter
   ○ B. type: linux install at the boot: prompt and press Enter
   ○ C. press Enter at the "Installation Options Screen"
   ○ D. press Alt+F1 and then the system will restart in installation mode

13. Which of the following is a protocol used to dynamically provide an IP address to a system?

   ○ A. NCP
   ○ B. DHCP
   ○ C. DNS
   ○ D. FTP

Post-Installation Configuration of Linux

Topics Covered in this Section

Describe various methods of specifying system configuration settings
Introduce the main utilities and menu headings used to configure a system
Discuss the difference between running utilities at the command line
and from a menu
Discover the capabilities of Linux in relation to hardware modems
and winmodems
Understand the need to re-install boot loaders and detail the methods
of installing them

In this section, you will learn about the text-based GUI utilities and X GUI utilities that are used to configure a system after the installation of Linux. You will also learn about hardware modems, winmodems, boot loader problems and how to re-install boot loaders.

Running Programs to Configure Your System

There are often many ways to specify settings to configure your system. Most of the time you can manually edit a text configuration file to specify settings. Other times, you may want to run a utility and specify settings with the utility, so that it will automatically edit a configuration file and put the settings in it for you.

When you decide to use a utility to specify system settings, you can usually choose between a (non-point-and-click) text-based GUI utility, such as the Setup Utility (shown in Figure 3-1), and a (point-and-click) X Windows GUI utility, such as the printconf-**gui** utility. If you do not have X Windows (a.k.a. **X**) installed on your system, you cannot run an X (X Windows) GUI utility. If you have X installed, you must have it running to be able to run an X GUI utility.

For example, if you set up Linux to boot to a virtual terminal (in text mode at a text prompt without a desktop), then X is not running. If X has been installed on the system, then you can run the command: startx to start X. Once X is running, you can open a terminal emulation window and run an X GUI utility at the command line, or run the utility from the Menu on the desktop (if the utility is available on the Menu).

Many X GUI utilities can be run from a menu on the GNOME or KDE desktop.

For example, the command: printconf-**gui** runs the binary for the Printer Configuration (**X GUI**) utility. To run this utility from a menu, you select: Menu ; System Settings ; Printing. These steps have the same effect as running the binary from the command line, but they take longer.

Many X GUI utilities can also be run by double-clicking on the icon for them.

For example, the Printer Configuration utility can also be run from the "Start Here" icon on the desktopwith the following steps: Start Here icon x 2 (double-click) ; System Settings icon x 2 ; Printing x 2. This also takes several steps.

However, some X GUI utilities are not on a GNOME or KDE desktop menu and are not available by selecting an icon; but they can still be run from the command line when X is running! In addition to this, the location of an item on a menu may change with the next release of Linux.

For example, you may be able to run a utility from the System Settings menu in one version of Linux, but this item may be located off of a different menu with the next version. It may not even exist on a menu in the next version; but you may still be able to run it from the command line!

To continue the example, an icon that is located in one (desktop or browser window) location may change to a different location with the next release of Linux.

In addition to running a utility at the command line, the following are locations and methods of running a (text-based GUI or X GUI) utility. All of the menu and icon locations may change from one Linux version to another, and may be different from one desktop type to another.

You can run utilities from:

> a menu on the GNOME desktop
> a menu on the KDE desktop
> one or more icons (at various locations) on a desktop
> one or more icons within a browser window

If you can run a utility from any of the above locations, you can also run the binary for it from the command line.

If you learn the command to run a utility at the command line, then you can run the utility regardless of the desktop that you are using, and usually regardless of the Linux version that you are running. In addition to this, running a utility at the command line is usually much faster than selecting an item from a series of menus (from a desktop) or a series of icons (on the desktop or in a browser window).

The name of a command (utility) may change from one version of Linux to another, but this is less likely to happen than the change of menu location or icon location.

In this course, we will usually just show the name of a utility (the name of the binary that runs the utility), so that you can run it from the command line, rather than describing every other location that can be used to run the utility (and may change).

To run a text-based GUI utility from the command line, you simply type in the name of the utility and press Enter. You do not need to have X running to be able to run a text-based GUI utility, such as the Setup Utility.

For example, to run the text-based version of the Printer Configuration GUI utility, named printconf-tui, you simply type in: printconf-tui and press Enter.

The **g** in printconf-**g**ui is used to indicate the X GUI version of the Printer Configuration utility and the **t** in printconf-**t**ui is used to indicate the text-based GUI version of the Printer Configuration utility.

X Windows requires a lot of system resources, such as memory, processor time and disk space. Many servers do not require X and so X is not installed on them. Servers do not require X to have their settings configured.

Linux is currently being used much more often as a server OS (without X) than as desktop OS (with X). You cannot run X GUI utilities while working on a system that does not have X installed.

Servers do not typically have X installed on them and are therefore configured with text-based utilities and also with commands that do not display a menu. Some settings on a server can also be configured with web-based utilities.

To run an X GUI utility from the command line, you can type in the name of the utility, a space, and then an "&" (ampersand) and press Enter.

For example, to run the X GUI version of the Printer Configuration utility, named printconf-gui, you type in: printconf-gui & and press Enter.

When running an X GUI utility at the command line, the space and the "&" (ampersand) are not absolutely required. However, if an X GUI utility is still running and you need to run another command at the command line (without opening another terminal emulation window), then you need to close the utility to be able to type in another command. Alternatively, you can open another terminal emulation window or go to a virtual terminal.

Typing a space and an "&" (ampersand) at the end of a command causes the command to execute in the "background". This causes the shell prompt to appear after you have run the command, so that you can type in more commands. The space between the name of the command and the "&" (ampersand) is not required, but will be used here for easier readability.

Using System Configuration Utilities

In order to run utilities that configure system settings you must either be logged in as the root user or use the su command to log in with the root user password.

If you log in to a desktop as a non-root user (recommended) and run a utility that configures system settings, you will be prompted for the password of the root user before you can access the utility.

If you log in to a desktop as a non-root user, open a terminal emulation window (to get a shell prompt) and run a utility that configures system settings, you will also be prompted for the password of the root user before you can access the utility.

If you have logged in to a desktop as a non-root user, open a terminal emulation window, run the su command to log in as the root user and run a run a utility that configures system settings, you will not be prompted for the password of the root user because you have already provided the password of the root user.

If you have logged in to a virtual terminal (without a desktop) as a non-root user and run a test-based GUI utility (from the command line) that configures system settings, you will be prompted for the password of the root user before you can access the utility.

If you have logged in to a virtual terminal (without a desktop) as a non-root user, run the su command to log in as the root user and run a utility (from the command line) that configures system settings, you will not be prompted for the password of the root user because you have already provided the password of the root user.

Post-Installation Configuration Utilities

The Kudzu Utility

The Kudzu utility is a hardware detection and configuration utility that is automatically run every time your system boots. When Linux is booting, you will see "Checking for new hardware" during the boot process. This is the Kudzu utility checking your system for new hardware components.

Support for most of your system components is installed during the installation of the Linux OS. However, over time hardware components will become defective or obsolete and will need to be replaced.

When a new (or replacement) hardware component is added to your system, the Kudzu utility will detect it and prompt you to ask if you want support for the component added to your system. If the component is a legacy non-PnP card, then Kudzu will prompt you for the settings being used by the card (IRQ, I/O port and DMA).

The Setup Utility

Running the command: setup at the command line displays the text-based Setup Utility. This text-based GUI utility provides a menu interface that allows you to run several other text-based GUI utilities. These utilities are used to change many system settings.

Figure 3-1 shows the opening screen of the Setup Utility. Selecting an item from this menu runs a binary that allows you to configure system settings.

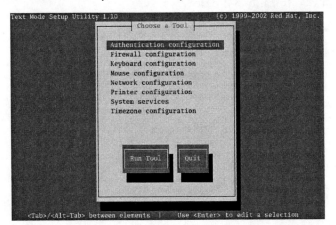

Figure 3-1: The Setup Utility

For example, selecting "Mouse configuration" from the opening screen of the Setup Utility runs the mouseconfig binary, which allows you to modify your mouse settings, such as type of mouse and mouse port.

Table 3-1 shows the menu items available in the Setup Utility, the binary that is run when you select an item, and the function of the binary.

Table 3-1 - The Setup Utility Menu Options

Menu Item	Utility	Function
Authentication configuration	authconfig	specify user authentication configuration
Firewall configuration	lokkit	specify firewall configuration
Keyboard configuration	kbdconfig	specify keyboard type
Mouse configuration	mouseconfig	specify mouse type and settings
Network configuration	netconfig	specify network settings
Printer configuration	printconf-tui	install printers
System services	ntsysv	specify automatic startup of services
Timezone configuration	timeconfig	configure time zone

Running setup and then selecting "Mouse configuration" is the same as running mouseconfig at the command line. Therefore, you can get to the items available in the Setup Utility more quickly by simply running the binary at the command line, rather than running setup and then selecting the item. However, if you cannot remember the name of the binary, you can run setup and then select the menu heading for it.

The System Settings Menu Heading

To configure some system settings from the desktop, such as your display, keyboard and mouse, you can use the System Settings menu heading, which is accessed by clicking on Menu at the bottom left of your screen.

Several items appear on the System Settings menu and the commonly used items are shown in Table 3-2 below.

Table 3-2 - System Settings Menu

Menu Item	Function
Date & Time	set the date and time
Display	specify screen resolution and color depth specify monitor specifications, such as model, Horiz. sync and Vert. sync specify graphics card specifications, such as card type and driver
Keyboard	specify the keyboard type
Mouse	specify mouse type and settings
Network	specify network card settings, such as device name and IP address specify networking settings, such as Hosts and DNS settings add and configure ISDN, modem, xDSL and wireless connections
Printing	add, delete, modify and configure printers
Sound Card Detection	view sound card specifications and test sound card

Linux and Modems

In Linux terms, there are two general "types" of modems: winmodems and hardware modems.

Winmodems are relatively inexpensive hardware components that do not include all of the functionality of hardware modems. Winmodems acquire the functionality of hardware modems through the use of software. They use proprietary (closed source) Windows software to accomplish the functionality of a hardware modem. They are a cheap method of providing a system with a modem through the combination of hardware and proprietary software. Many winmodems will not work with Linux.

Hardware modems are more expensive than winmodems and virtually all of them work with Linux.

If you have not yet purchased a modem and need one, be sure to get a good quality hardware modem. A hardware modem will likely be more expensive than a comparable winmodem, but will be well worth the price due to the time and frustration saved by not having to try to get an incompatible winmodem to work! A reputable hardware vendor will be able to show you which modems are hardware modems. The packaging of some winmodems show the word "winmodem" on them.

To determine if your existing modem, or one that you are about to purchase, is compatible with your distribution, see the **HCL** (Hardware Compatibility List) at the web site of your distribution, or go to the web site shown below.

For more information on getting modems to work with Linux, getting drivers for winmodems, and links to even more information on modems, go to:

> http://www.linmodems.org

To try and get an existing modem to work, do the steps below to set up your modem. These steps will cause the Network Configuration utility to probe your system for the modem and it will try to install support for it.

Installing Support for ISDN, Modem, xDSL and Wireless Connections

Support for ISDN, modem, xDSL and wireless connections is installed by doing the following steps:

Menu ; System Settings ; Network ; Add... ; select the device type ;

specify the settings required by the device that you have selected.

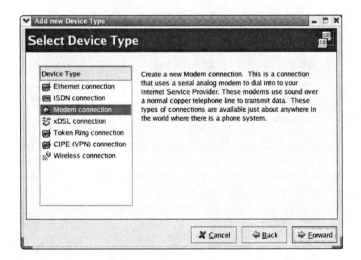

Figure 3-2: The Add new Device Type dialog box

Figure 3-2 shows the Add new Device Type dialog box. Notice the different devices that can be installed from this dialog box.

Setting Up a Modem to Access the Internet

If you are using a hardware modem and want to access the internet, do the steps below to set it up.

Prior to doing the steps below, contact your service provider for your the following information:

Phone Number: _____ (include a dialing prefix and area code if necessary)

Provider Name: _____ (such as: WorldWideISP - without spaces)

Login Name: _____ (such as: lancom1@worldwide.net)

Password: _____ (provided by your ISP)

To set up your modem to access the internet:

Menu ; System Settings ; Network ; Add... ; Modem connection ; Forward ;

At this point, the utility will probe your system for its modem. The Modem Device, Baud Rate, Flow Control and Modem Volume headings will be set up by default. These settings are typically correct, but can be changed if necessary. You may want to change the Modem Volume from Off (default) to another setting so that you can hear the modem dial. If you are not using touch tone dialing, deselect "Use touch tone dialing".

Forward ;

fill in the Phone Number, Provider Name, Login Name and Password fields ;

Apply ;

select your modem on the Network Configuration dialog box (if not already selected).

To test your connection:

Activate ; if you are prompted to save your changes, select Yes.

If your connection was established, you will see the word Active below the Status heading.

Re-Installing A Linux Boot Loader in the MBR

If you are having problems with Windows, you may need to re-install it to get it to work properly. You may also need to install Windows to upgrade it. It is fairly common to need to re-install or upgrade Windows.

If you are running a dual-boot or multi-boot system, are using a Linux boot loader (GRUB or LILO) and you have installed Windows after Linux (due to Windows problems or a Windows upgrade), then the installation routine of Windows will likely overwrite the Linux boot loader with its own boot loader. When you boot this system after installing Windows, the system will automatically run Windows (not display the GRUB or LILO screen) and you will not have access to Linux (the Linux partitions on the system). If you have not accidentally removed your Linux partitions during the Windows installation, you can restore your system so that you can access Linux.

To get access to Linux again, you must re-install your boot loader (GRUB or LILO) in the MBR. Fortunately, this is easier than it sounds. To re-install a Linux boot loader, you go into rescue mode and run a command that puts the boot loader back in the MBR.

Re-installing the GRUB Boot Loader

If you are using the GRUB boot loader, do the following steps:

Boot the system so that the Installation Options Screen appears ;

 To get to the Installation Options Screen, boot your system from CD I (or boot with the CD/Hard Disk Installation Boot Disk (floppy) with CD I in the CD-ROM drive).

at the boot: prompt, type in: linux rescue ; press Enter ;

at the Rescue dialog box select Continue ;

read the text of the next Rescue dialog box ; OK ;

chroot /mnt/sysimage grub-install *devicename*

Replace *devicename* in the above command with the device name of the hard disk that is used to boot the system, such as /dev/hda. The above command overwrites the existing MBR by installing the GRUB boot loader in the MBR.

exit ; remove CD 1 and the boot floppy (if you used one).

The system will automatically restart and you should see the GRUB boot loader menu.

Re-installing the LILO Boot Loader

If you are using LILO, do the same steps as described in "Re-installing the GRUB Boot Loader" above, except run the following chroot command in place of the one shown above:

chroot /mnt/sysimage lilo

The above command installs the LILO boot loader in the MBR. A device name is not required.

Re-Installing A Windows Boot Loader in the MBR

Linux boot loader software (GRUB or LILO) is installed in the MBR of the hard disk that is used to boot a system. In addition to this software, a boot loader requires other software components, such as programs and configuration files, that exist on a Linux partition.

If you are using a Linux boot loader and remove Linux from a system, then the software components required to display and use the Linux boot loader are removed from the system. When you boot a system after removing Linux, you will see an error message which indicates that the Linux boot loader was not able to run properly and display its menu.

If you are using a Linux boot loader and running a dual-boot Windows and Linux system, and then remove Linux, you will not be able to run Windows. You will just see a Linux boot loader error message after starting your system.

To be able to run Windows again, you can either install Linux, which will allow you to install a Linux boot loader (that will provide access to Windows), or you can install a Windows boot loader (if you do not need Linux on the system).

To install a Windows boot loader, boot from a Windows boot disk (floppy) that contains the Windows FDISK utility (not the Linux fdisk utility) and run the following command:

    FDISK /MBR

Shut your system down and then turn it on. The Windows boot loader will now allow you to run Windows.

To see the steps to create a Windows boot disk, search Help in Windows for "startup disk" and "boot disk". When a Windows boot disk is created, it may not automatically have the FDISK utility on it. Search Help in Windows for FDISK to see how to get this utility and put it on the boot disk.

 ## Section Review

1. Select three methods of running an X GUI utility.

    ☐ A. select the utility from a menu while working at a desktop
    ☐ B. run the binary for the utility at the command line
    ☐ C. run the guiload command at the command line and specify the name of the binary
    ☐ D. double-click on icons on the desktop or in a browser window

2. Which item can be selected from the System Settings menu to change the IP address of a network card and set up a modem to dial and ISP?

   ○ A. Net Config
   ○ B. NIC Properties
   ○ C. Network
   ○ D. Net/Modem Configuration

3. Which of the following are the most likely instances when you may need to re-install a boot loader (choose two)?

   ☐ A. when you install Linux after installing Windows
   ☐ B. when you install Windows after installing Linux
   ☐ C. when you create a new partition on an empty unpartitioned area of a disk
   ☐ D. when you have been using a Linux boot loader on a dual-boot Windows and Linux system and then remove all Linux partitions

4. The location of an item on a menu that runs a utility may change from one version of a distribution to another and from one distribution to another. T F

5. Which general type of modem is most likely not going to work with Linux?

   ○ A. winmodem
   ○ B. hardware modem
   ○ C. a dial-up modem
   ○ D. a cable modem

6. Which command can be run to display the X GUI version of the Printer Configuration utility.

   ○ A. printconf-tui
   ○ B. printconf-gui
   ○ C. printer-gui
   ○ D. configprint

7. A server must have X installed so that you can run an X GUI utility to configure the server. T F

8. Which methods can be used to modify system settings in a text configuration file (choose three)?

   ☐ A. use the boot loader to download configuration file updates
   ☐ B. manually edit a text file that contains configuration settings
   ☐ C. run an X GUI utility to specify configuration settings
   ☐ D. use a command to run a utility to specify configuration settings

9. You have booted a system to text mode (a virtual terminal shell prompt) and X Windows is installed on the system. What command is run to load X Windows?

    ○ A. xloader
    ○ B. startx
    ○ C. the X Window system cannot be loaded from a virtual terminal
    ○ D. xstart

10. All utilities that can be run from the command line can be selected from a menu while working at a desktop. T F

11. Which character is used at the end of a command to cause the program that is run with the command to run in the background, so that you can run additional commands at the shell prompt?

    ○ A. #
    ○ B. $
    ○ C. &
    ○ D. /

12. Select two methods that will allow you to run commands that configure system settings.

    ☐ A. log in as the root user (not recommended)
    ☐ B. log in as a non-root user
    ☐ C. log in as a non-root user, run the su - command, and then provide the password of the root user
    ☐ D. log in as root with the t (temp) option to temporarily work at the root user

13. What is the name of the utility runs and checks for new hardware each time a system boots?

    ○ A. Setup
    ○ B. Kudzu
    ○ C. Suconfig
    ○ D. Bootconfig

14. To re-install a Linux boot loader you do the following (choose two):

    ☐ A. boot into rescue mode from CD 1 and run the program to re-install the boot loader
    ☐ B. boot into rescue mode with the boot disk created during the installation process and run the program to re-install the boot loader
    ☐ C. boot from floppy and run FDISK /MBR
    ☐ D. boot into rescue mode from the CD/Hard Disk Installation Boot disk with CD 1 in the CD-ROM drive and run the program to re-install the boot loader

Chapter 4: Working with Desktops and Terminals

During the installation of Linux you installed the GNOME and KDE desktops. In this chapter you will learn about the components of these two desktops. This includes the icons on the desktop, the panel on the desktop, the menu in the panel, and the icons in the panel.

You will also learn how to create a terminal emulation window icon that provides a window with a shell prompt so that you can run commands and programs.

In this chapter you will also work with the windows that appear when you run a program or open a terminal emulation window. You will learn how to open, move, maximize, minimize, close, and change from one window to another.

By default, this distribution of Linux creates six virtual terminals when you boot the system. You will learn how to: log in and work in these terminals, move from one terminal to another, and to move from a virtual terminal to a desktop.

You will also learn the various methods of mounting a CD or floppy disk to make the filesystem of it accessible, and all of the methods of logging out, shutting down and rebooting a Linux system. This chapter also covers the differences between logging in as the root user and using the su command to log in as the root user.

The following commands are described in this chapter and are also used in the Hands-On Exercises:

mount	make the filesystem of a CD or floppy disk accessible
umount	properly end the use of a CD or floppy disk
eject	unmount and eject a CD
su	log in to work as the root user
sudo	run commands in a restricted manner as a user
login	log in to a Linux system
logout	logout of a Linux system
exit	exit out of shell session
poweroff	shut down a system and turn the power off
halt	shut down a system and not turn the power off
reboot	shut down a system and then restart the system
shutdown	properly shut down a Linux system
fdformat	format a floppy disk
mkfs	assign the ext2 filesystem to a disk
mkdosfs	assign the DOS/Windows filesystem to a disk

During the Hands-On Exercises of this section you will log in to each of the two desktops and use the icons and menus on them, access virtual terminals from a desktop, and use different methods of accessing the filesystem of a CD.

Chapter 4: Working with Desktops and Terminals

Topics Covered in this Chapter

Describe the components and user interface of the GNOME and KDE desktops

Discuss the methods of opening, closing and working with windows

Explain how to work at a terminal emulation window and create an icon for one

Detail the methods of accessing and working at virtual terminals

Learn the various methods of mounting a CD or floppy disk to make it accessible

Provide all of the methods of logging out, shutting down, or rebooting a Linux system

Discuss working as the root user in comparison to using the su command to log in as root

Do the steps to use icons and run programs on the two desktops, work in virtual terminals, and use different methods of accessing the filesystem of a CD

In this section, you will learn how to log in and work at the GNOME and KDE desktops. You will learn about the desktop icons, the menu and how to use the desktop interface.

You will also learn how to log in and work at the six virtual terminals that are available by default.

The GNOME and KDE Desktops

Figure 4-1 shows the GNOME desktop and Figure 4-2 shows the KDE desktop. These are the most commonly used desktops in a Linux environment.

The GNOME and KDE desktops are very similar to one another in this distribution of Linux. They both have the same Menu icon at the bottom left and they both have the same icons in the panel (across the bottom of the desktop) for Web Browser, Email, Word Processor, Create Presentations and Spreadsheet. They both also show the time in the bottom right corner.

With this version of this distribution, the Terminal Emulation Window icon shown in the panel in Figures 4-1 and 4-2 does not exist by default. It must be created for each user, when necessary.

On the desktop area above the panel, both desktops also have icons for Start Here and Trash. In this area, both desktops have an icon that provides access to the currently logged in user's home directory. This icon is called *"username's* Home" on the GNOME desktop and "Home" on the KDE desktop.

The features of the GNOME desktop will be described below and then the features of the KDE desktop will be described.

The GNOME Desktop

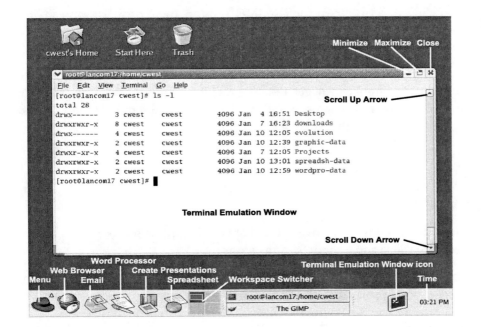

Figure 4-1:The GNOME desktop

The KDE Desktop

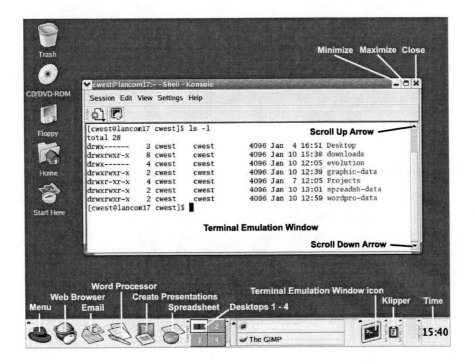

Figure 4-2:The KDE desktop

The GNOME Desktop

Below is a description of the GNOME desktop, the icons that appear on it, and the tasks that can be done when these icons are selected.

cwest's Home

Runs the Nautilus file manager and displays the contents of the home directory of the cwest user (/home/cwest). If you log in as a different user, then this icon will change to show the name of the new user.

Nautilus is a file manager utility that uses a web browser interface. It is used to view, copy, move and delete directories and files.

Start Here

Runs the Nautilus file manager and displays the Applications, Preferences, Server Settings and System Settings icons.

The Applications icon is used to access desktop productivity type programs, such as word processing and spreadsheet programs, and other applications. The Preferences icon allows you to specify settings such as the desktop background and fonts. The Server Settings icon is used to specify file server settings. The System Settings icon allows you to specify settings such as the date, time and screen resolution.

Trash

Directories and files deleted with the Nautilus file manager can be viewed and undeleted with this icon. Items deleted at the command line do not go into the trash and cannot be undeleted.

Deleted items that are in the trash can be permanently deleted by selecting:

> File ; Empty Trash ; Empty.

Icons on the GNOME Panel

The following items appear in the GNOME "panel", which is the grey bar that appears across the bottom of the screen. Icons for items, such as programs, can be added to the panel, moved to different locations and deleted. The panel itself can also be moved, such as to the left side, right side or top of the screen.

To see a description of an item in the panel, move your mouse cursor over top of the item (and do not click on the item).

Menu

This icon provides access to the GUI application software programs and utilities installed on the system. Items that can be accessed with the Start Here icon can also be accessed with this icon. Using the menu to select items is faster than selecting a series of icons (by double-clicking on the Start Here icon and then double-clicking on other icons).

Web Browser

Runs the Mozilla web browser.

Email - Evolution

Runs the Evolution email program.

Word Processor - Writer

Runs the word processing program named Writer by OpenOffice.org. Word processing documents created with this program have the filename extension of .sxw.

Create Presentations - Impress

Runs the presentation creation program named Impress by OpenOffice.org. Presentation files created with this program have the filename extension of .sxi.

Spreadsheet - Calc

Runs the spreadsheet program named Calc by OpenOffice.org. Spreadsheet files created with this program have the filename extension of .sxc.

Workspace Switcher

This item appears in the middle of the panel as a window that has four "panes" (by default). Each of these panes provides a "virtual desktop" (not virtual terminal). The top left window pane is selected by default. The top right, bottom left and bottom right window "panes" can also be selected. Each of these four window panes displays a different virtual desktop. This allows you to organize your applications (work tasks) into four areas.

For example, you could run a web browser and word processor in the top left pane (virtual desktop) to do research and writing tasks. You could then click on the top right pane and run graphics programs in this virtual desktop, you could click on the bottom left pane and run database programs, and click on the bottom right pane and run network monitoring utilities. To go from one virtual desktop (which is being used for a group of applications) to another, you click on the pane that represents the applications.

Terminal Emulation Window

You can open a terminal emulation window that provides a window in which commands can be run and the output of commands can be seen. You will create an icon that will be used to open terminal emulation windows in the Hands-On Exercises below. We will refer to this icon as the Terminal Emulation Window icon. Some Linux documentation uses the word xterm to refer to a terminal emulation window.

You can have several terminal emulation windows open at a time. This allows you to run commands in one window and also run commands to do other tasks in other windows, such as view documentation files or run a utility that shows the effect of a command on the memory of a system.

To close a terminal emulation window you can: click on the "X" in the top right corner of the window, type: exit and press Enter, or press Ctrl+d.

The window that appears in the middle of the screen in Figure 4-1 is a terminal emulation window that was "opened" by clicking on the Terminal Emulation Window icon. In Figure 4-1, the **ls** (list) command has been run and the output of the ls command can be seen.

Creating the Terminal Emulation Window Icon

The Terminal Emulation Window icon does not appear in the panel by default; it must be created.

To add the Terminal Emulation Window icon to the panel in GNOME:

right-click on a location on the panel that does not have an icon ; Add to Panel ;

Launcher from menu ; System Tools ; Terminal.

To move an icon on the panel to a different location: right-click on the icon ; Move.

To remove an icon from the panel: right-click on the icon ; Remove From Panel.

You will select the Terminal Emulation Window icon many times throughout this course so that you can run commands and see the output of commands.

The Minimize, Maximize and Close Buttons On A Window

In Figures 4-1 and 4-2, notice the three "buttons" (Minimize, Maximize and Close) at the top right of the terminal emulation window. These buttons are on every window on a GUI desktop.

The top right button is used to close a window, the middle button is used to maximize a window so that it fills the screen, and the left button is used to minimize the window so that it is still available, but is "in the background". These three buttons will be referred to many times during the Hands-On Exercises of this course.

Moving From Window To Window

To move from one window to another, press and hold down the Alt key, press the Tab key until the window that you need appears, and then let go of both keys.

Time

The time appears at the bottom right of the screen. Moving your cursor over top of the time shows the current date. Clicking on the time shows a calendar for the current month. Clicking on the time again causes the calendar to disappear.

The KDE Desktop

Below is a description of the KDE desktop. With the desktop setups currently used by this distribution, the GNOME and KDE desktops are extremely similar. Prior to version 8.0, the desktops had greater differences between them. The descriptions that you have just read for most of the GNOME desktop components are basically the same for the KDE desktop. The discussion below focuses on the KDE desktop items that are different from the GNOME desktop.

Home

Runs the Konqueror file manager and displays the contents of the home directory of the cwest user (/home/cwest) or other currently logged in user.

Similar in functionality to Nautilus, Konqueror is a file manager utility that uses a web browser interface.

Start Here

Runs the Konqueror file manager and displays four folders. These folders provide access to the same items that are seen as icons when you select the Start Here icon in GNOME.

Trash

Directories and files deleted with Konqueror can be viewed and undeleted with this icon. Items deleted at the command line do not go into the trash and cannot be undeleted.

To permanently delete a directory or file in the trash:

> right-click on the directory or file ; Delete ; Delete.

Icons on the KDE Panel

The following items appear in the KDE "panel", which is the grey bar that appears across the bottom of the screen. Icons for items can be added to the panel, moved to different locations and deleted.

To see a description of an item in the panel, move your mouse cursor over top of the item (and do not click on the item).

The Menu icon (at the bottom left) in GNOME is called the Start Application icon in KDE. For simplicity, we will refer to this item as "Menu" during the Hands-On Exercises, regardless of the desktop that you are using.

The Web Browser, Email, Word Processor, Create Presentations and Spreadsheet icons are the same in GNOME and KDE.

The item that is referred to as the Workspace Switcher in GNOME works the same as the window pane items numbered 1 through 4 in KDE and each one is a separate "virtual desktop".

Terminal Emulation Window

This icon works the same as in GNOME. We will refer to this icon as the Terminal Emulation Window icon. The window that appears in the middle of the screen in Figure 4-2 is a terminal emulation window that was "opened" by clicking on the terminal emulation window icon.

You will select the terminal emulation window icon many times throughout this course so that you can run commands, see the output of commands and do other tasks such as view documentation files and edit text files.

This icon does not appear in the panel by default; it must be created.

To add the Terminal Emulation Window icon to the panel in KDE:

> right-click on a location on the panel that does not have an icon ; Add ;
>
> Button ; System Tools ; Terminal.

To move or remove an icon from the panel, use the same steps as when using GNOME.

Klipper - Clipboard Tool

Items that have been cut or copied can be viewed in the Klipper - Clipboard Tool.

Time

This icon works the same as in GNOME.

GUI Desktop Mode and Text Mode

When you ran the installation routine earlier, you installed the GNOME and KDE desktops and your system was set up to boot into GUI desktop mode. When you boot your system, a GUI login dialog box appears. Once you log in, the GNOME or KDE desktop appears.

Rather than booting to a GUI desktop, your system can be set up to boot into text mode. With this setup, X Windows is not run (even though it is installed and can be run) and therefore a GUI desktop does not appear.

As you have installed X and the GNOME and KDE desktops on the system, you can make a minor modification to the system that causes it to either boot into text mode or boot to the GUI desktop.

Server systems are often installed without the software components that provide the GUI desktop. If you install a system without a GUI desktop, then you always boot into text mode and work at a virtual terminal.

Accessing Virtual Terminals

By default, this distribution of Linux creates six virtual terminals during the Linux boot process. This happens regardless of whether you have installed a X and a GUI desktop or not.

When you boot a system that is set up to boot into text mode (rather than GUI desktop mode), you see a "login:" prompt that allows you to access the first virtual terminal and log in. Once you log in, you are presented with a shell prompt at which you can run commands and programs.

When you boot a system that is set up to boot into GUI mode, you are presented with a GUI login dialog box. At this point, you can either log in and are then presented with a GUI desktop, or you can press a key combination to go to any of the six virtual terminals (and then log in at the virtual terminal to run commands and programs).

In other words, if you boot into GUI mode and see a GUI login prompt, you can go to a virtual terminal and log in without logging in to a desktop. There may be times when you do this because you do not need a desktop to do the tasks that you need to perform. Going to a virtual terminal from the GUI login prompt is faster than logging in (as a non-root user), opening a terminal emulation window, running: su - (to log in as root) and then entering in the password of the root user.

When you log in to a desktop, you can run multiple terminal emulation windows (of various sizes and locations on the screen) and you have access to utilities from the menu. When you log in to text mode, you have access to six virtual terminals, but you can only see one terminal at a time and cannot run X GUI utilities.

Some Linux documentation refers to virtual terminals as: virtual consoles, system consoles, text consoles and consoles.

Accessing a Virtual Terminal from the GUI Login or Desktop

When you boot into GUI mode and are presented with a GUI login dialog box, or when you have logged in to a desktop, you can press the following keys to go to a virtual terminal (any virtual terminal, from number 1 through 6):

    Ctrl+Alt+Fx   # replace the x in Fx with a number form 1 to 6

For example, to go to virtual terminal 1, press Ctrl+Alt+F1. When you press the Ctrl+Alt+Fx key combination for the first time, you are presented with a text "login:" prompt. At this point, you log in to the virtual terminal.

To go back to the GUI login prompt (if you have not yet logged in to the desktop), or to go to the GUI desktop (if you have logged in), press the following keys:

    Alt+F7   # go from a virtual terminal to the currently active
                     # desktop (if running)

Accessing Another Virtual Terminal from a Virtual Terminal

If your system is set up to boot into text mode, then you are presented with a text "login:" prompt after your system has booted. Once you log in, you are in virtual terminal 1.

To access another virtual terminal from any virtual terminal, you press the following keys:

    Alt+Fx   # replace the x in Fx with a number form 1 to 6

Summary of Key Combinations

To move from the GUI login dialog box, or from a desktop, to a virtual terminal:

    Press Ctrl+Alt+Fx and replace the x in Fx with a number from 1 to 6.

To move from any virtual terminal to another virtual terminal:

    Press Alt+Fx and replace the x in Fx with a number form 1 to 6.

If your system is set up to boot to a desktop, then to move from any virtual terminal to the GUI login dialog box (if you have not logged in) or to a desktop (if you have logged in):

    Press Alt+F7.

Logging In as the root User

As described in the installation section, it is not a good idea to log in as the root user when you are not doing system administration tasks, such as installing software and doing system maintenance.

It is also not a good idea to log in as root when you are doing relatively short system administration tasks, since it is easy to make a mistake (when logged in as root) that could damage a system, or erase all of the files on a system.

When working on a system, try to do as much work as possible using the *username* of a non-root user. This will reduce the risk of damaging a system by accidentally running a command as the root user (that should not have been run), and that a "regular" user would not have been able to run.

When you are logged in as a user, you can use the su command at the command line and then provide the root user password so that you can temporarily work as the root user.

Some people believe that you should never log in as the root user and only use the su command or the sudo command to do system administration tasks.

The su command allows you to log in as root and run commands until you end the "root user session" (by running the exit command, by pressing Ctrl+d or by running the logout command).

The sudo command is used to allow a user to have limited access to a system as root (or as another user).

The su Command

To do "day-to-day" non-administrative tasks, such as using a word processor or spreadsheet program, log in to a system as a non-root user. To do system administration tasks, log in as a non-root user and then use the su command (at a virtual terminal or in a terminal emulation window) to work as root and do system administration tasks.

 During this course, most of the tasks (Hands-On Exercises) that you do will be administrative tasks. Therefore, you will often use the su command (after logging in as a non-root user) to do these tasks. However, keep in mind that when you are not doing administrative tasks, do not run the su command (or log in as root).

The **su** (**s**uperuser) command is used to log in at the shell prompt (from a terminal emulation window or virtual terminal) as the root user. It starts another shell (a.k.a. subshell) within the existing shell (terminal emulation window or virtual terminal). After running this command you are prompted for the password of the root user, but you do not provide the name of the root user when you run this command. You can run the su command to log in to work as the root user, but you cannot log in with the user name of su. A user named su does not exist on the system.

The - (dash) option of the su command is used to provide an "environment" that is very similar to the environment that exists when you log in as the root user. Logging in *without* the - (dash) option is similar to the "environment" provided when you use the - (dash) option, but it is not "*as similar*".

For example, the directories in the PATH (environment variable) are very similar to those of the root user when you use the - (dash) option and they are *not* very similar when you do not use the - (dash) option.

When you use the - (dash) option, directory paths such as **/sbin** (**s**uperuser **binaries**) and /usr/**sbin** (superuser **binaries**) are in the PATH. These directories contain binaries (program files) for commands that are typically used for administrative tasks by the root user. When you do not use the - (dash) option, these directories are not in the PATH.

To continue the example, immediately after using the - (dash) option, your current directory is /root. Contrary to this, immediately after using su without the - (dash) option, your current directory is /home/*username*, where *username* is the name you logged in with, prior to running the su command. Therefore, we recommend using the - (dash) option when running the su command.

Using the su command to log in and work as the root user is sometimes referred to as: "su to root", "su as the root user" and "change to root". *We will use refer to this in the Hands-On Exercises as "su to root"*. When you see "su to root" in the Hands-On Exercises, type in: su - and press Enter. After this you will be prompted for the password of the root user.

When you use the su command to log in as the root user at a terminal emulation window (opened from a desktop), you are only working as the root user in that window, not in any other terminal emulation windows or virtual terminals (unless you use the su command in other terminal emulation windows or virtual terminals).

When you use the su command to log in as the root user at a terminal emulation window, the "root user session" (subshell) can be ended with the exit command or by pressing Ctrl+d. If you run the logout command in a terminal emulation window the window simply closes and you are still logged in with the user name that you used to log in to the desktop.

When you use the su command to log in as the root user at a virtual terminal, the "root user session" (subshell) can be ended with the logout command, the exit command or by pressing Ctrl+d.

When you use the su command to log in as the root user, or when you log in with the username of root, the shell prompt shows a # (pound) sign. When you are logged in as a non-root user, the shell prompt shows a $ (dollar) sign.

For security reasons, ***never*** log in to a desktop (at the GUI log prompt), or log in to a virtual terminal and start X, as the root user. Instead, log in to a desktop as a non-root user and use the su command to work as the root user.

The exit Command

If you have used the su command (at a virtual terminal or in a terminal emulation window) to log in and work as the root user, use the exit command to end the "su to root" session. No options are required with the exit command.

If you are logged in at a virtual terminal as a user (any user, including the root user) then the exit command will log you out and you will be at a text login: prompt. This is the same as running the logout command.

If you are working in a terminal emulation window (opened from a desktop) then the exit command will close the terminal emulation window, but you will still be "at" the desktop.

Methods of Logging In As the root User

You can log in to a desktop (at the GUI login prompt) as the root user (not recommended). In addition to this, you can log in to a desktop as a non-root user and open a terminal emulation window and use the su command to log in as root. As described above, we recommend using the - (dash) option when using the su command.

You can log in to a virtual terminal as root or you can log in as a non-root user and then use the su command to log in as root.

As described earlier, some people believe that you should never log in (to a desktop or virtual terminal) as the root user.

Mounting and Unmounting a Floppy Disk or CD

A floppy disk or CD must be mounted so that you can access the filesystem of it. This can be done from a desktop or from the command line (by running a command at a virtual terminal or by running a command in a terminal emulation window). Methods of mounting and unmounting a floppy disk or CD from a desktop and at the command line are described in detail below.

Mounting and Unmounting a Floppy Disk or CD from the Command Line

You cannot mount or unmount a floppy disk or CD from the command line unless you are logged in as root, or unless you have used the su command to log in as root.

Mounting and Unmounting a Floppy Disk from a Desktop

You can mount and unmount a floppy disk from a desktop (GNOME or KDE) while logged in as a non-root user (without being logged in as root or using the su command to log in as root).

You can mount and unmount a floppy from a desktop by using a floppy disk icon on desktop or by using a GUI utility, such as the Disk Mounter applet (available in GNOME).

Mounting and Unmounting a CD from a Desktop

You can mount and unmount a CD from a desktop (GNOME or KDE) while logged in as a non-root user.

A CD may contain a script file named **autorun** in its / (root) directory. If it does, then this file contains commands that can be "**auto**matically **run**" when the CD is put in the drive. The commands in the autorun script are only run if a desktop is running when the CD is put in the drive; and then only if you provide the password of the root user (at a GUI password prompt that automatically appears when the CD is put in the drive). You do not need to provide the password of the root user if you logged in to the desktop as the root user (not recommended).

When you are working at a desktop and a CD is put in the drive, then it is automatically mounted and a file manager window (presented by Nautilus if you are using GNOME or Konqueror if you are using KDE) appears showing the files on the CD. The CD is mounted regardless of whether or not it contains an autorun file.

If you are working at a desktop and run the mount command in a terminal emulation window (to mount a previously mounted and then unmounted CD), and the CD contains an autorun file, then you are asked if you want to run the autorun file and the file manager window appears.

If you are working at a virtual terminal (and a desktop is running), then a CD is automatically mounted when it is put in the drive. If the CD contains an autorun file, then you are asked if you want to run the autorun file (when you go to the desktop) and then the file manager window appears. If a desktop is not running, then a CD is not automatically mounted when it put in the drive.

If you are at a desktop and put in a CD that contains an autorun file (in its / (root) directory), then a GUI prompt appears requesting the password of the root user. You must provide the password of the root user to run the autorun file.

Mounting and Unmounting from the Command Line

If you have booted to text mode (and therefore a desktop is not running) and a CD is put in the drive, then the CD is not automatically mounted (because a desktop is not running) and you must run the mount command from the command line to mount the CD. You must be logged in as root or run the su command (to log in as root) to mount the CD.

If you have logged in to a desktop as root (not recommended), or used the su command (at a virtual terminal or terminal emulation window) to log in as root, and mount a floppy disk or CD from the command line (using the mount command), you cannot unmount it from the desktop (by using a floppy disk icon, or CD icon, or by using a GUI utility such as the Drive Mounter applet).

When the desktop is running and you put a CD in the CD-ROM drive, it will automatically be mounted (a default setting for both desktops). If you unmount the CD (by using the CD icon on the desktop or by using the umount command at the command line) and then mount the CD again from the command line, then you must unmount it from the command line.

 The above paragraphs provide a long explanation for something that doesn't happen that often, but if you find that you can't unmount a CD from the desktop, run the umount command from the command line to unmount it. *It can be very frustrating when you can't unmount a CD using the CD icon and you can't get the CD out of the drive when you press the eject button on the drive!*

Formatting and Assigning a Filesystem to a Floppy Disk

You must format a floppy disk prior to assigning a filesystem to it and you cannot format a floppy disk (to change the existing format of it, or change the existing filesystem of it) if it has been mounted. Doing the steps to format a floppy (described further below) are rarely required, as most floppy disks are sold "preformatted" (with a DOS/Windows format).

You must assign a filesystem to a floppy disk or CD prior to mounting it and you cannot assign a (different) filesystem to a floppy disk or CD if it is mounted.

The mount Command

The mount command is used to mount a partition on a hard disk, a CD, or a floppy disk, so that the filesystem on the item becomes accessible to the system. Several examples and further descriptions of the mount command are provided below.

When the mount command is run without any options, a list of the currently mounted devices, their mount points, and the filesystems being used by the devices appears - one line per device. This is a quick method of determining if a device, such as a CD or floppy has been mounted.

If a CD or floppy is not mounted and you run: mount without any options, then the device name of the CD or floppy does not appear in the list. If the CD or floppy is mounted, and you run: mount without any options, then the device name of the CD or floppy will appear in the list.

Using the mount Command to Mount a CD from the Command Line

A CD must be "mounted" so that the files on it can be accessed. Some desktops can be configured so that they automatically mount (automount) a CD when it is put in the CD-ROM drive. With this distribution, GNOME and KDE are configured by default to automatically mount a CD that is put in the CD-ROM drive.

If a desktop is not configured to automatically mount a CD when it is put in the CD-ROM drive, then the mount command is used to mount the CD. If a desktop is not running, then a CD is not automatically mounted when it is put in the drive. You must run the mount command to mount the CD.

A CD is referred to as /dev/cdrom and is mounted on the directory named cdrom, below the /mnt/ directory.

To mount a CD from the command line and make the filesystem on it available to your system, put the CD in the CD-ROM drive and run:

    mount /dev/cdrom /mnt/cdrom

Using the eject or umount Commands to Eject or Unmount a CD from the Command Line

The eject command is used to unmount a CD *and* eject it.

To unmount and eject a CD from the command line, run:

    eject cdrom

The umount command (not the unmount command) is used to unmount a CD, but *not* eject it.

To unmount a CD from the command line (and not eject it), run:

    umount /mnt/cdrom

You cannot unmount a floppy disk or CD if it is "busy". A floppy disk or CD is busy if you are accessing it in some way, such as by: running a program that is on it, opening a file on it, being "in" a directory on it (at the command line), or accessing it from within a GUI utility, such as the Nautilus or Konqueror file managers.

For example, if you run the following command, then you change directory to the floppy directory (below /mnt) and are "in" a directory on the floppy disk:

    cd /mnt/floppy

If you are "in" a directory on the floppy disk, then the system will consider that you are accessing the disk and therefore the disk will be "busy" and you will not be able to unmount it.

The same as above is true of using the following command to access the filesystem of a CD:

    cd /mnt/cdrom

In addition to the above examples of the **cd** (**c**hange **d**irectory) command, the system will consider that a floppy disk or CD is busy if you use the cd command (to change directory) to *any* directory on a floppy disk or CD.

To stop accessing the floppy disk or CD so that you can unmount it, use the cd command to change to any directory that is not on the floppy disk or CD.

For example, the following command changes to the root directory so that a floppy disk or CD is not being accessed (and is not busy):

    cd /

If you are using a GUI utility to view the filesystem of a floppy disk or CD, then the system will consider that the floppy disk or CD is busy and you will not be able to unmount it.

For example, if you run a file manager and do the steps to view the directory named floppy (below /mnt) or the directory named cdrom (below /mnt), then the system will consider the floppy disk or CD to be busy and you will not be able to unmount it. Either do the steps to view a directory that is not on the floppy or CD, or close the file manager, so that you can unmount the floppy disk or CD.

If you think that a floppy disk or CD is not being accessed and you try to unmount it and get a "device is busy" (or similar) message, then check all terminal emulation windows, virtual terminals and GUI utilities to see where the floppy disk or CD is being accessed.

If a CD is "busy" then you will not be able to eject it (in addition to not being able to unmount it).

Remember the above steps to stop a floppy or CD from being "busy". It is extremely frustrating when you cannot unmount a floppy or CD. Doing these steps can save you a lot of frustration and time!

Using the mount Command to Mount a Floppy Disk from the Command Line

A floppy disk must be "mounted" so that the files on it can be accessed. The mount command is used to mount a floppy disk. The floppy is referred to as /dev/fd0 and is mounted on the directory named floppy, below the /mnt/ directory.

To mount a floppy disk from the command line and make the filesystem on it available to your system, put the disk in the drive and run:

    mount /dev/fd0 /mnt/floppy

Using the umount Command to Unmount a Floppy Disk from the Command Line

The umount command (not the unmount command) is used to unmount a floppy. When this command is run, any files in the memory of the system that need to be written to the floppy are written. This includes files that have been saved to the floppy, copied to the floppy or moved to the floppy.

 Always unmount a floppy before removing it from a floppy drive. If data that needs to be written to a floppy is in the memory of a system , and you remove the floppy before the data is written, it will not be on the floppy. It will either be lost, or exist as files below the /mnt/floppy/ directory path on the hard disk (rather than on the floppy disk).

To unmount a floppy disk from the command line and cause the system to write all necessary files in memory to it, run:

    umount /mnt/floppy

Mounting and Unmounting a CD from the GNOME Desktop

When you put a CD in the CD-ROM drive, the GNOME desktop will automatically mount the CD by default and an icon for the CD will appear on the desktop. The Nautilus file manager will also automatically run and show you the contents of the CD.

If a file named autorun exists in the root directory of the CD, you will also be asked if you want to run the file. This file is used to automatically run a program on the CD, such as a program that shows some type of presentation that exists on the CD.

To unmount a CD from the GNOME desktop:

    right-click on the CD icon ; Eject.

Mounting and Unmounting a Floppy Disk from the GNOME Desktop

When you are working on the GNOME desktop, you can add the Disk Mounter "applet" (small GUI utility application software program) to the panel so that you can easily mount and unmount a floppy without using the command line.

To add the Disk Mounter "applet" to the panel:

> right-click on a location on the panel that does not have an icon ;
> Add to Panel ;

> Utility ; Disk Mounter.

The above steps add a Disk Mounter icon to the panel. The icon for the Disk Mounter applet looks like a floppy disk drive.

The Disk Mounter applet works like a button. To mount a floppy with the Disk Mounter:

> put the floppy in the drive ;

> click on the Disk Mounter (floppy disk drive) icon in the panel.

When you mount a floppy with the Disk Mounter, an icon representing the floppy disk appears on the desktop. Double-clicking on the floppy disk icon displays the contents of the floppy in the Nautilus file manager. Right-clicking on the floppy disk icon allows you to do several tasks, including formatting the floppy (and assigning a filesystem to it) and ejecting it (unmounting it).

To unmount a floppy with the Disk Mounter (not by right-clicking on the floppy disk icon on the desktop):

> click on the Disk Mounter (floppy disk drive) icon in the panel.

If a floppy is in the drive, but not mounted, clicking (once) on the Disk Mounter icon mounts the disk. The disk is not mounted by right-clicking on the Disk Mounter and selecting a menu item. When the floppy has been mounted, clicking (once) on the Disk Mounter icon unmounts it.

Mounting and Unmounting a Floppy Disk from the KDE Desktop

Unlike the GNOME desktop, the KDE desktop has a floppy disk icon and CD icon on the desktop at all times.

To mount a floppy disk with the floppy disk icon:

> put the floppy in the drive ; right-click on the floppy disk icon ; Mount.

After mounting the floppy, double-clicking on the icon for it displays the contents of it in the Konqueror file manager. Right-clicking on the icon for it allows you to do several tasks, including copying and moving the contents of it.

To unmount a floppy disk with the floppy disk icon:

> right-click on the floppy disk icon ; Unmount.

Mounting and Unmounting a CD from the KDE Desktop

When you put a CD in the CD-ROM drive, the KDE desktop will automatically mount the CD by default. The Konqueror file manager will also automatically run and show you the contents of the CD. If a file named autorun exists in the root directory of the CD, you will also be prompted for the password of the root user to run the file.

Right-clicking on the CD icon allows you to do several tasks, including copying and moving the contents of it.

To unmount a CD or eject (unmount and then eject) a CD from the KDE desktop:

> right-click on the CD icon ; select either Unmount or Eject.

Formatting a 1.44 MB (3-1/2") Floppy Disk

A floppy disk must be formatted and assigned a filesystem before it can accept files. Most floppy disks currently being sold are pre-formatted (i.e. they are formatted at the factory for you). These disks are also usually assigned the DOS/Windows filesystem so that they will work on a Windows system. These floppies can also be used on a Linux system because Linux can recognize the DOS/Windows filesystem.

The fdformat (floppy disk **format**) command is used to format a floppy disk. The option: /dev/fd0H1440 specifies the device name of fd0H1440 and this is the name of a file in the /dev/ directory. The **H1440** in fd0H1440 specifies that a High Density **1.44** MB floppy disk is being formatted.

To format a 1.44 MB (3-1/2") floppy, put the floppy in the drive, do *not* run the command to mount the floppy, and then run:

> fdformat /dev/fd0H1440

You must assign a filesystem to the floppy after running the above command.

The above command is rarely required because most floppies currently being sold have been formatted and they have also been assigned the DOS/Windows filesystem.

If you need to assign a filesystem to a floppy, do the steps below to assign either the ext2 filesystem or the DOS/Windows filesystem.

Assigning the ext2 Filesystem to a Floppy

The **mkfs** (**make** **fi**lesystem) command is run to assign a filesystem to a floppy. When you run this command without specifying a filesystem type, the ext2 filesystem is assigned to the floppy. The option: /dev/fd0 specifies the device name of fd0, which is a file in the /dev/ directory.

To assign the ext2 filesystem to a floppy, put the floppy in the drive, do *not* run the command to mount the floppy, and then run:

    /sbin/mkfs /dev/fd0   # run the **mkfs** binary in /sbin

If you are logged in as root or have used su to log in as root, you do not need to put /sbin/ at the start of the above command because the /sbin directory is in the PATH when you are logged in as root. More on this later.

The mkfs command (program) is a "front-end" that uses the mkfs.**ext2** program (by default) to assign the **ext2** filesystem to a disk.

The above command: mkfs /dev/fd0 could also be run as:

    /sbin/mke2fs /dev/fd0   # run the **mke2fs** (**make** **e**xt2 **f**ilesystem)
                                  # command in /sbin

The mke2fs in the above command runs the mke2fs command to assign the ext2 filesystem to the floppy. The mkfs (front end) uses the mkfs.ext2 program to assign the ext2 filesystem by default. The mke2fs program also assigns the ext2 filesystem. The **e2** in mk**e2**fs represents the **e**xt2 filesystem.

If you are logged in as root or have used su to log in as root, you do not need to put /sbin/ at the start of the above command because the /sbin directory is in the PATH when you are logged in as root.

The mkfs, mkfs.ext2, mke2fs and other programs for other filesystems, such as mkfs.**ext3** for the **ext3** filesystem, are in the /sbin/ directory.

In summary, when you run: mkfs /dev/fd0 the mkfs ("front-end" program) uses the mkfs.ext2 program to assign the ext2 filesystem to the floppy. When you run: mke2fs /dev/fd0 the mke2fs program is used to assign the ext2 filesystem to the floppy. The mkfs.ext2 and mke2fs files are identical files (same date, time and *contents*).

A floppy assigned the ext2 filesystem will work in a Linux system, or any system that can recognize the ext2 filesystem.

A floppy assigned the ext2 filesystem will *not* work in a Windows system because this OS does not recognize the ext2 filesystem (by default). There are software components that can be added to a Windows system to allow it to work with the ext2 filesystem.

A floppy assigned the ext2 filesystem will be able to utilize all of the benefits of the ext2 filesystem, such as maintaining permissions (user access) information. If you do not need to work with floppies on a Windows system, or if you have installed software that allows a Windows system to work with the ext2 filesystem, then you may want to run the above command to assign this filesystem to all of your floppies, so that they can utilize the benefits of this filesystem.

Assigning the DOS/Windows Filesystem to a Floppy

The **mkdosfs** (**make dos** filesystem) command is used to assign the DOS/Windows filesystem to a floppy. The option: /dev/fd0 specifies the device name of fd0.

To assign the DOS/Windows filesystem to a floppy, put the floppy in the drive, do *not* run the command to mount the floppy, and then run:

```
/sbin/mkdosfs  /dev/fd0        # run the mkdosfs (make dos filesystem)
                               # command in /sbin
```

If you are logged in as root or have used su to log in as root, you do not need to put /sbin/ at the start of the above command because the /sbin directory is in the PATH when you are logged in as root.

A floppy with the DOS/Windows filesystem will work in a Windows or Linux system, but it will not be able to utilize the benefits of the ext2 filesystem.

Shutting Down a Linux System

A Linux system needs to be shut down rather than simply turned off.

While the Linux OS is running there may be programs and processes running that need to finish, and there may also be files that are in memory that need to be written to disk. If you simply turn off a system that is running, these programs and processes do not get a chance to finish properly and files in memory will not have a chance to be written to disk. Therefore, you need to shut down a system rather than simply turn it off. When you shut a current (rather than a legacy) system down, then the power will automatically be turned off. When you shut an older system down, you may also need to turn off the power.

Always remember to save your work and close all programs that have been run from a desktop prior to shutting down or rebooting a system. If you have been working at one or more virtual terminals, make sure all programs in all virtual terminals have finished running prior to shutting a system down or rebooting it.

Shutting Down from the GUI Login Prompt

To shut a system down from the GUI login prompt, do the following:

>   Session (at the bottom of the screen) ; Shut down the computer ; OK.

Rebooting a Linux System

If a system is not working properly, due to a "hung" program or some other problem, you may need to reboot it so that the OS is started again. When you reboot a system, it goes through the process of shutting down and then it restarts and goes through the process of booting.

Rebooting from a Desktop

To reboot from a desktop, do the following:

>   Menu ; Log Out ; Restart the computer ; OK.

Rebooting from the GUI Login Prompt

To reboot a system from the GUI login prompt, do the following:

>   Session (at the bottom of the screen) ; Reboot the computer ; OK.

Shutting Down and Rebooting from a Virtual Terminal

The poweroff, halt, reboot and shutdown commands are used at a virtual terminal to shut down or reboot the OS. These commands can be run from a virtual terminal when a desktop is running, or from a terminal emulation window (when a desktop is running), but the latter is not recommended. If a desktop is running, shut down or reboot a system using the menu on the desktop.

The poweroff, halt and reboot commands can be run when you are logged in with any user name. You must be logged in as root or use su to log in as root to run the shutdown command.

The poweroff Command

To shut down a system and turn its power off when you are working at a virtual terminal, type: poweroff and press Enter.

The halt Command

To shut down a system and *not* turn off its power when you are working at a virtual terminal, type: halt and press Enter.

If you use the halt command on a system, then the system is stopped, but the power is not turned off and you can still see messages on the screen of the system. In this case, you may be able to see information that would help in diagnosing a problem with a system (prior to turning the power off and restarting the system).

The reboot Command

To shut down a system and restart it if you are working at a virtual terminal, run the following command:

```
reboot
```

The shutdown Command

In addition to the halt, poweroff and reboot commands, the shutdown command can be used to shut down a system, or shut down it down and then restart it.

The shutdown command provides more functionality than the halt, poweroff and reboot commands.

For example, if you run the shutdown command on a system that is being used as some type of server, so that you can do some maintenance on the server, all users that are logged in to the server can be notified of the shutdown. In addition to this, you can specify other options such as a time of day to shut down, or specify or an amount of time that will pass prior to the system being shut down.

The shutdown command cannot be run without options.

To shut down a system, run the following command:

```
shutdown -h now        # the h (halt) and now options of shutdown are used
```

To reboot a system, run the following command:

```
shutdown -r now        # the r (reboot) and now options of shutdown are used
```

To shut down a system in fifteen minutes (+15) and send the message: "System shutdown in 15 minutes. Please log out." to logged in users, run the following command:

```
shutdown -h +15 "System shutdown in 15 minutes. Please log out." &
```

The message: "System shutdown in 15 minutes. Please log out." will only appear on the virtual terminals of systems that are logged in to the system that is being shut down. If a user is working at a desktop (rather than a virtual terminal), the message will not appear. The message will also not appear in any terminal emulation windows that are open on the desktop.

Notice the "&" (ampersand) at the far right of the above shutdown command. When you run some commands (or use some options of some commands) without putting an "&" (ampersand) at the end of the command, then the command prompt does not appear until the command has completed.

If you ran the shutdown command with the +15 option (or other time option) and did not put an "&" (ampersand) at the end of the command, then the prompt would not appear until after the command had completed. In this case, the prompt would not appear for fifteen minutes. Therefore, you would not be able to run commands at the prompt (in the virtual terminal or terminal emulation window from which you ran the command) for fifteen minutes. (However, you could still run commands in other virtual terminals or terminal emulation windows.)

The "&" (ampersand) at the end of the above command causes the command to run in the background in a subshell, which causes the prompt to appear again so that you can run more commands.

The "&" (ampersand) can be used at the end of any command that does not cause the prompt to appear after running the command. This includes commands that run programs, such as a command to run a program to compile the source code of another program, which may take hours to compile.

The login and logout Commands

If you are at a virtual terminal and need to log in with a different user name, do the following:

> login *username* ; press Enter.

If you are at a virtual terminal and need to leave a system for a short period of time, do the following:

> logout ; press Enter.

Do not run the login and logout commands in a terminal emulation window (accessed from a desktop). Instead, do the following:

> Menu ; Lock Screen or Menu ; Log Out.

Locking the Screen or Shutting Down When Leaving a System

For security reasons, you should not go away from a Linux system while a virtual terminal or desktop is available for someone else to access.

If you are leaving a system for a short period of time and if a desktop is running, use the logout command to log out of all virtual terminals and then do the steps below to "lock your screen". This will prevent system access unless a password is provided. If you are logged in at a virtual terminal and go to the desktop and lock the screen, anyone can still do the steps to go to the virtual terminal and use it.

Shut the system down if you are leaving it for the day.

To lock your screen from the desktop:

> Menu ; Lock Screen ; a GUI login prompt appears.

To shut down from the desktop:

> Menu ; Log Out ; Shut Down ; OK.

Logging Out from a Desktop

To log in as a different user, log out as the current user. Once you log out, the desktop will not be available until someone logs in again.

To log out: Menu ; Log Out ; Log Out ; OK ; a GUI login prompt appears.

The User Name to Use for the Hands-On Exercises

If you did not create the cwest user during the Linux installation, then remember that when you see instructions to "log in as cwest", then log in with the non-root user name that you created when you installed Linux.

Also remember that if you see a reference to "your the home directory" or a directory path that includes the directory named cwest, replace cwest with the username that you created.

Hands-On Exercises

Using Figures 4-1 and 4-2 During the Hands-On Exercises Below

Figures 4-1 and 4-2 shown earlier in this section detail the components of the GNOME and KDE desktops. Use these figures to locate the desktop items that are described in the Hands-On Exercises below.

 Logging In to the GNOME Desktop

Boot your system so that the GUI login dialog box appears ;

click on Session (at the bottom of the screen) ; GNOME ; OK ;

below Username:, type in: *cwest* (or the user that you created during the installation) ; press Enter ;

below Password:, type in the password for the user ; press Enter.

 Creating a Terminal Emulation Icon

Right-click on an empty location (without an icon) on the panel (the grey bar across the bottom of the screen) ;

Add to Panel ; Launcher from menu ;

System Tools ; Terminal.

③ Opening A Terminal Emulation Window

Click on the Terminal Emulation Window icon that you just created to open a terminal emulation window.

Your current user name (cwest) appears in the border at the top of the window and also in the prompt at which you run commands. The prompt appears as: [cwest@lancomx cwest]$. This prompt is also referred to as the "command line" and "shell prompt".

You will use the Terminal Emulation Window icon throughout the course to open terminal emulation windows so that you can run Linux commands.

④ Re-Sizing and Moving A Window

Point to the bottom left corner of the window until your cursor changes shape to look like an "L" ; press and hold down your left mouse button and move the corner up and to the right (about a an inch).

Point to the bottom middle of the window until your cursor changes shape to look like an "_" ; press and hold down your mouse button and move the bottom border up (about a half an inch).

Point to the top border of the terminal emulation window ; press and hold down the left mouse button and move the window down (about a half an inch).

Now move the window back up to where it was.

⑤ Maximizing, Minimizing and Running Commands

The Close Window, Maximize Window and Minimize Window buttons are at the top right of the window. Move your cursor over top of (but do not click on) each of these buttons so that you can see the names of the buttons.

Click on the Maximize button to cause the terminal emulation window to fill the screen (except for the area taken up at the bottom of the screen by the panel). Move your cursor over top of the button that you just clicked. When you click on the Maximize button, its name changes to Unmaximize.

Click on the Minimize button (not the Unmaximize button) to cause the terminal emulation window to move "into the panel".

Notice that [cwest@lancomx:~] appears in the middle of the panel. This represents the terminal emulation window.

Hold down Alt and press the Tab key and let go. The terminal emulation window fills the screen again.

Run the following commands in the terminal emulation window. Press Enter after typing in each command.

```
]# ls  -la        #  press Enter to run the ls command and list of all of the
                  #  files in the cwest directory

]# man  ls        #  run the man command to see the "man page" (help)
                  #  for the ls command
```

press the PgDn key until you reach the end of the file ;

```
q                 #  type in:  q   and press Enter to go out of the man page
```

click on the Close Window button to close the terminal emulation window ;

click on the Terminal Emulation Window icon again ;

```
]# exit           #  the exit command is another way to close the window
```

click on the Terminal Emulation Window icon again ;

press Ctrl+d ; this also closes the window.

 Using the cwest's Home Icon

When you are using the GNOME desktop, you can tell who you are logged in as by the user name that appears in the *"username's* Home" icon on the desktop.

cwest's Home icon x 2 (double-click on the icon).

This icon provides quick access to the home directory of the cwest user. It runs the Nautilus file manager and displays the contents of the cwest directory, below the /home directory (i.e. the contents of /home/cwest).

Close this window.

 Using the Start Here Icon

Start Here icon x 2.

This provides access to icons for: Applications, Preferences, Server Settings and System Settings. You can also get access to these items from the Menu icon at the bottom left of the screen.

Close this window.

(8) Viewing the Names of the Items in the Panel

Move your cursor over top of (but do not click on) each item in the panel at the bottom of the screen ;

the name of each item will appear ;

move your cursor over top of (but do not click on) the Workspace Switcher icon.

Notice that the top left pane of this icon is darker than the other three panes.

(9) Using the Menu to Run Programs in the Panes of the Workspace Switcher

Click on the Menu (GNOME Menu) at the bottom left of the screen ;

Accessories ; Calculator ;

watch the dark top left pane in the Workspace Switcher window and move the Calculator around on the desktop ;

now run another program from the Menu (bottom left) ;

Menu ; Graphics ; PDF Viewer ; this program is used to view .pdf files ;

press Alt+Tab until Calculator is selected and then let go ; the Calculator appears again.

(10) Opening Programs in the Other Virtual Desktops

Click on the top right pane in the Workspace Switcher (in the middle of the panel.)

The other two programs no longer appear on the desktop. You have moved to another "virtual desktop". Now run a program in this virtual desktop.

Menu ; Office ; OpenOffice.org Draw ; look at your hard disk light to see if there is activity ; this program may take a minute to load ; click on Cancel when the opening dialog box appears ;

click on the bottom left pane in the Workspace Switcher ;

Menu ; Sound & Video ; CD Player ;

click on the bottom right pane in the Workspace Switcher ;

Menu ; Help.

The bottom right pane of the Workspace Switcher is currently selected.

Click on each of the other three panes and notice the programs that are running in each virtual desktop ;

now close all of the programs that you have opened in all of the Workspace Switcher panes.

⑪ Customizing Your GNOME Desktop

Menu ; Preferences ; notice the items on the menu at the right ;

Control Center ; this one heading provides access to the individual items on the Preferences menu ;

Background x 2 (double-click) ;

change some settings here if you would like to ; Close ;

minimize the Preferences window ;

in the middle of the panel, click on [Preferences] ; the window opens again ;

Mouse x 2 ; there are three "tabs" that appear at the top of this dialog box ;

the Buttons tab is currently selected ;

if you are left-handed, click on the box beside Left-handed mouse ;

click on the Cursors tab ; if you would like to change your mouse cursor, select a different one ;

read the note below the four cursor shapes ; Close ;

Theme x 2 ; the Application tab is selected ;

click on a different theme and watch the screen change ;

if you would like to change your theme, select a different one ;

Window Border (tab) ;

click on a different window border and watch the borders around windows and dialog boxes change ;

if you would like to use a different border, select a different one ; Close ;

close the Preferences window.

⑫ Logging Out of the GNOME Desktop and Logging In to the KDE Desktop

Menu ; Log Out ; Log Out ; OK.

Session ; KDE ; OK ;

log in as the cwest user ; No ; do not make KDE the default desktop.

⑬ Creating a Terminal Emulation Window Icon

Right-click on a blank area of the panel ;

Add ; Button ; System Tools ; Terminal.

Using the Icons on the Desktop

Notice that the KDE desktop has a CD/DVD-ROM icon and a Floppy icon even though you do not have a CD or a floppy inserted. These icons can be used to mount, unmount, view and do other tasks with a CD or floppy, as described earlier in this section.

> Home x 2 ; Konqueror runs and displays the files in /home/cwest ; close this window ;
>
> Start Here x 2 ; folders for Applications, Preferences, Server Settings and System Settings appear ;
>
> close this window.

 Viewing Icons in the Panel and Running Programs in Virtual Desktops

> Move your cursor over top of each of the icons in the panel ;

The item that was the Workspace Switcher on the GNOME desktop has numbers in each pane in the window.

> Point to (but do not click on) the 1 in the Workspace Switcher and "Desktop 1" appears ;
>
> use the Menu (bottom left) and run a program in Desktop 1 ;
>
> click on each of the other three desktops and run a program in each ;
>
> click from one desktop to another to change from one virtual desktop to another ;
>
> close all of the programs in the virtual desktops.

16 **Customizing Your KDE Desktop**

> Menu ; Preferences ; Look & Feel ; Background ;
>
> on the Background tab, click on the box beside the Color 1: heading ;
>
> click on a color in the box at the top left of the dialog box that opened ; OK ;
>
> do the same as above to change Color 2 ;
>
> Wallpaper tab ; No Wallpaper ; OK.
>
> Menu ; Preferences ; Peripherals ; Mouse ;
>
> if you are left handed, click on the circle beside Left handed ; OK.

⑰ **Logging Out of the KDE Desktop and Logging In to the GNOME Desktop**

Menu ; Logout ; Logout ; Session ; GNOME ; OK ;

log in as the cwest user.

⑱ **Using the su Command to Log In As the root User**

Open a terminal emulation window ; maximize the window.

Notice that the prompt includes the cwest user name and a $ (dollar sign).

Now run the following command at the shell prompt. You will use this command many times throughout this course.

]$ su -   # type: su, a space and then - (a dash) and press Enter

Running the above command is sometimes referred to in Linux documentation as "su to root", "su as the root user" and "change to root". It is a common method of logging in to a "subshell" as the root user, without actually logging in with the user name of root.

When you use the su command, you are only accessing the system as the root user at the location in which you ran the command (virtual terminal or terminal emulation window).

If you log in at a desktop as a non-root user (recommended) and then run the su command (in a terminal emulation window or at a virtual terminal), then any work that you do "at the desktop", such as using a word processor or spreadsheet program, is still done as the non-root user.

When you use the su command, we recommend that you always use the - (dash) option to get an "environment" that is very similar to the environment provided if you log in as the root user.

At the "Password:" prompt, type in the root user password ; press Enter.

Notice that the prompt now includes the root user name and a # (number sign).

The prompt shows the word "root" twice. The word "root" in "root@lancomx" represents the user named root. The word "root" *at the right of* "root@lancomx" represents the current directory, which is named root.

The directory name that appears in the prompt changes when you change into a different directory. The user name does not change unless you log in as a different user.

For security reasons, **never** log in to a desktop (log in at the GUI log prompt) as the root user.

]# ls -la   # files in the /root directory appear

click on the Terminal Emulation Window icon and open another terminal emulation window ; maximize the window.

You can have multiple terminal emulation windows open at once. The current terminal emulation window shows the user name of cwest at the left of the prompt and the current directory, named cwest at the right of the prompt. You will see the part of the prompt that shows the directory name change when you do some of the steps below.

]$ ls -la   # files in the /home/cwest directory appear

Alt+Tab to the "root user window" (the one with the # (number) sign) at the prompt.

You can work as the root user in one window and as the non-user (that you logged in with) in another window.

Minimize both terminal emulation windows ; notice how they appear in the panel.

 ## 19 Mounting a CD from the Desktop

Put CD 1 in your CD-ROM drive ; wait a few seconds and then close the Nautilus file manager window that opens ;

close the dialog box that asks if you want to run the autorun file.

For the duration of this course, unless otherwise specified, always close the window that opens when you put *any* CD (CD 1, 2 or 3) in the CD-ROM drive (or when you mount a CD with the mount command).

Push the eject button on your CD-ROM drive.

You cannot open the drive now that the CD has been automatically mounted by the desktop (the default configuration of the desktop).

Changing Into the cdrom Directory and Listing Files

Hold down Alt and press Tab until you can select the "root user window" ; once opened, the word "root" appears at the top left of the window ;

```
]# cd /mnt/cdrom        # change into the cdrom directory -
                        # the root directory of the CD
```

The following command will display the files in the cdrom directory, which is the root directory of the CD.

```
]# ls                   # files are listed alphabetically by default
```

Notice that the CD contains a file named autorun.

```
]# cd RedHat/RPMS        # change into the directory that contains
                        # the .rpm files

]# ls -l | less          # press the PgDn key and scroll to the bottom
```

These are all software packages that are included on CD 1.

```
q                       # exit out of the less command
```

 Trying to Unmount a CD that is Being Accessed

```
]# umount /mnt/cdrom     # try to unmount the CD - it is "busy"
```

minimize the terminal emulation window(s) so that the desktop appears ;

CD icon (on the desktop) x r (right-click) ; Eject ; Details ;

the CD is still "busy" ; OK.

22 **Changing Directory "Off Of" the CD So that You Can Unmount It**

Press Alt+Tab and select the "root window" ;

```
]# cd /                  # change directory so that you are not
                        # accessing the CD

]# umount /mnt/cdrom     # now you can unmount the CD

]# ls /mnt/cdrom         # no files appear because the CD is not mounted
```

If a CD is mounted, you cannot eject it by pressing the eject button on the CD-ROM drive. You must do the steps from the desktop or command line to unmount the CD before it can be ejected by pressing the eject button on the CD-ROM drive.

If you have mounted a CD from the command line you will not be able to unmount it from the desktop (by using the CD icon on the desktop). You must unmount it from the command line.

 Mounting a CD from the Command Line

The CD is not currently mounted, so you *could* (but don't) manually eject it if necessary. If you ejected the CD and put it back in again, the default desktop setup would cause the CD to be mounted again.

```
]# clear
```

This clears the screen - the output of the next command will be more readable.

Now run the mount command without any options to see the currently mounted partitions, mount points, and filesystems.

```
]# mount          # /dev/cdrom does not appear in the list
```

The command below mounts the CD.

```
]# mount /dev/cdrom /mnt/cdrom
```

The above mount command is commonly used to mount a CD while working in a virtual terminal (and a desktop is not running). By default, the GNOME and KDE desktops are set up to automatically mount CDs when they are put in the CD-ROM drive (with the distribution that you are using).

Unless otherwise specified, always close the window and dialog box that appear.

```
]# clear

]# mount          # /dev/cdrom now appears in the list
                  # because the CD is mounted
```

 Viewing Previous Commands and Output

If you need to see previous commands or the output of them, you can use the scroll bar and scroll arrows at the right of the terminal emulation window to scroll up to see a limited amount of previous commands and output.

Click on the Scroll Up Arrow at the top right of the terminal emulation window until you can see the output of the previous mount command (the output without /dev/cdrom in it).

Scrolling through previous commands and output can be extremely useful at times. Remember that you can scroll up (and then down) through commands and output in a terminal emulation window.

Ejecting a CD and Using the exit Command

```
]# ls  /mnt/cdrom     # files now appear because the CD is mounted
```

A few steps above, you ran a command that accessed the CD and listed the contents of the cdrom directory. This was done from the / (root) directory without changing directory "in" to the cdrom directory that is "on" the CD. Therefore, you are not currently "in" a directory "on" the CD and are not accessing the CD, and so you can unmount or eject it.

```
]# eject  cdrom       # this unmounts and ejects the CD
```

remove the CD and close the CD-ROM drive.

Notice that the name of the root user is at the left of the current shell prompt.

```
]# exit               # this logs you out of the subshell opened with
                      # the  su command
```

Notice that the cwest user name now appears at the left of the shell prompt.

```
]# exit               # when you are not "su", this closes the window
```

Alt+Tab to the "cwest window" and run the exit command to close the window.

 Accessing Virtual Terminals from the Desktop

In the steps below, you will log in to each of the six virtual terminals, run a command in each terminal and then switch between the terminals to see that something different is happening in each one.

```
Ctrl+Alt+F1           # virtual terminal 1 appears

log in as cwest ;

]# ls  -la            # files in the cwest directory (/home/cwest) appear

Alt+F2                # virtual terminal 2 appears
```

Alt+Fx is used to go from one virtual terminal to another.

```
Log in as cwest ;

]# su -               # log in with the password of the root user

]# ls  -la            # files in the /root directory appear

use Alt+F3 to move to virtual terminal 3 ; log in as cwest ;
```

now "su to root" again (run: su -   and log in with the password of the root user) ;

]# man ls   # view the man page of the ls command

use Alt+F4 to move to virtual terminal 4 ; log in as cwest ; su to root ;

]# cd /sbin   # change into the /sbin directory

]# ls -la

move to virtual terminal 5 ; log in as cwest ; do not su to root ;

]# setup   # run the Setup Utility - a text-based GUI utility

type in the root user password ; press Enter.

If you are logged in as a non-root user and run a utility that configures system settings, you must provide the root user password before the utility will run.

To close this utility later, press Tab twice to highlight "Quit" and press Enter.

Go to virtual terminal 6 ; log in as cwest ; su to root ;

]# top   # run the top command to see the processes
                         # currently running in memory

press Alt+F1 to go to virtual terminal 1 and see the output at this terminal ;

press Alt+F2 to go to virtual terminal 2 ;

now press Alt+Fx and replace x with the numbers 3 through 6 to move from one virtual terminal to another.

Unlike terminal emulation windows that are opened on a desktop, you cannot view more than one virtual terminal at a time. However, you can run commands or programs in all virtual terminals at one time (and still have the desktop running, and programs running on the desktop, and terminal emulation windows open on the desktop).

 27 **Going Back to the Desktop**

Alt+F7   # this key combination is used to go from
                         # a virtual terminal to the desktop

run a program from the menu ;

open a terminal emulation window.

You can run commands and programs in virtual terminals, and still run programs and open terminal emulation windows on the desktop.

Logging Out at Virtual Terminals

Always stop all programs in virtual terminals and log out of the virtual terminals before shutting your system down.

    Ctrl+Alt+F3   # go to virtual terminal 3

The Ctrl+Alt+Fx key combination is used to go from the desktop to a virtual terminal.

    q   # quit out of the man command

    Alt+F6   # the top command is running in this terminal

    q   # quit out of the top command

Notice the user name in the current prompt. The next command exits from the "su to root" session to the "cwest user session".

    exit   # go out of the subshell opened with the su command

The user name in the prompt changed from root to cwest.

    logout   # log out of virtual terminal 6

use Alt+Fx to go to virtual terminals 1 through 5 and run exit (if the terminal is in an "su session") and then run logout to log out of these terminals ; you should now be logged out of all virtual terminals ;

use Alt+Fx to go to virtual terminals 1 through 6 ; all of them look the same and all are ready to be logged in to.

 Shutting Down

Do not shut down the system from the command line (at a virtual terminal or in a terminal emulation window) when a desktop is running.

    Go to the desktop ; close all programs and windows ;

    Menu ; Log Out ; Shut Down ; OK.

Section Review

1. You have booted to text mode and are working at the shell prompt. Which of the following can be used to shut down a system properly (choose two)?

   ☐ A. logout
   ☐ B. shutdown now
   ☐ C. shutdown -h now
   ☐ D. poweroff

2. Which of the following programs is the default web browser of the GNOME and KDE desktops?

   ○ A. Netscape
   ○ B. Mozilla
   ○ C. Opera
   ○ D. Explorator

3. The environment that you get when you run the su command without a - (dash) is the same as the environment that you get when you run the su command with a - (dash). T F

4. What are two methods of closing a terminal emulation window?

   ☐ A. run the sulogout command
   ☐ B. run the exit command
   ☐ C. press Ctrl+d
   ☐ D. press Ctrl+c

5. If you are working at a desktop and need to leave your system temporarily, what is the most likely step you should do?

   ○ A. reboot the system
   ○ B. lock the screen
   ○ C. shut down the system
   ○ D. switch to a virtual terminal

6. Select the character that appears at the shell prompt by default when you use the su command to log in as the root user.

    ○ A. #
    ○ B. $
    ○ C. /
    ○ D. %

7. You can shut down a Linux system properly by simply turning the power off. T F

8. Several windows are open and maximized on the screen. Select the key combination that allows you to move to a different window.

    ○ A. Alt+Backspace
    ○ B. Alt+Tab
    ○ C. Ctrl+Tab
    ○ D. Ctrl+d

9. The Workspace Switcher in GNOME, or the items labeled Desktop 1 through 4 in KDE, allow you to access:

    ○ A. virtual terminals
    ○ B. virtual terminal emulation windows
    ○ C. four different web browser programs
    ○ D. virtual desktops

10. What is the default file manager for the GNOME desktop?

    ○ A. Nautilus
    ○ B. Kudzu
    ○ C. Konqueror
    ○ D. Explorator

11. You can view multiple virtual terminals at one time. T F

12. Which key combination allows you to move from virtual terminal 3 to virtual terminal 5?

    ○ A. Alt+F5
    ○ B. Ctrl+F5
    ○ C. Alt+F3
    ○ D. Shift+F5

13. Select the fist step that is used to start adding an item to the panel on a desktop.

    ○ A. double-click on the Add to Panel icon
    ○ B. right-click on the Menu icon
    ○ C. right-click on a blank area of the panel
    ○ D. double-click on a blank area of the desktop

14. The Trash icon on the GNOME or KDE desktop can be used to undelete files that have been deleted at the command line. T F

15. Virtual terminals are also referred to as (choose three):

    ☐ A. terminal emulation windows
    ☐ B. virtual consoles
    ☐ C. system consoles
    ☐ D. consoles

16. Your system is set up to boot into text mode and you have logged in to virtual terminal 1. You have put a CD in the CD-ROM drive. Which of the following commands is used to mount the CD in the CD-ROM drive.

    ○ A. load /dev/cdrom
    ○ B. mount /dev/cdrom /mnt/cdrom
    ○ C. mount /mnt/cdrom /dev/cdrom
    ○ D. mount /root/cdrom

17. Select the key combination that allows you to move from a desktop to virtual terminal 2.

    ○ A. Alt+F2
    ○ B. Shift+Alt+F2
    ○ C. Ctrl+Alt+F2
    ○ D. Ctrl+F2

18. Which command do you use to unmount a CD and cause the CD-ROM drive door to open?

    ○ A. umount cdrom
    ○ B. open cdrom
    ○ C. eject cdrom
    ○ D. open sesame

19. Which key combination is used to move from any virtual terminal to the currently running desktop?

     ○ A. Alt+F7
     ○ B. Ctrl+F7
     ○ C. Alt+Shift+F7
     ○ D. Ctrl+Backspace+F7

20. Which of the following statements are correct (choose two)?

     ☐ A. mkfs /dev/fd0   is used to assign the ext2 filesystem to a floppy
     ☐ B. mkfs /floppy   is used to assign the ext2 filesystem to a floppy
     ☐ C. mkdos /dev/fd0   is used to assign the DOS/Windows filesystem to a floppy
     ☐ D. mkdosfs /dev/fd0   is used to assign the DOS/Windows filesystem to a floppy

21. A floppy assigned the ext2 filesystem will not work in a Windows system by default because this OS does not recognize the ext2 filesystem. T F

22. You are working at a virtual terminal and a desktop is not running. You have mounted a CD in the CD-ROM drive and changed into the cdrom directory below /mnt/ to access the CD. When you try to unmount the CD, you get a message that states that it is busy. Select the command that will allow you to unmount the CD.

     ○ A. umount -nobusy /mnt/cdrom
     ○ B. shutdown cdrom
     ○ C. eject cdrom
     ○ D. cd /

23. You are working at either the GNOME or KDE desktop and have mounted a CD. Which steps would you take to cause the CD-ROM drive door to open?

     ○ A. right-click on the CD icon ; Eject
     ○ B. right-click on the CD icon ; Mount
     ○ C. double-click on the CD icon ; OpenEmUp
     ○ D. double-click on the CD icon ; Close CD

Chapter 5: The Linux Filesystem and the Shell Environment

During this chapter you will learn about the structure of the Linux filesystem and the shell environment.

The specifications for the Linux filesystem are provided in the Filesystem Hierarchy Standard (FHS). In this chapter you learn about this "standard" and the Linux filesystem hierarchy, including the default Linux directories that are located off of the root directory. You will also find out about Linux directory and file names, commonly used file extensions, hidden directories and files, and the difference between the full path to a directory or file and the relative path.

The Linux OS relies heavily on symbolic links, which are small files that point to other directories and files. Some distributions use symbolic links more than others. You will see why these links exist and learn about the benefits provided by these links.

This chapter also describes the benefits of mounting certain Linux directories on separate partitions and details the directories that should be mounted this way, and those that should not.

The shell "environment" is accessed by opening a terminal emulation window when running in GUI desktop mode or by booting to a virtual terminal in text mode. This chapter explains how to work effectively at the shell prompt, in the shell environment. It details the key features and benefits of the shell environment, the types of shell environments that are available, and the use and benefits of shell scripts.

The following commands are described in this chapter and are also used in the Hands-On Exercises:

cd	change directory
ls	list directories and files
pwd	print (display) the working directory
file	determine the "type" of a file
uname	display system information
man	display an on-line manual page
nl	number lines of output or a file
echo	echo (output) something to something else (by default, the screen)
clear	clear the screen and move the prompt to the top

The less, zless, bzless, more, zmore and bzmore commands are used to display the contents of a file or allow the output of a command to be scrolled through.

During the Hands-On Exercises, you will work at the shell prompt and learn how to use the cd command to move around the directory structure with absolute and relative paths. You will view the contents of all of the main directories that are located off of the root directory to see the files that are typically located in these directories.

You will also view many different types of files, including binary, script, configuration, hidden and compressed files, as well as various types of symbolic links.

The Linux Filesystem and the Shell Environment

Topics Covered in this Chapter

Discuss the Filesystem Hierarchy Standard (FHS) and the Linux filesystem

Learn the purpose of main Linux directories located off of the root directory

Detail the common file extensions and the benefits of hidden directories and files

Describe the difference between the absolute path and relative path

Discover the reasons for the use of symbolic links to directories and files

Understand the benefits of setting up directories as mount points of partitions

Explains the key features, benefits and types of shell environments

Do the steps to move around the directory structure, view the key files in the main directories, and view many different types of Linux files

In this chapter, you will learn about the main Linux directories, common filename extensions, the path to a directory or file, benefits of setting up directories as mount points and the shell environment.

During the Hands-On Exercises you use about ten new commands. You will learn several methods of changing directory, look at the main Linux directories, use the ls command to list the contents of directories and use the file command to see the "type" of a file. You will also use the less command to scroll through the contents of a file and also scroll through the output of a command.

The Filesystem Hierarchy Standard (FHS)

The Filesystem Hierarchy Standard (FHS) is a standard for the filesystem of UNIX-like systems, including Linux. This standard is maintained by the Filesystem Hierarchy Standard Group at http://www.pathname.com/fhs. This web site contains a document that outlines the requirements and guidelines for directory and file locations on UNIX-like systems. A filesystem that meets the requirements of the FHS standard is FHS "compliant".

The benefit of the FHS document is that it details guidelines that provide for a standardized filesystem hierarchy. This allows the programmers that provide new OS components, and updates to existing components, to know where these components should be located. It also allows support staff to know where the commonly used directories and files will be located. This includes the location of the kernel, the binaries that are used when you run commands, and text configuration files.

For example, directories that contain binaries, such as system administration commands, should always have the same directory name and the directory should always be in the same location. To continue the example, configuration files that provide system settings should always be in the same location.

In addition to the directory names, the names of commonly used binaries and configuration files are also a part of FHS. For example, the /bin directory should contain the cp binary that provides the copy command. FHS is a wonderful concept, but it is not always the practice!

The Filesystem Hierarchy

Linux uses a tree structured "hierarchy" for the organization of directories and the storage of files in the directories. The directory structure is "tree-like". It has a "root" directory, symbolized with a / (forward slash). All other directories "branch" off of the root. All directories that are off of the root are subdirectories of the root. The root directory is the "parent" of the subdirectories below it.

Directories are used to hold program files and data files in the same way as file folders are used to hold paper documents.

It is important to note that Linux treats all system components as a file.

For example, a directory is actually a file that contains the names of the files that are in the directory. Also, hardware components appear to the system as files.

Directory and File Listings

Running the ls command at the shell prompt allows you to get a listing of directories and files. The following is an example of a listing at the shell prompt of a directory named bin:

    drwxr-x---   22 root   root   4096 May 22 16:14 bin

The name of the directory (bin) appears at the far right. At the left of this name is the time (16:14). If the directory were *not* created this year, the year would appear in place of the time. Next at the left is the date (May 22). At the left of that is the size of the directory, which is 4,096 bytes (4 K). At the far left is a "**d**". This indicates that the item is a directory. The other items shown above, such as "rwxr-x---   22 root   root", are covered later, during the discussion of permissions.

The following is an example of a listing (from the ls command) of a file named grep.1.gz:

    -rw-r--r--   1 root   root   5907 Jul 17 2001 grep.1.gz

The name of the file appears at the far right (grep.1.gz). At the left of the name is the date that the file was created (July 17, 2001). At the left of that is the size of the file, which is 5,907 bytes (approximately 5.9 K). At the far left is a "-". This indicates that the item is a file. As mentioned above, the other items shown, such as "rw-r-r- 1 root root", are covered later.

The above file was created in 2,001. If the file was created this year, then the time that the file was created, in the form of hh:mm, would appear in place of the year.

When you run ls command and use the l option, as in: ls -l you see a series of characters at the left of each item in the directory listing. Table 5-1 shows the meaning of the far left character in a directory listing.

Table 5-1 - Leftmost Characters in a Listing

Character	Indicates
-	a file
d	a directory
l	a symbolic link (a.k.a. symlink) to another directory or file
c	a character device, such as a virtual terminal
b	a block device, such as a hard disk

When using the l option of the ls command, the - (dash) for file and the d for directory appear most often in the list that is output when the ls command is run. Remember that directory names have a "d" at the far left of them and files have a "-".

Linux Directory and File Names

Linux directory and file names are "case sensitive" and can be up to 255 characters in length. To avoid using one of the many (approximately twenty) "illegal" characters, use the letters a-z, A-Z and the numbers 0-9. To make commands easier to run, you may want to always use lower case letters for directory and file names.

Some programs will not work properly with directories and files that contain spaces. Therefore, it is best to avoid using spaces and use the - (dash) or _ (underscore) character instead, if necessary. A - (dash) is often useful to make a directory or file name easier to read.

A directory or file name can contain a suffix (a.k.a. extension). This is a . (dot) followed by one or more characters, such as ".o", ".ps" and ".png". It can even include another . (dot) followed by more characters, such as ".1.gz".

Common File Suffixes

There are several "standard" suffixes that are used for program files and data files. Below are a few examples of the many different suffixes.

.dat	**dat**a file
.txt	**text** file
.bak	**ba**ckup file
.db	**d**ata**b**ase file
.htm, .html	**h**ypertext **m**arkup **l**anguage (web page) file
.ps	**P**ost**S**cript file
.wav	audio file
.png, .jpg, .gif	graphic file
.lock	**lock**s a file that is in use so that it can not be written to
.o	**o**bject code file or module file
.h	**h**eader file of a C or C++ program
.c	**C** program source code file
.so	library file
.gz, .tgz, .bz2	compressed program and data files

Configuration files commonly use the following suffixes:

.conf, .cfg, .config and .cf

Determining the Type of a File When It Does Not Have a Suffix

Many Linux files do not have an suffix, but you often need to know the "type" of a file to understand what it does. The type of a file can be seen with the file command.

For example, the command: file inittab displays the output of: ASCII English text. Therefore, the inittab file is a text file.

Hidden Directories and Files

Almost all of the files that are used to configure settings on a Linux system are plain text files, as opposed to files that are coded or encrypted. Some Linux directories and files are prefixed with a . (dot). These files do not normally appear in directory listings when the directory is viewed with a GUI utility, such as Nautilus, or when viewed with a command that lists directories and files, such as the ls command.

These directories and files are commonly called "dot" directories and "dot" files and are "hidden" from regular directory listings. These directories and files typically contain configuration settings.

For example, each user's home directory contains a file called .bashrc that provides configuration settings for the bash shell.

As another example, when the KDE desktop is used, a directory named .kde is created in the home directory of a user that is using this desktop. This directory contains one or more directories and files that contain configuration settings for the KDE desktop.

The . (dot) and .. (two dots) Used to Represent Directories

When viewing directory listings with some utilities, a . (dot) and .. (two dots) appear at the start of the directory listing.

For example, when the **a** (show **a**ll items) option of the ls command is used to list files, as in: ls -a then a . (dot) appears as the first item in the list and .. (two dots) appear as the second item.

The . (dot) represents the current directory (a.k.a. working directory) and the .. (two dots) represent the parent of the current directory.

When you are at the shell prompt and working "in" the cwest directory, in the full path of /home/cwest, the cwest directory is the current directory and the directory named home is the parent of the current directory.

In the full path of /home/cwest, there are two / (slashes). One / (slash) is used to separate the home directory from the cwest directory. The other / (slash), at the left of home, is used to represent the / (root) directory. The / (root) directory is the parent of the home directory and the home directory is the parent of the cwest directory.

If you run the ls command with the a (all) option in the cwest directory, a . (dot) and .. (two dots) will appear in the listing. The . (dot) represents the cwest directory and .. (two dots) represent the home directory (which is the parent of the cwest directory.

The . and .. can be used with commands and utilities and can make running commands much easier.

For example, the .. can be used with the **cd** (**c**hange **d**irectory) command to move up one directory level. When you are in the cwest directory (/home/cwest), the command: cd .. moves you up one directory level into the directory named home (/home).

As another example, the . can be used with the **cp** (**copy**) command to represent the current directory.

Here's a situation: a file named memo.txt is in the misc directory, off of the / directory (/misc/memo.txt) and you are working in the cwest directory (/home/cwest). The following command copies the file named memo.txt from the misc directory to the cwest directory. The . (dot) at the end of the command below represents the current (cwest) directory.

    cp /misc/memo.txt .

The above command is the equivalent of the following command:

    cp /misc/memo.txt /home/cwest

and is a lot faster to type!

Do not confuse the . (dot) or .. (two dots), that are used to represent the current directory and the parent directory, with the . (dot) that is used to prefix the names of the hidden directories and files (that provide configuration settings). When you see the . (dot) and .. (two dots) in a directory listing, the dots that represent the current directory and the parent directory do not have names of directories or files at the right of them.

The Full Path to a Directory or File

The full path (a.k.a. absolute path) to a directory or file is the series of directories, starting at the root, that are required to access the directory or file. The full path to a directory ends in a directory name, and the full path to a file ends in a file name.

For example, the full path to the log directory below the var directory, below the root is: /var/log.

The full path to the boot.log file in the path of /var/log is: /var/log/boot.log.

In some Linux documentation, and when using some Linux utilities, a / is shown at the end (far right) of a directory path to indicate that the last item in the path is a directory name and not a file name. We will also use this at times to provide additional clarity as needed. When reading documentation, there are instances when it is obvious that a name is the name of a directory, and other times when it is not obvious. This depends on the context of the directory in the discussion.

For example, the / at the end of the following path: /etc/ppp/ indicates that ppp is a directory and not a file.

Symbolic Links to Directories and Files

A symbolic link (a.k.a. symlink, soft link, alias) is a small file that "points to" another directory or file, referred to as a target. Symlinks are a "shortcut" to a target directory or a target file.

The operation of the Linux OS relies heavily on symbolic links and they have many uses and benefits.

One benefit of a symlink is that it can allow an old command to point to a new command. The old command appears to exist, but the new command is actually run.

For example, the locate command in /usr/bin has been removed and replaced with the more secure **slocate** (secure **locate**) command. A file named locate in /usr/bin is a symlink to the slocate binary file in the same directory. The file named locate is only a few *bytes* in size and is a pointer to the slocate binary, which is about 30K in size.

You can still type in: locate and press Enter, but when you do, and the binary named locate is accessed, it points to the slocate binary and the slocate binary file is run to provide the command.

Another benefit of a symlink is that it allows you to easily view current documentation on a current command that has replaced an old command that has been removed.

For example, the locate.1.gz documentation file (man page) in /usr/share/man/man1 is a symlink that points to the slocate.1.gz file in the same directory.

The man command is used to view the contents of a man page file. Running: man *commandname* causes the man command to access the **man** (**man**ual) page file named *commandname.x*.gz and display the contents of the file (display help information on a command).

For example, the command: man locate causes the man command to display the contents of the locate.1.gz file (or the contents of the file to which the locate.1.gz points). Therefore, the symlink between locate.1.gz and slocate.1.gz causes the command: man locate to access the locate.1.gz file (which points to the slocate.1.gz file) and the slocate.1.gz file is displayed. Therefore, when you try to get information on the old command, you get information on the command that has replaced it!

 The man command can be used to see man "pages" for help on more than just commands. It can also display "manuals" (help) on other items, such as the bash shell and many different configuration files.

The man command and other methods of getting help with Linux are described in more detail later.

Another benefit of symlinks is the capability of providing compatibility between the many UNIX variants and the many Linux distributions. Linux is a ten year old "clone" of the thirty year old operating system named UNIX, and it must "work like" UNIX.

As mentioned earlier, there have been many different, but similar, versions of UNIX, such as AIX, BSD, DEC, HP-UX, SCO and Solaris. These are sometimes referred to as "variants" or "dialects" of UNIX. There are also many different, but similar, distributions of Linux. All of these different versions of UNIX and Linux work towards being compatible (POSIX compliant).

However, over time, the many different UNIX/Linux versions and distributions have used various similar (but different) directory and file names in various places. The kernel, and the commands and utilities that are used to administer a system, often expect certain directories and files to be located in a specific place, so that they can read information from them and write information to them. Symlinks allow a directory or file (target) to be accessed in more than one location.

For example, the script file named rc.sysinit is run when a system boots. This file is located in /etc/rc.d. However, there is a symlink to this file in /etc. The symlink named rc.sysinit in /etc points to the actual rc.sysinit script file in /etc/rc.d. This allows Linux OS components, such as utilities that have been written to work with various distributions of Linux, to access the file in either location, even though the actual script file is only in one location, which is /etc/rc.d.

To continue the example, the less command can be used to view the contents of a file. If you are in the /etc directory and run: less rc.sysinit to view the contents of rc.sysinit in /etc, you will actually see the contents of the file of the same name in /etc/rc.d! When you use the less command to access the rc.sysinit file in /etc, the symlink points to the file in /etc/rc.d and causes the command to display the file that is in /etc/rc.d.

The Default Linux Directories Located Off of the Root Directory

The / (root) directory contains several important main directories that are the "parent" of all of the subdirectories and files that exist on the system. These default directories were automatically created by the installation routine.

To conform to the FHS standard and to keep your filesystem concise and organized, it is recommend that you do not create any new directories directly off of the root. When you create directories for program files and data files, you should create them below the default directories. The descriptions below of the default directories located off of the root will allow you to understand the places where new directories should be created.

The following is a description of the main directories located off of the root directory on a typical Linux system. Most of these directories and the descriptions of their contents conform to the FHS standard. Do not remove any of these directories.

/boot

This directory contains the kernel program file and other files that are used to boot a system.

The file for the kernel is called vmlinuz. This file is a symbolic link to a file, which has the name vmlinuz-x.x.x-x, where the "-x.x.x-x" part of the file name is the kernel version number, such as 2.4.18-14.

If a new kernel is installed on the system, such as version 2.6.6-8, then the link for the vmlinuz file is changed from pointing to vmlinuz-2.4.18-14, to pointing to vmlinuz-2.6.4-8. This simple change allows the system to constantly use the same name for the kernel (vmlinuz), regardless of the kernel version.

/initrd

By default, this directory is empty, but it is used during the boot process. Do not put anything in this directory or remove it. If you remove this directory, your system will not boot and you will see a "kernel panic" error message.

/bin

This directory contains "essential" **bin**ary (program) files that provide you with basic command-line (non-menu) utilities. These utilities are commands that are run and do not provide a text-based GUI menu or an X GUI menu.

For example, this directory includes commonly used commands, such as cp (**c**opy files), ls (**l**ist files) and mkdir (**make dir**ectory).

The /usr/bin directory also contains "essential" command-line utilities.

/sbin

The **s**uperuser (a.k.a. su, root) **bin** directory contains **bin**ary files (commands) that are typically only used by the root user. These are considered to be system administration commands.

For example, /sbin contains the following: fdisk (partition a hard disk), halt (shut the system down), ifconfig (view and configure network settings), init (change the mode in which Linux is working) and runlevel (view the current mode).

The /usr/sbin directory also contains system administration commands.

/mnt

This directory is used to contain directories (subdirectories) that are used for mount points. The directories below /mnt are typically used for disk drives that use removable media, such as a floppy disk drives and CD-ROM drives.

For example, to provide a mount point for the CD-ROM drive in a system, the /mnt directory contains a subdirectory named cdrom. Also see the information on the /dev directory below.

In addition to directories that represent devices that use removable media, the /mnt directory can also contain directories that are the mount points for non-Linux partitions in a system.

For example, you could create a directory in /mnt named driveC and use this as the mount point for the first Windows partition (drive C:) that is on a disk in a dual-boot system. You will see the steps to do this later.

/dev

The device driver files for various hardware devices are located in this directory.

The mount command is used to mount a filesystem by assigning a mount point (such as a directory below the /mnt directory) to a hard disk partition or other disk device, such as a CD-ROM drive. After the partition or device has been mounted, it can be accessed by application software programs, utilities and commands.

For example, the command: mount /dev/cdrom /mnt/cdrom causes the device file named cdrom in the /dev directory to be mounted "onto" the cdrom directory below /mnt. The cdrom directory becomes the mount point for the CD and this allows you to access the filesystem of the CD. The files in the / (root) directory of the CD become accessible below /mnt/cdrom.

/etc

This directory contains many system configuration text files that are used by the OS.

/home

This is the parent directory for each user's "home" directory (except for the root user). When a user is created, a directory with the same name as the user is created below /home.

For example, when a user named cwest is created, a directory named cwest is automatically created below /home. The cwest directory is the parent directory for the user's data directories and files. The cwest user can create directories and create (save) data files below cwest.

/root

This is the home directory of the root user.

/lib

The /lib directory contains essential common **library** files that are used by various Linux OS programs.

/lost+found

The fsck (file **s**ystem **c**heck) utility is run to check and repair a filesystem. If this utility runs and finds parts of files (without names), it puts them in this directory.

/opt

This directory is commonly used as the parent directory for application software programs, such as word processors and spreadsheets. After a Linux installation, this directory may be empty.

/proc

The /proc directory is the parent directory of a "virtual filesystem". This directory does not actually exist on disk. It is created *in memory* when Linux boots. Among other things, the files in this directory contain current settings that are used by the kernel.

For example, the file named cpuinfo in this directory contains settings regarding the cpu (processor) in a system. The file named meminfo shows the way that memory is being used and the file named version contains information regarding the current version of the kernel.

/tmp

This directory is used to hold **temp**orary files, such as those created by application software programs and other programs.

Many programs automatically create temporary files when they are run and these files are commonly created in /tmp. These files are intended to exist only temporarily, for as long as the application is running. They are used by programs for their own internal purposes.

When you exit out of a program that has created "temporary" files, these files should automatically be deleted by the application that created them. If an application is running and it creates temporary files in /tmp and the power goes off, or a system hangs, then the application does not have the opportunity to exit and delete these files.

By default, users can create files in /tmp. You may find that users start keeping files in this directory if they are restricted in the disk space that is available to them. We recommend that you notify users that they should not create files in /tmp and any files that are created in the /tmp directory will *not* be "backed up" (to some kind of external storage) and that they will be deleted. With the distribution provided with this book, files created in /tmp are automatically deleted after a period of time (if they have not been accessed or updated).

/usr

This directory typically contains application software programs and utilities that can be shared across a network. It is the parent directory for many system components, including documentation files. It is the parent directory for the share directory (/usr/share), which is the parent for the doc, man and info directories. These three directories contain documentation regarding Linux OS components and provide an excellent example of a well-organized directory structure. You will see more on this in the Hands-On Exercises at the end of this chapter.

You are currently reading about directories located directly off of the / directory. Some of the subdirectories that commonly exist below /usr are described further below.

/var

This directory contains **var**iable length data files. This is data that changes (in size), as opposed to "static" data, which does not. It is the parent directory for subdirectories that contain several types of variable data files, including log files in /var/log, mail files in /var/mail and print (spooling) files in /var/spool.

Mounting Directories on Separate Partitions

When you installed Linux earlier in this course, you assigned the / (root), /boot, /home, /usr, and /var directories to partitions and each of these partitions was assigned a fixed amount of disk space. These partitions are commonly set up as mount points on Linux server systems.

In addition to the partitions used above, you can set up other directories (not just the ones off of the root) so that they are the mount points for hard disk partitions. However, this is not recommended for all directories that are off of the root.

For example, the Disk Druid component of Anaconda will not allow you to assign all directories that are off of the root to a partition. You can select and assign some directories to a partition, but not others. However, when you are using some partitioning utilities (other than Disk Druid), they may not stop you from assigning these directories to their own partitions.

Some directories should be kept in the / partition. They should not be assigned to their own partition. The files in these directories are required in the / partition for the system to function properly, such as during an attempt to go into rescue mode and "rescue" a system that is not booting properly.

The following directories are located off of the root and should not be set up as the mount point for a partition:

/bin, /dev, /etc, /lib, /mnt, /proc, /root and /sbin.

Benefits of Setting Up Directories as Mount Points of Partitions

As described in an earlier section, when a directory is a assigned as a mount point to a partition, the files in the directory (and its subdirectories) cannot exceed the size of the partition.

For example, when you installed Linux earlier, you assigned the /home directory to a partition with a fixed size. The maximum amount of space that can be taken up by directories and files in this partition can not exceed the size specified. The benefit of this is that the user or users that have home directories below /home can not fill the entire disk!

To protect from an attack on your system by a user on: your **LAN** (Local Area Network), your intranet (internal internet network) or on the internet, some directories are commonly assigned to their own partitions. This restricts the damage that can occur from a "denial of service" attack, where someone automatically creates files in these directories so that they become full. If the directory (partition) becomes full, the entire disk does not become full and the system can still function until these files are deleted.

The /home, /var and other "publicly available" (over a network) directories are commonly assigned to their own partitions to restrict the damage from a denial of service attack.

When you installed Linux earlier, you assigned the /var directory to a partition with a fixed size. If you installed the software components (packages) for a Web server or an FTP server on this system, many files (such as server log files) will be created in subdirectories below /var as these servers are being used. These files can become quite large. By restricting the size of /var you can increase the protection for your system by stopping files that are created in /var from using up all of the disk space on the system.

The "permissions" (a.k.a. capabilities) that users have to a partition (to which a directory points) can be set to read-only. This allows users to read files from the directory, but not write (save) files into the directory or delete files from the directory.

If all directories on a system were read-only, then users would not be able to save any of their work. However, when a directory is assigned to a partition, it can be mounted as read-only so that users cannot put files into the directory or remove files from the directory. This stops an attack where: "dangerous" programs are added to a directory, existing program files are replaced with "dangerous" program files, or program files are removed so that tasks can not be performed. Program files that cause damage to a system when they are executed (run) are "dangerous" files.

The /usr directory typically contains application software programs and utilities. Users do not need to save files into this directory. The /usr directory can be assigned to a partition (as you did during the installation) and then mounted as read-only to restrict users from saving files into it. This can also be done with other directories that users do not need to save files into.

Another benefit of assigning a directory as a mount point of a partition is that if the filesystem of a partition becomes damaged or corrupted, the damage only occurs to the space used by the partition and does not occur to the entire disk.

For example, if the filesystem of the partition to which the /var directory has been assigned becomes corrupted, the filesystems of all other partitions are not affected. If you cannot fix the filesystem of the /var directory structure with a disk repair utility, such as fsck, only the files on this single partition are lost (and can be restored from a backup).

Other Important Linux Directories

The following directories are also important to the operation of a Linux system. These directories are not located directly off of the root.

/usr/bin

The /bin directory contains essential command-line utilities and /usr/bin also contains files of this type.

In addition to /bin, /sbin and /usr/sbin, the /usr/bin directory contains many binary files that are commands. It also contains symlinks to binaries (of the same name, and of different names) in /bin and /sbin.

For example, the gzip command (binary) is used to "zip" up (combine) files and compress them into a single file. The gzip file in /usr/bin is a symlink that points the gzip file in /bin. If your current directory is the bin directory below /usr (/usr/bin) and you run the gzip command, the gzip symlink in the current directory will be accessed and because this file points to the gzip binary located in the /bin directory, the gzip binary in /bin will be executed.

/usr/sbin

The /sbin directory contains system administration commands and /usr/sbin also contains files of this type.

In addition to /bin, /sbin and /usr/bin, the /usr/sbin directory contains many binary files that are commands. It also contains symlinks to binaries in /sbin.

/usr/local

The local directory (below /usr) is a directory in which software programs are installed "locally". This directory is commonly used as the parent for application software programs.

/etc/skel

The **skel** (**skel**eton) directory contains directories and files that are automatically copied to the home directory of a user when the user is created. This directory commonly contains hidden configuration files for the bash shell and hiddden directories that contain configuration files for software programs that are being used.

For example, when you create a user named cwest, a directory named cwest is automatically created below /home. In addition to this, any directories and files in the skel (/etc/skel) directory are copied to the cwest (/home/cwest) directory. This process is used to provide users with the default directories and files that they require.

By default, there are only hidden (configuration) directories and files in the skel directory and not "unhidden" directories and files. For example, this directory contains the .bashrc file, which is used for the configuration of the bash shell and the .kde directory (if the KDE desktop is being used), which contains settings for the KDE desktop.

If you have other directories and files that you want all users to have, you can put them in the skel directory. In addition to configuration files, you can put data files, and even data directory structures that users will commonly need in this directory.

In an upcoming Hands-On Exercise, you will put data directories and files below the skel directory. When you create users, these directories and files will be copied below the home directories of the users.

/usr/share/doc

The **doc** directory is the parent directory for about 300 subdirectories that contain **doc**umentation information regarding software components. All of the subdirectories begin with the name of the software component and end in "-x.x.x", where the "x"s are numbers that show the current version number of the software.

For example, there is a subdirectory below doc named bash-x.xx. The x.xx in the directory name, such as 2.05, shows the current version of the **bash** (**B**ourne **A**gain **Sh**ell) installed on your system.

Each of the subdirectories below doc (/usr/share/doc), such as bash-x.xx contains documentation (text) files regarding the software components installed on your system. A huge amount of useful information is included in these directories in files such as README, FAQ, INTRO and NEWS. If you are having difficulty with a software component, or even if you just want to know more about it, this is a good place to look for help and information.

/usr/share/info

The info directory is the parent directory for "**info**mation" files. These files provide on-screen documentation regarding the Linux OS. After the installation that you did earlier, there are over 500 of these files. The number of info files installed is dependent on the number of software packages that you install. When you install some software packages, info files are also installed with the package.

The info command is used to display the contents of an info (help) file.

For example, when you run: info less you will see a description of the less command. Press "q" to quit out of info and get back to the shell prompt.

/usr/share/man

The man directory is the parent directory for several subdirectories that contain "**man**aul pages" (a.k.a. man pages). These "pages" are actually files that provide on-screen documentation regarding the Linux OS.

When you did the installation earlier, over 5,000 man page files were installed below the man directory! There are man pages for many topics, including system software components, commands and configuration files. The number of man pages (files) installed is dependent on the number of software packages that you install. When you install some software packages, man page files are also installed with the package. Most packages include one or more man page files. Fewer packages include one or more info page files.

As described earlier, the man command is used to display a man page and you press "q" to exit out of a man page.

The Home Directories of Users

When a user is created, a "home" directory is automatically created for the user. This directory is created below the directory path of /home.

For example, if you create a user with the name of cwest, then a directory named cwest is automatically created below /home. The full path to this directory is /home/cwest. The cwest directory is the parent directory for private data files created by the cwest user.

The exception to the above is the home directory for the root user. The home directory of the root user is not created below /home, it is created of off of the root (/) directory and is called "root". The path to the home directory of the root user is /root (root root). Be careful not to confuse the / (root) directory with the home directory of the root user (/root).

On most x86 keyboards, the ~ (tilde character) is located near the top at the left, beside the number 1 key. Linux uses the ~ (tilde) to represent the directory path to the home directory of a user. This character can be used with commands to do many tasks, such as view the contents of the home directory or change directory into the home directory.

For example, if you log in as cwest, then the command: ls ~ lists the files in the cwest directory, below /home. Running: ls ~ is the equivalent of running: ls /home/cwest.

The command: cd ~ is the equivalent of: cd /home/cwest and changes your current directory to the cwest directory, below /home.

The path to a user's home directory is maintained in the variable named: HOME.

The echo command is used (among other things) to "echo" (display) something to the screen, such as: the text in a script file that describes what a program is doing, display an error message, prompt you for information, or show the settings of a variable.

For example, every time a system boots, the following text appears on the screen:

> Press 'I' to enter interactive startup.

When a system boots, the rc.sysinit script file is run. It contains the following echo command, which causes the above (indented) text to appear on the screen:

> echo -en $"\t\tPress 'I' to enter interactive startup."

When using echo, the text to be output (from a script file) or the name of a variable, is prefixed with a $ dollar) sign.

When you log in as cwest and run: echo $HOME you see the output of: /home/cwest. The command: echo ~ also displays this output because the ~ represents the full path to the home directory of the user.

The Shell Environment - Overview

You can set up Linux to either boot to X Windows (X) as a "desktop system" or boot to a virtual terminal as a "non-desktop" system.

When you boot to X, you log in at a GUI login prompt and are presented with a GUI desktop, such as GNOME or KDE. These desktops provide you with a method of accessing the "shell" by using "terminal emulation".

Earlier, you created Terminal Emulation Window icons on the GNOME and KDE desktops. These icons provide access to a terminal emulation "window" that emulates the virtual terminal (text mode) of Linux.

In contrast to a "desktop" system, you can set up Linux as a "non-desktop" system. This type of system boots to a virtual terminal, where you log in at a text-based "login:" prompt . After logging in, you only see a text prompt, at which you can run commands. There is no desktop and you cannot run X GUI utilities.

Earlier, you used Ctrl+Alt+F1 to go from a desktop to virtual terminal 1 and then used Alt+Fx (replacing x with 1 through 6) to move from one virtual terminal to another. When you boot to text mode, you have access to these same virtual terminals, but you do not have access to a desktop.

You set up Linux to boot to X (GUI mode) when you need to use a "desktop" system to run application software programs. You set up Linux to boot to a virtual terminal (text mode) when you need a "non-desktop" system. This is done when you need some type of server, such as Web server, or when you need Linux to perform some other function, such as a router or firewall (or both).

When Linux is installed as a server, or other "non-desktop" system, you do not typically install X. This is because X is not required, and also because when X is installed and running, it uses a lot of system resources, such as memory, storage and processing time. A "non-desktop" system does not require a GUI desktop or the capability of running X GUI utilities (that can only be run when X is running).

There are many terms that are used to refer to a **virtual terminal**, such as: vt, virtual console, text console, console, console mode, text terminal, text mode, character device and character cell interface.

Some of the terms for a **terminal emulation window** are: terminal window, terminal mode, shell window, command line window, Xterm and xterm.

Working at the Shell Prompt in the Shell Environment

When you click on an icon on a desktop and open a terminal emulation window, or when you are working at a virtual terminal, you are at the shell prompt. When you are at the shell prompt, you are working in the shell environment.

The shell environment provides many powerful features that are described with the headings below.

Keyboard Macros

The shell allows you to create a keyboard macro and then run it so that you can easily repeat a series of keystrokes. This is the "recording" of a series of keystrokes that are typed at the shell prompt. After doing this, you can press a few keys to run all of the recorded keystrokes (commands). This allows you to quickly and easily repeat a series of commands with just a few keystrokes.

To begin recording a keyboard macro, press Ctrl+x and then "(" (the left bracket, without the quotation marks). Press Shift+9 to get the left bracket.

To stop recording a keyboard macro, press Ctrl+x and then ")" (the right bracket, without the quotes). Press Shift+0 to get the right bracket.

To run the macro, pressing Ctrl+x and then "e" (without the quotes).

To more easily remember how to create a macro, think of it as beginning with "(" and ending in ")" and that you press Ctrl-x prior to each bracket and then again with an "e" (execute) to run it.

The macro only lasts for your current "session" (until you log out).

Command History

Commands that are typed at the shell prompt are maintained by the system and become part of the command "history". You can have a previously run command appear at the shell prompt by pressing the Up Arrow key until the command appears. You can also view the list of commands in the command history by running the history command. When you do this, your previous commands appear with a unique sequential number at the left of each one. You can run a previous command by typing an ! (exclamation mark) and then typing the number that appears at the left of the command.

Input/Output Redirection

The default standard input (a.k.a. stdin) for Linux is the keyboard and the default standard output (a.k.a. stdout) is the screen. Input/output redirection is the capability of specifying that a command use something other than the defaults for standard input and standard output. You can specify where the input of a command is to come from and where the output of a command is to go to.

For example, input redirection allows you to specify that a command to take input (such as data) from a file. Output redirection allows you to send the output of a command to a file or to another command.

Control of Processes

The shell provides you with the capability of controlling processes, including processes that are "jobs".

Processes are programs that are run and load into the memory of a system after a system has booted and the kernel has loaded. The kernel loads several processes that it requires. Processes typically stay in the memory of a system until they are suspended (stopped and remain in memory) or killed (stopped and removed from memory). Processes that have been suspended can be resumed.

Processes provide services to a system and do other OS tasks that are not performed by the kernel.

Jobs are programs that are submitted to the system for processing (and become processes), such as the "job" of compiling a software program.

The shell can be used to start a process that you need, suspend a process that you need to stop temporarily, kill a process that is no longer needed, or kill a process that is no longer functioning properly.

Command Execution and Script Processing

The shell also allows a person doing administrative tasks to maintain a Linux system by running commands and executing shell scripts. The shell environment includes a command language interpreter that allows for the processing of commands and the processing of programming logic included in shell scripts.

Shell Scripts

Shell scripts are text files that contain statements to run commands, and usually also contain programming logic. They are "executed" (run like commands) to perform various tasks.

The command language interpreter of the shell provides a sophisticated programming environment that processes the programming logic included in shell scripts. This logic is basically the same as the logic found in any programming language and includes programming features, such as conditional loops and working with variables.

Linux relies heavily on shell scripts for many OS tasks. Shell scripts are automatically run when a system boots. These scripts do a wide variety of tasks such as mounting filesystems, checking for the availability of hardware components, starting system services and configuring the environment of the operating system.

Once a system has booted, you can run one of many existing scripts in the same way as you can run a command. You can also create your own scripts to automate tasks that you need to perform frequently. These scripts can do something as simple as run a single command, or as complex as checking for several system settings (variables) and performing multiple commands based on the settings of the variables.

Types of Shell Environments

There is more than one type of shell environment available with Linux. In the same way as you can choose from more than one GUI desktop, you can also choose from more than one kind of shell. The most common shell is the GNU Bourne Again Shell, called **bash**. Most Linux distributions use the bash shell by default, but another shell (environment) can be set up to be used if desired.

Some of the other shell types are: ksh, csh and tcsh. The ksh shell (**Korn shell**) is similar to the bash shell. The csh shell (**C shell**) provides an environment that is similar to working with the C programming language and is therefore popular with C programmers. The tcsh shell is an enhanced version of the csh shell. All of these versions of the shell are similar in functionality.

In addition to being able to use various types of shell environments, each of these environments can be customized to meet your needs by specifying settings in (text) configuration files. When any type of shell is used, the configuration files that specify the settings for a user are located in each user's home directory.

For example, the **bash** shell uses a text file named .**bash**rc (and some other files) in each user's home directory for custom user settings. The C shell (**csh**) uses a file named .**csh**rc and the enhanced C shell (**tcsh**) uses a file named .**tcsh**rc.

The echo command is used (among other things) to view the setting of a specific environment variable. The command: echo $SHELL shows the name of the current shell executable program file and the path to it.

The Shell Prompt

When you have used the su command to log in as the root user, with a host name of lancom17, and the current directory of man, then the default shell prompt appears as:

    [root@lancom17 man]#

Between the [ ] (square brackets), you can see your current user name, an @ (at) symbol, the host name, a space, and then the name of the current directory.

In the above prompt, the name of the current directory is "man". The full path to the man directory is /usr/share/man, but the prompt does not show the full path. The prompt only shows the name of the directory at the end of the path, which is the current directory.

The default prompt can be changed to display other information.

When you have used the su command to log in as the root user, or when you log in as the root user, the end (far right) of the prompt shows a "#" (number sign). When you are logged on as a non-root user, the end of the prompt shows "$" (dollar sign).

While doing system administration tasks, you will log in with various user names to test user setups and do other tasks. After logging in as a few different users, you may not remember who you are logged in as. The easiest way to see your current user name is simply by looking for it at the far left of the prompt.

The Use of]# and # During the Hands-On Exercises

Comments are used in virtually every text file that is a part of Linux. This includes text files that are: configuration files, script files and the source code of programs. A "#" sign sometimes appears at the left of configuration text in these files and then another "#" sign appears at the right of that, *on the same line*, to describe the configuration text.

For example, a configuration file may contain the following:

    #config-text   # the text here describes "config-text"

The line above is treated as a comment because it begins with a "#" sign. Removing the "#" sign from the left of "#config-text" above causes the "config-text" to be used by the system, rather than to be treated as a comment. The above line of text then appears as:

    config-text   # text here describes "config-text"

The text at the right of config-text (that begins with a "#" sign) is still treated as a comment and is not used by the system.

To provide concise descriptions of commands that you will run in the Hands-On Exercises, we will use a format that is similar to above.

When you are logged in as a non-root user, the shell prompt shows a "$" sign. When you have run the su command to log in as root, or when you are logged in as root, the shell prompt shows a "#" sign. To distinguish the shell prompt from a comment in the Hands-On Exercises, the prompt will be shown as "]#". Comments regarding commands will be shown at the right of the commands that you type in. The comments at the right of commands will begin with a "#".

Chapter 5: The Linux Filesystem and the Shell Environment

For example, the following shows the prompt of "]#" and indicates that you will type in: cd /etc   to use the cd command to change into the etc directory, below the /. Always press Enter after typing in a command. The text at the right of the command that begins with a "#" sign is a comment that describes what the command does.

```
]# cd /etc          # change into the /etc directory
```

There will be times when the output of a command is shown after you have run the command. This output will appear below the command and will not be preceded by "]#" or "#".

For example, the following requests that you run: echo $SHELL   and the output of this command: /bin/bash   appears below the command, without "]#" or "#" at the left.

```
]# echo $SHELL      # cause the contents of the SHELL environment variable
                    # to be output to the screen

/bin/bash           # the output shows the name of the shell executable
                    # file (bash) and full path to the shell (/bin/bash)
```

Typing Multiple Commands on One Line

The shell allows you to type in multiple commands on the same line by putting a ; (semicolon) in between them. The first command you type in will be run and then the next, and so on.

```
]# cd /etc ; ls     # change into the etc directory and then list the files in it
```

Commands Used in the Hands-On Exercises of this Section

Some commonly used commands, such as cd, pwd, nl and clear are described in detail below and are used in the Hands-On Exercises of this section. By reading about these commands below and then using them (quite a bit) in the Hands-On Exercises, you will gain an understanding of how they work and why they are used.

Some other commands, such as ls and man, are not described in detail below, but need to be used in this section. They will be described in detail in upcoming sections.

The cd Command

The **cd** command is used to **c**hange **d**irectory into a different directory so that you can "work" in a directory to do tasks such as copy, move and delete files. You must type in a space between cd and the text at the right of it.

After typing in cd, you can specify the full path to a directory or the name of one or more directories below the current directory. In addition to this, you can type in .. (two dots) to move up one directory level and also combine the .. (two dots) with directory names to move around the directory structure, as described below.

Examples of the cd Command

Below are examples of using the cd command and specifying the full path to a directory. These commands will allow you to change to a different directory when they are run from any directory.

The prompt (]#) and the comment (#) symbol are used in Hands-On Exercises, but will not usually be used when showing examples of a command.

cd /	change into the / (root) directory
cd /usr	change into the usr directory, below the / directory
cd /home/cwest	change into the cwest directory, below the path of /home
cd ~	change into /home/cwest when logged in as cwest
cd ~cwest	change into /home/cwest when not logged in as cwest

Below is an example of using the cd command and specifying a single directory below the current directory. Your current directory is the home directory, below the / (root). The full path to the current directory is /home. The following command will only work if the cwest directory is below the current directory:

cd cwest	change into the cwest directory, below /home

The full path to your current directory after running the above command is /home/cwest.

The following command does *not* work when used *instead of* the above command. This is because the / is not required in front of cwest. The / in front of the cwest directory name would only work if the cwest directory were off of the / directory.

cd /cwest	the system tries to change into a cwest directory below the /

Your current directory is cwest, below /home. The full path to your current directory is /home/cwest. You use .. (two dots), which represent the parent directory, to change up one directory level (to the parent directory).

    cd ..   the full path to your current directory is now /home

Your current directory is home and the full path to your current directory is /home. The cwest directory is below /home and the reports directory is below cwest. The following command changes directory from the home directory to the reports directory. This command will only work if the cwest directory is below the current directory and the reports directory is below the cwest directory.

    cd cwest/reports   change into the reports directory, below the
                                cwest directory

After running the above command, the full path to your current directory is /home/cwest/reports.

To change from the reports directory (/home/cwest/reports) to the skel directory, below the etc directory, which is below the / directory (/etc/skel), you use the following command.

    cd /etc/skel   the / precedes etc because the etc directory is
                                off of the /

Using the cd Command with an Absolute Path and a Relative Path

The absolute path to a directory is the full path, which specifies all directories from the / directory to the destination directory.

In this example, the cwest directory contains two subdirectories named reports and memos. The reports directory and the memos directory are considered to be "parallel" to one another in the directory "tree".

   The full path to the reports directory is: /home/cwest/reports.

   The full path to the memos directory is: /home/cwest/memos.

The reports and memos directories are on the "same level". They are both below the cwest directory and are parallel to one another.

When your current directory is reports (/home/cwest/reports) and you want to change into the memos directory. The following command uses the absolute (full) path to change from reports to memos.

    cd /home/cwest/memos   the absolute path is used with the cd command

---

However, this is a lot of typing, considering you are already in the reports directory, which is parallel to the memos directory.

The relative path to a directory is the path "relative" to your current position in the directory tree. The .. (two dots) are used in a relative path to represent the parent directory. These two dots can be used more than once, to represent the parent, the parent of a parent, and so on.

Your current directory is still reports (/home/cwest/reports). The following command uses the relative path to change from /home/cwest/reports to /home/cwest/memos. This command will only work if the memos directory is below the parent directory (of your current directory).

> cd ../memos   the relative path is used with the cd command

The above command uses .. (two dots) to represent the parent directory (cwest) and change into the memos directory, below the parent directory. It changes up one directory and then down into the memos directory.

When your current directory path is: /home/cwest/reports, then the command:

> cd ../memos

is the equivalent of:

> cd /home/cwest/memos

The .. (two) dots can be used more than once when specifying a relative path. This can be used with commands and is often seen when viewing symbolic links to a directory or file.

The next bit is trickier, but it provides a foundation for understanding many different things.

Continuinsg the above example, you want to use a relative path to change from the memos directory into the bbest directory. This is the home directory of the bbest user and is below /home.

> The full path to the bbest directory is: /home/bbest.

> The full path to the current directory is: /home/cwest/memos.

The following command uses two sets of .. (two dots). One set of dots represents the parent directory (cwest) and the other represents the parent of the parent directory (home). The command below moves into the parent (cwest), then into the parent of the parent (home) and then down into the bbest directory, below the home directory.

> cd ../../bbest   changes up two directory levels and then
>   down one

The Relative Path As Used with Symbolic Links

The following concepts are a bit tricky. You will do Hands-On Exercises further below that will help to illistrate these concepts.

Example of a Symlink that Points to a File of a Different Name in the Same Directory

The /boot directory has symbolic link (symlink) between a file named vmlinuz and a file in the *same directory* named vmlinuz-x.x.x-x (the "-x.x.x-x" represents the version number of the kernel that is being used by the system).

> This symlink appears as: vmlinuz -> **vmlinuz-x.x.x-x**

There is an arrow (->) in the line above. This indicates that the vmlinuz symlink file in /boot points to the vmlinuz-x.x.x-x binary (boot sector) file in /boot.

> /boot/**vmlinuz** points to /boot/**vmlinuz-x.x.x-x**

Example of a Symlink that Points to a Directory of the Same Name in a Different Directory

The /usr directory contains a symlink between a file named tmp (that appears as a directory) and a directory with the *same name* below the /var directory.

> The tmp symlink in /usr appears as: tmp -> **../var/tmp**

The arrow (->) in the line above indicates that the tmp symlink file in /usr points to the tmp directory in /var.

> /usr/**tmp** points to /var/**tmp**

The tmp symlink file (which appears as a directory) is in /usr and the usr directory is one directory level below the /.

The "../var/tmp" part of the above symlink uses one set of .. (two dots) to represent the parent directory (usr). If you break up "../var/tmp" into ".." and "/var/tmp", you can use the cd command to move into /var/tmp, the directory to which the symlink points.

For example, when you are "in" /usr/tmp and use the command: cd .. you move up one directory level to the /. When you use the command: cd /var/tmp you change into /var/tmp. The .. (two dots) shown for the symlink move you up one directory level to the root and then down into the path of /var/tmp.

The "real" tmp directory is below the var directory, which is below the parent of the current directory (/usr), which is the / directory. The "real" tmp directory is in the var directory, below the / directory.

When you access the tmp directory in /usr (/usr/tmp), you are actually accessing the tmp directory in /var (/var/tmp).

For example, if you run: cd /usr/tmp and change into the tmp directory below **/usr**, you are actually "working" in the tmp directory below **/var** (/var/tmp).

When you create a file in /usr/tmp, you are actually creating the file in /var/tmp. The tmp directory below /usr is not actually a directory; it is a symlink file that points to the tmp directory below /var. After creating a file in **/usr**/tmp and then viewing a listing of files in **/var**/tmp, you will see that the file you created is actually in **/var**/tmp!

This symlink allows the system to have a "directory" (which is a symlink file) in one location that points to a directory in another location.

This type of symlink is often used because different OS components (kernel, script files and binaries) of different variants of UNIX and distributions of Linux are expecting to find and use a directory (to create files in and to access files) in one location, such as /usr/tmp and others are expecting the directory to be in another location, such as /var/tmp! The symlink allows a system to appear to have the same directory in two locations, but actually use only one directory. The files that appear in a directory listing of /usr/tmp are actually located in /var/tmp.

Example of a Symlink that Points to a File of the Same Name in a Different Directory

The /usr/bin directory contains a symlink between a file named gzip (in /usr/bin) and a file with the *same name* in the /bin directory.

> The gzip symlink in /usr/bin appears as: gzip -> **../../bin/gzip**

The arrow (->) in the line above indicates that the gzip symlink file in /usr/bin points to the gzip binary in /bin.

> /usr/bin/**gzip** points to /bin/**gzip**

The gzip symlink file is in /usr/bin, which is two directory levels below the /. The symlink uses two sets of .. (two dots). One set of dots represents the parent directory (bin) and the other represents the parent of the parent directory (usr).

The "../../bin/gzip" part of the above symlink points to the gzip file in the bin directory. The symlink is in the /usr/bin directory, which is two directory levels below the /. Each set of .. (two dots) represents one of the two directories. One set represents the usr directory and the other set represents the bin directory. The "real" gzip binary file is in the bin directory, below the / directory.

When you are in the /usr/bin directory and run the gzip command, the system "sees" the gzip symlink file in your current directory (/usr/bin) and that it points to the file of the same name in /bin and then runs the binary file located in /bin.

This symlink allows the system to have a file (symlink) in one directory that points to a binary file in another directory. This is the equivalent of having the same command (binary) in two places.

The pwd Command

There will be times when you have used the cd command several times to move up and down to different locations in a directory structure. At this point, you may not remember exactly where you are. In other words, you do not know the full path to the current directory.

The default shell prompt shows your user name, host name and current directory name. It does not show the full path to the current directory. The pwd command allows you to see the full path to the directory in which you are working.

When you run the **pwd** (**p**rint **w**orking **d**irectory) command, it "prints" the full path to the "working" (current) directory "on" the standard output, which is the screen.

If you have used the cd command and changed into the path of: /usr/share/man, then your current directory is the man directory. By default, the shell prompt will only show the current directory name. When you run the pwd command, the output will be: /usr/share/man, which shows the full path to the current directory.

 The word "print" in the "**print working directory**" (**pwd**) command name is used to describe displaying the path on the screen. The pwd command "prints" the path on/to the "standard" (a.k.a. default) output, which is the screen.

By default, output goes to the screen, but it can be redirected elsewhere, such as to a file, another command or a device, such as a printer (which is represented on the system by a file). You will learn more about this in upcoming sections.

Many commands and utilities have options that allow you to "print" information. This usually means "print" to the screen and not on paper. In this case, the output appears on the screen, unless it has been redirected elsewhere, such as to a file.

For example, the fdisk utility has a "p" (print) option that has the description of "print the partition table". By default, this option does not send the settings of the partition table to the printer, it "prints" the settings to the default output, which is the screen.

Some Linux documentation, such as man pages, HOWTOs and README files, also use the word "print" to mean "display the output on screen".

The nl Command

The **nl** (**n**umber **l**ines) command is used to put line numbers at the left of each line in a file, such as a script or configuration file, or to put line numbers at the left of each line of output from a command. Each line will have a sequential number at the left, starting at "1".

This command is useful to get the total quantity of lines of output. It is also useful for putting line numbers at the left of output for documentation purposes. You can easily refer to a line by its number, rather than having to describe where to look!

The command: nl fstab causes the contents of the text file named fstab to be output to the screen with line numbers at the left.

The **ls** (list) command is used to display directories and files. The command: ls hda* lists all files beginning with "hda" and ending with any other characters. The "*" is used to represent "any other characters".

By adding "| nl" to the above command, as in: ls hda* | nl the output of the ls command is "piped" ("sent through the pipeline") with the | (vertical bar) to the nl command. The output will show a line number at the left of each file in the listing and therefore, the last file will show the total number of files. In this case, the output of the ls command is redirected ("through the pipeline") to the nl command with the | ("pipeline") character.

The echo Command

The echo command is used to "echo" (output) something, such as a message from a script file or the contents (value) of a variable. By default, the output is echoed to the standard output, which is the screen. When the echo command is used to display a message from a script file or the value of a shell variable, the message or variable must be prefixed with a $ (dollar) sign.

echo $HOME	displays the contents of the shell variable named: HOME the HOME variable contains the path to a user's home directory
/home/cwest	this is the output of the above command when you are logged in as cwest - it shows the full path to the home directory of the cwest user

The following echo command is in a shell script that is run when your system boots:

    echo -en $"\t\tPress 'I' to enter interactive startup."

The line above causes the following output to appear on the screen when your system boots:

    Press 'I' to enter interactive startup.

The clear Command

The clear command is used to remove all commands and output from a terminal emulation window, or from the display of a virtual terminal, and move the shell prompt to the top of the screen. This command is useful for making it easier to read the output of commands that you are about to run and is often used in shell scripts.

The screen can also be cleared by pressing Ctrl+l, which is faster than using the clear command.

The file Command

Although there are many filename suffixes (extensions) that are used to indicate the "type" of a file (such as .txt, .html and .conf), there are also *many* files that do not have suffixes. Binary files that provide commands and also many text files, such as some configuration files and script files, do not have filename extensions.

Many files contain "magic numbers", which are codes in the file that are used to represent various types of files. The file command is used to determine the type of a file using a "magic number" (that may be) in the file, and also by looking at other characteristics of the file.

When the file command is run "on" a file and a magic number is found in it, the text file named magic in /usr/share is referenced by the file command to determine the type of a file. The file named magic contains the codes and corresponding file types of many different types of files.

Do not edit the file named magic to add a magic number to a system. The following (path and) file is the "registry" of magic numbers being used by a system. This file is used to add a magic number to a system:

/usr/src/linux-x.x.x-x/Documentation/magic-number.txt

Replace the x.x.x-x in the directory named linux-x.x.x-x above with the version number of the kernel. The kernel version number can be seen by running: uname -r.

Examples of the File Command

file *filename*	replace *filename* with the name of a file
file sh	display the type of the file named sh
symbolic link to bash	this is the output of the above file command the file named sh is a symlink to the file named bash
file *	display the type of all files in the current directory
file * | less	same as above, except that "| less" allows you to scroll through the output - the output is "piped" (with the | symbol) to the less command

Notice the output of "symbolic link to bash" in the second example above. When the file command is used "on" a file that is a symlink, the output shows the type of the file and also shows the name of the file to which the symlink points (bash).

The uname Command

The uname (UNIX/Linux **name**) command is used to "print" (output) system information. By default, the output is "printed" to the screen.

The -r (**release**) option of the uname command displays the release (version) number of the kernel that you are currently using.

uname -r	the **-r** (release) option displays current kernel version number
x.x.x-x	this is the output of the above command - it displays the release number of the kernel in the form of x.x.x-x
uname -i	the -i option displays the hardware platform (that the kernel was compiled for)
uname -p	the **-p** option displays the **p**rocessor type being used in the system

The a (**all**) option displays all information that this command can display and includes: OS name, network node hostname, OS release number, OS version number (including the date of the kernel executable file), machine (hardware) type, host processor type and the hardware platform for which the current kernel was compiled.

uname -a	the **-a** option displays **all** of the information described above

The less Command

This command displays the contents of a text file, such as a script or configuration file. It also allows you to scroll through the output of a command. This command is also referred to as a "pager" because it allows you to scroll through a text file, or the output of a command, a "page" (screenful) at a time.

The less command allows you to view the contents of a file or the output of a command and scroll up and down through it. The more command is very similar to the less command, but you cannot scroll up when you use the more command.

less *filename*	replace *filename* with the name of a text file that you want to view
less inittab	display the contents of the text file named inittab

A | (vertical bar) is used to cause the output of the command at the left of the | (vertical bar) to be "piped" to the less command so that you can scroll through it.

ls -l | less	the output of: ls -l is "piped" into the less command
ls -l /etc | less	use less to view all items in the /etc directory
less *path*	replace *path* with a directory path to see all items in the path - a . (dot) and .. (two dots) can be used for the *path*
less /etc	same as: ls -l /etc | less but is much shorter
less .	view all items in the current directory
less ..	view all items in the parent directory (of the current directory)

To scroll up or down a line, press Up Arrow or Down Arrow, respectively. To go up and down a "screenful", press Page Up or Page Down, respectively. To go to the top, press Home and to go to the end, press End. To quit out of the less command, press q.

When using the less command to view a file, or the output of a command, you can search for text (in the file or in the output). To do a search, you press the / (slash) key, type in the text to be searched for and pressing Enter.

After you press Enter, the display will move to the first occurrence of the text that you typed in and all occurrences of the text will be highlighted. This is extremely useful for locating text so that you can see more information on something. You will do this many times throughout this course.

Once you have run the less command, or have piped the output of a command to it, you can get Help on using it by pressing the letter h. To exit out of Help, press q.

 The man command is used to view a man (manual) page (file) and the info command is used to view an info page. These programs have basically the same interface as using the less command. The same keys are used to scroll through text/output, get help, and quit out of man and info pages, as those that are used with the less command.

The more Command

The more command is basically the same as the less command, except that it is not as flexible and is used less often. For example, you can press the Spacebar to see the next screenful of information, but you cannot scroll up when using the more command. Therefore, less is more!

more *filename*	replace *filename* with the name of a text file that you want to view
ls -l | more	the output of: ls -l is "piped" into the more command

The zless and zmore Commands

The zless and zmore commands work the same as the less and more commands (respectively), except that they are used to view compressed files, such as files that have been compressed with the gzip program. Files compressed with the gzip program commonly have a .gz suffix.

The bzless and bzmore Commands

The bzless and bzmore commands work the same as the less and more commands (respectively), except that they are used to view compressed files, such as files that have been compressed with the bzip2 program. Files compressed with the bzip program commonly have a .bz2 suffix.

Causing the Prompt to Appear Again

When you run some commands in "not quite the right way", you may find that you are in a situation where it appears that you can not do anything at the shell prompt. This is usually indicated when the prompt does not appear or when you try to type text, but just keep hearing beeps each time you type. There are several ways that this can happen.

For example, you may have run a command without specifying enough of it to cause it to work correctly. In this case, you may need to specify more options, or the path to a directory or file. Sometimes you cannot type at the prompt if you have accidentally run a command that runs a program, and you are "in" the program, but are are not using the correct keystrokes to exit out of the program.

To make the prompt appear again, so that you can run more commands, try pressing "Ctrl+c" to stop the command that you typed in. If you used the Ctrl key on the left side of the keyboard and were not able to stop the command, try using the Ctrl key on the right side of the keyboard. Use "Ctrl+c" to try to stop a command first. If this does not work, then try pressing "Ctrl+z", using the Ctrl key on the left and then on the right.

If you are working in a terminal emulation window and the above steps do not provide a shell prompt (so that you can continue to run commands), then simply close the terminal emulation window. After this, select the "Terminal Emulation Window" icon to open a new terminal emulation window.

If you are working at a virtual terminal and these steps do not provide a shell prompt, then use Alt+Fx (and replace the x in Fx with a number from 1 to 6 - other than the number of the virtual terminal you are using) to go to another virtual terminal.

Hands-On Exercises

There are a lot of detailed Hands-On Exercises below. During these exercises, you will move around the system and look at information, but will not change anything on your system. If you are short of time, you can easily stop working through these exercises and continue later. Simply mark your place in the exercises and run the pwd command to see the current directory path. Write this path down at the location where you stopped.

When you start again, log in as cwest, open a terminal emulation window, su to root, and then use the cd command with the full path that was output by the pwd command.

For example, if the pwd command shows: /usr/sbin then run: cd /usr/sbin after logging in, opening a terminal emulation window and running the su command. This will allow you to continue the exercises where you left off.

① Logging in and Listing the Contents of the Home Directory

Boot to the GUI login dialog box ; log in as cwest ;

Password: *password* ; press Enter ;

click on the Terminal Emulation Window icon ;

click on the Maximize button at the top right of the terminal emulation window ;

```
]# su -        # "su to root" and provide the root user password
               # this is also shown as "su as the root user"
               # and "change to root"
```

Password: *password* ; press Enter.

At the start of future Hands-On Exercises, we will simply show:

> Log in to a desktop as cwest ; open a terminal emulation window ; su to root ;

in place of the above steps. Unless otherwise specified, always maximize a terminal emulation window when you open it (click on the Maximize button) and always use the GNOME (default) desktop.

Most of the work that you do in this course is done from the perspective of someone administering a Linux system. Therefore, you need to "su to root" most of the time to "see" the system and work on it from the perspective of an administrative user (as opposed to a non-root user). When not doing administrative tasks on a system, log in as a non-root user and do not run the su command to "su to root" (or log in as the root user at a virtual terminal).

After opening a terminal emulation window, notice that the shell prompt shows your current user name at the far left, then your host name and then the name of your current directory. Also notice that the border at the top of the window shows your current user name, hostname and directory.

When you open a terminal window, your current directory is your home directory (for any user name that you logged in with). This directory is represented by the ~ (tilde) symbol in the border at the top. You ran the su command to log in as root, so your current (home) directory is the directory named root, below the / (root) directory.

```
]# ls          # list all of the directories and files in the /root directory

]# ls -l       # the -l option of the ls command is used to get a
               # long (more detailed) listing

]# ls -la      # the -a option causes all directories and files to appear
               # this includes hidden (dot) directories and files
               # hidden directory and file names begin with a . (dot)
```

In this listing, looking from right to left, the names of directories and files (items) appear at the right. Next comes the time or the year. If the directory or file was *not* created this year, then the year will appear at the left of the item, in addition to the month and day. If the item was created this year, then the time appears instead of the year.

At the left of the month is the size of the item. The size of a directory does *not* indicate the total of the amount of space that the files in the directory are taking up. A directory name is actually a file that contains the names (and other information) of the directories and files that are in it. When a directory has a lot of items, the size beside the directory name increases to accommodate the names (and other information) of the items in the directory.

At the far left of the listing, the type of the item appears. Directories have a "d" at the left and files have a "-" at the left. On a color monitor, directories will appear in a different color from files.

 ## Changing Directory and Viewing the Contents of the / (Root) Directory

```
]# cd /        # change to the / (root, not /root) directory
               # notice that the shell prompt and the top window
               # border now show "/"

]# ls -l       # all of the directories off of the / appear
               # notice that no file names appear

]# ls -la      # also list the hidden (dot) directories and files
```

The top item in the listing is a . (single dot), which represents the current directory. The next item is .. (two dots), which represents the parent of the current directory. In the case of the / directory, it is both the current directory and the parent directory.

The .autofsck file appears because the a option of ls was used. This file is prefixed with a . (dot) and is a hidden file. It is used to tell the system information about running the fsck (file system check) utility when it boots.

 ## Using the cd Command to Move Around the Filesystem

The directory structure below the path of: /usr/share/man provides an excellent example of how directories are used to organize files. Now you will learn how to use the cd command by moving around this directory structure. After this, you will have a look at the contents of the directories that are located off of the root directory.

In the current screen output, notice that the usr directory is below the / (root) directory.

```
]# cd /usr       # change into the usr directory off of the / directory

]# ls -la        # there are no hidden directories or files in this directory
                 # the . and .. at the top of the list represent directories
                 # they do not represent hidden directories or files
```

Notice that the tmp symlink shows "-> ../var/tmp" at the right of it. This item, which is in the current directory (/usr/tmp), is a symbolic link (symlink) to the tmp directory below /var.

Also notice that an l (for symbolic link) appears at the far left of the name of the tmp directory. The .. (two dots) in ../var/tmp represent the parent of the current directory, which is the / directory.

In your directory listing, notice that there is a directory named share, below the current directory. The current directory is usr, as seen in the prompt.

```
]# cd /share     # an error message appears - the share directory
                 # is not below / (the root)

]# cd share      # a / is not required to change into a directory
                 # below the current directory
```

Notice that the prompt shows the current directory (share), but not the full path to the current directory.

```
]# clear         # run the clear command to clear the screen and
                 # move the prompt to the top
```

```
]# pwd          # this command "prints" the path to the working directory
                # look at the output above your current prompt

/usr/share      # this is the output of the pwd command

]# ls -l        # all of the items in the directory scrolled up
```

The | (vertical bar) is found above the \ (backslash) on your keyboard, usually on the right side of the keyboard above the Enter key.

```
]# ls -l | less     # press PgDn and look for the directory named
                    # man (below /usr/share)
```

The above ls command (with the l option) was piped to the less command so that you could scroll through the output of the command. The "| less" part of the above command is frequently used for this purpose.

Press "q" to quit out of the less command.

Multiple commands can be typed on the same line by putting a ; (semicolon) in between them. The first command that you type in will be run, then the next, and so on. This is not "piping" the output of one command to another command. A | (vertical bar) is used to "pipe" the output of one command to another.

```
]# cd man ; ls      # change into the man directory and list the files in it
                    # notice that the prompt changed from share to man

]# pwd              # your current directory is man, below /usr/share

/usr/share/man      # this output shows the full path to the current directory
```

 ## The manx Directories

In the last listing, notice the "man*x*" directories (below man) that end in a number (man1 through man9). These are the "man page" directories. They contain files that provide on-screen "manual pages" (a.k.a. man pages). You can view these man pages to get detailed descriptions of various the Linux OS components, such as commands and configuration files.

Each of these man*x* directories represents a different category of system information.

For example, the man1 directory contains files that describe "User programs", such as cd (change directory) and ls (list files). The man2 directory contains files that describe "System calls". The man3 directory contains files that describe "Library calls", and so on. The man command and the man directories are described in more detail in an upcoming chapter.

The man*x* directories provide an excellent example of a well organized directory structure. All man*x* directories are below one directory (the man directory, below /usr/share/) and each man*x* directory contains files that represents a different category of information.

```
]# clear              # run the clear command to clear the screen

]# ls -l              # the manx directories are listed again, in
                      # long format
```

press Ctrl+l to clear the screen ; you may want to do this often to make it easier to read the screen ;

```
]# ls -l              # notice the man1 directory

]# cd man1 ; ls       # all of the files in man1 end in .1.gz
```

The files in man1 end in .1.gz and the files in man2 end in .2.gz and so on. The **.gz** filename extension indicates that a file has been "zipped" (compressed) with the **gzip** command.

(5) Viewing a Directory Listing with more and less

```
]# ls -l              # all files are listed, but they take up more
                      # than one "screenful"
```

The " | more" part of the command below causes the output of "ls -l" to be "piped" into the "more" command.

```
]# ls -l | more       # the display stops after showing a
                      # "screenful" of information
                      # notice that "--More--" appears at the
                      # bottom of the screen.
```

Press the Spacebar and another "screenful" of files appears ;

press PgUp (or Page Up), PgDn (or Page Down), the Up Arrow and then the Down Arrow ;

the system beeps each time ;

press the Spacebar again ; the more command allows you to move down the listing, but you can not "scroll" up or down (move up or down one "screenful" or line at a time) ;

press "q" to quit out of the listing.

Now "pipe" the output of: ls -l   to the less command.

```
]# ls -l | less        # the display also stops after showing a
                       # "screenful" of information
```

press the Spacebar and another "screenful" of files appears ;

press Page Down and Page Up a few times ; you can scroll up or down a "screenful" at a time ;

press the Up Arrow and Down Arrow a few times ; you can scroll up or down one line at a time.

This is when "less" is (better than) "more"!

Scroll (up or down) until you see the file named: bash.1.gz ; this is the man page file that describes the Bash shell.

Notice that the size of the bash.1.gz file is quite large in comparison to many of the other man page files in the listing. This man "page" is extremely long and detailed. It contains about 150 "screenfuls" of information!

 ## 6 Viewing a Man "Page"

Press Page Down until you can see: find.1.gz ; this is the man page that describes the use of the find command ; press "q" to quit out of the listing.

Remember to press "q" to quit out of the less command when it is used in the steps below.

```
]# man  find        # run the man command to view the file
                    # named find.1.gz
                    # you do not need to specify the .1.gz
                    # extension of the file
```

Read the NAME, SYNOPSIS and the first paragraph below DESCRIPTION. Press Page Down to see the OPTIONS heading and read the first paragraph.

Press Page Down and some of the options (a.k.a. switches, arguments, parameters) of the command appear ;

press Page Down several times until you get to the end of the man "page", (the end of the find.1.gz file) ; press "q" to quit.

The system has been set up so that the man command can be run from any directory to see the man pages on various topics.

You specify the name of an item, such as "find", when you run the man command. The man command locates the file name (if it exists), such as find.1.gz, and displays the contents of the zipped (compressed) .gz file on the screen.

You are in the man1 directory and the file named find.1.gz is in this directory.

```
]# file find.1.gz          # display the type of the file named find.1.gz
```

The (rather long) output of the above command shows that the file contains "gzip compressed data".

 Viewing a Man "Page" Via a Symlink

Press the Up Arrow key at the shell prompt until the command: ls -l | less appears again ; press Enter.

press Page Down until you see the locate.1.gz file.

The "-> slocate.1.gz" at the right of locate.1.gz indicates that this file is a symbolic link to the slocate.1.gz file (in the same directory). Notice the size (at the left of the month name) of locate.1.gz. It is only a few bytes.

Press Page Down until you can see slocate.1.gz.

Notice the size of this file (at the left of the month). It is much larger than the symlink file.

Press "q" to quit out of the less command.

```
]# man locate      # run the man command to view the man
                   # page named locate
```

Notice that the name of the man page, SLOCATE(1), appears at the top left and top right. The "(1)" in "SLOCATE(1)" indicates that the man page is for category 1 of the man pages. This category describes "User programs" and the files for this category are in the man1 directory (your current directory).

Running: man locate   (above) did not show the man page for the locate command, it showed the man page for the slocate command. The locate.1.gz symlink points to the slocate.1.gz file. Accessing locate.1.gz (with: man locate) caused the system to use the symlink between locate.1.gz and slocate.1.gz to access the slocate.1.gz file and display slocate.1.gz.

Read the text below the "DESCRIPTION" heading for this man page.

The man page for the locate command (locate.1.gz) is a symlink (to slocate.1.gz) because the locate command has been removed from the system. The locate command no longer exists on the system because it was not secure. It has been replaced by the slocate (**secure locate**) command. Therefore, the man page describing the locate command points to the man page for the slocate command.

In addition to this, the binary file for the locate command has been replaced by a symlink that points to the binary file for the slocate command. Running the locate command actually runs the slocate command!

Press "q" to quit out of the man page.

```
]# man slocate              # run the man command to view the
                            # slocate man page
```

Running: man locate and running: man slocate displays the same man page.

Press "q" to quit.

 8 **Viewing the Symlink for locate and the Binary for slocate**

The symlink file for locate and the binary file for slocate are in /usr/bin. You can list a file that is in another directory by specifying the full path to the directory.

Press Ctrl+l (Ctrl+"el", not Ctrl+"one") to clear the screen ; do this often during the steps below and throughout this course ;

```
]# ls -l /usr/bin/locate    # the locate symlink points to the slocate
                            # binary, in the same directory
```

Notice that an "l" (for symlink) appears at the far left of the file name and that the file is very small.

press the Up Arrow key so that the above command appears again ;

press the left arrow key (not the Backspace key) a few times until your cursor is on the "l" in "locate" ;

type an "s" so that "locate" becomes "slocate" and press Enter to run the following command "on" the slocate binary ;

```
]# ls -l /usr/bin/slocate   # slocate and locate are in the same
                            # directory - notice the size of slocate
```

```
]# file /usr/bin/locate     # view the type of the file named locate
```

/usr/bin/locate: symbolic link to slocate

press the up arrow key again, and do the steps to add the "s" and run the following command:

```
]# file /usr/bin/slocate    # view the type of the file named slocate
```

Below is part of the output of the above command. The word "executable" indicates that this is a binary file.

/usr/bin/slocate: ... executable ...

Running the locate and slocate Commands

Now run the locate and slocate commands to locate files that contain the text of: vmlinuz

]# locate vmlinuz   # files in /boot that contain "vmlinuz" appear

press the Up Arrow so that the above command appears again ; press Home to move to the beginning of the text ; put an "s" in front of locate and run the following:

]# slocate vmlinuz   # the same files in /boot appear again

The locate command no longer exists. It has been replaced by a symlink (file). When you run the locate command, the symlink for it is accessed and the slocate (binary) is run.

10 Using .. (two dots) to Change Directory

Clear the screen (with Ctrl+l) ; run the pwd command ; your current (full) directory path should be: /usr/share/man/man1.

If your current directory is not man1, run the following command: cd /usr/share/man/man1

Notice that the name of the current directory (shown in the prompt) is man1.

]# cd ..   # this moved you up one directory level,
                           # to /usr/share/man - the prompt changed
                           # fromman1 to man

]# pwd   # you are "in" man, below /usr/share/

]# ls -l   # you are in the parent directory of the
                           # manx directories

]# cd man2   # change down one directory into man2

]# ls ; pwd   # all "man page" files in man2 end in .2.gz
                           # the output of pwd appears at the end of the list

The man2 directory contains man pages regarding "System calls". Notice the directory name at the end of the output of the pwd command and the current directory name shown in the shell prompt.

]# cd ../man3   # change up one level and then down into
                           # the man3 directory

The ".." (two dots) before "/man3" moved you up one directory level (to /usr/share/man) and then the "/man3" part of the command moved you down into man3. In the "../man3" part of the command, the / is used to separate the .. (two dots), which represent the parent directory, from the man3 directory name. In this case, the / is not representing the root directory.

It is very common to use the .. (two dots) to change directory (as shown above) and also to use them with other commands, such as the **cp** (**c**opy) and **mv** (**m**ove) commands. It can save you a lot of typing!

The above command: cd ../man3 is the equivalent of: cd /usr/share/man/man3

If you use: cd ../man3 then you are using a relative path.

If you use: cd /usr/share/man/man3 then you are using the absolute (full) path.

```
]# ls ; pwd              # the files in /usr/share/man/man3 appear
                         # notice the output of pwd

]# cd ../man4            # this moved you up one directory level and
                         # then down into man4
```

Use the Up Arrow key to run the command below.

```
]# ls ; pwd              # the files in /usr/share/man/man4 appear
                         # notice the output of pwd
```

The full path to the **man1** directory is: /usr/share/man/**man1**
The full path to the **man2** directory is: /usr/share/man/**man2**
The full path to the **man3** directory is: /usr/share/man/**man3**
The full path to the **man4** directory is: /usr/share/man/**man4**

The man1 through man9 directories are on the same directory "level", they are "parallel" to one another in the directory tree.

```
]# cd .. ; ls ; pwd      # move up one directory level ; list the files ;
                         # output the full path
```

Your current directory is now man (/usr/share/man), which is the parent directory of the man1 through man9 subdirectories.

 ## Viewing the File Named magic

Earlier, you ran the file command with: file find.1.gz to see the "type" of the find.1.gz file. The file named magic in /usr/share contains the information that is used by the file command to determine the type of a file.

```
]# cd .. ; pwd           # your current directory is now /usr/share

]# file magic            # view the type of the magic file

magic:  magic text file for file(1) cmd
```

The above output contains the text "magic text file for". Remember this text. You will search the file named "magic" for this text in a few steps.

In the above output, "file(1)" refers to the man page in category 1 (in the man1 subdirectory) for the command (cmd) named "file".

In addition to being used at the end of a command, the less command can also be used to display the contents of a text file.

```
]# less  magic          # read the first few lines of comments at
                        # the top of the file
```

You are using the less command ; press the / (slash) key ; this begins a search ;

type in the following text: magic text file for

press Enter ;

the text that you searched for appears highlighted at the top of the screen.

press the Up Arrow key a few times until you can see the following comment:

```
            # magic: file(1) magic for magic files
```

A few steps above, you ran the command: file magic and this caused the file command to search the contents of the text file named magic for a description of the file named magic (it searched for a description of itself).

When you ran: file magic the file command output the description (type) of the file and this description is on the line that is currently highlighted (on screen).

Whenever you run the file command "on" a file, the command looks in the file for its magic number (code) and also looks at other characteristics of the file. It then uses this information to search the file named magic for a description of the type of the file.

The file command is used to determine the type of a file by using a "magic number" (that may be) in the file and also by looking at other characteristics of the file.

```
q                            # quit out of less
```

Viewing the /boot Directory

This is the beginning of your look around the directories that are located off of the / (root).

Press Ctrl+l to clear the screen.

```
]# cd /boot ; ls -l
```

This directory contains the kernel executable program file and some other files that are used to boot the system.

Notice that the vmlinuz file (with a "z") is a symlink and is only a few bytes in size and that it points to a file named vmlinuz-x.x.x-x (with a "z") in the same directory. Also notice that there is a file named vmlinux-x.x.x-x (with a "x"). The files named vmlinuz-x.x.x-x and vmlinux-x.x.x-x are large files, in comparison to others in the directory.

 Viewing the Types of Files in /boot

An * (asterisk) can be used with a command as a "pattern" (a.k.a. "wildcard" character). When it is used without other characters, it represents all files. Using the file command with an * (asterisk) causes the command to provide a description of the type of all files. Clear the screen prior to running the next command.

   ]# file *

The file named vmlinuz is a symlink to vmlinux-x.x.x-x. The file named vmlinux-x.x.x-x is an executable binary (not script) file and the file named vmlinuz-x.x.x-x has the type of "x86 boot sector".

When you upgrade this system with a new kernel, then new vmlinux-x.x.x-x and vmlinuz-x.x.x-x files will be installed in /boot (with the new version number of the kernel in place of -x.x.x-x).

The name of the symlink file (vmlinuz) will not be changed, but its link will change and it will point to a new vmlinuz-x.x.x-x file. The symbolic link allows the system to keep using the same kernel program file name (vmlinuz), as the version number of the kernel changes. The system always uses the kernel name of vmlinuz, which points to vmlinuz-x.x.x-x.

The files named vmlinuz, vmlinuz-x.x.x-x and vmlinux-x.x.x-x are described in more detail later in the chapter that describes configuring, compiling and installing the kernel.

 Using the uname Command

   Press Ctrl+l and then get a long listing of the files in the current directory (/boot).

The -r (release) option of the uname command displays the release (version) number of the kernel that you are currently using.

   ]# uname -r

   x.x.x-x   # the output displays the release number of the kernel

The release number that is output matches the "x.x.x-x" part of the file names of vmlinuz-x.x.x-x and vmlinux-x.x.x-x in /boot.

Press Up Arrow and replace the "r" with an "i" to run the next command.

```
]# uname -i      # the -i option displays the hardware platform
                 # (that the kernel was compiled for)
```

The version of the kernel that you are currently using was compiled for a 386 system. This allows it to work on a 386 or greater processor.

```
]# uname -p      # the -p option displays your processor type
```

Later in this course you will compile the kernel. When you do this, you will compile it for the processor type being used by your system. If you are using a processor type that is higher than 386, then you will compile the kernel specifically for your processor type. This will provide you with a kernel that is optimized for your system.

```
]# uname -a
```

The -a (**all**) option displays all information that this command can display and includes (reading from left to right): OS name, network node hostname, OS release number, OS version number (including date of executable file), machine (hardware) type, such as i686, host processor type, such as i686, and the hardware platform that the current kernel was compiled for, such as i386.

 Viewing the /bin directory

The bin directory contains "essential" **bin**ary (program) files that provide you with "command-line utilities". These utilities are commands that are run at the command line (shell prompt) and do not provide a text-based GUI or X GUI.

```
]# cd /bin ; ls      # commonly used commands (binary files) appear
```

Notice the cp (**copy** files), ls (**list** files) and mkdir (**make dir**ectory) files. The /usr/bin directory also contains the same kind of files (command-line utilities).

```
]# file cp       # the output describes the file as "executable" - this is
                 # the cp binary file for the cp (copy) command
```

16 **Viewing the Current Shell and the Shell Executable Program Files**

The program files that provide you with your shell type are located in the /bin directory.

```
]# less .        # a . (dot) is used to represent the current directory
                 # this is similar to: ls -l | less  but is a lot faster!
```

This shows an * (asterisk) at the right of executable files and symink files that point to executable files.

Look for the ash, bash, bash2, bsh, csh, sh and tcsh files. These files are eithershell executable program files (that are run to provide a shell "environment"), or they are symlinks that point to a file that provides a shell "environment".

```
]# ls -l *sh*          # list all directories and files that contain the letters "sh"
```

Notice the "l" for "link" at the far left of some of the files. The only shell executable files (shells) that actually exist on the system are ash, bash (Bourne Again shell) and tcsh (enhanced C shell).

The bash2, bsh, csh and sh files are all symlinks that point to other shell executable files. The bash2 file points to bash; bsh points to ash; csh points to tcsh; and sh points to bash. Whenever one of these shells is referenced, such as in a script file, then the link to which the file points is used.

The bash shell is the default shell and is currently being used. The size of the bash executable file is over 500K and provides you with the shell "environment" (in which you are now working).

The shell variable named SHELL shows the shell that is currently being used by a system.

```
]# echo $SHELL      # display the shell currently being used

/bin/bash           # the executable named bash in /bin is being used

]# file bash        # this is an executable file
```

Shell script files are text files that are executable. When the name of the script (text file) is typed in and you press Enter, the commands in the text of the file are executed.

Shell script files begin with a statement that looks like a comment, but isn't. The statement specifies the name of the shell that the script is intended for and the directory in which the shell file is located.

For example, the following text is not a comment and is put at the start of a script for the bash shell:

```
#! /bin/bash
```

Some shell scripts begin with: #! /bin/**sh** (rather than: #! /bin/**bash**) and this indicates that the script is intended to be processed by a shell named "sh" in /bin. The **sh** is for the Bourne **sh**ell and **bash** is for the Bourne **A**gain **sh**ell.

Notice from your directory listing of /bin that the sh file is a symlink to bash. Therefore, scripts that begin with #! /bin/sh rather than #! /bin/bash will access the sh symlink file in /bin, that points to the bash binary in /bin, and use the bash shell. This allows scripts that begin with: #! /bin/**sh** to be executed when the sh shell is not being used.

Viewing the /sbin Directory

```
]# cd /sbin                    # change into the superuser (root) bin directory

]# less .
```

To generally see the "kind" of files (commands) in this directory, look for the fdisk, halt, ifconfig, init, runlevel and shutdown files. These are superuser (root user) binaries that are used for administrative tasks.

Now look for the telinit file and quit out of less.

```
]# ls -l telinit              # the telinit symlink points to the init binary
```

The telinit command was previously used to change from one runlevel to another, such as from runlevel 5 (GUI mode) to runlevel 3 (text mode). The telinit binary no longer exists and whenever you (try to) run the telinit command, you are actually running the init command (to change runlevel).

 Linux goes to great lengths to maintain "backward compatibility" with old commands. Some of this is due to providing the capability of using old commands and some of it is due the use of old script files that contain statements to run old commands.

```
]# file telinit

symbolic link to init          # the telinit file is a symlink

]# file init

... executable ...             # this is an executable binary program file
```

18 **The /usr/bin Directory**

The /bin and /sbin directories contain many binaries that are commands. The bin directory below /usr also contains binaries that are commands.

```
]# cd /usr/bin ; less .
```

Briefly scroll through the list and notice some of the names of the commands and symlinks that are in the current directory. Also notice that some of the symlinks point to files in other directories and that they use a relative path (with .. (dots)) to specify the directory path.

```
]# clear ; pwd ; ls -l gzip
```

As shown at the top of the screen, you are currently in /usr/bin.

The "l" at the far left of the listing of the gzip file indicates that it is a symlink. The path at the far right of the listing points to -> ../../bin/gzip. Therefore, the gzip symlink in /usr/bin points to the gzip binary in /bin.

The "../.." part of "../../bin/gzip" points the system up two directory levels, from bin to usr and then to the / (root). The "/bin/gzip" part of "../../bin/gzip" points to the file named gzip in the path of /bin.

In the steps below, you will see how to get a listing of only the symlink files in /usr/bin that point to binary files in /bin.

 ## 19 Using (the amazing) grep Command

A string of text is any series of letters, numbers and other characters that are found on the keyboard. The grep command allows you to specify a string of text and "grab" only the lines of output of a command that match the string.

In the command below, the output of the ls command is piped to the grep command. The grep command specifies the "../../bin" string of text. This allows you to grab only the output (of the list of files) that contains "../../bin" anywhere in the output, rather than viewing the entire list of files in the directory.

```
]# ls -l | grep ../../bin     # all of the symlinks that point to files
                              # in /bin appear
```

The output from the above command shows you all of the symlink files in /usr/bin that point to binary files in /bin.

The string of text that is "grepped" in the command below is "/sbin".

```
]# ls -l | grep /sbin        # the symlinks that point to files in /sbin
                              # and /usr/sbin appear
```

In the current directory (/usr/bin) , some of the symlinks point to a file of a different name in the same directory, others point to a file of the same name in a different directory, and others point to files of a different name in a different directory.

(20) Viewing the /mnt Directory

```
]# cd /mnt ; ls -l
```

The directory named cdrom is used as the mount point for the CD-ROM drive in your system and the directory named floppy is used as the mount point of the floppy disk drive.

```
]# ls -l cdrom        # this directory should be empty
]# ls -l floppy       # this directory should be empty
```

If you put files on a floppy (with a command or utility) and remove the floppy prior to unmounting it, and then shut down your system properly, the files that should have been written to the floppy may get written to (put in) the floppy directory below /mnt. This could occur because the floppy disk is no longer in the drive. If you ever forget to unmount a floppy and can't find the files that should be on it, check in /mnt/floppy!

(21) Viewing the /dev Directory

The **dev**ice driver files for various hardware devices are located in the **/dev** directory.

```
]# cd /dev
```

In the command below, the nl (**number line**) command is used with the | (vertical bar). The output of ls is "piped" into the nl command, which causes line numbers to appear at the left of each item that is output. The nl command can be used to number any output.

```
]# ls -l | nl          # there are over 7,000 device driver files in /dev!
```

Remember that you can press the Up Arrow key at the shell prompt to have previous commands appear.

Now add the less command to the above command so that you can scroll through the listing.

```
]# ls -l | nl | less
```

Notice the "**c**" at the far left of many of the files. These files represent "character devices". Search for the file named console. The "c" at the left of this file name indicates that it (the console) is a character device.

Press Page Down a few more times and notice that some other files have a "b" at the left, which stands for "**b**lock device".

Keep pressing Page Down and you will see that some of the files have an "l" at the left and are symlinks.

As mentioned earlier, the "*" in the command below is a "wildcard" character and it is used with the characters "hda". It causes the ls command to list all directories and files that begin with "hda" and end in any other characters.

```
]# ls -l hda*        # list all files beginning with "hda"
```

Notice the word "disk" in the middle of the listing. These are the device driver files that are used for each of the partitions that can exist on **hard disk** drive **a**. In this listing, all of the files that are listed are used to represent "block" devices.

```
]# ls -l hdb*        # list the device driver files for partitions on hdb

]# ls -l fd0         # this is the device driver file for the floppy drive
```

Notice the word "floppy" in the middle of the listing and that this file is a block device.

The "/dev/**fd0**" part of the command: mount /dev/**fd0** /mnt/floppy causes the device driver file named fd0 in the /dev directory to be mounted "onto" the floppy directory below /mnt. The fd0 device driver file allows you to access the filesystem of a floppy disk in the floppy drive.

 ## Viewing the /etc Directory

This directory contains many system configuration text files for the system, such as fstab, inittab and services.

```
]# cd /etc ; less .
```

Scroll down a few "screenfuls" and notice that many configuration files end in ".conf" and some others end in ".cfg" and ".config". Some configuration files in other directories end in ".cf". Some of the configuration files in /etc, such as fstab, do not have a filename suffix.

Use Page Down to view the entire list.

Viewing Some Configuration Files in the /etc Directory

]# less fstab

The **fstab** (**f**ile **s**ystem **tab**le) file defines device names, mount points and other filesystem settings that are used when the system boots.

In this file (at the left) you will see /dev/cdrom and /dev/fd0. The cdrom and fd0 device driver files are in the /dev directory.

At the right of /dev/cdrom and /dev/fd0 you see /mnt/cdrom and /mnt/floppy, respectively. The cdrom and floppy directories are mount points in the /mnt directory.

At the right of the /mnt/cdrom and /mnt/floppy statements are the settings used when these devices are mounted. These settings are used when the devices are mounted: manually (with the mount command), with an icon on the desktop, or when a CD is mounted automatically (such as when a desktop is running and you put a CD in the CD-ROM drive).

In the second column of text in this file you can see the word swap (for swap drive). At the left of this, you can see /dev/ and a device driver file name in the form of "hd**yn**". In hd**yn**, the **y** is the "position" of the drive (such as a, b or c) and the **n** is the partition **n**umber of the partition on the drive.

]# less inittab

The **inittab** (**init**ialization **tab**le) file specifies system initialization settings, including the runlevel (mode) to be used when the system boots.

Look down about 15 lines for: id:**5**:initdefault:

The number 5 in this statement tells the system to start in runlevel 5.

Notice the numbers below the line that begins with: # Default runlevel

Runlevels 0 through 6 are described here. Runlevel 3 is shown as "Full multiuser mode" and runlevel 5 is shown as " X11".

Runlevel 5 is GUI desktop mode with **X** (**X**11) running. When you boot into this mode, the GUI login prompt appears so that you can log in to a desktop.

Runlevel 3 is text mode. When you boot into this mode, you are presented with a login: prompt at a virtual terminal (and X is not running).

To change the default mode into which your system boots, simply edit this file (with a text editor) and change the 5 in the statement below to a 3.

id:**5**:initdefault:

Other settings in this file will be described later.

Use Page Down to view the entire file.

]# less services

This configuration file is used to specify the network services that are available to a system.

> Use Page Down to scroll to the bottom and briefly scan through the comments at the right of the names of the services.

> Use the file command to see the file type of the fstab, inittab and services files. These are all text files.

 Viewing the home Directory

The home directory below the / directory (/home) is the parent directory for user "home" directories (except for the root user). Users use their home directories as the parent directory for their private data files.

For example, the cwest directory below /home (/home/cwest) is the parent directory for the private data files created by the cwest user.

]# cd /home ; ls -l   # the home directory for the cwest user appears

When you create a user, a home directory for the user, with the same name as the user, is automatically created below /home.

Remember to replace "cwest" with the user that you created during the installation, if you did not create the cwest user.

]# cd cwest ; ls -la | less

All of the directories and files in /home/cwest appear. Most of the hidden (dot) directories and files are used specify configuration settings for a user. Some of them are used for other purposes.

Look for the .bashrc file, the .gnome directory and the .kde directory. These items provide a user with configuration settings for the shell, GNOME desktop and KDE desktop, respectively.

 Using the ~ (Tilde) Character to Access a Home Directory

The ~ (tilde) character is usually found above the ` (backquote) at the left of the number 1. It can be used at the command line to represent the "home" directory of a user.

If you are logged in with a non-root *username*, the command: cd ~   changes from any directory in the filesystem into the /home/*username* directory.

When logged in as root (or if you have used su to "go to root"), the ~ (tilde) represents the directory path of /root, which is the home directory of the root user.

```
]# cd /usr/share/man          # change into a directory that is not a
                              # home directory
```

Notice that the prompt shows a # (number sign) and the top border of the window shows a the path to the current directory (/usr/share/man).

```
]# cd ~ ; pwd                 # you are logged in as root and now
                              # you are in /root
```

Notice that a ~ (tilde) now appears in the top border of the window.

```
]# echo $HOME                 # the home directory of the current (root)
                              # user appears

]# echo ~                     # "echos" the "value" of the ~ character to
                              # the screen
```

Open another terminal emulation window (with the Terminal Emulation Window icon) **and maximize it**.

The prompt shows a $ (dollar sign) and the top border of the window shows a ~ (tilde). You are in the home directory of the cwest user (/home/cwest). You have not run the su command and therefore, you are working in this window as the cwest user.

```
]# cd /tmp ; ls               # change to a different directory and get a listing
```

Notice the directory name in the prompt (tmp) and the directory path (/tmp) in the top border of the window.

```
]# cd ~ ; pwd                 # when logged in as cwest, the ~ represents
                              # the path of: /home/cwest

]# echo $HOME                 # the home directory (path) of the current
                              # (cwest) user appears
```

Close the current terminal emulation window (**not** the one in which you are working as the root user) and clear the screen.

```
]# cd /usr/bin ; pwd          # notice the path in the top border of the window

]# cd ~ ; pwd                 # in this case, the ~ represents the path of: /root

]# cd ~cwest ; pwd            # change to the home directory of the cwest user
                              # "~cwest" represents the path of: /home/cwest

]# cd /etc ; pwd              # change into a directory other than /home/cwest

]# cd ~cwest ; pwd            # change into /home/cwest again

]# cd ~ ; pwd                 # change into /root again
```

Viewing the /proc Directory

This directory is the parent of a "virtual filesystem". The files in it actually reside in memory and contain current settings that are used by the kernel.

]# cd /proc ; less .

Press Page Down ; notice that the directories and files in this directory all have the current date ; they are created each time the system boots.

Scroll through this directory and look at the files named cpuinfo, meminfo and version.

]# less cpuinfo	# view the current settings of your cpu
]# less meminfo	# view the way that memory is being used # by your system
]# less version	# view Linux kernel version information

 Viewing the /var Directory

The /var directory is the parent directory for several types of system files, including log files (in /var/log), mail files (in /var/mail) and print (spooling) files (in /var/spool).

]# less /var   # use the path of /var with the less command
                    # to view /var from /proc

Look for the log, mail and spool subdirectories.

 Viewing the /etc/skel Directory

The skel directory, below /etc (/etc/skel) is used for "**skel**eton" files. These files are automatically copied to the home directory of a user when the user is created. Initially, all of the directories and files in this directory are hidden.

You can put directories and files in this directory that you want all new users to get. These directories and files could include data directories and data files that users will commonly need and configuration files for software programs that are used by all users.

]# cd /etc/skel ; ls	# no directories or files appear
]# ls -a	# the -a option displays all (hidden) directories files
]# ls -la	# the -l option was added to provide a long listing

By default, all directories and files in skel are hidden. They are prefixed with a . (dot). Notice that there are a few files that begin with ".bash".

```
]# ls -la ~ | less          # shows the hidden files in /root
                            # some files begin with ".bash"

]# ls -la ~cwest | less     # some files in /home/cwest begin
                            # with ".bash"
```

When a user is created, the directories and files in /etc/skel, such as those prefixed with ".bash", are automatically copied to the user's home directory. This provides the user with default configuration settings.

 Viewing the doc and info Directories Below /usr/share

```
]# cd /usr/share

]# ls -l | less             # look for the doc, info and man subdirectories

]# ls doc -l | nl | less    # list files in doc with line numbers at the left
                            # all of the items shown are directories
```

Briefly scroll through a few "screenfuls" and then press End.

The doc directory is the parent directory for over 300 subdirectories that contain **doc**umentation information regarding software components.

All of the directories below doc begin with the name of a software component and end in "-x.x.x", where the "x"s are numbers and letters that show the current version number of the software. These subdirectories contain text files regarding a software component.

Press Home ; look for the version number at the end of the directory name that begins with "bash-".

Write the version number here: _____.

31 Viewing the Contents of a doc Subdirectory

View your current directory path ;

Use the following command to change from your current directory into the /usr/share/doc/bash-x.xx directory. Replace the x.x.x with the version number of the bash- directory that you wrote down above.

```
]# cd doc/bash-x.x.x        # change into bash-x.xx, below doc

]# ls -l ; pwd
```

This directory contains **doc**umentation information regarding the bash shell.

```
]# less FAQ                 # view the text file named FAQ in the
                            # bash-x.xx directory
```

Read up to "Contents:" ; press "q" to quit ; clear the screen.

32 Viewing the Directory Named info Below /usr/share

```
]# pwd ; cd .. ; pwd        # the .. (two dots) represent the parent directory
```

When you use the .. (two dots) with the cd command (and do not specify another directory after the dots), they are used to move you up to the parent directory.

The doc directory is parallel to the info directory, below /usr/share.

The full path to the **doc** directory is: /usr/share/**doc**
The full path to the **info** directory is: /usr/share/**info**

You are currently in the doc directory (/usr/share/doc).

```
]# cd ../info              # change into the info directory, parallel to doc
                          # this is faster than typing: cd /usr/share/info

]# ls -l | less           # press Page Down and look at all of the files
```

All of the files are zipped (compressed) and end in .gz. Look for the file named tar.info.gz.

The info directory is the parent directory for "**info**mation" files. The info command is used to display the contents of an info file, such as the tar.info.gz file that describes the tar command. The ".info.gz" part of the filename does not need to be specified when you use the info command. (In the same way as the ".x.gz" part of a man page does not need to be specified when you use the man command).

```
]# info tar               # view the "info" on the tar command
                          # press "q" to quit
```

33 Creating and Running Keyboard Macro

Now you will do the steps to create and run a keyboard macro. This macro is pretty basic and short, so that you can see the results of all of it on the screen. In practice, you can use this feature to create a long series of complex commands that you need to run several times.

```
]# cd /root               # change directory "into" the /root directory
```

press Ctrl+l to clear the screen ;

press Ctrl+x and then Shift+9 to get the "(" left bracket ; this starts the recording of the macro ;

```
]# cd /bin                # change into the bin directory

]# ls -l mk*              # list the files beginning with "mk"
```

```
]# ls -l /etc/*.cfg        # without changing directory, list all files in /etc
                           # that end in ".cfg"
```

press Ctrl+x and then Shift+0 to get the ")" right bracket ; this stops the recording of the macro

```
]# cd /root                # change into /root so that you can see that the
                           # macro changes directory into the /bin directory
```

press Ctrl+l to clear the screen ;

press Ctrl+x and then e to "execute" the macro ; notice that the prompt now shows your current directory as bin ;

change to the /root directory ; clear the screen ;

do the steps to run the macro again ; clear the screen ; change to the /root directory ;

stay logged in to test your answers to the following questions.

 ## Section Review

After each of the following questions, write the answer to the question on the line provided and then run the command to test that you answered the question correctly.

1. Your current path is /root. On the single line below, write the two commands to change to the root (not /root) directory and then get a listing of the directories and files in it. Use the option to get a long listing and the option to show all files, including hidden files. Use the correct character as a separator between these two commands. Be sure to show this character, when necessary, as you answer all of the questions below and remember to run the commands to test them.

_____

2. Using an absolute (full) path, change into the log directory, below the var directory, which is below the root and get a long listing of the files in log, without showing hidden files (use only one option of the command that lists files). Write both of these commands on the same line with the correct separator between them.

_____

3. Your current directory is the log directory (below /var). View the contents of the rpmpkgs file in the log directory so that you can scroll up and down through the file. All of the files in the rpmpkgs file end in .rpm. These are the rpm (**R**ed Hat **P**ackage **M**anager) "packages" (software components) that have been installed on your system. Write the single command below.

_____

4. Change up one directory level to /var (do not use a full path), get a long listing of the files and display the full path to the current directory (three commands on one line).

_____

Notice that the mail directory below /var is a symlink to the mail directory below the spool directory (below the current directory). When you change into mail, you are actually (via the symlink), changing into /var/spool/mail.

5. Your current directory path is /var. Change down one directory into the mail directory (do not use an absolute path) and use the command to view the contents of the file named root, which is the mail file for the root user (two commands). After running the commands below, scan through the contents of the text file.

_____

The system has an email program called sendmail. The /var/mail directory, which is actually the /var/spool/mail directory, contains email text files. The text file named root in /var/mail is an email file. It contains email message(s)) that the system has automatically sent to the root user via the sendmail program. Each message is added to the end of the (same) text file. System error messages and other types of messages appear in this file. You should view the contents of this file periodically.

6. Change into the run directory, which is "parallel" to the mail directory using a relative path (one command). Do not use the directory named var in the command.

_____

7. Change into the doc directory, below the share directory, below /usr.

_____

8. Use the single character that represents the current directory, with the command that allows you to scroll up and down through a directory listing (or the contents of a text file), to view the contents of the doc directory. Do not exit out of the listing yet.

   _____

9. Look for the directory that begins with "grub-" and write the version number at the end of the file name here:_____. Exit out of the listing. Write the two commands to change into the grub-x.xx directory and get a long listing of the files in it (without using the command that allows you to scroll up and down through a directory listing).

   _____

10. View the contents of the file named README in the current directory so that you can scroll though the file.

    _____

11. Change into the proc directory below the / and view the file named meminfo.

    _____

12. Which of the following statements are correct (choose two)?

    ☐ A. a directory or file name can end in a suffix (filename extension)
    ☐ B. directory and file names are case sensitive
    ☐ C. directory and file names can not exceed 10 characters
    ☐ D. all programs can work properly with files that contain spaces

13. Select two symbols that appears in the prompt when you are logged in as the root user.

    ☐ A. #
    ☐ B. $
    ☐ C. ~
    ☐ D. @

14. What are two features of the shell environment?

    ☐ A. it restricts the amount of space that can be used by files
    ☐ B. it increases the amount of virtual memory in a system
    ☐ C. it allows you to control processes
    ☐ D. it allows you to create keyboard macros

15. Which of the commands below is used to see the "type" of a file?

○ A. echo
○ B. file
○ C. ftype
○ D. fileinfo

16. Select a benefit of the FHS standard.

○ A. it details guidelines that allow users to log in to multiple systems
○ B. it details guidelines that guarantee point to point protocol communication
○ C. it details guidelines that provide for a standardized filesystem hierarchy
○ D. it details guidelines that secure network cabling components

17. You need to check the current version of kernel. Which of the following will provide the information that you need?

○ A. uname -r
○ B. kernel -a
○ C. cd /linux ; less vnumber
○ D. cd /etc ; ls -l kernel

18. Which of the following statements correctly describe characteristics of symbolic links (choose two)?

☐ A. they are directory names that are used to point to themselves
☐ B. they are small files that point to a different directory or file
☐ C. they can point to directories and files in the same directory or in different directories
☐ D. they can only point to files in the same directory

19. When viewing a long directory listing, what two statements are correct?

☐ A. files have a "-" at the far left of them
☐ B. block devices have a "c" at the left of them
☐ C. directories have a "d" at the far left of them
☐ D. character devices have a "d" at the left of them

20. You need to view the contents of a text file in the virtual filesystem that provides information on the hardware settings of your system. Which directory (path) will contain this file?

○ A. /home
○ B. /etc
○ C. /proc
○ D. /lib

Chapter 5: The Linux Filesystem and the Shell Environment

21. Select the symbol that is used as a prefix for the names of hidden configuration files and directories and is also used to represent the current directory.

    ○ A. .
    ○ B. ..
    ○ C. ~
    ○ D. a

22. Which of the following is a characteristic of the /bin directory?

    ○ A. it contains "essential" GUI utilities
    ○ B. it contains "essential" commands, such as cp, ls and mkdir
    ○ C. it contains the kernel boot files
    ○ D. it contains utilities that can only be used the root (superuser) user

23. You are logged in as the cwest user. Select the command that will change your current directory to your home directory.

    ○ A. cd /home /cwest
    ○ B. cd /HOME/CWEST
    ○ C. cd /cwest
    ○ D. cd ~

24. You have had a problem with one of the hard disks in your system and the fsck program has been run to repair the filesystem on the disk. You can no longer locate an important file that you thought was backed up. Which directory may contain a part of this file?

    ○ A. /fsck.dump
    ○ B. /fsck.bak
    ○ C. /lost&found
    ○ D. /lost+found

25. Select two characteristics of the /usr directory.

    ☐ A. it is the parent directory for users that are assisting the root user
    ☐ B. it contains variable length data files
    ☐ C. it typically contains application software programs and utilities that can be shared across a network
    ☐ D. it is the parent directory for many system components, including documentation files in directories below the path of /usr/share

26. What are two benefits of setting up various directories as the mount points for separate partitions?

- ☐ A. it stops the directories in the /proc partition from exceeding the size of the CD
- ☐ B. the files in the directory can not exceed the size of the partition
- ☐ C. it restricts the damage that can occur from a "denial of service" attack
- ☐ D. it allows you to maintain user modules in base addresses

27. Select two "modes" to which Linux can boot.

- ☐ A. boot to a virtual disk emulator as an "emulation system"
- ☐ B. boot to X as a "GUI desktop system"
- ☐ C. boot to a hard card driver module as a "mod card system"
- ☐ D. boot to a virtual terminal as a "text mode non-desktop" system

28. Which of the following are correct regarding the /dev and /mnt directories (choose two)?

- ☐ A. the /dev directory contains device driver files for various hardware devices
- ☐ B. the /dev directory contains development modules for C programs
- ☐ C. the /mnt directory contains directories (subdirectories) that are used as mount points
- ☐ D. the /mnt directory contains maintenance text files

29. Which of the following are characteristics of shell scripts (choose two)?

- ☐ A. they are binary executable files
- ☐ B. they are executable text files
- ☐ C. they contain special terminal codes to represent internal devices
- ☐ D. the can contain text that is processed as programming logic

30. Which of the following are methods of clearing the screen when working at the shell prompt (choose two)?

- ☐ A. echo OFF
- ☐ B. clear
- ☐ C. Ctrl+l
- ☐ D. Alt+C

31. Which of the following is the full path to the directory that can contain directories and files that are automatically copied to the home directory of a user when the user is created?

- ○ A. /skel
- ○ B. /etc/skel
- ○ C. /usr/skel
- ○ D. /etc

32. Which of the following are benefits of symlinks (choose two)?

- ☐ A. they allow you to use old command names to run current commands
- ☐ B. they allow you to use the . (dot) with commands to represent the parent directory
- ☐ C. they assist in providing compatibility between the UNIX variants and Linux distributions
- ☐ D. they are normally hidden to provide additional security

33. Which of the following items describing filename extensions are correct (choose two)?

- ☐ A. .tar is commonly used for target files
- ☐ B. .gz is commonly used for compressed files
- ☐ C. .dat is commonly used for backup files
- ☐ D. .conf is commonly used for configuration files

34. Which of the following is characteristic of the /sbin directory?

- ○ A. it contains all of the common user GUI utilities
- ○ B. it contains the system binary startup script
- ○ C. it contains the mandatory library files
- ○ D. it contains utilities that are typically only used by the root (superuser) user

Chapter 6: Using Linux Commands

This chapter provides an overview of using fourteen "general purpose" Linux commands. It describes the components of a command, syntax of a command and using options and patterns. Several examples of each command are provided so that you can get a good idea of how each one works.

You will also learn about various methods of I/O (Input/Output) redirection to output commands to files, other commands and other locations.

The following commands are described in this chapter and are also used in the Hands-On Exercises:

ls	list directories and files
find	find directories and files
slocate	securely locate directories and files
grep	search directories and files for a string of text and restrict the output of a command so that it only displays lines of output that contain a specified string of text
cat	output the contents of a file
tac	output the contents of a file in reverse order
sort	sort output
head	output a limited amount of the start of a file and limit output (to an amount) at the start of output
tail	output a limited amount of the end of a file and limit output (to an amount) at the end of output
history	view the commands that you have previously used
touch	create a file or change the timestamp of a file
date	display the date
cal	display a calendar
look	look for words that begins with text that you specify

The zcat and bzcat commands are basically the same as the cat command, except that they are used on compressed files.

During the Hands-On Exercises, you will use the commands shown above to list files, output the contents of files, restrict the output of files and commands, search directories and files for text and find directories and files.

Using Linux Commands

Topics Covered in this Chapter

Learn various types of Linux commands and the evolution Linux Commands
Detail the components of a command and the syntax of a command
Show several examples for the use of fourteen Linux commands
Explain various methods of Input/Output (I/O) redirection
Provide keyboard shortcuts for working at the shell prompt
Learn how to use the Tab key to complete long commands
Use fourteen commands with many different options

This chapter provides an overview of using Linux commands. You will learn about the components of a command and using options and patterns. During this chapter you will learn several "general purpose" commands, as opposed to commands that are specifically used to work with printers, or commands that are used to work with users and groups.

During the Hands-On Exercises you will work with fourteen commands to see various options and how the commands can be used to work with one another.

Types of Linux Commands

There are many types of Linux commands and all of them can be run at the command line (a.k.a. shell prompt) during a shell "session".

There are commands that run binary programs, commands that run script files, commands that display text-based GUI utilities and commands that display X GUI utilities.

There are also shell "builtin" (a.k.a. built-in) commands. These commands are part of the shell environment. They are not run by executing a binary or script file (in a directory on the system). Built-in commands, such as cd, echo, exit, history and pwd are part of the shell executable file that you are using. They reside in memory and are loaded into memory as part of the shell binary file when a shell "session" is started.

When a shell "session" is started, the binary for the shell you are using is executed. If you are using the bash shell, then the binary named bash in /bin/ is executed when you start a shell session.

A shell "session" is started when you log in to a desktop and open a terminal emulation window or when you log in to a virtual terminal. A shell "session" is ended when you "exit" out of a terminal emulation window, close a terminal emulation window or log out of a virtual terminal.

There is a lot of Linux documentation that describes the use of Linux commands (and other Linux concepts). This includes man pages, the info command, the help command, HOWTOs and README files.

Some of this documentation uses the words "foo", "fu" and "bar" as sample names for commands, directory names, file names and other Linux components. These words are not real commands and files, but example words that are used to describe a command or concept.

For example, a README file may describe the use of the ls command and suggest that you run: ls -l /foo/bar.txt to list the file named bar.txt in the directory named /foo.

Using Linux Commands

As described earlier, Linux is "case sensitive". Therefore, you must type in commands in the "case" (upper case or lower case) that is required. This includes all parts of a command, including the command name, options, directory paths, file names, directory names and patterns (using the * and ? characters with other characters).

There are hundreds of "standard" Linux commands that are commonly used on a Linux system. Most of these commands have several options and some have thirty or more options. When describing a command, we will show the most commonly used options of it. The way that an option works with one command may not be the same as with another command.

For example, the -r option for one command may not provide the same output as the -r option for another command.

In addition to this, one command may do tasks that are similar to another command, but the options of one command may provide features that are not available in the command that is similar.

For example, the fdisk utility is commonly used to do partitioning tasks at the command line, but the parted utility can also be used to work with partitions. Although each of these utilities can be used for similar tasks, one utility may be "better" (or easier) to use for some tasks and the other utility may be "better" for other tasks.

Learning Linux Commands

The best way to learn commands is by using them with common options. You will do this many times during the Hands-On Exercises of this course. After you have an idea of what a command does, it is much easier to refer to Linux documentation, such as man pages, for more options and variations of a command.

The Evolution of Commands

As time passes, the functionality of many commands increases and some command options may be added and others may be removed.

For example, until a few years ago, the tar command did not have a -j option. The -j option was added to cause the tar command to be filtered through the bzip2 command (binary) when compressing data and to cause the tar command to be filtered through the bzip2 command (binary) when uncompressing data.

As another example, the locate command was not secure and so the slocate command was created and the locate command was removed and replaced with a symlink that points to the slocate command.

Seeing the Version of a Command

There will be times when you need to see the version of a command to see if it (the binary or script file) is current, or to see if you are using the correct version for the task you are trying to perform. The following will show the version of many commands:

    commandname --version

For example, running: ls --version   shows the version number (and some other information) for the ls command.

Understanding the Syntax of Linux Commands

The syntax (a.k.a. format) of a command shows how a command is used. Linux commands are not uniform. This is because the programming of the source code that creates the binaries for commands has been created and developed by many different people over a long period of time. Therefore, we are providing a generic method of describing commands in this chapter and this method will be used to describe many other commands throughout this course.

In this chapter, we will sometimes use the word "items" to refer to "directories and files", rather than constantly stating "directories and files".

For example, the statement: "*.gz is the [pattern] and represents all **items** ending in ".gz"" means: "all **directories and files** ending in ".gz"."

In some situations, such as in tables that describe options of commands, we will also abbreviate the word "**sub**directories" and use the word "**subs**" to refer to subdirectories.

Command Syntax

A command has a syntax or "format" that is used to describe the command name, the components of the command, and the order in which the components are used.

Below is the general syntax of a command:

    command [options] [path][pattern]

Below is the syntax of the ls command:

    ls [options] [path][pattern]

Notice that there is a space between command and [options] and between [options] and [path]. There is no space between [path] and [pattern].

Command Components

command	the name of a command
[options]	options that can be used with the command
[path]	an absolute or relative path or characters representing a path, such as a . (dot), .. (two dots) and ~ (tilde)
[pattern]	a single filename or wildcard characters used with other characters

Examples of a Command

The examples below show the components of a command, using the ls command.

ls	the "command" component of the ls command is used here
ls -l	"-l" is used as an [option] of the command options of most commands begin with a - (dash)
ls -la	"-l" and "-a" are used as [options] of the command
ls install.log	install.log is the [pattern] - in this case, a single filename
ls /var	/var is the [path]
ls *.gz	*.gz is the [pattern] - represents all items ending in ".gz" uses the * (asterisk) wildcard character
ls /etc/rc?.d	/etc/ is the [path] and rc?.d is the [pattern] there is no space between the [path] and [pattern] this example uses the ? (question mark) wildcard character to represent a single character rc?.d represents all items that begin with "rc", that have one character after "rc", and have the suffix of ".d" (items that end in ".d")

The following is a description of the optional components of a command, which are the [options], [path] and [pattern] components shown above.

Optional Parts of a Command

When [ ] (square brackets) are used around part of a command, such as [path], then you do not need to specify that part of the command in order for the command to work.

The [options] Part of a Command

The [options] component can be one or more options. Some options need to be prefixed with a - (single dash), some with -- (two dashes) and others do not require a dash or cannot be used with a dash. Sometimes options are also called switches.

Sometimes a space is required between options and some commands only allow you to use one option at a time - this will be stated when necessary. *The examples of a command that are provided in this book will indicate how many dashes are required and if options need to be separated by spaces.*

The [pattern] Part of a Command

The [pattern] (a.k.a. shell pattern) part of a command does not work the same with all commands. The examples of commands that are shown will help you to understand how a file matching pattern can be used with a command.

The [pattern] component of a command is used to represent a file matching "pattern". It can be one or more letters, numbers or other characters and may include wildcard characters. This can be the name of an item (directory or file) or part of the name of an item.

When the syntax of a command is shown and [ ] square brackets are not around the word "pattern", then a pattern (file specification) must be provided. A [path] can usually precede a [pattern]. When a [path] is not used with a command, the command will typically display output based on the files in the current directory.

The suffix (a.k.a. filename extension, extension) in the name of an item is the far right . (dot) and characters at the right of the . (dot).

For example, in the directory named rc.d, the ".d" is the suffix of the directory and in the file named speedbar.gz, the ".gz" is the suffix of the file.

Wildcard Characters in the [pattern] Part of a Command

Wildcard (a.k.a. wild-card) characters are used in a [pattern] to cause a command to work on multiple items and they represent characters in a pattern.

An * (asterisk) is used in a [pattern] to represent "all characters" in an item (when used alone) and "all *other* characters" in an item (when used with other characters, such as letters and numbers).

A ? (question mark) is used in a [pattern] to represent a single character. Multiple question marks can be used in a pattern to represent multiple characters, one character per question mark.

The following are examples of the [pattern] part of a command. The "items" is used to represent "directories and files".

*	all items (directories and files) - with or without a suffix
r*	items beginning with the letter "r"
boot*	items beginning with "boot"
mem	items contain "mem" anywhere in the name
*.png	items having the suffix of ".png" - that end in ".png" examples: app1.png and hello.png
?.cfg	items starting with only one character and ending in ".cfg" examples: b.**cfg** and 3.**cfg**
memo?.sxw	items beginning with "memo", having a single character after "memo", and having the suffix of ".sxw" examples: memo**1**.sxw and memo**h**.sxw - not memo23.sxw
memo??.sxw	items beginning with "memo", having a two characters (only) after "memo", and having the suffix of ".sxw" examples: memo**21**.sxw and memo**k9**.sxw - not memos.sxw
[a-z]*	items that begin with any lower case letter and end in any other characters
[A-Z]-list.dat	items that begin with any upper case letter and end in "-list.dat"
[a-zA-Z]report.sxc	items that begin with any lower case or upper case letter and end in "report.sxc"
[c-f]*	items that begin with the letters "c" through "f"
[Bb]ackup	items that begin with "B" or "b" and end in "ackup"
jan[0-9]	items that begin with "jan" and end in a number from 0 to 9
letters[3-7]	items that begin with "letters" and end in a number from 3 to 7

The [path] Part of a Command

The [path] part of a command is used to specify an absolute or relative directory path. It can be used with the [pattern] component of a command.

A . (dot) can be used to represent the current directory, and .. (two dots) can be used to represent the parent directory or be used when specifying a relative path.

The ~ (tilde) character represents the home directory of a user. The home directory is also referred to as a "user login directory" or "login directory".

The following are examples of the [path] part of a command:

.	the current directory
..	the parent directory
/bin	the bin directory below the / (root) directory
/var/log	the log directory below the /var/ directory
cwest	the cwest directory below the current directory
cwest/memos	the memos directory below the cwest directory, which must be below the current directory
../man2	the man2 directory, below the parent directory in this case, the man2 directory is "parallel to" and "on the same level as" the current directory
../../doc	the doc directory, below the parent of the parent directory
~	the home directory of the current user while logged in as cwest, this represents the cwest directory below /home while logged in as root, this represents the /root directory
~/downloads	the downloads subdirectory of the home directory of the current user - while logged in as cwest, this represents the path of: /home/cwest/downloads while logged in as root, represents the path of: /root/downloads
~cwest	while *not* logged in as cwest, represents the cwest home directory - a / (slash) is not required between ~ and cwest

Optional Parts of Options

When a command shows optional items in [ ] square brackets with a | (vertical bar) between the items, then only one of the options can be run at a time. The vertical bar represents the word "or". You can use one item "or" you can use another item.

For example, if you were using a command named "hello", and the syntax of the command showed:

```
hello [ a | b | c ]   run the hello command with option a, b, or c, but not
                      more than one of these options
```

Using a Command that Uses a String

Some commands can work with a "string" of text, which is a series of characters that can include letters, numbers and spaces. When you specify a string that contains one or more spaces, put a ' (single quote) at the start of the string and another at the end. You will see how to specify a "string" when you learn about the grep command later in this chapter.

Recurse, Recursive and Recursively

Some commands only "work on" (do tasks "in") the current directory, or "in" the last directory of a path, when a path is used with the command. They do not automatically "work on" subdirectories of the directory that the command has been used "on".

However, many commands have an option, such a **-r** or **-R** (for **r**ecursive), that causes the command to "work on" *subdirectories* of the directory (that the command has been used on). This includes *all* subdirectories below the directory. In short, it "works" from the directory (that the command has been used on) all the way down the directory tree, for all subdirectories that exist below the directory.

For example, the **rm** (**r**e**m**ove) command is used to remove files, but by default it does not remove files in subdirectories of the directory (that the command has been used on).

The **-r** (recursive) option of the **rm** (**r**e**m**ove) command causes the command to "*recurse*" and remove files in all subdirectories of the directory (that the command has been used on). The -r option causes the command to work "*recursively*".

Some commands, such as the find command, work recursively by default. The find command "works on" all subdirectories of the directory that the command has been used on, without having to use an option like the -r (recursive) option.

Input/Output (I/O) Redirection

While describing I/O redirection (below this heading), we will use the word "item" to represent something that provides input or output, such as a command, file or device (such as a printer).

When using the bash shell (and most Linux shells), the default standard input (a.k.a. stdin) is the keyboard and the default standard output (a.k.a. stdout) is the display screen (monitor). The keyboard and screen are the default input and output devices, respectively.

 Some Linux documentation shows that a command will "print" output.

For example, the man page of the ls command states that the **-h** (**h**uman-readable) option of this command will "print sizes in human readable format". In this case, the -h option "prints" to the default stdout device, which is the screen, not a printer.

The default output for errors is standard error (a.k.a. stderr) and by default this is the same as stdout (the screen). When you type in a command that does not work correctly, or the name of a command that does not exist, and an error message appears on the screen, the error (output) has appeared at stderr.

The number "2" is used to redirect errors from stderr to another "item" (other than the screen), such as a file.

For example, you have created a program named listit. The "2>" in the command:

    listit 2> listit-errors.log

causes any errors that are output from the listit program (command) to be put in a file named listit-errors.log.

The word "item" in Table 6-1 is used to represent something that provides input or output, such as a command, file or device (such as a printer). The symbols in Table 6-1 are used to redirect input and output from the standard input, standard output and standard error to an item (such as command, file or device).

Table 6-1 - Symbols used for Input/Output (I/O) Redirection

Symbol	Description
>	output to an item
>>	output to the end of (append to) an item
<	input from an item
|	"pipe" the output to an item

On an x86 keyboard, the > (greater than) and < (less than) characters are above the , (comma) and . (period) characters, respectively. The | (vertical bar) character is above the \ (backslash) character, which is often above the Enter key.

Examples of I/O Redirection

In the examples shown below, the example is shown on one line and a description of the example follows.

ls -l /home/cwest > home-dir-lists.txt

This command will provide a long listing of all files in /home/cwest and redirect the output to create a text (.txt) file named home-dir-lists.txt. The file named home-dir-lists.txt will be created in the current directory (the directory from which the command was run).

ls -l /home/bbest >> home-dir-lists.txt

This command outputs the listing of the bbest directory (below /home) and adds (appends) the output to the end of the file named home-dir-lists.txt in the current directory.

After running this command, the home-dir-lists.txt file will contain the output of the first example above and then the output of the above command.

hello < userdata.txt

You have created a program named hello that takes data input from a text file, sorts the data and prints it in a table. In the command above, the userdata.txt file is being input to hello program so that the data in userdata.txt can be processed by the hello program.

cat /var/log/messages | grep fsck

In this example, the cat command will cause the contents of the messages file in /var/log to be output to the screen. The "| grep fsck" part of the command causes the output to be piped to the grep command and the grep command will restrict the output so that only the lines of text that match "fsck" will be output to the screen.

cat /var/log/messages | grep fsck | less

Piping the output of a command to grep and then specifying a string of text, such as "fsck", to restrict the output of a command is a very common method of using the grep command.

The "| less" part of the above command causes the output to be piped to the less command so that the output can be scrolled through. The "pipeline" in the above command is the from the cat command to the grep command to the less command.

Using Quotation Marks While Working In the Shell Environment

There are three types of quotation marks (a.k.a. quotes) that are used "around" (at the start and end of) text while working in the bash shell. These quotes are used while doing tasks like running commands and scripts, and also when writing and testing scripts and source code.

A ' (single quote) is used around text so that the text is treated "as is".

the command: echo 'The current path is $PATH'

causes the output of: The current path is $PATH

A ` (back quote) is used around text so that the commands between the quotes are processed.

the command:

echo "The current output of the date command is: `date`"

causes the output of:

The current output of the date command is: Fri Feb 6 2:32 EST 2004

In the above command, a single backquote is at the start and the end of the word date (at the end of the line). This causes the date command to be run and the output of the date command is: Fri Feb 6 2:32 EST 2004.

A " (double quote) is used around text so that variables inside the quotes are processed and commands are not processed.

the command: echo "The current path is: $PWD and the date is: date"

causes the output of: "The current path is: /home/cwest and the date is: date"

The above command was run from the /home/cwest directory and therefore the $PWD variable caused the current path to be displayed. Single quotes were not used around the word date (or anywhere in the command) and therefore, the date command was not processed as a command.

On a most x86 keyboards, the ' (single quote) character is at the left of the Enter key and the " (double quote) character is above the single quote. The ` (backquote) character is above the Tab key and below the ~ (tilde) character.

The ls Command

The **ls** (list files) command is one of the most powerful and commonly used Linux commands. It is used to display information on directories and files in many ways. This command has more than forty options. Commonly used options and examples of these options are detailed below.

When you run the ls command without any options, you get an alphabetical (case sensitive) listing of all of the directories and files in the current directory. This listing does not include hidden files, which are prefixed with a . (period). It also does not show a . (period) to represent the current directory and .. (two periods) to represent the parent directory of the current directory.

Using the l option of the ls command displays the following output for a directory named common.

```
drwxr-xr-x   2 root   sales          4096  Oct  16  11:56  common
```

The drwxr-xr-x part of the listing shows one character for the type of the item, such as directory or file, and then the permissions. In the example above, the d indicates that the items is a directory. The rwxr-xr-x immediately at the right of the first character (the "d") shows the permissions.

The 2 at the right of the permissions is for the number of inodes being used by the directory.

The root at the right of the 2 shows the owner of the directory, which is the root user. The sales at the right of root is the group to which the directory has been assigned, which is the sales group.

The 4096 is the size of the directory. At the right of this is the date and time, shown as: Oct 16 11:56. At the far right is the directory name of: common.

If the above output was for a file and not a directory, then the same categories (or types) of information would appear, such as permissions, owner and group, but the leftmost character of the output would be a - (dash) rather than a d (for directory). Other characters can appear at the far left, such as c for character device and b for block device.

The Syntax of the ls Command

The following is the syntax of the ls command:

```
ls [options] [path][pattern]
```

Chapter 6: Using Linux Commands

Options of the ls Command

There are many options that can be used with the ls command and Table 6-2 shows the commonly used options. The word "items" will be used to represent "directories and files" for the remainder or this chapter, unless otherwise specified.

Table 6-2 - Common Options of the ls Command

Option	Description
-l	shows a long (more detailed) listing of items
-R	lists files recursively - only use the pattern of * or .* with this option
-d	use this option with the l option and specify a *directoryname* to see a long listing for only the single *directoryname* specified
-a	shows all items, including hidden items, which are prefixed with a . (period) also shows (at the top) a single . (dot) to represent the current directory and .. (two dots) to represent the parent directory of the current directory
-h	use this option with the l option to show "human readable" directory and file sizes, where k is kilobytes, M is megabytes and G is gigabytes
-F	shows the "type" of an item at the right of the name a / indicates a directory, an * indicates an executable (binary or script) and an @ indicates a symlink use this option with the l option for better readability if the l option is used with the F option, a / indicates a directory and an * indicates an executable (binary, script or symlink) with the l option, symlinks appear with "->" between symlink and target
-S	sorts items by Size with the largest items at the top use this option with the l option
-t	shows items sorted with the most recent time (including date) at the top - use this option with the l option
-X	shows items sorted alphabetically by suffix (a.k.a. filename extension) an suffix, such as .gz, .txt and .cfg indicates the "type" of an item use this option with the l option
-r	reverse the order of a sorted listing

Examples of the ls Command

ls	list of all non-hidden items sorted alphabetically in columns
ls -l	long (width-wise, detailed) list of all items, excluding . (dot) hidden items
ls -lR *	long listing of all items, excluding hidden items, recursively
ls -lR .*	long listing of all hidden items, recursively
ls -la	long listing of all items, including hidden items the a option causes . (dot) hidden items to appear and also causes a . (dot) representing the current directory and .. (two dots) representing the parent directory appear at the top of the list
ls -l install.log	long list for the file named install.log
ls *.png	list all items with a suffix of (that end in) ".png"
ls /var	list the contents of the var directory, which is off of the / (root) directory
ls data/?.sxw	list items in the data directory, below the current directory, that have a single character prior to the suffix of ".sxw"
ls r*	list all items in the current directory beginning with "r" *this also lists the contents of subdirectories that begin with "r"*
ls -l *ssh*	list all items that contain "ssh" anywhere in the name
ls -l *directoryname*	long listing of only the *contents* of a single *directoryname* does not display information for the *directoryname*
ls -ld *directoryname*	display information for the *directoryname* does not list the contents of the *directoryname*
ls -l | grep ^d	list only the names of directories does not show file names does not show the contents of the directories
ls -l | grep ^-	list only the names of files (that are not symlink files) does not show directory names or symlinks to files or directories
ls -l | grep ^l	list only the names of symlinks to files or directories does not show directory or file names
ls -lh	long list in "human readable" form - i.e. 4,794 bytes appears as 4.7k
ls -F	shows the "type" of an item at the right of the name a / indicates a directory, an * indicates an executable (binary or script) and an @ indicates a symlink use this option with the l option for better readability

Examples of the ls Command - Continued

ls -lF	long listing and "type" of an item at the right of the name with the l option, shows: / for directory, * for executable (binary, script or symlink) and symlinks appear with "->" between the symlink and target
ls -lS	long listing sorted by size with the largest at the top
ls -lSr	long listing sorted by size in the reverse order of the regular sort
ls -lt	long listing sorted with the most recent time at the top
ls -lX	long listing sorted alphabetically by filename suffix

The find Command

A Linux system consists of thousands of directories and files and you need to be able to find directories and files (by name or pattern) easily.

The find command is used to search for directories and files that match a name or pattern specified. The search is case sensitive. By default, this command works recursively.

The find command is commonly used with the -name option, which is used to specify a pattern (for directories and files). When using the -name option, always put ' ' (single quotes) around (at the start and end of) the pattern that you are searching for, even if the text does not contain a space. If you do not do this, then your search will not always provide the correct results. You may find some items, but may not find all items.

The find command works recursively by default and shows the path (absolute or relative) to the directory, file or pattern that was searched for.

This command is extremely powerful and has over forty options. The info command can be used to see examples of the use of this command.

On systems with large hard disks and many data files, the find command can take a long time to show all of its output if you search with a path of: / (all directories below the / directory). The amount of time that the find command takes to find a directory or file can be reduced by specifying a longer path.

For example, a path of: / will cause the find command to search all directories below the / directory. However, if you know that the directory (name) or file (name) that you are looking for is somewhere below the /var directory, then a path of: /var will restrict the search so that it only looks in /var and subdirectories of /var. The output when specifying /var will be displayed much faster if you simply specify the / directory, particularly on systems with many files.

The Syntax of the find Command

The following is the syntax of the find command:

    find [path] [options] ['pattern']

Options of the find Command

Table 6-3 shows the commonly used options of the find command. The word "items" represents "directories and files".

Table 6-3 - Common Options of the find Command

Option	Description
-name 'pattern'	find items that match the pattern
-type d	find directories only
-size +xk	find all files that are over x kilobytes in size replace x with a value for the size
-user 'username'	find all items "owned" by username also shows hidden directories and files

Examples of the find Command

In the examples shown below, the example is shown on one line and a description of the example follows.

find -name '*.gz'

Display items that begin with anything and end in ".gz" below the current directory (and subs of the current directory). No path was specified with this command.

find / -name 'inittab'

Find all items that have the name inittab. The path of / (the root directory) was specified. This command searches all directories below the / and therefore searches *all* directories. A search in all directories can take a long time. This command will find inittab, but does not find inittab.5.gz, ansi+inittabs and inittab.vim.

find /etc -name '*lpd'

Display items that begin with anything and end in "lpd" below the /etc directory (and subs).

find /usr/sbin -name '*group*'

Display items in /usr/sbin (and subs) that contain "group" anywhere in the name.

Examples of the find Command - Continued

find / -type d -name 'bin'

Find directories (only) with the name of "bin". Does not find sbin, cgi-bin or bin-test.

find / -type d -name '*bin'

Find directories (only) with the name of "bin", or that start with anything and end in "bin". Finds bin, sbin, cgi-bin or bin-test.

find -size +100k

Find all files in the current directory that are over 100k (1k = 1,024 bytes).

find -user cwest

Find all items "owned" by the cwest user. Also shows hidden directories and files.

The locate Command

The locate command was not secure and no longer exists. It has been replaced by a symlink that points to the slocate command.

The slocate Command

The slocate command is used to securely **locate** directories and files by searching a database of files. On a system with large disks and lots of files, this command is faster than the find command. However, the slocate database must be updated so that directories and files that have been created since the last update can be "slocated". By default, *with this distribution*, the slocate database is automatically updated daily.

The root user can use slocate to search for all directories and files on a system. Non-root users, which do not have permission to access the entire filesystem, can use slocate to search for directories and files to which they have permission.

Wildcard characters are not required when specifying a pattern with this command. It automatically provides output as though the pattern you are searching for has an * (asterisk) at the beginning and end of it.

For example, the following command will display all directories and files that contain ssh anywhere in the directory or file name. It will show: **ssh**, **sshd**, K25**sshd** and zsh.**ssh**.

    slocate ssh

The output of slocate can be limited by specifying a path in front of the pattern and by restricting the output by piping it to the grep command.

You must su to root or log in as root to update the slocate database with the U or u option.

Overall, the find command is a "better" command to use than the slocate command when you are working as the root user, and is more commonly used.

The Syntax of the slocate Command

The following is the syntax (a.k.a. format) of the slocate command:

    slocate [options] [path][pattern]

Options of the slocate Command

Table 6-4 shows the commonly used options of the slocate command.

Table 6-4 - Common Options of the slocate Command

Option	Description
-i	ignore the case (upper or lower) in the pattern while searching a search for the text "readme" would also find "README"
-u	update the slocate database from the / downwards
-U *path*	update the slocate database from the specified *path* downwards allows you to only update directories that you currently need to search and speeds up the update of the slocate database
-e *path, path*	exclude directories from the slocate database specify a *path* to each directory to be excluded use to exclude directories that should not be searched by users and when directories contain items that do not need to be searched

Examples of the slocate Command

slocate fstab	locate all directories and files that contain the text "fstab" examples of items found: **fstab**, **fstab**.5.gz, upd**fstab**.8.gz
slocate -i conf	locate all directories and files that contain the text "conf" or "CONF"
slocate *.conf	locate all files ending in .conf in all directories
slocate /etc/*.conf	locate all files ending in .conf in the /etc directory, but not in subdirectories of the /etc directory
slocate -u	update the slocate database from the / downwards
slocate -U /home	update the slocate database from /home downwards updates only the directories you currently need to search and speeds up the creation of the database
slocate -e /dev -u	exclude the path of /dev from the slocate database and update the slocate database from the / downwards

The grep Command

The grep command is an amazing and extremely useful command that can be used in two "forms". It is used to search files for characters (text) that *match* a string of characters, or it is used to restrict the output of something, such as a command, so that only the output that matches the string of characters is shown.

The string can consist of letters, numbers and other characters on the keyboard, such as: lancom, kudzu, sshd, network, host, id, succeeded, hda, kernel, 57 and 192.168.0. If a string contains spaces, then put ' (single quotes) "around" the string (at the start and end of it).

By default, grep will only match when the string matches the same case (upper or lower) of the characters that are being searched. The -i (ignore case) option can be used so that upper *and* lower case matches of the string will be output.

The grep commands is useful for locating a string of characters in a file, such as a configuration setting in a text file, a command name in the scripting logic (text) of a script file, and a variable name in the source code of a program.

The grep command is also useful for restricting output, such as the output of a command, so that the only output that is shown is the output that matches the string of characters specified with the command.

You will use both forms of the grep command many times during the Hands-On Exercises of this course.

The Syntax of the grep Command

The grep command has the following two "forms", or ways in which it can be used:

grep [options] '*string*' [path][pattern]

command-with-output | grep [options] '*string*'

The first form above searches for a string of characters in one or more files. The second form causes the output of a command to only show lines of text that match the string of text specified.

The "First" Form of the grep Command

The following "form" of the grep command will now be described:

grep [options] '*string*' [path][pattern]

By default, the output generated as a result of running the above form of the grep command shows: the path (absolute or relative) to a file (including filename) of the files that contain the '*string*' and the line of text (in the file) that contains the matching string. The -l option can be used so that only the path to the file (including filename) appears. With this option, the text that matches will not appear.

Also by default, any part of a directory name in a path that matches the string will appear, even if the path does not point to a file that matches the string). The "-d skip" option can be used so that directory names that match the string, but do not point to a file that matches the string, do not appear.

Options of the grep Command

Table 6-5 shows the commonly used options of the grep command.

Table 6-5 - Common Options of the grep Command

Option	Description
-r	recursive - search from the current directory, or the directory [path] specified, downwards
-l	only output the path (including filename) for files that contain match(es) for the string the text that matches the string will not appear when this option is used
-i	ignore the case of the string and output upper and/or lower case matches a search for 'path' would output "path", "PATH", "pATH", "paTH", patH", "Path", "PAth" and "PATh" as matches
-w	only output whole "words" (exact matches) and not "words" that contain more text than the string "grepping" for 'port' would not output "report" or "reported" or "reportedly"
-a	search for a string in a binary file as though it were a text file

The 'string' Component of the grep Command

If a *string* contains a space then it must be in ' ' (single quotation marks). If quotation marks are not used when a *string* contains a space, then the search is only done on the text in the string (from left to right) up to the first space.

The [path] Option of the grep Command

When you use grep to search for a string (of characters) in a file (rather than restrict the output of a command), you can specify a [path]. When specifying the [path], do not specify the / (root) directory. This will cause the command to search the entire filesystem and the command may "hang" (stop).

In an earlier section you learned about the type of files that are kept in the directories off of the / (root). When using grep, specify the path to a directory that may contain the file(s) that may contain the string you are looking for, such as /etc or /home.

The [pattern] Option of the grep Command

When specifying a [pattern], you can specify a single file name, use an * (asterisk) to represent all files, use   .* (dot asterisk) to represent . (dot) hidden configuration files, or use wildcard characters with other characters.

Examples of the "First" Form of the grep Command

For all of the examples below, the grep command searches for the *string* of characters that is specified with the command, such as lancom, kudzu, sshd, network and 57.

The grep command requires that certain command components be used alone and that other components be used together in order for it to work properly.

If you are "in" the directory that may contain the file(s) that you want to "grep", then either: use a [pattern], or use the **-r** (**r**ecursive) option with a [path] or a [pattern]. To search all files, when not using the -r option, use the * (asterisk) for the [pattern].

   grep *'string'* *   search all files in the current directory for the *string*
                             does not search subdirectories

When you use a [pattern], the -r option is not required (but can be used) and a [path] is not required (but can be used).

If you want to search subdirectories of the current directory, use the -r option. If you use the r option, you must specify a [path] or a [pattern]. If you want to search the current directory (and subs), then use a . (dot) to represent the [path] (to the current directory) or an * (asterisk) for the [pattern].

   grep -r *'string'* .   search all files in the current directory and subs for the *string*

   grep -r *'string'* *   search all files in the current directory and subs for the *string*

The following example uses the -r option and a pattern:

   grep -r *'string'* /etc   searches all files in /etc (the [path]) and subdirectories

The following are examples of specifying a [pattern] (and not a [path]):

   grep *'string'* inittab   searches a single file named inittab in the current directory
                                the [pattern] is inittab (a single file name)

   grep *'string'* *.conf   searches all files ending in ".conf" in the current directory
                                the [pattern] is *.conf

In the above examples, the -r option can be used and a [path] can be used in addition to the [pattern].

The following are examples of specifying a [path] and [pattern]:

grep 'string' /etc/hosts	searches the file named hosts in the /etc directory the [path] is /etc and the [pattern] is hosts
grep -r 'string' /var/boot.*	searches all files beginning with "boot." in /var the [path] is /var and the [pattern] is boot.* the -r option causes subs of /var to be searched

The following are examples of using the -l and -w options of the grep command:

grep -l bin *.doc	only output the path (including filename) for items that end in ".doc" that contain "bin" the text that matches the string will not appear when this option is used
grep -w 'port' *	only output items that contain the whole word "port", not "report" or "reported" or "reportedly"

The "Second" Form of the grep Command

The following "form" of the grep command will now be described:

    command-with-output | grep [options] 'string'

The above version of the grep command is fairly simple and is used very frequently. It is used to restrict the output of a command so that only lines of text that match the characters in the string appear. Some commands generate a huge amount of output. This form of the grep command is used to restrict the output to very specific information.

The "command-with-output" part of the above command represents a command that is run and provides some kind of output.

The "|" (vertical bar) in "| grep [options] 'string'" causes the output of the command to be "piped" to the grep command.

The "grep [options] 'string'" part of the above command causes grep to process the output and only display output that matches the 'string' that has been specified. The [options] that can be used here have been described above.

Examples of the "Second" Form of the grep Command

cat /etc/fstab | grep ext3	display the partitions in the /etc/fstab configuration file that are using the ext3 filesystem
ls -l | grep -i faq	display a listing of directory and file names that contain "faq" in any combination of upper and lower case letters
zcat *.gz | grep [Rr]eadme	display lines of text in .gz (compressed) files that contain "Readme" and "readme"
history | grep cat	show all commands in history that contain "cat", this will shows occurrences of the cat command

You will see many other examples of using this form of the grep command as you learn more Linux commands.

The zgrep and bzgrep Commands

The zgrep command works the same as the grep command, except that it is used on compressed files, such as files that have been compressed with the gzip program.

Files compressed with the gzip program commonly have the .gz suffix.

The bzgrep command works the same as the grep command, except that it is used on compressed files, such as files that have been compressed with the bzip2 program.

Files compressed with the bzip2 program commonly have the .bz2 suffix.

The cat Command

The cat command is used to output the contents of a text file to the screen, a file or a device.

The Syntax of the cat Command

cat [path]pattern

The pattern is not optional and can be a single file name.

Examples of the cat command

In the examples shown below, the example is shown on one line and a description of the example follows.

cat /etc/fstab

Output the fstab file in /etc to the screen

---

cat .bashrc > oldbash.txt

Output the file named .bashrc in the current directory to a file named oldbash.txt, that will be created in the current directory.

cat file1 file2 > file3

This command con"**cat**"enates (joins together) the contents of file1 and file2 (in the current directory) and creates file3 (in the current directory). In file3, the contents of file1 will appear above the contents of file2.

cat report* > allreports

This command uses the [pattern] of report* and joins the contents of all files beginning with "report" and creates a file named allreports.

The tac Command

The tac command works the same as the cat command, except that it outputs in reverse order. The letters "tac" are the reverse of "cat".

The zcat and bzcat Commands

The zcat command works the same as the cat command, except that it is used on compressed files, such as files that have been compressed with the gzip program.

Files compressed with the gzip program commonly have the .gz suffix.

The bzcat command works the same as the cat command, except that it is used on compressed files, such as files that have been compressed with the bzip2 program.

Files compressed with the bzip2 program commonly have the .bz2 suffix.

The sort Command

The sort command is used to sort input or output and is commonly used to sort the contents of a file. Many commands, such as ls, sort output automatically and have options to sort in reverse order and sort in other ways.

The Syntax of the sort Command

    sort [options] [path]pattern

When sorting files, the pattern is not optional and can be a single file name or any other pattern.

The **r** option of this command is used to sort in reverse order and the **n** option is used for a numerical sort. These two options can be combined.

Examples of the sort command

sort datafile	sort the file named datafile to the screen
sort datafile > sortedfile	sort datafile and output to a file named sortedfile
sort -r datafile > sortedfile	same as above, but sorts in reverse order
sort -rn datafile > sortedfile	same as above, but sorts in numberical order

The head Command

The head command is used to display the head (top) of: the contents of a file, or the output of a command. By default, this command causes the first ten lines of a file to be displayed, or the first ten lines of the output of a command. This is a quick way to send a part of the top of a file to the screen (standard output), or to another location, such as to another file or to a printer.

The -n option is used to specify a number of lines, other than the default number of ten. By default, -n is equal to 10 and therefore, the first 10 lines of a file appear if the -n option is not specified.

With the head command, the - (dash) in "-n25" or "-25" is used to indicate the beginning of the option and the quantity is specified with the option. The - (dash) is not indicating a negative number, it is simply indicating the quantity of lines to be displayed. The -n option of the head command works differently from the -n option of the tail command (described below).

This command is typically used when you need to see the top of some type of output, that will be longer than the number of lines that can be displayed on the screen, such as the top of a long configuration file or the top of a long listing of files.

The Syntax of the head Command

There are three forms of this command and the following is the syntax of them:

head [options] [path][pattern]

head [options] [path]*filename* [path]*filename* . . .

command-with-output | head

The -n option allows you to specify the number of lines to display. The default for -n is 10.

Examples of the head Command

head /etc/inittab	display the first 10 lines of the inittab text file in /etc
head -n25 lpd.conf	display the first 25 lines of the lpd.conf file in the current directory
head -25 lpd.conf	same as above - this shows that the "n" in "-n25" is not required
head -n5 *.txt | less	display the first 5 lines of all files ending in .txt in the current directory and pipe the output to less
head file1 file2	display the first 10 lines of file1 and then file2
ls -l | head	display the first 10 lines of output of the ls command the -n option is not available in this form of the command

The tail Command

The tail command is essentially the opposite of the head command.

This command is used to display the tail (end) of a file or the tail of the output of a command. By default, this command causes the last ten lines of a file to be displayed, or the last ten lines of the output of a command. This is a quick way to send a part of the top of a file to the screen (standard output) or to another location, such as a file or printer.

The -n option for the tail command is different from the -n option for the head command. A positive or negative number can be specified for -n with this command. A positive number, such as +15 will cause the output to show all lines from line 15 through to the end (of the file or output of a command). A negative number, such as -25 will show the last 25 lines (of the file or the output of a command). The default for -n is -10. In other words, the tail command shows the last 10 lines of output by default.

The -f option is used to cause the output of the tail command to display (or otherwise output) continuously. The display will change when the tail (end) of the output changes. This option is commonly used to view (or output to something, such as to a file or printer) the changes that occur to log files as the system is running.

If you use the -f option and do not put an & (ampersand) at the end of the command, the command (process) will run in the foreground and the prompt will not appear. To stop the continuous output of the command (process), press Ctrl+c and the prompt will appear again.

If you use an & (ampersand) at the end of the command, it will run in the "background" (as a process) until it is stopped (killed).

For example, the text at the end of the log (text) file named messages (in /var/log) changes when many different events occur on a system, such as when a user logs in or when a service is started, such as a web server.

Using the -f option allows you to see the last ten or the last -n (a number that you specify) lines of output continuously (usually the last -n lines of a file), *when new lines of output occur (such as when new lines are added to the end of the file)*.

To continue the example, you can open a terminal emulation window in the top half of the screen and run: tail /var/log/messages -f and open another terminal (emulation window) in the bottom half of the screen and do tasks that will cause the system to add text to the end of the log file (named messages). When an event occurs that causes a change to the messages file, the text that is added to the messages file will appear in the top window, immediately after the event occurs!

The cat command will show all of the text in the file and the end of the output will show the end of the file. In other words, the cat command shows the end of a file, without having to run the tail command. However, if you use the cat command on very long text files, such as long configuration files and long log files, you will have to watch all of the text in the file appear on the screen and wait to see the end of a file. If you use the tail command, you will see the desired text (almost) instantaneously and with much less clutter (it's easier on the eyes).

Use the tail command to quickly see the end of a file and control the amount of the file that is seen, or the amount of the file that is output (to a file or to a device, such as a printer). Use the -f option of the tail command to see the changes that dynamically occur to the end of a file, such as a log file.

The Syntax of the tail Command

There are three forms of this command and the following is the syntax of them:

tail [options] [path][pattern]

tail [options] [path]*filename* [path]*filename* . . .

command-with-output | tail

The . . . (three) dots in the second form of the tail command above means, and so on. In other words, you can continue to specify the [path]*filename* part of the command (for more than two times).

The -n option allows you to specify the number of lines to display. The default for n is 10.

The -f option is used to continuously display the output of the tail command.

Examples of the tail Command

tail +30 /etc/inittab

This command shows the contents of inittab (in /etc) from line 30 onwards. Do not put an "n" in front of the number when using the + (plus) sign (as in "+n30"). You can put an "n" in front of the number when using a - (minus) sign, but an "n" is not required in either situation.

tail /var/www/html/lancom/*.html | less

Let's say you are using the Apache web server and something is wrong with the html text of your web site. You think that there is an error in the text at the end of one of your .html files. The files that you need to check are in the path of: /var/www/html/lancom (the /lancom/ directory, below the parent directory for html files for the Apache web server, which is: /var/www/html).

The command above will display the tail (end) of all of the files ending in .html (*.html) in the path of: /var/www/html/lancom. The last ten lines of text for each file will appear after the line on which the filename appears. The filename will appear with "==>" at the left and "<==" at the right of it.

tail file1 file2

This command displays the last 10 lines of file1 and then the last 10 lines of file2.

find /lib -name '*.o' | tail

Finds all files below /lib (and subs) that end in .o and only displays the last ten files. The output will appear faster when it is "piped" to the tail command with: | tail than if it was not.

tail -25 /var/log/messages

This command will cause the last 25 lines of the file named messages (in /var/log) to appear on the screen. *This is a very common and extremely useful method of checking for system changes, error messages and unauthorized user access.*

tail -f /var/log/messages

This command will cause the last 10 lines of the file named messages (in /var/log) to appear on the screen. The -f option will cause the text to stay on the screen and the display will be updated whenever any text in the last ten lines of the file is changed! To stop the output, press Ctrl+c.

The above command is an excellent way of debugging changes that you are making to a system and checking for the system's response to something that you are doing, particularly if what you are doing is not working.

For example, if you are loading a driver for a hardware component, the above command will show if the driver loaded properly and details regarding the loading of the driver, such as the interrupt being used by a driver.

tail -30 /var/log/messages > messages-changes-*mmddyy*.txt

This command puts the last 30 lines of the messages file into a file named messages-changes-*mmddyy*.txt. The *mmddyy* part of the filename can be replaced with the month, day and year, respectively.

New text that is added to the end of the messages file will be added to the messages-changes-*mmddyy*.txt file. This command could be run every day, with a different *mmddyy* part of the filename to document the changes to the messages file.

The history Command

The Up Arrow and Down Arrow keys can be used to "scroll" through previous commands (in the history list), but this method is awkward to use if have been running a lot of commands and you need to run a long complex command that you used twenty minutes ago.

The history command shows a "history" of commands that have been previously used. The default maximum number of commands that are kept in "history" (that can be output with the history command) for the distribution you are using is 1,000. The number of commands in history is not the same for all distributions.

Commands can easily be run from history using the two methods described further below. This allows you to easily run long, complex commands.

When you exit out of a shell "session", then the last 1,000 commands (or less, if you have not yet run 1,000 commands) are saved to a file named .bash_history in each user's home directory. When you start a shell "session" again, the contents of .bash_history are put in "history" (into the "history list" in memory).

The $HISTFILESIZE and $HISTSIZE environment variables show the number of commands that are maintained in history. The default settings for these variables (for this distribution) is 1,000.

Running Commands from the Output of the history Command

Let's say you run the history command and history (the history list) shows you the following entries:

```
456  ls -l ~cwest
457  man inittab
458  mv /home/cwest/*.bak  /home/cwest/oldfiles
459  cd /root
460  ls /etc/*.conf
461  man bash
462  vi /etc/inittab
463  cd /home
464  mkdir common
465  cd common
466  mkdir letters
```

You can run a command from history by using an ! (exclamation mark) and specifying a number or by using a string that matches the beginning of a command.

To run a command using a number, type: !*n* and replace *n* with a number from the history list and then press Enter.

To run a command using a string, type: !*string* and replace *string* with a string of text that begins a command the history list and then press Enter. The most recent command that matches the string is run. Be sure to type in a string that is long enough to distinguish one command from a similar command, as described in the examples below.

Examples of Running Commands from history

The following examples are based on the output of the history command above (commands 456 through 466).

Typing: !l and pressing Enter runs the most recent command beginning with "l" (number 460, not 456), which is: ls /etc/*.conf.

Typing: !c and pressing Enter runs the most recent command beginning with "c" (number 465, not 463 or 459).

Typing: !ma and pressing Enter runs command number 461: man bash rather than the most recent command that begins with "m" (number 466).

Typing: !mv and pressing Enter runs command number 458.

Typing: !456 and pressing Enter runs command number 456. Using numbers at the right of the ! (rather than letters) is often the easiest method of running a command that is "in" history.

The Syntax of the history Command

To run the history command, simply type: history   and press Enter.

To see the last 25 commands in history (which will typically fill a "screenful"), run: history 25.

The history command is commonly "grepped" to get a list of commands that begin with a command name or to get a list of commands that contain certain text, such as the path to a directory.

Examples of the history Command

history	output history (the list of commands in the history list)

Let's say you ran the find command about an hour ago, but you can't remember exactly how you ran the command and you need to run it again.

history | grep find	show previous commands that contain "find"
history | grep usr	list commands that contain the text "usr", such as commands that referred to the /usr directory

The touch Command

The touch command is used to create a file or change the timestamp (date and time settings) of a file. We will be using it from time to time to quickly create files to see how various commands work.

Syntax of the touch Command

    touch [path]*filename*

Replace *filename* with the name of a file.

The date Command

The date command is used to display the current date.

The cal Command

The **cal** (**cal**endar) command is a simple and useful command that can show date information.

The Syntax of the cal Command

The following is the syntax of the cal command:

    cal [options] [month] [year]

The **-j** option causes the command to Julian dates, where each day is numbered sequentially from the start of the year. January 1st is day 1.

By default, the cal command shows the current month. The **-y** option allows you to see the calendar for an entire **year**.

The [month] component of the command is used to specify a number for a month. January is month 1. The [month] component cannot be used without specifying a [year].

The [year] component of the command is used to specify a year. If a year is not specified, then the command shows information for the current year.

Examples of the cal Command

All examples below show the date in "standard" format, except the example showing the use of the -j option. After using the -y option (in a terminal emulation window and outputting to the screen), you can use the scroll arrows in the right border of the window to scroll up to see all of the output.

cal	displays the current month
cal -j	displays the current month in "Julian" format
cal -y	displays the current year
cal -y 2006	displays the year 2006
cal 4 1944	displays April, 1944

The look Command

The look command is used to look for and display words that begin with a string that you specify. This is a quick way of checking the spelling of a word. Use as many characters in the string (as you think are correct) to reduce the amount of output.

    look *string*

    look recie   show all words that begin with recie

Keyboard Shortcuts for Working at the Shell Prompt

There are many keyboard shortcuts that can be used at the shell prompt. All of them can be seen by running the following command to see the "man page" for the bash shell: man bash. This man "page" consists of many screenfuls or "pages" of information on the bash shell. To quickly search for the beginning of the information on keyboard shortcuts in this file, type: /commands for moving   and press Enter.

The man page for bash describes many keyboard shortcuts in a "generic" way that can be used on any computer system. This is done because the keyboards of all computer systems are not the same. Some systems, particularly old ones, do not have Up Arrow, Down Arrow, Home and End keys and some do not have Ctrl and Alt keys. Therefore, this man page shows "generic" abbreviations and these can be translated to an x86 system.

For example, the bash man page uses "C-" to represent pressing the Ctrl key. The text "(C-a)" represents "Ctrl+a" and is used to move to the start of the current line. As your keyboard has a Home key, this key will be used instead of pressing Ctrl+a.

In the man page for bash, "M" stands for "Meta" key. This "generically" represents a key on the keyboard that is similar to the Alt key. On the keyboards of x86 systems, this key is typically the Alt key. Therefore, when the bash man page shows the text "(M-b)", interpret this as "Alt+b". This key combination is used to move backward one word.

The most commonly used keyboard shortcuts are shown in Table 6-6 below. In this Table, a "word" is any string of characters that begins and ends with a space. In the long run, learning these few shortcuts can save you a tremendous amount of time!

Table 6-6: Shell Prompt Keyboard Shortcuts

Keys	Description
Up Arrow	show the previous command
Down Arrow	show the next command
Home	move the cursor to the beginning of the command
End	move the cursor to the end of the command

Table 6-6: Shell Prompt Keyboard Shortcuts - Continued

Keys	Description
Alt+b	move the cursor back one "word"
Alt+f	move the cursor forward one "word"
Alt+d	delete from the current cursor position to the end of the "word" if your cursor is at the beginning of a "word", the word will be deleted
Alt+Backspace	delete from the current cursor position to the beginning of the "word" if your cursor is on the space after a "word", the previous word will be deleted
Ctrl+l	clear the screen and move the prompt to the top of the screen this is the same as running the clear command

Using the Tab Key at the Shell Prompt

Linux uses long names for several items, including command names, directory names, file names and variable names. Due to long directory and file names, the paths that you need to type to get information on something can be *very* long.

For example, the path (including filename) to a configuration file that is used when compiling the kernel on a 686 system is:

/usr/src/linux-2.4.18-14/configs/kernel-2.4.18-i686.config

You can use the Tab key to view and also complete (autocomplete) the names of several items, including commands, directories, files and variables. This is sometimes referred to as "command completion". Using the Tab key to view and complete the names of items can save a huge amount of time!

Using the Tab Key to Complete the Name of a Command

For example, typing: h and pressing Tab twice shows all commands that begin with the letter "h". This is useful if you know that a command begins with "h", but cannot remember the full name of it.

Adding an "i" to the command line, so that it shows: hi and pressing Tab twice shows fewer commands because there are fewer commands that begin with these two letters than with just the letter "h". From the few commands that are shown, you can see that the letters "hist" are enough to make the name of the history command unique from the other commands.

Adding "st" to the command line, so that it shows: hist and pressing Tab (once) causes the full name of the history command to appear, along with a space at the right of it. Using the Tab key like this is particularly useful when you need to run a command that has a long name.

The above methods can be used to view and run commands from any directory on the system. To do these steps, you do not need to be in the directory that contains the command.

Using the Tab Key to Complete the Names of Directories and Files

As mentioned above, the Tab key can also be used to view and complete the names of directories and files. If you do not type in enough characters for the name of a directory or file to be unique and press Tab twice, then you will see a listing of directories and files that match the characters that you have typed in. If you type in enough characters for the name of the directory or file to be unique and press Tab, then the shell will fill in the rest of the letters in the name for you.

The above method of using the Tab key can represent a substantial savings in time when long directory and file names are involved. It also increases your accuracy because the system will provide you with the correct directory and file names, rather than you having to type them in correctly. However, you must be in the directory that contains the directory of file, or specify the correct path to the directory or file, to use the Tab key in this way.

For example, your current directory is /root and you want to change into the backgrounds directory, in the path of:

    /usr/share/backgrounds

You type in: cd /u and press Tab. There is only one directory off of the / that begins with "u", so the shell adds the sr/ to what you typed in and the command now appears as:

    cd /usr/

Now you need the name of the share directory on the command line. You type in: s and press Tab and the system beeps because there is more than one directory below /usr/ that begins with s.

You press Tab again and all of the items that begin with "s" appear (the sbin, share and src directory names appear). You only need to type in "h" to uniquely identify the share directory from sbin and src directories.

You type in: h and press Tab and the now the command line shows:

    cd /usr/share/

Now you need the name of the backgrounds directory on the command line. You type in: b and press Tab and the system beeps.

You press Tab again and a few directories that begin with "b" appear. From this listing you can see that you only need to type in "ac" to uniquely identify backgrounds from the other three directories.

You type in: ac and press Tab and the now the command line shows:

    cd /usr/share/backgrounds/

Now you press Enter to change into the above directory path.

Here is a file name example that includes a path. You are in the /etc directory and want to use the cat command to view the contents of the anaconda-ks.cfg text file in the /root directory. You want to do this "from" the /etc directory, without using the cd command to change into the /root directory. Therefore, you will specify the path of /root in the command.

You type in: cat /r and press Tab. The shell automatically fills in "oot/" and the command line shows:

    cat /root/

because there is only one directory that begins with "r" below the / directory.

You type in: a and press Tab and the now the command line shows:

    cat /root/anaconda-ks.cfg

if there is only one file beginning with "a" in the directory!

You press Enter and the contents of the anaconda-ks.cfg file appear.

Using the Tab Key to Complete the Name of a Variable

The above examples describe using the Tab key to view and complete the names of commands, directories and files. The names are provided once you have typed in enough characters to make the name unique. The Tab key can also be used in the same manner with variables.

For example, the shell has a variable called LOGNAME that is used for your current login name. The echo command is used to display the setting of a variable. A "$" precedes the name of the variable when using the echo command.

Typing in: echo $L and pressing Tab twice shows six variable names that begin with "L".

Typing in: O (so that the command line shows: echo $LO) and pressing Tab causes the full variable name (LOGNAME) to appear. Pressing Enter shows the value of the LOGNAME variable.

There are lots of variables with long names and this is a good method of getting a listing of the one you need when you can not remember the full name.

The above methods of viewing and completing the names for commands, directories, files and variables can also be done with the names of other shell items.

Hands-On Exercises

During the exercises below, keep in mind that you use Ctrl+c or Ctrl+z to break out of commands that "hang". Try using the Ctrl key on the right hand side of the keyboard if the one on the left does not stop the command or program.

Also keep in mind that you can use the Up Arrow on the scroll bar in the right border of a terminal emulation window to scroll up to view previous commands and output. As soon as you start to type a command, the prompt at the bottom of the output will appear.

As described earlier, remember that you can use the Up Arrow and Down Arrow keys to scroll through previous commands to get to commands that you have already run, so that you can run them again, or edit them and run them again. Also remember to use Ctrl+l to clear the screen (often) so that the output of commands is easier to read.

 Logging In to Run New Commands

Log in to a desktop as cwest ; open a terminal emulation window ; su to root.

Unless otherwise specified, always maximize a terminal emulation window when you open it and always use the GNOME (default) desktop.

② Searching the bash Man Page

]# man bash	# look at the man page that describes the # bash shell # this is a very long man page with lots of # useful information
/commands for moving	# press / (slash) to search for "commands # for moving"

The text "(M-f)" means press Alt+f to move forward to the end of the next "word" and "(M-b)" means press Alt+b to move backward to the start of the previous "word". "(C-l)" means press Ctrl+l to clear the screen.

You can use the Home key to move to the start of a line and the End key to move to the end.

Try using these keyboard shortcuts as you work through the Hands-On Exercises.

q ; press "q" to quit out of the man command.

Using the Tab Key to Complete the Name of a Command

Do the steps below to see how "tab completion" (a.k.a. command completion) works when trying to run the history command.

]# h ; (type the letter "h") ; press Tab and the system beeps ;

press Tab again ; all of the commands that begin with "h" appear ;

i (type the letter "i" beside "h") ; press Tab and the system beeps ;

press Tab again ; all of the commands that begin with "hi" appear ; fewer commands appear.

From the output, you can see that the letters "hist" are enough to make the name of the history command unique from the other commands.

st (type in "st" at the right of "hi") ; press Tab.

The command is completed and a space is put at the end of the command name. This allows you to add more text to the command if you need to, such as adding "| grep ls" to this command.

Press Enter.

The history command runs and shows (up to) the last 1,000 commands that you have run. If you have run less than 1,000 commands, then this command will show you all of the commands that you have run so far.

 Using the Tab Key to Complete the Names of Directories In a Path

Do the steps below to change to the path of /usr/share/backgrounds (from any directory).

]# cd /u

press Tab.

There is only one directory off of the / that begins with "u", so the shell adds the sr/ to what you typed in and the command now appears as: cd /usr/.

Now you need the name of the share directory on the command line.

s ; press Tab.

The system beeps because there is more than one directory below /usr/ that begins with s.

Press Tab.

All of the items that begin with "s" below /usr/ appear. You only need to type in "h" to uniquely identify the share directory from the sbin and src (and any other) directories.

> h ; press Tab.

> Now the command line shows: cd /usr/share/

> Now you need the name of the backgrounds directory on the command line.

> b ; press Tab ; the system beeps ; press Tab ;

Items below /usr/share that begin with "b" appear. From this listing you can see that you only need to type in "ac" to uniquely identify the backgrounds directory from the other items.

> ac ; press Tab.

> Now the command line shows: cd /usr/share/backgrounds/

> Press Enter ; this changes your directory (path) into the above directory path.

⑤ Using the Tab Key to Complete a Directory Path and File Name

You want to use the cat command to view the contents of the anaconda-ks.cfg text file in the /root directory. You want to do this "from" the current directory, without using the cd command to change into the /root directory. Therefore, you will specify the path of /root in the command.

> cat /r ; press Tab.

The shell automatically fills in "oot/" and the command line shows: cat /root/ because there is only one directory that begins with "r" below the / directory.

> a ; press Tab.

Now the command line shows: cat /root/anaconda-ks.cfg because there is only one file beginning with "a" in the directory! This is much faster than typing in all of the characters of this command.

> Press Enter ; the contents of the anaconda-ks.cfg file appear.

⑥ "Catting a File" and "Grepping the Output"

Let's say that for some reason you only want to see the lines of text that contain "cwest" in the file named anaconda-ks.cfg.

> Press the Up Arrow ; now "grep" for the string "cwest" ;

> | grep cwest ; add this text to the previous command ; press Enter.

Now only the lines of text in the anaconda-ks.cfg file that contain the string "cwest" appear.

⑦ **Using the Tab Key to Complete the Name of a Variable**

The shell has a variable called LOGNAME that is used for your current login name. The echo command is used to display the setting of a variable. A "$" precedes the name of the variable when using the echo command.

]# echo $L

press Tab twice ; variables names that begin with "L" appear ;

O ; type in "O" (upper case oh), not 0 (zero) ; press Tab ;

the full variable name appears ; press Enter ; the value of LOGNAME (your current login name) appears.

⑧ **Using the l and a Options of the ls Command**

]# cd / ; ls   # list of all non-hidden items sorted alphabetically in columns

]# ls -l   # long (width-wise, detailed) list of all items,
                   # excluding . (dot) hidden items

]# ls -la   # long (width-wise, detailed) list of all items

In the above command, the -a option causes hidden . (dot) directories and files to appear and also causes a . (dot) representing the current directory and .. (two dots) representing the parent directory to appear at the top of the list.

⑨ **Using ls to List a Single File and to List Other Patterns**

Change into the bin directory below /usr ;

]# ls -l bzip2   # get a long list for the file named bzip2

change into the etc directory below the / ;

]# ls -l print*   # lists items that begin with "print" and end with
                    # anything else

]# ls -l *.conf   # lists items that begin anything and end with ".conf"

]# ls /home   # lists items below /home

without changing directory, get a long list of files in /lib that end in ".so" ;

use the Up Arrow key to repeat the above command and pipe the output to the less command ;

use "q" to quit out of the less command ;

repeat the above command, but change "ls" to "file" and remove the "-l".

---

(10) Listing Items in Directories and Using More Options of the ls Command

Your current directory should still be /etc.

Get a long list of all items, including hidden items, in the skel subdirectory of etc without specifying the full path to the skel subdirectory ;

get a long listing of all items in the boot directory below the / ; notice the sizes of the files ;

repeat the above command and add the -h option to make the output "human readable" ;

notice the change in appearance of the file sizes ;

]# ls -lS /boot	# long listing sorted by size with the largest at the top
]# ls -lSr /boot	# same as above, but in the reverse order
]# ls -lSrh /boot	# same as above, but with "human readable" sizes
]# ls -lt /boot	# long listing sorted with the most recent time at the top
]# ls -lX /boot	# long listing sorted alphabetically by suffix
	# look for the .b, .h, .img, .ja and .map suffixes

(11) Listing the "Types" of Items

After doing the following command, use the Scroll Up Arrow in the right border of the window to look at the top of the output.

]# cd /etc ; ls -F

A / indicates a directory, an * for an executable, and an @ for a symlink.

Use the Up Arrow key to edit the last command and change "etc" to "bin" ;

]# cd /bin ; ls -F   # this directory contains binaries and scripts

]# ls -lF

When the -l option is used with the -F option, an * indicates an executable (binary, script or symlink). Symlinks are indicated with "->" between the symlink and the target.

Use the Up Arrow key to get to the last command ; add "| less" to the command ; scroll to the bottom

⑫ Using ls to View Directory Information

Change into the /etc directory ;

]# ls -l | grep ^d   # lists all items have "d" at the far left

This displays only the names of directories (subs) in the current directory. It does not show "regular" (non-symlink) file names or symlink file names and it does not show the contents of the subdirectories.

]# ls -l | grep ^d | less

look for the directory named profile.d and directories that begin with "r" ;

scroll to the bottom.

The above two commands do not show the contents of the subdirectories that are listed. These commands only show directory names (subs of the current directory). This is because the characters "^d" in "grep ^d" cause the system to only display output that *starts* with the letter d.

When you run the ls command, a "d" for "directory" appears at the far left (start) of each line of output (when the item is a directory). The ^ (caret) at the left of "^d" indicates "start with" the letter "d". When using the ls command with the -l option, only directories start with a "d". Therefore, only directories appear when "| grep ^d" is used.

Later, you will use "^hd" to cause the shell to only display output that starts with "hd". In this upcoming exercise, you will run the dmesg command and "grep" for the string "^hd" so that only output that starts with hd (only output regarding devices (drives) that start with hd) appears. The plot thickens.

]# ls -l profile.d

When the -l option is used, the ls command displays a long listing of the *contents* of the profile.d directory. It does not display information on the directory itself.

]# ls -ld profile.d

When the -d option is used, the ls command displays information on the directory, it does not list the contents of the directory.

⑬ Listing Only Files and Only Symlinks

]# ls -l | grep ^-   # lists only the names of non-symlink files

]# ls -l | grep ^l   # lists only the names of symlinks to files or directories

Look at the size of the symlinks that appeared. These are all small files.

The /etc directory is commonly used for configuration files. Notice that the grub.conf symlink in /etc points to the grub.conf in /boot/grub. If you ran an editor and edited the grub.conf in /etc (to modify its settings) you would actually be modifying the grub.conf file in /boot (not the symlink in /etc).

 Distinguishing Between Items in the Current Directory and Items in Subdirectories

    ]# ls -l r* | less

Lists all items in the current directory beginning with "r". *This includes the contents of subdirectories that begin with "r".* The rc.d directory contains a few files and several subs.

> Notice items at the top of the list that have an "l" at the left ; these are symlinks that begin with "r" ;
>
> notice items that have a "-" at the left ; these are files that begin with "r" ;
>
> look for **rc.d:** at the far left, near the bottom ;
>
> /rc.d: # search for "rc.d:"

The **rc.d** that is highlighted at the far left is a directory name. It does not appear at the right side of the screen with a "d" at the far left to indicate that it is a directory. No information for the directory, such as date and size appears. The items that appear below the "rc.d:" at the far left are directories and files in the rc.d directory below /etc.

> /rpm: # search for "rpm:"

The rpm directory is also below the current directory.

 Searching for Files with the find Command

    ]# cd /usr/share/vim ; ls   # no items ending in .txt are in the current directory

The command below, displays items that begin with anything and end in ".txt", below the current directory and subdirectories of the current directory. The find command works recursively by default.

    ]# find -name '*.txt'   # always use ' ' single quotes around text to
                               # be searched for when using the -name option

A relative path to each item that ends in .txt appears. Your current path is /usr/share/vim. The . (dot) at the left of the path, in each line of output, represents the current directory (and the path to the current directory), which is /usr/share/vim. The full (absolute) path to each file (including the filename) is the combination of the current path (/usr/share/vim) and the path starting at the right of the . (dot) in each line of the output.

For example, the fill path to **./vim61/tutor/README.txt** is:

> /usr/share/vim**/vim61/tutor/README.txt**

```
]# find  -name  '*.txt'  | nl  | less
```

scroll to the bottom.

The following command shows all README.txt files below the current directory.

```
]# find  -name  'README.txt'  | nl  | less

]# find  -name  'c*.txt'  | nl  | less      # shows items beginning with "c"
                                            # and ending in ".txt"

]# find  -name  'c*'  | nl  | less          # shows items beginning with "c"
                                            # and ending in anything
```

(16) Specifying a Path with the Find Command

```
]# cd  /root ;  pwd

]# find  /proc  -name  'meminfo'
```

Finds items that have the name meminfo in /proc. A wildcard character is not used in the above command and so the output will only show exact matches. Files named meminfo.1 and big-meminfo will not appear.

```
]# find  /etc  -name  '*lpd'
```

Displays items that begin with anything (except a . (dot)) and end in "lpd" below the /etc directory (and subs).

To find items that begin with a . (dot), which are hidden items, put a . (dot) at the start of the pattern.

```
]# find  /etc  -name  '.bash*'       # display hidden items below /etc
                                     # that begin with ".bash"

]# find  /usr/sbin  -name  '*group*' # display items in /usr/sbin that contain
                                     # "group" anywhere in the item name
```

The command below shows all directories and files below /usr with *only* the text of "man" in the name and does not show names such as **man**path, commands and p**man**

```
]# find  /usr  -name  'man'
```

The command below shows all items below /usr that begin with man and end in the numbers 1 through 9, such as man1, man2 and man3. This command does not show files and directories that only have the text of "man".

```
]# find  /usr  -name  'man[1-9]'  | less

]# find  /usr/share  -name  'man[1-9]'   # shows only items below /usr/share

]# find  /usr/share  -name  'man[2-5]'   # shows only man2 through man5
```

The next command shows all items below the /usr that begin with man and end in the lower case letters "a" through "z" and the numbers 1 through 9. This will cause items such as mann, man1 and man2 to appear. It does not show files and directories that only have the text of "man".

```
]# find /usr -name 'man[a-z1-9]'
```

 17 Using Tab Completion to Specify a Path

```
]# cd /lib ; ls | nl        # many items, but which ones are subdirectories?

]# ls -l | grep ^d         # there are only a few subdirectories

]# cd m
```

press Tab and the rest of "modules" appears ; press Enter ;

```
]# ls

]# uname -r               # the subdirectory name shown with the ls
                          # command matches the kernel version shown
                          # with the uname command

]# cd 2
```

press Tab and the rest of the subdirectory (number) appears ; press Enter ;

```
]# ls                     # a directory named kernel exists below the
                          # current directory

]# cd k
```

press Tab and the rest of "kernel" appears ; press Enter ;

```
]# ls                     # a directory named drivers exists below the
                          # current directory

]# cd d
```

press Tab and the rest of "drivers" appears ; press Enter ;

```
]# pwd ; ls               # notice the subdirectory names

]# history | tail         # displays the last 10 items in "history"
```

From the output from the above command, notice that you used the cd command several times to get to the current directory (path). To get to this directory again, after going to a different directory, you could select each of the cd commands in history to get to this location, but this would be very slow.

(18) Using Tab Completion to Specify a Path on One Line (Revisited)

```
]# cd  /bin           # change to any other directory
```

Now we'll build up all of the path on one line, rather than using the cd command and pressing Enter after each directory name.

Let's say that you know that you need to go to a subdirectory below /lib/modules. In other words, you know the names of the first two directories in the path.

```
]# cd  /lib/m
```

press Tab ; "odules/" appears ; do not press Enter ;

press Tab ; there is only one directory below modules and so this directory name appears.

If there were more than one item (directory or file) below modules, you could press Tab again to see a listing of items and then start typing in the name of one.

Press Tab ; the system beeps ; there is more than one item below the current directory ;

press Tab ; a list of items below the current directory appears ;

k ; press Tab ; only one item begins with "k" and the directory name appears ;

press Tab twice ; the list of items below the current path (on the command line) appears ;

d ; press Tab ; the entire path that you need appears on one line ; press Enter.

Now if you wanted to change into this directory path later (hint, hint), you could do so by pressing the Up Arrow key and selecting the command or by "selecting the command from the list of commands in history", (or "selecting the command from the output of the history command", or "selecting the command from history").

There will be many times when you want to use a long directory path with a command, such as the cd command or ls command, after having specified it once. By specifying the path on a single line, you can easily get to it (using several methods shown below) so that you can use it again (with the same command or a different command). Learning these methods of working with commands will save you a ton of time!

Using the find Command to Search for Driver Files

```
]# ls ; pwd
```

The drivers directory is the "parent" directory for subdirectories that contain drivers (modules) for various hardware devices. These files have the .o suffix. The subdirectories of the drivers directory are basically the names of categories of hardware devices, such as cdrom, ide, scsi, sound, usb and video. These are categories for .o driver files.

```
]# find -name '*.o' | nl
```

After running the above command, driver files ending in ".o" below the current directory appear - lots of them!

```
]# find -name '*.o' | nl | less
```

Scroll down and look for the sound directory. Also look for the file named sound.o below the sound directory.

```
]# find -name '*.o' | grep /sound/
```

The above command restricts the output to the string of "/sound/". Now only the drivers for sound devices (below the sound directory) appear. Remember the quantity of items after running the following command.

```
]# find -name '*.o' | grep /sound/ | nl

]# pwd
```

The path is: /lib/modules/*kernelversion*/kernel/drivers

```
]# cd /root
```

Remember that you are in the /root directory while you are running the commands below.

```
]# find -name '*.o'            # there are no driver files below /root

]# find /lib/modules -name '*.o'   # the path of /lib/modules is used
```

The path in the above command (/lib/modules) is "long enough" to use to search for kernel driver (.o) files (rather than needing to specify the longer path of: /lib/modules/*kernelversion*/kernel/drivers).

Notice the quantity of items after running the following command. This is the same as the quantity that you needed to remember earlier.

```
]# find /lib/modules -name '*.o' | grep /sound/ | nl
```

After running the next command, you will be able to scroll through the list of drivers below the sound directory.

```
]# find /lib/modules -name '*.o' | grep /sound/ | nl | less
```

Above is a "pipeline". The find command is piped to the grep command is piped to the nl command is piped to the less command. Now that's output!

 Finding a Driver File

Let's say that you know the name of a driver file and want to find its location, or check that it still exists on the hard disk. In this example, the name of the driver file is sound.o.

You could use the path of: / to do a search in all directories below the root. However, you know that the driver is somewhere below /lib. By specifying a directory name below the / you can considerably reduce the amount of time that the find command takes.

Remember that you are (likely) working on a system with a "relatively" small amount of disk space and "relatively" few files. On a system with a large amount of disk space and many more data files, specifying a directory (or several) below the / can save a lot of time.

```
]# find /lib -name 'sound.o'      # the full path to the sound.o file appears
```

 Searching for Files by Size

```
]# ls -lS /boot            # see the sizes of items in /boot
]# ls -lSh /boot           # now in human readable form
]# find /boot -size +200k
```

The files that are over 200 k (200 x 1,024 bytes) appear.

The command below will cause only files that begin with "vmlinuz" to appear.

```
]# find /boot -size +200k -name 'vmlinuz*'
```

The next command will cause only files that begin with "vmlinu" to appear.

```
]# find /boot -size +200k -name 'vmlinu*'
```

The following command will display all files over 10k in and below /var/log. If you are working on a system where large log files can be created, such as a web server, you may want to run a command similar to below often to check for "runaway log files". You may want to change the size amount (as shown in the command below) from "+10k" to "+100k" or a higher amount.

```
]# find /var/log -size +10k
]# find /var/log -size +100k      # fewer - if any - files appear
```

You should be in /root. If not, run the cd command and the other commands shown on the same line below.

```
]# cd /root ; ls ; pwd
```

The following command displays all directories and files "owned" by the root user, including hidden directories and files. Directory and file ownership will be described in detail later.

```
]# find -user 'root'          # items in /root appear

]# find -user 'cwest'         # no items appear
```

The cwest user should not be the owner of any items below /root.

The next command should show (lots of) items below the path of /home/cwest, that are owned by the cwest user.

```
]# find /home/cwest -user 'cwest'
```

Now only show files that are owned by cwest that begin with ".bash".

```
]# find /home/cwest -user 'cwest' -name '.bash*'
```

 22 Creating Some Files To See How the slocate Command Works

```
]# cd ~cwest ; pwd

]# touch test123          # create a file named test123 in /home/cwest

]# cd /root

]# touch test123          # create a file named test123 in /root

]# slocate test123        # no files were found
```

The slocate database must be updated before the new file can be slocated. By default, *with this distribution*, the slocate database is automatically updated daily.

23 Updating the slocate Database and Trying to slocate Files

In the command below, the -e option will cause directories and files in the path of /root to be excluded from the update and the -u option will cause the system to update the database (with everything else) from the / directory downwards. The update may take a minute or two. You may want to keep reading until the prompt returns.

```
]# slocate -e /root -u

]# slocate test123
```

The file in /home/cwest was found, but not the one in /root because /root was excluded from the update.

```
]# slocate -u
```

Update the database without excluding any directories.

```
]# slocate test123        # now the file is found in both directories
```

 ## Using slocate While Logged In as a User

```
]# exit                   # end your "su to root" session
```

The prompt changes from having a # sign to having a $ sign. Now you are working as the cwest user.

```
]# cd ~ ; pwd             # change into /home/cwest - if not already there
]# slocate test123        # the full path to the file appears
```

The file only appears below the cwest home directory. The cwest user does not have permission to view items that are in the /root directory, therefore you cannot "slocate" the file that is in /root.

```
]# su -                   # log in with the password of the root user
]# slocate test123        # the file appears in /home/cwest and in /root
```

The root user has permission to slocate the file in any location.

Using grep to Search the Contents of Files

```
]# cd /root ; ls ; pwd    # change into /root - if not already there
```

A file named install.log should exist in the /root directory. This log (text) file contains a list of all (software) packages that were installed during the installation.

The package named bzip2 provides the system with the bzip2 compression utility.

Let's say you can't remember the name of the install.log file, but know that it is in the /root directory. The following command will check to see if the bzip2 package was installed during the installation.

```
]# grep bzip2 *           # search all files in the current directory for bzip2
```

The output will likely show two items. The line that does not show "-libs" is the line that represents the bzip2 package (file compression utility). The line that shows "-libs" is the package that contains libraries for the bzip2 program.

```
]# grep -r hosts /etc/*.conf    # searches for the string of "hosts" in
                                # items ending in ".conf" in /etc and subs
```

Using the -i (ignore case) Option of the grep Command

Clear the screen after running each commad below.

```
]# ls -l /etc/*.conf | nl        # dislpays a total of all ".conf" files
]# grep PATH /etc/*.conf | nl    # only a few ".conf" files appear
```

This command displays output for files that end in ".conf" that contain the text of "PATH" in upper case letters (only). Remember the number of lines of output.

```
]# grep -i PATH /etc/*.conf | nl   # more ".conf" files appear than above
```

The -i (ignore case) option causes the output to be displayed for files that contain the text of "PATH" in any combination of upper and lower case letters. Compare the number of lines of output in the last two commands.

 Viewing the Partition Settings in the fstab File

```
]# cat /etc/fstab        # shows the partition settings in fstab
```

The next command displays the partitions in the /etc/fstab configuration file that are using the ext3 filesystem.

```
]# cat /etc/fstab | grep ext3    # same as running: grep ext3 /etc/fstab
```

 Looking through Compressed (.gz) Files for a String

Change into the path of: /usr/share/man/man5 ; get a long listing and pipe it to less ; scroll to the bottom and notice that all of these man page files end in ".gz".

Lets' say you need to search for the text of "local machine".

```
]# zcat *.gz | grep 'local machine'
```

The zcat command works on compressed ".gz" files. Now try using cat rather than zcat.

```
]# cat *.gz | grep 'local machine'
```

The above command did not produce output because the .gz files are compressed.

```
]# zgrep 'local machine' *.gz    # zgrep works on compressed files
]# grep 'local machine' *.gz     # grep does not work on compressed files
```

Viewing the Files in /etc

After running the next command, briefly scan (visually look over) the filenames and notice the size of the file named inittab. The amount of text in the inittab file is more than a "screenful".

]# cd /etc ; ls -l | less

(30) **Using the cat Command with the nl Command**

At a screen resolution of 800 x 600, a terminal emulation window displays about 30 lines of text. The inittab file in the /etc/ directory is over 40 lines long. When you "cat out" the file with the command below, you will see the number of lines of output and the output will be longer than the screen can display. You will not be able to see the text that is at the top of the file.

]# cat inittab | nl   # the screen only shows the end of the file

Clear the screen often during the steps below to make the screen output easier to understand.

(31) **Viewing inittab with the less and head Commands**

]# less inittab   # this allows you to scroll through the text

To run the next command, press the Up Arrow key and then press Home. Delete the word: less and type in: head and then press Enter.

If you only need to see the text at the top of the file and do not need to see all of the file, then the next command will do the trick. It is also useful if you want to use the > (greater than) symbol to send the output to a file or device.

]# head inittab   # display the first 10 lines of the inittab text file in /etc
                      # this allows you to see a description of the inittab file
                      # and the author of the file

 Redirecting the Output of the head Command to a File

Now send the output (the top ten lines of inittab) to a file named top-of-inittab.txt in the /root/ directory.

]# head inittab > /root/top-of-inittab.txt

]# ls -l /root   # the top-of-inittab.txt file appears
                       # it was created with the command above

]# cat /root/top-of-inittab.txt

The top ten lines of inittab (from top-of-inittab.txt) appear.

You can redirect the output of files to other files so that you can document your system.

Listing and Viewing Configuration Files in /etc

The /etc directory contains many configuration files and many of these files have the filename suffix (a.k.a. extension) of: .conf.

The next command will output all of the *.conf files (more than a "screenful") and the command after that will only show the first ten files. If you only need to see the start of a listing of files, then the second command allows you to easily do this.

get a long listing of files that match the pattern of: *.conf in /etc.

All of the *.conf files scroll past and the top of the output cannot be seen.

```
]# ls -l *.conf | head
```

Displays only the first 10 lines of files ending in ".conf". Notice the size of the file named htdig.conf.

```
]# cat htdig.conf | nl      # this is a long file that cannot be displayed
                            # in a single "screenful"

]# head -25 htdig.conf      # display the first 25 lines htdig.conf
```

Viewing the Documentation Subdirectories

The command below will change you into the parent directory for documentation files. This directory is named doc and it contains documentation for many of the software components that are installed on your system.

```
]# cd /usr/share/doc

]# ls -l | nl               # there are over three hundred directories
                            # below the doc directory
```

After running the command below, briefly scan the directory names and press Page Down to scroll to the bottom of the list.

```
]# ls -l | nl | less        # notice the directory named
                            # vim-common-version
```

Listing the Contents of the vim-common-*version* Directory

The vim-common-*version* directory is the parent directory for information (documentation) on the vim (**vi im**proved) editor, which is also commonly referred to as the vi editor. This editor is a very powerful tool for working with text files (such as source code, configuration files and scripts) on a Linux system. It is one of the two most popular editors used with Linux. You will learn to work with this text editor later in this course.

```
]# cd vim              # start typing in the name of the
                       # vim-common-version directory
```

press Tab ; the remaining characters in the directory name appear ;

press Enter ; go into the vim-common-*version* directory ;

run the command that displays the **p**ath to the **w**orking **d**irectory.

Notice that you are in /vim-common-*version*/, below /usr/share/**doc**/

Run the command to get a long listing of the current (working) directory.

This directory contains information on the vi (vim) editor. Notice that this directory has a subdirectory named docs.

Change into the docs subdirectory (for the vi editor) ;

run the command to get a long listing of all files with the .txt suffix ;

now run the command again and "pipe" the output to the nl command.

There are over 100 text (.txt) files describing the vi editor are in this directory.

 Viewing the Top 10 Lines of Over 100 Files with One Command

The next command will allow you to get an overview of each of the text files in this directory by allowing you to scroll through the output of the first ten lines of each text file.

```
]# head *.txt | less
```

The head command indicates the start of each file (in the output on the screen) by putting the name of the file at the left of the screen between "==>" and "<==".

For example, the file named change.txt starts on the line below:

```
==> change.txt <==
```

Scroll through the output and scan some of the information for several of the files.

Running the above command: head *.txt | less with a pattern (such as *.txt) and "piping" the output (with the | "vertical bar") to the less command is extremely useful. It allows you to get an overview of many files in one listing, without having to open each file individually. This command is also useful for looking at the contents of many other files at once, such as source code or .html (text) files that are used for the content of a web site.

Now run the same command as above, but use the -n option so that you can see the first 20 lines of text in each file, rather than the default of 10 lines. If necessary, see the description of the head command earlier in this chapter.

Scroll through the output. Now you can see a bit more information on each file.

]# exit   # end the "su session"

]# exit   # close the terminal emulation window

Opening a Terminal Emulation Window - Half Screen Size

Open a terminal emulation window ; do not maximize it ; do not "su to root" ;

you are currently logged in as cwest ;

move the window to the top of the screen (if it is not already there) ;

use the side border(s) of the window to widen it so that it fills the width of the screen ;

use the bottom border to move the bottom of the window up so that it only fills half of the screen.

Using a + (Plus) Sign with the tail Command

In the next command, the text from line 30 onwards of the inittab file appears, rather than just the last 10 lines of the file. If you have permission to read a file, then you can read it and output the file with a command.

]# tail +30 /etc/inittab | less

As a user, you have permission to read the inittab file.

Using +n (where n is a number) is useful if you want to see output from a specific line number onwards, or if you want the output from a file or command to be put into a file from a specific line number onwards (by redirecting the output to a file with the > symbol).

(39) **Trying to Output the Contents of a File to which You Do not Have Permission**

]# tail -25 /var/log/messages   # you do not have "permission" to read
                                  # the messages file

"su as root" (or "su to root") ;

at the Password: prompt, type in the password of the root user and press Enter ;

now type in the above tail command again and output it to less.

The root user has permission to view the messages file.

If someone asks you to "tail the messages file", you now know exactly what to do.

(40) **Scrolling Up a Terminal Emulation Window**

Run the same command as above, but without piping the output to less.

Use the Up Arrow (at the right of the terminal emulation window) to scroll up to see all 25 lines of text that were output by the above command (scroll up until you can see the prompt again) ;

clear the screen (with Ctrl+l or the clear command).

(41) **Continuously Viewing the End of the messages File**

The command below will cause the last 10 lines of the messages file to appear *continuously*. When various events occur on a system, a description of the event is added to the end of the messages file. After text has been added to the end of the file, it will be displayed in the window in which the following command is running.

]# tail -f /var/log/messages   # notice that the prompt does not
                                 # appear again

(42) **Opening a New Window To Start a New "Session"**

Open another terminal emulation window and do the steps below to have it fill the bottom half of the screen ;

move the (entire) new window so that it is "flush" with the left of the screen (if it isn't already) ;

move the bottom border of the new window up so that the window is only about an inch deep ;

move the (entire) window down so that the top of it is just below the border of the top window ;

move the bottom border down to the top of the panel ;

move the right border so that the window is as wide as the screen ;

make sure you can see all of the top window ;

do the following commands in the bottom window.

In future, we will simply say "open a terminal emulation window so that it fills the top half of the screen and open another terminal emulation window so that it fills the bottom half of the screen".

 ## 43 Viewing the Results of an Authentication Failure and Starting a Session

The tail command should be running in the top window and the bottom window should be "active" (highlighted) so that you can run the following commands.

With the next command, you will "su to root" and type in the **wrong password**.

Watch the text at the bottom of the top window when you press Enter after typing in the wrong password for the root user below.

```
]# su -        # type in the wrong password for the root user
```

A line describing the "authentication failure" was added to the end of the messages file and appears in the top window. This represents the attempt to log in (authenticate) with the incorrect password.

The text that appears at the bottom (of the top), was added to the messages file (in /var/log) and then displayed by the tail command in the top window. Trying to log in with the wrong password was an "event".

Watch the top window when running the command below.

```
]# su -        # type in the correct password for the root user
```

Look for "ruser=cwest" in the text at the bottom of the top window. This indicates that the cwest user has opened (started) a session for the root user. This was another "event".

Watch the top window again when running the command below.

```
]# exit        # end the "su session"
]# su -        # type in the correct password again
```

 Viewing the Results of Starting and Stopping a Service

Now you will start a service and see the result in the top window.

"sendmail" is the name of a "service" that is loaded when you boot your system. It provides users with the capability of sending email. This service is used below to illustrate that when a service is stopped or started, these actions are events and they are added to the end of the messages file. Services are described in detail later.

Watch the top window again when you run the next two commands.

```
]# service sendmail stop
```

The results of this command were added to the end of the messages file.

```
]# service sendmail start
```

The results of this command were also added to the end of the messages file.

The starting and stopping of other services, such as a web server, are also put in the messages file. The messages file can also be "tailed" (with the tail command) to debug changes that you are making to a system (that aren't working) and to check for the system's response to something that you are doing, such as attempting to load a driver for a network card.

 "Catting Out" the messages File and Using grep

```
]# cat /var/log/messages | nl    # lots of output!
```

The following command "cats out" the messages file and restricts the output so that only lines of text in the messages file that contain the string "auth" appear so that you can see all "authentication failure" messages.

```
]# cat /var/log/messages | grep auth | nl
```

The next command does the same as above, but it is a bit shorter.

```
]# grep auth /var/log/messages | nl
```

Remember to check the messages file (in /var/log) if you think that your system is being accessed by someone that is not allowed access.

46 Stopping the tail Command

The bottom window should still be the "active" window. Watch the top window.

```
]# exit          # end the session for the root user in the bottom window
```

press Alt+Tab until the top window is selected ;

press Ctrl+c to stop the tail command (that was run with the -f option) ;

```
]# exit          # end the session for the root user in the top window
```

```
]# exit          # close the top terminal emulation window
                 # the bottom window is now selected
```

```
]# exit          # close the bottom terminal emulation window
```

47 Seeing the Default Number of Commands in history

Open a terminal emulation window ; maximize the window ; "su to root".

The following commands display the contents of two variables used to specify the number of commands in the history list.

```
]# echo  $HISTFILESIZE
```

```
]# echo  $HISTSIZE
```

Now run the history command to see a listing of the most recently run commands. Notice that each command has a number at the left of it.

```
]# history            # look at the commands in "history"
```

```
]# history | head     # see the first 10 commands in history
```

```
]# history | tail     # see the last 10 commands in history
```

```
]# history 25         # this shows the last 25 commands
```

48 Running Commands Using a String and a Number

In the next two commands, specify a string and a number of a command that can be run from the current directory.

Look for the lowest (most recent) command beginning with the letter "c". The following command runs it.

```
]# !string           # replace string with:  c
```

```
]# history 25
```

```
]# !n                # replace n with a number at the left of any command
```

The above step runs the command from history.

(49) Restricting the Output of history with the grep Command

]# history | grep find	# shows all commands in history that # contain "find"

use: !*n* and run one of the find commands (a long one) that searches below a path ;

press the Up Arrow key and the command that you just ran and not "!*n*"appears ;

]# history | grep find | tail	# shows the last 10 items that # contain "find"

use: !*n* and run another (different) one of the find commands that searches below a path ;

]# history | grep drivers	# displays the cd command(s) that # were used earlier to change to the # drivers directory

A cd command that changes to the following path should appear:

/lib/modules/*kernelversion*/kernel/drivers/

]# !*n*	# replace *n* with the number of a command that # changes to the drivers directory - that's fast!

Remember the above methods of using the history command so that you can use them in future Hands-On Exercises!

(50) Viewing Dates with the cal Command

]# cal	# displays the calendar for the current month
]# cal -j	# displays the current month in "Julian" format # the number for today is the number of days # since the beginning of the year
]# cal -y	# displays the calendar for the current year # you can scroll up to see all of it
]# cal 2007	# displays the calendar for the year 2007 # scroll up to see the year at the top

In the command below, replace *n* with the month you were born and *year* with the year you were born.

]# cal *n year*	# displays the month you were born

Now you can see what day of the week you were born on!

(51) Looking Up Words with the look Command

Let's say you can't remember how to spell "receivable".

```
]# look recie        # no output - no words (in the dictionary being used)
                     # appear for the string of "recie"

]# look recei        # shows several words, including receivable
```

clear the screen ; change to the /root directory ;

stay logged in to test your answers to the following questions.

 ## Section Review

After each of the following questions, write the answer to the question on the line provided and then run the command to test that you answered the question correctly.

1. Your current directory is /root. Do not change directory. Write the command to get a long list of items that begin with anything and end with ".conf" in the path of /etc, sorted by size with the largest item at the top and piped to the less command.

   _____

2. Write the command to get a long list of the "type" of items in the path of /lib and pipe the output to the less command. Do not use the file command.

   _____

3. Change into the path of /usr/share. Write the command to find all directory and file names below the current directory that contain **only** the text of "FAQ" (in upper case letters). **FAQ** stands for **F**requently **A**sked **Q**uestions. These files are text files that provide the answers to frequently asked questions about software components.

   _____

4. Now write the same command as above, but find all directory and file names that have the word "FAQ" anywhere in the name.

   _____

5. Change into the /root directory. Write the command to find all items below the path of /var that contain the text of "log" anywhere in the name of the item. Run this command from the current directory.

   _____

6. Documentation directories for software components are below /usr/share/doc. For example, the documentation for the grub boot loader is in a directory named grub-x.xx (where x.xx is the current version of grub). These directories contain documentation text files, such as README and NEWS.

   You are currently in a documentation directory for a program (this could be the documentation directory of any program below /usr/share/doc). You want to go to the web site of the program for some more information.

   Change into the grub-x.xx directory below /usr/share/doc. Write the grep command to search for the string of "www." in all files in the current directory. The answer is easy if you take it logically. Do not pipe the output of one command to another and do not specify more to the command than is required. Run this command from the grub-x.xx directory.

   _____

7. Your current directory is still the grub-x.xx directory below /usr/share/doc. Do not change directory and do not pipe the output of one command to another.

   Write the grep command to search for the string "networking configuration" in the path of /etc/sysconfig *and subs*. Remember that some options or components of a command *require* other options or components (hint, hint).

   _____

8. Change into the /etc directory. Write the command to output all of the contents of the fstab file in /etc to the screen. Do not use more text in the command than is required (do not specify anything that is not needed) and do not use a command that will allow you to scroll through the output.

   _____

9. Change into the /sbin directory. Write the command to output the top 10 lines of the lpd.conf file in /etc to the screen without changing directory and without piping the output of one command to another.

_____

10. Write the command that provides a long listing of all files in /etc that end in .conf. Also add the text that will cause the system to only display the top ten lines of output.

_____

11. Write the command to "tail the messages file" (in /var/log) with the option that will cause the last ten lines of text to stay on the screen, and will also cause the display to be updated, whenever any text is added to the end of the file. Remember to press Ctrl+c to stop this command.

_____

12. Write the command to "tail history" and show the last ten commands in history.

_____

13. Write the command to show the last 25 commands in history. Do not use the tail command or pipe the output of one command to another.

_____

14. Write the command to output all commands in history that contain the text "grep".

_____

15. Which command will cause only the first ten lines of output of the ls command to appear on the screen?

    ○ A. head | ls -l
    ○ B. ls -l | tail
    ○ C. ls -l | head
    ○ D. ls -l | cat

16. Select two methods of starting a shell "session", which will cause a shell binary (such as the bash executable in /bin) to be executed.

    ☐ A. opening a terminal emulation window
    ☐ B. executing the termshell script file
    ☐ C. running the shellbash command at the command line
    ☐ D. logging in to a virtual terminal

17. Some Linux commands are "case sensitive", but commands that run scripts are not. T F

18. Which pattern can be used to represent all directories and files that contain "log" anywhere in the name?

    ○ A. *log
    ○ B. log*
    ○ C. *log*
    ○ D. ?log?

19. The file named dirlist.txt in the current directory contains 50 lines. Which command will output only the lines that contain "/dev"?

    ○ A. find dirlist.txt | grep /dev
    ○ B. cat dirlist | grep dev
    ○ C. cat dirlist.txt | grep /dev
    ○ D. head dirlist.txt | grep /dev

20. The f option for one command produce basically the same results when this option is used in all other commands. T F

21. Which command concatenates (joins together) the contents of memo5 and memo7 (in the current directory) and creates memos (in the current directory)?

    ○ A. grep memo5 memo7 > memos
    ○ B. cat memo5, memo7 < memos
    ○ C. echo memo5 memo7 << memos
    ○ D. cat memo5 memo7 > memos

22. When specifying a string with the grep command, you need to use a ' (single quote) at the start and end of the string:

    ○ A. when the string has one or more spaces in it
    ○ B. any time you use a string
    ○ C. when the string is longer than six characters
    ○ D. when the string contains numbers

23. Select the pattern that can be used to list all directories and files that begin with "data" and end in any number from 3 through 7.

    ○ A. data3-7
    ○ B. data3*7
    ○ C. data3?7
    ○ D. data[3-7]

24. The r option of the find command is used to cause it to work recursively. T F

25. Which of the following character(s) will allow you to append (add) the output of a command to the end of a file?

    ○ A. >>
    ○ B. <
    ○ C. >
    ○ D. |

26. The syntax of a command named listit shows: listit [e | k]. The virtical bar between the "e" option and the "k" option indicates that:

    ○ A. you can run both options at the same time
    ○ B. you can run either the e option or k option, but not both at once
    ○ C. you can pipe the output of the e option to the k option
    ○ D. you can use the [(left square bracket) at the start of the e option and the] (right square bracket) at the end of the k option

27. You are logged in as the root user. Select the item that represents the path to a directory named common below the home directory of the cwest user.

    ○ A. ~/common
    ○ B. cwest~/common
    ○ C. ~cwest/common
    ○ D. ~/cwest/common

28. To have the find command work predictably when you use the -name option, you should always use a ' (single quote) at the start and end of the pattern that you are searching for. T F

29. Which of the following commands will redirect errors from a program named newprog to a file named newprog-errors.log?

   - ○ A. newprog < newprog-errors.log
   - ○ B. newprog < | newprog-errors.log
   - ○ C. newprog 2> newprog-errors.log
   - ○ D. newprog errors || newprog-errors.log

30. Select two correct statements regarding the three types of quotation marks.

   - ☐ A. a ' (single quote) is used around text so that variables inside the quotes are processed and commands are not processed
   - ☐ B. a ` (back quote) is used around text so that the commands between the quotes are processed
   - ☐ C. a ' (single quote) is used around text so that the text is treated "as is"
   - ☐ D. a " (double quote) is used around text so that the text is treated "as is"

31. You need to see the date that the reports directory, below the current directory, was created. Which command will display a long listing of information for the reports directory, but does not list the contents of the directory?

   - ○ A. ls -l reports
   - ○ B. ls -^d reports
   - ○ C. ls -ld reports
   - ○ D. ls -lh reports

32. Which type of command is not run by executing a file (on a disk in the system), but is a part of the shell executable file that you are using?

   - ○ A. a command that runs a GUI utility
   - ○ B. a builtin (a.k.a. built-in) command
   - ○ C. a command run by executing a binary
   - ○ D. a command run by executing a script file

33. You are working on a web server that uses log files in a subdirectory below /var. Your current directory is /root. You need to see the size and quantity of all files that are over 250 kilobytes. Which of the following commands will you use?

    ○ A. find -size +250k
    ○ B. find /var -size 250k
    ○ C. find /var -size +250k
    ○ D. find /var -size +250

34. Which item below will cause command number 756 to be run from history?

    ○ A. #756
    ○ B. ~756
    ○ C. *756
    ○ D. !756

35. Select the command that will list directories and files in the current directory that contain "readme" in the name, in any combination of upper and lower case letters.

    ○ A. ls -l | grep -c readme
    ○ B. list * | grep -r readme
    ○ C. ls -l | grep -i readme
    ○ D. grep -w *readme*

36. The Tab key can be used to complete (choose two):

    ☐ A. the name of a file
    ☐ B. text files at the 25th line of output
    ☐ C. the name of a variable
    ☐ D. the output of the cat command

37. Select the command that will sort the file named users.log to the default output.

    ○ A. sort users.log > screen
    ○ B. sort users.log
    ○ C. sort | users.log
    ○ D. sort users.log | grep screen

38. Select two correct statements regarding the wildcard characters that can be used in a [pattern].

   ☐ A. a ~ (tilde) is used to represent "all characters" in the suffix of all filenames

   ☐ B. an * (asterisk) is used to represent "all characters"

   ☐ C. a ? (question mark) is used to represent a single character

   ☐ D. a # (number sign) is used to represent "all characters" at the start of all filenames

39. Select the command that will cause only the last 20 lines of the file named boot.log to appear on the screen.

   ○ A. tail -20 boot.log

   ○ B. tail +20 boot.log

   ○ C. head -20 boot.log

   ○ D. cat -20 boot.log

Chapter 7: Getting Help with Linux

Linux documentation is available in many locations, such as manuals, files, web sites and by running commands. This chapter describes how to get help from documentation in these locations and by using commands.

In this chapter you will learn about the Linux Documentation Project, which provides access to many sources of Linux information, including hundreds of HOWTOs, FAQs and man pages. This site also provides access to guides (on-line books), the Linux Gazette (an on-line magazine) and LinuxFocus (an on-line magazine).

The following commands are described in this chapter and are also used in the Hands-On Exercises:

man	list man pages and display the contents of man pages
help	see the syntax of a command and get a brief description
info	display the contents of info pages
whatis	lists the man page names, numbers and descriptions for a *filename* (item) that is specified
apropos	lists the man page names, numbers and descriptions that contain the *string* of text that is specified
whereis	displays the full path, including filename, for binary, source code and man page files for an item specified

Getting Help with Linux

Getting Help with Linux

Topics Covered in this Chapter

Provide all of the locations in which help can be found for Linux
Understand the difference between the help option and the help command
Learn how to use the info command and navigate within an info page
Detail how the man command works and the categories of man pages
Compare using some options of the man command with using some other commands
Use all of the commands related to getting help with Linux

In this chapter, you will learn about many different sources of Linux help and the differences between all of the commands that provide help with Linux.

Linux Documentation

Linux documentation is available in many locations, such as manuals, files, web sites and by running commands. This chapter describes how to get help from documentation in these locations and by using commands.

When reading Linux documentation, keep in mind that some of it may be very general and not specific enough for the task you are trying to perform. It may relate to any version of Linux and may not provide the details that you require for the distribution or package (software component) that you are using.

On the other hand, some documentation may be too specific. It may only relate to tasks that are used for a specific distribution or package.

You should also check the date of the documentation (usually shown somewhere in the documentation). The information may only relate to older distributions or packages.

The Linux Documentation Project

The Linux Documentation Project is an organization devoted to developing good, reliable documentation for the Linux operating system.

The web site of the Linux Documentation Project (tldp) is located at: http://www.tldp.org. This is an excellent starting point for Linux Documentation.

This web site provides access to many sources of Linux information, including hundreds of HOWTOs, **FAQs** (answers to **F**requently **A**sked **Q**uestions) and man pages. This site also provides access to guides (on-line books), the Linux Gazette (an on-line magazine) and LinuxFocus (an on-line magazine).

HOWTOs

HOWTOs are technical documents that describe "how to" do a Linux task. They are written by anyone who wants to describe a Linux topic or provide the solution to a common problem

There are two types of HOWTOs, regular and mini. Regular HOWTOs typically provide more detail than the mini HOWTOs. The mini HOWTOs are shorter in length than the regular ones and tend to be specific rather than general.

Linux Web Sites

In addition to the Linux Documentation Project, there are many Linux web sites that provide help with Linux. This includes sites that provide access to documentation, news groups, mailing lists, free support and paid support.

A good starting point for Linux web sites is: http://linux.com.

Searching the Internet for Help

Another good way to get quick access to help is to go to a search engine, such as http://google.com and do a specific search for the information that you require.

You may want to include the word "linux" in some of your searches. For example, search for "linux modem drivers" rather than just "modem drivers".

Linux Users Groups

A great place to find out more about Linux and meet other people that use Linux is at a Linux Users Group. These groups get together and have discussions on lots of different Linux topics. There are over five hundred Linux Users Groups in over eighty countries. To locate a group in your area and find out the date, time and subject of the next meeting, go to one of the web sites below.

The web site of the Linux Users Groups WorldWide (**lugww**) is located at:

> http://lugww.counter.li.org

The web site of **GLUE**: Groups of Linux Users Everywhere is located at:

> http://www.ssc.com:8080/glue/

Installed Documentation Files

As seen earlier, when you install many software packages, a directory for the packages is created below /usr/share/doc. This directory contains documentation files for the package.

The help Option of Commands and Commands that Provide Help

There is a help option available with some commands and there are also several commands that provide help with Linux. These methods of getting help are described below.

The help Option of a Command

Many commands have a help option that displays a relatively short description of the command and the options that are used with it. This is useful if you have forgotten the letter or name of a command option.

Using the help Option

    command --help

Replace *command* with the name of a command. Use -- (two dashes) in front of help when getting help with most commands. However, only - (one dash) is used with some commands. If you cannot get help using two dashes, try using one.

Example of Using the help Option

    rm --help

The above command displays a relatively short description (in comparison to viewing the man page) of the rm command, including the options that are used with it and two examples.

The help Command

This command is used to get help on a **builtin** command (that is a part of the /bin/bash shell executable file).

The Syntax of the help Command

    help *builtin-command*

Replace *builtin-command* with the name of a bash builtin command.

Example of the help Command

    help echo

The info Command

The info command is used to get help from "info pages" (a.k.a. Texinfo manual, on-line info). These "pages" are in compressed (.gz) files in the path of /usr/share/info. Over five *hundred* info pages were installed when you did your Linux installation earlier.

Info pages can sometimes provide more information than man pages, including examples of using commands, but there are fewer of them.

 Info pages and man pages are files that contain one or more "pages" of help information. To save on disk space, info pages and man pages reside on disk in a compressed form. When the info command is used to view an info page, or when the man command is used to view a man page, the file is automatically decompressed (a.k.a. uncompressed) and displayed.

You can look "behind the scenes" and see the "codes" and the "layout" of info pages and man pages (files ending in .gz) with the zless, zmore and zcat commands.

The Syntax of the info Command

info *filename*

Replace *filename* with the text of an item that you want to get help on.

Example of the info Command

info find

Navigating While Using the info Command

Some info pages, such as the one for the mkdir command, do not have a Menu (of topics in the info page). Others, such as the one for the find command, are more detailed and provide a Menu.

If an info page has a Menu (or list of topics), then you put your cursor on the * (asterisk) at left of a topic and press Enter to see info on the topic. To go to go to the "top" of the info page (back to the opening screen that contains the Menu), press "t" (without quotes). To go to the next item on the Menu press "n". To go to the previous Menu item, press "p". To exit out of an info page, press "q".

Man Pages and the man Command

Man pages provide a tremendous amount of information regarding the Linux OS and Linux software components. They include information on many different items, such as commands, configuration files, the shell, and programming languages.

Documentation for the Linux OS, software programs and other OS components often refer you to man pages for additional information on a topic. Some man pages even refer you to other man pages!

When you install Linux, man page subdirectories are created below the directory path of /usr/share/man. After the Linux installation that you did earlier, over five *thousand* man pages were installed in subdirectories below /usr/share/man.

Anyone can create man pages and install them on a system so that they can be accessed by the man command.

For example, a company that has had custom software created for it can create man pages so that their employees can get help information that is specific to the custom software.

The man command is used to access the information in man pages and is described in detail further below.

The Categories of Man Pages

As described earlier, the FHS document describes the Filesystem Hierarchy Standard. This document describes the man pages ending with the numbers 1 through 8 and the location of the man page subdirectories (man1, man2, man3 and so on) below /usr/share/man. Although there are other man page subdirectories, the discussion below will focus on man1 through man8.

The man page subdirectories are organized by categories and are referred to by Section numbers. For example, the FHS document states that man1 describes "User programs". In this case, "User programs" are programs that users have the capability of running. This includes commonly used commands, such as cp (copy files), ls (list files) and mkdir (make directory).

Table 7-1 shows the Section Number, Man Page Subdirectory and Category for man pages, as described in the FHS document.

Table 7-1 - The Section Number, Man Page Subdirectory and Category for Man Pages

Section Number	Man Page Subdirectory	Category
1	man1	User programs
2	man2	System calls
3	man3	Library functions and subroutines
4	man4	Special files
5	man5	File formats
6	man6	Games
7	man7	Miscellaneous
8	man8	System administration

The FHS document states that all of the man page subdirectories, below /usr/share/man are optional.

The man.config File in /etc

The default configuration file for man is the file named man.config in /etc. This file is used to specify settings for the man command. The MANSECT statement in man.config is used by the man command to specify the order in which man page files are displayed when the man command is run.

The default MANSECT statement in /etc/man.config is:

MANSECT   1:**8**:2:3:4:5:6:7:9:tcl:n:l:p:o

In the statement above, notice that the number 8 appears after the number 1 and before the number 2.

For some topics, such as some commands and configuration files, there is more than one man page (file). For example, there is a man page file for mount named mount.2.gz in section 2 (the man2 subdirectory) and another one named mount.8.gz in section 8 (the man8 subdirectory).

If a man page file does not exist for section 1, but exists for 2 and 8, then the MANSECT statement in /etc/man.config causes the man page for 8 (rather than 2) to appear by default when: man *filename* (item name) is run.

Running: man mount causes the man page for section 8 to appear *rather than causing the man page for section 2 to appear*. Pressing "q" simply exits out of the first man page that appeared *and the other man page will not be displayed*.

To continue the example, running: man -a mount shows the "first" man page for the mount command (man page 8) and when you press "q", then the "second" man page for the mount command (man page 2) appears. This allows you to view all man pages for the *filename* (item name) of "mount".

The man Command

The man command is used to display the contents of man pages or list the names and descriptions of man pages.

The Syntax of the man Command

The following is the syntax of the man command:

man [*n*] [option] *filename | string*

The [n] option is used to specify a Section Number. For the examples below, only one [option] can be used at a time and a *filename* or a *string* must be specified. The | (vertical bar) between filename and string in the syntax above represents "or".

If a *filename* (item name) is specified, the *filename* will match the name of a file, ending in *x*.gz in one of the man*x* (man page) subdirectories (where *x* is the Section Number of the man page). The *filename* will be the name of a command, configuration file or other item for which a man page has been created.

Quotation marks will not work "around" text to specify a *string* that contains a space. You can search for more than one *string* at a time by putting a space between the first *string* and the next *string*. If you specify a *string* with the text of: web and at the right of that (after pressing the Spacebar) specify a *string* of: server then you will be searching for "web" and "server" (as two separate *strings*, that *could* be one after the other), *not* "web server" (not one string that *only* matches both words).

Unlike most Linux commands, the *string* of text can be any combination of upper and lower case letters. It does not need to be "case sensitive".

You can get help while viewing a man page by pressing "h".

You can search for text in a man page by pressing the "/" slash key, typing in some text and pressing Enter. The text that you entered will appear highlighted throughout the man page so that you can easily see it.

Pressing "/" and then the Up Arrow key shows the text that you searched for last, pressing Up Arrow again shows the text that you typed in prior to that, and so on. You can do this to modify the text so that you can search for something similar.

You can close the current man page by pressing "q".

Options of the man Command

Table 7-2 below shows the commonly used options of the man command. The following is a discussion of using options of the man command.

You need to distinguish between the *filename* of a man page, the Title heading *in* a man page, and the NAME heading *in* a man page to fully understand the options of the man command that are shown below.

Notice that the -f and -a options in Table 7-2 use a *filename* to represent an item for which you want to view the man page. This is the *filename* of an man page file, excluding the *.x*.gz extension (where *x* is the number of a section).

The *filename* of a man page (excluding the *.x*.gz suffix) is used as the Title heading "in" a man page and this appears at the top left and right of a man page, with the section number in brackets at right of the Title heading. The Title heading (which is the same as the *filename*, excluding the *.x*.gz suffix) may appear in upper or lower case letters.

For example, there are two man pages for the mkdir command. One is mkdir.1.gz in section 1 (the man1 subdirectory) and the other is mkdir.2.gz in section 2 (the man2 subdirectory). The Title heading that appears at the top left and right of the man page in section 1 is MKDIR(1) and the other is MKDIR(2).

When using the -f and -k options, you are specifically looking for an item that is a man page (file).

In addition to the Title heading, a man page has several other headings, including NAME, SYNOPSIS and DESCRIPTION.

The NAME heading shows the name of the item with a description at the right. Do not confuse the *filename* of a man page with the NAME heading.

The word "item' in the table below refers to an item that a man page has been created for, such as a command, configuration file or concept.

Table 7-2 - Common Options of the man Command

Option	Description
-f *filename*	lists the man page names, numbers and descriptions that contain the *filename* (item) that is specified the description is from the NAME heading in the man page
-a *filename*	displays the first man page for the *filename* (item) that is specified the *filename* appears in the Title heading at the top left and right of the man page pressing "q" exits out of the first man page that is displayed if there is more than one man page for the specified *filename*, then pressing "q" will show the next man page and so on

Table 7-2 - Common Options of the man Command - Continued

Option	Description
-k *string*	lists the man page names, numbers and descriptions that contain the *string* of text that is specified the *string* can be a *filename* (the name of an item) the description is from the NAME heading in the man page
[*n*] -K *string*	lists the man pages in Section Number *n* that match the *string* of text the *string* can be a *filename* (the name of an item) a Section Number is not required, but the "scope" of the search is reduced by specifying a Section Number each man page name that is found will appear and you can view it, not view it or quit out of the command

Examples of the man Command

In the examples below, the example is shown on one line and a description of the example follows.

man ls

Displays the *contents* of the manual page for the *filename* of "ls" (ls.*x*.gz). This displays the man page that describes the ls command. It displays the "first" man page that is found in the order specified by the MANSECT statement in /etc/man.config. Pressing "q" exits out of the man page and the shell prompt appears.

man -f mkdir

Lists the man page names and numbers for the *filename* (item) of "mkdir". This displays all of the man pages that describe the mkdir command.

The output of running: man -f mkdir is shown below.

```
mkdir (1) - make directories
mkdir (2) - create a directory
```

Notice the numbers in brackets. These indicate the Section Numbers of the man pages. There are two man pages (man page files ending in *x*.gz) that describe the mkdir command. One is the file named mkdir.1.gz in Section Number 1 (User programs - in the man1 directory) and the other is the file named mkdir.2.gz in Section Number 2 (System calls - in the man2 directory).

man 2 mkdir

Displays the *contents* of the man page for the mkdir command for Section Number 2. Running: man mkdir without specifying a Section Number would only show the first man page for the mkdir command. It would show mkdir.1.gz and not mkdir.2.gz.

If a Section Number is not specified, then the only man page that is displayed is the first *filename* that is found when the man command searches through the man page Section Numbers, in the order in which they have been specified in the MANSECT statement in /etc/man.config.

If there is more than one man page for the filename (item), and you do not specify a Section Number, then you may end up looking at the wrong man page and you may not see the information that you need.

When documentation refers you to a man page, it should state the man page number so that you can use it with the man command to view the correct man page. Referring to a man page without specifying a Section Number is a common problem.

For example, if the documentation says "see the man page for history for more details" and you run: man history then you will only see the BASH_BUILTINS man page for history (only one "screenful" of information). If the documentation says "see man 3 history for more details" and you run: man 3 history then you will see the man page for history for Section Number 3, which is about *twenty* "screenfuls" of information!

If you have been referred to a man page by some kind of documentation, and the documentation did not state a man page number, use: man -f *filename* (rather than: man -k *string* which may show more man pages than you need to see) to see a list of all man pages for the *filename* (item). This will allow you to see if there is more than one man page for the *filename* (item) and to locate the man page number for the man page that you need.

man -a mkdir

Displays the *contents* of the manual page(s) for the *filename* of "mkdir". In this case, the first man page for "mkdir" is for Section Number 1. Pressing "q" exits out of the first man page and then the contents of the next man page appears (from Section Number 2). Pressing "q" again exits to the shell prompt because there are only two man pages for this item. The -a option allows you to easily view the contents of multiple man pages on an item, one after the other.

man -k boot

Lists the man page names and **numbers** that contain the *string* of "boot", with a short description of each man page. The text of "boot" does not have to be "case sensitive".

Partial output of running: man -k boot is shown below.

```
boot-scripts [boot]    (7)    - General description of boot sequence
initrd                 (4)    - boot loader initialized RAM disk
perlboot               (1)    - Beginner's Object-Oriented Tutorial
reboot [halt]          (8)    - stop the system
```

Notice that the first item shows "boot-scripts [boot]". To see the man page for this item, you use the text in the "[ ]" square brackets (i.e. use "boot", not "boot-scripts"). Running: man 7 boot-scripts provides the output of: "No entry for boot-scripts in section 7 of the manual". Running: man 7 boot displays the man page for this item.

To see the man page for the other items shown above, use the man command with the item name that appears at the left, such as: man 4 initrd. The Section Number of the man page may not always be required, but if you use it, you will be sure to get the correct man page.

man 8 -K initrd

Lists the man pages in Section Number 8 (System Administration commands) that contain the *string* of "initrd". This provides a listing of man pages that contain information on initrd. If a Section Number is not used, all sections are searched and the output of the -K option can be quite long.

In the output shown below, notice that the three files are all in the same directory path, below the man8 directory. The 8 in the man8 directory is the Section Number. Also notice that the three files, pcinitrd.8.gz, hotplug.8.gz and mkboodisk.8.gz all have the number 8 in the file name and all end in .gz.

Partial output of running: man 8 -K initrd is shown below.

```
/usr/share/man/man8/pcinitrd.8.gz? [ynq] n
/usr/share/man/man8/hotplug.8.gz? [ynq] y
/usr/share/man/man8/mkboodisk.8.gz? [ynq] q
```

Each item in the listing prompts for [**ynq**], **y**es, **n**o or **q**uit. Responding with "n" lists the name of the next man page, if there is one. Responding "y" displays the *contents* of the man page. Pressing "q" while viewing a man page lists the name of the next man page, if there is one. Responding with "q" (at the [ynq] prompt) stops the listing of man pages.

In the output above, the response of "n" to the first prompt stopped the first man page, named pcinitrd.8.gz, from being displayed. The response of "y" at the next prompt caused the *contents* of the man page named hotplug.8.gz to be displayed. The letter "q" was pressed to exit out of this man page and the next prompt appeared. The last prompt was responded to with "q" and so the output stopped.

The whatis Command

Using the man command with the -f option is the same as using the whatis command.

For example, running: whatis mkdir is the same as running: man -f mkdir.

The whereis Command

The whereis command displays the full path, including filename, for binary, source code and man page files for an item specified.

For example, running: whereis mkdir shows the following output:

mkdir: /bin/mkdir /usr/share/man/man1/mkdir.1.gz /usr/share/man/man2/mkdir.2.gz

The mkdir binary is in /bin and the man pages are in the full path of:

/usr/share/man/man1/mkdir.1.gz
/usr/share/man/man2/mkdir.2.gz

The **whereis** command is useful for seeing if a binary, source code and man page file is installed and **where** the file **is** located.

The apropos Command

Using the man command with the k option is the same as using the apropos command.

For example, running: apropos mkdir is the same as running: man -k mkdir.

Hands-On Exercises

 1 **Logging In to Get Help Using Various Methods**

Log in to a desktop as cwest ; open a terminal emulation window ; su to root.

During the Hands-On Exercises below, you will be viewing man pages and info pages. Remember to press "q" to exit out of these pages when necessary.

 2 **Viewing the Man Page of a Builtin Command**

    ]# man cd

The "man page" that is displayed shows "BASH_BUILTINS(1)" at the top left and right. The "(1)" in "BASH_BUILTINS(1)" is the category of the man page that you are viewing. The "1" is for Section Number 1 (file in the man1 directory) and this category is for "User programs".

The man pages for category 1 are in compressed files with the suffix of ".1.gz" in the man1 directory below /usr/share/man. The man pages for category 2 are in compressed files with the suffix of ".2.gz" in the man2 directory below /usr/share/man, and so on.

The bottom of this page says "SEE ALSO" bash(1), and sh(1). The sh(1) man page (the file named sh.1.gz) is a symlink to the bash man page (bash.1.gz). To get more information on the builtin commands, see the man page for bash. Also, to get more information on the cd command, you can use the --help option of the cd command, as in: cd --help and also use the help command, as in: help cd.

Notice the other builtin commands on this man page, such as alias, echo, exit, help, history, logout, pwd, umask and unalias. The commands on this man page are a part of the shell executable file. The executable file for the bash shell is named bash and is in /bin.

 3 **Viewing Help for a Builtin in the bash Man Page**

    ]# man bash
    /cd

Above starts a search for "cd" in the bash man page. Keep pressing "n" (about seven times) until you see "cd [-L | -P] [dir]" at the left. This is the beginning of the description of the cd command.

④ Using the --help Option with a Builtin Command and a "Non-Builtin" Command

```
]#  cd  --help          #  the syntax of the cd command appears
                        #  cd is a builtin command

]#  rm  --help          #  a brief description of the usage of the rm
                        #  command appears - rm is not a builtin command
```

⑤ Using the help Command with a Builtin Command and a "Non-Builtin" Command

The help command is used to get help for builtin commands.

```
]#  help  cd            #  provides more information than using the --help option
```

This is the same text that you saw in the bash man page.

```
]#  help  rm            #  no help appears because rm is not a builtin command
```

Notice the output of the above command. It suggests that you use: help help (in case you used the command incorrectly), and suggests that you use the man command (with the -k option) or use the info command.

⑥ Viewing All of the Man Pages for an Item

```
]#  man  history        #  shows only the BASH-BUILTINS(1) page

]#  man  -f  history
```

This shows that there are many other man pages for history. Remember to use the -f option to see a list of all man pages for a *filename* (item).

```
]#  man  3  history
```

This shows the man page for history for Section 3, which is for "Library functions and subroutines". Remember to use a Section Number between "man" and the "*filename*" (item) to see the man page for a specific section.

If documentation suggests that you see a man page, but does not specify a section number to use with the man command, run: man -f *filename* (item) to see the numbers of all of the man pages and then run the man command to see the man page(s) that you need.

⑦ Viewing the Man Page of the find Command

```
]# man find        # a Section Number is not required to look at a
                   # man page in Section 1
```

The name of the item (the find command) appears at the top left and right. Notice the NAME, SYNOPSIS and DESCRIPTION headings. The NAME heading describes the command. SYNOPSIS shows the syntax of the command. DESCRIPTION provides a description of the command. Options of the command appear below the OPTIONS heading.

Scroll to the bottom of the page and see all of the options of this command. Notice that SEE ALSO (at the bottom) states that you can also see more information "on-line in Info". This means that you can see more information on the command by using the info command (by running: info find). Some other man pages state "full documentation for this command is maintained as a Texinfo manual". This also means that you can get more help on a command by running the info command.

⑧ Running the info command To View the Texinfo Manual for the find Command

```
]# info find
```

This is the "info page" (as opposed to "man page") for the find command.

Move your cursor on top of the * (asterisk) at the left of "Finding Files::" ; press Enter ;

move your cursor to the left of "Time::" ; press Enter ;

move your cursor to the left of "Age Ranges::" ; press Enter ;

scroll down until you can see both examples at the bottom ;

press "t" to go to the "top" (opening menu) ;

press "q" to quit.

Remember that "**p**" can be used to go to a **previous** page and "**n**" can be used to go to the **next** page.

⑨ Viewing the "First" Man Page for the mkdir Command

```
]# man mkdir       # only shows the contents of man 1 page
```

Pressinq q to exit out of the man page does not show any more pages.

---

⑩ Viewing all of the Man Pages for the mkdir Command

]# man -f mkdir

There are two man pages for this item. One is in Section 1 and another is in Section 2.

]# man 2 mkdir   # shows the man page that is in Section 2 (System calls)

⑪ Using the a Option of the man Command

]# man -a mkdir

Above displays the first man page for mkdir named MKDIR(1).

Press "q" and the next man page for mkdir, which is MKDIR(2) is automatically displayed ;

press "q" again to finish the display of these man pages.

⑫ Using find to See the Man Pages for mkdir

Use the find command to display (only) all files that begin with "mkdir" in all of the man*x* directories below the path of: /user/share/man. Write the command in the space provided below.

_____

The two man page files named mkdir.1.gz and mkdir.2.gz should appear.

⑬ Viewing a Man Page with the zless Command

Man page files are compressed and so the zless command is used to view them ("behind the scenes"), rather than using the less command.

]# zless /usr/share/man/man1/mkdir.1.gz

The second line shows: .TH MKDIR "1". The .TH is for Title heading, which is MKDIR. The "1" is for the Section Number and appears in brackets at the right of the Title heading (at the top left and right of the man page), as in: MKDIR(1).

Notice that "User Commands" appears at the end of the second line. This is the description of the commands that are in Section 1.

Below: .SH NAME is the text that appears below the NAME heading on the man page. This is the descriptive text that appears when you use the -f and -k options of the man command.

14 **Using the k Option of the man Command to Search for a String**

```
]# man -k boot
```

Above lists the man page titles (names), numbers and a short description for the *string* of "boot". This text does not have to be in the title at the top of the man page and the text does not need to be "case sensitive". Notice that several different section numbers (of man pages) appear in ( ) between brackets.

Now you can run the man command to view a man page by using the name of the man page at the left, such as "initrd" and the number.

```
]# man 4 initrd
```

Get a listing of the man pages for "boot" again and notice that some of the pages are in section 8 (something Klinger always wanted).

```
]# man -k boot
```

Use an upper case "K" in the command below.

```
]# man 8 -K boot
```

This causes the system to list man pages in Section Number 8 (only), that contain the text "boot".

Type "n" and press Enter at the first prompt so that the first man page is not shown ;

respond to the second prompt with "y" and the contents of the man page are displayed ;

press "q" to exit out of the man page and you are then prompted at the right of the next man page name ;

press "q" and press Enter to stop the listing.

15 **Looking at the man.config File**

```
]# less /etc/man.config     # look at the configuration file for man pages

/MANSECT                    # press Up Arrow three times
```

In the MANSECT statement, 8 appears after 1 and before 2. The MANSECT statement defines the order in which man pages are searched if the MANSECT variable is not set.

```
]# echo $MANSECT     # the MANSECT variable is not set
```

(16) Viewing Man Pages in the Order Specified by MANSECT

```
]# man mount        # notice the heading at the top left and right
                    # this is the man page for section 8
```

press "q" to quit out of this page ;

```
]# man -a mount     # the man page from section 8 appears
```

press "q" to quit out of this page ;

the man page from section 2 appears ;

press "q" to quit out of this page.

Man pages appear in the order specified by the MANSECT statement in /etc/man.config. Man page 8 appears before man page 2 due to the MANSECT statement.

(17) Viewing Man Pages on the exit Command in Many Sections

```
]# man -a exit      # shows the man page for section 1 (User programs)
                    # this is the BASH_BUILTINS man page
```

press "q" to quit out of this page;

the man page from section 2 (System calls) appears ; this describes the _exit or _Exit commands that can be used in a C program ;

press "q" to quit out of this page ;

man page 3 (Library functions and subroutines) for the exit command appears ;

press "q" to quit out of this page ;

man page n (Tcl Built-In Commands) appears.

Tcl is a scripting language that can be embedded in a program. It allows a program to have a GUI interface. The xconfig utility that you will use in the section that describes configuring, compiling and installing the kernel is a utility written using Tcl.

press "q" to quit out of this page (and any others that may appear).

(18) Using the whatis Command

Running the whatis command is the same as using the -f option of the man command.

```
]#  whatis  mkdir

]#  man  -f  mkdir
```

Both of the above commands provide the same output.

(19) Running the apropos Command

Running the apropos command is the same as using the -k option of the man command.

```
]#  apropos  mkdir

]#  man  -k  mkdir
```

Both of the above commands provide the same output.

(20) Using the whereis Command

The whereis command displays the full path, including filename for binary, source code and man page files, for an item specified.

```
]#  whereis  mkdir    #  shows the location of the binary file and the
                      #  two man pages
```

(21) Shutting Down

Close all programs and windows ; Menu ; Log Out ; Shut Down ; OK.

Section Review

1. Which of the following are correct statements regarding navigation when using the info command to view an "info page" that contains a menu of items (choose two)?

    ☐ A. type: p to go to the previous menu item
    ☐ B. type: t to go to opening screen (the menu)
    ☐ C. type: e to exit out of info
    ☐ D. type: / to go to the next menu item

2. Man pages can only be used to display information on commands. T F

3. Select the option of the man command that can be used with a *filename* (and not a *string* that is not a *filename*) to **list** the man page names, numbers and descriptions.

    ○ A. -a
    ○ B. -k
    ○ C. -K
    ○ D. -f

4. You have been reading some documentation at a web site about a utility that you have installed named fastback. The documentation for this program is in more than one manx directory. The documentation says "see man 5 fastback" for more information.

    Which command will you run so that you are sure to see the correct man page?

    ○ A. man fastback
    ○ B. manpage fastback 5
    ○ C. fastback 5
    ○ D. man 5 fastback

5. What is the name of the default configuration file for man in /etc?

    ○ A. man.config
    ○ B. man1.cfg
    ○ C. manconf
    ○ D. manpage.conf

6. Which of the following commands will show help information on the ls command (which is not a builtin command)?

   ○ A. help ls
   ○ B. ls help
   ○ C. ls --help
   ○ D. whereis help

7. Select the option of the man command that can be used with a *filename* (and not a *string* that is not a *filename*) to **display** the man pages that contain the *filename* (and will not prompt you to view an item). If there is more than one man page, then pressing "q" will display the next man page.

   ○ A. -a
   ○ B. -k
   ○ C. -K
   ○ D. -f

8. Select the commands that will display help information on the alias (builtin) command (choose two).

   ☐ A. help alias
   ☐ B. manpage alias
   ☐ C. alias --help
   ☐ D. alias info

9. Select the item that describes the man page directory structure and the categories of man pages.

   ○ A. the RHS filesystem
   ○ B. the DOC files document
   ○ C. the FHS document
   ○ D. the MANSECT statement in /etc/man.config

10. Which key is pressed to get help while viewing a man page?

   ○ A. ?
   ○ B. h
   ○ C. /
   ○ D. Tab

11. You have created a command (binary) named listit as well as a man page for it. The command fits in category 4.

    What should you use for the name and full path to the man page file that describes the command?

    ○   A.   /usr/bin/listit.4
    ○   B.   /usr/share/man/listit.4.gz
    ○   C.   /usr/share/man/man4/listit.4.gz
    ○   D.   /usr/share/man/man4/listit.gz

12. Which option of the man command can be used with a *string* (that can be a *filename*) to list the man page names, numbers and descriptions that contain the *string* (and will not prompt you to view an item)?

    ○   A.   -a
    ○   B.   -k
    ○   C.   -K
    ○   D.   -f

13. Select the name of the statement and variable that can be used to specify the order in which man page files are displayed when the man command is run.

    ○   A.   MANPATH
    ○   B.   SECTMAN
    ○   C.   MANCONFIG
    ○   D.   MANSECT

14. You have been reading some documentation at a web site about a program that you have installed named Anjuta (the binary name is anjuta). The documentation for this program is in more than one manx directory. The documentation says "see the man page for more information".

    Which command should you run so that you can quickly see a list of all man pages for the anjuta command (without being prompted to view the man pages)?

    ○   A.   man -f anjuta
    ○   B.   manpage -k anjuta
    ○   C.   man anjuta
    ○   D.   anjuta man

15. Using the man command with the -f option is the same as using the whatis command. T F

---

16. Which option of the man command can be used with a with a *string* (that can be a *filename*) to **list** man pages that match the *string*? This option will cause the man command to prompt you to respond with y, n or q.

   - ○ A. -a
   - ○ B. -k
   - ○ C. -K
   - ○ D. -f

17. Which command can be used to see "behind the scenes" in a man page?

   - ○ A. cat
   - ○ B. zless
   - ○ C. display
   - ○ D. less

18. What is the path to the parent directory of the documentation files that are often installed when a package is installed?

   - ○ A. /etc
   - ○ B. /binary/doc/readme
   - ○ C. /home/doc
   - ○ D. /usr/share/doc

Chapter 8: The VIM (Vi IMproved) Editor

During this chapter, you will learn about Linux text files, text editors and the use of the very popular vi editor.

The vi editor works in two "modes". You will see how to change between these modes and the tasks that can be done in each mode.

The vi editor also has several command-line commands. These commands are detailed along with the methods of using them.

You can run Linux commands and scripts from within the vi editor without having to exit out of it. This allows you to run commands to see information, such as get a directory listing, and it also allows you to test the changes that you have made to a file, such as a configuration file or script file.

The vi editor allows you to undo its commands, such as a command that has deleted text. It also allows you to redo commands if you change your mind. You can also delete (cut) and "put" (paste) text and this allows you to copy and move text from one location to another.

The following command is described in the chapter and is also used in the Hands-On Exercises:

vi   run the vi editor

During the Hands-On Exercises you will create a text file, use various keys to move around in the text, delete text and "put" text. You will also run commands from within the vi editor.

The VIM (Vi IMproved) Editor

Topics Covered in this Chapter

Discuss Linux text files and the benefits of the vi editor
Learn the difference between Normal mode and Insert mode
Describe changing from Normal mode to Insert Mode
Learn the use and purpose of command-line vi commands
Discover how to run Linux commands and scripts from within vi
Explain how to undo and redo commands and delete, put and copy text
Discuss methods of using shortcuts with commands
Detail the commonly used vi keys and commands

In this chapter, you will learn about Linux text files and various methods of using the vi editor. You will also discover how to change between the two "modes" used with this editor and how to use common command-line vi commands. You will also learn how to run Linux commands and scripts from within this editor.

During the Hands-On Exercises you will create a text file, enter text, use various keys to move around in the text and delete and "put" text.

Linux Text Files and the vi Editor

Linux is built on text and runs on text. The source code of programs, the script files that do system tasks, and the configuration files that specify system settings are all text. Therefore, you need a good text editor to view and edit these text files.

There are many text-based and GUI editors that can be used with Linux. The most commonly used editor for system administration tasks is the text-based VIM (Vi IMproved) editor. This editor is a revision of the earlier **vi** (**visual**) editor and is run with the command: vi or with the command: vi *filename* (replace *filename* with the name of the file that you need to edit). In addition to being called "VIM", this editor is also commonly referred to as "the vi editor". The reasons for the popularity of vi are described below.

With some Linux distributions, the vi editor is the only editor available when you boot a system into rescue mode to do steps to repair a system, such as edit and modify scripts and configuration files. This is due to its small requirement of disk space and memory. Being a text-based editor, it does not require the GUI environment of X. It can be run on a Linux system under any circumstances, such as at the console of a server (a virtual terminal) or while accessing another system remotely, such as via the ssh utility.

The vi editor allows you to execute Linux commands and scripts from within it. You can modify and save a script or configuration file; *stay "in" the editor* and run a command or script to test a modification that you just made. If the modification didn't work, you can continue to edit the file without having to run vi again.

By default, some Linux utilities use the vi editor from within them, to edit the configuration files that are used by the utilities. You can do some steps to change the default editor used by these utilities, but if you know how to use vi, then you don't need to!

The vi editor is an extremely powerful and flexible editor that has specific features that make it easier to create and edit the source code of programs, edit html files and work with multiple text files. However, it is not the easiest editor in the world to use.

Starting the vi Editor

To run the vi editor and start a new file, run: vi and press Enter.

To run the vi editor and open an existing file run: vi [path]*filename* and replace [path] with the path to the file and *filename* with the name of an existing file.

Normal Mode and Insert Mode

Unlike many other editors, by default the vi editor does not have menus from which you can select commands. It has the following two basic modes that are used to do tasks: Normal mode (a.k.a. Command mode) and Insert mode (a.k.a. Edit mode).

The documentation provided with the vi editor, such as its help system and tutorial, uses the term "Normal mode" and some other Linux documentation uses the term "Command mode" rather than "Normal mode". The same is true of the terms "Insert mode" and "Edit mode", respectively.

We will use the terms "Normal mode" and "Insert mode" rather than "Command mode" and "Edit mode", respectively.

Normal mode is used do things like move around in text, search for text and delete text. In this mode you can also run: "command-line vi commands", Linux commands and scripts. Command-line vi commands are preceded with a : (colon) and Linux commands and scripts are preceded with :! (a colon followed by an exclamation mark).

Insert mode is only used to edit (add and remove) text. It is not used to run commands.

Changing from Normal mode to Insert Mode

When you start the vi editor you are in "Normal mode". To change into "Insert mode" you type: i or press the Insert key. To change back into "Normal mode" you press the Esc key.

Using Command-Line vi Commands

The "command-line vi commands" are only run in Normal mode and they are *not* Linux commands or scripts. Many of these commands begin with a letter and some begin with the letters: w, q, d, u and p.

Commands that begin with:	Are used to:
w	write (save) a file
q	quit out of the program
d	delete text
u	undo changes
p	put (paste) text

The vi documentation uses the term "put" rather than "paste" to refer to "putting" text that you have deleted back into a file. To cut and paste text, you delete it and then "put" it.

Command-line vi commands are preceded by a : (colon). To run "command-line vi commands" in Normal mode, such as commands that begin with w, q, d, u and p, you type a : (colon) followed by the text required to run the command. If you are in Insert mode, you must press Esc to go into Normal mode before running command-line vi commands (or Linux commands or scripts).

Running a Command-Line vi Command

To run a command-line vi command in Normal mode, you type a : (colon), a letter that is used to start the command (such as w, q, d, u or p), and then the remaining text that is used to run the command.

For example, you have created a new file and are in Insert mode. Now you need to do the following to save the text that you have typed in:

> Press Esc (to go into Normal mode) ;
>
> type a ":" (hold down Shift and press ";" to get a colon) ;
>
> type a "**w**" and a space (this is a "**w**rite" (save) command) ;
>
> type in the name of the file and press Enter.

In this course, we are using a ; (semicolon) to separate items when describing commands. The semicolons shown below are not part of a command, they are used to *separate* the steps in a series of steps. All of the above steps can be shown as:

> Press Esc ; :w *filename* ; press Enter.

Running a Linux Command or Script

To run a Linux command or script in Normal mode, you type a : (colon) and then an ! (exclamation mark) followed by the text required to run the command.

For example, if you are in Normal mode and want to run a Linux command or script, do the following:

> Type a ":" to indicate the start of some type of command ;
>
> type an "!" to run a Linux command or script ;
>
> type in the name of a Linux command or script file (with or without options) ;
>
> press Enter.

For example, in Normal mode you type: :!ls to run the **ls** (list files) command and see a listing of files in the current directory.

After running a Linux command or script file, you will see the output of the command or script file and the system will "pause" until you press Enter to go back into the vi program.

If you need to run an executable file that is not in a directory in the PATH, then the name of the file must be preceded by the path to the file.

For example, a binary named greatprog is located in /home/cwest and the path of /home/cwest is not in the PATH. The path to the binary name of greatprog must be preceded by the path of /home/cwest. The path used to run the binary is: /home/cwest/greatprog.

To run the greatprog binary from within vi, you type in: :!/home/cwest/greatprog and press Enter. A . (dot) is not required between the ! (exclamation mark) and the path because the binary is not in the current directory.

The path to an executable must be specified *even if the file is in the current directory*. When the file is in the current directory, the executable is preceded by "./" (a dot and a slash). The . (dot) represents the current directory and the / (slash) is used to separate the directory (the . (dot)) from the file name of the executable.

If a / (slash) is not used between the . (dot) and the executable file name, then you are specifying the name of a hidden file (i.e. a . (dot) is immediately followed an executable file name appears to the system as a hidden file). A space can also be used to separate the . (dot) from the filename, but a / (slash) is commonly used and is commonly shown in documentation.

For example, you are logged in as cwest and are "in" your home directory (/home/cwest). You have compiled a program and created a binary named hello in your home directory, which is not in the PATH.

To run the hello program from the shell prompt, you type in: ./hello and press Enter.

To run the hello program from within the vi editor, you type in: :!./hello and press Enter.

To continue the example, you have used the su command to log in as root and you are in the /root directory. You have used the vi editor to create a script file named listit. You have saved the file and are still "in" the vi editor. You want to try to run the script before exiting out of the editor. This will allow you to quickly change the script (if it does not work correctly), without having to run the editor and load the file again.

You are "in" the /root directory and the script named listit is in /root. To run the script named listit, you type in: :!./listit and press Enter.

If you move the hello program or listit script to any directory that is in the PATH, then you do not need to type the path to the file prior to the file name, in order to be able to run the program or script. You will be able to run the program or script from any directory.

All of the commands that you have used in this course so far have been files in directories that are in the PATH (such as the /bin, /sbin, /usr/bin and /usr/sbin directories). The PATH is described in more detail in the next chapter.

Undoing and Redoing the Deletion of Text

In Normal mode, typing: u   causes the editor to undo your last change to the text in the file. This does not undo a previous vi command, or the effect of running a Linux command or script. If you continue to press: u   then each time that you do, a previous change is also undone. You can press: Ctrl+r   to redo something that you have undone.

Deleting, Putting and Copying Text

The dd command deletes the current line (the line that your cursor is on). The dw command deletes the current word.

To delete and put text (cut and paste text):

delete it with dd or dw ; move to the location in which the text should be "put" ;

type: p   and the deleted text will be "put" (pasted) at the destination.

When you use the **dw** (**d**elete **w**ord) command, it actually deletes from the current cursor location up to the next space. Therefore, to delete a complete word, position your cursor on the first letter of the word.

When you use: p   (a lower case "p") to "put" a *word* that was deleted with dw in front of a word, move to the *space in front of the destination*, rather than on the first letter of the destination.

When you use: p   (a lower case "p") to "put" a deleted *line* of text, it is put below the current cursor location.

If you use an upper case "P" to "put" a deleted word, you can put your cursor on the first character of a word and the deleted word will be put in front of the word with a space after it. You may find it easier to use an upper case "P" to "put" a deleted word.

To copy text:

delete it with dd or dw ; use: u   to undo the deletion ;

move to the destination and type: p   to "put" the text.

Using Shortcuts with Commands

After typing a : (colon) when in Normal mode, pressing the Up and Down Arrow keys allows you to scroll through previously typed commands.

After typing a : (colon) and the text required to specify a vi command, the Tab key can be used for "command completion", such as to specify a directory path when using the "**w**" ("**write**") command to save a file.

For example, typing: :w /e and pressing Tab completes the name of the etc directory. Another directory can then be specified if necessary and then the name of the file to be used for "writing" (saving) the file.

After typing: :! and the text required to specify the name of a Linux command, the Tab key can be used for "command completion", such as to specify a path at the right of the ls command. The Tab key can be used to specify a path to complete a command, but it cannot be used to complete the *name* of a command.

For example, typing: :!ls /e and pressing Tab completes the name of the /etc directory path.

To continue the example, typing: :!hist and pressing Tab does not complete the name of the history command.

When you are in Insert mode, the Home, End, Page Up, Page Down, Delete and arrow cursor keys work in vi the same as they do in "standard" word processors.

The Commonly Used vi (VIM) Keys and Commands

Table 8-1 is a Summary of Commonly Used vi (VIM) Keys and Commands. The first three items in this Table show the commands to move from Normal mode to Insert mode and vice versa. You do not need to press Enter after typing these commands.

Table 8-1 also shows the commands that can be run when you are in Normal mode. Commands are not run when you are in Insert mode. Press Enter after typing any commands that begin with a : (colon) (including Linux commands and scripts that are specified after typing: :!). You do not need to press Enter after typing commands that do not begin with a : (colon), except when using the / (slash) key to search for text.

For example, the :wq command begins with a : (colon) and the */text* command begins with a / (slash). You must press Enter after typing these types of commands.

To continue the example, the dd command does not begin with a : (colon) and you do not need to press Enter after doing this command.

Table 8-1 Summary of Commonly Used vi (VIM) Keys and Commands

Keys	Command Description
i	change from Normal mode into Insert mode
Insert	press the Insert key to do the same as above
Esc	change from Insert mode into Normal mode
:w *filename*	write (save) the current text and assign it a *filename*
:w	write (save) changes to a file that has been previously saved
:wq	write (save) to a file that has been assigned a name and quit
ZZ	a slightly faster method of doing the :wq command
:q	quit, when no changes need to be saved
:q!	quit without saving your changes
:!*command*	replace *command* with the name of a binary or script file to run a binary or script file put ./ between the ! and *command* if the file is not in a directory that is in the PATH
Ctrl+g	displays: filename, total number of lines in the file, the percentage (as "%age") down the file at the current cursor location and the current line number and column number
w	move forward one word
b	move backward one word
G	go to the last line in the file
1G	go to the first line in the file
*n*G	replace *n* with a number - go to the line number in the file line numbers do not need to be displayed to do this
:set **nu**	display line **nu**mbers at the left of the screen
:*n*	replace *n* with a line number to go to line number *n* line numbers do not need to be displayed to do this
dw	deletes the word at your current cursor location
*n*dw	replace *n* with a number - delete *n* words, one after the other
dd	deletes the line of text at your current cursor location
*n*dd	replace *n* with a number - delete *n* lines, the current line and downwards
p	put text deleted with dw at the *right* of the current cursor location put text deleted with dd *below* the current cursor location
P	put text deleted with dw at the *left* of the current cursor location put text deleted with dd *above* the current cursor location
u	undo your last change to the text in the file
U	undo all of the changes to a line of text
Ctrl+r	redo a change that you had undone

Table 8-1 Summary of Commonly Used vi (VIM) Keys and Commands - Continued

Keys	Command Description
/*text*	searches forward for the *text* that you specify type: n to go forward to the next occurrence of the text type: N to go to the previous occurrence of the text
?*text*	searches backward for the *text* that you specify type: n to go backward to the next occurrence of the text type: N to go to the previous occurrence of the text
:help	get help information on vi type: :q to get out of help

In addition to the above vi commands there are many other commands and capabilities of this program. To do a vi tutorial, run: vimtutor   at the command line.

Hands-On Exercises

 Using the vi Editor to Type Text Into a File

Open a terminal emulation window and maximize it.

```
]# vi                # the opening screen of the VIM - Vi IMproved
                     # editor appears
```

Type in: i or press the Insert key to go into Insert mode (a.k.a. Edit mode) ;

Notice that "-- INSERT --" appears at the bottom left.

Type in the following text, but do not type in text that appears at the right of the # (number) symbol or the # symbol itself) in the steps below. When you start typing, the text of the opening screen will disappear.

this is not the third line	# press Enter
this will become the first line	# type in some more text and press Enter
this is the number line	# type in another line of text and # press Enter
this is the line fourth	# type in another line of text and # press Enter

 Changing to Normal Mode and Saving the File

Press the Esc key to go out of Insert mode and into Normal mode (a.k.a. Command mode). Notice that "-- INSERT --" disappears from the bottom of the screen.

In the step below, type a ":", a "w" for "write", a space and the filename of sample.txt.

```
:w  sample.txt  ; press Enter
```

This writes (saves) the current file as "sample.txt" and now the name of the file appears at the bottom of the window.

---

③ Moving Around in the File

1G	# type "1" and an upper-case "G" to go to the top line of the file
G	# type an upper-case "G" to go to the end of the file
1G	# go to the top again

press: w (to move forward one word) a few times and put your cursor on the "t" in "third".

④ Deleting and Undoing the Deletion of Text

dw	# use the dw command to delete the word "third".
u	# type a "u" to undo the above command.

Press: b a few times to put your cursor on the "n" in "not".

Use the dw command to delete the word "not" in the first line of text.

⑤ Deleting and Putting Text to Move Text

Notice that the top line has the word "third" in it.

Use the dd command to delete the top line ;

move your cursor down one line ;

press: p to "put" (paste) the deleted line below the current line.

This puts the deleted ("third") line below the second line and *also moves the cursor onto the line that was just "put"* (the "third" line).

⑥ Deleting Text, Adding Text and Moving Around

Use the dw command to delete the word "number".

Go into Insert mode and type in the word "second" and a space.

Press the key that is used to change from Insert mode to Normal mode and look at the bottom of the terminal emulation window.

Press Ctrl+g to see the name of your file, total number of lines, and other information at the bottom of the screen. The two numbers at the bottom right (separated by a , (comma)) are the line number and then the column number. Watch these numbers change as you do the next few steps.

Press Home to go to the beginning of the line ; now move to the line that contains the word "fourth".

Press w a few times to move forward one word at a time.

Press End and then press b a few times to move backward one word at a time.

Use the dw command to delete the word "fourth" ; on the same line, move your cursor to the space *in front of* the word "line" ; press   p   to put the word "fourth" in front of the word "line" ;

Go into insert mode ; put a space between "fourth" and "line".

 Saving Your Changes to the File

Go into Normal mode ;

:w   # run the write command to save your changes

The above command saves the file with its current name.

8 **Adding Line Numbers On the Screen**

The command below will cause the editor to display line numbers at the left each line of text. These numbers are not saved with the file and will not appear when the file is opened later, until you run this command again.

Line numbers can be referred to when describing a file to someone, such as in a classroom environment. They can also be used so that you can easily go back to a line number quickly (by using the vi command: *n*G and replacing *n* with a number), after moving to somewhere else in the file. This is particularly useful in long text files so that you can return quickly to a specific line that may be hundreds of lines away!

Line numbers do not need to be displayed to use: *n*G to go to a line number.

:set nu   # add line numbers to the file

3G   # go to line number 3

1G   # go to line number 1

⑨ Deleting, Undoing and Searching for Text

Move your cursor to the first character of the second word on the second line.

2dw	# this deletes two words, one after the other
u	# undo the last change
3dd	# this deletes three lines - the current line and the # two lines below
u	# undo the last change
1G	# go to the top line of the file
/the	# search for the word "the" - your (flashing) cursor # moves to the beginning of the first match
n	# type: n to go to the next occurrence of "the"
n	# type: n again to go to the next occurrence of "the"
N	# type: N to go to the previous occurrence of "the"

⑩ Running Commands from Within the vi Editor

:!clear	# use: :! to run the clear command # the screen "pauses" until you press Enter
Press Enter.	
:!ls -l sa*	# use: :! to run the command: ls -la sa*

The sample.txt file that you have been working on should appear. The screen "pauses" until you press Enter.

Press Enter.

ZZ	# write (save) and quit out of vi # this is the same as doing: :!wq
cat sample.txt	# the contents of your first text file appear!

Section Review

1. In vi, you have used the dd command to delete a line of text. You are still in Normal mode. Which of the following will allow you to insert the deleted line of text above the current cursor location?

    - ○ A. i
    - ○ B. :!p
    - ○ C. p
    - ○ D. none of the above

2. You have run the vi editor and are in Insert mode. You need to see a long listing of the files in the /etc directory that begin with the letters "in". Which of the following will do this for you?

    - ○ A. :!ls -l /etc/in*
    - ○ B. press Tab ; :!ls -l /in*
    - ○ C. press Esc ; :!ls -l /etc/in*
    - ○ D. press Esc ; :qls -l /in*

3. Select the item that will allow you to search for the text of: network in the file that is in the vi editor. You are currently in Normal mode.

    - ○ A. /network
    - ○ B. /:network
    - ○ C. \network
    - ○ D. /:s network

4. Which of the following are correct statements regarding the vi editor (choose three)?

    - ☐ A. it only requires a small amount of disk space and memory
    - ☐ B. it can be used to search for text within a file
    - ☐ C. it allows you to execute commands from within it
    - ☐ D. it uses an automatic spelling checker

5. You are using the vi editor and have saved the text that you have entered in a file named dataset.txt. You go into Insert mode and make some more changes to the file. Which of the following is the most efficient method of saving the file?

    - ○ A. press Esc ; :w
    - ○ B. :w
    - ○ C. press Esc ; :w dataset.txt
    - ○ D. press Esc ; :!w

6. You have run the vi editor and retrieved a large configuration (text) file, which is over 200 lines long. You then run the command that puts line numbers beside each line of text. From working in this file earlier, you remember that the text that you need to edit is near the 144th line. You are currently at the top of the file. Rather than pressing Page Down several times to get to the desired location in the file, or searching for the text to edit, you use the following command:

   - ○ A. Go 144
   - ○ B. 144G
   - ○ C. 144g
   - ○ D. 144 Go

7. You are using vi, are in Normal mode, and want to delete the current line. Select item below that will allow you to do this.

   - ○ A. press Esc ; dd
   - ○ B. type: i ; dd
   - ○ C. :!dd
   - ○ D. dd

8. You have run the vi editor, are in Normal mode, and want to have numbers appear at the left of each line of text. Select the command that will do this for you.

   - ○ A. :set nu
   - ○ B. press Esc ; set nu
   - ○ C. nu set
   - ○ D. :put numb

9. A file named listit exists on your system. You have run: vi listit and modified a file. You then decide that you don't need the changes that you have made. Select the command that is used to quit vi without saving your changes.

   - ○ A. :!q
   - ○ B. :q!
   - ○ C. :Esc
   - ○ D. :q

Chapter 9: Understanding the PATH and Shell Configuration Files

During this chapter you will see the purpose of the PATH environment variable, and view the directory paths in it so that you can understand the reasons for them. All of the directory paths in the default PATH for the root user and non-root users are described in detail.

You will learn how to run binary and script files that are not in a directory that is in the PATH. You will also learn the difference between executables and builtin commands and how these relate to the PATH.

You will get an overview of all of the shell configuration files and the way in which they are processed. This includes the hidden bash configuration files and other bash configuration files.

The following commands are described in this chapter and are also used in the Hands-On Exercises:

alias	assign a string to a command
unalias	remove all aliases or a single alias
which	display the settings for an alias and the path to an executable

During the Hands-On Exercises, you will remove all directory paths in the PATH and then see what is required to execute programs that are not in the PATH. You will also view all of the shell configuration files, modify some shell configuration files, view alias settings, create temporary aliases, remove aliases and create permanent aliases in two locations.

Understanding the PATH and Shell Configuration Files

Topics Covered in this Chapter

Understand the PATH environment variable and the settings in it
Learn how to run binary and script files that are not in the PATH
Discuss the difference between executables and builtin commands
Get an overview of all shell configuration files and the processing of them
Learn the use and purpose of the alias, unalias and which commands
Do the steps to modify the PATH, view and modify shell configuration files,
and add temporary and permanent aliases

In this chapter, you will learn about the directory paths in the PATH, how to run executables that are in various locations, look at the contents of all of the shell configuration files and run commands that are related to the PATH and the shell configuration files.

The Bash Shell

The **bash** (**B**ourne **A**gain **Sh**ell) is the default shell for most Linux distributions. This chapter describes the PATH variable and shell configuration files that are used by the bash shell (for the distribution included with this book).

Other shells, such as the Korn shell and the C shell, are similar in the way that the PATH variable and shell configuration files work for them, but they are not the same.

The PATH Environment Variable

The PATH environment variable is an essential component of the shell. It is used to specify one or more directory paths that are searched when you run a command.

The PATH is searched by the shell to locate an executable file, so that it can be run *from any directory*. This allows you to run an executable without having to: change into the directory that contains the command, or specify the full path to the executable.

For example, if the PATH variable *did not exist* and you were in /home/cwest and wanted to run the ls command (in /bin), you would need to do either of the following to run this command:

```
cd  /bin ; ls        # change into /bin and run ls

        or

/bin/ls              # specify the full path to ls to run ls
```

However, when /bin is in the PATH and you run the ls command, the shell searches the directory paths in the PATH, finds /bin in the PATH, searches /bin for the ls executable and executes it.

The word "PATH" (in upper case) is being used to represent the PATH environment variable, which consists of one or more directory "paths". There are usually many directory paths in the PATH (variable) and each one is separated by a : (colon).

The words "*directory path*" (with "path" in lower case) are being used to represent a path that consists of one or more directories in a path.

For example, /bin is a "*directory path*" that represents the path to the bin directory below the / (root) directory (/bin). This directory path (/bin) is one of the directory path**s** in the PATH.

Do not confuse the path to a directory or file with the PATH (variable name). The path to a directory or file is used to specify the location of a directory or file. The PATH variable contains directory paths that are searched when you try to run an executable (without changing into the directory in which the executable is located, or without specifying the full path to the executable).

Running: echo $PATH shows the settings in the PATH variable (i.e. the directory paths in the PATH). These settings are used by the shell to search for executables (binaries, scripts, symlinks to binaries, and symlinks to scripts). Although symlinks to binaries and symlinks to scripts are just (very small) symlink files and not binary or script files, these symlinks still cause binaries and scripts to be executed. Therefore, we will refer to them as "executables", rather than stating "binaries, scripts, *symlinks to binaries*, and *symlinks to scripts*".

Running Binary and Script Files that are Not In a Directory that is in the PATH

Let's say you create a binary or script file in the current directory, and need to run it from the current directory. However, the current directory is not in the PATH. In this case, you must precede the name of the binary or script file with "./" or specify the full path.

For example, to run a binary or script named hello, which is in the current directory, use the following command:

        ./hello

The . (dot) in "./" represents the current directory and the / (slash) separates the . (dot) from the name of the file that you are trying to run (so that the . (dot) immediately followed by the file name does not appear to the system as a hidden file - as in: .hello).

You do not need to precede the name of a binary or script (that is not in a directory that is in the PATH) with "./" when you run it from a directory that is not your current directory. In this situation, precede the name of the binary or script with the directory path to the file (or change into the directory and precede the file name with "./").

For example, a binary or script named hello is in the /home/userprogs/bin directory path. This directory path is not in the PATH. Your current directory path is /usr/share/doc. To run the hello binary or script, use the full path, as shown in the following command:

/home/userprogs/bin/hello

In the above command, the full path of /home/userprogs/bin/ precedes the binary or script file named hello.

All of the commands that you have run in this course so far have been executables that are in directories that are in the PATH.

Examples of Directories In the PATH

The PATH when you log in as the root user, or "su to root", includes the following directory paths (and some others).

/bin, /sbin, /usr/bin and /usr/sbin

The above directories appear in the PATH with a : (colon) in between each, as shown below.

/bin:/sbin:/usr/bin:/usr/sbin

The ls command (executable) is in /bin; the shutdown command is in /sbin; the eject command is in /usr/bin; and the kudzu command (utility) is in /usr/sbin. When you run the any of these commands, the shell looks in the directory paths in the PATH to try and find the executable file. If the shell finds the file, then it runs the command. If it does not, then an error message appears.

The Default PATH for a Non-root User

The default PATH (directory paths in the PATH environment variable) for a non-root user are:

/usr/local/**bin**:/usr/**bin**:/bin:/usr/X11R6/**bin**:/home/*username*/**bin**

The above PATH consists of five directory *paths*. Each directory path in the PATH is separated from the next directory path by a : (colon).

The directory paths (in the PATH) allow non-root users to run the executable files that are in the directory at the end (far right) of each directory path *from any directory*.

For example, the above PATH contains the directory path of /usr/**bin**. The **bin** directory is at the end of the directory path. This allows users to run executables that are in the **bin** directory at the end of /usr/**bin**. Having /usr/bin in the PATH does not allow users to run executables in /usr, just in /usr/bin. If /usr was in the PATH, *without another directory name at the right of it*, then users would be able to run executables in /usr.

The default PATH for a non-root user is indented three paragarphs above. The text below is a description of the contents of each of the five **bin** directories at the end of each *directory path* in this PATH.

Directory Path	Contents of the Directory at the End of the Path
/usr/local/**bin**	used for binary files that are installed "locally"
/usr/**bin**	essential binary files, such as eject, find, head and info
/**bin**	essential binary files, such as cp, ls and mkdir
/usr/X11R6/**bin**	binary, script and symlink files for X, such as X, XFree86 and startx
/home/*username*/**bin**	used for binary files specific to a user

Below are comments on the /usr/local/bin, /usr/X11R6/bin and /home/*username*/bin directory paths.

The bin Directory at the End of /usr/local/bin

By default, the path of /usr/local/bin exists, but the bin directory at the end of this path does not contain any files. Binary files that should be run "locally" (not across a network) can be installed in this directory.

The bin Directory at the End of /usr/X11R6/bin

This directory contains X software components, such as X, XFree86, startx, xclock and xcalc.

When you start a shell session as a non-root user, the directory path of /usr/X11R6/bin is in the PATH. When you start a shell session as the root user, the path of /usr/bin/X11 is in the PATH (*in addition to the path of* /usr/X11R6/bin).

In the path of /usr/bin/**X11**, the **X11** is a symlink file that points to the bin directory below /usr/X11R6. Therefore, the path of /usr/bin/X11 is simply a symlink to the path of /usr/X11R6/bin. X software components are actually located in the bin directory below /usr/X11R6 and not the X11 directory below /usr/bin.

The directory paths of /usr/bin/X11 and /usr/X11R6/bin (in the PATH) provide users with access to X executable files in /usr/X11R6/bin, such as: the X symlink file that points to the XFree86 binary, the startx script and the X GUI utilities, such as xclock and xcalc.

XFree86 is the X server binary, the startx script is used to start the X server (run the XFree86 binary), xclock displays an analog clock and xcalc displays a calculator.

For example, if you are logged in to a virtual terminal (as the root user or a non-root user) and X (a desktop) is not running, the command **startx** will **start X** and the default desktop will appear. The paths to

/usr/X11R6/bin and /usr/bin/X11 allow you to run the startx script and other X executable files from any directory.

For example, if you are at a virtual terminal and need to start X to be able to use a desktop, you can run the startx script from any directory.

The bin Directory at the End of /home/*username*/bin

A home directory for a user is automatically created when you create a user. This creates the path of /home/*username*.

By default, a bin directory is *not* created below /home/*username*, *even though the path of /home/username/bin is in the PATH.* However, you can create a bin directory below a home directory and put the executables in it that should only be run by the user. This directory can be used for executables that only a single user requires.

When the settings (directory paths) in the PATH variable are viewed while logged in as cwest, then the path to the bin directory below the home directory of the cwest user is /home/cwest/bin. If the PATH were viewed while logged in as the bford user, then the path would be /home/bford/bin, rather than /home/cwest/bin.

The Default PATH When You Log In As root or "su to root"

The default PATH when you log in as root or "su to root" contains all of the directory paths that are in the default PATH for a user (the directory paths described above) and *also includes some others*.

The default PATH when you "su to root" is the same as the default PATH when you log in as root, except that when you "su to root", there is one additional directory path in the PATH (/usr/bin/X11). The other directory paths in the two PATHs (indented) below are the same, but in a different order.

The directory path at the far right of each of the PATHs shown below is /root/bin. The bin directory below /root is in the PATH for the same purpose as the bin directory below /home/*username*, as described above. As with each non-root user, the bin directory below /root was also not created by default when the root user was created (during the installation).

The default PATH when you "su to root" is shown below. It contains nine directory paths.

/bin:/sbin:/usr/bin:/usr/sbin:/usr/local/bin:/usr/local/sbin:**/usr/bin/X11**:/usr/X11R6/bin:/root/bin

The default PATH when you log in as root is shown below. It contains eight directory paths.

/usr/local/sbin:/usr/local/bin:/sbin:/bin:/usr/sbin:/usr/bin:/usr/X11R6/bin:/root/bin

Below is a description of the contents of the directory at the end of each directory path in the PATHs (indented) above, excluding the directory paths that are also in the PATH for a non-root user, which were described earlier.

Directory Path	Contents of the Directory at the End of the Path
/sbin	essential superuser binary files, such as fdisk, halt and mkfs
/usr/sbin	essential superuser binary files, such as groupadd, kudzu and useradd
/usr/local/sbin	used for superuser binary files that are installed "locally"
/usr/bin/X11	the X11 directory is a symlink to the bin directory below /usr/X11R6 (/usr/X11R6/bin), therefore, /usr/bin/X11 is a symlink that points to /usr/X11R6/bin the /usr/X11R6/bin directory path was described above

Below are comments on the above directory paths.

The sbin Directories

The "s" in the directory paths of /sbin, /usr/sbin and /usr/local/sbin above stands for superuser (the root user). These directories contain commands that are only required by the superuser (a.k.a. an administrative user).

The sbin Directory at the End of /usr/local/sbin

By default, the path of /usr/local/sbin exists, but the sbin directory (in the path of /usr/local/sbin) does not contain any files. Superuser binary files that should be run "locally" (not across a network) can be installed in this directory.

The X11 Directory at the End of /usr/bin/X11

As described for non-root users earlier, the X11 directory at the end of the path of /usr/bin/X11 is actually a symlink file that points to the bin directory in the path of /usr/X11R6/bin, which contains X software components, such as X, XFree86, startx, xclock and xcalc.

The /usr/bin/X11 directory path is in the PATH when you "su to root", but not when you log in as root.

The directory paths in the PATH for a non-root user, for the root user, and for when you su to root, will be very similar from one distribution to another, but will not likely be identical.

The PATH and Builtin Commands

Builtin commands can be run from any directory, regardless of the settings (directory paths) in the PATH because they are "built in" to the shell. They are a part of the shell binary file that is in memory. For the bash shell, this is the binary file named bash that is run when you start a "bash shell session" by opening a terminal emulation window or logging in to a virtual terminal.

Overview of the Shell Configuration Files and How They Are Processed

The executable file named bash in /bin causes the statements in the following configuration files (a.k.a. startup files) to be processed when a bash shell session is started:

```
/etc/profile
/etc/profile.d/*.sh files - these are files ending in .sh in the path of /etc/profile.d
~/.bash_profile
~/.bashrc
/etc/bashrc
~/.bash_history
```

Programming code in the bash executable file causes the statements in the /etc/profile file to be processed.

Statements in /etc/profile cause the statements in the files ending in .sh in the path of /etc/profile.d (/etc/profile.d/*.sh) to be processed.

When ~/.bash_profile is processed, statements in it cause ~/.bashrc to be processed.

Statements in ~/.bashrc cause the statements in /etc/bashrc to be processed.

The statements in ~/.bash_history (previous commands) are loaded into memory when a shell session starts so that they will appear when you run the history command.

When a shell session is ended, the statements in ~/.bash_logout are processed.

The Hidden Bash Configuration Files

The hidden bash configuration files are all prefixed with ".bash". These files are .bashrc, .bash_profile, .bash_history and .bash_logout and they are all located in the home directory of each user. Statements in these files are specific to a user and configure the shell environment for the user, as opposed to configuring the shell environment for all users.

When a ~ (tilde) is shown in the path of to a hidden bash configuration file, such as in the path of ~/.bashrc, it represents the home directory of any user.

The Shell Configuration Files

The purpose of each shell configuration file is described below. You will see the contents of each of these files during the Hands-On Exercises.

/etc/profile

Statements in this file create the PATH (specify the directory paths in the PATH variable) for all users and add additional directory paths to the PATH for the root user.

Some statements in this file assign values to several other variables, such as USER, HOSTNAME and HISTSIZE.

Some other statements in this file cause the .sh files in /etc/profile.d to be processed.

The .sh Files in /etc/profile.d

Among other things, the statements in the .sh files in /etc/profile.d cause the aliases named ll, l., ls, vi and which to be created.

 An **alias** is created by assigning a name (string of characters) to one or more commands, including options of the command. When the name of the alias is "run", the command(s) and options are run.

For example, if an alias named lsl is assigned "ls -la | less", then typing lsl and pressing Enter runs: ls -la | less (the ls and less commands).

The colorls.sh file in /etc/profile.d creates the aliases named ll, l. and ls. The vim.sh file in /etc/profile.d creates the alias named vi. The which-2.sh file in /etc/profile.d creates the alias for the which command.

To add an alias or function to the system for all users, create a file ending in .sh in /etc/profile.d and put the required statements in the file.

The ~/.bash_profile Configuration File

Statements in /etc/profile causes the statements in the .sh files to be processed. The statements in .bash_profile are processed after the statements in the .sh files in /etc/profile.d.

Statements in .bash_profile cause the statements in ~/.bashrc to be processed.

The .bash_profile file for a non-root user is slightly different from the .bash_profile file for a root user.

The bash configuration files do not contain line numbers at the left of each statement. Line numbers have been added to the left of each statement below with the nl command so that we can easily refer to each line.

The .bash_profile file for a Non-root User

The .bash_profile file for a non-root user contains the following statements:

```
1       # .bash_profile
2       # Get the aliases and functions
3       if [ -f ~/.bashrc ]; then
4              . ~/.bashrc
5       fi
6       # User specific environment and startup programs
7       PATH=$PATH:$HOME/bin
8       export  PATH
9       unset  USERNAME
```

Line 1 is a comment that identifies the file name.

Line 2 describes lines 3 through 5.

Line 3 is the beginning of an "if statement" and line 5 is the ending of the "if statement". Line 5 shows the letters "if" backwards to indicate the end of the "if statement" (fi).

Line 3 checks to see if a .bashrc file exists in the home directory of the user (represented by the ~ character), and if so, line 4 is processed. If the file does not exist, it is not processed.

Line 4 has a . (dot) and then a space in front of the path to the .bashrc file (~/.bashrc). The . (dot) causes the text in the .bashrc file (in the home directory of the user) to be processed.

Line 6 is a comment that describes lines 7 through 9.

Line 7 is the following statement: PATH=$PATH:$HOME/bin

This statement modifies the existing PATH by using PATH=. It adds the bin directory, below the home directory of a user ($HOME/bin), to the PATH.

The "$HOME/bin" part of the statement represents the path to the bin directory below home directory. For the root user, this path becomes /root/bin and for the cwest user, this path becomes /home/cwest/bin.

The "$PATH" part of the statement represents the existing settings (directory paths) in the PATH.

The "PATH=" part of the statement causes the existing PATH (represented by $PATH) to have the directory path represented by "$HOME/bin" to be added to the end of it. Notice the : (colon) between $PATH and $HOME/bin.

When you look at the directory paths in the PATH with a command, such as: echo $PATH the directory path of $HOME/bin appears at the far right of the PATH for all users.

For the root user, the far right directory path in the PATH is /root/bin.

For the cwest user, the far right directory path in the PATH is /home/cwest/bin.

 By default, the bin directory below the home directory of a user does not exist, but you can easily create it. If there is an executable that a user needs access to, you can put it in the bin directory below the home directory of the user.

If you install and program and need to add its directory path to the PATH for a user, you can add it at the right of the PATH statement on line 7 in .bash_profile. Use a : at the end of the existing statement, followed by the new directory path.

Line 8 uses the export command to put the PATH created by the PATH= statement on line 7 into memory. This replaces the previous PATH setting.

Line 9 uses the unset command to "unset" the USERNAME variable.

The .bash_profile file for the root User

The .bash_profile file for the root user contains the following statements:

```
1       # .bash_profile
2       # Get the aliases and functions
3       if [ -f ~/.bashrc ]; then
4              . ~/.bashrc
5       fi
6       # User specific environment and startup programs
7       PATH=$PATH:$HOME/bin
8       BASH_ENV=$HOME/.bashrc
9       USERNAME="root"
10      export  USERNAME  BASH_ENV  PATH
```

Lines 1 through 7 are the same for the root user as for a non-root user.

Line 8 sets the BASH_ENV variable to point to the .bashrc file below the home directory of the user.

Line 9 sets the USERNAME variable to the name of the root user.

Line 10 uses the export command to put the settings for the USERNAME, BASH_ENV and PATH variables, that are created in lines 7 through 9, into memory. This replaces the previous settings for these variables.

The ~/.bashrc Configuration File

The .bashrc file for a non-root user is the same as for the root user, except that for the root user this file contains three statements that create aliases for this user.

This file (for all users) contains a "# User specific aliases and **functions**" comment (heading). Statements for aliases and **functions** that a user requires are put below this comment.

 A **function** is created by assigning a name (string of characters) to two or more commands. The commands that have been assigned to the function are run when the function is run.

By default, non-root users do not have any statements that create aliases or functions below the "# User specific aliases and functions" comment in .bashrc. The root user has three statements that create aliases below this comment. These statements create the aliases named rm, cp and mv for the root user.

If you need to have an alias or function created for an individual user, put the statement for it below the "# User specific aliases and functions" comment in ~/.bashrc.

Statements in ~/.bashrc cause the bashrc file in /etc to be processed. The bashrc file in /etc is not prefixed with a . (dot). It is not a hidden file.

The .bashrc file for a Non-root User

The .bashrc file for a non-root user contains the following statements:

```
1    # .bashrc
2    # User specific aliases and functions
3    # Source global definitions
4    if [ -f /etc/bashrc ]; then
5            . /etc/bashrc
6    fi
```

Line 1 is a comment that identifies the file name.

Line 2 is a comment for text that can be created below this comment. This comment is like a heading for the statements that can appear below it. By default, no text that relates to this comment appears below this comment for a non-root user. However, text appears below this comment for the root user.

Line 3 is a comment for lines 4 through 6.

Line 4 checks to see if a file named bashrc (not .bashrc) exists below /etc, and if so, line 5 is processed, which causes the statements in the /etc/bashrc file to be processed. If the file does not exist, it cannot be processed.

Line 5 has a . (dot) and then a space in front of the path to the bashrc file (/etc/bashrc). The . (dot) causes the text in bashrc to be processed.

The .bashrc file for the root User

The .bashrc file for the root user contains the following statements:

```
1      # .bashrc
2      # User specific aliases and functions
3      alias  rm='rm  -i'
4      alias  cp='cp  -i'
5      alias  mv='mv  -i'
6      # Source global definitions
7      if [  -f /etc/bashrc ];  then
8             .  /etc/bashrc
9      fi
```

Lines 1, 2 and 6 through 9 are the same for the root user as for a non-root user.

Lines 3 through 5 create an aliases named rm, cp and mv, for each of the rm (**rem**ove), cp (**c**o**p**y) and mv (**m**o**v**e) commands, respectively.

The /etc/bashrc Configuration File

As described in the comments at the top of this file, it creates system-wide functions and aliases.

The ~/.bash_history Configuration File

The history command displays the commands in history (i.e. in the history list in memory).

The ~/.bash_history file contains up to 1,000 previously run commands. When you end a bash shell "session", the commands in the history list are saved to the ~/.bash_history file. The next time you start a shell session, the commands in the ~/.bash_history file are put into memory so that they can be accessed by using the Up and Down Arrow keys and the history command.

The ~/.bash_logout Configuration File

When you end a shell session, the .bash_logout file is processed. The .bash_logout file contains the following statements:

```
# ~/.bash_logout
clear
```

The first statement is a comment that describes the name of the file. The ~ represents the home directory (of any user).

The second statement simply causes the clear command to be run to clear the screen.

For example, when you log in as cwest and then run the su command and log in as the root user (at a virtual terminal or in a terminal emulation window), you start a shell session (open a subshell). When you run the exit command to end the shell session, the .bash_logout file is processed and this causes the screen to be cleared (and you are at the prompt for the cwest user, at the top of the screen).

The Settings in the PATH when a Shell Session is Started

The directory paths (for any user) in the PATH, immediately after starting a shell session, are created by the statements in /etc/profile and ~/.bash_profile.

The alias Command

The alias command is used to assign a string to a command. Options of a command, a [path], and a [pattern], can be specified with the command. The string is used to run the command with any options, path and pattern that has been specified.

This allows you to create a "command" (a short string of text) that runs a command with the options, path and pattern that you have specified. Therefore, you do not have to specify these items each time you run the command. This can save a lot of time if you are using the same command with the same options, path, or pattern repeatedly.

For example, the following ls command uses the -l (long), -h (human-readable), -S (Sort) and -r (reverse) options. This will allow you to quickly see large files at the end of the listing.

```
ls -lhSr
```

You may want to run a command like this repeatedly so that you can see the largest files in several directories.

The next command creates an alias using the string (name) of "**lslg**" (**for ls** large) so that you can run the ls command using the -l, -h, -S and -r options quickly.

> alias lslg='ls -lhSr'

Running: lslg will display the contents of the current directory, with the options specified. This is faster than running: ls -lhSr. A [path] and/or [pattern] can be used at the right of this alias.

When you create an alias, use a name for it that is in some way associated with its purpose, but is not too long. Examples are shown below.

The Syntax of the alias Command

The following is the syntax for one of the two forms of the alias command:

> alias [*string*='command [options]']

All of the text in the [ ] (square brackets) at the right of "alias" is optional. The alias command is run without options to see all of the aliases that have been created.

The = (equal sign) assigns the settings for 'command [options]' to the string.

The following is the syntax of the other form of the alias command:

> alias *string*

Above shows the settings of an alias when the string matches the string of an alias name. This is a method of seeing the settings of a single alias.

Examples of the alias Command

Descriptions follow each of the examples below.

alias

Displays the aliases that have been created.

alias cp

Displays the settings of the alias named cp.

alias ls='ls --color=tty'

This creates an alias named ls, which has the same name as the ls command. This alias is currently being used by your system. When you have run the ls command so far, you have actually run the alias to the ls command, which uses the --color=tty option of this command. This option causes the screen output to appear with different colors for various items, such as directories, hidden files and symlinks.

alias ll='ls -l --color=tty'

Assigns the string of "ll" to "ls -l --color=tty". Running the "command": ll causes the ls command to be run with the -l and --color=tty options. The file named colorls.sh in /etc/profile.d contains a statement that automatically creates this alias for all users.

alias l.='ls -d .* --color=tty'

Assigns the string of "l." to "ls -d .* --color=tty". When this alias is run, the -d and --color=tty options of the ls command are used with the pattern of ".*". The file named colorls.sh in /etc/profile.d contains a statement that automatically creates this alias for all users.

alias rm='rm -i'

This creates an alias named rm, which has the same name as the **rm (rem**ove) command. Whenever the rm alias is run, the **-i** (interactive) option of the rm command is used. This alias is automatically created when you log in as root or su to root. It is not automatically created for non-root users.

The **rm (rem**ove) command is used to remove directories and files. The **-i** (interactive) option of the rm command causes the system to prompt you before removing any directories or files. You must type 'y" and press Enter for each item that you want to remove.

When you are working as a non-root user, the rm alias is not automatically created. However, when you are working as the root user, the rm alias with the -i option is automatically created.

The root user has permissions to all directories and files. If this user ran the rm command incorrectly (and the rm alias with the -i option was not being used), all of the files on the system could easily be removed without any prompting.

For example, the following command would erase all of the items below the root, due to the accidental space in the path between the first / (slash) and the rest of the path.

        rm -r / home/cwest/old-files

The **-r (r**ecursive) option is used in the above command. This tells the command to remove all items (subdirectories and files) below the path specified with the command. The command was intended to remove all directories and files below the old-files directory.

However, the shell only "sees" the above command up to the first /, due to the space at the right of it. It runs the command as: rm -r / rather than using the path of: /home/cwest/old-files. The command: rm -r / tells the system to remove all items below the / directory, which is everything!

When working as root and being prompted prior to having this command delete everything provides you with additional protection and allows you to change your mind.

When a user is logged in as a non-root user, the user does not have permissions to all directories and files. The user cannot accidentally delete everything if a mistake is made. Therefore, the user does not automatically have an alias for the rm command that adds the -i option to the command.

In addition to the rm alias, there is also a cp alias and an mv alias for the cp and mv commands, respectively. These aliases are also are automatically created when you log in as root or su to root. These aliases are not automatically created for non-root users. The cp and mv aliases also add the -i (interactive) option to each of these commands.

When you log in as root or su to root your home directory is /root. The .bashrc file in /root contains a comment regarding aliases followed by three statements that set up aliases for the rm, cp and mv commands, as shown below.

```
# User specific aliases and functions
alias rm='rm -i'
alias cp='cp -i'
alias mv='mv -i'
```

The above three statements are not in the .bashrc file for non-root users. Therefore, aliases for rm, cp and mv are not set up by default for non-root users. An error in running the rm, cp or mv command when logged in as a non-root user will not cause as much damage as an error made by the root user.

The unalias Command

The unalias command is used to remove all aliases or a single alias.

The Syntax of the unalias Command

The following is the syntax of the unalias command:

unalias [-a | *aliasname*]

The -a option removes all aliases. Use the -a option or replace *aliasname* with the name of an alias.

Examples of the unalias Command

unalias -a

Removes all aliases that currently exist.

unalias ls

Removes the alias named ls. The default alias for ls uses the --color=tty option of the ls command. This causes the ls command to display output with various colors. Removing this alias stops the ls command from showing output with colors. Colored output can be difficult to read on some types of monitors and also on some overhead display systems, such as those that are used to display computer output on a large screen in a classroom.

The which Command

The which command is used to display the settings for an alias and also the path to an executable. The name of an alias or executable is used at the right of the which command.

Example of the which Command

By default the root user has an alias named rm that is created due to a statement in ~/.bashrc.

The command: which rm provides the output of:

```
    alias rm='rm -i'                    # the alias settings for the alias named
rm
     /bin/rm                            # the location of the rm executable
```

The which command is similar to the whereis command (described earlier), but is not the same. The whereis command displays the path for binary, source code and man page files, but does not show information regarding aliases.

 ## Hands-On Exercises

 ### 1 Logging In To View the PATH and Configuration Files

Log in to a desktop as cwest ;

open a terminal emulation window and maximize it ;

stay logged in as the cwest user.

```
]# echo $PATH          # see the directory paths in the PATH variable
                       # below is the output of the command

     /usr/local/bin:/usr/bin:/bin:/usr/X11R6/bin:/home/cwest/bin
```

All of the directory paths end in with a directory named **bin** and none of the them end in **s**bin (for superuser **bin**aries).

Displaying Binaries in Directories in the PATH

Each of the directory paths in the above PATH (output) are described below, in the order in which they appear.

```
]# ls /usr/local/bin        # by default, there are no files in this directory

]# whereis eject            # shows that eject is in /usr/bin and also shows
                            # the path to eject.1.gx (the man page file for
                            # the eject command)

]# whereis ls               # shows that ls is in /bin
                            # also shows the path to the ls man page

]# whereis X                # shows that X is in /usr/X11R6/bin
                            # X is a symlink to the XFree86 server binary

]# ls /home/cwest/bin       # by default, this bin directory does not exist
```

 Removing the directory paths in the PATH and Trying to Run Commands

```
]# ls -la          # the ls command currently works

]# echo $PATH      # there are currently directory paths in the PATH
                  # notice that the /bin directory path is in the PATH
```

Directory paths are separated from one another by a : (colon). The /bin directory path is the third directory path in the PATH.

```
]# PATH=          # removes all directory paths from the PATH

]# echo $PATH     # there are no longer any settings in the PATH
```

You ran the ls command above. It is in /bin.

```
]# ls -la          # the ls command no longer works
                  # ls is in /bin and /bin is not in the PATH

]# /bin/ls
```

Specifying the full path to ls allows you to run the command from any directory. This is a common method of running an executable if the directory path of the executable is not in the PATH.

```
]# cd /bin ; ls
```

Changing into /bin also allows you to run the ls command.

```
]# cd ~ ; pwd      # the ~ represents the path to the home directory

]# PATH=/bin       # assign the directory path of /bin to the PATH variable

]# echo $PATH      # /bin is now in the PATH, but no other directory paths

]# ls -la          # now you can run programs in /bin
```

```
]# eject cdrom        # an error message appears - eject is in /usr/bin
                      #  and this directory path is not currently in the PATH
]#  PATH=$PATH:/usr/bin
```

This **adds** /usr/bin to the existing PATH (represented by $PATH) and assigns it (by using the = sign) to the variable named PATH. You will see something very similar to this when viewing the .bash_profile file below.

```
]#  echo  $PATH      #  /usr/bin is now also in the PATH

]#  eject  cdrom     #  the command works because /usr/bin is now in
                     #  the PATH
```

Your PATH currently contains two directory paths.

```
]#  exit             #  this ends the shell session and closes the
                     #  terminal emulation window
```

 Starting another Shell Session for the cwest User

Open a terminal emulation window and maximize it ;

run the command to display the settings (directory paths) in the PATH variable.

All of the original directory paths are now back in the PATH.

Starting a shell session by opening the terminal emulation window caused the statements in all of the shell configuration files to be executed. This includes the statements in /etc/profile and ~/.bash_profile that put the directory paths in the PATH.

(5) **Starting a Shell Session for the root User**

Keep the terminal emulation window for the cwest user open. Notice that cwest appears in the border at the top left of the window.

Open another terminal emulation window and maximize it ; su to root ;

```
]#  echo  $PATH      #  the directory paths for the root user appear
                     #  notice the directory paths that end in sbin
```

Alt+Tab to the cwest terminal emulation window. The PATH for cwest does not contain any directories named sbin. Notice the last directory path in the PATH.

The last directory path in the PATH for cwest and root is the path of ~/bin.

Alt+Tab back to the root terminal emulation window.

The PATH for the root user includes all of the directory paths that are available to a non-root user, including the last directory path of ~/bin. Non-root users and the root user have a path to the bin directory below their home directories.

The PATH for the root user also includes three directory paths that end in an sbin directory and a /usr/bin/X11 directory.

```
]# ls -l /usr/bin/X11    # the X11 symlink points to /usr/X11R6/bin
                         # as describe earlier
```

The three directory paths that end in sbin are: /sbin, /usr/sbin and /usr/local/sbin.

```
]# whereis fdisk       # shows that fdisk is in /sbin

]# whereis kudzu       # shows that kudzu is in /usr/sbin

]# ls /usr/local/sbin  # by default, no files are in this directory
```

Binaries for the superuser are kept in directories named sbin.

Now you will start working with aliases.

 6 Viewing the Aliases for root and cwest

Clear the screen.

```
]# alias              # the aliases for the root user appear
```

Alt+Tab to the cwest (terminal emulation) window ; clear the screen ;

```
]# alias              # the aliases for the cwest user appear
```

Non-root users have five aliases, but do not have aliases named cp, mv and rm. Notice the settings of each of the aliases.

Alt+Tab to the root (terminal emulation) window.

The root user has eight aliases. The same five as a non-root user, plus the aliases named cp, mv and rm. Notice that the cp, mv and rm aliases all have the -i option.

7 Using the Alias Named rm

```
]# touch test.txt     # create a file named test.txt

]# rm test.txt        # the -i option of the rm alias causes the prompt
                         # to appear
```

type: y and press Enter.

The -i option of the rm alias protects the root user from accidentally removing directories and files, by prompting prior to deleting an item.

⑧ Running the rm Command as cwest

Alt+Tab to the cwest window ; notice that this user does not have an alias named rm ;

use the touch command to create a file named test.txt as the cwest user ;

remove the test.txt file.

The cwest user is not prompted prior to the file being removed because the rm alias with the -i option does not exist for this user.

⑨ Using the which Command

Alt+Tab to the root window ;

]# which ls

The alias command that created the alias for ls appears. The path to the ls executable also appears.

]# alias ls   # the settings for the ls alias (only) appear

]# which l.

The -d and --color=tty options and the pattern (.*) used by the l. alias appear.

]# l.   # use the l. alias

run the which command again for each of: rm, cp and mv ; all of these aliases use the -i option.

⑩ Removing an Alias

]# which ls   # this alias uses the --color=tty option

]# ls /etc   # on a color monitor, some items appear in color

]# unalias ls   # removes the ls alias

]# alias   # the ls alias no longer appears

]# ls /etc   # all output is now only in black and white

---

(11) Creating an Alias

```
]# alias lslg='ls -lhSr'    # create an alias named lslg

]# alias                    # the lslg alias appears in the list

]# lslg                     # run the ls command with the options
                            # specified in the lslg alias

]# lslg /etc                # use a path with the lslg alias

]# lslg /var/log/mess*      # use a path and pattern with the lslg alias
```

The aliases that you add at the shell prompt are temporary. They only last until the end of the shell session.

```
]# exit                     # end the "su to root session"

su to root ;

]# alias                    # the lslg alias no longer appears in the list
```

(12) Viewing Aliases in .bashrc

```
]# cat .bashrc
```

The .bashrc file in /root contains three alias statements below the "# User specific aliases and functions" comment. These statements create the rm, cp and mv aliases. Each of these aliases causes the -i option of the command to be used with each command.

```
]# cat ~cwest/.bashrc       # ~cwest is used rather than /home/cwest
```

The .bashrc file in ~cwest (the home directory of the cwest user) does not have any alias statements below the "# User specific aliases and functions" comment.

(13) Making an Alias Permanent for the root User

Aliases are typically added below the "# User specific aliases and functions" statement in ~/.bashrc.

The steps below will back up the .bashrc files in /root and ~cwest prior to editing them.

```
]# cp .bashrc .bashrc.bak

Alt+Tab to the cwest window ;
```

Chapter 9: Understanding the PATH and Shell Configuration Files

]# cp .bashrc .bashrc.bak

Alt+Tab to the root window ;

]# vi .bashrc   # run vi to edit the .bashrc file for the root user in /root

press i to go into Insert mode ;

add the following statement on the blank line below the last of the three alias statements in this file:

alias lslg='ls -lhSr'

press Enter to put a blank line after the above statement ;

press Esc to go into Normal mode ;

hold down Shift and type ZZ to save and exit ;

]# cat .bashrc   # your new alias should appear

]# alias   # the lslg alias does not currently exist

You need to start a new shell session for the new alias to be created.

]# exit   # end the "su to root session"

su to root ;

]# alias   # the lslg alias was created by the statement in .bashrc

]# lslg /boot   # test the new alias

(14) Adding the lsla Alias to the cwest User

From the /root directory, run the vi editor and specify the path to the .bashrc file in the home directory of the cwest user.

Remember to press i to go into Insert mode, Esc to go into Normal mode (after editing the file) and use ZZ to save the file and exit.

Add following alias below the "# User specific aliases and functions" comment (after putting a blank line below the comment):

alias hi='history 25'

save the file and exit out of vi ;

"cat out" the .bashrc file that you just edited to see if you made the edit correctly ;

"cat out" the .bashrc file in /root and compare the alias statements in it to the one you just added to the .bashrc file in ~cwest ;

Alt+Tab to the cwest window ; run the alias command.

You need to start a new cwest shell session for the new alias to be created.

]# exit

open a terminal emulation window and maximize it ;

run the alias command ; the hi alias should appear ;

run the alias named hi ; the last 25 commands in the history list appear.

Now you can quickly see the end of the history list so that you can run long commands from it (as described in an earlier chapter) or so that you can see the commands that you have used recently.

The root user has the lslg alias and the cwest user has the hi alias.

Add the alias named hi to the .bashrc file of the root user ;

test the new alias to see that it works ; run some commands from the history list, such as the command to run vi and edit .bashrc in ~cwest.

In a later chapter, you will add an alias to the .bashrc file in /etc/skel so that whenever a new user is created, the alias statement will be in ~/.bashrc for the user. Therefore, each new user that is created will be able to use the alias.

Now you will start looking at the settings in the bash configuration files.

 Seeing the User ID of the Current (root) User

Alt+Tab to the root window ;

change into the /etc directory ;

]# id -u

The -u option of the **id** command causes the user id the current user to appear. The id of the root user is 0 (zero). This value and the id command will be seen in an "if statement" in /etc/profile below.

 Viewing the/etc/profile File

The bash binary causes the statements in the /etc/profile configuration file to be processed.

]# nl profile | less

The comment at the top of the file is the path to the filename you are looking at. The next two comments describe the file.

Lines 4 through 12 create the PATH for all users.

Lines 13 through 18 add directory paths to the PATH for the root user (in addition to the directory paths that were added by lines 4 through 12).

Line 14 uses the id command with the -u option to check to see if the id of the current user is "0". The back quotes around id -u cause the id command to be run with the -u option so that the current user id number can be compared to 0 (with the = 0 part of the statement).

If the id of the current user is 0, then the script continues and adds the paths in statements 15 through 17 to the PATH. Therefore, the root user gets the directory paths (all ending in sbin) that are shown in lines 15 through 17 added to the PATH. Non-root users do not get these directory paths added to the PATH.

Line 19 adds /usr/X11R6/bin to the PATH.

Lines 23 through 27 assign values to several variables.

Line 31 uses the export command "export" (set) the settings for the PATH, USER and other variables to the shell.

Lines 32 through 36 cause the statements in the .sh files in /etc/profile.d to be processed.

 Listing the .sh Files in /etc/profile.d

Change into the profile.d directory below the current directory ;

]# ls -l

The .csh files are used to configure the C Shell. The .sh files are used to configure bash shell.

]# ls -l *.csh   # configuration files for the C Shell

]# ls -l *.sh

As described above, the /etc/profile configuration file causes the *.sh files in this directory to be processed.

 Grepping for "alias" Statements in the .sh Files

]# clear ; alias   # see the current aliases

]# grep alias *.sh   # search for "alias' in all files ending in ".sh"

All of the statements in the .sh files that contain the word "alias" appear. Notice the three filenames of colorls.sh, vim.sh and which-2.sh at the left of the output.

grep alias ~/.bashrc   # search for "alias' in /root/.bashrc

The aliases specific to the root user appear. The .sh files and ~/.bashrc provide the aliases for users.

 Viewing the "alias" Statements in the .sh Files

]# less colorls.sh   # notice the statements that create
                            # the ll, l., and ls aliases

---

use less to look for the alias statement in vim.sh that creates the alias for vi ;

use less to look for the alias statement in which-2.sh that creates the alias for which.

 Listing the Hidden Configuration Files in the Home Directory of the root User

]# cd /root

]# ls -l .bash*

The four hidden bash shell configuration files appear, as well as the .bashrc.bak file that you created earlier when you backed up the .bashrc file.

 Viewing the ~/.bash_profile File

]# nl .bash_profile

Line 1 is a comment that shows the name of the file.

Lines 2 through 5 cause the statements in the ~/.bashrc configuration file to be processed.

Line 6 is a comment that is like a heading for the statements below it.

Line 7 is the statement: PATH=$PATH:$HOME/bin

The "$HOME/bin" part of the statement represents the path to the bin directory below home directory. For the root user, this path becomes /root/bin and for the cwest user, this path becomes /home/cwest/bin.

The "$PATH" part of the statement represents the current settings (directory paths) in the PATH.

The "PATH=" part of the statement causes the existing "$PATH" (variable) to have the directory path represented by "$HOME/bin" to be added to it. Notice the : (colon) between $PATH and $HOME/bin.

For all users, the directory path of $HOME/bin appears at the right of all directory paths in the PATH.

If you install and program and need to add its directory path to the PATH for a user, you can add it at the right of the PATH statement in line 7. Use a : at the end of the above statement followed by the directory path.

Lines 8 and 9 specify settings for the BASH_ENV and USERNAME variables, respectively.

Line 10 exports (out of the script) the (values of the) USERNAME, BASH_ENV and PATH variables.

Viewing the ~/.bashrc File

]# clear ; nl .bashrc

The three statements below the "# Source global definitions" comment cause the statements in /etc/bashrc to be processed.

 Viewing the /etc/bashrc File

]# less /etc/bashrc

Read the three comments at the top of the screen. This file will be described in more detail later.

 Viewing the ~/.bash_history File

]# cat .bash_history

The commands from the last shell session appear. When you started this session, these commands were put in memory so that they could be accessed with the history command.

 Viewing the ~/.bash_logout File

```
]# cat .bash_logout        # the clear command is at the bottom of the file
                           # there is currently text on the screen

]# exit
```

The clear command in ~/.bash_logout causes the screen to be cleared when a bash shell session ends, including when you end an "su to root session" (that is run in a subshell).

Change into the /etc directory.

 Creating a .sh File for an Alias Named lsld

In an earlier chapter, you saw the syntax of three commands that use a ^ (caret) to list directories only, symlinks only and files only.

You want all users to be able to easily run the following command, which provides the output of **ls** using the -l option and shows **directories only (lsld)**. Therefore, you will create a file in /etc/profile.d named lsld.sh that causes an alias named lsld to be created when all users start a shell session.

]# ls -l | grep ^d

Change into the profile.d directory below /etc ;

Run the vi editor and specify the file name of lsld.sh (put the file name on the same line as the vi command to run the editor) ;

go into insert mode and type in the following comment and statement (make the text "flush left" (do not indent it) and put a blank line after the comment):

outputs a long listing of directories only

alias lsld='ls -l | grep ^d'

go into Normal mode ; save the file and exit (it was named when you ran vi with the file name on the same line as the command) ;

"cat out" the lsld.sh file to see if you edited it correctly ;

You need to start a new shell session for the new alias to be created.

]# exit

 ## (27) Testing the lsld Alias

Open a terminal emulation window and maximize it ;

run the alias command without any options ; the lsld alias exists for the cwest user ;

su to root ; run the alias command again ; the lsld alias also exists for the root user ; the .sh files below /etc/profile.d create aliases for all users ;

change into the /usr directory path ;

run the lsld alias to get a listing in the current directory ;

run the alias command and specify the name of the new alias ; the settings for the new alias (only) appear ;

running: lsld is much faster than running: ls -l | grep ^d.

Due to the syntax of the lsld alias, it only works "in" the current directory. It does not work with a path or pattern at the right of the alias name.

If you put a pattern, such as /etc at the right of lsld, then "ls -l | grep ^d" (the command from the lsld alias) will be combined with "/etc" and the shell will "see" the command: ls -l | grep ^d /etc and "/etc" is not an option of the grep command.

(28) Creating an Alias to Show Non-Symlink Files (Only)

Change into the directory in which .sh configuration files are created ;

use vi and create a file named **lslf**.sh (for **ls** long listing of **f**iles) ;

put the following three lines of text in the file:

```
#  outputs a long listing of non-symlink files (only)
#  does not show directory names or symlinks

alias  lslf='ls  -l  |  grep  ^-'
```

"cat out" the file to see that it looks correct.

(29) Creating an Alias to Show Symlinks (Only)

Use vi and create a file named **lsll**.sh (for **ls** long listing of **l**inks) ;

put the following three lines text in the file:

```
#  outputs a long listing of symlink files (only)
#  does not show directory names or non-symlink file names

alias  lsll='ls  -l  |  grep  ^l'
```

"cat out" the file to see that it looks correct ;

exit out of the current subshell ; su to root ;

run the alias command to check that all of the new aliases are there ;

change into the /boot directory path ; clear the screen ;

run the lsld alias and directories (only) should appear ;

run the lslf alias and non-symlink files (only) should appear ;

run the lsll alias and symlink files (only) should appear ;

the contents of the /boot directory now appear in three categories of items!

(30) Staying Logged in for the Section Review

Alt+Tab to the cwest window and run the exit command to close it ;

clear the screen ; you should be in a root user window ;

change to the /root directory ;

stay logged in to test your answers to the following Section Review questions.

Section Review

After each of the following questions, write the answer to the question on the line provided and then run the command to test that you answered the question correctly.

1. Run the alias command to see the syntax of the color option that is used with the alias named ls.

   Write the command to remove the alias named ls and then run this command to test your answer. Always test your answers.

   _____

2. Run the ls command. No colors should appear in the output.

   Write the command to assign the alias name of lslh to the ls command so you will get a long listing in human readable form when the alias is run. Include the --color option (as seen above when you looked at the alias named ls) so that your output with show colors. Run this alias on the /lib directory.

   _____

3. Write the single command to see the settings of the alias named mv and the path to the binary named mv.

   _____

4. You have used su to log in as root and your current directory is /root. Write the command to get a long listing of all of the hidden configuration files (only) in your home directory (and the backup of one of these files).

   _____

5. Select the character that is used to separate directory paths (not directories) in the PATH.

   ○ A. #
   ○ B. :
   ○ C. /
   ○ D. ;

---

6. The default path for the root user (and when you su to root) contains:

    ○ A. directory paths that end in root
    ○ B. directory paths that end in rbin
    ○ C. directory paths that end in sbin
    ○ D. directory paths that end in tmp

7. You have created a binary named snow. It is in the directory path of /home/userprogs/bin and this directory path is not in the PATH. Your current directory is /boot. Which two items will allow you to run this binary?

    ☐ A. cd /home/userprogs/bin ; ./snow
    ☐ B. cd /home/userprogs/bin ; snow
    ☐ C. /home/userprogs/bin/snow
    ☐ D. ./home/user/bin/snow

8. The ~ in the path of ~/.bashrc represents:

    ○ A. any directory that is the current directory
    ○ B. the /home directory
    ○ C. a comment pointing to the bash configuration file
    ○ D. the home directory of a user

9. Somehow the PATH variable does not contain any directory paths, but you can still run the cd command. Why is this possible?

    ○ A. the cd binary is in the current directory
    ○ B. cd is an AUTOPATH variable
    ○ C. cd is a built-in command
    ○ D. cd is a part of the kernel executable

10. The alias command is the best way of adding a directory path to the PATH. T F
     F

11. Which of the following are hidden bash configuration files (choose two)?

    ☐ A. /etc/profile
    ☐ B. ~/.bashrc
    ☐ C. /etc/bashrc
    ☐ D. ~/.bash_logout

12. The name of an alias can be assigned to a command and the following components of a command so that the alias name can quickly be used repeatedly (choose three).

    ☐ A. one or more options so that the options are used with the alias
    ☐ B. a comment so that the comment appears when the alias is run
    ☐ C. a path so that the pattern can be used with the alias
    ☐ D. a pattern so that the pattern can be used with the alias

13. The ~/.bash_history file contains commands that are run when a user logs out. T F

14. Which option of the alias command can be used to remove all aliases?

    ○ A. -r
    ○ B. -ra
    ○ C. -a
    ○ D. -rm

15. You need to run the binary named hello in the directory path of /home/cwest, but this directory path is not in the PATH. Your current directory is /var/log. Select the item that will allow you to run this binary.

    ○ A. /var/log/hello
    ○ B. ./hello
    ○ C. /home/cwest/hello
    ○ D. cd /home ; hello

16. Select the file that should be used to add a directory path to the PATH for a single user (only).

    ○ A. ~/.bash_profile
    ○ B. /etc/profile
    ○ C. a .sh file in /etc/profile
    ○ D. ~/.bashrc

17. You have created several users using the default settings and configuration files. You want to add an alias to the system that will be created when all users (current and future) start a shell session. Which is the most efficient method of adding the alias?

    ○ A. put the alias statement in the ~/.bash_profile file for the existing users and any new users that you create
    ○ B. put the alias statement in the ~/.bashrc file for the existing users and any new users that you create
    ○ C. put the alias statement in a .sh file in /etc/profile.d
    ○ D. put the alias statement in the .bashrc file in /etc/skel

18. All hidden bash configuration files all begin with:

    ○ A. .bash_
    ○ B. .bash
    ○ C. .csh
    ○ D. .bsh

19. You need to add the directory path of: /home/userprogs/bin to the default PATH statement of: PATH=$PATH:$HOME/bin in the appropriate shell configuration file for a single user (only). Which of the following represents the text that you will add immediately to the right of the PATH statement in the file so that the user will have this directory path in the PATH?

   ○ A. /home/userprogs/bin
   ○ B. ;/home/bin
   ○ C. # /home/userprogs/bin
   ○ D. :/home/userprogs/bin

20. Which option of the which command can be used to remove an alias?

   ○ A. -rm
   ○ B. -r
   ○ C. -x
   ○ D. none of the above

21. Select two files that add directory paths to the PATH.

   ☐ A. ~/.bash_profile
   ☐ B. ~/bash_history
   ☐ C. /etc/profile
   ☐ D. /etc/.bashrc

22. A comment in the ~/.bashrc file states that part of the file is used for user specific aliases and functions. T F

23. The default path for a non-root user contains:

   ○ A. directory paths that end in sbin
   ○ B. directory paths that end in bin
   ○ C. directory paths that end in home
   ○ D. directory paths that end in usr

24. A non-root user needs to be able to run a script that you have created from any directory (to which the user has access). Which of the following will allow the user this capability?

   ○ A. create a directory named bin below the user's home directory and copy the script into it
   ○ B. create a directory named bin below /root and copy the script into it
   ○ C. copy the script into /tmp
   ○ D. copy the script into /var/log

Chapter 10: Adding a Disk and Partition to a Linux System

In this chapter you are provided with an overview of all of the steps to add a hard disk and partition to a Linux system so that the partition is automatically mounted when the system boots.

You will use the dmesg command in conjunction with the grep command to determine if a hard disk that you have added to a system is "seen" by the system when the system boots.

You will learn how to use options of the fdisk utility at the command line and also how to go "in" to the fdisk utility to see existing partitions, add a new partition and remove a partition.

You will also find out how to use the mkfs command to assign a filesystem to a partition and how to use the e2label command to assign a label to a partition.

This chapter also details the columns of settings in the /etc/fstab file. You will edit this file to add settings for the partition that you create with fdisk. You will also see the relationship between the /etc/mtab file and the /etc/fstab file.

You used the mount and umount commands to earlier to mount and unmount floppy disks and CDs. The mount command is used here to mount a partition on a directory that you have created as a mount point. The umount command will be used to do the opposite.

The df command displays disk space usage for all currently mounted partitions and block devices, excluding the swap partition. You will use various options of this command to view disk space usage information for mounted partitions.

The following commands are described in the chapter and are also used in the Hands-On Exercises:

dmesg	view hard disk and CD-ROM drives that are "seen" by a system
fdisk	view, add, remove and modify hard disk partitions
mkfs	assign a filesystem to a partition
e2label	assign a label to a partition
mount	view currently mounted partitions, mount additional partitions and the filesystems of removable media
umount	unmount partitions and the filesystems of removable media
df	displays disk space usage for currently mounted partitions and removable media

During the Hands-On Exercises you will create a partition, assign it a filesystem, assign it a label, add a statement for it to fstab, and reboot to test that it is automatically mounted during the boot process.

If you are working on a dual-boot system that has Window installed on it as well as Linux, you will also do the steps to add access to the Windows partition from "within" Linux.

Adding a Disk and Partition to a System

Topics Covered in this Section

Provide all of the steps required to add a disk and partition to a system
Learn how to use the fdisk utility at the command line and also how to work "in" this utility
Describe several other commands that are used to work with partitions
Detail the contents of the fstab file and how this file relates to mtab
Do the steps to add a partition to a system so that it is automatically booted
Set up a Linux to access a Windows partition on a dual-boot system

In this chapter you will learn about the commands and files that are used to work with, view, create and modify partitions. You will add a partition to your system and set it up so that it is automatically mounted during the boot process. You will also create a mount point for a Windows partition and edit the fstab file to have the partition automatically mounted.

Adding a Disk and Partition to a System - Overview

The steps below describe adding a new disk to a system and having one or more partitions on the disk automatically accessible after the Linux OS boots. Below is an overview. The commands mentioned in the steps below are described in more detail further below.

When you installed Linux earlier, you left some unpartitioned (empty) disk space so that you could create a partition in this chapter. All of the steps below, except physically attaching the disk, will be done using this unpartitioned disk space.

Step 1 - Attach the new hard drive to the system and do steps to "set up" the drive and have the drive "seen" by the system. The steps that are required depend on the hard drive type and are detailed in the manufacturer's documentation.

Step 2 - Use the dmesg command to see if the drive was attached and set up correctly. If the drive is available to the OS, it will appear in the output of the dmesg command.

The steps below are used whether you have added a new disk to the system or are adding a new partition to an existing disk.

Step 3 - Use the fdisk utility to create a partition on the disk.

Step 4 - Use the mkfs command to assign a filesystem to the partition.

Step 5 - Use the mkdir command to create a mount point for the partition.

Step 6 - Use the e2label command to assign a label to the partition. This step is optional. You can specify the device name of a partition in fstab rather than use a label.

Step 7 - Use a text editor and add a statement to /etc/fstab so that the partition is automatically mounted when the OS boots.

Step 8 - Use the mount command so that it reads the settings that you made in fstab to mount the partition on the mount point that you created. This tests that the mount point works prior to rebooting the system.

Step 9 - Use the df command to see the settings of the new partition, including the size, space used, space available and percentage of space used. This checks that you specified the correct size when you created the partition.

Step 10 - Reboot the system to test that the partition is mounted automatically.

Details on Steps 2 through 10 are provided below.

Using dmesg to View Hard Disk Drives

When you attach a new hard drive to a system, you do steps to "set up" the drive and have the drive "seen" or "recognized" by the system. The steps that are required depend on the hard drive type and are detailed in the manufacturer's documentation.

When Linux boots, the drive should be detected by the system. If the drive was not attached and set up correctly, Linux may not be able to access the drive and you will not be able to do the additional steps to add it to your system.

After attaching a new drive to a system, watch the system when it boots, you may be able to see output that indicates that the new drive is "seen" by the system. If you did not see this information, you can use the dmesg command to see if the drive was attached and set up correctly.

The dmesg Command

The dmesg command displays a tremendous amount of system information and is described in more detail in an upcoming chapter. It is described here because it can be used to view the drives (hard disk and CD-ROM drives) that are accessible by the OS.

Example of the dmesg Command

dmesg | grep ^hd

Shows IDE disks that were "seen" by the OS when the system booted. A description of the disk appears at the right of each disk device name (such as hda, hdb and hdc).

The ^ (caret) that appears in the above command is used so that only lines that *begin* with "hd" (have "hd" at the far left margin) appear. If the ^ (caret) is not used, then all lines that contain the letters "hd" would appear and this would provide more information than you require.

To view other types of drives, replace the "**hd**" in "grep ^**hd**" in the above command with the two letters that identify the drive type.

For example, to see SCSI drives, replace the "**hd**" in "grep ^**hd**" with **sd** and to use the following command:

```
dmesg | grep ^sd
```

Below is sample output of the command: dmesg | grep ^**hd**

```
hda: Maxtor 6L060J3, ATA DISK drive
hdb: QUANTUM FIREBALL EX12.7A, ATA DISK drive
hdc: MATSHITA CR-588, ATAPI CD/DVD-ROM drive
hda: 117266688 sectors (60041 MB) w/1819KiB Cache, CHS=7299/255/63, UDMA(33)
hdb: 24901632 sectors (12750 MB) w/418KiB Cache, CHS=1550/255/63, UDMA(33)
hdc: ATAPI 32X CD-ROM drive, 128kB Cache
```

The fist three lines describe the hda, hdb and hdc drives. hda and hdb are hard disks and hdc is a CD-ROM drive.

The fourth and fifth lines in the above output show the disk sizes of hda and hdb and contain the word "Cache". These lines represent cache memory that is installed on the IDE controller (that is attached to the inside or outside of the hard disk). The last line shows the speed (32X) and cache size of the CD-ROM drive.

The fdisk Utility

The fdisk utility has options that can be used at the command line to provide hard disk and partition information. In addition to this, you can run the fdisk command and specifying a disk device name to go "in" to the fdisk utility to view and modify partition settings.

You will learn how work "inside" the fdisk utility in the Hands-On Exercises below.

The fdisk and parted utilities are commonly used to view, modify and create partitions. The parted utility was described in detail earlier. Other utilities are also available to do these tasks.

You can use a utility to view a mounted partition, but do not use a utility to modify a mounted partition. If you need to make a change to a partition, such as resize it, use the umount command to unmount the partition.

If you have installed a new disk in a system then it will not be mounted when you boot the system and you can do the steps to create partitions on it and add these partitions to your system.

The fdisk utility can be used to completely remove all partitions and data on a hard disk. Always make sure that you have two reliable backups of all of the hard disks attached to a system prior to using this utility.

Test your backups to make sure you can restore from them!

Examples of the fdisk Command

fdisk

This displays usage (help) information for fdisk. To use fdisk to view or modify the settings of a hard disk you run fdisk and specify the path to the device that you need to work with, such as /dev/hda.

An example of the output of: fdisk (without options) appears below and shows the usage of the command.

```
Usage: fdisk [-l] [-b SSZ] [-u] device
    E.g.: fdisk /dev/hda    (for the first IDE disk)
          or: fdisk /dev/sdc    (for the third SCSI disk)
          or: fdisk /dev/eda    (for the first PS/2 esdi drive)
          or: fdisk /dev/rd/c0d0  or: fdisk /dev/ida/c0d0   (for RAID devices)
```

fdisk /dev/hda

Runs the fdisk utility so that you can view or modify the partitions on the first IDE hard disk (/dev/hda).

fdisk -l

The file named partitions in /proc contains very detailed information on all of partitions on the disks in a system. The information in this file is difficult to read and interpret.

The -l option of fdisk displays the information in /proc/partitions (for all partitions on all hard disks) in "human readable" form.

To view or modify the settings of a single disk, you run fdisk and specify the path to the device name. Once this is done, you are "in" the fdisk utility. When you are "in" fdisk, you can use the "**p**" option to "**p**rint" the partition table. This "prints" the partition table of the (single) disk that you specified when you started the utility, to the default output (the screen).

The output displayed with the p option (in fdisk) is the same as when you use the -l option of fdisk from the command line, except that when the -l option is used from the command line, all partitions on all disks appears. Therefore, the output shown below is the same as if you viewed the partition table of each disk from within fdisk.

An example of the output of: fdisk -l   appears below.

Disk /dev/**hda**: 255 heads, 63 sectors, 7299 cylinders
Units = cylinders of 16065 * 512 bytes

Device	Boot	Start	End	Blocks	Id	System
/dev/hda1	*	1	2550	20482843+	c	Win95 FAT32 (LBA)
/dev/hda2		2551	2563	104422+	83	Linux
/dev/hda3		2564	2818	2048287+	83	Linux
/dev/hda4		2819	7299	35993632+	f	Win95 Ext'd (LBA)
/dev/hda5		2819	2883	522081	82	Linux swap
/dev/hda6		2884	2940	457821	83	Linux
/dev/hda7		2941	2978	305203+	83	Linux
/dev/hda8		2979	3003	200781	83	Linux

Disk /dev/**hdb**: 255 heads, 63 sectors, 1550 cylinders
Units = cylinders of 16065 * 512 bytes

Device	Boot	Start	End	Blocks	Id	System
/dev/hdb1		1	100	803218+	83	Linux

Below is a description of the partition output (shown above) for the first hard disk (hda).

The above output indicates that there are two hard disks are in the system. The heads, sectors, cylinders and units for each disk appear above the partition information of each disk.

The first hard disk (hda) has a Windows partition on hda1 and the * (asterisk) below the Boot heading indicates that this is the partition from which the system boots.

This disk also has Linux partitions on hda2, hda3, hda5, hda6, hda7 and hda8. Partitions 5 through 8 are in the Extended partition. At the right of hda5 you can see that this is the Linux swap partition.

In the Id column of the first disk, the c is for a "Win95 FAT32" partition, which is actually a Windows 2000 Professional partition. The f in the Id column is for a "Win95 Ext'd" partition. This partition was actually created with the Linux installation routine. All partitions on both disks, excluding the first partition on the first hard disk, were created with the Linux installation routine.

The 83 in the Id column for partitions 2, 3, 6, 7 and 8 is the Id (number) of a Linux partition. This does not indicate whether or not the partition is ext2, ext3 or any other filesystem type. When you run the mount command without any options, the filesystem type of each partition is displayed.

The 82 in the Id column is the Id (number) of a Linux swap partition.

The paragraph below is a description of the partition output (shown above) for the second hard disk (hdb).

The second hard disk (hdb) has a Linux partition on hdb1. The 83 in the Id column indicates that this is a Linux partition.

fdisk -l /dev/sdd

This example of the fdisk command shows that the path to a device can be specified at the right of the -l option. The /dev/sdd shown above represents the fourth SCSI hard disk. Using a path to a device with the -l option is useful on a system that has a lot of hard disks, such as a system with a lot of SCSI disks. This provides output on a specific disk (rather than long output that shows all disks).

The mkfs Command

The mkfs command is used to assign a filesystem to a partition. If files exist on the partition, this command will remove them.

mkfs -t ext3 /dev/*patitiondevicename*

In the example above, replace *partitiondevicename* with the device name of the partition, such as hda6. The -t option specifies the filesystem type of ext3 and the command assigns the ext3 filesystem to the partition. The system will use default settings for other options that could be specified with mkfs, such as block size.

After running the mkfs command, its output shows several settings that were used when a filesystem was assigned to the partition. One of these settings shows an amount of space (in blocks and as a percentage of the partition) that is "reserved for super user". By default, part of a partition is reserved for the "super user" (root).

The e2label Command

The e2label command is used to assign a label to a partition, such as the path to the mount point of the partition. A label is easier to remember than a partition number.

For the ext2 and ext3 filesystem, you cannot use a label that is longer than 16 characters. Therefore, you cannot use a directory path that is longer than 16 characters for a label.

You can use a label of /home/common, but a label of /home/common/sales is too many characters.

e2label /dev/*patitiondevicename* /home/common

The example above assigns the label of /home/common to the partition of /dev/*patitiondevicename* . Replace *partitiondevicename* with the device name of the partition, such as hda10.

The /etc/fstab Configuration File

The **fstab** (filesystem **table**) configuration (text) file in /etc is read when a system boots, and when some commands are run (such as the mount command). It specifies the settings to be used when mounting a partition, such as /boot, or a block device, such as a floppy disk or CD. It is read by software components of the system but not written to.

Each line in the file represents a partition or block device. There are six columns in this file. Column 1 shows the name of a partition or block device and the other columns are used to specify settings for the partition or block device.

An example of the contents of an fstab file appears below. Six column numbers have been added above the contents of the file for the descriptions of each column further below.

1	2	3	4	5	6
LABEL=/	/	ext3	defaults	1	1
LABEL=/boot	/boot	ext3	defaults	1	2
none	/dev/pts	devpts	gid=5,mode=620	0	0
LABEL=/home	/home	ext3	defaults	1	2
none	/proc	proc	defaults	0	0
none	/dev/shm	tmpfs	defaults	0	0
LABEL=/usr	/usr	ext3	defaults	1	2
LABEL=/var	/var	ext3	defaults	1	2
/dev/hda5	swap	swap	defaults	0	0
/dev/cdrom	/mnt/cdrom	iso9660	noauto,owner,kudzu,ro	0	0
/dev/fd0	/mnt/floppy	auto	noauto,owner,kudzu	0	0

Column 1 - The Partition/Device Name Column

This column shows a LABEL or device name for a partition or block device. A label is assigned to a partition with the e2label command (described above).

"LABEL=" appears at the left of the /, /boot, /home, /usr and /var partitions that you created during the Linux installation.

Look for /dev/hda5 near the bottom of Column 1. The hda5 in /dev/hda5 is the device name (represented by a file named hda5 in /dev) for the hda5 partition. The **hd** in **hd**a5 represents an AT-API (IDE or EIDE) drive. The **a** in hda5 represents the AT-API disk drive attached to the Primary Master. The **5** in hda5 represents the first logical partition in an Extended partition. Column 2 shows that /dev/hda5 is the swap partition (a.k.a. swap drive).

Column 2 - The Mount Point Column

This column shows the mount point of the partition or device in Column 1.

For example, /boot is the mount point of LABEL=/boot and /mnt/cdrom is the mount point for /dev/cdrom. The boot directory below the / is the mount

point for the /boot partition. The cdrom directory below the /mnt directory
is the mount point for /dev/cdrom.

Column 3 - The Filesystem Type Column

This column shows filesystem being used by the partition or device.

Column 4 - The Mount Options Column

This column shows options that are used to mount the filesystem that is
being used by the partition or device. If there is more than one option, it is
separated from the next option by a , (comma).

When "defaults" appears in this column, the default options of rw, suid, dev,
exec, auto, nouser and async are used.

The **rw** option is used to specify that a partition be mounted **read write**.
This allows data to be read from and written to the partition.

The **ro** option is used to specify that a partition be mounted **read only**. This allows
data to be read from the partition, but prevents data from being written to it.

Column 5 - The Dump Frequency Column

Dump is the name of an backup utility. This column is used to specify a
value when using the dump utility, or when using a utility that is similar to
the dump utility, that accesses the value in this column.

This column indicates the dump (backup) frequency of: 0 for never, 1 for
daily and 2 for every other day. This is how often filesystem information is
"dumped" (output) to a backup device.

In our example fstab file above, the /, /boot, /home, /usr and /var partitions
have the number 1 and all other partitions have the number 0. Use the
value of 1 for all partitions that you add to fstab, unless you need to specify
a different number to be used by the dump utility.

Column 6 - The fsck Order Column

This column shows the order in which a **fsck** (filesystem check) is done on
the partitions, such as when fsck is run during the boot process.

The / partition has the value of 1 and is checked first. Other partitions
are assigned numbers from 2 through 9 and are checked in numerical
order after the / partition. If more than one partition has the same number,
it is checked in the order in which it appears in the fstab file. The number
0 is used to cause the fsck to ignore the partition.

In our example fstab file above, the / has the number 1 and the /boot, /home, /usr
and /var partitions have the number 2. All other partitions have the number 0.

The mtab File

The **mtab** (**m**ount **tab**le) configuration (text) file in /etc contains the settings for the currently mounted partitions and block devices.

When you mount a partition or block device, this file is updated with the partition or device name and the settings for the partition or device name.

When you run the mount command without any options, the partitions and block devices and most of their settings in mtab are displayed.

An example of the contents of an mtab file appears below.

```
/dev/hda7     /              ext3      rw                  0 0
none          /proc          proc      rw                  0 0
usbdevfs      /proc/bus/usb  usbdevfs  rw                  0 0
/dev/hda2     /boot          ext3      rw                  0 0
none          /dev/pts       devpts    rw,gid=5,mode=620   0 0
/dev/hda8     /home          ext3      rw                  0 0
none          /dev/shm       tmpfs     rw                  0 0
/dev/hda3     /usr           ext3      rw                  0 0
/dev/hda6     /var           ext3      rw                  0 0
```

The mount Command (Revisited)

The mount command is used to: view the currently mounted partitions, mount additional partitions, and mount the filesystems of removable media. Once you have mounted a partition or the filesystem of removable media, then the filesystem becomes available to the system.

When you use the mount command to a mount floppy disk, the filesystem of the floppy becomes available below /mnt/floppy. When you use the mount command to a mount CD, the filesystem of the CD becomes available below /mnt/cdrom.

Examples of the mount Command

mount

Displays the currently mounted partitions and filesystems.

mount /dev/fd0 /mnt/floppy

Mounts the device name of /dev/fd0 on the mount point of the floppy directory below /mnt. This allows the filesystem of the floppy to be accessed below /mnt/floppy. The "/dev/fd0" part of this command is required if a statement for the /mnt/floppy mount point is not in Column 2 in fstab.

The contents of the / (root) directory of the floppy appear in the floppy directory below /mnt.

For example, the command: ls -l /mnt/floppy shows the contents of the root directory of the floppy.

mount /mnt/floppy

If the /mnt/floppy mount point has been specified for /dev/fd0 in fstab, then this command can be used to mount a floppy, without specifying the device name of /dev/fd0.

In other words, if a statement for /mnt/floppy exists in Column 2 in fstab, then the settings for this device, such as the /dev/fd0 device name, are used when the floppy is mounted.

mount /dev/cdrom /mnt/cdrom

Mounts the device name of /dev/cdrom on the mount point of /mnt/cdrom so that the filesystem of a CD can be accessed below /mnt/cdrom. The / (root) directory of the CD appears in the cdrom directory below /mnt. The "/dev/cdrom" part of this command is required if a statement for /mnt/cdrom mount point is not in fstab.

mount /mnt/cdrom

If the /mnt/cdrom mount point has been specified for /dev/cdrom in fstab, then this command can be used to mount a CD without specifying the device name of /dev/cdrom.

mount /dev/hda9 /home/common

Mounts partition 9, located on hda (the first IDE hard disk), on the mount point of the common directory, below /home.

mount /home/common

Mounts the partition that has the mount point of /home/common in fstab. This command uses the settings specified on the same line as the /home/common mount point in fstab.

The umount Command (Revisited)

The umount command is used to unmount partitions and the filesystems of removable media. Once you have unmounted a partition or the filesystem of removable media, then the filesystem is no longer available to the system.

You cannot unmount a partition if it is "busy" and you should **never** modify the settings of a partition if it is mounted. Some utilities will not allow you to modify (including delete) a partition if it is mounted, but others will not. For example, you can use fdisk to delete a partition that is mounted, but do not do this.

A partition is busy when it is being used by the OS or when it is being accessed by a user. Some partitions, such as /, are always being used by the OS and are always busy.

If you need to modify a partition that is being used by the system (busy), then boot into Rescue Mode to make the modifications. When going into Rescue Mode, select the Skip option, rather than the Continue or Read-Only options) so that no partitions are mounted and therefore you can modify all partitions.

 The GNU Parted utility, run with the parted command, allows you to make a lot of different modifications to partitions, such as resizing and copying partitions.

Examples of the umount Command

umount /mnt/floppy

Unmounts a floppy disk and causes the files in memory that need to be written to the floppy to be written. Do not remove a mounted floppy disk without unmounting it first.

A floppy drive light is on when the floppy is being written to or read from. When you unmount a floppy, the OS may need to write data that is in memory to the floppy. Do not remove a floppy from a floppy drive while the floppy drive light is on (while it is being accessed).

umount /mnt/cdrom

Unmounts a CD so that it can be removed from the drive. If you need to unmount *and* remove a CD from the drive, then use the eject command (without any options). This will unmount the CD *and* open the CD-ROM drive door.

umount /dev/hda9

Unmounts the hda9 partition. If there are directories and files in the mount point directory that was used for hda9, they will no longer be visible below the mount point directory.

umount /home/common

Unmounts the partition that has the mount point of the common directory below /home.

The df Command

The df (**d**isk space **f**ree) command displays disk space usage for all currently mounted partitions and block devices, excluding the **swap** partition. The output of this command shows the device name, total size, space used, space available, percentage space used and the partition on which the device name is mounted.

As described earlier, the **swap** partition is disk space that is used as though it is RAM (memory) in the system.

Partition information for the swap partition can be seen with the fdisk command, but the output of this command does not show the amount of space used and "free" on the swap partition.

The top command is used to see the top processes running in memory and the free command is used to see memory size and usage information. These commands are described in detail later.

The top command also shows the available, used and free amounts of space on the swap partition (on the fifth line). The free command also shows this information (on the fourth line).

The Syntax of the df Command

The following is the syntax of the df command:

df [options] [/dev/*partitiondevicename* | *pathtopartition* | *partitionlabel*]

An example of a *partitiondevicename* is hda2. The full path to the partition is /dev/hda2.

An example of the *pathtopartition* is /mnt/floppy.

An example of the *partitionlabel* is /var.

Options of the df Command

Table 10-1 - Common Options of the df Command

Option	Description
-h	displays output in human readable format
-T	displays the filesystem Type of each partition
--sync	causes buffered data to be written to disk before displaying output

The –sync option causes data that is in memory to be written to disk prior to providing the output of the df command. This option causes the command to produce accurate (current) space usage output.

Examples of the df Command

df	shows information on all currently mounted partitions and block devices
df -h	same as above, but in human readable format sizes are shown in K (kilobytes), M (megabytes) and G (gigabytes)
df -hT	same as above, but adds a new column named "Type" that displays the filesystem type of each partition
df -h --sync	same as above, but causes data in memory to be written to disk prior to displaying output
df -h /dev/hda7	shows information for the hda7 partition (only), using the /dev/**partitiondevicename** of /dev/**hda7**
df -h /mnt/floppy	shows information for the floppy disk (only), using the **pathtopartition** of **/mnt/floppy**
df -h /boot	shows information for the /boot partition (only), using the **partitionlabel** of **/boot**

When you installed Linux earlier, you specified a size of 100 MB for the /boot partition. The boot directory is the mount point of the partition to which it points, such as hda2 (/dev/hda2).

When you use a utility (such as a command or GUI file manager) to display directories and files in a mount point directory, such as /boot, you are looking at the entire contents of the partition to which the mount point was assigned. All directories and files below the mount point are in the partition to which the mount point was assigned. The maximum size of the directory is restricted in size by the size of the partition.

For example, the /boot directory cannot contain more than 100 MB of directories and files because the partition to which it points in not larger than 100 MB. When you use a utility to view all of the directories and files in /boot, you are looking at all of the items that are in the 100 MB partition to which /boot has been assigned, such as hda2 (/dev/hda2).

An example of the output of the command: df -hT appears below. The device names of the partitions appear at the left and the mount points appear at the far right.

You created the mount points of /, /boot, /home, /usr and /var during the Linux installation and specified the size of these partitions

Filesystem	Type	Size	Used	Avail	Use%	Mounted on
/dev/hda7	ext3	289M	77M	196M	29%	/
/dev/hda2	ext3	99M	9.2M	84M	10%	/boot
/dev/hda8	ext3	190M	11M	169M	6%	/home
none	tmpfs	125M	0	124M	0%	/dev/shm
/dev/hda3	ext3	1.9G	1.6G	246M	87%	/usr
/dev/hda6	ext3	433M	43M	368M	11%	/var
/dev/cdrom	iso9660	644M	645M	0	100%	/mnt/cdrom

The CD in the CD-ROM drive has been mounted and appears at the bottom of the above output. If the CD was not mounted, then it would not appear in the output.

Adding Access to a Windows Partition on Dual-Boot System

When Windows is installed on an x86 system, it is typically installed on the first partition of the first hard disk, which is hda1. The steps below allow you to access this partition from "within" Linux. By default, you will not be able to run Windows programs, but you will be able to access data files that you have created with Windows applications. Many Linux applications can read data files created with Windows applications.

You will do the steps described below during the Hands-On Exercises.

Step 1 - Use the mkdir command to create a mount point for the partition below /mnt/. In our example, we will user a directory named driveC.

Step 2 - Use a text editor and add a statement to /etc/fstab so that the partition is automatically mounted when the OS boots.

In our example, we will use the following statement. This causes /dev/hda1 to be mounted on the driveC directory using the vfat filesystem.

> /dev/hda1   /mnt/driveC vfat   auto, owner, users 0 0

Step 3 - Use the mount command so that it reads the settings that you made in fstab to mount the partition on the mount point that you created. This tests that the mount point works prior to rebooting the system.

Step 4 - Use the df command to see the settings of the partition.

Step 5 - Reboot the system to test that the partition is mounted automatically.

Hands-On Exercises

 Logging In to Add a Partition to a System

Log in to a desktop as cwest ; open a terminal emulation window ;
su to root ;

]# cd /etc ; cat fstab	# the settings in this configuration file appear
]# ls -l fstab	# notice the date and time
]# ls -l mtab	# the current date and the time that you # booted appear
]# clear ; cat mtab	# shows the currently mounted partitions
]# mount	

When you run the mount command without any options, the partitions and
block devices and most of their settings that exist in mtab are displayed. A
line for /dev/cdrom does not appear in the output of mount.

 Mounting a CD and Seeing the Changes in mtab

Put CD 1 in the CD-ROM drive.

The desktop automatically mounts the CD. You logged in to the desktop as
the cwest user. Therefore, the CD is mounted by the cwest user, not root.

]# ls -l mtab

The time changed because the file was updated when the CD was mounted.

]# cat mtab   # view all of the contents of mtab

A line for /dev/cdrom (the mounted CD) appears.

]# clear ; cat mtab | grep /dev/cdrom

The following items appear at the right of /mnt/cdrom:

iso9660 ro,nosuid,nodev,user=cwest 0 0

]# cat fstab | grep /dev/cdrom

The following items appear at the right of /mnt/cdrom:

iso9660 noauto, owner, kudzu, ro 0 0

The options (settings) at the right of /mnt/cdrom in fstab were used when the CD was mounted. The results of these settings are seen when you "cat out" mtab. The "owner" setting in fstab became "user=cwest" in mtab.

```
]# mount              # a line for /dev/cdrom (the mounted CD) appears
```

③ Viewing the Drives "Seen" by the System

If you have installed a new hard disk and it is "recognized" by the system, the following command will show it. Replace the "hd" in the following command with the two letters that represent your disk, such as "sd" for a SCSI disk, if the disk that you installed is not an AT-API disk.

```
]# dmesg | grep  hd    # more information than is required appears

]# dmesg | grep  ^hd   # the hard disk(s) and CD-ROM drive appear
```

If a disk appears here, it was "recognized" by the system during the boot process.

④ Viewing the Contents of /proc/partitions and Using the -l Option of fdisk

Get a long listing of the partitions file in /proc and notice the date and time.

The /proc directory is a virtual filesystem that is created in memory each time you start your system. It contains many files that contain system information and settings. The file named partitions in /proc contains information on all partitions on all hard disks that are "seen" by a system.

Clear the screen ; "cat out" the contents of the partitions file in /proc.

```
]# fdisk -l    # displays many of the partition settings in /proc/partitions in
               # human readable form - all partitions on all hard disks
```

The -l option of fdisk shows output for all disks in a system. If you have several disks in your system, such as a server system with multiple SCSI drives, then the output can be quite long. In the command below, replace *diskdevicename* with the device name of the hard disk on which Linux is installed, such as hda.

```
]# fdisk -l /dev/diskdevicename
```

Specifying /dev/*diskdevicename* with the fdisk command is useful if there is more than one hard disk in the system.

Running fdisk to Create a New Partition

When you installed Linux earlier, you left some space available in the Extended partition of hda so that you could create another partition later. Well, now's the time!

Rather than physically adding a disk to your system, you will use the unpartitioned free space that you left available during the Linux installation that you did earlier. You could, however, install a new disk in your system and do all of the steps below to: create a partition on it, assign it a filesystem and a label, and add a partition on the disk to your system by editing fstab.

You need a directory on your system named common that will be used as the parent directory for user data files. *The Filesystem Hierarchy Standard suggests that you use the default directories off of the / directory for all programs and data rather than creating any new directories off of the /.*

User home directories and user data files are kept below /home. Therefore, we will use the /home directory as the parent directory for the common directory. This directory will be the parent directory for common user data files.

In the command below, replace *diskdevicename* with the device name of your hard disk, such as hda. The disk device name does not include the partition number. A *partitiondevicename* is the device name of a hard disk, plus the number of the partition on the hard disk, such as hda8.

 Be sure to specify the correct name for the *diskdevicename* below.

Also, when creating the partition below, be sure to specify the correct partition number. This will be a partition number for a new partition, not an existing partition.

If you are creating a partition on the first IDE hard disk in a system, then replace *diskdevicename* with hda.

```
]# fdisk /dev/diskdevicename    # go "in" to the fdisk utility

m                               # type:  m  and press Enter
                                # displays help on fdisk commands
                                # notice the descriptions of n and p

p                               # "prints" the partition table to the screen
```

Notice the number below the End heading for the last partition in the list. You will create a partition immediately after the last partition in the list.

Also notice the number of cylinders at the top right, on the first line of the output. Compare the number below the End heading for the last partition with the number of cylinders at the top. This indicates whether or not you have free space on the disk.

```
n                 # type:  n  and press Enter
```

The number that appears at the right of "default" is the cylinder number immediately after the last existing partition.

Press Enter to accept the default number. Notice the output of "Using default value *nnnn*", where *nnnn* is the number that will be used.

Notice the +size, +sizeM and +sizeK settings. We want to create a 50 MB partition. Therefore, we will specify +50M. You can create a larger partition if you have the disk space for it.

```
+50M              # type in:  +50M  and press Enter
p                 # see your new partition - at the end of the list
```

For the new partition, notice the numbers below Start, End and Blocks.

A *partitiondevicename* is the combination of the disk device name and the partition number, such as hda9.

Write the partition device name of the partition that you just created below:

/dev/_____

You will need the *partitiondevicename* in the steps below.

Below the Id heading, the number 83 appears. This indicates a Linux non-swap partition. The filesystem type on the partition has not yet been specified.

```
m                 # notice the descriptions of l, q and w
l                 # if you needed to specify a different Id, you would use
                  # one of these numbers - look at the descriptions
                  # for 5, b, c, e, f, 82 and 83
```

If you have Windows installed on your system, then b, c, e or f will appear when you "print" the partition table to the screen. The number 82 is used for Linux swap partitions and 83 is used for Linux non-swap partitions.

```
p                 # look at the numbers below the Id heading
```

If you typed "q" now, then you would quit out of fdisk without saving any of the changes that you have made. If you think you have made a mistake, type "q" and do the steps to create the partition over again. Otherwise, do the step below to write the settings of the new partition to disk.

```
w                 # write the changes to disk and exit out of fdisk
```

If you create, delete or modify partitions with fdisk, you must use: w to write the changes, rather than: q to quit (without writing the changes).

Read the messages that appeared after you did the step above. You must reboot your system for the new partition to be recognized.

If you still have a CD in the drive, run: eject and remove it from the drive.

Close all terminal emulation windows and programs ; Menu ; Log Out ;
Restart the computer ; OK ;

log in as cwest ; open a terminal emulation window ; su to root.

 6 **Assigning a Filesystem to the New Partition**

]# fdisk -l   # your new partition should appear

In the command below, replace *partitiondevicename* with the name that you
wrote down above, such as hda9. This command assigns the ext3 filesystem to
the partition. The -t option specifies the filesystem type of ext3. The system
will use the default settings for other options that could be specified with the
mkfs command, such as block size.

]# mkfs -t ext3 /dev/*patitiondevicename*

Read through the output of the mkfs command. Notice the amount of space
(in blocks and as a percentage of the partition) that is "reserved for the super
user". When you see output of the df command below, it will show that some
space on your new partition is used. Some of this is the space that has been
"reserved for the super user".

7 **Creating a Mount Point and Mounting the Partition**

The command below creates a mount point (directory) named common
below /home for your new partition.

]# mkdir /home/common   # create the directory named common
                               # below /home

Get a long listing of /home to see that you created the directory in the right place.

In the step below, replace *patitiondevicename* with the name of your partition.

]# mount /dev/*patitiondevicename* /home/common

Once a statement for the partition has been added to fstab, then the partition will
automatically be mounted during the boot process. Also, if you ever need to
mount the partition from the command line, then the "/dev/*patitiondevicename*"
part of the above command will not be required because a statement for the
partition is in fstab.

]# mount   # shows that the new partition has the
                               # ext3 filesystem

]# umount /home/common   # use the path to the mount point to
                               # unmount the partition

Assigning a Label to the Partition

The e2label command below assigns the label of /home/common to the /dev/*patitiondevicename* partition.

    ]# e2label /dev/*patitiondevicename* /home/common

There is no output after running the above command.

    ]# mount /home/common

This command did not work because a statement for the partition is not in fstab.

You were able to mount the partition with (a few steps ago):

    mount /dev/*patitiondevicename* /home/common

but are not yet able to mount it with: mount /home/common.

 Backing Up fstab and Adding a Setting to It for the New Partition

You need to make a backup of fstab prior to editing it. In the step below, the file named fstab is copied to the file named fstab.bak. Both files will exist in the /etc directory.

    ]# cp /etc/fstab /etc/fstab.bak

Run vi and load /etc/fstab. Add the following statement on a blank line at the end of fstab. Press Tab between each "chunk" of text, except press Spacebar once between "1" and "2".

    LABEL=/home/common /home/common ext3 defaults 1 2

Save and exit out of vi.

 Mounting the Partition Using the Settings in fstab

The following command will now mount the partition to which /home/common points because the settings for it exist in fstab.

    ]# mount /home/common

After adding a new partition to fstab, always mount it with the mount command (without using /dev/*partitiondevicename*) before shutting down or rebooting. This tests that the new partition can be mounted properly with the settings in fstab, prior to having the boot process mount it for you.

    ]# mount   # the new partition appears
    ]# df -hT   # the new partition has the ext3 filesystem, points to
                   # /home/common and has some space used

Notice the size of the partition. The common directory will be used for common user data files. Users will not be able to create more files in the common directory (the new partition) than the number of megabytes that you specified when you created the partition for this directory.

(11) Ensuring that You can Create a File in the New Partition

Change into the common directory below /home ;

use the touch command to create a file named test.txt in the new partition ;

get a long listing of the common directory ; the test.txt file should appear ;

```
]#  umount  /home/common        #  you are "in" the directory, so you
                                #  cannot unmount it
```

change to the /root directory ; run the above command again ;

get a long listing of /home (without changing directory) ; the common directory appears ;

get a long listing of the common directory below /home (without changing directory) ; no files appear because you have unmounted the partition to which the common directory points ;

```
]#  mount  /home/common
```

get a long listing of the common directory below /home again ; the test.txt file appears because the partition is mounted.

(12) Checking that the Partition Mounts After Rebooting

Close all terminal emulation windows and programs ;

select the items from the Menu to reboot (a.k.a. restart) your system.

Watch the screen as your system boots. When a list of partitions appears below "Checking filesystems", you should be able to see your new partition as: /home/common. This list of partitions appears because the **fsck** (filesystem **check**) command is being run to check the filesystems on them.

Log in as cwest ; open a terminal emulation window ;

```
]#  cd  ../common      #  change into the common directory, which is
                       #  parallel to the cwest directory (below /home)
```

Get a long listing of the common directory ; the test.txt file appears.

You did not use the mount command to mount the common directory. It was automatically mounted during the boot process due to the statement that you put in fstab for it.

13 Creating a File in the New Partition

Use the touch command to *try* to create a file named test1.txt.

You can "see" the files in common, but you do not have permission to create a file in this directory (more on this later).

su to root ;

change into /home/common ; use the touch command to create a file named test1.txt ;

get a long listing of the current directory ; the test1.txt file should appear ;

]# rm test1.txt

When you are working as root, you can create files in the common directory (the new partition).

]# df -hT   # the new partition that is mounted on /home/common appears

14 Adding Access to a Windows Partition on a Dual-Boot System

If you are using a dual-boot Windows/Linux system, the following steps set up access to a Windows partition from "within" Linux.

The next command creates a directory named driveC. This will be the mount point for the hda1 (Windows) partition. The full path is used below and therefore the command will create driveC in /mnt/ when it is run from any directory.

]# mkdir /mnt/driveC

]# ls -l /mnt   # check that the driveC (mount point) directory exists

Run vi and load /etc/fstab. Add the following statement on a blank line at the end of fstab. Press Tab between each "chunk" of text, except press Spacebar once between "0" and "0".

/dev/hda1   /mnt/driveC   vfat   auto, owner, users   0 0

When the Linux boots, this statement will cause the hda1 partition to be automatically mounted on the driveC directory, using the vfat filesystem.

If you have other Windows partitions, create mount points for them below /mnt and add statements for them to fstab.

The next command causes the mount command to look in fstab for the settings for the /mnt/driveC mount point and then the command mounts the hda1 partition on /mnt/driveC. This checks that the settings in fstab are correct before rebooting the system.

```
]#  mount  /mnt/driveC

]#  mount                  #  the partition, mount point and settings for
                           #  hda1 appear

]#  df  -hT  |  grep driveC   #  shows disk space information for the
                              #  Windows partition

]#  cd  /mnt/driveC  ;  ls  -l
```

The files in the root directory of the Windows partition appear. This partition is referred to as drive C: in Windows. Now you can access the filesystem of the Windows partition!

 Shutting Down

Close all programs and windows ; Menu ; Log Out ; Shut Down ; OK.

 Section Review

1. The label of /boot has been given to the hda2 partition and a LABEL=/boot statement with the correct settings has been added to fstab. Select the command that can be used to unmount the partition.

    O A. umount /boot
    O B. umount /dev/boot
    O C. umount -r /boot
    O D. umount /boot/hda2

2. You can use a utility to view a mounted partition, but you should not use a utility to modify a mounted partition. T F

3. When you are "in" fdisk, what do you use to get a listing of partitions on a disk?

    - ○ A.   l for list the partition table
    - ○ B.   s for show the partition table
    - ○ C.   p for print the partition table
    - ○ D.   d for display the partition table

4. Which file is read during the boot process for the settings that are used for partitions?

    - ○ A.   /proc/mtab
    - ○ B.   /proc/filesystems
    - ○ C.   /etc/fstab
    - ○ D.   /root/inittab

5. Select the command used to put a filesystem on a partition.

    - ○ A.   mkfs
    - ○ B.   fdisk
    - ○ C.   fstab
    - ○ D.   dmfs

6. You need to create a partition on the third SCSI disk in a system. Select the command that you need to use to start fdisk.

    - ○ A.   fdisk /dev/hdc
    - ○ B.   fdisk /dev/sdc
    - ○ C.   fdisk /dev/scc
    - ○ D.   fdisk /dev/scsic

7. The -h option of fdisk displays the information in /proc/partitions (for all partitions on all hard disks) in "human readable" form. T F

8. Which of the following commands will work?

    - ○ A.   e2label /home/common /dev/hda9
    - ○ B.   e2label /dev/hda9 /home/common/sales
    - ○ C.   e2label /dev/hda9 /home/common
    - ○ D.   e2label /dev/hda /home/common

9. The top and free commands can be used to see the amount of space used on a swap partition. T F

10. A new hard drive has just been installed in your system and you have not booted the system since it was installed. After booting the system, which command can be used to see if the hard drive was "seen" by Linux during the boot process?

   O A. mount
   O B. lsdisk
   O C. dmesg
   O D. dlist

11. Select the command that is run to test the settings in fstab after it has been edited to add a statement for a new partition.

   O A. mkfs
   O B. mounttab
   O C. mtest
   O D. mount

12. You can always modify a mounted partition without having any problems with the partition. T F

13. Select the command that will show the SCSI hard disks installed in a system.

   O A. dmesg | grep ^sd
   O B. dmesg | grep ^sc
   O C. dmesg | grep ^hd
   O D. fdisk | grep ^sd

14. Which option of the df command is used to display the filesystem type of a partition?

   O A. -fstype
   O B. -t
   O C. -T
   O D. -l

Chapter 11: Using Filesystem Commands

During this chapter you will learn that an X GUI or text-based GUI file manager will not always be available to use for file management tasks, and the benefits of using commands to perform these tasks.

You will also find out about several filesystem commands and the options that are commonly used with them. You will see the subtle differences between how an option that can be used with one command works a bit differently from the same option for a different command.

The following commands are described in this chapter and are also used in the Hands-On Exercises:

mkdir	make (create) a directory
rmdir	remove (delete) an empty directory
cp	copy directories and files from one location to another
mv	move directories and files from one location to another and rename a single directory or a single file
rm	remove directories and files
du	show the disk space usage of directories and subdirectories

A Case Study scenario is introduced in this section regarding a fictitious company named RMG Inc. This company requires data directory structures to be created for its Production and Sales Departments.

During the Hands-On Exercises you will use all of the commands described in this chapter to create the data directory structures for this company and copy and move data files into the directories that you create.

Using Filesystem Commands

Topics Covered in this Chapter

Learn the options of several filesystem commands

See many examples of using these filesystem commands

Introduce the RMG Inc. Case Study Scenario

Detail the data directory structures required by this company and the data files that are required in each directory

Do the steps to create the data directory structures required by RMG Inc. and copy and move data files into these directories

In this chapter, you will learn about several filesystem commands and their options, create data directory structures, copy and move files, and use the du command to see the disk space usage of these directories and subdirectories.

X GUI File Managers and Text-Based GUI File Managers

X GUI and text-based GUI file managers can be used to do most of the filesystem management tasks that are described in this chapter. However, when you are working on a server and a desktop is not available, an X GUI file manager, such as Nautilus or Konqueror cannot be used. Furthermore, a text-based GUI file manager may not have been installed and is therefore unavailable.

When you boot into Rescue Mode, a desktop is not running and so an X GUI file manager cannot be used and a text-based GUI file manager is not available (by default with this distribution). Therefore, there will be many times when you will need to use the commands described below.

The filesystem management commands described in this chapter are commonly used and are extremely fast and powerful.

By default, the root user has aliases for the cp, mv and rm commands and these aliases all use the -i (interactive) option to help prevent you from making mistakes while using these commands.

Due to the permission restrictions of non-root users, they can only make mistakes in the limited areas of the system to which they have permission. In addition to this, non-root users may only want to use an X GUI file manager rather than using filesystem commands. Therefore, non-root users do not have the cp, mv and rm aliases with the -i (interactive) option by default. If you feel it is necessary for your environment, you can easily change this by creating one or more .sh files in /etc/profile.d that cause these aliases to be created for all users.

The mkdir Command

The **mkdir** (**make dir**ectory) command is used to make (create) a directory.

The Syntax of the mkdir Command

The following is the syntax of the mkdir command:

mkdir [options] [path]*directoryname*

The -p option of this command is used to cause all parent directories in the specified [path] to be created if they do not exist above the *directoryname*.

Examples of the mkdir Command

mkdir letters

Creates the directory named letters below the current directory. A relative path (the current directory) is being used with this example.

mkdir /home/common/creative

Creates the directory named creative below /home/common. An absolute path is being used in this example. This command can be run from any directory to create the creative directory below the path of /home/common.

mkdir -p userdata/reports

Creates the directory named reports below the directory named userdata in the current directory. If the userdata directory does not exist, then the -p option causes it to be created.

The example above shows a relative path. The -p option works the same as described above if an absolute path is used.

The rmdir Command

The **rmdir** (**re**move **dir**ectory) command is used to remove a directory if the directory is empty (if it does not contain subdirectories or files).

The Syntax of the rmdir Command

The following is the syntax of the rmdir command:

rmdir [options] [path]*directoryname*

The -p option of this command is used to cause the parent directory in the specified [path] above the *directoryname* to be removed if it is empty. Each additional empty parent directory above that is also removed.

The rm command can also be used to remove a directory structure (multiple directories) by using the -r option and specifying the name of a parent directory (rather than the *directoryname* at the end of the [path]). The directories do not need to be empty to be removed.

Examples of the rmdir Command

rmdir memos

Removes the directory named memos below the current directory, if it is empty. A relative path (the current directory) is being used with this example.

rmdir /home/datafiles/jan

Removes the directory named jan (if it is empty) below the [path] of /home/datafiles. An absolute path is used in this example and therefore this command can be run from any directory.

rmdir -p progs/userprogs/anjuta

Removes the directory named anjuta (if it is empty) below progs/userprogs. The progs directory is in the current directory. If the userprogs directory is empty, then the -p option causes it to be removed as well. If the anjuta and userprogs directories are empty, and the progs directory is empty, then the -p option causes progs to be removed as well.

The example above shows a relative path. The -p option works the same as described above if an absolute path is used.

The cp Command

The **cp** (**copy**) command is used to copy directories and files from one location to another.

The Syntax of the cp Command

The following is the syntax of the cp command:

    cp [options] source destination

The source can be a [path] or [pattern] or both. The destination can also be a [path] or [pattern] or both.

 By default, the root user has an alias named cp that causes the -i option to be used when the cp command is used. This causes the system to prompt you for each existing file that you are trying to copy a file (with the same name) over top of, unless you use the -f option. Therefore, when you are working as the root user, you must type: y and press Enter to copy a file over top of an existing file, unless you use the -f option.

When you try to copy a source directory to a destination directory with the same name, an error message appears. When you do this and use the **-r** (**recursive**) option, then the source directory (name, files and subs) is copied *below* the destination directory.

Keep the above comments in mind when looking at the options of the command below.

For example, the -i option below shows "only used when copying files, not directories". This is because you cannot copy a source directory to a destination directory (that has the same name) without the using the -r option, and when the -r option is used, the source directory is copied below the destination directory. The -i option is not required because no files are going to be copied over top of existing files.

Options of the cp Command

Table 11-1 - Common Options of the cp Command

Option	Description
-i	**i**nteractive - prompts prior to copying a file over top of an existing file only used when copying files, not directories
-f	**f**orce the copy of files over top of existing files without prompting only used when copying files, not directories
-b	**b**ackup - creates a backup copy of each *destination* file in the destination directory (when a source file has the same name as a file in the destination) the backup file has the same name as the copied file, plus a ~ (tilde) at the end of the file name only used when copying files, not directories
-r	**r**ecursive - copy a directory and its contents below the destination directory only used when copying directories (and their contents), not files
-v	**v**erbose - displays a message describing the actions of the command

Examples of the cp Command

cp memo1.sxw memo2.sxw

Copies memo1.sxw to a new file named memo2.sxw.

cp report-jan.sxc ../feb/report-feb.sxc

Your current directory is named jan and the report-jan.sxc file is in the current directory. The feb directory is parallel to the current directory. This command copies report-jan.sxc into the feb directory and the destination file is named report-feb.sxc. The file is renamed in the destination.

If a file named report-feb.sxc exists in the feb directory *and the -b option is used in the above command,* then the existing report-feb.sxc file would be renamed to report-feb.sxc~ and the report-jan.sxc would be put in feb with the name of report-feb.sxc.

cp /home/cwest/*.txt .

Your current directory is /home/bbest. This command copies all files ending in ".txt" in /home/cwest to the current directory (bbest). A . (dot) is commonly used with the cp command to represent the current directory.

cp -r letters /home/data

The directory named letters is below the current directory. This directory contains files and subdirectories (which contain files).

The above command copies the directory named letters and everything in it (due to the -r option) to the directory named data, below /home. Therefore, the letters directory and the directory structure below letters is copied to /home/data.

The directory named data now contains the directory named letters and all of the files and subdirectories in letters. This is an example of copying files rather then moving them. Therefore, the directory named letters (and everything in it) still exists below the current directory.

The mv Command

The **mv** (**m**ove) command is used to move files from one location to another and is also used to rename a single directory or a single file.

The Syntax of the mv Command

The following is the syntax of the mv command:

    mv [options] source destination

To move items to a destination directory, the destination directory must exist. It will not automatically be created.

By default, the root user has an alias named mv that causes the -i option to be used when the mv command is used. This causes the system to prompt you for each existing file that you are trying to move a file (with the same name) on top of, unless you use the -f option. Therefore, when you are working as the root user, you must type: y and press Enter to move a file over top of an existing file, unless you use the -f option.

When you move a directory to a directory with the same name, then the source directory (name, files and subs) is moved *below* the destination directory. Unlike the cp command, this happens without specifying the **-r** (recursive) option. The mv command does not have a -r option.

Options of the mv Command

Table 11-2 - Common Options of the mv Command

Option	Description
-i	interactive - prompts prior to moving a file over top of an existing file only used when moving files, not directories
-f	force the move of files over top of existing files without prompting only used when moving files, not directories
-b	backup - creates a backup copy of each *destination* file in the destination directory (when the source file has the same name as a file in the destination) the backup file has the same name as the moved file, plus a ~ (tilde) at the end of the file name only used when moving files, not directories
-v	verbose - displays a message describing the actions of the command

Examples of the mv Command

mv graphic1.sxi /home/cwest/gr-data

Moves the file named graphic1.sxi from the current directory to the gr-data directory below /home/cwest. The file no longer exists in the current directory.

mv /home/common/*.sxw /home/backup

Moves all files ending in ".sxw" from the common directory below /home to the backup directory below /home. The moved files no longer exist in /home/common.

mv /home/bford/mar* .

Your current directory is /home/common/ss-data. This command moves all files beginning with "mar" in /home/bford to the current directory. A . (dot) is commonly used with the mv command to represent the current directory. The moved files no longer exist in /home/bford.

mv reports /home/common/may

Your current directory contains the directory named reports and this directory contains files and subdirectories that contain files. This command moves the reports directory (structure) into the may directory below the path of /home/common.

mv graphic1.sxi graphics.sxi

Moves the file named graphic1.sxi in the current directory to the name of graphics.sxi in the current directory. The graphic1.sxi file no longer exists. This command *renames* the graphic1.sxi file to the new name of graphics.sxi.

mv april last-april

A directory named april exists below the current directory. This directory contains files and subdirectories that contain files. This command *renames* the directory named april to the new name of last-april. The directory named april no longer exists. All files and subdirectories that were below april are now below last-april.

The rm Command

The **rm** (**rem**ove) command is used to remove directories and files.

The Syntax of the rm Command

The following is the syntax of the cp command:

rm [options] [path][pattern]

By default, the root user has an alias named rm that causes the -i option to be used when the rm command is used. This causes the system to prompt you for each item (directory or file) that you are trying to remove, unless you use the -f option. Therefore, when you are working as the root user, you must type: y   and press Enter for each item, unless you use the -f option.

If there are a lot of items to be removed with the rm command, responding to each item can take a long time and be very tedious. Therefore, the -f option can be used so that you are not prompted for each item. However, if you make a mistake, then you can end up instantly removing a part of your filesystem. You can accidentally remove *all* of your filesystem if the -r option is used with the -f option. The -r option is only used with the rm command when you are removing directories (i.e. only when you are specifying a directory name at the end of the [path] and a [pattern] is not used).

Notice the (accidental) space after the first slash in the following command. The following command will remove all directories and subdirectories on a system without prompting!

rm -rf / home/bford

The accidental space at the right of the first slash causes the command to work on the / (root) directory and therefore, the -r and -f options of the command cause all items below the / directory to be deleted (*even if the -i option is part of an alias for the rm command*).

Use extreme caution when using the -r and -f options of the rm command, particularly when you are working as the root user.

We recommend that you only use the -r and -f options when specifying a directory below the current directory. In other words, do not use these options with an absolute path and only use them when specifying a relative path to a directory below your current directory. This will limit the amount of the filesystem that could be removed if you made a mistake.

For example, the bford user is no longer working on the system and you need to remove the directories and files in the bford directory below /home. There may be hundreds or thousands of directories and files below the bford directory. If you used the rm command without the -r and -f optons, you would have to type: y and pressing Enter to remove each item and this would not be feasible.

Rather than specify the absolute path of /home/bford with the rm command, you change into /home and specify the relative path of bford, as shown in the command below. Therefore, you are not in any danger of removing any directories below the / directory or the entire filesystem.

        rm -rf bford

Options of the rm Command

Table 11-3 - Common Options of the rm Command

Option	Description
-i	interactive - prompts prior to removing directories and files
-f	force the removal of directories and files without prompting
-r	recursive - remove a directory and all of its contents only used when removing directories, not files
-v	verbose - displays a message describing the actions of the command

Examples of the rm Command

An absolute path is not used in any of the examples below for the reasons described in the above Caution icon. We recommend that you change into the parent directory of the items that you need to remove and use a relative path (rather than an absolute path) with the rm command. As described earlier, use extreme caution when running the rm command with the -r and -f options.

rm mgccc-quote.sxw

Removes the mgccc-quote.sxw file in the current directory.

rm common/tticc-fax.sxi

You are in /home and a directory named common exists below /home. This command removes the tticc-fax.sxi file located in the path of /home/common.

rm -r jan

The jan directory is below your current directory. This command removes the jan directory recursively (i.e. the jan directory and all items in it). By default, the alias named rm causes the system to prompt you for each item below jan. You must type: y and press Enter to remove each item. If there are a lot of items below a directory, add the -f option to the command.

rm -rf wp-data

The wp-data directory is below the current directory. This command removes the wp-data directory recursively without prompting for each item in the data directory.

Use extreme caution when using the -r and -f options together.

The du Command

The **du** (disk space **u**sage) command shows the disk space usage of directories and subdirectories and provides a summary of the total disk space used, by directory.

The Syntax of the du Command

The following is the syntax of the du command:

    du [options] [path][pattern]

Options of the du Command

Table 11-4 - Common Options of the df Command

Option	Description
-h	displays output in human readable format
-s	displays a summary for the path and/or pattern specified

Examples of the du Command

du

Displays the disk space usage (sizes) for all subdirectories in the current directory, and all subdirectories below them, with the total space used on the last line of output. This is the space used by all items in subdirectories, shown for each subdirectory (rather than sizes being shown for each file). Hidden directories (prefixed with a . (dot)) are shown by default.

When this command is run in a home directory, such as cwest, many items usually appear because there are typically hidden directories below a home directory and many subdirectories below these hidden directories.

du -h

Same as above, but in human readable format (K (kilobytes), M (megabytes) and G (gigabytes)).

du -hs

Same as above, but only shows the last line of output (a summary).

du -hs *

Shows the summary for all items below the current directory. This is very useful.

du -h /boot

Displays total space used in /boot and each subdirectory of /boot in human readable format.

If /boot has two subdirectories named lost+found and grub, then the output shows three items. The total space used in /boot/lost+found, total space used in /boot/grub and then total space used in /boot.

The total space used in the directory that is specified with the command, such as /boot, appears last and includes the space used in the subdirectories of the directory.

RMG Inc. - Case Study Scenario

RMG Inc. is a company that makes greeting cards. They need to have two of their departments set up on a server (your system) so that users attached to the server can share data files. The two departments are the Sales Department and the Production Department.

The users in each department work with three software programs. They use a graphics program that works with files that have a .sxi suffix; a spreadsheet program that works with files that have a .sxc suffix; and a word processing program that works with files that have a .sxw suffix.

When you installed Linux earlier, you installed three OpenOffice.org application software programs. These are the **I**mpress graphics presentation program, that uses .sxi files; the **C**alc spreadsheet program, that uses .sxc files; and the **W**riter word processing program, that uses .sxw files.

Data files with the suffixes of .sxi, .sxc and .sxw are on CD 3 and will be used during this Case Study. You will put these files in various directories on your system and use the Impress, Calc and Writer programs to access these files locally, and also access them from a server "over the network".

Your Mission (Should You Choose to ...)

As the administrator of the server that will be used by the Sales and Production Departments, you have been asked to create data directories for user private data and for the common data files of users in the Sales and Production Departments. After creating these data directories you will put the necessary files in them.

The directory structures that are required and the files that go in them are detailed below.

The User Data Directories and the Parent Data Directory for the Sales and Production Departments

User private data will be kept in three data directories below each user's home directory.

All common user data for the Sales and Production Departments will be kept in the common directory below /home. You created the partition for the common user data files and assigned the common directory as the mount point for this partition in the last chapter.

Private User Data

Template files are documents that are pre-formatted with blank areas that can be filled in with personal data, customer data or supplier data.

Users will be provided with user template data files so that they can more easily create the documents that they require. These template files will be put in three directories below their home directories. These directories will be **gr**-data, **ss**-data and **wp**-data, for **gr**aphic, **s**pread**s**heet and **w**ord **p**rocessing documents, respectively.

Each user requires three template data files for each of the three programs that they will be using.

For the graphics program, these files are: calendar.sxi, clock.sxi, reminder.sxi.

For the spreadsheet program, these files are: daily-report.sxc, weekly-report.sxc, monthly-report.sxc.

For the word processing program, these files are: letter.sxw, memo.sxw, invoice.sxw.

The User Data Directories

The user data directories with the template data files are shown below.

```
/home/cwest/
        gr-data/
                calendar.sxi, clock.sxi, reminder.sxi
        ss-data/
                daily-report.sxc, weekly-report.sxc, monthly-report.sxc
        wp-data/
                letter.sxw, memo.sxw, invoice.sxw
```

Common User Data

User data files that are "common" (shared) will be kept below the parent directory named common, below /home (/home/common).

Each department will have a directory below /home/common for shared data files.

The directory for the Production Departmentwill be named prod and the path to this directory will be /home/common/prod.

The directory for the Sales Department will be named sales and the path to this directory will be /home/common/sales.

The prod and sales directories are parallel to one another. They are both below /home/common. They are on the same directory "level".

Production Department Data

The prod directory (/home/common/prod) is a parent directory for the five common Production Department subdirectories described below.

Current greeting card orders that have been put into production will be kept below the current-orders directory. These files include word processing documents (.sxw files) and the costing (spreadsheet) documents (.sxc files) that describe the specifications of the orders.

Graphics, spreadsheet and word processing data that will be shared amongst users in the Production Department will be kept in the shared-**gr**-data (shared **gr**aphics data), shared-**ss**-data (shared **s**pread**s**heet data) and shared-**wp**-data (shared **w**ord **p**rocessing data) directories, respectively.

Template files for new printing press plates, new schedules, notification emails and starting date letters will be kept in the masters directory.

The Production Department Data Directory Structure

The Production Department data directory structure with data files is shown below.

```
/home/common/prod/
        current-orders/
                dsb-costing.sxc, dsb-order.sxw, egcc-costing.sxc,
                egcc-order.sxw, espcc-costing.sxc, espcc-order.sxw,
                itt-costing.sxc, itt-order.sxw
        shared-prod-gr-data/
                datcc-card.sxi, patnc-card.sxi
        shared-prod-ss-data/
                batch-costs.sxc, item-costs.sxc
        shared-prod-wp-data/
                blanket-order.sxw, single-order.sxw
        masters/
                new-plate.sxi, new-schedule.sxc, notify-email.sxw,
                start-date-letter.sxw
```

Sales Department Data

The sales directory (/home/common/sales) is a parent directory for the five common Sales Department subdirectories described below.

Current quotes that have been sent to customers will be kept below the current-quotes directory. These files include word processing documents (.sxw files) and the accompanying graphics documents (.sxi files) that describe various greeting card products.

As with the Production Department, graphics, spreadsheet and word processing data that will be shared amongst users in the Sales Department will be kept in the shared-gr-data, shared-ss-data and shared-wp-data directories, respectively.

Template files for new contracts, month end reports, greeting card graphics, and new quotes will be kept in the templates directory.

The Sales Department Data Directory Structure

The Sales Department data directory structure with data files is shown below.

```
/home/common/sales/
        current-quotes/
                jcjc-card.sxi, jcjc-quote.sxw, nmcc-card.sxi, nmcc-quote.sxw
        shared-sales-gr-data/
                lancom-card.sxi, mgccc-card.sxi
        shared-sales-ss-data/
                03-month-end.sxc, 04-month-end.sxc
        shared-sales-wp-data/
                lancom-quote.sxw, mgccc-quote.sxw
        templates/
                contract.sxw, month-end.sxc, new-card.sxi, new-quote.sxw
```

Hands-On Exercises

 ### 1   Logging In to Create the RMG Inc. Data Directories

Log in to a desktop as cwest ; open a terminal emulation window ; su to root.

Your current directory is /root.

Use caution when doing the exercises below. Doing it right the first time is easier than doing it over. Sometimes *much* easier than having to do it over. Also, use the Tab key whenever possible to complete the names of items.

Without changing directory, get a long listing of the common directory below /home ; this directory does not yet contain the prod and sales directories.

Your current directory is still /root. The command below uses the absolute path to create the prod directory. When an absolute path is used, the directory can be created from any directory, as long as you have permission to create the directory in the destination (parent) directory.

]# mkdir /home/common/prod

Change into the common directory below /home ; get a long listing ; the prod directory should appear.

The path to your current directory is /home/common. The next command uses a relative path to create the sales directory below the current directory.

]# mkdir sales

get a long directory listing and the prod and sales directories should appear.

 ### 2   Copying Data Files into /home/cwest, /home/common/prod and /home/common/sales

You need to copy the user data files in the user directory on the CD to the home directory of the cwest user (/home/cwest). You also need to copy the Production Department data files in the prod directory on the CD to /home/common/prod and the Sales Department data files in the sales directory on the CD to /home/common/sales.

Put CD 3 in your CD-ROM drive ; it will be mounted automatically by the desktop ;

change into the cdrom directory below /mnt ; get a long directory listing ;

```
]# cd hello
```

press Tab ; change into the hello-linux-data directory ;

get a long listing of the current directory ;

the prod, sales and user (sub)directories should appear ;

change into the user directory ; get a long listing ; user data files appear ;

```
]# cp * /home/cwest          # copy all files in the user directory
                             # to /home/cwest
```

without changing directory, get a long listing of the files in /home/cwest ;
the user data files that were copied from the user directory should appear ;

```
]# cd ../prod ; ls -l        # use a relative path to change into the
                             # prod directory
                             # the prod directory is parallel to the
                             # user directory
```

```
]# cp * /home/common/prod    # copy all files in prod to
                             # /home/common/prod
```

without changing directory, get a long listing of the files in /home/common/prod ;
the common data files for the Production Department should appear ;

the sales directory on the CD is parallel to the prod directory ; use the cd
command with the relative path to the sales directory, to change into the
sales directory (see the last cd command above) ; get a long listing ;

copy all of the files in the current directory (the sales directory on the CD),
to /home/common/sales (see the last cp command above) ;

get a long listing of /home/common/sales ;

change into /home/cwest ;

run the command to see the path to your current directory ; get a long listing ;

use the command: eject to eject the CD ; remove the CD and close
the drive door.

The following three chmod commands change the permissions of the data
files to the default permissions that they would have if they were created by
the root user. This will be described in more detail in the next chapter.

```
]# chmod 644 /home/cwest/*
```

```
]# chmod 644 /home/common/prod/*
```

```
]# chmod 644 /home/common/sales/*
```

Now that you have copied the data files to the correct parent directories (cwest,
prod and sales), you will create subdirectories for these files and move the data
files into the subdirectories.

---

③ **Creating Subdirectories for the User Template Data Files**

Your current path should be: /home/cwest.

]# mkdir gr-data   # create the subdirectory for graphics data

create the ss-data and wp-data directories below the current directory ;

get a long listing to see that the correct directory names appear.

④ **Moving the User Template Data Files Into Subdirectories**

The user template data files exist in /home/cwest and we need to put them in the above subdirectories and not also have them in /home/cwest. Therefore, we will move the files into the subdirectories rather than copy them.

You need to move the files with the .sxi suffix into gr-data, the files with the .sxc suffix into ss-data and the files with the .sxw suffix into wp-data.

Do not use an * (asterisk) as a wildcard character to represent all files when using the mv command below. This wildcard character will also represent all subdirectories. If you use this character, then you will end up moving all subdirectories (in the current directory) into the destination directory that you specify.

Also, do not use an * (asterisk) with other characters if it will specify a pattern that matches a subdirectory name. If you do, then the subdirectory will be moved into the destination directory that you specify. Best to use the suffix of a file name if you use the *. This will stop the pattern from matching the name of a subdirectory.

]# mv *.sxi gr-data

get a long listing of the current directory ; the .sxi files are no longer in this directory ;

]# ls -l gr-data   # the .sxi files are now in this directory

move the .sxc files into ss-data ; get a long listing of the current directory and ss-data ;

move the .sxw files into wp-data ; get a long listing of the current directory and wp-data ;

make sure that only .sxi files are in gr-data, only .sxc files are in ss-data and only .sxw files are in wp-data and also make sure that there are no .sx? (**.sx**i, **.sx**c or **.sx**w) files in /home/cwest.

Creating Subdirectories for the Production Department Data Files

Change into the prod directory below /home/common ; get a long listing ;

create the following directories below the prod directory:

current-orders, shared-prod-gr-data, shared-prod-ss-data,

shared-prod-wp-data, masters

get a long listing ;

Earlier, you created an lsld alias by creating a file named lsld.sh in /etc/profile.d. This alias gives a listing of directories only. This alias should still exist.

Run the alias command to see if the lsld alias still exists ; the other aliases that you created earlier should also still exist ;

for the lsld alias, look at the syntax at the right of the = (equal) sign to see what this alias does ;

now run the lsld alias to get a listing of directories only.

Make sure you have created all of the above directories and that the names of them are correct.

6 **Moving the Production Department Data Files Into Subdirectories**

Do not use an * (asterisk) as a wildcard character to represent all files when using the mv command below. This wildcard character will also represent all directories. If you use this character, then you will end up moving all subdirectories (in the current directory) into the destination directory that you specify.

Remember to use the Tab key whenever possible to complete the names of items.

```
]# ls -l itt*            # these two files need to go into current-orders

]# mv itt* current-orders  # moves itt-order.sxw and itt-costing.sxc

get a long listing  ;  now run the lslf alias get a long listing of files only.
```

Using wildcard characters whenever possible (check the output of the above listing), but not using a * (single asterisk), or an * with a pattern that matches a subdirectory name, and not moving more files than necessary, move the following files into current-orders:

dsb-costing.sxc, dsb-order.sxw, egcc-costing.sxc, egcc-order.sxw,

espcc-costing.sxc, espcc-order.sxw

When checking your work in a step further below, remember that itt-order.sxw and itt-costing.sxc were also moved to the directory containing the above files.

Move the following files into shared-prod-gr-data:

datcc-card.sxi, patnc-card.sxi

Move the following files into shared-prod-ss-data:

item-costs.sxc, batch-costs.sxc

Move the following files into shared-prod-wp-data:

single-order.sxw, blanket-order.sxw

Move the following files into masters (do not use a * (single asterisk) to represent all files or in a pattern that matches a subdirectory name):

new-plate.sxi, new-schedule.sxc, notify-email.sxw, start-date-letter.sxw

]# ls -l current-orders   # check that this directory contains the correct files

repeat the above command for all of the other directories above and check that each directory contains the correct files ;

also make sure that there are no .sx? (**.sx**i, **.sx**c or **.sx**w) files in /home/common/prod.

⑦ Creating Subdirectories for the Sales Department Data Files

Change into the sales directory below /home/common ; get a long listing ;

create the following directories below the sales directory:

current-quotes, shared-sales-gr-data, shared-sales-ss-data,

shared-sales-wp-data, templates

us the lsld alias to get a long listing of directories only.

Make sure you have created all of the above directories and that the names of them are correct.

⑧ **Moving the Sales Department Data Files Into Subdirectories**

Remember the earlier comments regarding using an * (asterisk) as a
wildcard character with the mv command.

Run the lslf alias get a long listing of files only.

Move the following files into current-quotes:

   jcjc-card.sxi, jcjc-quote.sxw, nmcc-card.sxi, nmcc-quote.sxw

Move the following files into shared-sales-gr-data:

   lancom-card.sxi, mgccc-card.sxi

Move the following files into shared-sales-ss-data:

   03-month-end.sxc, 04-month-end.sxc

Move the following files into shared-sales-wp-data:

   lancom-quote.sxw, mgccc-quote.sxw

Move the following files into templates (do not use a * (single asterisk) to
represent all files):

   new-card.sxi, new-quote.sxw, contract.sxw, month-end.sxc

```
]# ls -l current-quotes     # check that this directory contains the
                            # correct files
```

repeat the above command for all of the other directories above and
check that each directory contains the correct files ;

also make sure that there are no .sx? (**.sx**i, **.sx**c or **.sx**w) files in
/home/common/sales.

⑨ **Using the du Command in the cwest Directory**

Change into /home/cwest ;

```
]# du | less        # disk space usage for items in and below cwest appears
                    # the total space used by all items appears last

]# du -h | less     # uses the human readable option

]# du -hs           # uses the summary option - only shows the
                    # total (last line)

]# du -hs ??-data   # shows a summary by subdirectory
```

(10) Using the du Command in the Common Directory

Change into /home/common ; get a long listing ; there are only subdirectories ;

```
]# du -h              # disk space usage for each subdirectory appears
                      # the total space used by all subdirectories appears last

]# du -hs             # uses the summary option - only shows the total

]# du -hs *           # shows a summary by subdirectory

]# ls -lR prod | less
```

All of the subdirectories below prod and the files in each subdirectory appear. The prod directory has five subs and each one contains files. The subdirectories below prod do not contain any subdirectories.

```
]# du -h prod            # same as running:  du -h /home/common/prod
```

Shows total space used by the files in the subdirectories of prod and shows the total space used by all directories and files in prod on the last line.

```
]# du -hs prod           # uses the summary option - only shows the
                         # total for each item

]# ls -lR sales | less
```

All of the subdirectories below sales and the files in each subdirectory appear.

```
]# du -h sales           # same as running:  du -h /home/common/sales
```

Shows total space used by the files in the subdirectories of sales and shows the total space used by all directories and files in sales on the last line.

```
]# du -hs sales          # uses the summary option - only shows the
                         # total for each item

]# du -h /boot
```

Shows the space used in subdirectories of /boot and the total space used in /boot at the end.

(11) **Using the du Command with the sort Command**

```
]#  du  -h
]#  du  -h  |  sort          # this didn't quite work right
```

The output of du is piped to the sort command.

```
]#  du  -h  |  sort  -n       # the n (numeric) option of the sort command
                             # was needed
```

Now the listing shows directories sorted by the space that they are using.

```
]#  du  -h  |  sort  -rn      # the r (reverse) option of sort is used here
```

(12) **Creating Multiple Directories with One Command**

Run the alias command.

When you are working as the root user, the alias names of cp, mv and rm are all aliases for commands of the same name. These aliases cause each of these commands to automatically use the -i (interactive) option.

Your current directory should be /home/common.

```
]#  mkdir  -p  one/two/three
```

The -p option causes all three directories to be created below the current directory.

(13) **Copying Files into Subdirectories**

The steps below copy a file in the current directory into subdirectories using a relative path. The file is copied to a new name in each subdirectory.

```
]#  touch  test.txt

]#  cp  test.txt  one/test1.txt       # copies test.txt to one with the name
                                      # of test1.txt

]#  cp  test.txt  one/two/test2.txt

]#  cp  test.txt  one/two/three/test3.txt
```

The one, two and three directories now have a file in each.

(14) **Renaming a File with the mv Command**

Get a long listing ; the file named test.txt appears ;

```
]#  mv  test.txt  test.bak     # renames test.txt to test.bak
```

get a long listing ; the file named test.bak appears.

]# rm test.bak

Copying a Directory Structure to a New Location

]# mkdir data

get a long directory listing ;

]# cp -r one data   # copies one (and the directory structure
                                    # below one) to data

Copies the directory named one and everything below it (due to the -r option) to the directory named data. Data now contains the directory named one and one contains test1.txt. The directory named one contains the directory named two and so on.

]# clear ; ls -lR data   # the directories and files below data appear

Renaming a Directory with the mv Command

]# mv data test-data   # renames data to test-data

The directory structure (files and directories) that were below data are now below test-data.

]# clear ; ls -lR test-data   # the directories and files below test-data appear

17 Removing a Directory Structure and Being Prompted

Get a long listing ; you copied, rather than moved, the directory named one to below data (which became test-data) ; the one directory still exists ;

]# ls -R one   # the directories and files below test-data appear

The rm command below will demonstrate how the recursive option of it works. You will "descend" into the one directory, then the two directory, and then the three directory. You will then be prompted for the removal of files and directories from the bottom up! Type: y   and press Enter each time you are prompted. If there were a lot of files below the one directory, this would take a long time.

]# rm -r one   # remove the directory named one and all
                                  # items below it

(18) Removing a Directory Structure Without Being Prompted

]# ls -lR test-data   #   the directories and files below test-data appear

]# rm -rf test-data ; ls -l

The test-data directory and all its subdirectories and files are instantly removed! The **-r** (recursive) option causes the entire directory structure below test-data to be deleted. The **-f** (force) option stops the **-i** (interactive) option from prompting you. Use the -r and -f options of the rm command with extreme caution.

(19) Shutting Down

Close all programs and windows ; Menu ; Log Out ; Shut Down ; OK.

Section Review

1. You are in /home and a directory named userprogs exists below /home. Select the command that removes the thisisit file located in userprogs.

    ○ A.   rm -r /userprogs/thisisit
    ○ B.   rm userprogs/thisisit
    ○ C.   rm /data/userprogs/thisisit
    ○ D.   rn /home/thisisit

2. Your current directory is /home/cwest. Select the command that will copy the files ending in ".txt" from the backup directory below /home/common to your current directory.

    ○ A.   cp /home/cwest/*.txt /backup
    ○ B.   cp /home/common/backup/*.txt .
    ○ C.   cp /home/common/backup/*.txt /cwest
    ○ D.   cp /home/common/backup/*.tst .

3. Your current directory has a subdirectory named memos, which contains files and subdirectories. You need to move memos and its contents to below /home/data/june. Select the command that will do this.

   ○ A. mv memos /home/data/june
   ○ B. mv memos home/data/june
   ○ C. mv memos /home/june
   ○ D. mv -r memos /home/data/june

4. The old-data directory is below /home/backup and your current directory is /home. Select the command that removes the old-data directory, files in old-data and all subdirectories (and their contents) below old-data.

   ○ A. rm -r old-data
   ○ B. rm -r /home/backup
   ○ C. rm -i /home/old-data
   ○ D. rm -r backup/old-data

5. Your current directory is /home/cards. There are no directories below your current directory. Which command will create two directories below the current directory (one below the other)?

   ○ A. mkdir -v data/sales
   ○ B. mkdir -r data/sales
   ○ C. mkdir -p data/sales
   ○ D. mkdir /home/data/sales

6. There is a directory named weekly below the current directory and it is empty. Which two commands can be used to remove the weekly directory?

   ☐ A. rm -r weekly
   ☐ B. mkdir -r weekly
   ☐ C. rmdir weekly
   ☐ D. rmvdir weekly

7. The progs directory exists below your current directory and it contains files and subdirectories. You need to rename this directory to old-progs. Which of the following commands will do this?

   ○ A. mv progs ./old-progs
   ○ B. mv -r progs old-progs
   ○ C. rn progs old-progs
   ○ D. mv progs old-progs

8. Which option causes the cp, mv and rm commands to prompt you?

   O A. -i
   O B. -r
   O C. -f
   O D. -p

9. Your current directory is /root. A directory named common exists below /home. Select the command that will create a directory named promo below common.

   O A. mkdir promo
   O B. mkdir /home/promo
   O C. mkdir home/common/promo
   O D. mkdir /home/common/promo

10. Your current directory is com-data below /home. A directory named sept-backup exists below the current directory and this directory contains files and subdirectories. Select the command that removes sept-backup and its contents without prompting.

    O A. rm -rf sept-backup
    O B. rm -rf /home/sept-backup
    O C. rm -r sept-backup
    O D. rm -rn com-data/sept-backup

11. Which command displays the disk space usage (sizes) for all subdirectories in the current directory, and all subdirectories below them, with the total space used on the last line of output?

    O A. df
    O B. du
    O C. rm
    O D. dc

12. Select the option that causes the rm command to make a backup of any files that you delete before deleting them.

    O A. -b
    O B. .bak
    O C. -c
    O D. none of the above

Chapter 12: Users, Groups, Permissions and Attributes

In this chapter, you will learn how users access Linux servers and the process that is used to allow users at RMG Inc. to access an NFS file server. You will also learn how users can be added to a group so that they acquire the permissions of the group on the server.

All of the permissions that can be assigned to users and groups are detailed in this chapter, including the methods of creating users and groups and assigning them permissions. The attributes that can be assigned to files and the method of assigning them are also described.

Important text files that contain user, group and password information are also detailed.

The following commands are described in this chapter and are also used in the Hands-On Exercises:

useradd	create a user
userdel	delete a user
usermod	modify the settings of a user
passwd	assign a password to a user and change an existing password
chage	specify password settings for a user
users	view the users currently logged on to a system
groupadd	create a group
groupdel	delete a group
groupmod	modify the group id number or group name of a group
chgrp	change the group name for directories and files
groups	displays all of the groups to which the currently logged in user belongs, or the names of the groups to which a specific user belongs
chown	change the user name and group name of directories and files
chmod	change the mode (a.k.a. permission settings) for a directory or file
chattr	assign attributes to files and remove attributes from files
lsattr	view the attributes of a file
id	view ID information for users and groups
umask	view the current umask setting or specify a umask setting

During the Hands-On Exercises, you will create users and groups and add users to groups. You will also assign permissions, users and groups to the directory structures of the Production and Sales Departments of RMG Inc.

Users, Groups, Permissions and Attributes

Topics Covered in this Chapter

Discuss the permission settings that can be assigned to directories and files

Detail the system text files that are used when working with users and groups

Learn the default and common permission settings for directories and files

Provide descriptions of the commands related to users, groups and permissions

Describe the default umask settings and the scripting logic that provides the default umask

You will do the steps to create the users and groups for the Production and Sales Departments at RMG Inc. and assign these users and groups permissions to the prod and sales directory structures. After this, you will run application software programs to test the permissions of the users in each department.

Overview of Creating Users and Groups for Linux Servers

There are many types of Linux servers to which users need a user account (user name) in order to be able to access the server for various tasks.

For example, a user needs an account to upload and download files to and from a Web Server or FTP server, and also to work with files in the filesystem of an **NFS** (Network File System) file server.

The concepts and tasks covered in this chapter apply to all of these servers.

Every service provided by a Linux server can protect itself and the server from unauthorized access by running under a restricted username and/or by requiring user authentication.

For example, the apache web runs as the user "apache" by default. Anyone can connect to the web server, but they are restricted by the server to the files and folders (usually) below /var/www/html. FTP servers, on the other hand, require user authentication. Users are required to log in using the optional "anonymous" user, or a user that is valid on the system running the server. NFS services provide access to files and folders based on user and group ids.

User accounts (user names) are created and assigned passwords so that users can access Linux servers. These accounts are assigned permissions to directories and files so that they can access them.

In addition to users, you can create groups and assign users to groups. When a user is assigned (added) to a group, the user becomes a member of the group. The permissions assigned to a group are acquired by the members of the group.

There are several permissions that can be assigned to directories and files, and there are also attributes that can be assigned to files. The permissions and attributes are used to allow access to, and to restrict access from, directories and files.

In this chapter, you will learn how to create users and groups and add users to groups. You will also learn how to assign permissions to directories and files, and remove permissions from directories and files. In addition to this, you will learn how to assign attributes to files and remove attributes from files.

The RMG Inc. Case Study Continued

We will be using an NFS file server for the RMG Inc. Case Study example in this chapter.

Each user in the two departments of RMG Inc. uses an x86 (PC) system. Each PC contains a network card and network cabling connects all of the PCs, including the server.

In an upcoming chapter you will do the steps to set up the NFS file server so that part of the filesystem of the server (/home/common and subs) is accessible to the users that you create in this chapter. Some of the permissions that users will have to the file server will be acquired through membership to the groups that you create in this chapter.

Once you have set up the NFS file server, you will use the users created in this chapter to access it. This will demonstrate how users access an NFS file server and will also demonstrate that the users, groups, permissions and attributes that you have set up work correctly.

In the last chapter, you created the directory structure for the Production and Sales Departments of RMG Inc. and put data files in the directories that you created.

In this chapter, you will create users for each person in the two departments and create a group for each department. The group named prod will be created for people in the Production Department and a group named sales will be created for the Sales Department.

The users in the Production Department will be added to the prod group and the users in the Sales Department will be added to the sales group.

You will assign user names and group names to directories and files, to allow and restrict user access to the directory structures that you created in the last chapter. You will also assign attributes to files to restrict access to some of the files in the directory structure.

The directory structure for the two departments exists below /home/common. The Production Department will use files in the directory structure below /home/common/prod and the Sales Department will use files in the directory structure below /home/common/sales. There are five subdirectories below each of the prod and sales directories that contain data files for each department.

Accessing the Filesystem of an NFS File Server

In our RMG Inc. Case Study example, users will be logging in at workstations and accessing files on an **NFS** (Network File System) file server.

Users in the Production Department (the prod group) will log in to their workstations and have access to the directory structure below /home/common/prod and users in the Sales Department (the sales group) will log in to their workstations and have access to the directory structure below /home/common/sales. Users in prod will have limited access to a directory below the sales directory. Similarly, users in sales will have limited access to a directory below the prod directory.

In an upcoming chapter, you will do some steps to allow a user at a workstation to access part of the filesystem of an NFS server (rather than all of it). You will put some settings in /etc/fstab at a workstation and some settings in /etc/exports at the server, so that when a user logs in at the workstation, the user will automatically have access to part of the filesystem of the server. The user will have limited access to the prod and sales directory structures (on the server) below /home/common.

The common directory below /home on the server contains the prod and sales directory structures. The common directory below /home on the workstation is empty. It is the mount point for the common directory below /home on the server.

In the classroom, every student is creating the directory structures below /home/common and therefore, this directory is not empty. When you do the Hands-On Exercises in the upcoming chapter, you will work in pairs and use one of your systems as the workstation and the other as the server. You will use the mv command at the workstation system to move the common directory to a new name and then create the common directory again so that it will be empty.

Your system will be set up as the NFS file server in an upcoming chapter and you will create the users and groups on this server in this chapter. You will create the users needed for each department and a group for each department, and then add the appropriate users to each group.

For example, a user named showe will be created at the server and added to the prod group at the server. Therefore, several users and two "non-system" groups will exist at the server.

To access the server, a user is also created at the user's workstation.

For example, the showe user (only) is created at the workstation. Therefore, the showe user exists at the server and also exists at the workstation. Several users exist at the server and only one user exists at the workstation. Other users could be created at the workstation, but in our example, they are not required.

To access the filesystem of an NFS server from a client, a user does not log in to the server. Instead, the user logs in to his or her workstation with his or her username and (due to the settings in /etc/fstab and /etc/exports) *the same user name (and user id) at the server* provides the user with access to the filesystem of the server (the directory structures below /home/common on the server).

The user has access to the filesystem of the server according to the permissions assigned to the user through the username of the user and any groups to which the user belongs. The user, group permissions and attributes part of the setup is done in this chapter. The setup of the NFS server, such as putting settings in /etc/fstab and /etc/exports, is done in an upcoming chapter.

When a user logs in at a workstation, the settings in /etc/fstab and /etc/exports cause part of directory structure (part of the filesystem) of the server to "appear" as part of the directory structure of the filesystem in the workstation.

For example, when a CD is not mounted, the cdrom directory below /mnt is empty. When a CD is mounted, the filesystem of the CD "appears" below /mnt/cdrom. The directories and files on the CD exist below /mnt/cdrom and can be accessed with commands and applications.

To continue the example, when a user logs in to a workstation, the settings in /etc/fstab and /etc/exports cause the /home/common directory at the workstation (which is empty at the workstation) to have the prod and sales directory structures (which are at the server) below it. This allows the user to access the directories and files in prod and sales (which are at the server) with commands and applications.

In summary, workstations have a directory named common below /home, but they do not have a directory structure below /home/common. The common directory is empty. The common directory below /home (at the workstation) is the mount point for the directory structure on the filesystem of the server.

The server has the prod and sales directories below /home/common and these are the only directories below common. There are five directories with several files below each of the prod and sales directories. The directory structure (five subdirectories) below prod is primarily for the users in the prod group and the directory structure (five subdirectories) below sales is primarily for the users in the sales group.

If a user logs in to a workstation without the settings in /etc/fstab and /etc/exports, then the user does not have any directories below /home/common. The prod and sales directory structures do not exist. However, when a user logs in at a workstation (and the settings in /etc/fstab and /etc/exports exist) and the same user name exists at the server, then the user automatically has access to the sales and prod directory structures. The user did not log in to the server. The user logged in to the workstation and the settings at the workstation and at the server cause part of the filesystem on the server to become accessible. The prod and sales directory structures that exist on the server automatically exist below /home/common. These directories on the server automatically become part of the filesystem of the workstation.

By default, when you create a user, a home directory is created for the user. Unless a user is physically logging in at the server (by using the keyboard at the server), then the user does not require a home directory on the server and the user will have a home directory on the workstation. When you create a user, but do not need to create a home directory for the user, such as a user that you create on a server, you can create the user without creating a home directory.

In the classroom, you will be using your system as both a server and a workstation. You will be creating users and groups and doing all of the steps to set up the permissions and attributes for the users and groups on the server. Therefore, you will also be creating each of the user names that are required to log in from each workstation. However, in our example, you only need one user name at a workstation.

Therefore, during the Hands-On Exercises you will create home directories for the prod and sales users when you create them and this will allow you to test the user names that you create at your system (use the system as both a server and a workstation).

If you were not using your system as both a server and a workstation, you would not need to create home directories for users at both the server and the workstation. You would likely only create the home directory for the user when you create the user at the workstation (and not when you create the user at the server). Therefore, home directories would only exist on workstations.

Permissions, Users And Groups

Permissions

A permission for a directory or file is a capability of doing something to a directory or file, such as changing into a directory, deleting a file or creating a file.

The read Permission

The read (r) permission for a file allows the contents of the file to be read, but does not allow the contents of the file to be modified and does not allow the file to be deleted.

The read (r) permission for a directory allows the contents of the directory to be viewed, such as with the ls command. The x permission is required to change into a directory. When not "in" a directory, a user must have the x permission (in addition to the r permission) to list the contents of a directory. Therefore, when you assign the r permission for a directory, also assign the x permission. A user requires the r and x permissions to *effectively* "work" with files in a directory.

The write Permission

The write (**w**) permission for a file allows the contents of the file to be modified.

The write (**w**) permission for a directory allows: the creation of files in the directory, the deletion of files from the directory, the creation of directories in the directory, and the deletion of directories from the directory.

The execute Permission

The execute (**x**) permission for a binary or script file allows the file to be executed (run). This permission is used on binary and script files so that they are executable.

The execute (**x**) permission for a directory allows a directory to be "changed in to", such as with the cd command. When you assign the x permission for a directory, also assign the r permission.

Other Permissions

In addition to the r, w and x permissions, users can acquire permissions through Set User ID, Set Group ID and the "sticky" bit. These permissions are described further below.

Users

A user (a.k.a. user account) is used to log in and work on a system.

When you install Linux, the root user (a.k.a. superuser) is created automatically by default and you assign this user a password. When you did the Linux installation earlier in this course, you created a non-root user and assigned this user a password.

You can create more users during the installation process, or create users afterwards with the useradd command or with a GUI utility.

The useradd command replaces the adduser command (believe it or not). The adduser command no longer exists, but a file named adduser exists and is a symlink to useradd. When you try to run the adduser command, the symlink (from adduser to useradd) causes the useradd command to run.

Groups

A group is a name that is created and then the name is assigned user names. The group name can then be assigned to directories and files. Each directory and file has a group name.

Users that have been assigned to a group are members of the group. Permissions for a group can be specified for directories and files. The users that are members of a group acquire the permissions that the group has been assigned to a directory or file.

Assigning a group to a directory or file and specifying the permissions of the group to the directory or file is a method of easily assigning permissions to multiple users for directories and files.

A user can be a member of more than one group.

A group cannot have another group as a member.

Directory and File Owner Types and Understanding the Permission Settings

There are four directory and file owner "types". These are **u** (user), **g** (group), **o** (other) and **a** (all). The type of **all** is used to refer to all users (u, g and o) and is abbreviated with **a**.

By default, when you create a user, a Primary Group is created for the user and the name of this group is the same as the user's name. When the cwest user was created during the installation, a Primary Group named cwest was also created. Therefore, there is a cwest user and a cwest group. When the Primary Group name for a user is the same as a user's name, it is sometimes called a "user private group".

By default, the user that creates a directory or file is the owner of the directory or file. The Primary Group of the user that creates a directory or file is the group (owner) of the directory or file. With the default of the user name and Primary Group name of the user being the same, then the owner of the directory or file and the group of the directory and file are the same name.

For example, the showe user is in the showe (user private) group and this group is the Primary Group of the showe user. The showe user creates a directory named yes. A long listing of the directory shows the following:

```
drwxrwxr-x   2 showe    showe      1024 Mar 19 12:23 yes
```

A "d" is the first character at the left of the output above. The first character is used to indicate the type of the item, such as d for directory, - (dash) for file and l for symlink. The rwxr-x--- at the right of the "d" are the permissions of the directory. When discussing permissions for a directory or file, we will not show the first character of an item (the d, - or l). Therefore, the permissions of the yes directory are rwxrwxr-x, not **d**rwxrwxr-x.

The showe user created the yes directory and is therefore the owner of the directory. The showe user has the Primary Group of showe and therefore this group is the "group owner" of the directory.

In the output above, the user name of showe appears at the right of the permissions of rwxrwxr-x. The group name of showe appears at the right of showe.

The permissions of the directory are rwxrwxr-x. The **u** (user, owner) of the directory is showe and the **g** (group) of the directory is showe. Therefore, the permission settings for the directory are rwxrwxr-x, showe, showe.

Any users that are not the user owner or members of the group owner of a directory or file are "other". The type of **other** is abbreviated with **o**.

Permissions are shown in three groups of three, one after the other. The first three permissions are for the u (user, owner) of the directory or file. The second three permissions are for the g (group) of the directory or file and the third (the last) three permission are for o (other).

The permissions of **r** (read), **w** (write), **x** (execute), **s** (suid or sgid) and **t** (sticky bit) can appear for a directory or file. A - (dash) in a listing of permissions indicates no permission.

The yes directory has the permission settings of rwxrwxr-x, showe, showe. The first three permissions (for the u of the directory) are rwx, the second three permissions (for the g of the directory) are rwx and the last three permissions (for o, other) are r-x.

This indicates that the u of the directory (showe) has **rwx** (**r**ead, **w**rite and e**x**ecute) to the directory, the g of the directory (showe) has **rwx** to the directory and o has **r-x** (**r**ead and e**x**ecute) to the directory. Therefore, for the yes directory, the showe user has the rwx, users in the showe group (which only has the showe user as a member) have the rwx and all other users have rx. Other users are users that are not the showe user and are not in the showe group.

Here is another example. This time we're looking at a file. A long listing of the file shows the following:

-rwxrw-r--   1 jbeck   sales   1024 Mar 19 12:23 gtr.txt

The - (dash) at the far left of the output above indicates that gtr.txt is a file and this - (dash) will not appear when showing the permissions of the file. The rwxrw-r-- at the right of the - (dash) are the permissions of the file.

In the output above, the user name of jbeck appears at the right of the permissions of rwxrw-r--. The group name of sales appears at the right of jbeck. The jbeck user is the u (owner) of the file and the sales group is the g of the file.

An example of the *permissions* of a directory or file are rwxrw-r-- and an example of the *permission settings* of a directory or file are rwxrw-r--, jbeck, sales.

We will use the phrase *permissions* to refer to the nine permissions of a directory or file (rwxrw-r--).

We will use the words *permission settings* to refer to the permissions, u and g of a directory or file (rwxrw-r--, jbeck, sales).

The abbreviations of **u** (**u**ser), **g** (**g**roup), **o** (**o**ther) and **a** (**a**ll) are used with some of the commands that are used to specify permission settings. We will also use these abbreviations when discussing permissions. Keep mind that the **o** abbreviation is for **o**ther, not for owner.

With the permission settings of rwxrw-r--, jbeck, sales for a directory or file, the u of the file is jbeck and has the permissions of rwx, the g of the file is sales and has the permissions of rw- and the o of the file has the permissions of r--. The users that are members of the sales group have rw-. "Other" users are users that are not the jbeck user and are not in the sales group.

The user that creates a directory or file is automatically assigned as the owner (u) of the directory or file, and by default, the Primary Group of a user is also automatically assigned as the g of the directory or file. Also by default, the Primary Group name of a user is the same as the user's name. Therefore, when a user creates a directory or file, the user's name is the u of the file and the user's name (which is the user's Primary Group name) is also the g of the directory or file.

The u and g of a directory or file are referred to in some Linux documentation as the ownership of the directory or file.

In a list of the nine permission settings for a directory or file, such as rwxrw-r--, each setting in the list can be referred to as a "flag" and the flag can be off or on. When a flag is on, a letter, such as r, w or x appears. When a flag is off, a - (dash) appears.

For example, in the list of permissions of rwxrw-r--, the r, w and x flags are on for u (rwx); the r and w flags are on and the x flag is off for g (rw-); and the r flag is on and the w and x flags are off for o (r--).

Some Linux documentation refers to the permissions, user (owner) and group of a directory or file, such as rwxrw-r--, jbeck and sales, as attributes. We will refer to these items as permission settings.

Files can be assigned attributes which are not the same as the permissions, user and group of a directory or file. Attributes, such as i, a, S, d and A, can be assigned with the chattr command and these attributes can be viewed with the lsattr command. These attributes are also sometimes referred to as flags and are considered to be on or off. We will refer to the attributes of a file as attributes.

The /etc/passwd File

The file named passwd in /etc is a text file that serves as the database for system passwords. Each line in the file represents an account (a.k.a. user) on the system, such as a user account or a system account.

 There are several "system accounts" (users), such as bin, daemon, ftp, gopher, halt, mail, news and shutdown. There is even an account with the name of "nobody". These accounts are used by the system for various purposes. The system requires that these accounts exist so that they can do tasks, such as provide services to the system.

There are also "system groups" that are used by the system for various purposes. Some system accounts are also system groups with the same name.

The passwd file is read by the system when a user account (a.k.a. user) attempts to log in.

The file named passwd has the permission settings of rw-r--r--, root, root. The r to the o of the file enables users to read from the file, but does not allow users to write to the file.

Below is the entry for the root user in the passwd file:

    root:x:0:0:root,,,:/root:/bin/bash

Below is the entry for the cwest user in the passwd file:

    cwest:x:500:500:Chris West:/home/cwest:/bin/bash

Each line in the passwd file consists of seven fields, each separated from the next with a : (colon), in the same way as directory paths in the PATH are separated with a : (colon).

The seven fields are described below using the entry for the cwest user shown above as the example.

The first field in the above entry is the ID name field (a.k.a. user account name) and shows "cwest".

The second field is the password field and it contains an "x". When a system is using encrypted "shadow passwords" in /etc/shadow, then the second field is an "x". If not, then this field contains an encrypted (a.k.a. coded) password.

The third field is the **UID** (User **ID**) number field and it contains "500". This is the UID number of the user.

Each account on a system has a UID number. The root user has the UID of 0 and the first non-root user is typically given the number 500. The user that you created during the Linux installation (cwest) was assigned the number 500. By default, each additional user is given the next number above 500.

System accounts, such as bin, daemon and shutdown, typically have UID numbers below 100.

The fourth field is the **GID** (Group **ID**) number field and it also contains "500".

By default, when a user is created, a group is also created with the same name as the user. This group is referred to as the user's Primary Group. Therefore, the cwest user is in the Primary Group named cwest and this user has the UID of 500 and the GID of 500.

The fifth field is the comment field and it contains "Chris West". This field can be used for the "full name" of a user or for other comment text.

The sixth field contains the path to the user's home directory, which is "/home/cwest".

The seventh field contains a command that is executed by the binary named login when a user logs in. By default, this field contains "/bin/bash". This causes the binary named bash in /bin to be executed when a user logs in. A different shell executable, or a binary that runs an application, or the name of a script can be put in place of "/bin/bash".

The /etc/shadow File

The file named shadow in /etc is a text file that serves as the database for user names, encrypted passwords and other user password settings, such as the minimum number of days before a password can be changed and the maximum number of days after which a password must be changed.

Each line in the /etc/shadow file represents a user or system account and shows several settings for the account.

If the second field in each statement in /etc/passwd (not /etc/shadow) contains an "x", then a system is using encrypted "shadow passwords" and these encrypted passwords are maintained in the corresponding second field in /etc/shadow.

For example, if the entry for cwest in /etc/passwd has an "x" in the second field, then the entry for cwest in /etc/shadow will have the encrypted password of cwest in the second field.

A user account must be assigned a password before it can be used. If a password has not been assigned to a user, then !! (two exclamation marks) appear in the second field in the statement for the user in /etc/shadow and the user cannot log in. If the user has been assigned a password, then the encrypted version of the password appears in the second field, rather than !!.

The file named shadow has the permission settings of r--------, root, root. Therefore, only the root user can read the contents of the /etc/shadow file. However, the passwd binary can read and write to the /etc/shadow file, as described below.

Below is the entry for the tsawyer user in the /etc/shadow file. This user has not been assigned a password yet, so !! appears in the second field.

    tsawyer:!!:12127:10:20:5:22:12687

The settings at the right of !! are all password settings, such as the minimum number of days before a password can be changed (10). Some default password settings are specified in /etc/login.defs and some password settings can be specified with the useradd command. All password settings can be specified with the chage command.

The /etc/skel Directory

By default, the /etc/skel directory consists of hidden files, including the bash configuration files named .bashrc, .bash_profile and .bash_logout. This directory may also include hidden files and directories that provide configuration information for software components that have been installed on the system.

Other directories and files that are required by a user are also put below /etc/skel, such as user template data files for applications.

When you create a user, the contents of /etc/skel are copied to below the user's home directory.

The /etc/login.defs File

This file contains default settings that are used when a user or group is created. The statements that are used as defaults, and that are commonly modified for users, are described below.

PASS_MAX_DAYS   99999

This sets the maximum number of days the password can be used without being changed. The default number of 99999 sets the maximum so high that there is no restriction on the maximum number of days. Therefore, users are not forced to change their passwords.

PASS_MIN_DAYS   0

This sets the minimum number of days between password changes. This statement is used to stop a user from immediately changing his or her password back to a previous password and continuing to use an old password. The default value of 0 allows users to change their passwords at any time.

By specifying a number higher than 0 (zero), such as 10 (days), a user is forced to use a new password for a minimum of 10 days.

PASS_MIN_LEN   5

This sets the minimum length of a password of 5 characters. Some organizations require longer passwords and modify this default setting.

PASS_WARN_AGE   7

This specifies that a user will be warned that his or her password will expire in 7 days.

CREATE_HOME   yes

This causes a home directory to be created for a user by default. The home directory will be created below /home and will have the same name as the user.

The /etc/group File

A user can be added to one or more groups when the user is created with the useradd command. After a user has been created, the user can also be added to a group with the usermod command.

The file named group in /etc is a text file that serves as the database for system groups. Each line in the file represents a group on the system, such as a group named prod for the users in the Production Department or a "system group".

There are several "system groups", such as bin, daemon, ftp, gopher, mail and news. These groups are used by the system for various purposes. The system requires these accounts so that they can do "system" tasks, such as provide services to the system.

Some system groups are also system accounts (user names) with the same name (i.e. some system groups have the same name as a system account).

The group file is read by the system when a user logs in and has the permission settings of rw-r--r--. This enables the system (and users) to read from the group file (so that a user can log in), but does not allow users to write to the file.

Below is the entry for the sales group in the /etc/group text file:

    sales:x:chynde,psimon,jbeck

Field 1 in the above entry is the group name (sales).

Field 2 is the password field and it contains an "x". When a system is using encrypted group "shadow passwords" in /etc/gshadow, then the second field is an "x". If not, then this field contains an encrypted password.

For the sales group, the three names at the right of the "x:" (in the above example) are users that are in the sales group.

The group name that appears for a directory or file, such as in a long listing of a directory or file, is derived from the /etc/group file. The system "sees" the number of the group for each directory and file and cross-references the number with the group name in /etc/group and displays the group name.

The /etc/gshadow File

By default, groups do not have passwords and do not typically need passwords. The groupadd and groupmod commands are usually all that is required to create groups and modify the settings of groups. However, a group can have an administrator to modify settings of the group and the group can have a password to prevent unauthorized changes to group settings.

The **gpasswd** (**g**roup **passw**ord) command is used to assign passwords to groups and administer groups. If a group is assigned a password, then the password for the group and some settings for the group are maintained in /etc/gshadow.

The useradd Command

The useradd command is used to create a user account.

A command named adduser (not useradd) was formerly used to create users and so a file named adduser in /usr/sbin is symlink to the useradd binary in the same directory. Therefore, when you try to run the adduser command, you actually run the useradd command. (Just like the locate and slocate commands that were described earlier).

When a new user is created with the useradd command, the following events occur:

The user gets the default system settings and/or any settings specified by options of the command, including the settings in /etc/login.defs. If useradd command settings are specified that override default settings, then these are used rather than the default settings.

A home directory is created for the user. By default, this directory is /home/*username*, where *username* is the name of the user that has been created.

The contents of /etc/skel are copied to the user's home directory. This includes any subdirectories of /etc/skel and their contents.

By default, (if the -g option of useradd is not used) a Primary Group with the same name as the user is automatically created. A statement for this group is added to /etc/group.

If the user is added to any supplementary groups (with the -G option of useradd), the user name is added to the statement for the group in /etc/group.

A statement (single line) for the user account is added to each of the /etc/passwd and /etc/shadow files.

If you create a user without the -p (password) option of useradd, then !! appears in the second field of the /etc/shadow file. To allow the user to log in, you must run the passwd command and assign the user a password. Once this is done, the !! in the second field of /etc/shadow are removed and replaced with the encrypted version of the password that you assigned to the user.

The Syntax of the useradd Command

The following is the syntax of the useradd command:

    useradd [options] *username*

Options of the useradd Command

There are about twenty options that can be used with the useradd command. Many of these options allow you to override the default user configuration settings.

For example, when you create a user, a home directory is created for the user below /home and the directory is the same name as the username. An option of the useradd command allows you to specify a different directory (path) for the home directory for a user. Another option of useradd allows you to specify a different default shell for a user.

Table 12-1 shows the commonly used options of the useradd command.

Table 12-1 - Common Options of the useradd Command

Option	Description
-c	add a **c**omment for a user - put the comment between " " commonly used to specify a "full name" for a user
-g	specify the initial login **g**roup (a.k.a. Primary Group) for a user with a group name or GID number only a *single* group name or GID number can be used the group name or GID number must exist prior to using this option
-G	specify one or more supplementary **g**roups for a user separate multiple groups with a , (comma) and no space only a group name and not a GID number can be used the group name must exist prior to using this option
-d	specify the full **d**irectory path to a home directory, other than the default of /home/*username*
-s	specify the full path to a **s**hell binary the default of path to the shell binary is /bin/bash
-e	specify a date in the form of mm/dd/yyyy for an account to **e**xpire
-p	specify an encrypted **p**assword for a user when the account is created only use this option with an encrypted password
-M	do not create a ho**m**e directory for a user
-n	do not create a Primary Group **n**ame with the same name as the user
-u *uid*	replace *uid* with a user id number to specify the UID of the user

Comments on Options of the useradd Command

For the -d option, if the full path specifies an ending directory name below a parent directory that exists, then the ending directory is automatically created and becomes the home directory for the user. If the full path specifies an ending directory name below the name of a parent directory that does not exist, then the ending directory is not automatically created, an error message appears, and the user is not created.

For example, if the full path specified with the -d option is /home/www.abc.com, then the directory is automatically created because /home exists.

However, if the full path is /home/websites/www.abc.com and the websites directory does not exist, then the www.abc.com directory is not automatically created, an error message appears, and the user is not created. If the websites directory exists, then the www.abc.com directory is created and the user is created.

The -e option is commonly used when you know that a user will no longer need an account after a certain date.

For example, if you are creating user accounts for ten people that are coming in to temporarily type data into a database for thirty days, you would use this option to specify the last date that these users should be able to log in.

If you use the -p option and specify an unencrypted password, then the password is stored in /etc/shadow as "clear" (unencrypted) text and you will not be able to log in with the password. You must specify an encrypted password with the -p option and then use the unencrypted version of the password to log in.

The -p option is useful if you are using a program to automate the process of adding users to a system. The program will handle the encryption of the password. However, if you are not using such a program, create users with the useradd command and then run the passwd command to assign passwords to your users. A script can be used to automate the process of creating users with useradd and then assigning passwords with passwd.

Examples of the useradd Command

useradd -c "Becky Ford" bford

This creates a user account named bford and adds a comment of "Becky Ford" for the user, which specifies the "full name" of the user. The default user account settings are assigned to the user. This is the second user to be created and by default this user acquires the next sequential number above 500 for the UID number.

A group name was not specified by using the -g option above. Therefore, a group name with the same name as the user is automatically created. This is the second user and group to be created and by default the user and group both acquire the next sequential number above 500 for the UID and GID number, respectively. The UID and GID numbers will be the same.

The -g option is used to specify the initial login **g**roup (a.k.a. Primary Group) for a user. This option was not used in the example above. Therefore, by default, a group is automatically created at the same time as the user and this group has the same name as the user.

When the -g option is not used, the user name and the Primary Group name for the user are the same and the UID and GID numbers are the same. *This is important to remember for the discussion below regarding some scripting logic in /etc/bashrc that specifies the default umask setting for a user.*

The statement in /etc/passwd for the bford user account appears as:

    bford:x:501:501:Becky Ford:/home/bford:/bin/bash

The first 501 in the above statement is the user id (UID) number. The second 501 is the group id (GID) number of the Primary Group of the user. The first and second numbers are the same. Therefore, the primary group name for this user is the same name as the user.

The statement in /etc/group for the bford group (the Primary Group name of the bford user) appears as:

    bford:x:501

useradd -c "Tom Sawyer" -G mississippi tsawyer

This command creates a user account named tsawyer using the default system settings. The -g (lower case "g") option was not used and therefore a group name with the same name as the user was automatically created. The tsawyer user has the Primary Group name of tsawyer.

The -G option causes tsawyer to be added to the supplementary group named mississippi. Therefore, this user is in two groups. The Primary Group name for the tsawyer user is tsawyer and the supplementary group name for this user is mississippi.

By default, the first non-root user is assigned the UID of 500. The tsawyer user is the eighth user to be added to the system. Therefore, the UID number of this user is 507.

The statement in /etc/passwd for the tswayer user account appears as:

tsawyer:x:507:507:Tom Sawyer:/home/tsawyer:/bin/bash

When the tsawyer user was created, the tsawyer group was also created and the user was added to the mississippi group.

The statement in /etc/group for the tsawyer group (the Primary Group name of the tswayer user) appears as:

tsawyer:x:507

When the mississippi group was created, it was assigned the GID of 17000 and this number appears in the statement for the mississippi group in /etc/group, as shown below. The tsawyer user is a member of the mississippi group and therefore this user name also appears in the statement for the group.

mississippi:x:17000:tsawyer

This example is the same as above, except that the -u option has been used to specify a UID number for the user.

The word item will be used to represent directories and files in the discussion below. Utilities, such as the ls command (with the -l option) can be used to see the u (owner) and g of an item (directory or file). You have seen these names appear many times beside an item when getting a long listing with the ls command.

Let's say you are using an NFS file server. You have created a user named tsawyer at the server and have assigned this user appropriate permissions to part of the filesystem of the server. You need to create a user named tsawyer at a workstation so that the tsawyer user (at the workstation) can access the filesystem of the server as tsawyer, with the permissions of tswayer (at the server).

When you create the tswayer user at the workstation you should use the -u option of useradd to specify the same UID number for the user at the workstation as at the server. Therefore, the UID number for the u (owner) of items created by tsawyer on the server will match the UID number in /etc/passwd (at the server). This will cause the correct user name to appear as the owner of items when using a utility to view items on the server. It is important to have the workstation UID number(s) match the server UID number(s).

For example, the tsawyer user was created at the server prior to being created at the workstation. When the tsawyer user at the server was created, the user acquired the next available UID number, which was 507. When you use the useradd command (shown above) and also use the -u option and create the tsawyer user at the workstation, the user is assigned the UID of 507. Therefore, the UID number for the user in /etc/passwd at the workstation matches the UID number of the user in /etc/passwd at the server.

The entry in /etc/passwd at the workstation and server is:

tsawyer:x:507:507:Tom Sawyer:/home/tsawyer:/bin/bash

 You may decide not to create home directories for users at the server and only have home directories on workstations. If so, then "/home/tsawyer" will only appear in /etc/passwd at the workstation and not in /etc/passwd at the server. The -M option of useradd is used to stop the creation of a home directory when you create a user.

When a utility needs to display the user name (owner) of an item, it "looks" at the item and "sees" the UID number (not name) of the user that created the item. The utility then "looks" in /etc/passwd for the user name that matches the UID number of the item and displays the name of the user beside the item.

When the UID number in /etc/passwd at the workstation and server are the same, and a long listing is done for an item that has been created by tsawyer the server, the user number of 507 is found in /etc/passwd (on the same line as the name tsawyer) at the server and the correct user name (tsawyer) appears beside the item.

If a user other than tsawyer has 507 (in /etc/passwd at the server), then that user name will appear when a long listing of files is done *at the server* on the filesystem of the server!

For example, tsawyer has UID of 507 in /etc/passwd at his workstation, but bford has the number of 507 in /etc/passwd at the server. When tsawyer is working at his workstation and gets a long listing of an item that he created, his name will appear beside the item (because the system will use the /etc/passwd file on the workstation). However, if root gets a long listing of the item at the server, the name of bford (from the /etc/passwd file on the server) will appear.

When a user is deleted, the statement for the user in /etc/passwd is automatically removed. If a user with the UID of 507 creates an item and then the user is deleted, the name of the user will no longer appear beside the item in a long listing. The UID number (507) will appear in place of the user name.

The above concept is also true for GID numbers. If a user is in the group named prod at the workstation and the group named prod at the server, both groups need to have the same GID number.

When a group is deleted, the statement for it in /etc/group is automatically removed. If an item is created by a member of a group and then the group is deleted, then the name of the group will no longer appear beside the item in a long listing. The GID number will appear in place of the group name.

**useradd -c "Web Master 1" -d /home/www.lancom-tech.com **

-G webmasters webmaster1

The \ at the end of the first line above is used to indicate that the above two lines must be typed on one line (without typing in the \).

You have created a group named webmasters. This group will be used by people that will be administering web sites on the system. Each web site will exist below /home and each web administrator will be given the name of webmaster*x*, where *x* is a number. Users will log in with the user name of webmaster*x*, rather than a user name that is some variation of their real name.

The above command creates a user named webmaster1 and this user will be administering the web site content for the web site of http://www.lancom-tech.com. The content of this web site will exist in /home/www.lancom-tech.com.

Alternatively, all of the web sites on the system could be created below a parent directory named sites or websites, below /home. This parent directory could be created below /home or below another directory path.

The default parent directory for a *single* domain on an Apache web server is /var/www. However, you can configure an Apache server for multiple domains on a single server and specify the path to the directory that contains the web site content for each domain (such as the path of /home/websites/www.lancom-tech.com for the domain of lancom-tech.com).

After running the above command to create the webmaster1 user, the following occurs:

A user account named webmaster1 is created and a Primary Group named webmaster1 is created. The user account name appears at the far right of the above command. This is the twentieth user to be created and therefore, the user acquires the UID of 519 by default.

The **-c** option assigns the comment of "Web Master 1" in the comment field in /etc/passwd.

The **-d** option assigns the user the full home directory path of /home/www.lancom-tech.com. This full path specifies a directory that is directly below /home and /home exists. Therefore, the www.lancom-tech.com directory is created automatically. The full path to the home directory is put in the sixth field in the statement for the user in /etc/passwd.

The **-G** option assigns the user to the supplementary group named webmasters. This group was created prior to running the above command. The primary group of the webmaster1 user is webmaster1 and this user also belongs to the supplementary group named webmasters.

The userdel Command

The **userdel** (**user del**ete) command is used to delete a user. This removes the user name from the system. Without the -r option, this command does not remove the home directory structure of the user or any directories or files that the user has created (in any location).

The -r option is used to remove the home directory of a user and all directories and files in it.

The Syntax of the userdel Command

The following is the syntax of the userdel command:

    userdel [option] *username*

Examples of the userdel Command

Example	Description
userdel webmaster1	deletes the webmaster1 user account
userdel -r slaurel	deletes the slaurel user account and the /home/slaurel directory structure

 If a user is deleted without using -r option (to remove the home directory), the next user created (with the same user id) will have access to the previous user's home directory and any folders and files owned by that user elsewhere on the system.

For example, if a user is created with a user id of 501 and that user creates directories and files in any location including the home directory, after that user is deleted, the next user created will also be number 501 and will own the directories and files of the previous user.

For the distribution provided with this book, you will likely also need to remove the orbit-*username* directory and its contents from below /tmp when you delete a user.

The usermod Command

The **usermod** (**user mod**ification) command is used to **mod**ify the settings of a **user**.

The Syntax of the usermod Command

The following is the syntax of the usermod command:

    usermod [options] *username*

Options of the usermod Command

The -c, -g, -G, -d, -s, -e and -u options of the usermod command are the same as for the useradd command.

Table 12-2 shows the common options of the usermod command.

Table 12-2 - Common Options of the usermod Command

Option	Description
-L	"lock" the password of an account so that no one can log in using the account name
-U	"unlock" the password of an account so that someone can login using the account name

If you use the -G option to add a user to a supplementary group and the user is already a member of one or more other groups, be sure to also specify the all of the other groups. If you do not specify all groups, then the user will be added to the single group specified and removed from the other groups! Use a , (and no space) between all of the groups to which a user should be a member when using the -G option.

Examples of the usermod Command

usermod -u 507 tsawyer

Changes the UID number of the tsawyer user to 507.

For example, the UID of tsawyer at a server is 507, but the GID of the user at a workstation is not 507, but needs to be.

usermod -L cwest

Locks the password for the cwest user so that this user can no longer log in. If a user attempts to log in as cwest, the error message that appears is the same error message that appears when a user does not exist.

Use the -L option to lock an account when you know that a user will not need to log in for a period of time or when you do not want a user to log in for a period of time.

The -L option causes usermod to put an ! (exclamation mark) in front of the encrypted password in the /etc/shadow file.

usermod -U cwest

Unlocks the password for the cwest user so that this user can log in.

The -U option causes usermod to remove the ! from in front of the encrypted password in the /etc/shadow file.

The passwd Command

The **passwd** (**passw**ord) command is used to assign a password to a user and change an existing password.

If an encrypted password is not assigned to a user when the user is created, then you must assign a password to the user before the user account can be used. The passwd command allows you to do this.

When creating passwords, we recommend that you use at least six characters, use some numbers and also use a mixture of upper and lower case letters. If you type a letter of a password in upper case when you create a password, then you must also type it in upper case when using the password.

When creating passwords, use a password that you can remember, but do not use a word that would easily be associated with you, such as the name of your favorite pet.

Passwords do not "echo" (display) on the screen as they are typed in. All passwords that you type in must be confirmed by typing them in a second time. This ensures that you actually typed in what you thought you typed in!

Once you have typed in a password for the first of the two times and pressed Enter, the system will warn you if it considers the password to be "bad", such as by being too short, too simplistic or based on a dictionary word. If you get a message indicating that a password is "bad", press Enter at the second prompt for the password and run the passwd command again and create a password that is not "bad".

The Syntax of the passwd Command

The following is the syntax of the passwd command:

    passwd [options] [*username*]

At the command line, a user (including root) can simply type passwd and press Enter to change his or her password.

Only the root user can specify a [*username*] with the passwd command to change the password of another user.

If you require users to change their passwords, be sure to teach them this command (if they are not using a desktop) or how to access a GUI utility that will allow them to change their passwords.

Changing a Password with a GUI Utility

To use a GUI utility to change the password of the currently logged in user from the GNOME or KDE desktop:

Menu ; Preferences ; Password.

Examples of the passwd Command

passwd

This command is used by all users to change the password of the user that they are currently logged in as. If you are a non-root user, this command prompts you for the current password, then prompts you for the new password, and then prompts you to retype the new password. If you are the root user, this command does not prompt you for the current password. It prompts you for the new password, and then prompts you to retype the new password.

passwd bford

The root user (only) can change the password of any user. In this case, the root user is changing the password of the bford user.

After running the above command, the root user is prompted for the new password and then prompted to retype the new password. The root user is not prompted for the current password of the user. Therefore, the root user does not need to know the existing password of a user to change the user's password.

The chage Command

The **chage** (**ch**ange **age**) command is used to specify password settings for a user. This includes a setting for the expiry date of a password and several other settings.

By default, users do not have an expiry date on their passwords and this situation is not very secure. Users often provide passwords to other users for various reasons, such as to provide temporary access when a person is off on vacation or away due to illness. Therefore, passwords should be forced to expire so that if one user gives a password to another, there is a limit to the time that it can be used. User passwords can also have other settings, as described in the options and examples below.

The -l option of the chage command can be used by any user to see his or her password settings. All other options of the chage command can only be used by the root user.

The Syntax of the chage Command

The following is the syntax of the chage command:

    chage [options] *username*

Common Options of the chage Command

Table 12-3 shows the common options of the chage command.

Table 12-3 - Common Options of the chage Command

Option	Description
-l	list (display) the password age settings of a user
-m *days*	specify the **m**inimum number of *days* between password changes
-M *days*	specify the **m**aximum number of *days* between password changes
-W *days*	specify the number of *days* prior to a required password change that a user will be **w**arned that the password must be changed
-I *days*	specify the number of *days* of account **i**nactivity, after a *password* (not *account*) has expired, before the account is locked
-E *yyyy-mm-dd*	use *yyyy-mm-dd* to specify the date that a user *account* (not *password*) **e**xpires when the account expires, it becomes locked

Comments on Options of the chage Command

The default setting for -m is 0, for -M is 99999, -W is 7, -I is -1 and -E is Never. The default settings for the -m, -M and -W options are acquired from the PASS_MIN_DAYS, PASS_MAX_DAYS and PASS_WARN_AGE statements, respectively, in /etc/login.defs. The PASS_MIN_LEN (minimum password length) and some other user settings can also be specified in /etc/login.defs.

The -m option sets the minimum number of days between password changes. This statement is used to stop users from immediately changing their passwords back to a previous password and continuing to use an old password. The default value of 0 allows users to change their passwords at any time.

By specifying a number higher than 0 (zero), such as 10 (days), a user is forced to use a new password for a minimum of 10 days.

The -M option is used to force a user to change his or her password.

The -W option is used to warn a user that he or she will need to change his or her password by the end of the number of days specified with the command.

If a password (not account) has expired, then a user can still change his or her password and log in. The password has expired, but not the capability of changing the password and logging in. When a user attempts to log in after a password has expired, the user is prompted for the old password and then the new password twice.

However, if a password has expired, the account should not be left available for someone to log in indefinitely. The -I option is used to limit the amount of time (of inactivity) that a user can log in and change his or her password after the password has expired. If the number of days specified with the -I option has passed, then the account becomes locked.

The -E option is used to specify the date when an account (not password) expires. This option is commonly used when you know that a user will no longer need an account after a certain date.

For example, if you are creating user accounts for ten people that are coming in to temporarily type data into a database for thirty days, you would use this option to specify the last date that these users should be able to log in.

If the -I or -E options are used and an account has become locked, then only the root user can unlock the account.

If the -I option caused an account to become locked (and you do not want to specify a date with the -E option because the user will be working for the organization indefinitely), the root user can unlock the account by using the chage command with the -M option (and any other desired options).

If the -E option caused an account to become locked, the root user can unlock it by using the chage command again with -E option and specifying a date in the future.

Examples of the chage Command

chage -M 20 -m 10 -W 5 -I 3 cwest

Sets the maximum days between password changes to 20, the minimum days between password changes to 10, and causes the user to be warned 5 days before the password must be changed. After the maximum days of 20, if there is no activity (i.e. a user does not log in) for three days, then the -I setting of 3 causes the account to become locked.

chage -l cwest

Displays the password age and expiry date settings for the cwest user. With the settings of the first example above, the output of this command appears as:

Minimum:	10
Maximum:	20
Warning:	5
Inactive:	2
Last Change:	Mar 16, 2004
Password Expires:	Apr 05, 2004
Account Expires:	Never

chage cwest

Starts the command in interactive mode and you are prompted for each of the above password settings for the cwest user, except for the Password Expires setting. The Password Expires setting is automatically produced by adding the maximum days setting to the current date. You *can* specify a date for the Last Change setting when using this command in interactive mode.

chage -E 2004-04-20 bford

Sets the account (not password) of the bford user to expire on April 20, 2004. This user will be moving to a different server after this date and will no longer need access to this system.

The users Command

The users command is run (without any options) to see a list of users currently logged on to a system.

The groupadd Command

The groupadd command is used to create a group. Users that are members of the group acquire the permissions that have been assigned to the group for the directories and files to which the group has been assigned.

The Syntax of the groupadd Command

The following is the syntax of the groupadd command:

    groupadd [options] *groupname*

The -g *gid* option is used to specify a **gid** (**g**roup **id**) number for a group. If this option is not used, then the group acquires the next available GID number (which is typically used for the Primary Group number of a user when a Primary Group is automatically created for a user).

If you do not use the -g *gid* option and the next available GID number is used, then the next time you create a user (and allow the system to automatically create a Primary Group for the user), then the UID number will be one number less than the GID number. The UID and GID numbers for a user will not be the same (i.e. they will not be "in sync"). The UID and GID numbers do not have to be the same, but it makes things easier to manage.

For example, the next available UID number on a system is 503 and the next available GID number is 503. When you create your users, you are allowing the system to automatically create a Primary Group for the user that is the same name as the user.

If you create a group without using the -g option, then the next available GID number of 503 is used for the new group. The next time you create a user, the UID number for the user will be 503, but the GID number will be 504 because 503 was used for the new group that you created. The user will have the UID of 503 and GID of 504 and this appears confusing.

We recommend that you use the -g option and specify a number that is well above the number of users that will be created, such as 10000. You may want to use 10000 for the first group, 11000 for the second, 12000 for the third, and so on.

Example of the groupadd Command

groupadd -g 16000 webmasters

This creates the group named webmasters with the GID number of 16000.

The groupdel Command

The **groupdel** (**group del**ete) command is used to delete (remove) a group.

You cannot delete a group if any users have the group as their **g** (primary **g**roup name). You must first change the g for these users to a different primary group. This can be done with the usermod command.

The Syntax of the groupdel Command

The following is the syntax of the groupdel command:

groupdel *groupname*

Example of the groupdel Command

groupdel acctng

This removes the group named acctng. This group cannot be deleted if any users have it as the **g** (primary **g**roup name).

The groupmod Command

The **groupmod** (**group mod**ification) command is used to modify the group id number or group name of a group.

The Syntax of the groupmod Command

The following is the syntax of the groupmod command:

groupmod [options] *groupname*

Options of the groupmod Command

Table 12-4 shows the options the groupmod command.

Table 12-4 - Common Options of the groupmod Command

Option	Description
-g *gid*	specify a *gid* number to change the **g**roup id (GID) number of the group
-n *groupname*	specify a *groupname* to change the **n**ame of the group

Examples of the groupmod Command

groupmod -g 15000 creative

This changes the group id (GID) number of the group named creative to 15000.

groupmod -n today yesterday

This changes the group name of the group named yesterday to the name of today.

The chgrp Command

The chgrp (**ch**ange **gr**oup) command is used to change the **g** (**g**roup name) for directories and files.

The Syntax of the chgrp Command

The following is the syntax of the chgrp command:

chgrp *groupname* [path][pattern]

A GID number can be specified in place of *groupname* above.

The -R (**r**ecursive) option changes ownership for all directories and files from the specified location (relative or absolute path) downwards.

The -R option only works with an * (asterisk) for the pattern (i.e. not *.sxi, *.txt or *letter*).

A group must exist before using the name of the group or the GID number of the group with this command.

Examples of the chgrp Command

chgrp prod gr-data

Changes the **g** (**g**roup name) for the directory named gr-data, in the current directory, to prod.

chgrp dataentry *.sxc

Changes the **g** (**g**roup name) for the all files in the current directory ending in .sxc to dataentry.

chgrp -R prod current-orders

This command changes the g to prod for the current-orders directory and all directories and files below the current-orders directory.

chgrp -R sales *

The -R (**r**ecursive) option causes this command to change the g to sales for all directories and files in and below the current directory.

An absolute or relative path can be used prior to the pattern of * (an asterisk). However, only the pattern of * (an asterisk) and not a pattern such as *.sxi, *.txt or *letter* can be used with the -R option.

The groups Command

The groups command displays all of the groups to which the currently logged in user belongs, or the names of the groups to which a specific user belongs.

A user name can be specified with this command to see the groups to which the user belongs.

Example of the groups Command

groups cwest

If the cwest user is a member of the prod and sales groups, then the following output appears:

```
cwest: prod sales
```

The chown Command

The **chown** (**ch**ange **own**ership) command is used to change the user name and group name of directories and files.

The Syntax of the chown Command

The following is the syntax of the chown command:

chown [options] *user.group* [path][pattern]

You can specify user or group or both. A UID number can be used in place of a user name and a GID number can be used in place of a group name. If you are only specifying a group, precede the group name with a . (dot). A : (colon) can be used in place of a . (dot).

The -R (**r**ecursive) option changes ownership for all directories and files from the specified location (relative or absolute path) downwards.

The -R option only works with an * (asterisk) for the pattern (i.e. not *.sxi, *.txt or *letter*).

Users and groups must exist before using the names of them with this command.

Examples of the chown Command

The directories and files shown in the following examples are below the current directory. A full path or other form of a relative path can also be used.

chown hfinn letters

Changes the user name of the letters directory to the user name of hfinn.

chown .acctng reports

The . (dot) in .acctng indicates the group named acctng. This command changes the group name of the reports directory to the group name of acctng.

chown lstevens.mktng sept

For the sept directory, changes the user name to lstevens and the group name to mktng.

chown showe.support *.sxi

Changes the user to showe and the group to support for all files ending in .sxi below the current directory.

chown -R .prod prod

The . (dot) in .prod indicates the group named prod. This command changes the g to prod for the prod directory and all directories and files below the prod directory.

chown -R bford.sales *

The -R (**recursive**) option causes this command to changes the u to bford and the g to sales for all directories and files in and below the current directory.

An absolute or relative path can be used prior to the pattern of * (an asterisk). However, only the pattern of * (an asterisk) and not a pattern such as *.sxi, *.txt or *letter* can be used with the -R option.

The chmod Command

The **chmod** (**ch**ange **mod**e) command is used to change the mode (a.k.a. permission settings) for a directory or file.

The Syntax of the chmod Command

The following is the syntax of the chmod command:

chmod [options] *mode* [path][pattern]

The *mode* is the set of permissions that are specified with the command. The permissions can be specified using symbolic mode or numeric mode.

The -R (**recursive**) option changes permissions for all directories and files from the specified location (relative or absolute path) downwards.

The -R option only works with an * (asterisk) for the pattern (i.e. not *.sxi, *.txt or *letter*).

Specifying Permissions with Symbolic Mode

The syntax of the chmod command (above) shows *mode* between [options] and [path][pattern]. When using the chmod command you can either specify the *mode* by using symbolic mode or numeric mode.

Symbolic mode uses a combination of letters (symbols) and the + (plus) sign, - (minus) sign and = (equals sign). Symbolic mode uses the following syntax.

ownertype[+ | - | =]*permissions*

The *ownertype* is abbreviated with **u** for **u**ser, **g** for **g**roup, **o** for **o**ther, and **a** for **a**ll.

The *permissions* are abbreviated with **r** for **r**ead, **w** for **w**rite, **x** for e**x**ecute, - (dash) for none, **s** for **s**uid or **s**gid, and **t** for sticky bit.

The = sign is used to "set" all permissions. The u, g, o or a that is used with the = sign is assigned the specified permissions and previous permissions no longer exist, unless they were assigned again with the = sign. When the = sign is used, a - (minus) sign or nothing can be put at the right of the = sign to remove all permissions.

Examples of Specifying the Mode with Symbolic Mode

The syntax of the chmod command above shows *mode* between [options] and [path][pattern]. Below are examples of specifying this *mode* using symbolic mode.

Example	Description
u+x	assign the execute permission to **u**ser this is commonly used to quickly assign the x permission to a script file
g-w	remove the **w**rite permission from **g**roup
o=-	remove all permissions from **o**ther
o=	remove all permissions from **o**ther
go-rw	remove the **r**ead and **w**rite permissions from **g**roup and **o**ther
o-wx	remove the **w**rite and e**x**ecute permissions from **o**ther
o+r	assign the **r**ead permission to **o**ther
ug+x	assign the e**x**ecute permission to **u**ser and **g**roup
a=rw	assign **a**ll (u, g and o) the **r**ead and **w**rite permissions u, g and o will only have the read and write permissions
ug=rw,o=r	assign **u**ser and **g**roup the **r**ead and **w**rite permissions and assign **o**ther the **r**ead permission
-w	remove **w**rite from user, group and other (all)
+rx	assign **u**ser, **g**roup and **o**ther (all) the **r**ead and e**x**ecute permissions

Permissions can be assigned to, or removed from, "all" (u, g and o) by using a + sign or - sign without putting u, g, o or a at the start of it, as in the last two examples above. When permissions are assigned or removed like this, the permissions are assigned or removed up to the permissions specified by the current umask setting. The umask is described in detail further below.

For example, if the umask is set to 022, then the w (2) permission is "masked" for g and o. If an item has no permissions and you assign +rwx, then the permissions will be rwxr-xr-x, rather than rwxrwxrwx; even though w was assigned to g and o. The umask stopped the w permission from being assigned.

The umask has the opposite effect when permissions are removed by using a - sign without putting u, g, o or a at the start of it.

To continue the example, if the umask is set to 022, then the w (2) permission is "masked" for g and o. If an item has all permissions and you assign -rwx, then the permissions will be ----w--w-, rather than ---------. Even though w was removed from g and o, the umask stopped the permission from being removed.

You may decide not to use the + or - sign as described above and use another method, such as using a= and specifying the permissions.

More examples of using symbolic mode are shown with the chmod command examples below.

Specifying Permissions with Numeric Mode

The syntax of the chmod command (above) shows *mode* between [options] and [path][pattern]. When using the chmod command you can either specify the *mode* by using symbolic mode or numeric mode.

When using the chmod command, a three or four digit number can be used for the *mode* between [options] and [path][pattern]. A three digit number can be used when assigning the r, w and x permissions. A four digit number is used when assigning Set User ID, Set Group ID and the "sticky" bit (as described further below).

Table 12-5 shows the Numeric Representations of Permissions. The first three numbers below the Number column are the numbers for each of three permissions of r, w and x. Then next number is 0 and is used to explicitly assign no permissions.

The Number Combination column shows the numbers that are used to represent a combination of permissions (multiple permissions).

For example, assigning a directory or file the number 7 results in the permissions of rwx. The 7 is the combination of the number 4 (the number for the r permission), the number 2 (the number for the w permission) and the number 1 (the number for the x permission).

The permissions of **rwx** correspond to the numbers **421**, respectively. The r is 4, the w is 2 and the x is 1. The total of these three numbers is 7.

By remembering the first four items in the Table below, you can work out the numbers that represent the various combinations.

Table 12-5 - Numeric Representations of Permissions

Number	Corresponding Permission	Number Combination
4	r--	
2	-w-	
1	--x	
0	---	
7	rwx	7 = 4 + 2 + 1 (r is 4, w is 2 and x is 1)
6	rw-	6 = 4 + 2 (r is 4 and w is 2)
5	r-x	5 = 4 + 1 (r is 4 and x is 1)
3	-wx	3 = 2 + 1 (w is 2 and x is 1)

A four digit number can be used for *mode* and it can begin with 0 (zero). The "leading" 0 is used when assigning Set User ID, Set Group ID and the "sticky" bit (as described further below). The next three numbers specify one or more permissions, each number is for u, g and o, respectively.

A three digit number can also be used for *mode* and each of the three numbers specify one or more permissions. When using a three digit number, each number is for u, g and o, respectively.

For example, when the number 0754 is assigned to a directory or file, the 7 is for u and translates to rwx, the 5 is for g and translates to r-x and the 4 is for o and translates to r--. The resulting permissions appear in a long listing as: rwxr-xr--. The number 754 could be used in place of 0754. A four digit number is not required unless you are assigning Set User ID, Set Group ID or the "sticky" bit.

To continue the example, when the three digit number of 640 is assigned to a directory or file, the 6 is for u and translates to rw-, the 4 is for g and translates to r-- and the 0 is for o and translates to ---. The resulting permissions appear in a long listing as: rw-r-----.

Examples of Specifying the Mode with Numeric Mode

The syntax of the chmod command above shows *mode* between [options] and [path][pattern]. Below are examples of specifying the *mode* using numeric mode.

Example	Permissions	Description
600	rw-------	rw for u, no permissions for g and o
644	rw-r--r--	rw for u, r for both g and o the default permission for files that are created when umask is set to 022
664	rw-rw-r--	rw for both u and g, r for o the default permission for files that are created when umask is set to 002
700	rwx------	rwx for u, no permissions for both g an o the default permission setting for home directories
755	rwxr-xr-x	rwx for u, r-x for g and o a common permission setting for binaries and scripts the default permission for directories that are created when umask is set to 022
775	rwxrwxr-x	rwx for both u and g, r-x for o the default permission for directories that are created when umask is set to 002

More examples of using numeric mode are shown with the chmod command examples below.

Examples of the chmod Command Using Symbolic Mode

The directories and files shown in the following examples are below the current directory. A full path or other form of a relative path can also be used.

chmod go-w private

Removes the w permission for g and o for the private directory. If the directory had the permissions of rwxrwxrwx, then the above command would cause the permissions to become rwxr-xr-x.

chmod a=rw *.sxi

Assigns **all** (u, g and o) the r and w permissions (only) for all files ending in .sxi. The permissions of the files ending in .sxi become rw-rw-rw-, regardless of the prior permissions.

For example, if a file had the permissions of rwxr–r-x, then its permissions become rw-rw-rw-.

chmod u+x listit

Add the x permission for u for the file named listit. In this case, the file named listit is a script file that had the commonly acquired permissions of rw-rw-r--. This command changes the permissions to rwxrw-r-- so that the user (owner) of the file can execute the script file.

This is a very common method of quickly assigning a script file the x attribute so that the user of the file (usually you) can run the script.

Examples of the chmod Command Using Numeric Mode

chmod 0700 data

Sets the permissions on the data directory to rwx------. The u of the directory has rwx (7) to the directory and g and o have --- (0) and --- (0) (no permissions), respectively. The leading 0 in 0700 is not required. The number 700 can be used for the *mode* rather than 0700.

The permissions of rwx------ (700) are the default permissions settings for the *home directory* of a user. The home directory of a user is owned by the user and the u of the directory has all permissions. Therefore, a user has all permissions to his or her home directory and g and o have no permissions to it.

chmod 755 gr-data

Sets the permissions on the gr-data directory to rwxr-xr-x. The u of the directory has rwx (7), the g has r-x (5) and o has r-x (5). Therefore, all users have (at least) the r and x permissions to the directory and can change into it and view the contents of it. The r and x permissions to a directory are required to effectively work with files in a directory.

chmod -R 740 creative

The -R (recursive) option causes this command to set permissions to rwxr----- for the creative directory and all items (directories and files) below it. The u of the items has rwx (7), the g has r-- (4) and the o has --- (0). A relative path is used here to specify the creative directory in the current directory and an absolute path can be used. No pattern is used with the path in this example.

chmod -R 644 *

The -R (recursive) option causes this command to set permissions to rw-r--r-- for items in the current directory, all subs and all files in subs and so on. The u of the items has rw- (6), the g has r-- (4) and the o has r-- (4).

An absolute or relative path can be used prior to the pattern of * (an asterisk). However, only the pattern of * (an asterisk) and not a pattern such as *.sxi, *.txt or *letter* can be used with the -R option.

The chattr Command

The chattr (**change attributes**) command is used to assign (set) attributes to, and remove (clear) attributes from, files on an ext2 or ext3 filesystem.

Some Linux documentation refers attributes as the permissions, u and g of a directory or file. However, the attributes assigned and removed with chattr are not the permissions, u and g of a directory or file. The attributes assigned and removed with this command are described below.

The ls command cannot display file attributes that have been assigned with the chattr command. The lsattr (**list attr**ibutes) command is used to view the attributes of a file.

The Syntax of the chattr Command

The following is the syntax of the chattr command:

chattr [options] [+ | - | =]*attribute* [path][pattern]

The + (plus sign) is used to add one or more attributes to a pattern and the - (minus sign) is used to remove one or more attributes from a pattern.

The = (equals sign) is used to "set" the attributes for a pattern. After using the = sign, the pattern will only have the attributes specified with the = sign.

The -R (**recursive**) option changes the attributes of files from the specified location (relative or absolute path) downwards.

The -R option only works with an * (asterisk) for the pattern (i.e. not *.sxi, *.txt or *letter*).

Attributes Used with the chattr Command

Table 12-6 shows the attributes that are implemented in the current version of the Linux kernel.

Table 12-6 - Attributes of the chattr Command

Attribute	Description
i	**i**mmutable - see the description below
a	**a**ppend - see the description below
S	**S**ynchronize - changes to the file are immediately written to disk
d	**d**ump - exclude the file from being backed up when the dump command is used to do a backup
A	**a**time - the **atime** (access **time**) record of the file is not modified when the file is accessed or modified

The **i** (immutable) and **a** (append) attributes can only be assigned and removed by the root user.

When a file has the i attribute, no user can modify the contents of it, delete it, rename it (by moving it to the same directory with a different name), change the permissions of it, or change the u and g of it. The root user must remove the i attribute before any of these tasks can be done.

A file with the i attribute can be moved to a different directory (even though an error message appears and the file still exists in the source directory - therefore, it is not really moved, it is copied).

A file with the i attribute can be copied to the same directory or a different directory.

Once a file with the i attribute has been moved or copied, the file will not have the i attribute in the destination directory.

A file with the i attribute cannot have a file (with the same name) copied onto it or moved onto it.

The i attribute is typically given to "template" files that contain information that can be retrieved and then copied from, to a different file, and/or saved to a different file name.

When a file has the a attribute, a user can only append to the contents of it and no user can delete it, rename it, change the permissions of it, or change the u or g of it. The root user must remove the a attribute before any of these tasks can be done.

A file with the a attribute cannot be moved, but it can be copied. Once copied, the file will not have the a attribute in the destination directory. A file with the a attribute cannot have a file (with the same name) copied onto it or moved onto it.

The **A** (atime) attribute can be used to reduce disk I/O if you are working on a laptop system with a slow hard disk and files are being accessed frequently.

The **c** (compress), **s** (zero the contents of a file when it is deleted) and **u** (undelete) attributes are not implemented in the version of the Linux kernel provided with this distribution, but may be implemented in future versions.

Examples of the chattr Command

chattr +i *.sxc

Add the **i** (immutable) attribute to all files in the current directory ending in .sxc.

chattr -i *.sxc

Remove the **i** (immutable) attribute from all files in the current directory ending in .sxc.

**chattr +aS   * **

Add the **a** (append) and **S** (synchronize) attributes to all files in the current directory.

**chattr -R +i   * **

The -R (recursive) option causes this command to add the **i** (immutable) attribute to all files in and below the current directory.

An absolute or relative path can be used prior to the pattern of * (an asterisk). However, only the pattern of * (an asterisk) and not a pattern such as *.sxi, *.txt or *letter* can be used with the -R option.

The lsattr Command

The lsattr (**l**ist **attr**ibutes) command is used to view the attributes of a file on an ext2 or ext3 filesystem that have been assigned with the chattr command.

The Syntax of the lsattr Command

The following is the syntax of the lsattr command:

    lsattr [options] [path][pattern]

The **-a** (**all**) option is used to list all directories and files, including hidden directories and files.

The -R (recursive) option is used to list attributes recursively. The -R option only works properly when it is used without a pattern.

Examples of the lsattr Command

lsattr

List the attributes (that have been assigned with the chattr command) for all files, excluding hidden files, in the current directory.

lsattr -a

List the attributes for all files, including hidden files, in the current directory.

lsattr *.sxi

List the attributes of all files in the current directory that end in .sxi.

lsattr -R

The -R (recursive) option causes this command to list the attributes of all files in and below the current directory. Do not use a pattern with the -R option.

The id Command

The id command shows ID information for users and groups. If it is used without any options, it shows information for your currently logged in user ID.

The Syntax of the id Command

The following is the syntax of the id command:

    id [options] *username*

Options of the id Command

Table 12-7 shows the commonly used options of the id command.

Table 12-7 - Common Options of the id Command

Option	Description
-u	display the UID for a user
-g	display the GID number of the initial login group (a.k.a. Primary Group) for a user
-G	display the supplementary group numbers for a user
-n	display the name rather than the number use this option with the -u, -g and -G options

Examples of the id Command

id psimon

For the psimon user, this displays the UID number, user name, GID number and group name. This command produces the following output:

    uid=505(psimon) gid=11000(sales) groups=11000(prod)

id root

For the root user, this displays the same categories of information as above, but also shows more groups because this user is in several groups. This command produces the following output:

    uid=0(root) gid=0(root) groups=0(root),1(bin),2(daemon),3(sys),4(adm),6(disk),10(wheel)

id -g psimon

For the psimon user, displays the GID number only, which is 11000.

id -gn psimon

For the psimon user, displays the GID name only, which is sales.

The Default Directory and File Permissions and the Default umask Setting

Linux uses the default numeric mode setting of 777 for the permissions that are assigned to a directory, when a directory is created and a umask setting does not exist. However, by default a umask setting exists.

The default umask setting used by the kernel is 0022 and is specified in the file named fs_struct.h in /usr/src/linux-*kernelversion*/include/linux. The umask setting is used to "mask" or "block" the default directory and file permissions so that only the result can "show through". This setting is removed (deducted) from the default directory permissions and the default file permissions and creates a different default set of directory and file permissions.

The default mode setting of 777 for a directory is "masked" by the setting of 0022 and the result is 755 (777-22). The permissions of 777 have the mask of 0022 removed from them. Therefore, the default permissions for a directory are rwxr-xr-x (755). A user requires a minimum of r and x to change into a directory and view the contents of a directory. In addition to r and x, these default permissions provide w for u (the owner of the directory).

Linux uses the default numeric mode setting of 666 for the permissions of a file, when a file is created and there is no umask setting. However, by default a umask setting exists.

The default setting of 666 for a file is "masked" by the setting of 0022 and the result is 644 (666-22). The permissions of 666 have the mask of 0022 removed from them. Therefore, the default permissions for a file are rw-r--r-- (644). The u has rw and both g and o have r. The x permission is not included in these default permissions. The x permission is not needed as frequently (for files) as the r and w permissions because it is only required for binary and script files.

In summary, the default permissions assigned to a directory when it is created are 777, less the default umask of setting of 0022 (777-22). This results in the permissions of rwxr-xr-x (755).

The default permissions assigned to a file when it is created are 666, less the default umask of 0022 (666-22). This results in the permissions of rw-r--r-- (644).

However, the default umask setting of 022 is not always used by default! With this distribution and some other distributions, an "if statement" in the /etc/bashrc shell configuration file is used to specify the default umask setting for a user. The if statement in /etc/bashrc causes the umask setting to either be 0002 or 0022. This is described in more detail below.

The umask Command

The umask (UNIX **mask**) command is used to view the current umask setting and can be used to specify the current umask setting.

The umask setting specifies a "mask" that is used "over" the default directory and file permissions. If the umask has a value greater than 000, then the umask reduces the default directory and file permissions.

A umask setting (change) that is made at the command line with the umask command only lasts for the current shell session.

New items (directories and files) that are created, and items that are copied, will acquire their permissions based on the specified umask setting.

New items that are created, and items that are copied, acquire their permissions up to the permissions that are allowed by the umask setting (as described in detail below).

Directories and files that are moved are not affected by the umask setting.

New items that are created, and items that are copied, acquire the u and g of the user that created the items or did the copying, unless sgid has been assigned to the parent directory (sgid is described in detail below).

Directories and files that are moved have the same permissions, u and g in the destination as at the source.

Some programs and utilities modify the umask setting while they are running so that directories and files that are created by them acquire their permissions based on the specified umask setting.

The Syntax of the umask Command

The following is the syntax of the umask command:

    umask [options] *mode*

The *mode*, such as 002 and 022, is specified in numeric mode rather than symbolic mode. The *mode* specified with umask results in a *mode* that is assigned as the default set of permissions that are "masked" from the default permissions for a directory or file, when a directory or file is created or copied (but not moved).

For example, the if umask is set to 022, then this number is used as the default set of permissions that are masked from the default directory permissions of 777. This results in the default permissions of 755 (777-22) being assigned to a directory that is created.

To continue the example, if umask is 022, then this set of permissions is masked from the default file permissions of 666. This results in the default permissions of 644 (666-22) being assigned to a file that is created.

The -S (symbolic) option of the umask command is used to show the permissions, in symbolic mode, that will be assigned to a directory that is created.

The Effect of the umask Setting on the Default Directory and File Permissions

By default (with this distribution), the umask setting for a user is either 002 or 022. The setting that a user acquires (002 or 022) is determined by scripting logic in the /etc/bashrc configuration file and this scripting logic is described further below.

The umask mode, such as 002 and 022 and the resulting mode (assigned as default settings when a directory or file is created), such as 775 and 755 can appear with a "leading" 0 (zero). For example, 002, 022, 775 and 755, may appear as 0002, 0022, 0775 and 0755, respectively.

When you run the umask command without any options, then the current umask setting appears. The umask settings in the /etc/bashrc file are 002 and 022, not 0002 and 0022. However, when you run umask to see the current umask setting, and the setting is 002, then 0002 appears. When you run the umask command with a setting of 022, then 0022 appears.

Most of the time, we will show the umask setting and the mode with just three digits (i.e. without a leading 0).

The Default Permissions for Directories and Files When umask is 002

When the umask setting is 002, then the 777 for directories is masked by 002. The 777 for directories has the umask of 002 subtracted from it and results in the mode of 775 (777-2). The umask of 002 produces the mode of 775 for directories and this causes directories that are created to have the permissions of rwxrwxr-x (775). Therefore, both u and g have all permissions and o has r and x. The w for o is masked.

Also, when the umask is 002, then the 666 for files is masked by 002. The 666 for files minus the 002 umask results in 664. The umask of 002 produces the mode of 664 for files and this causes files that are created to have the permissions of rw-rw-r-- (664). Therefore, both u and g have r and w and o has r.

In summary, when umask is 002, then the default permissions assigned to directories that are created are rwxrwxr-x (775) and the default permissions assigned to files that are created are rw-rw-r-- (664).

 Each of the three digits in the umask is for u, g and o, respectively. The umask of 00**2** masks the **o** of an item that is created. The umask of 022 masks the g and o of an item that is created. The umask of 200 masks the u of an item.

The permissions of **rwx** correspond to the numbers **421**, respectively. The r is 4, the **w is 2** and the x is 1. The total of these three numbers is 7.

When the umask is set to 002, then the 2, which represents w is masked from the o of the item.

For example, a *directory* that is created with a umask setting of 000 has the permissions of rwxrwxrwx. When the umask is set to 002, then the 2, which represents w to o is masked and the result is rwxrwxr-x.

To continue the example, when the umask is set to 022, then the 22, which represents w to g and o is masked and the result is rwxr-xr-x.

As another example, a *file* that is created with a umask setting of 000 has the permissions of rw-rw-rw-. When the umask is set to 002, then the 2, which represents w to o is masked and the result is rw-rw-r--.

To continue the example, when the umask is set to 022, then the 22, which represents w to g and o is masked and the result is rw-r--r--.

The Default Permissions for Directories and Files When umask is 022

When the umask setting is 022, then the 777 for directories is masked by 022. The 777 for directories has the umask of 022 subtracted from it and results in the mode of 755 (777-22). The umask of 022 produces the mode of 755 for directories and this causes directories that are created to have the permissions of rwxr-xr-x (755). Therefore, u has all permissions and both g and o have r and x.

Also, when the umask is 022, then the 666 for files is masked by 022. The 666 for files minus the 022 umask results in 644. The umask of 022 produces the mode of 644 for files and this causes files that are created to have the permissions of rw-r--r-- (644). Therefore, u has r and w and both g and o have r.

In summary, when umask is 022, then the default permissions assigned to directories that are created is rwxr-xr-x (755) and the default permissions assigned to files that are created is rw-r–r– (644).

Examples of the umask Command

umask

This command displays the current umask setting in numeric mode. By default, this number will either be 0002 or 0022.

umask 0002

This command changes the umask setting to 0002 for the current session.

With a umask of 002, the mode for directories is 775 (777 - 2) and the mode for files is 664 (666 - 2).

Directories that are created will have the permissions of rwxrwxr-x (775) and files will have rw-rw-r-- (664).

For example, you are logged in as root and your current umask setting is 022. With this setting, directories that you create will have the default permissions of rwxr-xr-x and files that you create will have the default permissions of rw-r--r--.

However, you are creating directories and files in a directory that will be accessed by users that have a umask setting of 002. In this case, you want the directories and files to have the settings that occur when umask is 002. Therefore, you run the umask command and set the umask to 002 until you have finished creating the directories and files for the users.

umask -S

Based on the current umask setting, this command displays the permissions, in symbolic mode, that will be assigned to a directory (not file) that is created.

When umask is 022, the permissions for a directory are rwxr-xr-x (755 = 777 - 22) and the output of the above command will be:

```
u=rwx,g=rx,o=rx
```

The Scripting Logic in /etc/bashrc that Specifies the Default umask Setting

For the distribution that is being used with this book, the default umask setting is determined (and specified) by scripting logic in lines 6 through 10 of the /etc/bashrc (bash configuration file). If this scripting logic did not exist, then the default umask would be 022 (as specified in the fs_struct.h file described above).

For example, if lines 6 through 10 in /etc/bashrc were "commented out" (by putting a # symbol at the start of each line), or if these lines were removed, then the default umask setting would be 022.

For this distribution, the default umask setting for any user (root or non-root) is determined by the scripting logic in lines 6 through 10 of /etc/bashrc. The comments on lines 4 and 5 and the scripting logic in lines 6 through 10 are shown below.

```
4    # by default, we want this to get set.
5    # Even for non-interactive, non-login shells.
6    if [ "`id -gn`" = "`id -un`" -a `id -u` -gt 99 ]; then
7    umask 002
8         else
9    umask 022
10   fi
```

Line 6 is the start of an if statement and line 10 is the end of it. Line 10 shows "fi", which is the reverse of "if" and indicates the end of the if statement.

If the conditions of the if statement on line 6 are met, then line 7 is processed (umask 002). If not, then line 8, which shows "else", causes line 9 to be processed (umask 022).

If the conditions between the [ ] square brackets on line 6 are met, then a user will get the umask setting of 002 shown on line 7. If the conditions are not met, then a user will get the umask setting of 022 shown on line 9.

The if statement on line 6 and the conditions between the [ ] square brackets are shown below.

```
if [ "`id -gn`" = "`id -un`" -a `id -u` -gt 99 ]; then
```

The above text from line 6 translates to: "if the **g**roup **n**ame is equal to (=) the **u**ser **n**ame and (-a) the **u**ser id number is greater than 99; then".

If these conditions are met, then the user gets the umask setting of 002. If not, the user gets the umask setting of 022.

The id command is used three times in the statement above to produce the group name, user name and the user id number, respectively.

"`id -gn`" runs the id command with the **g** (**g**roup) and **n** (**n**ame) options and produces the group name.

"`id -un`" runs the id command with the **u** (**u**ser) and **n** (**n**ame) options and produces the user name.

"`id -u`" runs the id command with the **u** (**u**ser) option and produces the user number.

Summary of the Conditions on Line 6

If the Primary Group name of the user logging in is the same as the user name *and* the user id number is greater than 99, then the umask for the user is set to 002.

If the Primary Group name of the user logging in is different from the user name, then the umask for the user is set to 022. If the group name and user name are the same, but the user id number is not greater than 99, then the umask for the user is set to 022.

The Default umask Setting When Logged In as root with the Default root User Settings

When the root user was created during the Linux installation, a Primary Group name with the same name as the user name was created and the user was assigned the user id of 0 (zero).

When logged in as root, the Primary Group name (root) is the same as the user name (root), but the user id number (0) is not greater than 99. The conditions on line 6 are not met and so the user gets the umask setting of 022 (from line 9). Running umask at the command line shows 0022. By default, the root user has a umask setting of 022.

The Default Directory and File Permissions When umask is 022

When logged in as a user with a umask setting of 022, the mode for *directories* that are created is 755 (777 - 22), which appears as rwxr-xr-x. The permissions of r and x are required to effectively work in a directory (change into a directory and view the files in it). The umask of 022 provides the mode of 755 (rwxr-xr-x), which provides the r and x permissions for u, g and o (all users). It also provides w to the u (owner) of the directory.

When logged in as a user with a umask setting of 022, the mode (permissions) for *files* that are created is 644 (666 - 22) which appears as rw-r--r--. This provides u with rw, and g and o with r.

The Default umask Setting When Logged In as cwest with the Default cwest User Settings

When the cwest user was created during the Linux installation, a Primary Group name with the same name as the user name was created and the user was assigned the user id of 500.

By default, users are assigned user id numbers starting at 500 and this number increases by one for each additional user that is created. Therefore, unless you specify otherwise (when creating a user), all user ids will be greater than 99.

When logged in as cwest, the primary group name (cwest) is the same as the user name (cwest) and the user id number (500) is greater than 99. The conditions on line 6 are met and so the user gets the umask setting of 002 (line 7). Running umask at the command line shows 0002.

By default, all non-root users will have a umask of 002.

The Default Directory and File Permissions When umask is 002

When logged in as a user with a umask setting of 002, the mode for *directories* that are created is 775 (777 - 2), which appears as rwxrwxr-x. The permissions of r and x are required to effectively work in a directory. The umask of 002 provides the mode of 775 (rwxrwxr-x), which provides the r and x permissions for u, g and o (all users). It also provides w to the u (owner) and g of the directory.

When logged in as a user with a umask setting of 002, the mode for *files* that are created is 664 (666 - 2), which appears as rw-rw-r--. This provides both u and g with rw, and o with r.

Set User ID and Set Group ID

Set User ID can be assigned to a binary and is not intended for any other type of file or directory.

Set Group ID can be assigned to a binary or a directory.

Set User ID for a binary, Set Group ID for a binary and Set Group ID for a directory are described below.

Set User ID for a Binary

A binary can be assigned the **s** (set UID) permission in the third position of the **u** (user) permissions of the binary. When the s permission is assigned to the u of a binary, the binary "has" Set User ID (a.k.a. SUID, **suid**, setuid bit).

The "s" or "S" for suid appears in the same position for the u of a binary as the x for execute. If a binary does not have x for user and you assign it suid, then an upper case "S" appears rather than a lower case "s". Both "s" and "S" have the same effect. We will use a lower case "s" to represent suid.

A binary file, such as a binary in the /bin directory for a command, commonly has the permissions of rwxr-xr-x. If a binary with these permissions is assigned the s permission, then the permissions will become rwsr-xr-x. The x that was in the third position of the u permissions changes to an s. The s permission includes the x permission.

The s permission for the u of a file is only assigned to a binary (program) file. It is not intended for any other type of file and is not intended for a directory.

The effect of suid for a binary is that when the binary is executed, *it is executed with the permissions of the u (user) of the file*. The "set user id" (suid) "sets" (s) the "effective" user id (uid) of the file to the u of the file, which is the user name (owner) assigned to the file. The "effective" UID of the process that is started when the program is run (the binary program running in memory) is the name of the u (user, owner) of the file. You will see the "effective" UID of a process in a later chapter.

For example, a binary has suid and the u of the binary is root. When a user executes the binary, the program runs with the permissions of the root user (for as long as the program is running). This allows a user to execute a binary and have greater permissions than normal to do some tasks. The "effective" UID of the process (the binary program running in memory) is the root user.

To continue the example, the passwd binary in /usr/bin is run to assign user passwords and change user passwords. This binary has the settings of r-s--x--x, root, root. The s in the third position of the u permissions indicates that this file has suid. The u (user, owner) of the file is root. When a non-root user executes this binary, it runs with the permissions of the root user.

When a non-root user runs the passwd command to change his or her password, the passwd binary needs to write the new (encrypted) password in the text file named shadow in /etc/. However, a non-root user does not have permission to write to this file.

When a non-root user runs the passwd binary, *the binary* (not the user) has the permissions of root (due to the "set user id"). The user id of the binary has been "set" to root, and so the binary has the permissions of the root user, so that it can write to the /etc/shadow file.

A non-root user that runs the passwd command does not become the root user. Instead, the passwd binary runs with the permissions of the root user (and the passwd program can only do what it has been written to do). The passwd binary only allows a non-root user to change his or her own password, not the password of another user.

Set Group ID for a Binary

A binary can be assigned the **s** (set uid) permission in the third position of the **g** (**g**roup) permissions the binary. When the s permission is assigned to the g of a binary, the binary "has" Set Group ID (a.k.a. SGID, **sgid**, setgid bit).

 The "s" or "S" for sgid appears in the same position for the g of a binary as the x for execute. If a binary does not have x for group and you assign it sgid, then an upper case "S" appears rather than a lower case "s". Both "s" and "S" have the same effect. We will use a lower case "s" to represent sgid.

A binary file commonly has the permissions of rwxr-xr-x. If a binary with these permissions is assigned the s permission, then the permissions will become rwxr-**s**r-x. The x that was in the third position of the g permissions changes to an s. The **s** permission includes the **x** permission.

The s permission for the g of a file is only assigned to a binary (program) file. It is not intended for any other type of file. The s permission can also be assigned to the g of a directory.

The effect of sgid for a binary is this: when the binary is executed, *it is executed with the permissions of the g (group) of the file*. The "set group id" (SGID) "sets" (S) the "effective" group id (GID) of the file to the g of the file. The "effective" GID of the process that is started is the name of the g (group) of the file.

For example, the slocate binary in /usr/bin appears as rwxr-**s**r-x, root, **slocate**. The u (user, owner) of the file is root and this user has rwx permissions. The g (group) of the slocate file is **slocate**. The name of the binary is slocate and the name of the g of the binary is also slocate. The slocate group has r-**s** permissions to the slocate binary and therefore, this binary has SGID. It has the s permission for the slocate group. When a user runs the slocate command, the command runs with the permissions of the slocate group.

Set Group ID for a Directory

A directory can be assigned the **s** (set uid) permission in the third position of the **g** (**g**roup) permissions of a directory. When the s permission is assigned to the g of a directory, the directory "has" Set Group ID (a.k.a. SGID, **sgid**, setgid bit).

 The "s" or "S" for sgid appears in the same position for the g of a directory as the x for execute. When umask is 0002 or 0022 and a directory is created, then the g (group) permissions for the directory are rwx or r-x. Therefore, directories commonly have x for other.

However, if a directory does not have x for other and you assign sgid to it, then an upper case "S" appears rather than a lower case "s". Both "s" and "S" have the same effect. We will use a lower case "s" to represent sgid for a directory.

The "set group id" (sgid) "**sets**" (S) the "effective" group id (GID) of the directory to the g of the directory. The effect of sgid for a directory is that files created in the directory acquire the same group name as the group name of the directory.

For example, the current-orders directory exists below /home/common/prod. The g of the current-orders directory is prod. You want all directories and files that are created in this directory to be accessible by the prod group. Therefore, you assign sgid to the directory (which has the g of prod).

When any user creates a directory or file in this directory, the g of the item will be prod (rather than the g of the user that creates the item). This will allow all users in the prod group to access the item. The u of the item will be the name of the user that creates the item.

RMG Inc. Case Study Example of Assigning SGID to a Directory

For the RMG Inc. Case Study, you created a directory named prod below /home/common/. This is the parent directory for shared data directories for the Production Department. The prod directory has five subdirectories that will be used for shared data by members of the Production Department.

During the Hands-On Exercises below you will create a group named prod and also create the users for the Production Department. The users in the Production Department will be added to the prod group. This will make them members of the prod group.

The users in the prod group should not be able to create directories and files in /home/common/prod. They should only be able to create directories and files in subdirectories of prod. They will primarily be creating files in the subs of prod, rather than directories. Now we will discuss what happens when files are created and then we will discuss what happens when directories (subs) are created.

Files that are Created in a Directory that has SGID

By default, each user has a Primary Group that is the same name as the user. If a user named cwest creates a directory or file in his or her home directory, then the u of the directory or file is cwest *and the g of the directory or file is also cwest.*

By default, when the users in the prod group create files in subs of prod, the u of the file will be the name of the user (this is fine) *and the g of the file will also be the name of the user* (this is not what we want).

If the g of a file is the name of a user, then other users in prod will not be able to access (read from and write to) the file. The g of the file needs to be prod.

The g of a file can be changed manually by running the chown or chgrp commands, but this is a tedious solution. By assigning sgid to the directory, then files that are created in the directory will automatically be assigned the g of the directory. If the g of the directory is prod, then files created in the directory will automatically have the g of prod and all users in the prod group will have access to them!

During the Hands-On Exercises you will assign the prod group name to the g of the prod directory and also assign prod to the g of the five subs in the prod directory. You will also remove all permissions that o has to the prod directory and its five subs.

The showe user in the prod group. This user changes into the current-orders directory below prod and creates a file. By default, the u of the file is showe and the g of the file is also showe. The showe user can access the file, but other users in the prod group cannot.

To allow all users in the prod group to be able to access the files in the subs of the prod directory, that are created by users in the prod group, you will assign sgid to each directory below prod. The g of each sub of prod will be prod.

The sgid on the directory will cause all directories and files created in a sub of prod *by anyone* to have the g of prod (the name of the g of the *directory* is assigned to the g of the directory or file), rather than the g of the Primary Group name of the user (which is the same as the user name).

Therefore, if you are logged in as showe and create a file in a sub of prod, the u of the file will be showe, but the g of the file will be prod and all users in the prod group will have access to the file. The default permission settings on a file that is created are rwxrw-r–, *username*, prod. The g of the file has rw. Therefore, the prod group (which is the g of the file) will have rw to the file. o does not have access to the directory, so the r permission for o cannot be used by "others".

Directories (Subdirectories) that are Created in a Directory that has SGID

By default, when a user in the prod group creates a directory in a sub of prod, the u of the directory will be the name of the user (this is fine) *and the g of the directory will also be the name of the user* (this is not what we want).

If the g of a directory is the name of a user, then other users in prod will not be able to change into the directory. They will not have access to the contents directory. All permissions to the o of the parent directory (prod) have been removed. Therefore, even though a directory that is created in a sub of prod will have r and x to o, others will not be able to access it because they cannot change into the prod directory.

By assigning sgid to prod and to subs of prod, directories that are created in the subs can automatically be assigned the g of the directory. The g of the directory is prod and therefore, directories created in a sub of prod will automatically have the g of prod and all users in the prod group will have access to them!

The showe user in the prod group. This user changes into the current-orders directory below prod and creates a directory. The u of the directory is showe. With sgid on the parent directory, the g of the directory will be prod. All users in the prod group will be able to access the directory. In addition to this, because the parent directory has sgid, directories created in the directory also have sgid. Therefore, sgid on a directory works recursively on directories created in directories that have sgid!

The Sticky Bit (Permission)

A directory can be assigned the **t** (sticky bit) permission in the third position of the **o** (other) permissions of the directory. When the t permission is assigned to the o of a directory, the directory "has" the "sticky" bit.

When the sticky (**t**) bit (a.k.a. t permission, restricted deletion flag) is assigned to the o of a directory, only the owner of a file in the directory can delete or rename the file. The owner of a file is the user that created the file. Therefore, when this permission is used, only the person that creates a file can delete it or rename it. This permission is typically assigned to "world-writeable" directories in which multiple users can create files, such as the /tmp directory.

The "t" or "T" for sticky bit appears in the same position for the o of a directory as the x for execute. When umask is 0002 or 0022 and a directory is created, then the o (other) permissions for the directory are r-x. Therefore, directories commonly have x for other.

However, if a directory does not have x for other and you assign the sticky bit to it, then an upper case "T" appears rather than a lower case "t". Both "t" and "T" have the same effect. We will use a lower case "t" to represent the sticky bit.

The /tmp directory appears as rwxrwxrwt, root, root. The root user has rwx, the root group has rwx and other (all other users) have rwt. The "t" in "rwt" (for the o of /tmp) is the "sticky bit". Therefore, all non-root users can create files in /tmp and only the user that creates the file can delete or rename the file. Other users can view the contents of the file, but cannot delete or rename it.

The Linux kernel ignores the t permission when it is assigned to a file.

Assigning the s and t Permissions

The s permission is assigned to the u of a binary to make the binary suid.

The s permission is assigned to the g of a binary to make the binary sgid. The s permission is assigned to the g of a directory to make the directory sgid.

The t permission is assigned to the o of a directory to assign the sticky bit to a directory.

Assigning the s or t Permission Numerically

To assign the s or t permission when specifying the *mode* for a directory of file numerically, use 4, 2 or 1 as the first digit of the four digits. Use 4 as the first digit for suid (for a binary), 2 as the first digit for sgid (for a binary or directory) and 1 as the first digit for the sticky bit (for a directory). Use the remaining three digits to specify the other permissions that are required for the file or directory.

For example, to assign the s permission to the u of a binary so that it has suid, use four digits for the mode and make the first digit the number 4. Use the remaining three digits to specify the other permissions that are required for the file. In this case, the remaining three digits are 555. The permissions on the *binaryfilename* after running the following command are r-**s**r-xr-x.

    chmod 4555 *binaryfilename*

To assign the s permission to the g of a binary so that it has sgid, use four digits for the mode and make the first digit the number 2. In this case, the remaining three digits are 755. The permissions on the *binaryfilename* after running the following command are rwxr-**s**r-x.

    chmod 2755 *binaryfilename*

To assign the s permission to the g of a directory so that it has sgid, use four digits for the mode and make the first digit the number 2. In this case, the remaining three digits are 750. The permissions on the *directoryname* after running the following command are rwxr-**s**---.

    chmod 2750 *directoryname*

To assign the t permission to the o of a directory so that it has the sticky bit, use four digits for the mode and make the first digit the number 1. In this case, the remaining three digits are 777. The permissions on the *directoryname* after running the following command are rwxrwxrwt. These are the default permissions of the /tmp directory.

> chmod 1777 *directoryname*

Assigning the s or t Permission Symbolically

When you assign the s or t permission symbolically, the permission is added to the existing permissions. If the x permission exists (where the s or t is being added), then the s or t replaces the x permission. If not, S or T (in caps) appears in the third position of u, g or o.

To assign the s permission to the u of a binary so that it has suid, use the following command.

> chmod u+s *binaryfilename*

To assign the s permission to the g of a binary so that it has sgid, use the following command.

> chmod g+s *binaryfilename*

To assign the s permission to the g of a directory so that it has sgid, use the following command.

> chmod g+s *directoryname*

To assign the t permission to the o of a directory so that it has the sticky bit, use the following command.

> chmod o+t *directoryname*

The Effect on Permissions when Directories and Files are Moved, Copied and Created

In the following discussion, the word items is used to refer to directories and files; sgid to a directory is not involved; and a user has the permissions necessary to move, copy and create files.

It is very important to understand what happens with the permissions, users and groups when items are moved, copied and created. All three of these acts affect permissions, users and groups differently.

Moving Items

When an item (directory or file) is moved with the mv command, the permissions, u and g of the item at the destination are the same as at the source location. The permissions, u and g of the item are not changed. A umask setting does not have an effect on items that are moved.

Copying Items

When an item (directory or file) is copied with the cp command, the permissions of the item can be affected by the current umask setting. Also, the u and g of the item become the u and g of the user that copies the item.

Some versions of the cp binary preserve the permissions, u and g of a directory or file in the destination when a directory or file is copied. The version of the cp binary with this distribution does not do this.

However, there is a **-p** (**p**reserve) option of the cp binary that is provided with this distribution. This option causes the permissions (but not the u and g) of a directory or file to be "preserved" so that they are the same in the destination as in the source.

The man page for the cp command with this distribution states that the permissions, ownership (u and g) and timestamp (date and time) will be preserved when the -p option is used.

However, the permissions and timestamp are preserved, but the ownership (u and g) is not (even though the man page states that the ownership is preserved)! When an item is copied with the cp command (with or without the -p option), the u and g of the item in the destination will be the same as the u and g of the user that copied the item.

When items are copied with the cp command (without the -p option), the umask setting is *applied* to the items that are copied. The items will have permissions *up to* the permissions allowed by the umask.

For example, a file has rw-rw-r-- (664). It has w to u and g, but not o. When the file is copied and the umask setting is 022 (which stops the w permission for g and o), then the file will have rw-r--r--. The w permission for g is "masked" (blocked) by the umask setting. The w permission for o did not exist and therefore the umask setting did not have an effect. The file will have permissions *up to* the permissions allowed by the umask.

To continue the example, a file has rw-r--r-- (644). It has w to u, but not g and o. When the file is copied and the umask setting is 022 (which stops the w permission for g and o), then the file will still have rw-r--r--. The w permission for g and o did not exist and therefore the umask setting did not have an effect.

To continue the example, a file has r-------- (600). When the file is copied and the umask setting is 022, then the file will still have r--------.

Creating Items

New directories are commonly created with the mkdir command. New files can be created in many ways, such as running a text editor and creating a file, running a script that creates a file, and running an application and saving a file.

When a new directory is created in a directory, it acquires the default directory permissions of 777, less the current umask setting. If the umask setting is 002, then the directory acquires the permissions of 775. If the umask setting is 022, then the directory acquires the permissions of 755.

When a new file is created in a directory, it acquires the default directory permissions of 666, less the current umask setting. If the umask setting is 002, then the file acquires the permissions of 664. If the umask setting is 022, then the file acquires the permissions of 644.

When a new directory or file is created, it acquires the u and g of the user that created it (unless the directory has sgid). Therefore, the user that creates a directory or file becomes the u (owner) of the directory or file and the g of the directory or file becomes the g of the user that created it.

When a directory has sgid and a new directory or file is created in it, the new item acquires the g of the parent directory, not the g of the user that created the directory.

For example a directory has sgid and the g of the directory is prod (the prod group). When any user creates a directory or file in the directory, the g of the item will be prod (which is the g of the parent directory). The u (owner) of the item will be the name of the user that created the item.

When you create a user with the useradd command, the directories and files below /etc/skel are copied to the home directory of the user.

The umask setting is *applied* to the items that are created in the home directory of the user. The items will have permissions *up to* the permissions allowed by the umask.

For example, a directory below /etc/skel has rwxrwxr-x (775). When a user is created with useradd and the umask setting is 022, then the directory that is created below the home directory of the user will have rwxr-xr-x (755).

To continue the example, a directory below /etc/skel has rwxr-xr-x (755 = 777 - 022). When a user is created with useradd and the umask setting is 022, then the directory that is created below the home directory of the user will still have rwxr-xr-x.

When you create a user with the useradd command, the files below /etc/skel and the files in subs below /etc/skel are also copied to the home directory of the user.

The umask setting does not affect the files below /etc/skel (and files in subs of /etc/skel) that are copied to the home directory of the user. The permissions (not the u and g) that the files have in /etc/skel have, are the same in the home directory (and subs) of the user as they are in /etc/skel. The permissions in the destination are the same as in the source.

When the useradd command is run, the files /etc/skel and subs are copied to the home directory of a user by the useradd binary, not the cp binary. If the files were copied with the cp binary, then the umask would be applied to the files and the u and g of the files would be the u and g of the user that ran the cp command.

When you create a user with the useradd command, the u and g of the directories and files that are copied from below /etc/skel to the home directory of the user are the same as the u and g of the user that has been created.

By default, the user name is the same as the primary group name. Therefore, the username and group name of the user are the u and g of the directories and files that are copied from /etc/skel to the home directory of a user. This allows the user to be able to access the directories and files.

The Permissions on the Items in a User's Home Directory that are Copied from /etc/skel

When you create a user with the useradd command, the items (directories and files) below /etc/skel are copied to the home directory of the user.

The umask setting is *applied* to the directories (not files) that are created in the home directory of the user. The directories will have permissions *up to* the permissions allowed by the umask.

For example, a directory below /etc/skel has rwxrwxr-x (775). When a user is created with useradd and the umask setting is 022, then the directory that is created below the home directory of the user will have rwxr-xr-x (755).

To continue the example, a directory below /etc/skel has rwxr-xr-x (755). When a user is created with useradd and the umask setting is 022, then the directory that is created below the home directory of the user will still have rwxr-xr-x.

When you create a user with the useradd command, the files below /etc/skel and the files in subs below /etc/skel are also copied to the home directory of the user.

The umask setting does not affect the files below /etc/skel (and files in subs of /etc/skel) that are copied to the home directory of the user. The permissions (not the u and g) that the files have in /etc/skel have, are the same in the home directory (and subs) of the user as they are in /etc/skel. The permissions in the destination are the same as in the source.

When the useradd command is run, the files /etc/skel and subs are copied to the home directory of a user by the useradd binary, not the cp binary.

If the files were copied with the cp binary, then the umask would be applied to the files and the u and g of the files would be the u and g of the user that ran the cp command.

When you create a user with the useradd command, the u and g of the directories and files that are copied from below /etc/skel to the home directory of the user are the same as the u and g of the user that has been created.

By default, the user name is the same as the Primary Group name. Therefore, the username and group name of the user are the u and g of the directories and files that are copied from /etc/skel to the home directory of a user. This allows the user to be able to access the directories and files.

Permissions Required by the u (Owner) of a Directory or File

A user that is the u (owner) of an item (directory or file) must have a permission assigned to the u of the item for the user to have any permissions to the item. If the u of an item has no permissions and the g and o has rwx permissions, the u still has no permissions, even if the user is a member of the g of the item.

Here is a scenario. A user is the u (owner) of an item, but the u does not have any permissions to the item. The user is a member of the g of the item and the g has r to the item. The user does not have r to the item, even though the user is a member of the g of the item and the g has r to the item.

For example, an item has the settings of ---r-----, bford, prod. The bford user is the u (owner) of the item and u does not have any permissions to the item. The bford user is a member of the g of the item (the prod group), which has r to the item. However, bford still does not have r to the item.

To continue the example, if the item has the settings of -w----r--, bford, prod, then bford has w to the item and o has r to the item, but bford does not have r to the item.

The concept described above also applies to the w and x permissions for the u (owner) of an item.

The u (owner) of an item can assign all permissions to the u of the item, even if the u has no permissions to the item.

By default, the chmod binary is in /bin and users can use this utility. If a user knows how to change permissions, and the user has access to a utility that allows the user to change permissions, then a user that is the u of the item can change the permissions of the u to the item to any and all permissions.

A system can be set up so that non-root users do not have access to a utility that allows them to change the permissions of any item.

In summary, the u (owner) of an item must have r to the u of the item to have the r permission; and must have w to the u of the item to have the w permission; and must have x to the u of the item to have the x permission; regardless of the permissions of g and o to the item.

Permissions Required for the g (Group) of a Directory or File

When a user is not the u (owner) of an item (directory or file), but is a member of the g of the item, then the g must be assigned a permission to the item for the user to have any permissions.

Here is a scenario. A user is **not** the u (owner) of an item and the u of the item has no permissions (or any set of permissions, including all permissions). The user is a member of the g of an item. The g of the item does not have any permissions. The o of the item has the r permission. The user does not have r to the item, even though o has r to the item. (If the user was the u (owner) of the item, then the item would require r for u for the user (owner) for the user to have r to the item, as described above).

For example, an item has the settings of ------r--, bford, prod. The mwong user is not the u (owner) of the item and is a member of the g of the item (the prod group). The o of the item has r the permission. However, mwong still does not have r to the item.

The concept described above also applies to the w and x permissions for the g (group) of an item.

In summary, if a user is not the u (owner) of an item, but is a member of the g of an item, then the item must have r to the g of the item for the user to have r to the item; and must have w to the g of the item to have the w permission; and must have x to the g of the item to have the x permission, regardless of the permissions for o. (If the user was the u (owner) of the item, then the item would require one or more permissions for the u (owner) to have one or more permissions, as described above).

Permissions Required for the o (Other) of a Directory or File

When a user is not the u (owner) of an item (directory or file) and is not a member of the g of the item, then the o must be assigned a permission to the item for the user to have any permissions.

Here is a scenario. A user is **not** the u (owner) of an item and is **not** a member of the g of the item. The u and/or g has no permissions (or any set of permissions, including all permissions). The user only has permissions that are assigned to the o of the item.

For example, an item has the settings of rwxrwxr--, bford, sales. The mwong user is not the u (owner) of the item and is not a member of the g of the item (the sales group). The o of the item has r the permission. Therefore, mwong has r to the item.

The concept described above also applies to the w and x permissions for the o (other) of an item.

In summary, if a user is not the u (owner) of an item and is a not a member of the g of an item, then the item must have r to the o of the item for the user to have r to the item; and must have w to the o of the item to have the w permission; and must have x to the o of the item to have the x permission.

Additional Comments on Permissions and Attributes

In the following discussion, all references to "user" are for a non-root user, the word "item" is used to represent "directory and file" and the user has r and x to the parent directory of the items.

A user requires r and x to a directory to effectively "work" on files in a directory.

The permissions of r and x are required for a user to effectively "work" with files in a directory. These permissions allow a user to change into a directory and view the contents of the directory. The discussion below is an example of a situation where a user does not require the r and x permissions to read the contents of a file in a directory.

If a directory has no permissions, except for the x permission for o, then a user can change into the directory, but cannot get a listing of the files in a directory and therefore, cannot see the names of the files in the directory.

If a file in the directory has no permissions for g and o, and the user is not the u (owner) of the file, then the user cannot open the file. If the user is the u (owner) of the file and the file has the r permission for u (and g and o have no permissions), then the user can open the file in read-only mode (if he or she knows the name of the file).

In other words, if the directory has x to o (only) and a user is the u (owner) of a file in the directory and the u has r to the file, then the user can open and read the contents of the file in read-only mode. The x (only) to the directory and the r to the file combine to allow the user to read the contents of the file.

Therefore, if a program was written to automatically access a file for a user (because the user does not know that the file exists in the directory), then the program or the user would be able to read the contents of the file *without having the r permission to the directory.*

Conversely, if a directory has no permissions, except for the r permission for o, then a user cannot change into the directory, and cannot get a "proper" listing of the files in a directory. When the user gets a listing of the directory (by specifying a path to the directory), the user will see the names of the files in the directory and "Permission denied" beside each one, regardless of the user's permissions to the files.

If a file in the directory has rwxrwxrwx, cwest, cwest, then the cwest user cannot open and read the contents of the file (or do anything with the file). The r to o (only) of the directory and rwx to the u of the file do not combine to allow the user to read the contents of the file (or do anything with the file).

If a user has w to a directory, then the user can create items in the directory and can also delete all of the items in the directory, regardless of the permission settings (not attributes) of the items.

If a user does not have w to a directory, then the user cannot create files in the directory. However, if a user has r and w to (an existing) file in the directory, then the user can read the file and write to the file.

Only the root user can use the useradd, usermod, userdel, groupadd, groupmod and groupdel commands to make changes to a system. All of the binaries for these commands are in /usr/**s**bin.

The commands used to do the tasks below are shown in ( ) brackets. These tasks can also be done by GUI utilities.

Only the root user can change the u (owner) of an item (with chown).

The u (owner) of an item can change the g of the item to a group (primary or supplementary) to which the user is a member (with chown or chgrp).

For example, the permission settings of an item are rwxrwxr-x, cwest, prod. The cwest user is the u (owner) of the item and is a member of the prod and sales groups. The cwest user can change the g of the item from prod to sales and vice versa.

The u (owner) of an item can change the permissions of the item to any permissions (with chmod).

The i attribute is commonly assigned (with chattr) to a file so that it cannot be deleted or renamed. However, the contents of a file with the i attribute cannot be modified.

Only the root user can change the i and a attributes of a file.

The u (owner) of a file, with the r permission, can change the attributes of a file to any attributes (other than a or i).

A user with the r permission to a file can view the attributes of the file (with lsattr).

Other than a user password, only the root user can modify password settings (with chage).

Any user can see his or her password settings (with the -l option of chage).

The passwd, users, groups, id and umask commands can be run by any user.

The Red Hat User Manager Utility

If a desktop is running on a system, such as a non-server system, then the Red Hat User Manager (GUI) utility can be used to manage users and groups. You can use this utility to create, delete, modify and view the settings of users and groups.

To run the Red Hat User Manager utility: Menu ; System Settings ; Users and Groups.

As described earlier, for security reasons you should never log in to a desktop as the root user.

When you are logged in to the desktop as a non-root user and you do the steps to run the Red Hat User Manager utility, you are prompted for the password of the root user. Figure 12-1 shows the Query dialog box that requests this password. If this password is not provided, then the utility will not appear.

Figure 12-1 - The Query dialog box of the Red Hat User Manager utility

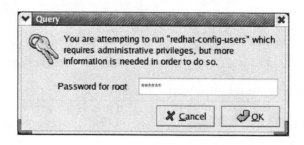

The opening screen of the Red Hat User Manager utility is shown in Figure 12-2. By default, the Users tab (at the left, below the Add User button) is selected when you run this utility. In this Figure, the bford user is selected.

To see group information, select the Groups tab (at the right of the Users tab).

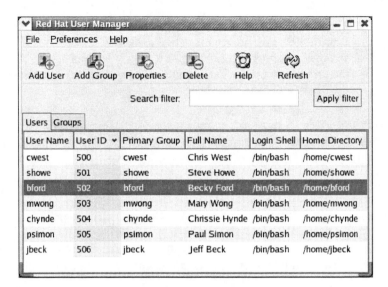

Figure 12-2 - The Red Hat User Manager utility with the Users tab selected

The Add User and Add Group Buttons

The Add User and Add Group Buttons appear near the top of the Red Hat User Manager utility.

To add a new user, select the Add User button and provide the settings for the user.

When adding a user with the Add User button, you can select "Specify user ID manually" and specify a UID number for the user (if necessary).

To add a new group, select the Add Group button and provide the settings for the group.

When adding a group with the Add Group button, select "Specify group ID manually" and provide a GID number for the group, such as 10000. This will stop the group from acquiring a GID number that is the next available number above 500 (i.e. a number that "should" only be used for users).

Selecting "Specify group ID manually" and providing a GID number for the group is the same as using the -g option of the groupadd command when you create a group with this command.

The Users Tab of the Red Hat User Manager Utility

When you run the Red Hat User Manager utility, the Users tab below the Add User button is selected by default. This tab shows the current user names and several settings for the user.

 This Users tab is basically showing the contents of /etc/passwd, except that the x that represents the use of shadow passwords does not appear and the primary group *name* appears, rather than the *number* (GID) for the primary group. The /etc/passwd file only shows the GID number of the Primary Group.

To modify the settings of a user, select the name of a user and then select Properties button. After a user has been created, the UID of the user cannot be changed with this utility.

To delete a user, select the name of a user and then select the Delete button.

The Groups Tab of the Red Hat User Manager Utility

The Groups tab shows the current group names, and the group id and members of each group. By default "system" groups are not shown, but can be displayed.

 The Groups tab is basically showing the contents of /etc/group, except that the x that represents the use of shadow group passwords does not appear.

To modify the settings of a group, select the name of a group and then select the Properties button. After a group has been created, the GID of the group cannot be changed with this utility.

Figure 12-3 - The Red Hat User Manager utility with the Groups tab selected

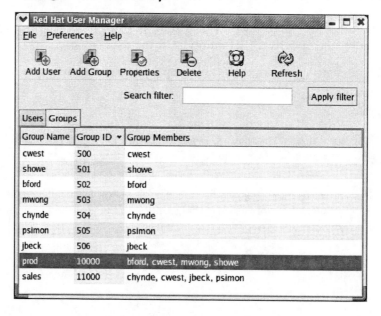

To delete a group, select the name of a group and then select the Delete button.

Figure 12-3 shows the Red Hat User Manager utility with the Groups tab selected. In this Figure, the prod group is selected.

By default, the "system" users and groups, such as bin, daemon, ftp, gopher, mail and news do not appear in the Red Hat User Manager utility. This allows you to focus on "non-system" users and groups.

To see the "system" users and groups: Select Preferences ; deselect "Filter system users and groups".

If you run the Red Hat User Manager utility and then do any work on users or groups at the command line (such as add a user or group, delete a user or group, or modify the settings of a user or group) and then go back to the Red Hat User Manager utility, then select the Refresh button to have the changes that were made at the command line appear.

Hands-On Exercises

 Logging In to Work with Permissions, Users and Groups

> Log in to a desktop as cwest ; open a terminal emulation window ; do not su to root.
>
>]# cd / ; ls -l

All items show "root, root" and so the u (owner) is root and g is root for all of the directories off of the / (root) directory. Therefore, non-root users, such as cwest, are in the category of o "other".

Look at the permission settings on the bin directory. They are: rwxr-xr-x. The u permissions are rwx, the g permissions are r-x and the o permissions are r-x. Therefore, root has the u permissions of rwx and the g permissions of rwx and o (any other user) has r-x permissions in /bin.

The permissions of r-x appear for "other" for all items below the / (root), except the lost+found and root directories. As cwest, you are in the category of "other", and have r-x to all directories except lost+found and root.

The permissions of --- appear for "other", for the lost+found and root directories. cwest does not have any permissions in /lost+found or /root (the home directory of the root user).

```
]# cd /root              # cwest cannot change into the home
                         # directory of the root user

]# cd /bin ; ls -l       # cwest can change into /bin and see the
                         # files in this directory
```

The permission settings on most files in this directory are rwxr-xr-x (755), root, root. The category of o has r-x and cwest is in the category. The x permission allows a user to execute a binary. Therefore, cwest can execute the binaries in this directory.

```
]# touch  test.txt
```

Only root can create files in this directory or any directory off of the root, except /tmp.

 Permissions on /etc/shadow and Set User Id on the /etc/passwd File

```
]# ls -l /etc/shadow     # notice the permissions on the shadow file

]# cat /etc/shadow       # cwest does not have permission to view
                         # the contents of the shadow file
```

The /etc/shadow file contains encrypted user passwords and has the permission settings of r--------, root, root. Users cannot view or modify this file *directly* (which is a good thing!). They *can* modify it by using the passwd command. Only the root user can modify this file, or a non-root user that runs a binary with the permissions of the root user. This is where **suid** (**set user id**) comes in.

```
]# whereis passwd        # the passwd binary is in /usr/bin

]# ls -l /usr/bin/passwd # notice the permissions on the passwd binary
```

The passwd binary (not the passwd text file in /etc) has the permission settings of r-**s**--x--x, root, root. The "s" in the r-**s** for the u (owner) of the file indicates that the file has **s**uid ("set" **u**ser id). In this case, set user id is set to the root user because root is the owner (**u**) of the passwd binary. Therefore, when a non-root user executes this binary to change his or her password, the binary executes with the permissions of the owner of the file, which is root.

When a non-root user runs the passwd binary, the binary needs to see the old user password in /etc/shadow, to verify that the user should be able to change the password. It then needs to write the new password into the /etc/shadow file. With suid on the binary and root as the user, the binary runs with the permissions of the root user and the binary can read from and write to /etc/shadow.

The Set Group Id on the /usr/bin/slocate File

]# whereis slocate

]# ls -l /usr/bin/slocate   # notice the permissions on the slocate binary

The slocate binary has the permission settings of rwxr-**s**r-x, root, **slocate**. The "s" in the r-**s** for the g (group) of the file indicates that the file has s**g**id ("set" group id). The g of the file is the **slocate** group. In this case, set group id is set to the slocate group which is the **g** of the slocate binary. Therefore, when a non-root user executes this binary to securely **locate** files, the binary executes with the permissions of the g of the binary, which is the slocate group.

The Sticky Bit on /tmp

]# cd / ; ls -ld tmp   # shows the permission settings for /tmp

The permissions settings are rwxrwxr**wt**, root, root. Therefore, the permissions for o are r**wt**. The cwest user, and all other non-root users, have r**wt** permissions in tmp. You can read from and write to files in /tmp. The "t" in r**wt** is for sticky and indicates that the directory has the "sticky" bit. Only the owner of a file (i.e. the user that creates a file) in this directory can delete it or rename it.

]# cd /tmp ; touch test.txt ; ls -l test.txt

The permission settings of test.txt are rw-rw-r--, cwest, cwest. Therefore, cwest is the owner (u) and g of the file. The u and g permissions are both rw- and so cwest can read the file and write to the file. The o permissions are r--. Therefore, "others" have the read permission to the file, but no other permissions.

However, with the permission settings of rwxrwxr**wt**, root, root, on the /tmp directory, then o (all users) have w to the directory. The w permission to a directory (when it does not have the sticky bit) allows a user to delete all files in a directory, regardless of the permission settings on the files. If this directory did not have the sticky bit, all users would be allowed to delete all files, regardless of the permission settings on the files.

The cwest user created test.txt and is the owner of the file. Therefore, no other non-root user can delete or rename the test.txt file in /tmp (even with the w permission on the directory) because the directory has the sticky bit. The system "knows" the name of a user that is logged in, and that the owner of the test.txt file is cwest, and that the /tmp directory has the "sticky bit". Therefore, no other non-root user can delete or rename the file.

]# rm test.txt

(5) **Viewing Permissions on Directories Below /home**

```
]# cd /home ; ls -l        # the common and cwest directories appear
```

The home directory of cwest has the permission settings of rwx------, cwest, cwest. The six - (dashes) at the right of rwx indicate that **g** (group) and **o** (other) have no rights to the cwest directory. Therefore, cwest is the only non-root user that has access to the cwest home directory. cwest is the u and g of the directory and o has no permissions to this directory.

The r and x permissions are required on a directory to read the contents of a directory and change into a directory. These permissions are required to effectively "work" in a directory. No other non-root users can change into the cwest home directory or view the contents of it.

The u and g of the cwest directory are the same name. When the cwest user was created during the installation, the Primary Group name of cwest was assigned to the cwest user. By default (when the -g option of useradd is not used), the **g**roup name is the same as the **u**ser name.

Look at the permission settings on the common directory below /home. You were logged in as root when you created the common directory in the last chapter. Therefore, the u (owner) and g of the directory are both root.

By default, the root user has a umask setting of 022. This setting causes directories to have the permissions of rwxr-xr-x (755 = 777 - 22). Therefore, the common directory has the permission settings of rwxr-xr-x, root, root. The r-x permissions to o allows all users to change into this directory and view the contents of it.

```
]# cd cwest ; ls -l        # notice the permission settings on the
                           # three ??-data directories
```

You were logged in as root when you created the **??**-data (**gr**-data, **ss**-data and **wp**-data) directories and moved files from /home/cwest into these directories. These directories have the same permissions as the common directory because the umask of the root user is 022.

Although the ??-data directories have r and x to other, these directories are below the cwest home directory, which has no permissions to other. No non-root users can access the cwest directory and therefore, no non-root users can access the ??-data directories below cwest, regardless of the permission settings on the ??-data directories.

```
]# clear ; ls -lR ??-data    # notice the permission settings on the files
```

In the last chapter, you *created* the ??-data directories and then *moved* the files into these directories.

The directories were *created* while working as root with a umask of 022. The default umask of a non-root user is 002. If the directories were created with a umask of 002 (rather than 022), then they would have permissions of 775 (rwxrwxr-x), rather than 755 (rwxr-xr-x).

By default, when files are *moved*, they have the same permission settings in the destination as they had in the source. All of the files that were moved from /home/cwest into the ??-data directories have the permission settings of rw-r--r--, root, root. These files had these settings in the source directory and were moved (rather than copied or created) and therefore have these same settings in the destination directory.

The cwest user needs to be the u and g of the ??-data directories, and the files in these directories, in order to be able to work with these items.

In the last chapter, you created the prod and sales directories below /home/common and also created several subdirectories below each of these directories. You also moved files into these subdirectories. These steps created the prod and sales directory structures below /home/common.

You will use the chmod command below to change the permissions of the ??-data directories (below /home/cwest), the prod and sales directory structures, and the files in these directories. You will also use the chown command to change the u and g of these directories and files. This will allow the appropriate users to access these directories and work with the files in them.

 Creating a Directory and File with a umask of 002

Your current directory is cwest and you are logged in as cwest.

    ]# umask

Your current umask setting (as cwest) is 0002.

    ]# mkdir testdir ; ls -ld testdir

The testdir directory has rwxrwxr-x (775) 775 = 777 (default directory permissions) - 002 (umask).

    ]# touch testfile.txt ; ls -l testfile.txt

The testfile.txt file has rw-rw-r-- (664) 664 = 666 (default directory permissions) - 002 (umask).

    ]# rmdir testdir ; rm testfile.txt

If you had run the umask command and (temporarily) changed the umask setting for the root user to 002, prior to creating the directories in the last chapter, then the directories that you created would have the permissions of 775. You were logged on as root when you created the directories and therefore, the u and g of the directories is root, root.

The files that you moved into directories in the last chapter have the same permissions (644) in the destination directory as the source directory and the same u (root) and g (root) as in the source directory.

 Viewing Permissions of /etc and Some Files in It

]# ls -ld /etc

As cwest (o, other), you have r-x to the /etc directory and can change into it. However, you do not have the w permission in this directory, so you cannot remove files, create files, or modify the contents of files.

]# cd /etc ; clear

]# ls -l shadow

As described above, cwest cannot read this file. Non-root users cannot see the encrypted passwords in this file.

]# ls -l passwd   # cwest can read the contents of this file

]# cat passwd

The settings in /etc/passwd for cwest appear at the end. The UID of cwest (in the third field) is 500 - remember this.

]# grep cwest passwd   # same as running: cat passwd | grep cwest

]# grep root passwd

The settings for the root user appear. The UID of root is 0 - remember this.

The grep command is commonly used to see the settings of an individual user in /etc/passwd, particularly if you have many users (many statements in /etc/passwd).

]# ls -l group   # cwest can read the contents of this file

]# cat group

Many "system" groups exist and the Primary Group of cwest appears at the end. The root group has scrolled by.

]# grep cwest group   # the group name and GID number appear

The cwest group in /etc/group is the Primary Group of the cwest user. By default, this group was created when the cwest user was created. Therefore, the user name of cwest and the Primary Group name of cwest are the same. Remember this.

```
]# grep root group
```

The Primary Group of the root user appears and the supplementary "system" groups (at the left) to which the root user is a member appear. The root user name and the Primary Group name of this user are the same. Remember this.

```
]# ls -l bashrc          # cwest can read the contents of this file
```

 ## 8 Viewing the Statements in bashrc that "Set" the umask

```
]# clear ; head -12 bashrc | nl      # lines 6 through 10 set the
                                     # default umask for a user
```

If the (primary) **group name** and **user name** are the same **and** the **user id** (UID) is greater than 99, then the umask is set to 002 (which appears as 0002 when the umask command is run without any options).

You will now get the settings that are checked in the if statement in line 6.

```
]# id -gn ; id -un ; id -u       # shows primary group name, user
                                 # name and user id
```

The primary group name (cwest) and user name (cwest) are the same and the user id (500) is greater than 99. Therefore, according to the scripting logic in line 6, the umask will be 0002.

```
]# umask                 # the umask of 0002 should appear
```

The directory permissions of 777, less the umask of 002 result in the mode of 775 (rwxrwxr-x) for directories that are created when umask is 002.

```
]# umask -S              # uses the symbolic option of umask

u=rwx,g=rwx,o=rx         # this is the output when the -S option
                         # is used
```

The above output shows the default permissions that will be assigned to directories, but does not show the permissions that will be assigned to files.

When you created a directory and file earlier in these exercises, with the umask of 002, the directory permissions were 775 (rwxrwxr-x) and the file permissions were 664 (rw-rw-r--).

⑨ Changing to root and Viewing Statements in bashrc Again

```
]# su -                  # su to root and log in with the password of root
```

```
]# clear ; head -12 /etc/bashrc | nl
```

Have a look at line 6 again. If group name = user name -a (and) user id number -gt (greater than) 99, then the umask is set to 002. If not, a user will get the umask setting of 022 (line 9).

While working as the root user, get the settings that are checked by the if statement on line 6.

```
]# id -gn ; id -un ; id -u       # shows primary group name, user
                                 # name and user id
```

The group name (root) and user name (root) are the same, but the user id (0) is not greater than 99. Therefore, the umask for root is 022 (same as 0022).

```
]# umask                 # the umask of 0022 should appear
```

The directory permissions of 777, less the umask of 022 results in the mode of 755 (rwxr-xr-x) for directories that are created when umask is 022.

```
]# umask -S              # uses the symbolic option of umask
```

```
u=rwx,g=rx,o=rx          # this is the output when the -S option is used
```

⑩ Creating a Directory and File When umask is 022

You are working as root and your current directory is /root.

```
]# mkdir testdir ; ls -ld testdir
```

The testdir directory should have the permissions of rwxr-xr-x (755 = 777 - 22) due to the umask of 022.

```
]# touch testfile.txt ; ls -l testfile.txt
```

The testfile.txt file should have the permissions of rw-r--r-- (644 = 666 - 22) due to the umask of 022.

```
]# rmdir testdir ; rm -f testfile.txt       # the -f option of rm used - you
                                            # will not be prompted
```

(11) **Changing Back to cwest and Viewing Some Permissions Again**

```
]#  exit              #  exit out of the root user subshell
```

You are currently logged in as cwest.

```
]#  cd ~ ; ls -l      #  the ??-data directories have rwxr-xr-x, root, root

]#  ls -lR ??-data    #  the files in the ??-data directories have
                      #  rw-r--r--, root, root
```

When you are logged in as root, you can create directory structures and create files, but if other users need access to the directories and files that you have created, then you must do the steps to provide users with the permission settings to use them.

If you change the umask setting to the appropriate setting for users (such as 002) while working as root and creating directories and files, then you do not need to change the permissions for directories and files later, but you will need to change the u and g of the directories and files.

Now you will do the steps to provide users with access to the directories and files that you created in the last chapter.

You will start by modifying the settings of the ??-data directories and the files in them.

The cwest user was created during the installation and no ??-data (template data) directories existed below /etc/skel. If these three directories existed in /etc/skel prior to the creation of the cwest user, then you would not need to do the steps to change the permissions, u and g of these directories and the files in them.

You will modify the permission settings of the directories and files in the prod and sales directory structures (below /home/common) so that users in the prod and sales group will be able to access these directory structures.

You will put an alias in a bash configuration file in /etc/skel, create the ??-data template directories in /etc/skel, modify settings in /etc/login.defs, create groups, create users and then test the setup.

(12) **Testing the Permissions of cwest to the ??-data Directories and the Files in Them**

>]# ls -ld ??-data   # notice the permission settings on these directories

You were logged in as the root user when you created the gr-data, ss-data and wp-data directories below cwest. Therefore, the u and g for these directories is root.

>]# ls -lR ??-data   # gr-data contains a file named calendar.sxi

The root user is also the u and g for the files in the gr-data, ss-data and wp-data directories.

>]# cd gr-data ; touch testfile.txt

The cwest user does not have w (write) to gr-data.

>]# rm -f calendar.sxi

The cwest user is o and o does not have w to the directory w is required to remove files from a directory.

>]# cd ..   # your current directory should be /home/cwest

minimize the terminal emulation window.

(13) **Running the Writer, Impress and Calc Programs for the First Time**

You will test the permissions of users and groups by double-clicking on .sxw, .sxi or .sxc files in the steps below.

However, the Writer, Impress and Calc programs need to be run from the desktop the first time any user runs one of these programs. When this is done, the programs request some setup information that is written to hidden files in the home directory of the user.

If you try to run these programs for the first time by double-clicking on a .sxw, .sxi or .sxc file (without providing the setup information), the program will likely either: not load the file, or will load the file and hang.

After logging in as any user, remember to run these programs for the first time by using the icon for the program in the panel at the bottom of the desktop, and then respond to the prompts. After running each program, close it without saving the current file. After doing this, you should be able to run these programs without a problem by double-clicking on a .sxw, .sxi or .sxc file.

By moving your mouse cursor over the icons in the panel, you can see the names of the Writer, Impress and Calc programs. Clicking once on one of these icons launches the application. The application will not launch instantly. It will take a short time before loading and requesting the setup information. Wait for the application to load without double-clicking.

After launching the Writer program from the desktop for any user for the first time, click on Cancel. The next time you launch the program, select "Remind me to register later" and then click OK. Close the program without saving the file.

After launching the Impress program from the desktop for any user for the first time, click on: Do not show me this again ; Next ; Next ; Create ; OK. Close the program without saving the file.

After launching the Calc program from the desktop for any user for the first time, select "Remind me to register later" and then click OK. Close the program without saving the file.

In the steps below, you will log in as each of the users that you create to test the users. Once the above steps have been done for the first time for every user, you should be able to test the permissions of users and groups by double-clicking on .sxw, .sxi or .sxc files.

Remember to do these steps for each user that you test.

Do the above steps for all three programs for the cwest user now.

 ### Testing the User and Group Permissions of the cwest User

cwest's Home (icon on the desktop) x 2 (double-click on the icon) ;

gr-data folder x 2 (double-click on the gr-data folder) ;

gr-data appears in the top border of the window ; calendar.sxi x 2 ;

the Impress program should run ; notice that (read-only) appears at the right of the filename in the top border of the window ;

File ; Save As ... ; do not change the filename ; Save ; Yes ;

an error message appears because you cannot write to the file (you do not have w to the file) ;

if you had w to the directory, you would still not be able to save the file (with the same name) ; OK ;

File ; Save As ... ; remove the existing filename ; File name: *test.sxi* ; Save ;

an error message appears because you cannot create a file in gr-data (you do not have w to the directory) ; if you had w to the directory, you would be able to create the file (save it with a new name) ;

OK ; close the Impress application window and the gr-data window (showing the files in gr-data) ; if necessary, Alt+Tab to the terminal emulation window ;

cwest needs to be made u and g of the ??-data directories and files and the permissions of these items needs to be modified.

15 Changing the User and Group for the ??-data Directories

su to root ; change into /home/cwest ; ls -ld ??-data.

The **change own**er command is used below to change the u and g of the ??-data directories. The first cwest in the command below is for u and the second is for g. A . (dot) is used between the user name and group name. The ?? (question marks) are is used to represent the gr, ss and wp in each of the three user template data directories. This allows you to change the user and group of all three directories at once.

]# chown cwest.cwest ??-data

The chgrp command can also be used to change the g of a directory or file. However, the chown command allows you to change both the u and the g.

]# ls -ld ??-data   # now cwest is the u and g for these directories

]# ls -l ??-data   # cwest also needs to be the u and g of the files
                          # below each of these three directories

change into the gr-data directory ;

]# chown cwest.cwest * ; ls -l

change up one directory level to the path of /home/cwest.

Rather than changing into the other two directories and running the chown command above, you can use the -R option in the command below to change the u and g for the ??-data directories and all of the files in them. If there were subdirectories in the ??-data directories, then these subdirectories and the files in them (and subdirectories in them, and files in them, and so on) would also be changed to cwest.cwest.

```
]# chown -R cwest.cwest ??-data

]# ls -ld ??-data
```

Notice that the permissions for the ??-data directories are: rwxr-xr-x (755). This is because these directories were created when you were logged in as root with a umask of 022.

```
]# ls -l ??-data          # cwest is now the u and g for the files
```

Notice that the permissions for the files in the ??-data directories are: rw-r--r-- (644). These are the permissions that the files had in /home/cwest prior to being moved into the ??-data directories.

⑯ Changing the Permissions on the ??-data Directories

The command below changes the **mod**e (permissions) for the three ??-data directories to the same permissions that occur when a user creates a directory (with a umask of 002), which are: rwxrwxr-x (775).

```
]# chmod 775 ??-data      # changes the ??-data directories only

]# ls -ld ??-data         # now the permissions should be: rwxrwxr-x
```

⑰ Changing the Permissions of Files in the ??-data Directories

```
]# ls -l ??-data
```

The current permissions on the files in the ??-data directories are: rw-r--r-- (**644**).

The command below changes the **mod**e (permissions) for the files in the three ??-data directories to the same permissions that occur when a user creates a file (with a umask of 002), which are : rw-rw-r-- (**664**).

The command below does not change the permissions on the ??-data directories, just the files in the directories. You want the directories to have the permissions of 775, not 664.

The * at the end of the command specifies that all files in the ??-data directories be changed. If the "/*" at the end of the command was not used, then the ??-data directories would be changed (rather than the contents of the directories).

```
]# chmod 664 ??-data/* ; ls -l ??-data
```

Adding the lsl Alias to the cwest User

```
]# cd /etc/skel ; ls -la
```

The .bash_logout, .bash_profile and .bashrc user shell configuration files are in this directory. There are likely other hidden directories and files in this directory that provide configuration information for other software components.

When a user is created, the contents of /etc/skel are copied to the user's home directory. If directories and files exist below /etc/skel, they are also copied to the user's home directory.

In an earlier chapter, you created an alias named lsl in the .bashrc file in the home directory of the cwest user. Now you will add this alias to the .bashrc file in /etc/skel so that when a user is created, the user will automatically have the alias.

```
]# clear ; cat ~cwest/.bashrc     # now you can see the lsl alias that
                                  # you created earlier
```

You could put this alias in a .sh file in /etc/profile.d. However, you will put it in .bashrc to demonstrate that new users can be given an alias using this method.

The items in /etc/skel are copied the home directories of users. Therefore, all users that you create will have this alias until you remove it from /etc/skel/.bashrc. If you did not want some new users to have this alias, you could remove it prior to creating them.

Your current directory is /etc/skel. Run the vi editor and specify the filename of .bashrc to load the file and edit it.

Remember to press i to go into Insert mode when you need to add text, Esc to go into Normal mode (after editing the file), and use ZZ to save the file and exit. Keep these keys in mind while you are doing editing further below.

Add the following alias below the "# User specific aliases and functions" comment (after putting a blank line below the comment):

```
alias lsl='ls -lhSr'
```

save the file and exit out of vi ;

"cat out" the .bashrc file that you just edited to see if you made the edit correctly.

Viewing and Setting the umask

A few steps from now, you will create the user template data directories below /etc/skel and put the template data files in them. But first, you will view the current umask settings then change the umask.

You are currently logged in as the root user and are in /etc/skel.

    ]# umask   # the umask should be 0022 (same as 022)

    change to the home directory of the root user ;

    ]# mkdir testdir ; touch testfile.txt ; ls -l

With a umask of 022, testdir is rwxr-xr-x (755) and testfile.txt is rw-r--r-- (644).

    ]# umask 002   # change umask from 022 to 002 for the directories
                       # to be created below

    ]# umask   # check the current umask setting - for the root user,
                       # this setting will be in effect for the current shell
                       # session only

    ]# mkdir testdir1 ; touch testfile1.txt ; ls -l

When a group is created with the same name as the user and the UID is greater than 99, umask is set to 002. With a umask of 002, testdir1 is rwxrwxr-x (775) and testfile1.txt is rw-rw-r-- (664). These are the default permissions of a user.

Compare the permissions of the testdir and testdir1 directories.

Compare the permissions of the testfile.txt and testfile1.txt files.

You can remove multiple directories with one rmdir command by putting a space between each directory name. This method of specifying multiple items can also be used for other commands, such as rm and mkdir.

    ]# rmdir testdir testdir1 ; rm -f testfile.txt testfile1.txt ; ls -l

 Creating the User Template Data Directories in /etc/skel

The directories and files that exist in /etc/skel are copied to the home directory of a user when the user is created. You want each user to get the three ??-data (user template data) directories and the files in them. Now you will create these directories in /etc/skel and put the appropriate files in them.

You are logged in as root and have changed the default umask from 022 to 002 (the default umask of users). You will create the directories below /etc/skel with the umask of 002 so that they will have the same permissions as the default permissions of users.

You should be in the skel directory below /etc.

```
]# mkdir gr-data ss-data wp-data ; ls -l
```

The permissions of the above directories are rwxrwxr-x (775) due to the umask setting of 002.

The data files in the ??-data directories below /home/cwest have not been modified since they were put in these directories. Therefore, these files can be put in the ??-data directories below /etc/skel to provide template data files for users.

```
]# ls -l ~cwest/??-data
```

The permission settings on the files are rw-rw-r–, cwest, cwest.

```
]# cp ~cwest/gr-data/* gr-data
```

Copy using a relative path for the source and destination. You are copying existing files rather than creating new files.

```
]# ls -l gr-data
```

The permission settings on the files in /etc/skel/gr-data are rw-rw-r--, root, root. You are logged in as root and you copied the files. Therefore, the u and g of the files is root. If you moved the files, then they would have the same permission settings in the destination as in the source. If umask was set to 022 (the default for root), then the files would have rw-r--r-- (644 = 666 - **22**) rather than rw-rw-r-- (664 = 666 - 2).

```
repeat the above two steps to copy the appropriate files into the ss-data
and wp-data directories and see that they were copied properly ; make
sure you copy the correct files to the correct directories.

]# clear ; ls -lR
```

All ??-data directories are rwxrwxr-x, root, root and all files in them are rw-rw-r--, root, root.

The gr-data directory should contain: calendar.sxi, clock.sxi and reminder.sxi

The ss-data directory should contain: daily-report.sxc, monthly-report.sxc and weekly-report.sxc

The wp-data directory should contain: invoice.sxw, letter.sxw and memo.sxw

---

When root has a umask of 002 and a user is created, the ??-data directories that are created below the home directory of the user will have rwxrwxr-x (775). Although o has r-x to the ??-data directories, o has --- (no permissions) to the home directory of the user. The home directory is the parent directory for the ??-data directories. Therefore, o cannot access the ??-data directories.

When you create a user with the useradd command, the current umask is applied to the directories below /etc/skel that are put below the home directory of the user. However, the umask is not applied to the files in /etc/skel and the files in the subs that are put below the home directory of the user. The permissions on the files in /etc/skel and the files in the subs will be the same at the destination as at the source.

When a user has a primary group name the same as the user's name and the UID of the user is greater than 500, then the default permissions for a directory created by a user are 775 and files are 664.

If you set the permissions on the directories that you create below /skel to 775, and the permissions of the files to 664, and set the umask to 002 prior to creating a user, then the directories and files will have the default user permissions below the user's home directory.

If you do not set the umask to 002 and use the umask of 022, then the directories will have rwxr-xr-x, but the files will still have the same permissions at the destination. Permissions on the directory of rwxr-xr-x are fine because the user is the u and g of the directory and therefore, as the u of the directory, the user has rwx to the directory, regardless of the setting for g.

After running the command above, you can see that the u and g the /etc/skel/??-data directories and their files is root. When you create a user, the items below /etc/skel that are put below /home/*username* will automatically have the u and g of *username* (the name of the user that you create). This allows the user to access the items without you having to modify the u and g with the chown command (as you had to do for the cwest user above).

When you create users below, you will allow the system to create a Primary Group for the user that has the same name as the user. When the bford user is created, the permission settings for the home directory of this user will be rwx------, bford, bford.

The u of bford has the permissions of rwx, The g of bford has --- and o has ---. Therefore, the user has all permissions and the g and o have no permissions.

Viewing the Password Settings of the cwest User

]# chage -l cwest

The password settings of cwest appear. These are the default settings in /etc/login.defs.

The cwest user was created during the Linux installation, using the default password settings in /etc/login.defs.

21 Backing Up the login.defs File and Modifying the Default Settings in login.defs

Do the steps below to create a back up copy of the login.defs file in the /etc directory prior to modifying it.

You are currently working as root and are in the /etc/skel directory.

]# cd ..   # change up one directory level into /etc

]# cp login.defs login.defs.bak

Make a backup of login.defs named login.defs.bak.

Now you will look at and modify some settings in the login.defs file prior to creating users.

Run the vi editor and load the login.defs file ; move your cursor down to the following statement, which sets the maximum number of days that a user can use a password.

PASS_MAX_DAYS   99999

Change the 99999 to 20 ; this will force users to change their passwords at least every twenty days.

The following statement is used to stop passwords from being changed prior to a specified number of days. The default value of 0 allows users to change their passwords at any time. This statement is used to stop a user from changing his or her password back to a previous password and continuing to use an old password.

For the next setting, change the 0 to 10 ; this will stop users from changing their passwords back to a previous password for 10 days.

> PASS_MIN_DAYS   0

Notice the following statement. This sets the minimum length of a password to 5 characters. Change the value of 5 to 6.

> PASS_MIN_LEN   5

The next statement specifies that a user will be warned that his or her password will expire in 7 days. Change the value for this statement to 5.

> PASS_WARN_AGE 7

Scroll down and read the comment above the UID_MIN and UID_MAX statements ;

scroll down and read the comment above the GID_MIN and GID_MAX statements ;

scroll down until you see the following statement.

The next statement causes a home directory to be created for a user by default. Leave this statement as is.

> CREATE_HOME   yes

Save the login.defs file and exit out of vi.

 ## Viewing and Modifying the Password Settings for cwest

>]# chage -l cwest

Modifying login.defs did not modify the settings of cwest. The settings in login.defs are only used when new users are created.

The command below sets the **maximum days** between password changes to 20, the **minimum days** between password changes to 10, and causes the user to be **warned** 5 days before the password must be changed.

>]# chage -M 20 -m 10 -W 5 cwest

>]# chage -l cwest

Now cwest has the same settings as the current defaults in login.defs.

Viewing Ownership and Permissions for the prod and sales Directory Structures

Change into /home ; get a long listing ;

change into the subdirectory named common ; get a long listing ; the prod and sales directories appear ; these are the parent directories of the prod and sales directory structures that you created in the last chapter.

You were logged in as root when you created the prod and sales directory structures and put files in subdirectories of prod and sales.

]# ls -lR | less

Scroll through the listing. All items have the u and g of root. All directories have permissions of: rwxr-xr-x and all files have permissions of: rw-r--r--. The permission settings of these items needs to be changed to suit the needs of the users in the Production and Sales Departments.

You need to create users for the people in the Production and Sales Departments. You also need to create a prod group for the Production Department users and a sales group for the Sales Department users.

Once this has been done, you can change the u, g and permission settings for the items in the prod and sales directory structures. You cannot assign a user or group name to a u or g setting for an item until the user or group exists.

 Creating the prod Group for the Production Department

Now you will create a group named prod for the Production Department, prior to creating the users for the department. This will allow you to use the -G option of the useradd command to add users to the group (as a supplementary group, rather than the Primary Group) when the users for this department are created.

```
]# grep prod /etc/group          # the prod group does not exist

]# groupadd -g 10000 prod        # create the group named prod with
                                 # the GID number of 10000

]# grep prod /etc/group          # the settings of the prod group appear
```

Adding cwest to the prod Group

The cwest user is in the Production Department and does not need to be created, but this user needs to be a member of the prod group. The usermod command is used to modify user settings.

]# usermod -G prod cwest

The prod group is now a supplementary group for cwest.

]# grep cwest /etc/group

The Primary Group of cwest appears and the prod group appears with cwest as a member.

 Creating the Production Department Users

You have decided to create user names using the first letter of the first name and all of the last name.

Steve Howe, Becky Ford and Mary Wong are in the Production Department and will be assigned the user names of showe, bford and mwong.

]# useradd -c "Steve Howe" -G prod showe

]# grep showe /etc/passwd

The settings of the showe user appear. The x in the second field indicates that shadow passwords are being used. The UID and GID numbers in the third and fourth fields are the same. Therefore, the user name and Primary Group name are the same. The path to the home directory is in the sixth field and the default shell is in the seventh field.

]# grep showe /etc/shadow

The !! in the second field indicates that the user has not been assigned a password. The 10, 20 and 5 are from the PASS_MIN_DAYS, PASS_MAX_DAYS and PASS_WARN_AGE settings that you made in login.defs.

]# grep showe /etc/group

The prod and showe groups appear.

The prod group has showe as a member. This group is a supplementary group for showe.

The showe group in /etc/group is the Primary Group of the showe user. The GID number of the showe group in /etc/group is the same as the number in the third field in /etc/passwd (for the showe user).

Repeat the above useradd command to create the bford (Becky Ford) and mwong (Mary Wong) users. Use the -c option to specify the user's full name and the -G option to specify the prod group as a supplementary group.

    ]# tail /etc/passwd   # the new users appear at the end

    ]# tail /etc/shadow

The new users have not been assigned passwords. The !! in the second field for the new users indicates that the users have not been assigned a password. The second field of cwest shows the encrypted version of the cwest password.

The 10, 20 and 5 for the new users are from the PASS_MIN_DAYS, PASS_MAX_DAYS and PASS_WARN_AGE settings that you made when you edited /etc/login.defs.

    ]# tail /etc/group

The members of the prod group appear at the right of prod. Remember that this is a method of seeing the members of a group. The Primary Groups for the cwest, showe, bford and mwong users also appear.

 ## Creating Passwords for the Production Department Users

    ]# passwd showe

    repeat the above command for bford and mwong.

    ]# cat /etc/shadow

The !! that was in the second field has been replaced with the encrypted version of the passwords that you just assigned to the users.

    ]# chage -l showe

The default password settings from login.defs appear.

    Repeat the above command for bford and mwong.

28 **Setting Up the Permission Settings for the prod Directory Structure**

You will be guided through the process of setting up the permission settings for the prod directory structure below. After doing this, you will set up the permission settings for the sales directory structure, with just a brief description of each of the tasks that need to be performed.

The cwest user will be working as the system administrator for the prod and sales groups. Therefore, cwest will be the u (owner) and the prod and sales directories below common.

> You should be in the common directory below /home ;
>
> get a long listing of the common directory ;
>
>]# ls -lR prod | less   # root is the u and g of all items below prod
>
> get a long listing of the common directory after running each of the next two commands ;
>
>]# chmod 750 prod   # change the permissions on prod to rwxr-x---

Now o will not have any permissions to prod. Numeric mode (750) was used with chmod command above.

>]# chown cwest.prod prod
>
> Change the u of prod to cwest and the g of prod to prod.

The cwest user now has rwx to prod.

The prod group now has r-x to the prod directory. The prod group does not have w to the directory and therefore, users (members) in the group cannot create directories or files in prod. Users in prod should only be able to create directories and files in the subs of prod, not in prod.

>]# ls -lR prod | less   # root is still the u and g of all items below prod
>
>]# chown -R cwest.prod prod/*
>
> For the five subs of prod and the files in these subs, change the u to cwest and the g to prod.
>
>]# ls -lR prod | less

Now cwest is the u and prod is the g of all items below prod.

```
]# cd prod

]# ls -lR | less
```

There are five subs of prod and no files in prod. There are only files in the subs of prod. Notice the permissions of o for directories and files.

The five subs of prod have r and x for o and the files in the directories have r for o. You will be assigning the t (sticky bit) to o for the subs of prod further below. This will cause the x on the subs to change to t. Therefore, you do not need to remove the x from o in this case.

If you removed the x from o and then assigned the sticky bit, then an upper case "T" would appear rather than a lower case "t". The "case" (upper or lower) of the "t" does not matter. Both indicate that the sticky bit is on the directory.

The permissions of the files in the five subs are currently rw-r--r--. When you remove the r from the o of the files with the command below, o will have no permissions to the files in the subs.

```
]# chmod -R o-r *
```

Remove the r permission from the o of the subs of prod and remove r from the files in the subs.

```
]# ls -lR | less      # now o has no permissions to the subs and files
```

Now o only has x to the subs of prod and no permissions to the files in the subs of prod. The symbolic mode of o-r was specified above.

The users in the Production Department need w to four of the five subs of prod. Therefore, the prod group needs w to these subs. You will assign w to all subs and then remove w from one. This is easier than assigning w to each of the four individually.

The users in prod also need w to all files in the subs of prod, except in masters. You will assign the w to the g of all files and then remove the w from the files in masters.

```
]# chmod -R g+w *
```

Add the w permissions to the g (prod) of the subs and to the g (prod) of the files in the subs.

```
]# ls -lR | less
```

Now g (the prod group) has w to the five subs and all of the files in the five subs.

The masters directory contains "master" template files that will be maintained by the cwest user, which has rwx to the subs of prod, as the u (owner) of the subs.

The members of prod do not require the w permission to the masters directory. They should not be able to modify the master template files. They only need to be able to read (run a program and open) the files in masters and then save these files into other directories.

```
]# chmod -R g-w masters
```

Remove the w permission from the g of masters and the g of the files in masters.

```
]# ls -lR | less
```

The g (prod) of the masters directory does not have w and the g (prod) of the files in masters does not have w.

In the masters directory, the users in prod (other than cwest) will only be able to read the files and save them into other directories. They will not be able to modify the files and save them back into masters (with the same name or with a different name). They will also not be able to create directories and files in masters or delete directories and files in masters.

 ## Assigning the i Attribute to Files in masters

Change into the masters subdirectory and get a long listing.

The g of the files (prod) only has r and therefore users will be able to read these files, but not write to them. However, as an additional precaution, you will assign the i (immutable) attribute to the files in masters.

```
]# lsattr              # the files have no attributes

]# chattr +i *         # assign the i attribute to all files in masters
```

get a long listing of the current directory ; the ls command does not display attributes ;

```
]# lsattr              # all files have the i attribute
```

change up one directory level ; get a long listing ; the g of each directory is prod and o has x (only) for each directory.

Assigning SGID and the Sticky Bit to Directories

Files that are created in the subs of prod need to accessible to the prod group. By assigning sgid to the subs of prod, files that are created in the subs will automatically have the g of the directory (prod) assigned to them. This will allow users in the prod group to access the files, based on the permissions of the g of the parent directory and the g of the files. Directories that are created in subs of prod will also have the g of prod.

```
]# chmod g+s *          # assign sgid to all subs of prod

]# ls -l                # g now has s (sgid) for all subs of prod
                        # o has x to the subs of prod

]# chmod o+t *          # assign the sticky bit to all subs

]# ls -l          # o now has t (the sticky bit) for all subs of prod
```

Users will not be creating files in masters, therefore this directory does not need the sticky bit.

```
]# chmod o-t masters ; ls -l    # remove the sticky bit from masters

]# chmod o-x masters ; ls -l    # remove the x from o for masters

exit ; you are now working as cwest and are in the home directory of cwest ;

change into the current-orders directory below /home/common/prod  ;

]# touch test.txt ; ls -l
```

The test.txt file has the u of cwest and the g of prod, rather than the g of cwest. The sgid on the directory causes the g of the file to be prod rather than cwest.

```
]# mkdir -p a/b/c ; ls -lR
```

The g is prod for the a, b and c directories due to the sgid on the parent directory. These three directories also have sgid. Therefore, any files created in these directories will have the g of prod. The u will still be the name of the user that creates the file.

The o of prod (below /home/common) has no permissions. Therefore, o does not have any permissions for any subs of prod or files in subs of prod.

```
]# rm -f test.txt ; rm -rf a
```

(31) Viewing Users and Groups in the Red Hat User Manager

Menu ; System Settings ; Users and Groups ; *password* ; OK.

The Users tab is selected and the users that you have created appear . The Primary Group for each user is the same as the user name and other user settings that are in /etc/passwd appear.

bford (select this user) ; Properties button ; select each of the tabs in the User Properties dialog box ; user settings can be modified here ;

the Groups tab (in the User Properties dialog box) shows that the user is a member of the prod group ; Cancel ;

Groups tab (from the opening screen) ; this is basically the same as /etc/group ; the Primary Group names for a users appears ; the GID number of the prod group and the members in this group also appear ;

prod (select this group) ; Properties button ; Group Users tab ; users in the group appear and users can be added to the group here ; cancel ;

Preferences (menu) ; deselect "Filter system users and groups" ; now all groups appear.

The Add User button can be used to create users and the Add Group button can be used to create groups.

Close the Red Hat User Manager ; close all windows (terminal emulation and programs).

(32) Testing the Permissions of the Users that You Created

Menu ; Log Out ; Log Out ; OK ; Username: *bford* ; Password: *password* ;

run the Writer, Impress and Calc programs for the first time from the icons in the panel and respond to the prompts as described earlier ; remember to do this step for all of the users that you test ;

bford's Home (icon) x 2 ; when the user was created, the three ??-data subs were created for the user ;

ss-data folder x 2 ; the window now shows ss-data in the top border ; when the user was created, the files in the ??-data directory were also created for the user ;

monthly-report.sxc x 2 ; the Calc (spreadsheet) program runs ; close the program ;

at the ss-data window, below the Bookmarks menu heading select "Up" ; select "Up" again ;

an icon appears on all folders except bford and common ; this indicates that bford does not have permissions in these folders ;

mwong folder x r ; Properties ; Permissions tab ; mwong is the u (owner) the folder (her home directory) and only the owner has permissions (rwx) to the folder ;

notice the text view and number view settings ; Close ;

common folder x 2 ; prod x 2 ; shared-prod-wp-data x 2 ; blanket-order.sxw x 2 ;

the Writer (word processor) program runs ; "(read-only)" does not appear in the top border ;

File ; Save As ... ; trillium-order.sxw ; Save ; close the Writer program ;

at the shared-prod-wp-data window, select Up ; masters folder x 2 ;

Edit ; Select All Files ; press the Delete key ; Delete button ; you do not have permission to delete the files in masters ; click on Stop several times ;

click on a blank area of the window to deselect the files ; new-plate.sxi x 2 ;

the Impress (graphics presentation) program runs ; (read-only) appears in the top border ;

File ; Save As ... ; do not change the filename ; Save ; Yes ;

you do not have permission (in masters) to save the file with the same name ; OK ;

File ; Save As ... ; *trillium-plate.sxi* ; Save ; OK ;

you do not have permission to save the file in masters with a different name ; OK ;

File ; Save As ... ; *trillium-plate.sxi* ; at the top right of the dialog box, click on the folder with the up arrow on it ;

current-orders folder x 2 ; Save ; (read-only) no longer appears in the top border ;

close the Impress program ;

at the masters window, new-plate.sxi x r (right-click on the file) ; Properties ; Permissions tab ;

File owner shows cwest and file group shows prod ; Owner has Read and Write (rw) and Group has Read (r) ; notice the settings at the right of text view and number view: ; Close ;

select Up ; current-orders x 2 ; trillium-plate.sxi x r ; Properties ; Permissions ;

you are logged in as bford, so this user appears as the owner ; the prod group appears beside file group ; notice the permission settings ; other members of prod have rw to this file ; Close ;

close all windows ;

Menu ; Log Out ; Log Out ; OK ; log in as the showe user ;

run the three programs from the icons in the panel and respond to the prompts as described earlier ;

showe's Home x 2 ; Up ; Common x 2 ; prod x 2 ; current-orders x r ; Properties ; Permissions tab ;

the group of the folder is prod and this group has rwx to current-orders ;

notice the text view and number view settings ; the folder has sgid and the sticky bit ; Close ;

current-orders x 2 ; trillium-plate.sxi x r ; Properties ; Permissions tab ;

the owner of the file is bford ; the group is prod ; the group has rw ; Close ;

with the trillium-plate.sxi file selected, press the Delete key ; Delete button ;

bford is the owner and the current-orders folder has the sticky bit ; only the bford user can delete the file ; Stop ;

trillium-plate.sxi x 2 ; File ; Save As ... ; do not change the name ; Save ; Yes ;

showe can modify and save the file, but cannot delete the file ; close all windows ;

do the steps to log in to the desktop as mwong ;

run the three programs from the icons in the panel and respond to the prompts as described earlier ;

mwong's Home x 2 ; gr-data x 2 ; this user also got the ??-data directories and files ; close the window ;

desktop x r (right-click on an empty area of the desktop) ; New Terminal ;

```
]# cat  .bashrc        # the text of the lsl alias that you put in
                       # /etc/skel/.bashrc appears

]# alias  lsl          # the settings for the lsl alias appear

]# lsl                 # the alias works and mwong is the u and g
                       # of the ??-data directories

]# lsl  gr-data        # mwong is the u and g of the files in
                       # the ??-data directories

]# users               # mwong is the only user currently logged
                       # in to the system

]# groups
```

The groups to which the current user is a member appear - the mwong Primary Group and prod supplementary group.

```
]# groups  showe
```

The groups to which the showe user is a member appear.

 ## Commenting Out the cwest User and prod Group

```
su to root  ;

]# cd  /home/common/prod/current-orders

]# ls -l              # cwest appears as the u of several files

]# vi  /etc/passwd
```

put a # and a space at the left of the entry for cwest ; this "comments out" the user ; save the file ;

```
]# ls -l
```

Now the UID number appears in the listing rather than the cwest user name. If a user is deleted, then the UID number will appear rather than the user name.

Without changing directory, edit /etc/passwd again and remove the # and the space at the left of cwest ;

edit /etc/group and "comment out" the prod group ; save the file ;

```
]# ls -l              # the GID of prod appears
```

If a group is deleted, then the GID number of the group will appear rather than the user name.

Edit /etc/group again and remove the # and the space at the left of prod ; get a long listing again.

When a long listing is done, the system "sees" the UID and GID numbers for items in the directory, it then "looks" in the passwd and group files for the names that match the numbers, and then displays the names. If the names do not exist, then the UID and GID numbers are displayed rather than the names.

 Shutting Down

If you are not doing the optional exercises below, close all programs and windows ; Menu ; Log Out ; Shut Down ; OK.

 Optional Exercises

Now that you have set up the prod group, you can set up the sales group.

 Logging In to Do the Optional Exercises

Login in as cwest ; su to root.

Create the group named sales with the GID number of 11000.

"grep" the group file in /etc to see that the new group exists.

 The cwest user is currently a member of the prod group and also needs to be a member of the sales group. If you use usermod to add cwest to the sales group and only specify the sales group, then the user will be removed from the prod group!

Add the cwest user to the both the sales group and the prod group with a single command.

Create the Sales Department users named chynde (Chrissie Hynde), psimon (Paul Simon) and jbeck (Jeff Beck). Use the -c option to specify the user's full name and the -G option to specify the sales group as a supplementary group.

"cat out" the passwd and shadow files in /etc to see the settings of the new users.

"grep" the group file in /etc for psimon to see the groups for this user and the members of sales.

Run the command required to see the password settings of a user in the sales group.

Assign passwords to the members of the sales group.

Change the permissions on the sales directory (only) below /home/common to rwxr-x---.

Change the owner and group of the sales directory (only) to cwest and sales, respectively.

For the five subs of sales and the files in these subs, change the u to cwest and the g to sales.

Assign sgid to all subs of sales.

Assign the sticky bit to all subs of sales, except the templates directory.

Remove all permissions from o for the templates directory.

Remove the r permission from o for the other four directories.

Assign the w permission to g for all subs of sales and all files in subs of sales, except the templates directory and the files in this directory.

Assign the i attribute to the files in templates.

Log in as each of the new users to see that the user names work.

Run the three programs for each user by using the icons in the panel and responding to the prompts as described earlier.

Test that the permissions that you set up worked by double-clicking on files and saving files (as you did earlier).

As a user in sales other than cwest, try accessing files below the prod directory structure.

As the cwest user, try accessing files in the prod and sales directory structures.

As a user in the sales group, other than cwest, try accessing files in the prod and sales directory structures. The user should be able to access files in the sales directory structure, but not in the prod directory structure.

Add rx to the o of sales (below /home/common/) and add r to the o of the current-quotes subdirectory of sales (this directory has t for o, which includes x).

The files in current-quotes have r for o. Files that are created with the default user umask of 002 have 664, which provides rw-rw-r--. Therefore, o has r by default for any files that are created by users in the sales group.

Now users in the prod group can read the files in current-quotes. They cannot save files in this directory, but they can save them in other directories to which they have permission, such as their home directories, or four of the five subs of the prod directory structure. They cannot delete files from this directory.

However, any "other" user also has the same access to current-quotes as a user in the prod group.

Section Review

In the questions below, the word "item(s)" will be used to refer to directories and files.

1. If a user has rx to a directory, what right does the user require to (an existing) file in the directory so that the user can read the file and write to the file?

   ○ A. r
   ○ B. w
   ○ C. x
   ○ D. t

2. A user named mwong cannot log in to the system. You need to see the password settings of this user. Which command will do this for you?

   ○ A. setpass -l mwong
   ○ B. passview mwong
   ○ C. chage -l mwong
   ○ D. userpass -s mwong

3. A directory has the permission settings of rwxr-s---, root, creative. The directory has:

   ○ A. sgid
   ○ B. suid
   ○ C. the sticky bit
   ○ D. none of the above

4. By default, when you create a group, a number is automatically assigned to the group and this number is the next available number above 500. You need to create a group named creative for the Creative Department, but do not want the group number to automatically be assigned to the group. You have decided to use the GID number of 15000 for the group. Which command will allow you to do this?

   ○ A. addgroup -G 15000 creative
   ○ B. groupadd -g 15000 creative
   ○ C. groupmod -g 15000 creative
   ○ D. groupadd creative -g 15000

5. Which of the following statements are correct (choose three)?

    □ A. a group can be a member of another group
    □ B. when a user is added to a group, the user becomes a "member" of the group
    □ C. the root user is created automatically by default during the installation process
    □ D. a user "account" is a user name and its associated settings

6. When an item is moved with the mv command, the permissions at the source are the same in the destination, but the u and g become the u and g of the user that moved the file. T F

7. A directory has the permission settings of rwxr-x---, jbeck, sales. Select the correct statements regarding these permissions (choose three).

    □ A. sales is the g (group) of the directory and has the rx permissions
    □ B. o has all permissions
    □ C. o has no permissions
    □ D. jbeck is the u (owner) of the directory and has the rwx permissions

8. Which option of the useradd command can be used to specify a supplementary group for a user?

    ○ A. -G
    ○ B. -s
    ○ C. -d
    ○ D. -c

9. A binary has the permission settings of rwxr-sr-x, root, slocate. When the binary is executed, it runs with the permissions of the slocate group. T F

10. Which are the permission settings of the file named passwd in /etc?

    ○ A. rw-r--r--, root, root
    ○ B. rw-r--rw-, root, cwest
    ○ C. rw-rw-rw-, users, root
    ○ D. rwxr--rwx, root, others

11. You have backed up the home directory of the bford user and now you need to delete the user and remove the home directory (structure) with the same command. Which command should you use?

    ○ A. userrem -r bford
    ○ B. deluser -h bford
    ○ C. userdel -M /home/bford bford
    ○ D. userdel -r bford

12. A directory has the permission settings of rwxr-sr-x, root, drafting. When a user (with sufficient permission) creates a file in this directory, the file will have:

- ○ A. the g of root
- ○ B. the g of drafting
- ○ C. the o of root
- ○ D. the o of drafting

13. You are logged in as the jbeck user and want to change the password of the psimon user. Which command will allow you to do this?

- ○ A. passwd -su psimon
- ○ B. passwd psimon
- ○ C. chagepass psimon
- ○ D. none of the above

14. After creating a user with the useradd command (without using the -p option), you must run the userpass command to assign the user a password before anyone can log in as the user. T F

15. Select the most secure password from the list below.

- ○ A. ABC123
- ○ B. WestChris
- ○ C. Lo7Tr3
- ○ D. RR77SS

16. The permissions set on the /etc/passwd file allow all users to read the file and the permissions set on the /etc/shadow file only allow the root user to read the file. T F

17. Which permissions, when assigned to a directory, allow a user to effectively work in a directory by allowing the user to change into the directory, and view the contents of the directory (choose two)?

- ☐ A. r
- ☐ B. w
- ☐ C. x
- ☐ D. t

18. When a user is created, the user is assigned some default password settings in /etc/login.defs. Which command can be used to modify these password settings?

- ○ A. chage
- ○ B. chpasswd
- ○ C. passchage
- ○ D. passdefs

19. When a system is using encrypted "shadow passwords" in /etc/shadow, then the second field in the /etc/shadow file is an "x". T F

20. The user named frodo is the u of the directory named elvenwood and the group named root is the g of this directory. You need to change the g of the directory to elves. The elvenwood directory is below your current directory. Which two commands will allow you to do this?

    - ☐ A. chgrp .elves elvenwood
    - ☐ B. chgrp elves elvenwood
    - ☐ C. chown .elves elvenwood
    - ☐ D. chown elves elvenwood

21. A directory has the permission settings of rwxrwxrw**t**, root, root. The directory has:

    - ○ A. suid
    - ○ B. sgid
    - ○ C. the sticky bit
    - ○ D. none of the above

22. The user named hfinn has the UID number of 523 on an NFS file server. You have created this user at a workstation and the user was automatically assigned the next available UID number, which was 502. You want the UID number at the workstation to be "in sync" with the UID number at the server. Which of the following commands will you run at the workstation to do this?

    - ○ A. useradd -u 502 hfinn
    - ○ B. usermod -u 502 hfinn
    - ○ C. usermod -u 523 hfinn
    - ○ D. moduser -u 523 hfinn

23. You are working as the root user and need to see the groups to which the bford user is a member. Which two commands below will allow you to do this?

    - ☐ A. groups
    - ☐ B. groups bford
    - ☐ C. cat /etc/passwd
    - ☐ D. grep bford /etc/group

24. When using the chmod command to symbolically specify the mode for a file, which item will assign the user the read and write permissions and assign the group and other the read permission?

    ○ A. ug=rw,o=r
    ○ B. u=r,go=rw
    ○ C. u=rw,o=r
    ○ D. u=rw,go=r

25. Which two of the following statements regarding default permissions are correct?

    ☐ A. when umask is 002, the default permissions for a directory are rwxrwxr-x
    ☐ B. when umask is 002, the default permissions for a file are rw-r--r--
    ☐ C. when umask is 022, the default permissions for a directory are rwxrwxr-x
    ☐ D. when umask is 022, the default permissions for a file are rw-r--r--

26. A directory named userdata is below your current directory and you need to change the mode of this directory so that the group of the directory and other of the directory do not have the w permission. Which command will do this?

    ○ A. chown go-w userdata
    ○ B. chage go=w userdata
    ○ C. chmod go-w userdata
    ○ D. chmod go=w userdata

27. A directory has the permission settings of rwxrwxrw**t**, root, root. When any user creates a file in this directory:

    ○ A. only the root user or the user that created the file will be able to delete it
    ○ B. the file will have the u of the directory and the g of the user that creates the file
    ○ C. the file will have the g of the directory and the u of the user that creates the file
    ○ D. none of the above

28. By default, UID numbers that are assigned to users are greater than 99. T F

29. You do not want the root user or any user to remove any files in the current directory. What can you do so that the files cannot be deleted?

    ○ A. remove the w permission from the u, g and o of the parent directory
    ○ B. set the umask of the parent directory to 222
    ○ C. use the chattr command to assign the i attribute to all files in the current directory
    ○ D. use the lsattr command to assign the i attribute to all files in the current directory

30. The -a option of the ls command can be used to view the attributes of files, such as the i attribute. T F

31. Which command can be used to display the UID number, GID number, user name and group name of a user?

    ○ A. umask
    ○ B. uid
    ○ C. userid
    ○ D. id

32. The default permissions for a home directory are:

    ○ A. 700
    ○ B. 775
    ○ C. 600
    ○ D. 664

33. Which command will allow you to change the u of the subdirectory named checklist to mbolan?

    ○ A. chown checklist mbolan
    ○ B. chgrp .mbolan checklist
    ○ C. chown mbolan checklist
    ○ D. chmod mbolan checklist

34. The current umask setting is 027 and you create a directory. What will be the permission settings on the directory?

    ○ A. rwxr-x---
    ○ B. rwxr--r--
    ○ C. r-xr-xr-x
    ○ D. rwxrwx---

35. When you change the umask setting, the change stays in effect until you change it again; even if you log out and log back in again. T F

36. The umask setting of 002 masks the:

    ○ A. w permission to u
    ○ B. x permission to g
    ○ C. w permission to o
    ○ D. r permission to o

37. A binary has the permission settings of r-s--x--x, root, root. The binary has:

    ○ A. sgid
    ○ B. suid
    ○ C. the sticky bit
    ○ D. none of the above

38. You need to change the u and g of all items below the current directory to cbrown and creative, respectively. Select the command that will do this.

    ○ A. chown -R cbrown.creative *
    ○ B. chown cbrown.creative *
    ○ C. chmod -r cbrown.creative *
    ○ D. chown -R cbrown.creative

39. When a user is created with the useradd command, the files in /etc/skel and subs that are copied to the home directory of the user:

    ○ A. always have the default file permissions, less the current umask setting
    ○ B. have the same permissions (not the same u and g) in the destination as in the source
    ○ C. have the same u and g in the destination as in the source
    ○ D. none of the above

40. The default umask setting is either 002 or 022. T F

41. An item has the settings of r---w-rwx, bilbo, hobbits. The bilbo user is in the hobbits group. Which permission(s) does the bilbo user have to the item?

    ○ A. r, and the bilbo user can assign the u of the item all permissions
    ○ B. rw, and the bilbo user can assign the u of the item all permissions
    ○ C. rwx, and the bilbo user can assign the u of the item all permissions
    ○ D. none of the above

42. Which file contains the scripting logic that determines the default umask setting for a user?

   - ○ A. /etc/login.defs
   - ○ B. /etc/bashrc
   - ○ C. /etc/.bash_profile
   - ○ D. /etc/skel/.bashrc

43. When a file is created with an application (that does not assign setuid or setgid), the file acquires the default the permissions, less the current umask setting, and the u and g become the u and g of the user that created the file (unless the parent directory of the file has sgid). T F

44. When a user is created with the useradd command, the items in /etc/skel and subs that are copied to the home directory of the user:

   - ○ A. have the u and g of root
   - ○ B. have the u and g of the user that ran the useradd command
   - ○ C. have the u and g of the user that is created
   - ○ D. none of the above

45. The u (owner) of an item cannot change the permissions of the item. T F

46. Which command will remove the group named history from the system?

   - ○ A. groupdel history
   - ○ B. delgroup history
   - ○ C. grouprem history
   - ○ D. group -r history

47. An item has the settings of r---w-rwx, lvanpelt, peanuts. The cbrown user is in the peanuts group. Which permission(s) does the cbrown user have to the item.

   - ○ A. rw
   - ○ B. w
   - ○ C. rwx
   - ○ D. none of the above

48. The file named shadow in /etc contains default password settings, such as the minimum number of days before a password can be changed. T F

49. By default, which items occur when you create a user (choose two)?

    ☐ A. the files in /skel are put below the user's home directory

    ☐ B. a statement for the user is added to the /etc/passwd and /etc/shadow files

    ☐ C. the user is added to a Primary Group that has the same name as the user

    ☐ D. the user is added to a Primary Group named everybody

50. Which permission, when assigned to a directory, allows a user to create items in the directory and also delete all of the items in the directory, regardless of the permission settings (not attributes) of the items?

    ○ A. r

    ○ B. w

    ○ C. x

    ○ D. t

51. You have a group named parts with a GID number of 14000 on an NFS file server. This group also exists at a workstation, but with a different GID number. You want the GID number at the workstation to match the GID number at the server. Which command will you run at the workstation to accomplish this?

    ○ A. groupdel parts ; groupadd 14000 parts

    ○ B. groupchage -u 14000 parts

    ○ C. groupmod 14000 parts

    ○ D. groupmod -g 14000 parts

52. The execute (**x**) permission is assigned to a binary or script file to allow the file to be executed (run).   T   F

53. An item has the settings of r---w---x, hello, linux. The lstevens user is not in the linux group. Which permission(s) does the lstevens user have to the item?

    ○ A. rwx

    ○ B. rw

    ○ C. x

    ○ D. none of the above

54. The useradd command was used prior to the adduser command.   T   F

55. Select two of the characteristics of the default settings in the /etc/passwd file when a user is created.

   ☐ A.   two !! appear in the second field until the user is assigned a password
   ☐ B.   the UID number and the GID number are the same
   ☐ C.   the default group name is others
   ☐ D.   the default shell is /bin/bash

56. Which are the permission settings of the file named shadow in /etc?

   ○ A.   ------r--, users, root
   ○ B.   ---------, root, root
   ○ C.   r--------, root, root
   ○ D.   r-xr-xrwx, root, everybody

57. The g and o of a directory or file are referred to in some Linux documentation as the ownership of the directory or file. T F

58. Which file contains default password settings that are used when a user is created and that can be seen with the -l option of the chage command?

   ○ A.   /etc/passwd
   ○ B.   /etc/login.defs
   ○ C.   /home/common/pass.defs
   ○ D.   /etc/skel/.bash_profile

59. A binary has the permission settings of rwxr-sr-x, root, slocate. The binary has:

   ○ A.   sgid
   ○ B.   suid
   ○ C.   the sticky bit
   ○ D.   none of the above

60. Which option of the useradd command can be used to specify a "full name" for a user?

   ○ A.   -g
   ○ B.   -c
   ○ C.   -d
   ○ D.   -s

61. When a utility needs to display the user name (owner) of an item, it "looks" at the item and "sees" the UID number (not name) of the u (owner) of the item. In which file does the utility "look" for the user name that matches the UID number?

    ○ A. /etc/shadow
    ○ B. /etc/login.defs
    ○ C. /etc/passwd
    ○ D. /etc/skel/.bashrc

62. You need to change the mode of all items below the current directory to 644. Select the command that will do this.

    ○ A. chown -X 644 *
    ○ B. chmod -R 644 all
    ○ C. chagemod -R 644 *
    ○ D. chmod -R 644 *

63. The u (owner) of an item can change the g of the item to a group (primary or supplementary) to which the user is a member. T F

64. The current umask setting is 027 and you create a file. What will be the permission settings on the file?

    ○ A. rwxr-x---
    ○ B. rwxr--r--
    ○ C. r-xr-x---
    ○ D. rw-r-----

65. A binary has the permission settings of r-s--x--x, root, prod. When the binary is executed, it runs with the permissions of the prod group. T F

66. You have run the ls command with the -l option and see a number rather than a name for the u (owner) of a file. What may have happened?

    ○ A. the group of the u (owner) may have been removed from the system (deleted)
    ○ B. the u (owner) may have been removed from the system (deleted)
    ○ C. the /etc/shadow file may have become corrupted
    ○ D. the user may have logged out of the system

67. Which statement in /etc/login.defs is used to stop a user from immediately changing his or her password back to a previous password and continuing to use an old password?

- ○ A.   PASS_MAX_DAYS
- ○ B.   NO_SET_BACK_DAYS
- ○ C.   PASS_MIN_DAYS
- ○ D.   PASS_MIN_MONTHS

68. You need to see if a user named jbeck is a member of the prod group. Which command will display this information?

- ○ A.   grep prod /etc/group
- ○ B.   cat /etc/passwd
- ○ C.   grep /etc/groups | prod
- ○ D.   less | /etc/group.mems

69. When an item is copied with the cp command that is included with this distribution (without the -p option), the permissions at the source may be different from the destination (depending on the source permissions and the current umask setting), and the u and g become the u and g of the user that copied the file. T F

Chapter 13: Backing Up Your System

During this chapter you will learn the importance of doing system backups and where to get more information regarding backup hardware, software, strategies and procedures.

The main focus of this chapter is the on tar command and how it can be used to combine files into a single tar file (backup file) and how options of this command can be used to compress and decompress a backup tar file.

You will see several examples of using the tar command to create a tar file, extract files from a tar file and view the contents of a tar file.

The -z and -j options of the tar command can be used to cause this command to compress a tar file by using the gzip and bzip2 programs, respectively. These two programs can also be used on their own to compress and decompress (uncompress) files. The gunzip and bunzip2 programs can also be used to decompress files. The gzip, gunzip, bzip2 and bunzip2 programs are also described in this chapter with examples.

The zip and unzip commands can also be used to compress and decompress files and are also described here.

The following commands are described in this Chapter and are also used in the Hands-On Exercises:

tar	combine and compress directories and files into a single file
gzip	compress and decompress files
gunzip	decompress files
bzip2	compress and decompress files
bunzip2	decompress files
zip	compress and decompress files
unzip	decompress files

During the Hands-On Exercises, you will use various options of the tar command to combine and compress files into a single file and also view the contents of a tar file. You will also open two terminal emulation windows, run the top command in one window and the tar command in another. This will allow you to see the gzip and bzip2 programs working "in the background" to compress and decompress files when the -z and -j options of the tar command are used.

Backing Up Your System

> ### Topics Covered in this Chapter
>
> Discuss the importance of doing system backups
> Learn how the tar command be used to do backups and distribute files
> Describe several examples of using the tar command to work with tar files
> Discuss other file compression and decompression programs
> Use various options of the tar command to combine and compress files

In this chapter, you will learn about doing system backups, the tar command, and other file compression and decompression programs.

During the Hands-On Exercises you will use the tar command to back up your home directory and the prod and sales directory structures that you created below /home/common.

Backing Up a Workstation or Server

Backing up a Linux workstation and server data to some type of removable media is extremely important. Massive amounts of data can easily be lost through hardware failures and operator errors, such as a hard disk crash or the incorrect use of the rm command. If you make regular daily backups of your system, you have made an excellent investment in time and backup hardware costs, and have taken out insurance against a possible disaster.

There are many software and hardware solutions for data backup. However, one of the easiest ways to do a backup, such as to tape or other removable media, is to use the tar command.

Scripts can be created to automate the backup process by running the tar command to back up the necessary data files. This chapter focuses on the use of the tar command to do backups.

A popular and powerful network backup software solution named **AMANDA** (**A**dvanced **M**aryland **A**utomatic **N**etwork **D**isk **A**rchiver) is included on CD 2. This software consists of four packages (.rpm files) and allows you to create an archiver server to back up networked systems. This includes systems using various versions of Linux, UNIX and Windows. This software works with either the dump or **tar** commands. Later in this course you will learn how to install software packages that exist as .rpm files on CD 1 and CD 2.

AMANDA is comprised of four software packages and one is named amanda-server-*version*. When this package is installed, documentation regarding its use is installed in the path of:

/usr/share/doc/amanda-server-*version*

Getting More Information on Backup Solutions

There is a tremendous amount of information available over the internet regarding backup hardware, software, strategies and procedures. To access this information, do a search of the Internet for "linux backup" and similar text. This will provide *many* links to information on backing up a Linux system.

In addition to this, you can go to The Linux Documentation Project at http://www.tldp.org and see the following:

    Introduction to Backing Up and Restoring Data
    Linux Administration Made Easy - Chapter 8: Backup and Restore Procedures
    Linux Complete Backup and Recovery HOWTO

The tar Command

The tar (tape **ar**chive) command allows you to combine any number of directories and files, from one or more directories, into a single file (a.k.a. tarfile). As the word "archive" implies, the tar command is used to back up a system by combining files and putting them onto some type of removable storage device. This command was originally written to archive data to tape (as in *tape* **ar**chive), but it can also write data to other types of media, such as hard disk or CD. Very large capacity tapes are commonly used as a backup media.

In addition to archiving files by combining them into a single file, the -z and -j options of the tar command can be used to "zip up" (compress) the files that are put into an archive. These two options can also be used to "unzip" (decompress) files when they are being extracted (removed) from an archive. Files that are put in a tarfile are not always compressed.

In addition to being used to back up and restore files, the tar command is also used to combine and compress files. This allows files be emailed to someone as efficiently as possible and also allows them to be downloaded quickly from a server.

Files that have been put into a tarfile with the tar command have been "tarred". A software package (or other set of files) that has been "tarred" (into a single file) is often referred to as a "tarball" (a tar archive file). The tar command is also used to "untar" a tarball (or tarfile) and extract the files in it to one or more directories.

Linux software programs in either source code form or as binary files are tarred, compressed and exist for download as tarballs (with the suffixes of .tar.gz, .tgz or .tar.bz2) in thousands of locations around the world. During the upcoming chapter on installing software, you will untar the files in a "tarball" that contains source code, compile the code and install it.

In the past, Linux OS components and application software programs were only available as "tarballs". Now many distributions deliver software as "packages" rather than "tarballs". They use either **.rpm** (**R**ed Hat **P**ackage **M**anager) files or some other method of packaging the software. As mentioned earlier, you will also install "packages" that are in .rpm files during the chapter on installing software.

The terms tarfile and tarball can be used interchangeably. However, we will typically use the word "tarball" to refer to the files of a *software package* that have been compressed and put into a single file. A tarball may contain any number of files.

For example, a tarball could contain only a few files and consist of the compiled version of a driver for a hardware component and a few documentation files that describe how to install it. A tarball could also contain hundreds or thousands of source code files that are required to compile a complex software package.

We will use the word "tarfile" to refer to *any* file that has been created with the tar command, including a tarball. A tarfile may can contain one or more files, and may or may not have been compressed. However, a tarfile typically contains many files and is often compressed.

When you use the tar command, suffixes are not automatically added to the end of the name of the tarfile that you are creating. You must provide the appropriate suffix when using the tar command. Use the .tar suffix for files that will be put in an archive, but will *not* be compressed. Use the .tar.gz or .tgz suffix for files that are "tarred" and compressed with the -z option of the tar command and use the .bz2 suffix for files "tarred" and compressed with the -j option.

A tarfile that has not been compressed takes up more space than the sum of the files in it and therefore tar files are also often compressed.

Options of the tar Command

A - (dash) is not required prior to specifying options with this command, but it is best to use it so that you don't accidentally start using other commands without using a - (dash) in front of options. Table 13-1 shows the commonly used options of the tar command.

Table 13-1 - Common Options of the tar Command

Option	Description
-c	create an archive with the filename specified
-z	the -z option (with the **-c** (**c**reate) option) causes the tar command to use the g**z**ip program to compress the files into the tarfile
	the -z option (with the **-x** (e**x**tract) option) causes the g**z**ip program to decompress a tarfile that was compressed with the -z option - use this option on files with a suffix of .tar.gz or .tgz
-j	the -j option (with the **-c** (**c**reate) option) causes the tar command to use the bzip2 program to compress files into a tarfile
	the -j option (with the **-x** (e**x**tract) option) causes the bzip2 program to decompress a tarfile that was compressed with the -j option - use this option on files with a suffix of .bz2
-v	display **v**erbosely (with more detail) the files being put in an archive, the files being extracted from an archive, or the existing files in an archive
-f	precede the **f**ilename of the archive being created, extracted or displayed with this option
-p	preserve the **p**ermissions during backup and during restore
-x	e**x**tract files from a tarfile
-P	archive the absolute **P**ath with each file when creating an archive
	restore a file to its original (absolute) **P**ath when extracting files from an archive - the absolute path must have been archived when the archive was created
-t	display the files in a tarfile - use with the -v option to see more information
-k	**k**eep (and do not overwrite) existing files when extracting from a tarfile
-r	add files to the end of (append to) an existing tarfile
-d	display the **d**ifference between the files in a directory and those in a tarfile

Overview of Options of the tar Command

The -z option of the tar command can be used to compress and decompress files with the gzip program. The -j option of the tar command can be used to compress and decompress files with the bzip2 program. The gzip and bzip2 programs can also be used independently as commands to compress and also decompress files. The gunzip and bunzip2 programs can also be used to decompress files.

The **-c** (**c**reate) option of the tar command (along with some other options) is used to create a tarfile. The **-x** (e**x**tract) option (along with some other options) is used to remove files from a tarfile.

The -z option of the tar command can be used to compress files into a tarfile or extract files from a compressed tarfile. Rather than using the -z option, the -j option can also be used to compress files into a tarfile or extract files from a compressed tarfile.

The -z Option of the tar Command

When used with the -c option to *create* a tarfile, the **-z** option automatically causes the ***gzip*** program to be used "in the background" to zip up (compress) the files that are being added to the archive. When creating a file with the -z option, use .tar.gz or .tgz as the suffix for the file.

Using the -z option to compress files into a tarfile takes longer than not using this option, but it creates a smaller file.

When used with the -x option to *extract* files from a tarfile, the **-z** option automatically causes the ***gzip*** program to be used "in the background" to unzip (decompress) the files that are being removed from the archive.

The -z option of the tar command is used to unzip files with the suffixes of .tar.gz or .tgz. Most Linux software packages that are available for download from the internet are compressed and many have the .tar.gz or .tgz suffixes.

The -j Option of the tar Command

When used with the -c option to *create* a tarfile, the **-j** option automatically causes the ***bzip2*** program to be used "in the background" to zip up the files that are being added to the archive. When creating a file with the -j option, use .tar.bz2 as the suffix for the file.

Using the -j option to compress files into a tarfile takes longer than not using this option, but it creates a smaller file. Using the -j option takes longer than using the -z option and also creates a smaller file.

When used with the -x option to *extract* files from a tarfile, the **-j** option automatically causes the **bzip2** program to be used "in the background" to unzip the files that are being removed from the archive.

The -j option of the tar command is used to unzip files with the suffix of .tar.bz2. In addition to .tar.gz and .tgz files, many Linux software packages that are available for download have the .tar.bz2 suffix.

 You will do steps during the Hands-On Exercises below to see the gzip program being used "in the background" to compress or decompress a tarfile when the -z option of the tar command is used.

You will also do these steps to see that the bzip2 program is used to compress or decompress a tarfile when the -j option of the tar command is used.

Specifying the Data to be Archived by the tar Command

A path, pattern, or path and pattern is used with the tar command to indicate the data to be archived. The pattern can be a single file name.

When a directory path (only) is specified, then the command works recursively (it will also work on subdirectories of the specified path) and it tars all files, including hidden files.

For example, if you specify the path of: /home   then the command will tar all files in /home and subdirectories of /home, including hidden files.

When a pattern of a * (single asterisk) is specified (with or without a path), then the command works recursively, but it does not tar hidden files.

For example, if you specify the path and pattern of: /home/*   then the command will tar all files in /home and subdirectories of /home, excluding hidden files.

When a pattern that is *not* a * (single asterisk) is specified (with or without a path), then the command does not work recursively and it does not tar hidden files.

For example, if you specify the path and pattern of: /home/*.sxi   then the command will only tar all .sxi files in /home.

Tarring Files with Relative and Absolute Paths

If you want files to be restored from an archive file into their original path, specify an absolute (full) path for the source of the files, use the -P option when you create the archive, and use the -P option when you untar the tarfile.

In other words, when creating a tarfile, specify all directories from the / (root) directory to the directory or pattern being "tarred" and use the -P option. Also, use the -P option when using the tar command to "untar" the tarfile so that its files are restored to their original directories. This causes the absolute path that was "tarred" with each file to be used as the path to which the file will be restored.

When using the -P option to restore files, be sure that they do not overwrite existing files that you require (and that are more current than the files in the archive). If you are restoring files onto a system that contains data, rather than to a new storage device, do a complete backup prior to doing the restore. The **-k (keep)** option can be used to keep existing files rather than overwriting them.

Also, use the -t option (with the -v and -f options) of the tar command to view the contents of a tarfile prior to untarring it. This will allow you to see the path that was archived with each file and the files that you are about to restore. Always do a test to make sure that you can restore any backups that you create.

When you use the tar command to create an archive and "tar" files into a tarfile, the path to each file is included in the tarfile with the file name (and the contents of the file). However, by default, the path to the file does not include the / (root) directory, even if you specify the full path to the source of the files. Therefore, by default, the relative path to each file is archived with the file, rather than the absolute path.

For example, a file named memos.sxw is located in /home/cwest. You change into the /home/cwest directory and tar the memos.sxw file with the following command:

```
tar  -cjvf bu-111204.bz2 /home/cwest/memos.sxw
```

The absolute path to the file (/home/cwest) and the filename was specified with the above tar command. However, the path to the file (that is included in the tarfile) is: home/cwest/memos.sxw and not: /home/cwest/memos.sxw. The -P option of the tar command must be used to cause the tar command to archive the absolute path to the file (so that the / (root) directory is included as part of the path in the tarfile).

After doing the above command, the / that represents the / (root) directory is not included in the tarfile. Therefore, when you use the tar command to untar the file (from any directory other than the / directory), its contents will not be put in the absolute path of /home/cwest and its contents will not be put back in the directory from which it originated. Instead, it will be put in a relative path below the directory from which it was untarred.

To continue the example, if you put the bu-111204.bz2 file (the tarfile containing the memos.sxw file) in the /test directory and run the tar command (in /test) to extract the files from it, it will be put in the relative path of: home/cwest/memos.sxw below the path of /test. In other words, the file will be put in the path of /test/home/cwest/memos.sxw.

The full path to the file will be: /test/home/cwest/memos.sxw and not: /home/cwest/memos.sxw.

To continue further, if you put the tarfile in /home/cwest (the directory in which the file in the tarfile originated) and untar it from this directory, then the relative path of: home/cwest/memos.sxw that was tarred in the bu-111204.bz2 file will be appended (added on to the end of) to the current path of /home/cwest. The resulting full path to the file will be: /home/cwest/home/cwest/memos.sxw (not likely what you intended).

The -P option of the tar command causes the command to archive the absolute Path with each filename. This will cause the / (root) directory to be included in the path to the file (in the tarfile).

For example, if you change into /home/cwest and run the tar command using the -P option (with the other required options), to tar the file named memos.sxw (in /home/cwest), the path to the file in the tarfile will be: /home/cwest/memos.sxw and not: home/cwest/memos.sxw. When you put the tarfile containing memos.sxw *in any directory* and untar it with the -P option, then the file will be untarred into its absolute directory path of: /home/cwest/memos.sxw (which is where you are likely going to want it).

If you want to be able to easily restore tarred files to their original location, use the -P option and specify the absolute path when creating a tarfile. Also use the -P option when untarring a tarred file so that the files in the tarfile are restored to their original location. As described above, use caution when untarring files with the -P option to ensure that you do not overwrite existing files.

Examples of Using the tar Command to Archive Files

tar -cvf bu-092604.tar /home/cwest

This example puts all of the directories and files in the path of /home/cwest in a file named bu-092604.tar. This includes hidden files. The bu-092604.tar file is created in the directory from which the tar command was run. To create a tarfile in a directory other than the current directory, precede the name of the tarfile with a path.

In the filename of bu-092604.tar, the **bu** stands for **b**ackup and the numbers 092604 represent the date of September 26, 2004.

tar -czvf common-data.tar.gz /home/common

In this example, the -z option causes all of the files in the path of /home/common to be compressed into a file named common-data.tar.gz. The .tar.gz suffix was assigned to the file (rather than just .tar) to indicate that the files in it were compressed with the gzip program. The suffix of .tgz could be used in place of .tar.gz above.

When the -z option is used with the -c option, files are zipped (compressed) into the file that is created. When the -z option is used with the -x (extract) option, files are unzipped (uncompressed) from the tarfile.

The full path to the directory is specified in the command above, but the -P option is not being used and so the relative path of: home/common and not the absolute path of: /home/common   will be tarred with each filename.

If this file is untarred, it will create files in the relative path of home/common, below the directory in which the tarfile exists. If the file is put in the / (root) directory and is untarred from this directory, then it will create files in the original path of /home/common.

tar -czvf common-sxw-files.tar.gz /home/common/*.sxw

This example is the same as above, except that it uses *.sxw for the pattern. This will cause all files in the common directory that end in ".sxw" to be tarred and compressed into the file named common-sxw-files.tar.gz. Files in subdirectories of common will not be included in the archive because the *.sxw pattern was used.

tar -cPzvf bu-cwest-120702.tar.gz /home/cwest

This example uses the -P (Path) option to cause the tarfile to include the full path to each file that is in it. As required when using the -P option, the full path to the cwest directory is also specified.

After running this command, the tarfile contains the absolute path of: /home/cwest/*filename*   for each *filename* in the tarfile, rather than the relative path of: home/cwest/*filename*.

To have files restored to their original location, the -P option must also be used when untarring a file that has been tarred with the -P option (or the file must be untarred from the root directory). As described earlier, use caution when untarring files with the -P option to ensure that you do not overwrite existing files. Depending on the circumstances, you may or may not want to use the -k option (to keep existing data) when using the -P option .

For example, the -k option will not be required if you are doing a restore to a disk that does not contain any data or does not contain the data that you are restoring. This option will also not be required if you want to overwrite existing data with old data.

tar -cPjvf bu-cwest-120702.tar.bz2 /home/cwest

In this example, the -j option is used and the .tar.bz2 suffix was assigned to the file to indicate that the files in it were compressed with the bzip2 program.

tar -cpvf /dev/*devicename* --label="Backup on `date '+%Y-%B-%d'`." /home

The (lower case) -p option shown in this example is used to preserve permissions. It is an example of backing up the /home directory and its subdirectories to a tape device named /dev/*devicename*. The *devicename* is replaced by the name of the tape device.

For example, /dev/st0 could be used for SCSI tape 0, if you are using a SCSI tape drive that has the number 0. The device must be mounted and you must have permission to access the device.

The file name at the right of the -f option is "/dev/*devicename*", which is the name of a tape backup device. The backup device is treated like a file. The --label option is used (rather than a file name) to identify the backup on the tape. The label of "Backup on `date '+%Y-%B-%d'`." would become "Backup on 2004-April-28." if the backup was done on April 28, 2004.

In this example, the -z or -j options were not used and so the data will not be compressed.

When the date command is run without any options, the date and time are displayed . Alternatively, the output of the date command can be formatted using several items that are prefixed with % (a percent sign). These items can be used to restrict the amount of output from the date command and to format the appearance of the output. Some of these items are shown below.

```
%Y    four digits for the year, such as 2004
%B    the full month name, such as April
%d    the number of the day of the month, such as 28
```

In the above command, the --label of "Backup on `date '+%Y-%B-%d'`." uses the date command within ` ` (back quotes). The formatting of the output of the date command is: +%Y-%B-%d and this is between ' ' (single quotes).

When the date is April 28, 2004, then the result of: `date '+ %Y-%B-%d'` is: 2004-April-28. When a (default) long listing is done of items that use this date format, the items will be sorted by year, then by month and then by day of month.

In the example above, the date command is used for the label of the backup on tape. However, the date command can also be used in this manner to name a file.

For example, in the following command, the text of:

> bu-`date '+%Y-%B-%d'`.tar.bz2

will cause the name of the tarfile to be:

> bu-**2004-May-17**.tar.bz2

if the date is: May 17, 2004.

> tar -cPjvf bu-`date '+%Y-%B-%d'`.tar.bz2 /home/cwest/*

You will put a command similar to the above command in a script that automates the process of doing a backup in the upcoming chapter on scripting.

Examples of Using the tar Command to Extract Files from an Archive

tar -xPzvf bu-cwest-120702.tar.gz

The -P option was used when the bu-cwest-120702.tar.gz file was created. This example extracts the files from bu-cwest-120702.tar.gz and restores them to their original location. If the -P option is *not* used with this command, then the directory structure is created below the current directory.

tar -xPjvf bu-cwest-120702.bz2

This is the same as above, except that the -j option is used because the file has the .bz2 suffix.

tar -xPkjvf bu-cwest-120702.bz2

This command is the same as above, except that the **-k** option is used. The option cases the tar command to "**keep**" files that already exist.

For example, if a file named memos.sxw, in the path of /home/cwest was in bu-cwest-120702.bz2 and a file named memos.sxw exists on the hard disk in the path of /home/cwest, then the tar command will keep the existing file on the disk and not replace it with the file in bu-cwest-120702.bz2.

Examples of Using the tar Command to View the Files in an Archive

tar -tvf letters.tar | less

This example uses the -t option and displays the contents of the letters.tar file. The output of the command is "piped" to the less command so that the output can be scrolled through.

All of the directories and files in the letters.tar file and the path to each of them will appear. If the -P option was used when the tarfile was created, then the path to each file begins with the / (root) directory. If this option was not used, then the / directory (only) is omitted from the path to each item.

The -z or -j options are not used because the file does not have a suffix of .tar.gz, .tgz or .tar.bz2.

tar -tzvf letters.tar.gz | less

This command is the same as above, except that the -z option is used because the file has the .tar.gz suffix. If the file had the .bz2 suffix, then the same command would be used, except that the -z would be replaced with a -j.

The gzip and gunzip Commands

When you use the **-c** (**c**reate) and **-z** (gzip) options of tar (with other options, such as the -v and -f options), you create a file and zip (compress) it. The gzip command is automatically used "in the background" by the tar command to compress the tarfile.

When you use the **-x** (e**x**tract) and **-z** (unzip) options of tar (with other options, such as -v and -f), you extract files from a tarfile and unzip (uncompress) them. In this case, the gzip command is automatically used "in the background" by the tar command to unzip the file.

The gzip command can be used on its own to compress a .tar file, as shown in the following example:

    gzip wpdata.tar

After running the above command, the wpdata.tar file becomes a compressed and automatically acquires the file name of: wpdata.tar.gz and the wpdata.tar file no longer exists. The gzip command adds the .gz to the end of the file name.

The gunzip command can be used to decompress (uncompress) a .tar.gz or .tgz file and make the file a .tar file.

The following is an example of using gunzip to decompress a .tar.gz file. This file could have been created by using the tar command with the -z option, or by using the tar command (without the -z option) and then using the gzip command to compressed the .tar file.

    gunzip wpdata.tar.gz

After running the above command, the wpdata.tar.gz file becomes decompressed and automatically acquires the file name of: wpdata.tar and the wpdata.tar.gz file no longer exists. The gunzip command removes the .gz from the end of the file name.

If you need to extract the files from the wpdata.tar file, use the tar command, as described above.

The bzip2 and bunzip2 Commands

There will be occasions when you need to extract and unzip an archive of files that are in a compressed file that ends in .tar.bz2. This can occur when you download Linux software (tarballs) from the internet. Files that have the .tar.bz2 suffix may have been zipped with the bzip2 program or with the tar command, and files with this suffix can be unzipped with the bunzip2 program and the tar command. The bzip2 and bunzip2 programs are faster than the gzip and gunzip programs and provide better compression.

 Older Linux systems may have an older version of tar installed that does not support the -j option (the use of the bzip2 program). If you are working with older systems that do not have current versions of the tar and bzip2 binaries, use the -z option rather than the -j option, or install current versions of the tar and bzip2 programs.

The following is an example of using the bzip2 command to compress a .tar file:

    bzip2 wpdata.tar

After running the above command, the wpdata.tar file becomes a compressed and automatically acquires the file name of: wpdata.tar.bz2 and the wpdata.tar file no longer exists. The bzip2 command adds the .bz2 to the end of the file name.

The bunzip2 command can be used to decompress (uncompress) a .tar.bz2 file and make the file a .tar file.

The following is an example of using bunzip2 to decompress a .tar.bz2 file. This file could have been created by using the tar command with the -j option, or by using the tar command (without the -j option) and then using the bzip2 command to compress the .tar file.

    bunzip2 wpdata.tar.bz2

After running the above command, the wpdata.tar.bz2 file becomes decompressed and automatically acquires the file name of: wpdata.tar and the wpdata.tar.bz2 file no longer exists. The bunzip2 command removes the .bz2 from the end of the file name.

If you need to extract the files from the wpdata.tar file, use the tar command, as described above.

The zip and unzip Commands

The tar command archives directories and files and an option of it (-z or -j) can be used to cause the gzip or bzip2 program to compress the archive. The tar command is also used to extract files from an archive and can be used to cause gzip or bzip2 to decompress files. In other words, the tar command uses additional programs to compress and decompress files.

The zip command can archive directories and files and the unzip command can extract files that have been created with the zip command. The zip command can compress files and the unzip command can uncompress zipped files *without* the use of another program (such as gzip or bzip2).

The zip and unzip commands are not used as often in Linux environments as the other commands described above. They are more commonly used in a Windows environment. The zip and unzip commands work on files that typically have the .zip suffix.

 Hands-On Exercises

 Logging in to Use the tar Command

> Log in as cwest ; open a terminal emulation window ; su to root ; change into the home directory of the cwest user.
>
>]# tar -cf bu-cwest.tar /home/cwest   # back up all items below cwest

The -v option was not used and so the files that were backed up did not appear.

A path was not specified at the left of the tarfile name of bu-cwest.tar above. Therefore, the tarfile was created in the current directory, which is also the directory that is being "tarred". The output of the above command shows that the bu-cwest.tar file is the archive file and that it was "not dumped". This indicates that the backup file (tarfile) that you created was not backed up (dumped). The items in the cwest directory were backed up, but not the tarfile that was being created.

You can specify a path at the left of a tarfile name so that the file is created in a different directory, but for simplicity we are not doing this here.

>]# ls -lh   # write the size of the .tar file here: _____
>
>]# rm bu-cwest.tar

② Viewing the Contents of a Tarfile as It is Being Created

```
]# tar -cvf bu-cwest.tar /home/cwest
```

The -v option shows the names of all of the directories and files that were tarred. A pattern was not used at the right of the /home/cwest path above and so all items, including hidden items, were tarred. Use the up arrow at the right of the terminal emulation window to scroll up and see the hidden items that are prefixed with a . (dot).

```
]# rm  bu-cwest.tar
```

③ Using an * to Tar Non-Hidden Items

```
]# tar -cvf bu-cwest.tar /home/cwest/*
```

An * (asterisk) is used in the pattern above. This causes the tar command to only tar non-hidden items.

```
]# ls -lh          # write the size of the .tar file here: _____
```

The hidden items take up a lot of space.

④ Viewing the Contents of a Tarfile

```
]# tar -tvf bu-cwest.tar        # the contents of the tarfile appear
```

Look at the path to each item at the right of the output. A / (slash) representing the root directory does not appear at the left of "home" in the path to each item.

```
]# rm  bu-cwest.tar
```

⑤ Tarring with the Absolute Path

```
]# tar -cPvf bu-cwest.tar /home/cwest/*
```

The output of the tar command now shows a / at the left of "home". The -P option is used to cause the absolute path to be included in the backup.

```
]# tar -tvf bu-cwest.tar        # now a / appears at the left of "home"
```

You used the -tvf options above. The -t option allows you to display the files in the tarfile. In the next tar command below, you are using the same options, except that you are replacing the "t" with an "x" so that you can extract the files from the tarfile. *It is a good idea to use the -t option to check the contents of a tarfile prior to using the -x option to extract items from a tarfile.*

Extracting Files from a Tarfile

>   ]# ls -l

Your current directory is /home/cwest. Notice that a home directory does not currently exist below cwest.

>   ]# tar -xvf bu-cwest.tar

The -v option causes the files that are being extracted to appear.

7 **Viewing the Restored Files and Removing Them**

>   ls -l   # look for the home directory below cwest

A home directory now exists below /home/cwest and the contents of the bu-cwest.tar file (/home/cwest) were restored to /home/cwest/home/cwest. In other words, the command above restored the files in the path of /home/cwest to the path of /home/cwest (your current directory). The -P option was not used above and so a relative path was used when the files were extracted from the tarfile. The -P option was used when the bu-cwest.tar file was created, but the -P option was not used when the contents of the file were extracted.

>   ]# cd home ; ls -l ; pwd

A cwest directory is now below /home/cwest/home.

>   ]# cd cwest ; ls -l ; pwd

The contents of /home/cwest/home/cwest appear.

>   ]# cd .. ; cd .. ; pwd   # change into the "real" cwest directory

Your current directory path should be /home/cwest. If you are not currently in the path of /home/cwest, change into this path. Do not run the rm command below from the root directory.

>   ]# ls -l ; pwd

A home directory should be below your current directory and your current directory path should be /home/cwest. Do not use a / in the command below.

>   ]# rm -rf home ; ls -l

Removes the home directory below /home/cwest.

⑧ **Removing a File and Restoring It**

Change into the gr-data directory below the current directory ; get a long listing ;

remove the clock.sxi file ; get a long listing.

The clock.sxi file will be restored with the next tar command.

Change up one directory level and get a listing.

The bu-cwest.tar file should appear. Be sure to use the **-k (keep)** option in the command below so that existing files are not overwritten. The -P option causes the absolute path in the tarfile to be used.

```
]#  tar  -xPkvf  bu-cwest.tar          #  existing files were not overwritten

]#  ls  -l                             #  a home directory was not created
                                       #  in /home/cwest

]#  ls  -l  gr-data                     #  the clock.sxi file was restored

]#  rm  bu-cwest.tar
```

⑨ **Creating a Directory for Archive Files**

When using the tar command below, you will precede the names of the tarfiles that you create with the path of /home/archives. The archives directory will be used to hold the tarfiles that you will create. The directory name of "archives" is an example of a "backup related" directory name. A different name could be used. Also, the archives directory could be created in a different location. In some environments the archive tarfiles may be in a directory on a backup server hard disk and in others the archives may only exist on tape.

```
]#  mkdir  /home/archives
```

Change into the common directory below /home.

```
]#  ls  -lR  |  less
```

The prod and sales directory structures below common appear. This is the directory structure you created earlier. Scroll to the bottom to see the directory names and the files in them.

⑩ Backing Up the Common Directory

Now tar up the common directory structure without using compression. Other options could also be used in the command below.

]# tar -cPvf /home/archives/bu-common.**tar** /home/common

Get a long listing in "human readable" form of the archives directory below /home to see the .tar file that you just created.

The command below tars up the common directory structure with the -z option. This causes the tarfile to be compressed by the gzip program. The .tar.gz or .tgz suffix is used when the -z option is used. Be sure to add the -z option and use the .tar.gz suffix in the command below.

]# tar -cP**z**vf /home/archives/bu-common.**tar.gz** /home/common

Get a listing of /home/archives again ; the .tar.gz file was compressed with gzip.

The next command uses the -j option, which causes the tarfile to be compressed by the bzip2 program. The .tar.bz2 suffix is used when the -j option is used. Be sure to replace the -z option with the -j option and use the .tar.bz2 suffix in the command below.

]# tar -cP**j**vf /home/archives/bu-common.tar.**bz2** /home/common

Get a listing of /home/archives again ; the .tar.bz2 file was compressed with bzip2.

The .tar file is relatively large in comparison to the two compressed files and the .tar.bz2 file was compressed more than the .tar.gz file.

⑪ Copying a Directory Structure and Preserving Permissions

Your current directory path should be /home/common and the sales and prod directory structures exist below this path.

The next command copies the sales directory structure to a new directory structure named test to make a backup of the sales directory structure. If the next tar command does not work properly, you can restore the contents of the sales directory structure.

]# cp -rp sales test   # uses -r (recursive) and -p (preserve permissions)

Clear the screen and get a long listing.

Removing the sales Directory Structure

```
]# rm -rf sales          # files in sales/templates were not removed
]# ls -lR sales
```

The files in sales/templates cannot be removed because they have been assigned the **i** (immutable) attribute. However, they could be removed after removing the **i** (immutable) attribute from them with the chattr command.

```
]# lsattr sales/templates
```

The i attribute appears for each remaining file.

```
]# lsattr test/templates
```

The files in test/templates that were copied from sales/templates above do not have any attributes and can be removed with the rm. You will do this further below.

 Viewing an Archive and Restoring from It

Now look at the contents of the bu-common.**tar.bz2** file.

```
]# tar -tjvf /home/archives/bu-common.tar.bz2 | less
```

This shows you the contents of the bu-common.tar.bz2 tarfile. The prod and sales directory structures are in this file. You could extract files from any of the three files that you created in /home/archives.

Now that you have seen that you are going to extract files from an archive that contains the desired files, the "t" in the above command can be replaced by an "x", as shown in the following command. The -P and -k options are also used below. Be sure to use the -k option if you need to keep existing files rather than overwrite them with data that may be older. Do not use: | less in the command below.

```
]# tar -xPkjvf /home/archives/bu-common.tar.bz2
```

Scroll up to the top of the output of the last command (i.e. until you see shell prompt and the last command that you ran). The directories and files below the sales directory were restored, except for sales/templates. Scroll down to see that existing items below the prod directory structure were not restored. This is seen from the output of "Cannot open: file exists".

```
]# ls -lR sales | less
```

All of the files that were removed from the sales directory structure should have been restored. If they were, do the following step to remove the test directory structure.

```
]# rm -rf test ; ls -l      # the test directory structure was removed
```

Setting Up to View the Programs Used by the tar Command to Compress Files

The following steps demonstrate that the tar command uses the gzip and bzip2 programs "in the background" to compress and decompress tarfiles.

"Unmaximize" the current terminal emulation window by clicking on the middle button in the top right of the window ;

move and size this window so that it only fills the top two thirds of the screen ; make the window as wide as the screen ;

]# top   # this command will be described in detail later in the course

The top command shows the top processes that are running in memory in "real time". These are the processes that are using the most processing time.

If necessary, move the bottom border of the window (not the entire window) down so that you can see eight lines of output below the column headings, such as PID, USER and PRI. The names of the processes running in memory appear below the COMMAND heading at the right. The process (program) named top should appear below the COMMAND heading.

open another terminal emulation window ; su to root ;

move the bottom border of the window up so that it can only display about four lines ;

now move and size this window so that it only fills the area at the bottom of the screen, below the top window ; both windows should be visible and they should not overlap one another.

 Viewing the Use of the gzip Program by the tar Program

The following command tars and compresses the contents of doc directory structure below /usr/share into a tarfile. The doc directory structure is only being used in this example to provide the tar command with enough data so that you can see the tar and gzip programs in the top window. A smaller amount of data may not allow you enough time to see this.

These steps are being done to demonstrate that the tar command uses the gzip program "in the background" to compress an archive when the -z option of the tar command is used. Immediately after running the following command, look for "tar" and "gzip" in the top window, below the COMMAND heading at the right.

Your current directory should be /root. The next command will take roughly four minutes or less, depending on your system.

```
]# tar  -cPzvf  /home/archives/test.tar.gz  /usr/share/doc
```

The activity of the tar command appears in the bottom window and the activity of processes in memory appears in the top window.

The tar and gzip programs should appear below the COMMAND heading in the top window. The -P option was used in the above command, but is not used when extracting files from the tarfile below because we do not need to restore these files into the absolute path.

```
]# ls  -lh  /home/archives/test.tar.gz
```

write the size of the file here: _____

The next command will restore the doc directory structure (that was below /usr/share) into your current directory (/root). Watch for "tar" and "gzip" in the top window after running the command below. Once you have seen that the gzip program is used to decompress the tarfile, press Ctrl+c to stop the tar command.

Make sure your current directory is the /root directory and not the / directory.

```
]# tar  -xzvf  /home/archives/test.tar.gz

]# ls                # you are in /root - the usr directory should appear

]# ls  -lR  usr      # some of the data from the archive was restored in /root
```

Do not use a / in the command below and run the following command from the /root directory, not the / directory.

```
]# rm  -rf  usr
```

 Viewing the Use of the bzip2 Program by the tar Program

Now you will replace the "z" in the last two tar commands with a "j" so that the bzip2 program appears in the top window rather than the gzip program. Be sure to use the correct suffix on the tarfile below and watch for the "tar" and "bzip2" in the top window. The next command will take roughly seven minutes or less, depending on your system.

```
]# tar  -cPjvf  /home/archives/test.tar.bz2  /usr/share/doc

]# ls  -lh  /home/archives/test.tar.bz2
```

write the size of the file here: _____

Compare the sizes of the last two tarfiles that you created. The bzip2 program provides better compression than the gzip program and also takes longer to compress files.

The next command will restore the doc directory structure into your current directory (/root). Watch for "tar" and "gzip" in the top window. Once you have seen that the gzip program is used to decompress the tarfile, press Ctrl+c to stop the tar command.

Make sure your current directory is the /root directory and not the / directory.

```
]# tar -xjvf /home/archives/test.tar.bz2
```

```
]# ls -lR usr        # some of the data from the archive was restored
```

The usr directory is currently in the /root directory. Do not use a / in the command below and run the following command from the /root directory, not the / directory.

```
]# rm -rf usr
```

Without changing directory, remove the test.tar.gz and test.tar.bz2 files from /home/archives.

Do the steps to shut your system down.

Section Review

1. Select the filename suffix that is commonly used when the tar command is used to create a tarfile that is not compressed.

   ○ A. .gz
   ○ B. .tar
   ○ C. .tfi
   ○ D. .bak

2. Select two statements that are correct regarding files that have the .tar.gz suffix.

   ☐ A. they are compressed
   ☐ B. they are decompressed
   ☐ C. they have been created with the tar command
   ☐ D. they always include software utilities

3. Which set of options precede the name of a .tar file so that you can view the contents of it in as much detail as possible?

   ○ A. -tvf
   ○ B. -xf
   ○ C. -zdf
   ○ D. -jvf

4. The gunzip command can be used to decompress a file that has the filename suffix of .tar.gz, but it cannot be used to extract files from the resulting .tar file. T F

5. A directory structure containing data files has been tarred and compressed with the gzip utility and has the .tar.gz suffix. Which option of the tar command must be used with the -t, -v and -f options to view the contents of the tarfile?

   ○ A. -x
   ○ B. -z
   ○ C. -c
   ○ D. -j

6. Select two filename suffixes that are most commonly seen when looking for Linux tarballs that are available for download from the internet.

    ☐ A.   .tar
    ☐ B.   .rgm
    ☐ C.   .tar.gz
    ☐ D.   .tar.bz2

7. When you use the tar command to create a tarfile and do not specify a filename suffix, the appropriate suffix is automatically appended to the name of the tarfile that is created. T F

8. In addition to using the -c, -v and -f options used to create a tarfile, select the option that is used to cause a tarfile to be compressed with the bzip2 program.

    ○ A.   -j
    ○ B.   -x
    ○ C.   -z
    ○ D.   -b

9. Which two filename suffixes are commonly used for tarfiles that have been compressed with the -z option of the tar command?

    ☐ A.   .tar.bz2
    ☐ B.   .tar.gz
    ☐ C.   .tar
    ☐ D.   .tgz

10. All tarfiles are compressed. T F

11. When using the tar command with the -P option to restore from an archive, which option is used if you do not want to overwrite existing files?

    ○ A.   **-s** for **stop**
    ○ B.   **-h** for **halt**
    ○ C.   **-k** for **keep**
    ○ D.   **-w** for **whoops**

12. Select the filename suffix that is commonly used for tarfiles that have been compressed with the -j option of the tar command.

    ○ A. .tar.gz
    ○ B. .tgz
    ○ C. .tar
    ○ D. .tar.bz2

13. Which option of the tar command precedes the filename of the tarfile?

    ○ A. -z
    ○ B. -j
    ○ C. -f
    ○ D. -v

14. Select two programs that are used "in the background" when the -z and -j options of the tar comand are used.

    ☐ A. zip
    ☐ B. bzip2
    ☐ C. tzip
    ☐ D. gzip

Chapter 14: The X Window System

In this chapter, you will learn about the operations of the X Window System, its main software components and recent versions. You will also learn about important X directories, X files, man pages and documentation files.

The XF86Config file is the main configuration file for the X Server. Settings that configure X are made in several "sections" of this file and the purpose of each of these sections is described.

The XF86Config file can be configured manually with a text editor or it can be modified by using several utilities. An overview of the utilities that can be used to configure the XF86Config file is provided here.

Some utilities cannot be used to configure X while X is running, and X must be started after configuration changes have been made so that the changes can take effect. Therefore, a procedure for stopping X, configuring it, and then starting it again without rebooting a system is detailed.

The following commands are described in this chapter and most of them are also used during the Hands-On Exercises:

XFree86 -configure	create a "basic" XF86Config.new configuration file
xf86config	create an XF86Config file
Xconfigurator	modify XF86Config settings
setup	modify keyboard and mouse settings in XF86Config
X -showconfig	display X Server name and version number
xset -q	display the current X Server configuration settings
init	change to a different runlevel
runlevel	display the current and previous runlevels

During the Hands-On Exercises, you will look at the main X directories and X files, configure X using a GUI utility and configure X by manually editing the XF86Config file.

The X Window System

> ### Topics Covered in this Chapter
>
> Provide an overview of the X Window System and its main components
> Learn about the X Server and the XFree86 Project
> Understand the latest two major software versions of X
> Discuss important X directories and X binary, script and text configuration files
> Discover the purpose of each of the sections in the XF86Config file
> Learn about the utilities that can be used to configure X
> Provide a procedure for stopping X, configuring it and restarting it
> You will look at the contents of the main X directories, run a GUI utility
> to configure X and manually edit the XF86Config file

The X Window System (a.k.a. **X**, X11, X Windows) is the standard underlying set of *graphic* software components that provide basic graphic operations to UNIX and Linux operating systems. This provides developers with a standard set of functions that are used to build GUI software, such as the GNOME and KDE desktops.

X Windows was created by a group of over one hundred companies, including HP, IBM, Intel and Sun Microsystems. This group is called The Open Group (TOG) and you can find out more about this group at: http://www.opengroup.org.

X.org is the organization that is dedicated to maintaining the X Window System code (program source code) and the engineering of future enhancements to it. This organization periodically provides official updates of the source code to the general public free of charge. It also governs the X11R6 specifications, which are the specifications of the X Window System.

The X Window System provides the foundation for a GUI desktop, such as GNOME or KDE. The GUI desktop works with a window manager to provide the "look and feel" of the desktop environment.

You can get more information on the X Window System at: http://www.x.org.

The benefit of this standard X Window System is that developers can create *portable* software applications that are designed to run in a network environment. This allows developers to create a single application and have it run on a huge variety of systems with different video display hardware, rather than having to create different versions of the application for different hardware environments.

Window Managers

A window manager is used with your GUI desktop to control the appearance, placement and other characteristics of a window. Among other things, a window manager allows you to specify how windows are resized and how to switch between windows. Sawfish and Window Maker are popular window managers and there are several others.

 GNOME is the default GUI desktop for this distribution and the Metacity window manager is the default window manager. Some distributions use GNOME and Sawfish as the defaults and others use a different default GUI desktop and window manager.

For detailed information on over thirty window managers and comparisons between them, you can go to the "Window Managers for X" site at: http://www.xwinman.org.

The benefit of window managers is that they allow several different GUI desktops to be used with Linux (one of each at a time). This gives you the capability to choose your own desktop appearance and functionality, to get the look and feel that you want and need!

The X Protocol

In the mid-1980s, the X Protocol was developed to provide a standard graphical user interface for Unix systems, and this protocol also works for Linux systems. The X Protocol provides a common windowing system that works on virtually all Unix/Linux platforms, from huge mainframe computers to minicomputers to PCs!

The X protocol works in a client-server relationship. Any application, such as a utility or program, that makes a request of the X Server is called an X Client. The X Client makes a request for a display operation, such as opening a window, and the X Server performs the tasks required to deliver the requested display operation.

X runs on a system as a server. X Clients and the X Server are commonly running on the same system. However, systems can be clients that are not running the X Server and are remotely accessing an X Server that is on a different system.

For example, a terminal is accessing a remote server through some type of cabling system. The terminal is not running an X Server. The remote system is running an X Server. The terminal can run X Clients that are accessing the remote X Server.

The X Server

The X Server is the main component of the X Window System. XFree86 is an implementation of the X Window system and includes drivers for your graphics card and support for your monitor, graphics card, keyboard and mouse.

X Server (a.k.a. X11 Server) software manages the monitor, graphics card, keyboard and mouse. When you are using Linux on a PC, the X Server (XFree86) software can be set up to run automatically when the PC boots up. This is the usual default setting when X is installed on a system.

When you work at a Linux PC and run a GUI application, such as a word processor, your application is an X Client of the X Server software *that is running in your PC.* In this case, the X Server is not server software that is running on a remote network server; it is a server that is running in your PC.

As of this writing, the current version of the **X** Window System is Version **11**, Release **6.6** (X11R6.6). The "**X11**" in the version number of "**X11**R6.6" appears as a directory below the /etc directory (/etc/**X11**). The X Window System is sometimes referred to as "X11".

The "**X11R6**", in the version number of "**X11R6**.6" appears as a directory below the /usr directory (/usr/**X11R6**).

The directory names of X11 and X11R6 are used because they follow the naming convention of the X11R6 specification of the X Window System. These directories hold program and configuration files for the X Window System and are described in detail below.

An X session is started when your system boots and runs X. This is also referred to as a "session". When a user logs out, the session ends.

The X Server and the XFree86 Project

The XFree86 Project produces the X Server named XFree86. This is a freely distributed open source implementation of the X Window System, as defined by the X11R6 specifications of X.org.

XFree86 consists of the X Server software, X Client software, and software documentation. In the name XFree86, the X is for the X Window System, the Free is because it is distributed for free (including the source code) and the 86 represents any x86 type of PC processor, such as a 486 or Pentium. However, XFree86 also works on Alpha, PowerPC, Sparc and other platforms.

As of this writing, the most current version of XFree86 is 4.3.0. We will use 4.x when generally referring to any version of 4. The previous version of XFree86 was 3.3.6. We will use 3.x when generally referring to any version of 3. Version 3.3.6 is still available and is used in the rare instances when a graphics card or monitor does not work with version 4.x.

XFree86 Version 3.x

As of this writing, the latest 3.x version of XFree86 is 3.3.6. There will be no *updates* or additional drivers for this version. If there is an *upgrade* for 3.3.6 it will be to version 3.3.7 and it will only be a "bug fix" upgrade.

XFree86 Version 4.x

As of this writing, the latest 4.x version of XFree86 is 4.3.0. If your graphics card is not supported by version 4.x, you can: change to version 3.x, upgrade your graphics card to one that is supported, or wait until your card is supported by 4.x. The XFree86 Development Team (of the XFree86 Project) is now only focusing on version 4.x of XFree86.

The graphics card driver that you get with any version of XFree86 may not be an "accelerated" (fast) driver. However, the web site of the manufacturer of your graphics card may provide an accelerated driver for your card. We recommend that you go to the web site of your manufacturer and see if they have drivers for your card that are better than those provided by XFree86. If you install a driver that was specifically designed by the manufacturer of your graphics card, you may find a dramatic improvement in the speed of your video display!

You can download the current XFree86 Server, versions 3.x and 4.x, as well as XFree86 drivers (for graphics cards) from http://www.xfree86.org. However, whenever you are downloading software that *may* also be provided by your distribution of Linux, such as graphics card driver software, check the web site of your distribution first. It is usually better to download the software from the web site of your distribution (i.e. Red Hat, Debian or other), because the version at their site may have been modified (optimized) to work with your distribution.

For example, if you are using the Red Hat distribution of Linux and need to download a current XFree86 driver, and the driver is at http://www.xfree86.org as well as at http://www.redhat.com, then download it from http://www.redhat.com. This will ensure a smooth installation when using XFree86.

If the web site of your graphics card manufacturer has drivers for XFree86, contact them and ask if their drivers will work better than those provided by the web site of your distribution.

Whenever you download software, be sure to get the instructions for installing the software from the web site.

For more information on XFree86, the XFree86 Project and hardware that is supported by this software, you can go to: http://www.xfree86.org.

The X Directories

/usr/X11R6

The X11R6 directory (below /usr) is the parent directory for various subdirectories that contain X files. The names of the directories indicate the types of files in the directory.

For example, the **bin** directory contains many **bin**ary files for X. The **lib** directory contains **lib**rary files, the **man** directory contains **man** page files, and the **doc** directory contains X **doc**umentation.

Some of the subdirectories of /usr/X11R6 are described below.

/usr/X11R6/bin

This directory contains the main X Server program file, named XFree86, some X configuration utilities, and X Client files (X GUI programs).

The bin directory contains a file named X, which is a symlink to the XFree86 (X Server) binary. The bin directory also contains X GUI programs, such as xclock, xclipboard and xcalc.

Keep in mind that any application that runs on an X server is called an X Client. The directory path of /usr/X11R6/bin is in the PATH for all users. This allows all users to run the X GUI programs. Users may be able to run X configuration utilities that are in the bin directory, but they will not have permission to write to the XF86Config (configuration) file in /etc/X11. Therefore, users are not able to make configuration changes.

/usr/X11R6/include

This directory contains software development files for the X Window System.

/usr/X11R6/lib

This directory holds **library files** for the X Window System. These files provide program code for commonly used software routines.

Library files contain program code in binary form. They are kept in library directories, that usually have the name lib. These files provide a collection of commonly used software routines (program code) to software programs. More than one program will use the code in a library. This is an efficient method of providing common code to multiple programs because it saves disk space and RAM.

/usr/X11R6/lib/X11

This directory is the parent directory for directories that provide support for functions of the window manager.

/usr/X11R6/lib/X11/doc

This directory is used for documentation ("readme files") related to the X Window System. Most of the files in this directory begin with "README" and have a filename suffix that describes the contents of the file.

For example, the file named README provides an overview of XFree86 version 4.x. The file named DESIGN is approximately 100 pages and describes the design of XFree86 version 4.x and information on the settings in XF86Config (the X configuration file). The file named README.ati describes using the XFree86 ATI driver for ATI video adapters (graphics cards).

/usr/X11R6/man

The man directory is the parent directory for eight subdirectories named man[1-8] (i.e. man1, man2, up to man8). These subdirectories contain many man pages regarding X.

For example, you can display information on the XFree86 server by running: man XFree86. This shows the contents of the file named XFree86.1x.gz, in the man1 directory, below /usr/X11R6/man/.

Running: man XF86Config provides a description of the XF86Config configuration file, including settings that can be made in "sections" of the file (as described further below).

/etc/X11

The X11 directory, and some subdirectories of this directory, hold all of the default configuration files for all of the components of the X Window System. The main XFree86 configuration file is XF86Config and this file is in /etc/X11.

Users can create text files in their home directories that override some of the default configuration settings, such as their default desktop.

The XF86Config Configuration File

The X Window System uses the X Server named XFree86. This server is configured by the settings in the XF86Config text file. Settings in this file can be specified by running various Linux utilities and settings can also be specified by manually editing this file.

The easiest way to modify the settings in your XF86Config file is to use a GUI utility that is available from the menu on the desktop. However, you may need to manually edit this file to specify settings that cannot be selected in a utility. Therefore, all of the sections in XF86Config are described below so that you will know how to modify them manually if you need to.

Comments in the XF86Config File

The XF86Config file uses the # sign to indicate the start of a comment and there are many comments in this file. Some comments describe the contents of the file and other comments are statements in the file that configure settings. If the # sign is removed from the left of a statement, then the settings of the statement will be used.

For example, the following comment describes the file:

    # File generated by anaconda.

The following comment is a statement that can be used to configure a setting:

    #   Option "AutoRepeat" "500 5"

The system will treat the above statement as a comment until the # sign is removed. If the # sign is removed, then the settings of the statement will be used. This allows commonly used settings to be included in the file and to be available for use by removing the # sign.

Sections in the XF86Config File

The XF86Config file has "sections" that begin with the heading of **Section "<section-name>"** and end with **EndSection**. Between these two headings are indented statements that provide settings for the X Server.

The following is an example of a "section" of XF86Config. This settings in this section are for a PS/2 type of mouse.

```
Section "InputDevice"
        Identifier          "Mouse0"
        Driver              "mouse"
        Option              "Device"  "/dev/input/mice"
        Option              "Protocol"  "IMPS/2"
        Option              "Emulate3Buttons"  "yes"
        Option              "ZAxisMapping"  "4 5"
EndSection
```

The "<section-name>" is "InputDevice". The statements that are indented below the section name specify the type of input device and provide "parameters" (settings) for the device. The word Identifier specifies that the device named "Mouse0" is being configured. Driver is used to specify the software driver named "mouse". The section ends with the word EndSection.

Manually Editing the XF86Config File

To manually edit the XF86Config file in /etc/X11: open it with a text editor, modify the settings that you need to change, or add new settings, and then save the file.

The XF86Config file exists in /etc/X11. Always back up this file before editing it or running a utility that will modify it. Use the cp command to copy the file to the same name, but with a .bak or other filename suffix. You may want to copy the file to the same directory or a different directory.

You need to "su to root" to be able to write changes to the XF86Config file, but you don't need to stop X to edit this file. However, you do need to stop X and start it again to have the changes take effect.

Be very careful when manually editing the XF86Config file. A simple error could stop your X Server from loading.

For example, if you have typed "Optioin" rather "Option", your X Server may not load. If your X Server does not load after manually editing a configuration file, check it for errors. If you can not find any errors, put your backup of the file in /etc/X11 and then try to load the X Server again (by logging in again or running startx).

During the Linux installation, XFree86 version 4.x was installed by default. At this time, the installation routine attempted to configure XFree86 to work with your graphics card, monitor, keyboard and mouse. Most configuration problems occur with graphics cards and monitors. If you have an older graphics card or monitor, XFree86 version 4.x may not work correctly (but this is rare). If you cannot configure XFree86 version 4.x with the Linux utilities or by manually editing the configuration file, you may need to install XFree86 version 3.x.

For information on installing XFree86 version 3.x, go to: http:// www.xfree86.org or the web site for your distribution of Linux.

For information on the sections in XF86Config and editing the settings in this file, see man 5x XF86Config.

The Sections of XF86Config

The XF86Config file consists of the following sections and examples of important sections are provided below.

ServerFlags

This section is used to specify miscellaneous X server settings. It is not created by default and if it is created, settings in it may be overridden by statements in the ServerLayout section.

The Ctrl+Alt+Backspace key combination can be used to kill the X Server. This immediately stops the X Server and any clients (GUI applications) that are running on it. Any work that has not been saved will be lost.

The Ctrl+Alt+Keypad-Plus and Ctrl+Alt+Keypad-Minus keys can be used to "cycle" forward or backward through monitor resolutions, when multiple resolutions have been specified. This changes the monitor resolution, but changing the resolution may result in a display that does not show the entire desktop.

For example, if you change to a lower resolution, then the desktop will be larger than the screen and you will not be able to view the entire desktop on the screen. To see areas of the desktop that are not currently in view, you move your mouse cursor to the area that is not shown and it will "pan" into view. This is called "desktop panning".

If you want to do "desktop panning" then you will likely want to be able to use the Ctrl+Alt+Keypad-Plus and Ctrl+Alt+Keypad-Minus keys can be used to "cycle" forward or backward through monitor resolutions. However, if you do not want users to change to resolutions that stop the system from displaying the entire desktop, you may want to disable the Ctrl+Alt+Keypad-Plus and Ctrl+Alt+Keypad-Minus keys.

The ServerFlags section can be used to prevent a user from stopping a server with Ctrl+Alt+Backspace and to prevent cycling through monitor resolutions with the Ctrl+Alt+Keypad-Plus and Ctrl+Alt+Keypad-Minus keys.

You may want to disable the use of the Ctrl+Alt+Backspace key combination as described below. However, before doing this, be sure that your X Server and all other components of the system are working correctly.

The Ctrl+Alt+Backspace key combination can be useful at times to shut down the X Server and many users will never use this key combination. You may want to tell them *not* to use it, so that they don't accidentally lose work!

To prevent a user from stopping the X Server with Ctrl+Alt+Backspace, add the following text to XF86Config:

```
Section "ServerFlags"
        Option "DontZap"  "on"
EndSection
```

To prevent a user from cycling through monitor resolutions with the Ctrl+Alt+Keypad-Plus and Ctrl+Alt+Keypad-Minus keys, put the following in the ServerFlags section:

```
Option "DontZoom"  "on"
```

ServerLayout

This section is used to specify settings for the X Server when it starts. An example is below:

```
Section "ServerLayout"
        Identifier    "Anaconda Configured"
        Screen 0      "Screen0"   0 0
        InputDevice "Mouse0"  "CorePointer"
        InputDevice "Keyboard0"  "CoreKeyboard"
EndSection
```

The Identifier heading shows that the server is configured and the Screen heading identifies the default screen to be used. Some systems have more than one monitor attached.

There are two InputDevice statements and this is the quantity most commonly found. The first statement is for the mouse and the second for the keyboard. CorePointer and CoreKeyboard indicate that the Mouse0 and Keyboard0 devices are the preferred devices.

Files

This section is used to specify files that are used when the X Server starts. Below is an example:

```
Section "Files"
        FontPath    "unix/:7100"
EndSection
```

The FontPath statement specifies the settings for fonts.

Module

This section is used to specify the names of **modules** to load from the /usr/X11R6/lib/modules directory structure. Do not manually edit this section to "comment out" or delete existing statements that load the default modules.

Modules (a.k.a. loadable modules) are driver files and other types of files that add functionality, services and features to the X server. They can be loaded into memory to be used when they are needed and unloaded when not needed. This provides tremendous flexibility and reduces the overall memory that is required.

InputDevice

This section is used to specify settings for input devices. There can be more than one InputDevice section. Each one is used to specify settings for an input device, such as a mouse, keyboard or drawing tablet. There are usually two of these sections, one for your keyboard and one for your mouse. Others can be added for additional devices.

Below is an example of this section for a standard PS/2 mouse attached to a PC:

```
Section "InputDevice"
        Identifier      "Mouse0"
        Driver          "mouse"
        Option          "Device"  "/dev/input/mice"
        Option          "Protocol"  "IMPS/2"
        Option          "Emulate3Buttons"  "yes"
        Option          "ZAxisMapping"  "4 5"
EndSection
```

The Option of "Device" "/dev/input/mice" specifies the path to device file. The Option of "Protocol" "IMPS/2" specifies that the IMPS/2 protocol be used for the mouse.

Linux can work with a three button mouse, but a lot of PC mice are just two button mice. Pressing both mouse buttons at once becomes the equivalent of pressing the third mouse button. The setting of Option "Emulate3Buttons" "yes" is used to specify that a two button mouse emulate (act like) a three button mouse, when both buttons are pressed at once.

There is a file named README.mouse in /usr/X11R6/lib/X11/doc that describes setting up serial, bus and PS/2 mouse support for XFree86 version 4.x. It describes settings for many different types of mice, with examples of statements that are used in the InputDevice section for these mice.

Monitor

This section is used to specify settings for your monitor. There can be more than one Monitor section if you are using more than one monitor. The VendorName and ModelName statements are optional.

An example of a Monitor section is shown below:

```
Section "Monitor"
        Identifier          "Monitor0"
        VendorName          "Monitor Vendor"
        ModelName           "Monitor Model"
        HorizSync           30.0 - 67.0
        VertRefresh         50.0 - 120.0
        Option              "dpms"
EndSection
```

Be very careful when manually editing the Monitor section. Incorrect settings could damage or destroy your graphics card or monitor. This is less likely to occur on current hardware than on legacy hardware.

In particular, be sure that you are specifying the correct range of values for HorizSync and VertRefresh if you are editing this section. See the manual for your monitor for correct range of settings to use.

Device

This section is used to specify graphics card settings. There may be more than one Device section if more than one graphics card is in the system.

The example below is for a system that is using an ATI graphics card. The Driver setting is used to specify the driver file to be used for the card.

```
Section "Device"
        Identifier          "ATI Mach64 3D RAGE II"
        Driver              "ati"
        VendorName          "ATI Mach64 3D RAGE II"
        BoardName           "ATI Mach64 3D RAGE II"
EndSection
```

Screen

This section is used to indicate to the system which graphics card works with which monitor. This section "binds" (combines) graphics card(s) to monitors(s), so that the server knows which components to use together. Remember that there can be more than one graphics card in a system and more than one monitor attached to a graphics card. There is always one of these sections and there may be more if needed.

In the Section "Screen" below, the DefaultDepth setting is 16, which represents 16 bpp (bits per pixel) and produces 64,000 colors. This section has three SubSections named Subsection "Display" and each of these specify settings for Depth and Modes.

```
Section "Screen"
        Identifier "Screen0"
        Device    "ATI Mach64 3D RAGE II"
        Monitor   "Monitor0"
        DefaultDepth    16
        SubSection "Display"
            Depth    24
            Modes    "1024x768" "800x600" "640x480"
        EndSubSection
        SubSection "Display"
            Depth    16
            Modes    "800x600" "640x480"
        EndSubSection
        SubSection "Display"
            Depth    8
            Modes    "640x480"
        EndSubSection
    EndSection
```

When **DefaultDepth** is **16** (as shown above), then the SubSection "Display" that shows **Depth 16** will be used for the Depth and Modes (resolutions) settings. The first resolution that appears at the right of Modes (below Depth 16) is used for the default resolution. Therefore, when DefaultDepth is 16, the default resolution will be 800x600.

The only other resolution for Depth 16 is 640x480. If you press Ctrl+Alt+Keypad-Plus, then the screen resolution becomes 640x480. If you press these keys again, the resolution will go back to 800x600.

If more than one screen resolution has been specified beside Modes, in Section "Screen", then the Ctrl+Alt+Keypad-Plus and Ctrl+Alt+Keypad-Minus key combinations can be used to "cycle" forward or backward from one screen resolution to another.

If you change to a lower resolution, then the desktop will be larger than the screen and you will not be able to view the entire desktop on the screen. To see areas of the desktop that are not currently in view, you move your mouse cursor to the area that is not shown and it will "pan" into view. This is called "desktop panning".

If you are using an application, such as a CAD (Computer Aided Design) program that is displaying a large amount of information on the screen, you may want to have all of the data "on the desktop", but you may not want to see all of the desktop at once. To see other areas of the desktop, you would use your mouse cursor to "pan" to areas that are not in view.

The DontZoom option of the ServerFlags can be used to stop someone from using the Ctrl+Alt+Keypad-Plus or Ctrl+Alt+Keypad-Minus keys to "cycle" through the existing screen resolutions.

Unless you have used the DontZoom option in the ServerFlags section, pressing the Ctrl+Alt+Keypad-Plus or Ctrl+Alt+Keypad-Minus keys will "cycle" through the screen resolutions that appear at the right of Modes. Pressing one of these key combinations once will change from the current resolution to the next resolution at the right.

You could run the GUI utility from the desktop that is used to specify depth and resolution settings and select other resolutions. Alternatively, you could manually edit XF86Config and add other valid resolutions beside the Modes setting (below Depth 16, or for any Depth) and these resolutions would become available to your system. The first resolution at the right of Modes becomes the default resolution that is used when X is started.

For the example Section "Screen" above, if you used a text editor and changed the DefaultDepth (not Depth) setting from 16 to 24, then the SubSection "Display" that shows Depth 24 will be used for the depth and resolution settings. The first resolution that appears at the right of Modes (below Depth 24) will be used for the default resolution. Therefore, the default resolution will be 1024x768.

The Ctrl+Alt+Backspace key combination is used to stop (kill) the X Server. If you manually edit XF86Config, log out (from the desktop), log in, and do not get the settings that you have specified, use the Ctrl+Alt+Backspace key combination to kill X and cause the server to automatically restart. This will force the system to use the new settings.

The /etc/inittab file has the following statement:

```
x:5:respawn:/etc/X11/prefdm  -nodaemon
```

The number **5** and the word **respawn** in the above statement causes X to automatically restart whenever you are in runlevel 5 and X is killed. More on this bebow.

DRI

This section is used to specify **DRI** (**D**irect **R**endering **I**nfrastructure) settings. DRI is used to provide support for 3D software programs so that they can use the accelerated capabilities of 3D graphics cards. This also applies to providing accelerated support for 2D graphics cards. The Module section (described earlier) is used to load a DRI module for these capabilities and the DRI section is used to specify settings for it.

If you are using DRI, you can find out more about specifying settings for this section in the README.DRI file in /usr/X11R6/lib/X11/doc directory

You can also find out more information about DRI at: http://dri.sourceforge.net.

Viewing Information on Your Current X Server

To see the settings for you current X Server, such as name and version number, run the following command:

```
X -showconfig
```

An example of the output of X -showconfig is shown below:

```
XFree86 Version 4.2.0 (Red Hat Linux release: 4.2.0-72) / X Window System
(protocol Version 11, revision 0, vendor release 6600)
Release Date: 23 January 2002
    If the server is older than 6-12 months, or if your card is
    newer than the above date, look for a newer version before
    reporting problems.  (See http://www.XFree86.Org/)
Build Operating System: Linux 2.4.18-11smp i686 [ELF]
Build Host: daffy.perf.redhat.com

Modular Loader present
OS Kernel:  Linux version 2.4.18-14 (bhcompile@stripples.devel.redhat.com)  (gcc version 3.2 200209)
03 (Red Hat Linux 8.0 3.2-7) #1 Wed Sep 4 13:35:50 EDT 2002
```

The main things to note in the above text are that the current X Server software running in the system is XFree86 and the version number is 4.2.0.

The current XFree86 Server configuration can be seen by using the following command:

```
xset -q
```

This displays settings for your keyboard, pointer (mouse or other pointing device), screen saver and font paths. An example of the output of xset -q is shown below:

```
Keyboard Control:
  auto repeat: on   key click percent: 0   LED mask: 00000000
  auto repeat delay: 500   repeat rate: 30
  auto repeating keys:    00ffffffdffffbbf
          fa9ffffffdffdff
          ffffffffffffffff
          ffffffffffffffff
  bell percent: 50   bell pitch: 400   bell duration: 100
Pointer Control:
  acceleration: 2/1   threshold: 4
Screen Saver:
  prefer blanking: yes   allow exposures: yes
  timeout:  0  cycle:  0
Colors:
  default colormap: 0x20   BlackPixel: 0   WhitePixel: 65535
Font Path:
  /home/cwest/.gnome2/share/cursor-fonts,unix/:7100,/home/cwest/.gnome2/share/fonts
Bug Mode: compatibility mode is disabled
DPMS (Energy Star):
  Standby: 7200   Suspend: 7200   Off: 14400
  DPMS is Enabled
Font cache:
  hi-mark (KB): 1024  low-mark (KB): 768  balance (%): 70
```

Using Utilities to Configure the X Server

You specified settings for your video card, monitor, mouse and keyboard during the installation of Linux and these settings are maintained in the XF86Config file in /etc/X11.

The installation routine usually does an excellent job of configuring the settings in the XF86Config file. However, after the installation you may discover that you need to modify the XF86Config file to accommodate a change in hardware or to add some settings.

You can either configure the XF86Config file by manually editing it, or you can use a software utility to modify the settings in this file. Manually editing XF86Config can be a bit tricky and may not be necessary if you are making a simple change, such as adding a new screen resolution. Fortunately, there are several software utilities that can be used to modify XF86Config.

You need to work as the root user (su to root) to run the non-GUI utilities that modify XF86Config or to manually edit this file. If you run a GUI utility from the desktop, you need to provide the password of the root user before you can access the utility.

Stopping the X Server

Some Linux utilities that modify XF86Config cannot be run when the X Server is running. Therefore, you must stop X prior to running these utilities.

Other Linux utilities that modify or create an XF86Config file can be run without stopping X, but you must stop and then start X to have the changes in the file take effect. If you manually edit XF86Config, you must also stop and then start X to have the changes take effect. You do not need to restart (reboot) a system to stop and start X.

Changing the Runlevel to Stop and Start X

Linux uses several runlevels and these are represented by the numbers 0 through 6. The runlevels are used to control the "mode" of the system and the (system) services that are being run. There is also a runlevel that is used to stop a system (runlevel 0) and another runlevel to reboot a system (runlevel 6).

Linux typically operates in either runlevel 3 (text mode) or runlevel 5 (GUI mode). When a system is "in" runlevel 3, X *is not* running and the system is in "text mode". In this case, you log into the system at a text login prompt and work at one or more virtual terminals.

When a system is "in" runlevel 5, X *is* running and the system is operating in "GUI (desktop) mode". Your system is currently set up to boot into runlevel 5 and start X. In this case, you log in at a GUI login screen and work in "GUI mode" (at a desktop). Runlevels are described in much more detail later.

You can use the init command at the shell prompt (typically at a virtual terminal) to change your current runlevel. When you are in runlevel 5 and run: init 3 the system will stop X, stop some of the services that are running, and change to runlevel 3 (text mode).

 Earlier versions of Linux used the telinit command to change from one runlevel to another. The telinit binary file has been replaced with the telinit symlink file, which points to the init command (binary).

You can also stop X by pressing the Ctrl+Alt+Backspace key combination while in GUI mode. However, a statement in the inittab file in /etc/ automatically causes X to start again and also causes the GUI login screen to appear.

The /etc/inittab text file contains the number **5** and the word "**respawn**" in the following statement:

    x:**5**:**respawn**:/etc/X11/prefdm -nodaemon

The above statement causes X to be restarted (respawned) when you are in runlevel **5**. If you install X during the installation process (and you did), then the system is set up to operate in runlevel 5 by default.

When you press Ctrl+Alt+Backspace and kill X, the number **5** and the word "**respawn**" in the above statement causes X to automatically start *if you are in runlevel 5* (which you are). Therefore, you must kill X without having it "respawn", or you will constantly be presented with the GUI login screen whenever you press Ctrl+Alt+Backspace.

Running: init 3 will change your system to runlevel 3, stop (kill) X and also stop some other services. This allows you to stop X and modify XF86Config without being presented with the GUI login screen.

A Procedure to Stop X, Modify the XF86Config File and Start X

The steps below are not used if you are running a GUI utility from the desktop menu to modify X settings.

The steps below allow you to stop X without having to reboot your system. Once X is stopped, you can either manually edit XF86Config, or run a utility to configure XF86Config, and then start X to have the changes take effect.

Save all of the work being done on the desktop. If you stop X while an application is running and your work has not been saved, you will lose the work.

Press Ctrl+Alt+F1 to go to virtual terminal 1.

Log in as a non-root user and then "su to root".

Run the command: init 3 to change into runlevel 3. This will kill X (shut down the GUI desktop) and will also cause a few system services to shut down; but the system will not be shut down. When the services have been shut down, there will be no more activity on the screen, but the prompt will not appear again until you press Enter.

Press Enter once the services have shut down so that the prompt appears again.

Change into the /etc/X11 directory and copy XF86Config to XF86Config.bak. You may want to copy the file to a new name in the same directory or to a different directory, such as directory that you have set up for important system files. You may also want to use a filename suffix other than .bak.

Do the steps to modify XF86Config by manually editing this file or by running a utility to modify the settings in it.

Run the command: init 5 to change into runlevel 5. This will start X and cause it to process the changes in the XF86Config file. It will also cause some services to start. You will then be presented with the GUI login screen.

Log in with a non-root user name and password. Your configuration changes should have taken effect. However, you are still logged in at virtual terminal 1 as the root user.

Go to virtual terminal 1 again and press Enter to so that the prompt appears again.

Run the command: exit to end the root user session and then run the command: logout to log out as the non-root user that you used to log in with at virtual terminal 1.

Press Alt+F7 to go to the desktop. Done!

Utilities That Can Be Used to Configure X

The utilities that can be used to configure XF86Config are described below. Some of these utilities cannot be run when X is running and this is indicated for each utility.

Using GUI Utilities to Configure X Settings

Monitor, video card, keyboard and mouse settings can be made from the desktop with the Display Settings, Keyboard, and Mouse Configuration (GUI) utilities. When you modify settings with these utilities, the changes are automatically written to the XF86Config file in /etc/X11. This is an easy alternative to manually editing the XF86Config file. However, although you can specify commonly modified settings with these utilities, you cannot specify all of the settings that can be made in XF86Config.

For example, the above GUI utilities will not allow you to specify the settings in the ServerFlags section of XF86Config that disable the Ctrl+Alt+Backspace, Ctrl+Alt+Keypad-Plus and Ctrl+Alt+Keypad-Minus keys.

The Display Settings GUI Utility

You can run the Display Settings GUI utility from the desktop to change the settings for your monitor resolution, color depth, monitor type and video card type.

The following steps take you to the Display Settings dialog box:

Menu ; System Settings ; Display

As with the Red Hat User Manager utility that you ran earlier, you must provide the password of the root user at the Query dialog box to be able to access the GUI utilities that modify the display, keyboard and mouse settings.

After changing settings at the Display Settings dialog box, such as changing the screen resolution, you must log out and then log in again for the changes to take effect.

The Display tab allows you to specify the resolution and color depth settings. Figure 14-1 shows the opening screen of the Display Settings dialog box with the Display tab selected.

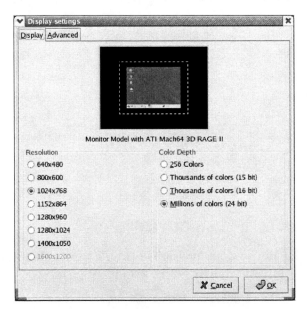

Figure 14-1 - The Display Settings dialog box with the Display tab selected

The Advanced tab allows you to specify monitor and video card settings. Figure 14-2 shows the Display Settings dialog box with the Advanced tab selected.

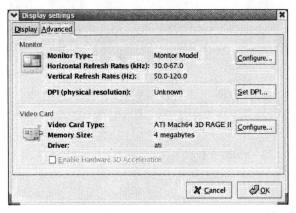

Figure 14-2 - The Display Settings dialog box with the Advanced tab selected

Below Monitor, the Configure... button allows you to specify the monitor model name, horizontal refresh rate and vertical refresh rate.

Also below Monitor, the Set DPI... button allows you to specify the DPI (physical resolution).

Below Video Card, the Configure... button allows you to specify the video card type, memory size, driver and special options.

The Keyboard GUI Utility

You can run the Keyboard GUI utility from the desktop to specify your keyboard type with the following steps:

> Menu ; System Settings ; Keyboard

Figure 14-3 shows the Keyboard dialog box.

Figure 14-3 - The
Keyboard dialog box

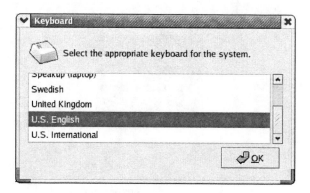

The Mouse Configuration GUI Utility

You can run the Mouse Configuration GUI utility from the desktop to specify settings for your mouse with the following steps:

> Menu ; System Settings ; Mouse

Figure 14-4 shows the Mouse Configuration dialog box.

Figure 14-4 - The Mouse
Configuration dialog box

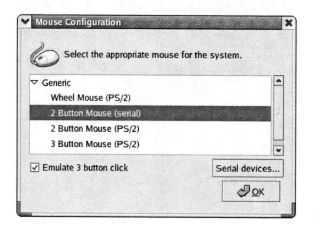

Using the -configure Option of XFree86 to Create a XF86Config.new File

The XFree86 binary (which provides the XFree86 Server) has a -configure option. If you want to quickly create a generic XF86Config file for XFree86 (a.k.a. X, X Windows) and do not want to use a configuration tool to create or edit the file, then you can run: XFree86 -configure to create this file. You may need to do this if your XF86Config file has been deleted and you do not have a backup.

The command: XFree86 -configure does not prompt you for any settings. It causes XFree86 to probe your graphics card, monitor and mouse, and put the settings that were determined from the probe into a file named XF86Config.new in /root. This provides a "minimal" or "basic" set of configuration settings that can be modified. After this, you can put XF86Config.new in /etc/X11 and rename this file as XF86Config (to remove the .new suffix on the filename).

You can only run the -configure option of XFree86 when X is not running.

The file named X in /usr/X11R6/bin is a symlink to the file named XFree86, in the same directory. The file named XFree86 is the main binary for X. The -configure option is available whenever you are using the XFree86 Server (regardless of your distribution).

Using xf86config to Create an XF86Config File

If you want to create an XF86Config file, but do not have access to a GUI utility, you can use the xf86config utility. This text-based utility simply displays text describing an item to be configured and then the options that can be selected for the item. You type in a response that corresponds with an option and then press Enter. This process continues until you have selected all of the options for your monitor, graphics card, keyboard and mouse. After responding to the prompts and prior to creating the XF86Config file, the utility prompts you for the path in which to create the file. This utility is run by typing xf86config at the command line and pressing Enter.

Figure 14-5 shows an example of the text that appears when the xf86config utility is run. To respond to the text, you type in a number that represents your mouse protocol type and press Enter. After this, you are prompted for more information regarding your mouse, keyboard, graphics card and monitor.

The xf86config utility does not "probe" your graphics card, monitor or mouse for their settings and therefore does not present you with suggested settings. You must know the make, model and various settings for your graphics card, monitor and mouse prior to running this utility.

Figure 14-5 - An
example of text output
from xf86config utility

```
First specify a mouse protocol type. Choose one from the following list:

1.  Microsoft compatible (2-button protocol)
2.  Mouse Systems (3-button protocol)
3.  Bus Mouse
4.  PS/2 Mouse
5.  Logitech Mouse (serial, old type, Logitech protocol)
6.  Logitech MouseMan (Microsoft compatible)
7.  MM Series
8.  MM HitTablet
9.  Microsoft IntelliMouse

If you have a two-button mouse, it is most likely of type 1, and if you have
a three-button mouse, it can probably support both protocol 1 and 2. There are
two main varieties of the latter type: mice with a switch to select the
protocol, and mice that default to 1 and require a button to be held at
boot-time to select protocol 2. Some mice can be convinced to do 2 by sending
a special sequence to the serial port (see the ClearDTR/ClearRTS options).

Enter a protocol number:
```

For your monitor, you will need to specify the vertical refresh rate and horizontal sync rate. If you specify monitor settings that are beyond the capabilities of your monitor, you may damage or destroy your monitor. This is less likely to occur on current hardware than on legacy hardware. If you need to use the xf86config utility, see your monitor manual for its settings.

The xf86config utility is a part of XFree86 and is available whenever you are using the XFree86 Server (regardless of your distribution).

X can be running when you use this utility, but as always, X must be started again to read the new settings.

The Xconfigurator Utility

As described above, Red Hat Linux version 8.0 now has GUI utilities that are run from the desktop to configure settings in the XF86Config file. Prior to version 8.0, the Xconfigurator utility was commonly used to configure X. Therefore, although this utility is no longer exists in 8.0, there will still be older systems on which you can run this utility to configure X. This utility is run by typing Xconfigurator at the command line and pressing Enter.

The Xconfigurator utility is a text-based GUI utility that probes your monitor and graphics card for their settings and offers these as settings for your system. It then allows you to specify alternative settings for these items and also allows you to specify depth and screen resolution (mode) settings. It does not allow you to modify mouse and keyboard settings. These settings can be modified by manually editing the XF86Config file or by using another utility.

The settings specified with Xconfigurator are automatically written to the XF86Config file in /etc/X11.

After specifying settings with this utility, you are asked if you want to test the settings. If you do not stop X prior to running this utility, you will not be able to test your new configuration settings. Therefore, stop X prior to running this utility so that you can test your new settings.

The Setup Utility

The Setup utility was described earlier, during the post-installation configuration section. It is run by typing setup at the command line and pressing Enter.

The setup utility has the Keyboard Configuration and Mouse Configuration menu options. These options allow you to quickly change the settings of these items. X does not need to be stopped prior to selecting these options, but it must be stopped and then started prior to the changes taking effect.

Hands-On Exercises

① Logging In to Work with X

Log in as cwest ; open and maximize a terminal emulation window ;
do not su to root ;

change into the X11R6 directory below /usr ; this is the parent directory
for various subdirectories that contain X files ;

get a long listing ; change into the bin directory.

② Viewing Files in /usr/X11R6/bin

```
]#  echo  $PATH      # /usr/X11R6/bin is in the PATH - also for the root user

]#  less  .          # the . (dot) used with less represents the
                     # current directory
```

scroll down until you can see X ; this is a symlink to XFree86 ;

look for the XFree86 binary ; notice the size of this file ; this is the X
Server binary ;

look for the startx script file ; when X is not running, this file can be
used to start X ;

look for xf86config ; this is a utility for configuring X ; quit out of less ;

```
]#  ls  -l  x*  |  less    # use a lower case "x" with the * (wildcard character)
```

look for xcalc, xclipboard and xclock ; these are GUI X programs.

③ Running X Client Programs

Programs that you run "on" an X Server are X Clients.

```
]#  xcalc              # the X calculator appears
```

Alt+Tab to the terminal emulation window ; the prompt did not appear
because you did not use an & (ampersand) at the right of the command ;

press Ctrl+C to get the prompt back ; this stops the xcalc program (process) ;

]# xcalc &   # the calculator *and* the prompt now appear

Alt+Tab to the terminal emulation window ; repeat the above step to run the xclipboard and xclock programs ;

minimize the terminal emulation window ;

move the calculator to the far right of the screen ; move the clock to the middle of the screen ;

close all three of these programs ; Alt+Tab to the terminal emulation window.

④ Viewing Files in /usr/X11R6/man

Without specifying a full path, change into the man directory, which is parallel to your current directory ;

get a long listing ; these are the man page directories for X ;

]# find -name *.gz | nl | less   # get a listing of all of the man
                                  # pages for X

at the right of ./man1/, look for XFee86, Xserver and xf86config ;

/XF86Config   # search for "XF86Config" - this file is in man5

press End   # there are a lot of man pages for X!

quit out of less.

⑤ Viewing Some of the Man Pages for X

Change to the home directory of the cwest user.

The X man pages can be viewed by any user from any directory.

]# man X   # this man page provides an overview of X

]# man X.Org   # the X.Org and X Project Team are described
                     # notice the full members at the bottom

]# man XStandards   # this "page" describes the X standards

Viewing the Man Page for the XF86Config File

The man page for the XF86Config file describes the file and the settings that can be made in it.

]# man XF86Config

/serverflags   # search for "serverflags"

press n to go to the occurrence of serverflags ;

/dontzap   # read the description of Option "DontZap"
                      # also read the description of Option "DontZoom"

 ### Viewing Some Documentation Files in /usr/X11R6/lib/X11/doc

The /usr/X11R6/lib/X11/doc directory is used for documentation ("readme files") related to the X Window System.

]# cd /usr/X11R6/lib/X11/doc ; less .

Several documentation files appear and most of them are prefixed with "README". Notice that there are files named DESIGN, README and README.mouse.

]# less README   # provides an overview of XFree86

]# less DESIGN   # describes changes between the 3.x and 4.x X Server

]# less README.mouse

This file describes setting up many different types of mice, with examples of statements that are used in the InputDevice section of XF86Config.

]# less README.ati

This file describes using the XFree86 ATI driver for ATI video adapters (graphics cards).

8 Changing Into /usr/X11R6/bin

]# pwd   # your current path should be /usr/X11R6/lib/X11/doc

change up three directory levels ; your current path should be /usr/X11R6 ;

change into the bin directory below the current directory ;

run the command to see your current path, which should be /usr/X11R6/bin ;

```
]# echo $PATH          # all users have /usr/X11R6/bin in the PATH
]# whereis startx      # startx is in the current directory
]# file startx         # this is a script that can be used to start X
```

⑨ Viewing the Current Settings for X

```
]# whereis X           # X is in the current directory
]# file X              # this file is a symlink to the XFree86 binary
]# whereis XFree86      # X and XFree86 are both in /usr/X11R6/bin
]# X -showconfig       # the same as running:  XFree86 -showconfig
```

This shows the current X Server version number and release date.

```
]# whereis xset ; file xset    # xset is a binary in the current directory
]# xset -q
```

This displays settings for your keyboard, pointer (mouse or other pointing device), screen saver fonts.

⑩ Viewing the XF86Config File in /etc/X11

```
]# cd /etc/X11 ; ls -l XF*     # the XF86Config text file is the main
                               # Free86 configuration file
]# less XF86Config
```

Scroll through this file and notice the name of each "Section". A section named ServerFlags does not currently exist in this file.

Scroll up until you can see the top of the "Screen" section.

The setting for DefaultDepth (not Depth) is your current color depth. Below SubSection "Display", look for the SubSection that matches your DefaultDepth. The Modes setting below Depth shows the resolutions that are currently available.

During the installation of Linux you were asked to select the resolution of 800x600. Other resolutions may also appear. In the steps below, you will select at least one more resolution for your system.

Write your current DefaultDepth and Modes below.

DefaultDepth: _____   Mode(s): _____

Quit out of less ; close all terminal emulation windows and programs.

All of the steps that you have done so far have been done as the cwest user.

⑪ Using the Display Settings GUI Utility

Menu ; System Tools ; the Display, Keyboard and Mouse menu items appear ; selecting these items runs GUI utilities to configure X ;

Display ; type in the password for the root user at the Query dialog box.

The item selected below Color Depth should match the DefaultDepth setting that you wrote down above.

You wrote down your current Modes setting(s) above. If 640x480 is already one of your current Modes, then select a resolution that you do not currently have as one of your Modes in the step below. Do not select a resolution that your monitor is not capable of displaying.

Below resolution, select 640x480 ; OK ; read the Information dialog box ; OK ;

Menu ; Log Out ; Log Out ; OK ;

the GUI login screen should appear and your screen resolution should have changed.

⑫ Viewing the Changes to Your System

Log in as the cwest user ; your desktop size currently matches your screen resolution (i.e. you should currently be able to see all of your desktop) ;

open a terminal emulation window ; use less to view the XF86Config file in /etc/X11 ;

scroll down to the section named "Screen" ; notice your DefaultDepth ; look for the Depth setting that matches this ; below this and beside Modes, the new resolution of 640x480 should appear ;

if you had a setting of 800x600, it has likely been removed ; quit out of less.

Changing to a Higher Resolution

Run the Display Settings GUI utility again ; do not change your Color Depth ;

select 800x600 ; you may need to move your mouse cursor to the side border of the dialog box and move it up so that you can see the OK button ; OK ; OK ;

use less to look at the "Screen" section in your XF86Config file again ; you will likely have two resolutions now (800x600 and 640x480) ;

quit out of less ; close the terminal emulation window ; log out and then log in as cwest again.

Your screen resolution should have changed to 800x600 and all of the desktop should be visible on the screen.

Using Ctrl+Alt+Keypad-Plus and Ctrl+Alt+Keypad-Minus Key Combinations

Use the + (plus) and - (minus) keys on the numeric keypad at the right of your keyboard when you see "Keypad-Plus" and "Keypad-Minus", respectively below.

Press the Ctrl+Alt+Keypad-Plus key combination ; your screen resolution changes ;

If you only have the resolutions of 640x480 and 800x600, then you are currently at 640x480. The entire desktop is not likely visible on the screen.

Move your mouse cursor to the bottom of the screen, top of the screen, left of the screen and right of the screen ; this is called "desktop panning" and is useful if you have a large amount of information, such as a huge CAD drawing, on the screen ;

Press Ctrl+Alt+Keypad-Plus again ; your screen resolution changes ; if you only have two resolutions in XF86Config, then you are back to 800x600 ;

Press Ctrl+Alt+Keypad-Minus ; do this again until you are back at 800x600.

Using the Keypad-Plus key moves "forward" to the next screen resolution and using Keypad-Minus moves "backward" to the previous screen resolution.

If your users do not need to do "desktop panning", you may want to disable the Ctrl+Alt+Keypad-Plus and Ctrl+Alt+Keypad-Minus key combinations.

Viewing a Statement in the /etc/inittab File

Open a terminal emulation window and maximize it ; use less to view the inittab file in /etc ;

press End to go to the end of the file ; look for the following statement:

x:5:respawn:/etc/X11/prefdm -nodaemon

The 5 is for runlevel 5 and the word respawn causes X to be restarted when you kill X.

]# man inittab	# read the paragraph below the DESCRIPTION heading
/respawn	# read the description of this item
]# runlevel	# as cwest, you do not have /sbin in your PATH
]# /sbin/runlevel	# specify the full path to the runlevel binary

Even though you are not logged in as root, you have sufficient permissions to run this binary by specifying the absolute path to it!

The output of the runlevel command should be: N 5 and the 5 (at the right) indicates the current runlevel. Therefore, your current runlevel is 5. The "N" indicates "none". This indicates that there has not been a previous runlevel. More on this below.

When your current runlevel is 5 and you kill X with Ctrl+Alt+Backspace, the respawn statement in /etc/inittab causes X to automatically be restarted whenever you kill it.

16 **Killing X with Ctrl+Alt+Backspace**

Close the terminal emulation window ;   press Ctrl+Alt+Backspace ; the GUI login screen appears ; X has been "respawned" (restarted) ;

press Ctrl+Alt+Backspace ; the GUI login screen appears again.

Some utilities do not allow you to configure X while X is running. However, when you kill X with Ctrl+Alt+Backspace, it just restarts again. Therefore, you can do the steps described below to kill X (without it restarting), configure X, and then start X.

For any X configuration changes (that have been made in any way) to take effect, X must always be restarted.

(17) **Using the init Command to Change Your Runlevel**

Press Ctrl+Alt+F1 to go to virtual terminal 1 ; log in as cwest ; su to root ;

]# init 3   # change to runlevel 3 - shut down X and some other services

There may be a short pause before you see the services being shut down.

Press Enter to have the prompt appear ; press Alt+F7 to try to go to the desktop ; the desktop should not appear ;   press Ctrl+Alt+F1 to go to virtual terminal 1 ;

]# runlevel   # the current runlevel appears at the right - previous at the left

(18) **Backing Up XF86Config and Adding the ServerFlags Section to It**

]# cd /etc/X11   # this directory contains XF86Config

]# cp XF86Config XF86Config.bak   # back up the XF86Config file

]# vi XF86Config   # run vi to edit the file

press i to go into insert mode.

To stop a user from using Ctrl+Alt+Backspace to kill X you will add the ServerFlags section to XF86Config with the DontZap option.

To stop a user from changing the screen resolution with Ctrl+Alt+Keypad-Plus and Ctrl+Alt+Keypad-Minus you will add the DontZoom option to the ServerFlags section.

On the second blank line after the first line in the file, add the following text. Be very careful to type in the text exactly as shown. Indent the Option statements by pressing Tab once. You can use any number of spaces wherever spaces are shown. Put a blank line between the section that you are adding and the next section.

```
Section  "ServerFlags"
    Option  "DontZap"  "on"
    Option  "DontZoom"  "on"
EndSection
```

Press Esc ; press ZZ to save and exit ;

]# init 5   # change to runlevel 5 - the GUI login screen appears

log in as cwest ; the desktop appears.

(19) Logging Out of Virtual Terminal 1

Press Ctrl+Alt+F1 ; press Enter so that the prompt appears ;

run the exit command to exit out of the root user subshell ;

run the logout command to logout as the cwest user ; press Alt+F7 to go to the desktop.

(20) Testing the New Settings in XF86Config

Press Ctrl+Alt+Backspace ; X should not be killed and the GUI login screen should not appear ;

press Ctrl+Alt+Keypad-Plus and Ctrl+Alt+Keypad-Minus ; the screen resolution should not change ;

all done for now! ; do the steps to shut down your system from the menu.

Section Review

1. What text file contains settings for the X Server?

    - ○ A. XConfig
    - ○ B. XF86Config
    - ○ C. x.config
    - ○ D. xserver

2. Select three characteristics of the X Server.

    - ☐ A. it can be set up to run automatically when a system starts
    - ☐ B. it manages the monitor, graphics card, keyboard and mouse
    - ☐ C. it can only be operated in runlevel 3
    - ☐ D. the XFree86 binary provides an X Server when it is run

3. Which directory path is in the PATH for all users?

    ○ A.   /usr/X11R6

    ○ B.   /usr/X11R6/bin

    ○ C.   /etc/X11

    ○ D.   /usr/X11R6/man

4. Your XF86Config file contains the following section. What is the default screen resolution that will be used by the system?

```
Section "Screen"
        Identifier "Screen0"
        Device    "ATI Mach64 3D RAGE II"
        Monitor    "Monitor0"
        DefaultDepth    24
        SubSection "Display"
            Depth    24
            Modes    "1024x768" "800x600" "640x480"
        EndSubSection
        SubSection "Display"
            Depth    16
            Modes    "800x600" "640x480"
        EndSubSection
EndSection
```

    ○ A.   1024x768

    ○ B.   800x600

    ○ C.   640x480

    ○ D.   none of the above

5. A system is currently running in "text mode" (without X). Which command will cause X to be started?

    ○ A.   runlevel 5

    ○ B.   init 5

    ○ C.   xstart 5

    ○ D.   init 3

6. Select the file that contains the statement the causes the X Server to respawn when it is stopped.

   ○ A. /etc/XConfig
   ○ B. /etc/X11/XF86Config
   ○ C. /etc/X/init
   ○ D. /etc/inittab

7. X Clients and the X Server rarely run on the same system. T F

8. In the XF86Config, which of the following indicate the end of a section?

   ○ A. the # symbol
   ○ B. End
   ○ C. EndSection
   ○ D. SectionEnd

9. Which organization is dedicated to maintaining the X Window System code and the engineering of future enhancements to it?

   ○ A. X.org
   ○ B. XWin.org
   ○ C. XWS.com
   ○ D. X11R6.edu

10. You have copied a working XF86Config file to a backup file in the same directory named XF86Config.bak and then manually edited the XF86Config file. You run the init command to change to runlevel 5 and the X Server "hangs" due to a configuration problem in XF86Config. You need to do some research to determine the cause of the problem, but you need to get the system working immediately. Select the best solution to this problem.

   ○ A. reboot your system and the X Server will automatically use the XF86Config.bak file
   ○ B. change to a virtual terminal and log in, change to runlevel 3, copy XF86Config.bak to XF86Config, change to runlevel 5
   ○ C. run the Xconfigbak utility so that it copies the XF86Config.bak file to the XF86Config file and automatically restarts the X Server
   ○ D. press Ctrl+Alt+Backspace to kill the X Server and then start it again with the -autobak option so that it uses the XF86Config.bak file

11. The XFree86 X Server can only be run on x86 systems. T F

12. What is one of the main benefits of the X Window System?

    ○ A. it allows the use of several different mouse consoles
    ○ B. users can access remote printers through text-based utilities
    ○ C. developers can create portable applications designed to run in a
          network environment
    ○ D. multiple partitions can be created within a single filesystem

13. Which directory commonly contains the XF86Config file?

    ○ A. /etc/X11
    ○ B. /X11
    ○ C. /sbin/X11R6
    ○ D. /proc

14. Which type of files contain program code in binary form that provide a
    collection of commonly used software routines to software programs?

    ○ A. text configuration files
    ○ B. X coder files
    ○ C. script files
    ○ D. library files

15. The GUI desktop works with a window manager to provide the "look and
    feel" of the desktop environment. T F

16. Which item provides a common windowing system that works on virtually
    all UNIX/Linux platforms?

    ○ A. the XF96Config file
    ○ B. the X virtual manager
    ○ C. the X protocol
    ○ D. the X terminator

17. Which command will show the name and version number of the current X Server?

    ○ A. Xversion
    ○ B. X -showconfig
    ○ C. Xlist
    ○ D. Xvdisplay

18. Which section of XF86Config can be used to disable the Ctrl+Alt+Backspace key combination?

    ○ A. ServerFlags
    ○ B. ServerLayout
    ○ C. XControl
    ○ D. XKeys

19. Which is the current version of XFree86?

    ○ A. 2.x
    ○ B. 3.x
    ○ C. 4.x
    ○ D. 5.x

20. Which key combination can be used to change the screen resolution?

    ○ A. Ctrl+Alt+Backspace
    ○ B. Ctrl+Alt+Insert
    ○ C. Alt+F7
    ○ D. Ctrl+Alt+Keypad-Plus

21. Select three popular window managers.

    ☐ A. Sawfish
    ☐ B. GNOME
    ☐ C. Window Maker
    ☐ D. Metacity

Chapter 15: Creating and Running Linux Scripts

In this chapter, you will learn how to use a text editor to create a script, make it executable, and run it like any other Linux command. You will get an overview of shell script syntax, the benefits of using comments in scripts, and the types of shell variables.

Conditional expressions are used in scripts to compare items and test for conditions. Many different types of conditional expressions are described, including those used for directory and file comparison, numerical comparison, string comparison, and logical operators. Several examples of all of these conditional expressions are also presented.

Control structures are used with conditional expressions to control the processing of the statements in scripts. The syntax of all of the control structures that can be used in scripts are discussed, with examples that illustrate their use.

The following control structures are described in this chapter:

```
for . . . in . . . do
if . . . then
if . . . then . . . else
if . . . then . . . elif
while . . . do
until . . . do
case . . . in . . . pattern
```

During the Hands-On Exercises you will create a directory for scripts that is in the PATH. You will then use the vi editor to create several scripts, use the chmod command to make them executable, and then run these scripts to test them.

Creating and Running Linux Scripts

Topics Covered in this Chapter

Provide an overview of the process of creating and running shell scripts

Discuss the syntax used in scripts and the use of different types of quotation marks

Define the types of variables, positional parameters and special parameters

Explain the different types and uses of conditional expressions

Detail all of the control structures used to control the processing of statements in scripts

Learn the use of continue and break statements in a control structure

Do the steps to create and run several scripts using various control structures

Overview of Shell Scripts

Shell scripts are text files that contain statements to run commands, and usually also contain variables and programming logic. They are run like commands to perform various tasks.

Linux shell environments, such as bash and tcsh, include a command language interpreter and high-level programming language. This allows for the processing of programming logic included in shell scripts.

The command language interpreter of the shell provides a sophisticated programming environment that processes the programming logic included in shell scripts. This is basically the same as the logic found in any programming language and includes programming features, such as control structures, conditional expressions and various types of variables.

Linux relies heavily on shell scripts for many OS tasks when it boots and also after the system has started. Shell scripts are automatically run when a system boots to do a wide variety of tasks, such as mounting filesystems, starting system services and configuring the environment of the operating system. Once a system has booted, you can run one of many existing scripts in the same way as you run a command.

You can also create your own scripts to automate tasks that you need to perform frequently. These scripts can do something as simple as run a single command, or as complex as checking for several system settings and performing multiple commands based on these settings.

The syntax and programming logic for scripts in one Linux shell is similar to the logic used in another, but not always the same. We will describe the syntax and programming logic used with the bash shell in this chapter.

Creating and Executing Scripts

One method of creating and executing a script is to simply put one or more commands in a text file and then run: bash *scriptfilename* and replace *scriptfilename* with the name of the text file. This works, but requires that you type in "bash" every time you run a script.

The more common method of creating and executing a script is to put the statement: #!/bin/bash at the top of the a text file, make the file executable and then execute the script by typing the name of the script and pressing Enter. These steps are described below.

The statement: #!/bin/**bash** at the top of the script indicates that the file is a script file and that it is to be processed by the **bash** shell binary file in the /bin directory path. Unlike when a # appears at the start of most statements in a text file, the # at the start of this statement does not indicate that the statement is a comment.

Some existing scripts on the system begin with: #!/bin/sh and will still work properly because the file named **sh** in /bin is a symlink to the **bash** binary file named bash in /bin. Scripts that begin with #!/bin/**sh** may have originally been created for the Bourne **sh**ell (**sh**) and scripts that begin with #!/bin/**bash** have been created for the Bourne **again sh**ell (**bash**).

To make a script file executable, run the following command and replace *scriptfilename* with the name of the script file.

        ]# chmod u+x *scriptfilename*

This assigns the x permission to the **u** (**u**ser) of the file. Depending on the purpose of the script, you may also want to assign the x permission to the **g** (**g**roup) and **o** (**o**ther) of the file.

To execute a script file that is in the *current directory*, use one of the following methods:

        ]# . *scriptfilename*   # a space is the separator between the dot and
                                        # the *scriptfilename*

        ]# ./*scriptfilename*   # a / is the separator between the dot and
                                        # the *scriptfilename*

If a space is used between the dot and the *scriptfilename*, then the file does not need to be made executable. If a / is used between the dot and the *scriptfilename*, then the file must be made executable. The . in the above examples represents the current directory.

The first example above can also be used in a script, to cause the script to execute another script.

A script file can be put in a directory that is in the PATH. If this is done and the script file has been made executable, then the script is run in the same way as a command is run. Simply type the name of the script file and press Enter.

    ]# *scriptfilename*   # the *scriptfilename* is run like a binary file

To allow the root user to run a script, you can put it in an sbin directory that is already in the PATH. To allow all non-root users (and the root user) to run the script, you can put it in a bin directory that is already in the PATH. To allow a single user to run a script, you can do the steps described below.

By default (with this distribution), the PATH for every user contains a directory path that points to a directory named bin below the home directory of each user. Also by default, this directory does not exist!

To allow a single user (only) to run a script, you can create a bin directory below the home directory of the user and put the script in it. Then that user (only) will automatically be able to run the script by simply typing the name of the script and pressing Enter. Make sure the user has the x permission to the script through u, g or o.

Typically, script files: contain #!/bin/bash as the first statement; they are made executable; and are put in a directory that is in the PATH of a user, so that a user can run the script from any directory on the system.

 Do not name a script after any type of control structure, such as if, while or case, or after any environment variable, binary, builtin command or script command, such as init, USER, test or echo.

Using Comments In a Script File

When you are creating a script file, you know what you are trying to achieve and understand all of the statements that you have put in the file. However, a few months later, you may not remember why you created the script in the way that you did. In addition to this, other people may need to understand what the script does and how it works. Therefore, it is good practise to comment scripts for your future reference and for the benefit of others. In a script (as well as in a configuration file), comment statements begin with a # symbol,

Using Quotation Marks in Scripts

There are three types of quotation marks that are used in scripts.

A ' (single quote) is used around (at the start and end of) text so that the text is treated "as is".

> the command: echo 'The current path is $PATH'

> causes the output of: The current path is $PATH

When single quotes are used, $PATH is not replaced by the value of the environment variable named PATH and the directory paths in the PATH are not displayed.

A ` (back quote, a.k.a. backtick) is used around text so that the command(s) between the quotes are processed. There are backquotes around the date command in the example below. These cause the date command to be run from within the script.

> the command: echo "The date is: `**date**`"

> causes the output of: The date is: **Fri Feb 6 2:32 EST 2004**

Rather than using `  ` (back quotes) around a command, you can precede the command with "$(" and end it with ")" as shown below for the date command, which is the equivalent of the above command.

> echo "The date is: $(**date**)"

A " (double quote) is used around text so that variables inside the quotes are processed and commands are not processed. The following command has been run from the /home/cwest directory. If a ' (single quote) was around the word date, then the result of the date command would appear.

> the command: echo "The current path is: **$PWD** and the date is: date"

> causes the output of: The current path is: **/home/cwest** and the date is: date

More examples of using the different types of quotation marks are shown below.

Shell Variables

Shell variables are also simply referred to as variables and there are two types of them. Their names consist of letters, numbers and _ (underscore) characters. They cannot begin with a number and cannot contain a - (dash).

"Code" the names of your user-created variables by abbreviating words that would describe the variable. Make them as meaningful as possible, without being too long.

Environment Variables

Environment (a.k.a. keyword) variable names typically only have upper case letters whereas the names of user-created variables can use a mix of upper and lower case letters.

The three examples below are from statements that are in the /etc/profile script (that configures the shell). They are examples of assigning values to variables in a script. Each statement assigns a value to each of the variables named HISTSIZE, HOSTNAME and USER.

The value of a variable can be displayed with the echo command. A $ sign is used at the start of a variable when using the echo command and " " (double quotation marks) are used around the $ sign and the variable, as in: echo "$HOSTNAME" and in: echo "$hello".

The following statement simply assigns the value of 1000 to the environment variable named HISTSIZE.

    HISTSIZE=1000

In a script, the statement: echo "$HISTSIZE" displays the output of: 1000

The next statement runs the binary named hostname in the /bin directory and the result of this command is assigned to HOSTNAME. Notice the ` ` (backquotes) at the start and end of the path and name of the binary file.

    HOSTNAME=`/bin/hostname`

If the hostname is: lancom57.lancom.com then the command: /bin/hostname produces the name of: lancom57.lancom.com and assigns this name to the HOSTNAME variable.

Then in a script, the statement: echo "$HOSTNAME" displays: lancom57.lancom.com

The statement below runs the id command with the -u (user) and -n (name) options and assigns the result of the command to the environment variable named USER.

    USER="`id -un`"

If the user name is: jbeck   then the command: id -un produces the name of: jbeck

Then in a script, the statement: echo "$USER" displays: jbeck

Environment variables are "exported" (with the export command) to the shell from within a script so that they are available to the shell (and programs that are run in the shell).

For example, the HISTSIZE, HOSTNAME, USER and other environment variables are exported from the /etc/profile file when a bash shell session is started.

The following statement in the /etc/profile file uses the export command to export the variables that were assigned values in the file. This causes the variables to be available to the shell.

```
export PATH USER LOGNAME MAIL HOSTNAME HISTSIZE INPUTRC
```

User-Created Variables

User-created variable names are assigned values by using an = sign between the variable name and the value. Do not put spaces before or after the = sign.

The following statements in a script assign the variable named var1 the value of hello and the variable named var2 the value of linux.

```
var1=hello
var2=linux
```

In the same script, the statement: echo "$var1" "$var2" displays: hello linux

Using " " when Assigning Values to Variables and Viewing Variables

Use " " (double quotes) when assigning a value that contains one or more spaces, or Tab characters, to a variable.

The following assigns the value of "Monday and Tuesday" to a variable named days:

```
days="Monday    and    Tuesday"
```

When the value of a variable contains more than one adjacent space or Tab character, use " " (double quotes) around the value. If this is not done, all adjacent blank spaces are reduced to a single space. The following displays the value of the variable named days:

```
echo "$days"
```

In the same script, the statement: echo "$days" displays: Monday and Tuesday

Conditional Expressions

Below are some examples of conditional expressions used when comparing items, strings and numbers.

Directory and File Comparison Expressions

-e item	true if the item exists
-f item	true if the item exists and is a file
-d item	true if the item exists and is a directory
-s item	true if the item exists and has a length greater than zero
-x item	true if the item exists and is executable

Numerical Comparison Expressions

-eq	true if one number is equal to another
-ne	true if one number is not equal to another
-gt	true if one number is greater than another
-ge	true if one number is greater than or equal to another
-lt	true if one number is less than another
-le	true if one number is less than or equal to another

String Comparison Expressions

$string1 = $string2	true if string1 is equal to string2
$string1 != $string2	true if string1 is not equal to string2
-n $string	true if the string is non-zero bytes (has something in it)
-z $string	true if the string is zero bytes (has nothing in it)

Logical Operators - NOT, AND and OR

! expression	true if expression is false the ! represents the logical **NOT**
expression1 **-a** expression2	true if expression1 **and** expression2 are both true the -a represents the logical **AND**
expression1 **-o** expression2	true if expression1 **or** expression2 is true the -o represents the logical **OR**

Below the heading "Numerical Comparison Expressions", notice that "**-eq**" is used for "**eq**ual to" in a numerical comparison expression and below the heading "String Comparison Expressions", the "=" sign is used for "**eq**ual to" in a string comparison expression.

Also, notice that "-**ne**" is used for "**n**ot **e**qual to" in a numerical comparison expression and "!=" is used for "**n**ot **e**qual to" in a string comparison expression.

To see a listing of about thirty conditional expressions, such as the ones shown above, search the bash man page for "CONDITIONAL EXPRESSIONS" (use all upper case letters) and then press "n" (lower case) twice. Be sure to use a lower case "n" after typing in the text that you are searching for in upper case letters.

Examples of several of the above conditional expressions are shown two headings below.

Shell Syntax and Other Special Characters

In addition to fairly basic shell script statements that run commands, there is a syntax used for more detailed statements and there are other special characters that can be used in a script. The following statement is an example of this.

```
[ -f /etc/profile.d/lang.sh ] &&  . /etc/profile.d/lang.sh
```

The statement above is from the S05kudzu script in /etc/rc.d/rc5.d. The **[-f /etc/profile.d/lang.sh]** part of the above statement tests to see if a file named lang.sh exists in /etc/profile.d and is a file. If so (if true), the **&&** part of the statement (which is the **AND** part of the statement) causes the text at the right of it to be processed. If not, then the text is not processed. The **. /etc/profile.d/lang.sh** part of the statement causes the scripting logic in the file named lang.sh to be processed. The . (dot) that appears prior to the path to the lang.sh file causes the scripting logic in the lang.sh file to be processed. It allows you to run a script from within a script. This is the same as executing a script by typing a . (dot), a space and the name of a script at the shell prompt to execute a script.

If the **&&** in the statement above were replaced by **||** (representing **OR**) then the command on the right would only be processed if the condition on the left were not true.

For the syntax of shell script statements and to see a other special characters used in shell scripts, such as the ones shown above, search the bash man page for "SHELL GRAMMAR" (use all upper case letters).

Examples of Conditional Expressions

Test conditions can be put between [ ] square brackets. A space is required "around" (at the left and right of) each square bracket, unless a ; (semicolon) is used at the right of the] right bracket. For simplicity, put a space around (at the left and right of) both square brackets even when the right square bracket is followed by a ; (semicolon).

[-f /var/run/confirm]

Tests to see if the file named confirm exists in /var/run and is a regular file.

[-d "$adir"]

Tests to see if the value in the variable named adir is a directory.

[-x /bin/tar]

Tests to see if the file named tar exists in /bin and is executable (has the x permission).

[$RETVAL -eq 5]

Tests to see if the value in the variable named RETVAL is equal to 5.

[$rc -gt 0]

Tests to see if the value in the variable named rc is greater than zero.

[$string1 = $string2]

Compares string1 and string2 and if they are equal, the condition is true.

[-n "$CONFIRM"]

Tests to see if the value of the string in the variable named CONFIRM has a length greater than zero bytes. This tests to see if the variable has something in it.

[! -x file1]

The ! represents a logical NOT. This conditional expression tests to see if the file named file1 is not executable (-x). The condition is true if file1 is not executable.

[-f /etc/raidtab -a -f /proc/mdstat]

This is an example that uses a logical AND, which is represented by the -a. It tests to see if /etc/raidtab and /etc/mdstat exist and are files (-f). If *both* raidtab and (-a) mdstat exist and are files, then the condition is true.

[-f /var/run/utmpx -o -f /var/log/wtmpx]

This is an example that uses a logical OR, which is represented by the -o. It tests to see if /var/run/utmpx and /var/log/wtmpx exist and are files (-f). If *either* of utmpx or (-o) wtmpx exist and are files, then the condition is true.

Positional Parameters and Special Parameters

A variable cannot begin with a number. However, there are *positional parameters* that are one or more numbers (digits) and *special parameters* that are a single character.

Positional parameters are used in shell scripts to allow you to refer to: the name of a command, and the command-line arguments that are typed in with the command. These parameters begin with the number 0, which is used for the name of a command, and they increase by a single number for each item (separated by a space) that is typed at the right of a command. These parameters are referred to as "*positional* parameters" because their numbers refer to the position of the argument on the command line.

Special parameters are a single character, such as @ and #.

When a command (script) is run, the command has the parameter name of 0 (zero).

In a script, the following statement will display the name of the script: echo "$0"

When one or more items are typed in at the right of a command, each of these items is separated by a space. These items are referred to as command-line arguments. The names for these arguments are numbers. The name of the parameter for the first command-line argument is 1. The name of the parameter for the second command-line argument is 2, and so on.

In a script, this statement displays the first command-line argument: echo "$1"

When referring to a command-line parameter above 9, put { } curly braces around the number.

In a script, this statement displays the tenth command-line argument: echo "${10}"

The *special* parameter named @ contains all of the command-line arguments that were typed in with the command.

In a script, this statement displays all of the command-line arguments: echo "$@"

The *special* parameter named # contains the number of command-line arguments.

In a script, this statement displays the number of command-line arguments: echo "$#"

Let's say you created a script named **dispargs** (for **disp**lay **arg**uments) that contained the echo statements shown in Table 15-1 below, and then ran the script with the three command-line arguments of blue, bird and sky.

    ]# dispargs blue bird sky

Table 15-1 shows the results of running the echo command several times from within the script named dispargs. The echo statements in this script display the positional parameters 0, 1, 2 and 3 and the special parameters @ and #.

Table 15-1 - Script Commands, Screen Output and Comments

Script Statement	Screen Output	Comments
echo "$0"	dispargs	the name of the script is displayed
echo "$1"	blue	the first command argument
echo "$2"	bird	the second command argument
echo "$3"	sky	the third command argument
echo "$@"	blue bird sky	all command arguments
echo "$#"	3	the number of arguments

Control Structures

Control structures (a.k.a. program constructs) are used in scripts to control the execution of the statements in a script. In the following descriptions of control structures, the text in bold and italics is the text that you modify to specify the *condition* to be tested and the *statements* that need to be executed.

A *condition* is tested for true or false. There may be multiple items that are tested for *condition*. If the condition is true, the value of 0 (zero) is returned and if false, a non-zero value is returned.

The for ... in ... do Control Structure

The for ... in ... do control structure has the following structure:

```
for loop-index in argument-list
do
     statements
done
```

The *argument-list* could include the following:

```
items listed within the script
items represented by a variable, such as $aliases
items represented by a special character, such as an *
command-line arguments (items typed at the right of the script name
when the script is run)
```

When the for ... in ... do structure is processed, the value of the first item in the *argument-list* is assigned to the name that is used for the *loop-index* and the *statements* between the do statement and the done statement are processed. When the done statement is processed, the next item in the argument-list is assigned to the name used for the *loop-index* and the *statements* between do and done are processed again. This process is repeated for each item in the *argument-list*.

For simplicity and easier readability, lines 1 and 2 of the above structure are often combined, with a ; in between them and this results in the following structure:

```
for loop-index in argument-list ; do
    statements
done
```

Examples of the for ... in ... do Control Structure

The birdlist (Bird Listing) Script

```
for bird in robin bluebird crow ; do
    echo "$bird"
done
echo "End of the list of birds."
```

The name of the *loop-index* is **bird** and there are three arguments (robin, bluebird and crow). These arguments are contained in the script, as opposed to being command-line arguments. The loop executes once for each of these arguments and runs the statement: echo "$bird" each time.

The first time through the loop, the word robin is assigned to **bird**. The statement: echo "$bird" causes the word robin to appear on the screen. The second time through the loop, the word bluebird is assigned to bird and the word bluebird appears on the screen. The third time, the word crow appears on the screen. When there are no more arguments, the loop is finished and the "echo" statement after "done" is processed.

```
]# birdlist          # this runs the above script, named birdlist

robin                # this is the output of the above script
bluebird
crow
End of the list of birds.
```

The dirlist (Directory Listing) Script

```
for i in * ; do
    echo "$i"
done
echo "End of the directory listing."
```

The name of the *loop-index* is **i** and an * is used to represent all directories and files in the current directory.

For each directory and file in the current directory, the statement: echo "$i" is run and displays the name of the directory or file.

The current directory contains three items: a script file named dirlist, a file named memo.sxw, and a directory named reports.

```
]# dirlist              # runs the dirlist script

dirlist                 # this is the output of the above script
memo.sxw
reports
End of the directory listing.
```

The arglist (Argument Listing) Script

```
for  arg  in  "$@"  ; do
     echo  "$arg"
done
echo "End of the list of command-line arguments."
```

This script is run with one or more command-line arguments. The name of the *loop-index* is **arg** (for command-line **arg**uments). The command-line arguments that are typed in at the right of the name of the script are put in the special parameter named @.

The loop executes once for each command-line argument in the @ parameter and runs: echo "$arg".

The first line of the above script is:

```
for  arg  in  "$@"  ; do
```

The **in "$@"** part of the "for statement" above can be "implied" (and therefore, not included) and this statement can be reduced to:

```
for  arg  ; do
```

The (slightly more) streamlined version of the arglist script appears below:

```
for  arg  ; do
     echo  "$arg"
done
echo "End of the list of command-line arguments."
```

The following command runs the arglist script with the three arguments of 7, 12 and 305.

```
]# arglist  7  12  305    # runs the arglist script with three arguments

7                         # this is the output of the above script
12
305
End of the list of command-line arguments.
```

The name of the *loop-index* in the above example is **arg**. It could also be some other name, such as i, adir, afile, auser, var, number or list.

Examples of Other for ... in ... do Statements

for i in 2 3 4 5 6 ; do

The statements below this example will be repeated for each of the numbers 2, 3, 4, 5 and 6. This statement is used in the /etc/rc.d/rc.sysinit script.

for i in /etc/profile.d/*.sh ; do

The statements below this example will be repeated for each file in the path of /etc/profile.d that ends with ".sh". If there are five files that end in .sh in /etc/profile.d, then the statements below this example will be processed five times. This statement is used in the /etc/profile script.

for afile in /var/lock/* /var/run/* ; do

The * at the end of the path of /var/lock and /var/run causes the statements below this example to be repeated for each item (directory and file) in the path of /var/lock and also for each item in the path of /var/run. This statement is used in the /etc/rc.d/rc.sysinit script.

The if ... then Control Structure

The if ... then control structure has the following structure:

```
if condition
    then
        statements
fi
```

If the *condition* is true, then the *statements* are processed. If the *condition* is not true, continue with the statements that are below the "fi" (end of the if) statement.

Notice the way that the above statements are indented and that the structure begins with "if" and ends with "fi", which is the word "if" backwards. All control structures that begin with "if" end in "fi".

For simplicity and easier readability, lines 1 and 2 of the above structure are often combined, with a ; in between them and this results in the following structure:

```
if condition ; then
    statements
fi
```

Any of the conditions below the heading "Examples of Conditional Expressions" (shown earlier in this chapter) can be used for the *condition* part of the above control structure.

Example of the if . . . then Control Structure

```
if [ -x /bin/ping ] ; then
    echo  The ping file exists in /bin and is executable.
fi
```

The **condition** to be tested is: [-x /bin/ping] which uses -x to see if the file named ping exists in /bin and that it is executable. If so, the echo statement is processed. If not, then the statements below "fi" are processed.

The if . . . then . . . else Control Structure

The if . . . then . . . else control structure has the following structure:

```
if condition ; then
    statements
else
    statements
fi
```

If the **condition** is true, then the **statements** between "then" and "else" are processed, and then the statements below "fi" are processed.

If the **condition** is not true, then the statements between "else" and "fi" are processed, and then the statements below "fi" are processed.

Any of the conditions below the heading "Examples of Conditional Expressions" (shown earlier in this chapter) can be used for the **condition** part of the above control structure.

Example of the if . . . then . . . else Control Structure

The variables named string1 and string2 have been assigned the values of bin and home, respectively.

```
string1="bin"
string2="home"
if [ $string1 = $string2 ] ; then
    echo  "string1 is equal to string2"
else
    echo  "string1 is not equal to string2"
fi
```

The **condition** to be tested is: [$string1 = $string2] and if the values for the two strings are equal, then the first echo statement is run. If not, then the second echo statement is run.

In this example, the value of string1 is bin and the value of string2 is home. The two strings are not equal and so the second echo statement is run.

The if ... then ... elif Control Structure

The if ... then ... elif control structure has the following structure:

```
if condition ; then
        statements
    elif condition ; then
        statements
fi
```

The above structure contains a "nested" (indented) **condition** that begins with "elif" (for "**else if**") on the third line. This control structure can contain multiple "nested" conditions by adding more "elif **condition** ; then" statements (with the **statements** to be processed below them).

The above structure has two statements that test a **condition**. If the first **condition** (on the first line) is true, then the **statements** between "then" and "elif" are processed, and then the statements below "fi" are processed.

If the first **condition** is not true, then the second **condition** (on the third line) is tested. If the second **condition** is true, then the **statements** between "then" and "fi" are processed, and then the statements below "fi" are processed.

The above control structure can also include an "else" statement. The control structure below is the same as above, except that the third last and second last statements have been added.

```
if condition ; then
        statements
    elif condition ; then
        statements
else
        statements
fi
```

If the first **condition** is not true and the second **condition** is not true, then the **statements** between "else" and "fi" are processed, and then the statements below "fi" are processed.

Any of the conditions below the heading "Examples of Conditional Expressions" (shown earlier in this chapter) can be used for the **condition** part of the above control structure.

The while ... do Control Structure

The while ... do control structure has the following structure:

```
while condition ; do
    statements
done
```

While the **condition** is true, then the **statements** are processed. When the **condition** becomes false, continue with the statements that are below the "done" statement.

Example of the while ... do Control Structure

```
i=3
while [ $i -ge 0 ] ; do
    echo The value of i is "$i".
    i=$(($i-1))
done
echo "End of the while ... do control structure."
```

The variable named i is initialized to 3. While the value in the variable named i is **greater than or equal to (-ge)** 0 (zero), process the echo statement that is below the while statement and then the next statement decreases the value of the variable named i. The first time through the loop, the value of i is 3, then next time, the value is 2, and so on. When i is -1, the test condition is no longer true and the echo statement after the done statement is processed.

The output of running the above script is:

```
The value of i is 3.
The value of i is 2.
The value of i is 1.
The value of i is 0.
End of the while ... do control structure.
```

The until ... do Control Structure

The until ... do control structure has the following structure:

```
until condition ; do
    statements
done
```

The while ... do and the until ... do control structures are similar. For the the until ... do control structure, *until* the **condition** is true (as opposed to *while* the **condition** is true), the **statements** are processed. Once the **condition** is true, continue with the statements that are below the "done" statement.

Example of the until ... do Control Structure

```
i=0
until [ $i -eq 3 ] ; do
    echo The value of i is "$i".
    i=$(($i+1))
done
echo "End of the until ... do control structure."
```

The variable named i is initialized to 0. Until the value in the variable named i is equal to (**-eq**) 3, process the echo statement that is below the until statement and then the next statement increases the value of the variable named i. The first time through the loop, the value of i is 0, then next time, the value is 1, and so on. When i is 3, the test condition becomes true and the echo statement below the done statement is processed.

The output of running the above script is:

```
The value of i is 0.
The value of i is 1.
The value of i is 2.
End of the while ... do control structure.
```

The continue and break Statements

Each of the following three types of control structures end with a "done" statement. The "done" statement is the end of the loop.

```
for ... in ... do
while ... do
until ... do
```

When a "continue" statement is encountered in one of these three control structures, the loop terminates and control is transferred to the "done" statement (at the end of the loop) and the script continues to loop, if it has not completed. The statements between the "continue" statement and the done statement are not processed, but the looping continues, if it has not completed.

When a "break" statement is encountered in one of these three control structures, the loop terminates and control is transferred to the "done" statement and the script does not continue to loop. The statements between the "break" statement and the done statement are not processed.

Example of a Script that Contains the break and continue Statements

The line numbers at the left of the script below are for the purposes of discussion only.

```
1    for i in 1 2 3 4 5 6 7 8 ; do
2        if [ $i -lt 4 ] ; then
3            echo "A continue statement occurred below here."
4            continue
5        fi
6
7        echo $i
8
9        if [ $i -gt 6 ] ; then
10           echo "A break statement occurred below here."
11           break
12       fi
13   done
14   echo "End of the continue and break script."
```

The for loop on line 1 is set up to loop once for each of the numbers 1 through 8. The first three times through the loop, line 2 is true because i is less than 4 and therefore, the echo statement on line 3 is processed three times, as well as the continue statement on line 4. The continue statement on line 4 transfers control to the done statement on line 13. The continue statement stops lines 5 through 12 from being processed and the loop continues at line 1 again.

When i becomes 4, line 2 is no longer true and lines 3 through 5 are no longer processed. Line 7 causes the value of i, which is 4 to be output. Line 9 is not true and so lines 10 through 12 are not processed. This same sequence of events occur when i is 5 and 6.

When i becomes 7, line 7 is processed and the value of i is output. Also, line 9 is true and lines 10 through 12 are processed. This causes the echo statement on line 10 to be processed. The break statement on line 11 transfers control to line 13 and exits out of the loop. The for loop on line 1 was set up to continue until 8, but only reaches 7 because line 11 was processed.

The output of running the above script is:

```
A continue statement occurred below here.
A continue statement occurred below here.
A continue statement occurred below here.
4
5
6
7
A break statement occurred below here.
End of the continue and break script.
```

The case . . . in . . . pattern Control Structure

The case . . . in . . . pattern control structure has the following structure:

```
case test-string in
    pattern
        statements
        ;;
    pattern
        statements
        ;;
    pattern
        statements
        ;;
    . . .
esac
```

This control structure is used to cause **statements** to be processed based on a pattern and it can be used with or without a menu.

In the example below, this control structure is used with a menu that requests a response from a user. The user input that is typed in at the prompt becomes the **test-string** and when the **test-string** matches a pattern in the control structure, the **statements** below the pattern are processed.

The ;; (two semicolons) below **statements** are used to end the **statements** that appear for each pattern.

The ". . ." that is shown above the last statement (esac) is used to indicate that there can be more than three sets of patterns and **statements**.

Example of the case ... in ... pattern Control Structure

The line numbers at the left of the script below are for the purposes of discussion only.

```
1    clear
2    echo -e "              \n  USER MENU\n"
3    echo "    a. List the contents of your home directory"
4    echo "    b. Show the path to the current directory"
5    echo -e "    c. Show the name of the host\n"
6    echo -e "Type in a, b or c:   \c"
7    read  response
8    case "$response" in
9        a)
10           ls -l ~
11           ;;
12       b)
13           pwd
14           ;;
15       c)
16           hostname
17           ;;
18       *)
19           echo "The $response response is not an option."
20           ;;
21   esac
```

Lines 1 through 6 clear the screen and display a menu. When the -e option of echo is used with "\n" then a "NEWLINE" (a.k.a. hard return, pressing Enter) occurs for each "\n". The "\n" causes a blank line to appear on the screen. This is used in lines 2 and 5. When the -e option of echo is used with "\c" then a "NEWLINE" does not occur. This is used on line 6 so that the flashing cursor that awaits the response appears on the same line as the text that prompts for the response.

Line 7 is used to read the response typed in at the keyboard. Lines 8 through 21 contain the case ... in ... pattern control structure.

Lines 9, 12, 15 and 18 are the "pattern" part of the control structure. The) bracket at the right of the pattern is part of the control structure. The statements on lines 10, 13, 16 and 19 are the *statements* that are processed when a "pattern" is provided. There can be more than one line of *statements* for each pattern. The ;; (two semicolons) on lines 11, 14, 17 and 20 are used to end the *statements* that appear for each pattern.

If the value of the response is the letter a, then the statement on line 10 is processed. If the value is b, line 13 is processed. If the value is c, line 16 is processed. The * is used for the pattern on line 18. This is the "catchall" pattern. If a user does not type in a valid pattern, such as a, b, or c, then the * is used for the pattern and the statement on line 19 is displayed.

As shown, this script will be displayed once and one response will be processed. The script does not cause the menu to be displayed again after one response.

The menu that appears when the above script is run is shown below:

USER MENU

    a. List the contents of your home directory
    b. Show the path to the current directory
    c. Show the name of the host

Type in a, b or c:

Using Functions

A function is a name to which one or more commands or statements are assigned. This can be done at the shell prompt or in a script. When creating a function, the name of the function is followed by () two enclosed brackets.

To run the function at the shell prompt, type in the name of the function without the brackets and press Enter. To run the function in a script, type in the name of the function without the braces. Arguments can be used at the right of a function name at the shell prompt and in a script.

The script named functions in /etc/rc.d/init.d contains several functions. These functions are used by over forty scripts in the /etc/rc.d/init.d directory.

The following text in /etc/rc.d/init.d/functions creates a function named **checkpid()**. This allows the function to be defined once and used many times in the same script or in other scripts.

```
# Check if $pid (could be plural) are running
checkpid() {
local i
    for i in $* ; do
        [ -d "/proc/$i" ] && return 0
    done
    return 1
}
```

There are several functions that are created in the /etc/rc.d/init.d/functions file. These are used to do various tasks, such as start a process, determine the process id of a service and kill a process.

Many of the scripts in /etc/rc.d/init.d contain the following statement:

```
#  Source function library.
.  /etc/rc.d/init.d/functions
```

The . (dot) at the start of the statement above causes the text in the file named functions to be processed. This allows the scripts in /etc/rc.d/init.d to use the functions defined in the script named functions.

Testing and Debugging Scripts

It is a good idea to build scripts gradually. You may want to create small files that do a "logical section" of the script. Test each "logical section" as you create the script and then gradually add the text of the "logical sections" together into the create the final script.

To help debug the script, use echo statements in "logical statements" that display some text to the screen to show that the logic of the script works.

Hands-On Exercises

 Logging In to Create and Run Scripts

Log in as cwest ; open a terminal emulation window ; su to root.

]# echo $PATH

The last (far right) directory path in the PATH should be /root/bin, even though this directory does not exist yet.

Create a directory below /root named bin ; change into this new directory.

You will create scripts in /root/bin and these will automatically be in the PATH. Therefore, the scripts can be run by simply typing in the name of the script and pressing Enter. The scripts in /root/bin will only be available to the root user.

Creating a Script that Runs Commands

The text of the scripts below is indented, but when you type this text in, type the text that is only indented once flush left. Type the text that is indented twice only once, and so on. Put blank lines in the script files as shown. Create all of the scripts in /root/bin.

```
]# vi smscript        # run vi and create a file named smscript
```

Type the following text into the file named smscript:

```
#!/bin/bash

# smscript - a small script that runs a few commands

clear
echo "Show the Linux version number."
uname -r
echo
echo "Show the date."
date
echo
echo "Show the sizes of the subs of /home, sorted."
du -s /home/* | sort -n
echo
echo "Show the disks installed in the system."
dmesg | grep ^hd
```

```
]# chmod u+x smscript
```

You are currently logged in as root and created the file named smscript as root. Therefore, the u and g of the file is root. The above command assigns the x permission to the u of the file, which is root.

To allow some or all users to run the script, you would put it in a directory that is available to a group of users, or in a directory that is available to all users, and that is in the PATH for some or all users. You would also assign x to the g of the file, or to the o of the file. If you assigned the x to the g of the file, you would assign a group name to the file so that users in the group could execute it. If you assigned x to the o of the file, all users could execute it.

```
]# smscript           # run the script named smscript
```

③ **Creating a Script to Do a Backup of /home/common**

Use vi to create a file named bucommon and type in the following text:

#!/bin/bash

\# bucommon - back up /home/common

\# this is a script to back up the directory structures below /home/common
\# and put the backup file in /misc/archives

\# the backup file name will begin with bu-, followed by the current date
\# and will have the suffix of .tar.bz2

tar -cPjvf /misc/archives/bu-`date '+%Y-%B-%d'`.tar.bz2 /home/common/*

A directory off of the / named misc (/misc) should exist ; if a directory named archives does not exist below this directory, create it ;

assign the x permission to the u of the bucommon file and then run it ;

list the files in /misc/archives to check that the backup file (with today's date) was created ;

]# tar -tjvf /misc/archives/bu-   # press Tab so that the rest of the
                                    # backup file name appears at the
                                    # right of the command

④ **Creating a Script that Shows Command-Line Arguments**

Use vi to create a file named dispargs and type in the following text:

#!/bin/bash

\# dispargs - display arguments

\# this is a script to display command-line arguments and other parameters
\# run this script with three command-line arguments

\# the positional parameters named 0, 1, 2 and 3 are used
\# as well as the special parameters named @ and #

clear
echo "The name of the command, the parameter named 0, is: $0"
echo
echo "The first argument, the parameter named 1, is: $1"
echo
echo "The second argument, the parameter named 2, is: $2"
echo
echo "The third argument, the parameter named 3, is: $3"
echo
echo "All arguments, the parameter named @, are: $@"
    echo
    echo "The number of arguments, the parameter named #, is: $#"

Assign the x permission to the u of the file and then run it with three arguments, such as:

]# dispargs blue green red

Compare the script with the output and notice the values that are displayed for the parameters of 0, 1, 2, 3, @ and #.

 5 **Creating the arglist (Argument Listing) Script**

Use vi to create a file named arglist and type in the following text:

```
#!/bin/bash

#  arglist - argument listing script

for  arg  in  "$@"  ;  do
    echo  "$arg"
done
echo "End of the list of command-line arguments."
```

The "@" in the statement: for arg **in** "**$@**" represents all command-line arguments.

Assign the x permission to the u of the file and then run it with three arguments, such as:

]# arglist sun moon stars

Now edit the arglist file and remove **in** "**$@**" from it so that the script appears as shown below:

```
#!/bin/bash

#  arglist - argument listing script

for  arg  ;  do
    echo  "$arg"
done
echo "End of the list of command-line arguments."
```

Run the script with five arguments.

The **in** "**$@**" in the "for" statement of the script is "implied" and is not required.

⑥ **Creating a Script Using the case . . . in . . . pattern Control Structure**

Use vi to create a file named commandmenu and type in the following text:

```
#!/bin/bash

#  commandmenu - run commands from a menu

clear
echo  -e "\n              USER MENU\n"
echo  "    a.  List the contents of your home directory"
echo  "    b.  Show the path to the current directory"
echo  -e "    c.  Show the name of the host\n"
echo  -e "Type in a, b or c:   \c"
read  response
case "$response" in
    a)
        ls  -l  ~
        ;;
    b)
        pwd
        ;;
    c)
        hostname
        ;;
    *)
        echo "The $response response is not an option."
        ;;
    esac
```

Assign the x permission to the u of the file and then run it ;

type in: a and press Enter ;

run the script again and type in: b   and press Enter ;

repeat this for c ; run the script again and type in something other than a, b or c.

A Script to Determine the Type of an Item (Directory or File)

The script below uses an if . . . then . . . else control structure within a for . . . in . . . do control structure. The * in the "for" statement causes the statement to loop through all of the directories and files in the current directory. The "if" statement tests to see if the contents of the variable named adir is a directory (-d). If it is, then the name of the directory and "is a directory" appears. If it is not, then the name of the file and "is a file" appears.

Create a two subdirectories named "one" and "two" below the current directory (/root/bin).

Use vi to create a file named dirlist and type in the following text:

```
#!/bin/bash

#  dirlist - directory listing

#  this states the type of each item in the current directory

clear
for  adir  in  *  ; do
    if  [  -d  "$adir"  ]  ;  then
        echo  "$adir is a directory"
        echo
    else
        echo  "$adir is a file"
        echo
    fi
done
echo "End of the directory listing."
```

Assign the x permission to the u of the file and then run it.

The name of each item in the directory should appear with either "is a directory" or "is a file" at the right of it.

(8) Creating a Function at the Shell Prompt

```
]# dateshow() {          # start creating the function
> clear                  # a ">" prompt appears, do not type in ">"
> date
> }                      # the right curly bracket ends the function

]# dateshow              # this runs the function
```

The dateshow function is only available during the current shell session.

(9) Creating a Function in a Script

Use vi to create a file named functscript and type in the following text:

#!/bin/bash

functscript - function script

dateshow() {

    clear
    date

}

dateshow

Assign the x permission to the u of the file and then run it.

(10) Using a Function Located in a Different Script

Edit the script named functscript and remove the last line (the dateshow statement) ;

run the script named functscript.

The function still exists in the script, but it is no longer executed by the dateshow statement.

Use vi to create a file named functuse and type in the following text:

#!/bin/bash

functuse - function use

. /root/bin/functscript

dateshow

Assign the x permission to the u of the file and then run it.

The statement: . /root/bin/functscript runs the script named functscript from within the script named functuse. This creates the function named dateshow so that is function can be used by the script named functuse. The statement: dateshow runs the function that was created with the script named functscript.

In the next chapter, you will see the contents of the script named functions in /etc/rc.d/init.d. This script contains seventeen functions that are used to control system services. There are about forty scripts in /etc/rc.d/init.d that use the functions in the script named functions. The functions are defined once in the script named functions and are used repeatedly by the other scripts in /etc/rc.d/init.d.

You may also want to create and run some of the other scripts that are shown earlier in this chapter.

 Shutting Down

Close all programs and windows and shut down your system.

 Section Review

1. Which two statements will cause the name of the host to be displayed?

   ☐ A. echo `hostname`
   ☐ B. echo 'hostname'
   ☐ C. echo "hostname"
   ☐ D. echo $(hostname)

2. You are working as the root user and have just created a script named listhomes in a directory that is in the PATH. You want to run the script by simply typing the name of the scripts and pressing Enter. Select the command that will allow this user to be able to run the script.

   ○ A. chown u+x listhomes
   ○ B. chmod u-x listhomes
   ○ C. run u+x listhomes
   ○ D. chmod u+x listhomes

3. Select the item that describes what the conditional expression below is used to test.

    [-f /etc/hosts]

   ○ A. tests to see if hosts exists in /etc and is a directory
   ○ B. tests to see if hosts exists in /etc and is a file
   ○ C. tests to see if hosts exists in /etc and is executable
   ○ D. tests to see if hosts exists in /etc (only)

4. Select two numerical comparison expressions.

   ☐ A. -gr
   ☐ B. -lt
   ☐ C. -eq
   ☐ D. -en

5. Which command will cause the variables that were assigned values in a script to be available to the shell after the script has been processed?

   ○ A. export
   ○ B. commshell
   ○ C. sendval
   ○ D. valexp

6. What will be the output of the following script statement when you are logged in as bford?

    echo "Your user name is: $USER"

   ○ A. echo "Your user name is: $USER"
   ○ B. "Your user name is: $USER"
   ○ C. echo Your user name is: USER
   ○ D. Your user name is: bford

7. Which two items are correct regarding logical operators?

   ☐ A. !! is used to represent the logical NOT
   ☐ B. -a is used to represent the logical AND
   ☐ C. & is used to represent the logical AND
   ☐ D. -o is used to represent the logical OR

8. Select the only three control structures that can be "interrupted" by a "continue" or "break" statement.

   ☐ A. while . . . do
   ☐ B. case . . . in . . . pattern
   ☐ C. until . . . do
   ☐ D. for . . . in . . . do

9. Select two correct statements regarding positional parameters and special parameters.

   ☐ A. # represents the number of command-line arguments
   ☐ B. @ represents the last command-line argument
   ☐ C. 0 represents the name of the script (command) that was run
   ☐ D. 1 represents the name of the script (command) that was run

10. The following condition is true, if:

   [-f /etc/cups/cupsd.conf -o -d /var/log/cups]

   ○ A. cupsd.conf is a file in /etc/cups or if cups is a directory in /var/log
   ○ B. cupsd.conf is a file in /etc/cups and if cups is a directory in /var
   ○ C. cupsd.conf is a file in /etc/cups and if cups is not a directory in /var/log
   ○ D. cupsd.conf is not a file in /etc/cups or if cups is not a directory in /var/log

11. When a "break" statement is encountered in a control structure that ends in "done", the loop terminates after processing the statements between the "break" statement and the "done: statement. T F

12. Which control structure is most commonly used to display a menu of options?

   ○ A. until . . . do
   ○ B. if . . . then . . . else
   ○ C. case . . . in . . . pattern
   ○ D. for . . . in . . . do

13. Select the character that is used as a "catchall" pattern in a case . . . in . . . pattern control structure.

   ○ A. !
   ○ B. *
   ○ C. #
   ○ D. @

14. Which item describes the conditional expression below?

   [$string1 = $string2]

   ○ A. it deducts string1 from string2 and if they contain any text that is similar, the condition is true
   ○ B. it compares string1 and string2 and if they are not equal, the condition is true
   ○ C. it compares string1 and string2 and if they are equal, the condition is true
   ○ D. it compares string1 and string2 and if both contain text, the condition is true

15. Which two control structures end with the word "done"?

    - ☐ A. while ... do
    - ☐ B. for ... in ... do
    - ☐ C. if ... then
    - ☐ D. case ... in ... pattern

16. Which statement (in a script) will cause the script named functions to be processed?

    - ○ A. . /etc/rc.d/init.d/functions
    - ○ B. #! /etc/rc.d/init.d/functions
    - ○ C. runcomm /etc/rc.d/init.d/functions
    - ○ D. proc /etc/rc.d/init.d/functions

17. By default, the PATH variable contains a directory path to a directory named bin, below each user's home directory. T F

18. The following statement is in the /etc/rc.d/rc.sysinit script. Select two items that describe what it does.

    ktag="`cat /proc/version`"

    - ☐ A. executes the ktag command using options in the /proc/version file
    - ☐ B. tests to see if the file named /proc/version exists
    - ☐ C. runs the cat command so that it outputs the contents of /proc/version
    - ☐ D. assigns the output of the cat command to the variable named ktag

19. Control structures that begin with "if" end with the "efi". T F

20. A script named listit is located in the current directory and the current directory is not in the PATH. Which two commands will allow you to run the script?

    - ☐ A. listit
    - ☐ B. run listit
    - ☐ C. ./listit
    - ☐ D. . listit

21. Which two statements regarding numerical and string comparison operators are correct?

    - ☐ A. -ne is used when doing a string comparison
    - ☐ B. -ne is used when doing a numerical comparison
    - ☐ C. != is used when doing a numerical comparison
    - ☐ D. != is used when doing a string comparison

Chapter 16: Runlevels, the Boot Process, Services and Processes

In this chapter, you will learn about the runlevels or "modes" in which a Linux system can operate and how these can be configured to run the services that are required for each runlevel.

We will discuss the boot process of a Linux system, from selecting the OS on a boot loader menu through to the login prompt. During this process, the kernel is loaded, the init binary is executed, and several script files are processed to initialize the system. You will learn the purpose of each of these scripts and the system components and services that they set up in the memory of a system.

Several system services are described, and then the initialization process and directory structure that is used to start these services is detailed.

Linux allows incredible control over the processes that are running in memory. You can use commands to monitor the memory of a system and view a large amount of information on each process that is running. This allows you to locate processes that are not working properly, so that you can remove them from memory and then start them again if necessary. This can be done without having to reboot a system.

The following commands are described in this chapter and are also used in the Hands-On Exercises:

ntsysv	configure the default setting for a service in a runlevel
serviceconf	configure the default setting for a service in a runlevel
	immediately start, stop and restart services
chkconfig	configure the default setting for a service in a runlevel
	add a service to the init scripts directory structure
	delete a service from the init scripts directory structure
service	view and control the settings of services
init	change from one runlevel to another
runlevel	view the current and previous runlevel
ps	view information on the status of processes
top	view information on the top processes
	stop a single process by pid and remove it from memory
kill	stop a single process by pid and remove it from memory
killall	stop one or more processes by name and remove them from memory
nice	start a process with a specific priority
renice	change the priority of an existing process
free	display memory statistics

During the Hands-On Exercises, you will view the scripts that are used during the boot process and use commands to: configure the default settings for a service, immediately start and stop services, change the current runlevel, view the current runlevel setting, view the status of processes, stop processes and view memory statistics.

Runlevels, the Boot Process, Services and Processes

Topics Covered in this Chapter

Discuss the runlevels in which a Linux system can operate
and the runlevels used to halt a system and reboot a system
Detail the steps that occur during the Linux boot process
Describe the purpose of the scripts used in the boot process
Introduce several commonly used system services
Explain the need to configure the default settings for services
Learn the benefits of controlling the processes running in memory
Use commands to configure and control services, change and view
runlevels, view and control processes, and display memory statistics

The Runlevels or "Modes" of Linux Operation

Linux can operate in various "modes", which are referred to as runlevels. A runlevel is represented by a number and the default number (runlevel) is specified in /etc/inittab. Linux only operates in one runlevel at a time. The two most commonly used modes are "text mode", which is runlevel 3, and "GUI mode", which is runlevel 5.

Each service uses system resources, such as memory and CPU time. Services that are not required for a runlevel should not be started so that system resources are used efficiently. This is also useful for keeping a system more secure by not running some processes that could allow an "attack" from another system. The services that are required by a system in one runlevel may not be required in another runlevel and they are set up to start or not start for each runlevel.

For example, there is a service named lpd that allows a system to print. The lpd binary in /usr/sbin is executed to start the lpd process, which runs in the background. A process that runs in the background is referred to as a daemon. Therefore, the lpd daemon provides the printing service. This service may be required by a system in one runlevel, but not in another.

To continue the example, the lpd printing service may not be required when the system is booted in text mode (and is working as some type of server), but this service may be required when the system is booted in GUI mode (and is working as a workstation in runlevel 5). Therefore, the system will be configured to not start the lpd service when it is operating in runlevel 3 and also be configured to start the lpd service when it is operating at runlevel 5.

Runlevels are all specified by a number from 0 through 6. Runlevel 1 can also be referred to by using an upper or lower case "s". Table 16-1 shows the Linux Runlevels.

Table 16-1 The Linux Runlevels

Runlevel	Description of the Runlevel
0	Halt - stops all processes in an orderly manner and shuts down - do not set the default runlevel in /etc/inittab to 0
1, S, s	Single user mode - used for system maintenance - only one user can access the system - no network or other services are activated - X is not running and only a few processes are running
2	Multiuser mode - multiple users can log in - all filesystems are mounted - all processes are started, except X, xinetd, at and NIS/NFS
3	Multiuser mode - multiple users can log in - all filesystems are mounted - X is not running - text mode and text login
4	Not used by default
5	Multiuser mode - multiple users can log in - all filesystems are mounted - X is running - GUI mode and GUI login
6	Reboot - stops all processes in an orderly way and reboots the system - do not set the default runlevel in /etc/inittab to 6

Table 16-1 shows general descriptions for each runlevel for this distribution. The "modes" and settings described above for each runlevel are the same for many distributions, but not the same for all distributions. See the documentation of your distribution for specifics on each runlevel.

The most commonly used runlevels are 0, 3, 5 and 6. Runlevel 0 halts (shuts down) the system. Runlevel 6 reboots the system, which is the same as runlevel 0, except that the system starts again after shutting down. Runlevel 3 is text mode (without X) and 5 is GUI mode (with X).

Most Linux systems operate in either runlevel 3 (text mode) or runlevel 5 (GUI mode). Linux servers usually operate in runlevel 3 and workstations usually operate in runlevel 5.

For example, a server does not typically have X installed because it does not require a GUI desktop to operate, and X requires a lot of system resources (memory, processor time and storage). Commands to administer a server are run at the shell prompt and GUI utilities (that require X) are not used. Therefore, runlevel 5, which provides GUI mode, is not required.

Workstations typically require a GUI desktop (provided by X) and therefore operate in runlevel 5.

The default runlevel setting for a system is specified in the inittab file in /etc. The default setting is usually either 3 (text) or 5 (GUI).

Changing the Default Runlevel by Editing inittab

To change the default runlevel (**initdefault**), you log in as root and edit the inittab file and simply change the number at the left of **initdefault** to the desired number. In the statement below, the runlevel is 5. To change the default to 3, simply change the 5 to a 3. After this, the system will boot in text mode.

id:5:**initdefault**:

The word **init** is in **init**default and appears in directory and filenames that are related to system startup. This word usually stands for **init**ialization (such as during a system startup).

The rc.sys**init** file is processed during startup and scripts in the directory named **init**.d are also processed during startup.

The runlevel of 0 causes the system to halt and 6 causes the system to reboot. Do not specify 0 or 6 as the default in inittab or the system will boot and then halt (if set to 0), or it will constantly boot and then reboot (if set to 6).

The Linux Boot Process Overview

When an x86 system boots, the Linux boot loader is loaded from the MBR of the hard disk that is used to boot the system. When the Linux operating system is selected from the the boot loader menu, the Linux kernel (/boot/vmlinuz-*version*) is loaded.

After this, the initrd (boot loader **initialized RAM disk**) image (/boot/initrd-*version*.img) is loaded and a small script within initrd loads some kernel modules that are required to boot. The kernel then executes the binary named **init** (**init**ialization), which is located in /sbin. The init binary is the first process and is sometimes referred to as the "parent of all processes". The init binary then processes the statements the /etc/inittab file.

The /etc/inittab File

The main tasks performed when the /etc/inittab (**init**ialization **table**) file is processed are shown below:

it sets the default runlevel (mode), such as 3 for text mode or 5 for GUI (X) mode
it causes the **rc.sysinit** script in /etc/rc.d to be processed
it causes the **rc** script in /etc/rc.d to be processed
    the **rc** script (through a symlink) causes the /etc/rc.d/**rc.local** file to be processed
it creates the virtual terminals numbered 1 through 6
if in runlevel 3, a text login screen appears so that you can log in to a virtual terminal
if in runlevel 5, the GUI login screen appears so that you can log in to a desktop

The steps done by the **rc.sysinit** and **rc** scripts (in /etc/rc.d) are described in detail below.

The virtual terminals created by inittab are the ones that are accessed with Alt+F**x**, where **x** is a number from 1 through 6).

You will see the contents of /etc/inittab, /etc/rc.d/rc.sysinit, /etc/rc.d/rc and other files used during the boot process during the Hands-On Exercises.

The Tasks Done by the rc.sysinit Script File

The rc.sysinit (**r**un **c**ommand **sys**tem initialization) script in /etc/rc.d is run from within inittab (when inittab is processed by init). The rc.sysinit script performs many **system initialization** tasks. The main tasks are described below.

    the hostname of the machine is set
    the functions script is run
    a "Welcome to Red Hat Linux" banner is printed
    the proc filesystem is mounted
    sysctl is run to configure certain kernel parameters
    the keyboard map is loaded
    the system font is set
    USB Devices are initialized
    the filesystem is checked to determine if fsck should be run or not
    the user and disk quotas are determined
    the ISA PnP devices are configured
    the LVM (Logical Volume Manager) is loaded
    swap partitions are setup using swapon
    the /etc/mtab file is cleared
    the /etc/mtab~ or /etc/mtab~~ file is cleared
    the /proc and other parts of the proc filesystem are put into /etc/mtab
    the depmod binary is run to create a module dependencies
    if used, RAID is initialized and also LVM if set up with RAID
    the filesystems are mounted

The rc.sysinit script also causes the messages that the kernel has put in memory during startup to be written to the log file named /var/log/dmesg. These kernel messages can be viewed by running: dmesg | less. The dmesg command is described in more detail in the chapter on log files.

The Tasks Done by the rc Script File

The script named rc in /etc/rc.d is used to run the "init scripts" that start and stop services for the runlevel being used by the system. These scripts are often referred to as "the System V runlevel scripts", "the Sys V init scripts" or "the scripts that provide SysV services".

 System V was a "commercial" version of UNIX. The "V" in "System V" is the Roman numeral for five, as in "System Five". Linux conforms to the way in which System V initialization scripts work. We will refer to these scripts as "init scripts".

The **rc** (**r**un **c**ommand) script in /etc/rc.d is run from within inittab (when inittab is processed by init) and it starts the services that have been set up to be started for the default runlevel specified in /etc/inittab.

The method, directory structure and files used to control services are described a bit further below.

Linux System Services

There are many services that can be installed on a Linux system. When you installed Linux earlier, you selected items that installed several services. You can also install services after installing Linux. In a later chapter, you will turn on the NFS File Server service, which was installed when you installed Linux, and you will also install the Apache Web server (service).

Some examples of services are provided below. The Daemon heading shows the name of the binary that is run to provide the service. Notice that the name of the service is not always the same name as the daemon. Binary files for daemons often end in "**d**" for **d**aemon.

Service	Daemon	Description
lpd	lpd	line printer daemon that provides the printing service
cups	cupsd	Common UNIX Printing System - an alternative to lpd
email	sendmail	an email service
http	httpd	the Apache Web Server service
nfs	nfsd	the NFS File Server service
bind	named	the Domain Name Service

Some services use more than one daemon and some also use more than one daemon of the same name (several different processes with the same name).

The Init Scripts Directory Structure

The rc.sysinit, rc and rc.local scripts are in /etc/rc.d.

The init.d directory, in the path of /etc/rc.d/init.d, contains the scripts that are used to control services, such as starting and stopping services. This directory contains several scripts, such as lpd and gpm.   The lpd script is used to control the lpd process. The binary for the **lpd** (**l**ine **p**rinter **d**aemon) is in /usr/sbin. The gpm script is used to control the service of mouse support when you are using a virtual terminal (accessed with Ctrl+Alt+F*x*). The binary for the gpm service is also in /usr/sbin.

If you only have a few services installed, you will only have a few files in the init.d directory. If you install more services, then you will have more files in this directory.

Each file in the init.d directory is a script that is used to control a different service (except for a few, such as halt and killall). The script for a service is used to do tasks such as start and stop the daemon(s) (binary file(s)) that provide the service.

For example, a script file named lpd is in /etc/rc.d/init.d. When this script file is run (executed) to start the lpd service, it runs the lpd daemon (binary) in /usr/sbin. The lpd daemon runs as a process and provides the lpd service.

Below is a summary of the init scripts directory structure.

/etc/rc.d/
    init.d   contains the scripts used to control services

    rc0.d   contains symlinks for runlevel **0** that point to scripts in init.d
             these symlinks cause all services to stop and the system to halt

    rc1.d   contains symlinks for runlevel **1** that point to scripts in init.d
             these symlinks cause all services to stop

    rc2.d   contains symlinks for runlevel **2** that point to scripts in init.d
             these symlinks cause some services to start and some to stop

    rc3.d   contains symlinks for runlevel **3** that point to scripts in init.d
             these symlinks cause some services to start and some to stop

    rc4.d   contains symlinks for runlevel **4** that point to scripts in init.d
             these symlinks cause some services to start and some to stop

    rc5.d   contains symlinks for runlevel **5** that point to scripts in init.d
             these symlinks cause some services to start and some to stop

    rc6.d   contains symlinks for runlevel **6** that point to scripts in init.d
             these symlinks cause all services to stop and the system to reboot

The rc0.d, rc1.d, rc2.d, rc3.d, rc4.d, rc5.d and rc6.d can collectively be referred to as the rc?.d directories or as the rc[0-6].d directories. *The rc?.d directories only contain symlinks.* All of these symlinks point to corresponding scripts in /etc/rc.d/init.d, except for the symlinks named S99local, which is located in rc2.d through rc5.d. The S99local symlinks point to the script named rc.local in /etc/rc.d and causes this script to be processed.

The Files in the Init Scripts Directory Structure

The symlinks in the rc?.d directories all begin with either the letter "K" or "S". After these letters, each script has a two digit number, followed by the name of the service.

The "**K**" in the symlink filename indicates that a service should be **killed** (stopped) and the "**S**" indicates that a service should be **started**.

The two digit number specifies the order in which the symlinks are processed, which specifies the order in which services are stopped and started.

For example, let's say that you booted into runlevel 5 and that the rc5.d directory contains two symlinks named S60**lpd** (which points to the script named **lpd** in init.d) and S85**gpm** (which points to the script named **gpm** in init.d).

The "S" in the names of each of these symlinks indicated that these services should be started. The S60lpd symlink points to the lpd script in init.d. Due to the "S", the lpd symlink causes the lpd script to start the lpd service.

If the S60lpd symlink began with a "K" (K60lpd) and you changed into runlevel 5 (from another runlevel, rather than when the system started), then the lpd script in init.d would kill the service by killing the daemon that provides the service.

The S60lpd symlink has the number **60** and the S85gpm symlink has the number **85**. The 60 is lower than the 85 and this causes the lpd service to be started before the gpm service.

Now let's say you need to change into runlevel 3 so that the system can function as a server. You can do this without restarting the system by running the init command, as in: init 3. When you do this, you are changing from runlevel 5 to runlevel 3.

Let's say that you have configured the lpd service so that it does not start in runlevel 3 and that the gpm service still does (if it is not already running). In this case, the symlinks in rc3.d for these two services are K60lpd and S85gpm.

When your system changes from runlevel 5 to runlevel 3, the symlinks in rc3.d are processed. The K60lpd symlink causes the lpd script in init.d to be processed so that the lpd service is killed; the S85gpm symlink causes the gpm script in init.d to be processed so that the gpm service is started (if it is not already started).

The symlinks in the rc?.d directories begin with either "K" or "S" and then this letter is followed by a two digit number. The scripts that are used to control services, such as the scripts named lpd and gpm in init.d, contain a comment statement near the top of the file that is similar to the one shown below, which is from the gpm script in init.d.

```
# chkconfig 2345 85 15
```

The chkconfig command is used to turn services on, turn services off, and to view the settings of services for each of the runlevels. The above statement indicates (to the chkconfig command) the runlevels in which the service should be started by default (2345), the number to be used in the name of the symlink when the service is turned on (85), and the number to be used when the service is turned off (15).

For example, the above statement shows "2345" and this specifies the runlevels in which the service will be started in by default. The symlinks in the rc2.d through rc5.d directories will begin with "S". The "85" in the statement above is the number used for the "S" script and the "15" is used for the "K" script.

For the gpm service, the name of the "S" symlink is "S85gpm" and the name of the "K" symlink is "K15gpm". If this service has been configured to be "on" in runlevels 2, 4 and 5, then the rc2.d, rc4.d and rc5.d directories will each contain a symlink named S85gpm. If this service has been configured to be "off" for runlevel 3, then the rc3.d directory will contain a symlink named K15gpm.

The lpd service uses the same number (60) for the "S" script as for the "K" script.

Each script in the init.d directory is used to control a service, such as starting, stopping and restarting a service. Each script contains the programming logic required to do these tasks for the service that the script represents. These scripts also use functions in the script file named functions in the init.d directory.

Utilities Used to View Available Services and Turn Them On and Off

When your system boots, it boots into the default runlevel specified in inittab. The services that need to be started for the specified default runlevel are started at that time.

When a system changes to runlevel 0, all services are stopped and the system shuts down.

When a system changes to runlevel 6, all services are stopped and the system reboots (restarts).

When a system changes from one runlevel to another (that is not runlevel 0 or 6), such as when the init command is used to change from runlevel 5 to runlevel 3, then the services that are not required in runlevel 3 are stopped and those that are required in runlevel 3 (and are not already running) are started.

The chkconfig, ntsysv and serviceconf commands are used to specify the services that are started and stopped for each runlevel. Changes made in these three utilities do not take effect until the current runlevel is changed, either by restarting the system or using a command, such as init to change to a different runlevel. However, the service command can be used to start, stop and restart services without restarting a system or changing the runlevel of a system.

For example, let's say you are in runlevel 5 and the lpd service is not running. You run one of the above three utilities and set the default for the lpd service to "on" for runlevel 5. This does not start the service until the system is restarted or until the system changes into this runlevel. However, if you restart your system in runlevel 5, the service will be started; or if you change to a different runlevel and then back to runlevel 5, the service will be started.

The chkconfig, ntsysv and serviceconf commands can only be used to display and modify the default settings of the services that have been installed on your system (by turning the default setting to on or off for each runlevel). They are not used to add a service to your system. Services are added (installed) in the same way as packages (software programs) are installed.

The chkconfig, ntsysv and serviceconf utilities are described below. They all display the status (on or off) of the services that are installed on your system and can be used to turn a service on or off. The serviceconf utility can also be used to start, stop and restart a service.

The ntsysv Command

The ntsysv command runs the ntsysv (text-based GUI) utility. The "**sysv**" in "nt**sysv**" stands for "System V". This utility does not require X to run.

A service can be turned on by putting an * (asterisk) at the left of it and turned off by removing the *. Pressing the Spacebar toggles the * on and off.

By default, this utility configures services by setting them to on or off for the current runlevel (only). To configure services in one or more other runlevels, use the --level option.

For example, you are working in runlevel 5 and need to set up a service so that it starts when the system is in runlevel 3. The following command runs the utility so that you can modify the settings of a service for runlevel 3:

    ntsysv --level 3

Figure 16-1 shows the ntsysv utility. The services that are "on" for the current runlevel have an * (asterisk) at the left of them.

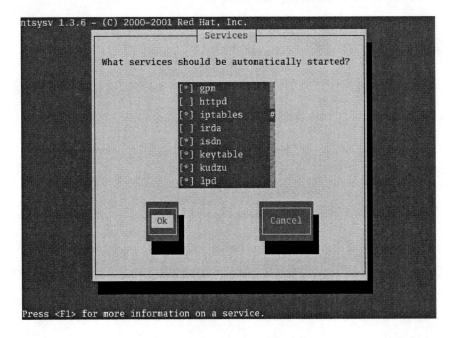

Figure 16-1 - The ntsysv utility

The serviceconf Command

The **serviceconf** command runs the **Service Configuration** (X GUI) utility, which allows you to turn services on or off for runlevels 3, 4 and 5. Turning a service on for a runlevel does not start the service until the system changes into the runlevel for which the service was turned on (by restarting the system in the runlevel or changing into the runlevel). The same is true for turning a runlevel off. However, this utility can also be used to start, stop and restart services by selecting the Start, Stop and Restart buttons. This utility requires X to be running.

To configure a service for a runlevel, select the runlevel (3, 4 or 5) from the Edit Runlevel menu. After this, click on the box at the left of the name of the service so that a check mark appears. Be sure to select the Save button prior to closing this utility. If you save changes to xinetd services, xinetd is restarted. If you save changes to other services, they are not restarted.

Figure 16-2 shows the Service Configuration utility. When a service is selected, a description of the service appears at the bottom of the utility. The gpm service is selected and its description appears at the bottom.

Figure 16-2 - The Service Configuration utility

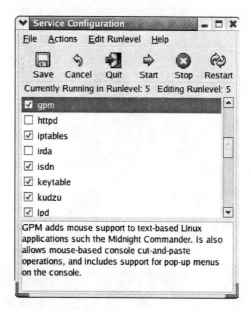

The chkconfig Command

The chkconfig command is used to turn services on and off in runlevels 2 through 5. This command is also used to add a service to the init scripts directory structure, delete a service from the init scripts directory structure, and list the services and their status (on or off) for each runlevel. This command does not require X and provides a very quick method of viewing and modifying service settings.

Examples of the chkconfig Command

In the examples below, replace *servicename* with the name of a service, such as lpd or gpm.

chkconfig --list

This lists all of the services and the status (on or off) of each service for the runlevels 0 through 6. The output of this set of options is commonly "piped" to the less command.

chkconfig --list *servicename*

This command displays the same information as above, but for one service only.

chkconfig *servicename* on

This command turns the *servicename* on for runlevels 2 through 5. After running this command, the symlinks in rc2.d through rc5.d for the *servicename* will begin with "S".

chkconfig *servicename* off

This command turns the *servicename* off for runlevels 2 through 5. After running this command, the symlinks in rc2.d through rc5.d for the *servicename* will begin with "K".

chkconfig --level 35 *servicename* on

This command turns the *servicename* on for runlevels 3 and 5. After running this command, the symlinks in rc3.d and rc5.d for the *servicename* will begin with "S". Other runlevels and combinations of runlevels can also be specified in place of 3 and 5.

chkconfig --level 3 *servicename* off

This command turns the *servicename* off for runlevel 3. After running this command, the symlink for the *servicename* in rc3.d will begin with "K". Other runlevels and combinations of runlevels can also be specified in place of 3.

chkconfig --add *servicename*

Adds the symlinks for the *servicename* to the rc?.d directories. The script that runs the service must exist in init.d and have a chkconfig statement similar to the following (described above).

```
# chkconfig 2345 85 15
```

chkconfig --del *servicename*

Removes the symlinks for the *servicename* from the rc?.d directories. The script that runs the service must exist in init.d and have a chkconfig statement similar to the one described above.

The service Command

The service command is a script file in /sbin that is used to control services. This command is used to view the status of services, start a service that is not currently running, and stop a service that is no longer required.

This command is also used to restart a service that is already running. When a service is restarted, it is stopped and then started again. This is often done after modifying the settings in a configuration file for a service. The service is stopped so that it can be started, and then it is started so that the new settings in a configuration file will be read.

Examples of the service Command

service --status-all

This displays the status of all services. The status can be "running..." or "stopped". The output of this option is commonly "piped" to the less command.

service --status-all | grep *servicename*

This displays: *servicename* (pid 631) is running... for the *servicename* specified.

service *servicename* status

This displays: *servicename* (pid 631) is running... or: *servicename* is stopped for the *servicename* specified.

service *servicename* start

This starts the *servicename*.

service *servicename* stop

This stops the *servicename*.

service *servicename* restart

This stops the *servicename* and then starts it again. This is often done after modifying the configuration file of a service, so that the modified configuration file is read when the service starts.

The init Command

As described earlier, the init binary is run during the boot process. This binary can also be run as a command. It is used to change from one runlevel to any other runlevel.

For example, a system is working in runlevel 5 as a workstation in GUI mode, and now it needs to be working as a server in runlevel 3 without X running. The init command is used to change from runlevel 5 to runlevel 3.

The following command will change to runlevel *x*. Replace *x* with the desired runlevel.

    init x

The telinit command was formerly used to change from one runlevel to another. This command has been replaced by a symlink named telinit that points to the init binary.

The runlevel Command

The runlevel command displays your current runlevel and previous runlevel. When this command is run without any options, two items appear.

If you have not changed runlevel since the system booted, then the letter "**N**" (for **None** - no previous runlevel) appears at the left and the current runlevel appears at the right. If you change the runlevel and then run the runlevel command, the previous runlevel appears at the left and the current runlevel appears at the right. If you have used "s" or "S" to change to runlevel 1 (single user mode), then "s" or "S", rather than 1, will appear for this runlevel.

Overview of Processes

Linux is an extremely stable operating system that rarely crashes and therefore, rarely needs to be restarted or rebooted. If a program (process) crashes, it can usually be removed from memory by running a command to remove the process from memory, without having to restart or reboot the system. These features make the OS extremely popular and convenient!

When Linux boots, the init binary is executed and it becomes a process that stays in memory for as long as the system is running. The init process is often referred to as the "parent of all processes" and it starts many other processes when a system boots.

Most of the processes that are run by init have the owner (user name) of root and the UID of 0, which is the user id number of the root user. Some other processes have the owner name of a "system" user.

For example, the lpd (line printer daemon) process runs with the owner name of lp and the xfs (X Font Server) process runs with the owner name of xfs.

Each process running in memory is assigned a unique number. This number is referred to as the **process id**, or **pid**. The pid of the process named init is 1. There are commands that display the pid of the processes in memory.

Each time a program is run, such as a binary, script or command, it starts a new process. Sometimes a program starts one or more other processes. In other words, a program (process) other than init can start a process. In this case, init is the parent of the process (the program), but the program can also run one or more other processes.

Each process, except init, has a parent process. The number of the parent process is referred to as the **ppid (p**arent **p**rocess **id**). The ppid of init is 0 because init does not have a parent process. The ppid of any process started by init is 1 because the pid of init is 1. Since init starts many other processes, there are many processes that will have the ppid of 1.

The ppid of a process that is run by another process (other than init), is the pid number of the parent process. In other words, if the pid of a process is 1536 and this process (rather than init) runs another process with the pid number of 1562, then the ppid of 1562 is 1536. There are commands that display the ppid of a process.

Linux allows you to use commands to view a large amount of information regarding the processes that are running in memory. It also allows you to control the processes in memory by removing them from memory or changing their priority.

When you run a command at the shell prompt with a & (ampersand) at the end of the command, the job number of the process appears in [ ] and the process id appears at the right. The & at the right of the command causes the command to run in the background and the shell prompt appears after running the command.

For example, running the command: xclock & may show the output of: [1] 2062. The "[1]" is the job number and the "2062" is the process ID.

The ps Command

The **ps** (**p**rocess **s**tatus) command is used to view a large amount of information on the status of the processes that are running in memory. It shows a "snapshot" of the processes when the command is run. The output of the command is not updated. The top command shows the top processes in memory and its output is updated frequently.

This command has many options that are used to view information on processes in many different ways. Commonly used options are described below.

Figure 16-3 shows the output of the ps command when it is run with the -aux options. Notice the column headings across the top and that init is at the top right and the number 1 appears below the PID heading for this process. The init process is the "parent of all processes".

```
USER      PID %CPU %MEM   VSZ  RSS TTY     STAT START   TIME COMMAND
root        1  0.0  0.3  1264  416 ?       S    08:32   0:04 init
root        2  0.0  0.0     0    0 ?       SW   08:32   0:00 [keventd]
root        3  0.0  0.0     0    0 ?       SW   08:32   0:00 [kapmd]
root        4  0.0  0.0     0    0 ?       SWN  08:32   0:00 [ksoftirqd_CPU0]
root        5  0.0  0.0     0    0 ?       SW   08:32   0:02 [kswapd]
root        6  0.0  0.0     0    0 ?       SW   08:32   0:00 [bdflush]
root        7  0.0  0.0     0    0 ?       SW   08:32   0:00 [kupdated]
root        8  0.0  0.0     0    0 ?       SW   08:32   0:00 [mdrecoveryd]
root       13  0.0  0.0     0    0 ?       SW   08:32   0:00 [kjournald]
root       69  0.0  0.0     0    0 ?       SW   08:32   0:00 [khubd]
root      163  0.0  0.0     0    0 ?       SW   08:32   0:00 [kjournald]
root      164  0.0  0.0     0    0 ?       SW   08:32   0:00 [kjournald]
root      165  0.0  0.0     0    0 ?       SW   08:32   0:00 [kjournald]
root      166  0.0  0.0     0    0 ?       SW   08:32   0:00 [kjournald]
root      167  0.0  0.0     0    0 ?       SW   08:32   0:00 [kjournald]
root      457  0.0  0.3  1324  476 ?       S    08:32   0:00 syslogd -m 0
root      461  0.0  0.3  1264  416 ?       S    08:32   0:00 klogd -x
rpc       478  0.0  0.3  1404  488 ?       S    08:32   0:00 portmap
rpcuser   497  0.0  0.4  1444  528 ?       S    08:32   0:00 rpc.statd
root      582  0.0  0.3  1256  420 ?       S    08:32   0:00 /usr/sbin/apmd -p
```

Figure 16-3 - The output of the ps -aux command

The Column Headings of the ps Command

Below is a description of the main column headings that appear when the ps command is run with the -aux options. These column headings appear in Figure 16-3.

USER - The user name of the owner of the process.

PID - The process id number.

%CPU - The percentage of the total amount of CPU time that is being used by the process.

%MEM - The percentage of the total amount of memory that is being used by the process.

VSZ - The amount of virtual memory used.

RSS - The related kernel function.

TTY - The name of the terminal (virtual terminal or terminal emulation window) that is running the process. Virtual terminals are tty*x*, where *x* is a number. Virtual terminal 1 is tty1, virtual terminal 2 is tty2 and so on. Terminal emulation windows are pts/0 for the first window that is opened, pts/1 for the second and so on. This is useful for showing you "where" a process is running.

STAT - The **state** (a.k.a. status) of a process. The codes used for this column are shown below.

Codes used in the STAT (state) Column

R - running
S - sleeping
W - has no resident pages
< - a high priority process
N - a low priority process
D - uninterruptible sleep (usually I/O)
R - runnable (on run queue)
T - traced or stopped
Z - a defunct ("zombie") process
L - has pages locked into memory (for real-time and custom I/O)

START - The time that the process was started.

TIME - The amount of time that the process has run since it was started in hour:minute format.

COMMAND - The name of the command that started the process.

Commonly Used Options of the ps Command

The following discussion of options refers to using the a, u and x options together rather than individually. The a, x and l options are also commonly used together, as shown in the examples below.

The **-a** (**all**) option shows all processes, including the processes of other users. The processes are grouped by virtual terminals and terminal emulation windows. In other words, all of the processes that are running in a terminal (virtual terminal or terminal emulation window) are grouped together. This allows you to see which programs are running on a terminal-by-terminal basis.

The **-u** (user name) option shows all processes running in the current terminal by user name. The user name beside a process is the name of the user that started the process and this user is the owner of the process.

The **-x** (not e**x**clude) option shows all processes currently running on a system.

Examples of the ps Command

The output of the ps command, such as when it is used with the -aux and -alx options, is commonly "piped" to the less command.

ps -aux

This is one of the most commonly used sets of options. The PID column shows the number of the **process id (pid)**. The output of this command is often piped to grep using the name of a process. This is commonly done to get the **pid (process id)** number or **ppid (parent process id)** of a process. The pid and ppid numbers can be used with commands to control processes.

ps -aux | grep gpm

Displays output for the process named gpm (only). Commonly used to get the pid number of a process, which appears in column 2.

ps -axl

The -l (long format) option is often used with the -ax options. One of the main benefits of using this option is that in addition to the PID column, it shows a **PPID (parent process id)** column that displays the parent process id of a process. The parent process id for a process is the number of the process that started the process.

For example, init is the first process and has the pid number of 1. It does not have a parent and so its ppid number is 0. Many processes are run by init and these processes have the ppid of 1 (which is init). However, init is not the only process that runs other processes. Many processes run other processes.

You can use the kill command and specify the pid of a process to stop some processes. However, this does not always work to stop a process. Sometimes you need to kill the parent of a process to kill a process. In this case you use the ppid number of the parent process to kill the process (and the parent process). Do not kill the parent process if the parent process is number 1, which is the init process.

ps -axl | grep lpd

Displays output for the process named lpd (only). Commonly used to get the pid number (column 2) or ppid number (column 4) of a process. The pid number is often used with commands to kill a process.

ps *pid*

Replace *pid* with the process id number shown in the PID column. This shows information on a specific process.

ps --User *username*

Replace *username* with the name of a user, such as root or cwest. This shows the processes that are running for a specific user.

ps --Group *groupname*

Replace *groupname* with the name of a group, such as root (the "system" group named root). This shows the processes that are running for a specific group.

ps -eH

Displays all processes (-e) in a hierarchy (-H) with the parent process (init) flush left and the child processes indented below parent processes.

The top Command

The top command shows the top processes in memory by CPU usage and a large amount of statistical information that is updated frequently. This utility is interactive and accepts keystrokes while it is running so that you can change the display of information.

Table 16-2 shows some of the keys that can be used when working with the top utility. To use one of the keys below, type in the key *but do not press Enter*, except as described for the k key. Use the case (upper or lower) of each letter as shown.

For example, use a lower case "h" for help information and an upper case M to sort by memory usage.

Table 16-2 - Keys for the top Command

Keys	Description
h	get help information
q	quit out of help
M	sort by memory usage
P	sort by CPU usage
N	sort by process id
i	toggle on/off the display of idle processes
k	kill a process - you are prompted for a *pidnumber*
	type in a *pid* number and press Enter to kill the process

Figure 16-4 shows the top utility. Notice the statistics in the top three lines. Look for the number of users in the top line and the breakdown of the processes in the second line. The fourth and fifth lines show memory statistics, including swap space statistics. Current processes appear below the PID, USER and other headings. Notice the X, slocate, top, and init commands (processes) below the COMMAND heading.

```
 4:01pm  up  7:29,  2 users,  load average: 0.97, 0.63, 0.58
98 processes: 94 sleeping, 4 running, 0 zombie, 0 stopped
CPU states: 48.1% user,  4.9% system,  0.0% nice, 46.9% idle
Mem:   126116K av,  123944K used,    2172K free,       OK shrd,    3208K buff
Swap:  265032K av,   36032K used,  229000K free                  54028K cached

  PID USER      PRI  NI  SIZE  RSS SHARE STAT %CPU %MEM    TIME COMMAND
  807 root        7 -10 27516  11M  5248 S <  24.2  9.3   39:51 X
  957 cwest      20   0  9100 8680  5740 R    21.2  6.8    1:34 gnome-terminal
 2194 cwest      15   0  1680 1680   392 D     4.1  1.3    0:00 slocate
 2186 root       16   0  1036 1036   820 R     1.3  0.8    0:03 top
  865 cwest      15   0  5792 5500  4532 S     1.1  4.3    0:40 metacity
    5 root       15   0     0    0     0 SW    0.1  0.0    0:00 kswapd
  867 cwest      15   0  5004 4012  3844 S     0.1  3.1    0:01 gnome-settings-
 2057 cwest      15   0  1484 1484  1120 S     0.1  1.1    0:00 bash
    1 root       15   0   448  416   396 S     0.0  0.3    0:04 init
    2 root       15   0     0    0     0 SW    0.0  0.0    0:00 keventd
    3 root       15   0     0    0     0 SW    0.0  0.0    0:00 kapmd
    4 root       34  19     0    0     0 SWN   0.0  0.0    0:00 ksoftirqd_CPU0
```

Figure 16-4 - The top utility

If your system is running slower than you think it should be, or is not working properly in some other way, you can run this utility and look for processes that are using a large amount of resources, such as CPU time (below the %CPU heading) and processes that are taking a large percentage of memory (below the %MEM heading). Your system may have one or more processes that are not working properly and that need to be killed (stopped).

To kill a process in top, type: k   and type the number of the process ; press Enter

type the number of the signal to use to kill the process and press Enter, or

press Enter to use the default signal of 15.

There are sixty-three signals that can be used to kill a process. A listing of them can be seen by running: kill -l   (using the letter "l", not the number 1). Some of the commonly used signals that can be used to kill a process are shown in Table 16-3.

Table 16-3 - Signals Used to Kill Processes

Signal	Description
1	SIGHUP (signal to hang up and start the process again)
HUP	same as above
9	kill (forcibly terminate a process)
15	term (software termination signal - the default)

Signal 1 (SIGHUP) will cause some processes to stop and then start. Signal 9 is used to force a process to be killed when other signals will not kill it. Signal 15 is the default used by top.

The kill Command

The kill command is used to kill a process that is not working properly or is no longer required. A number can be used with the kill command to send a "signal" to kill a process. Some of the common signals used with the kill command are shown in Table 16-3 above.

The *pid* number and *ppid* number of a process that needs to be killed can be seen with the ps command and the top command, as described above. If the process (only) cannot be killed, you may need to use the *ppid* number to kill the parent process. The name of a process or filename of a process is not used with this command.

You must be the owner of a process or the root user to kill a process with the kill command.

Examples of the kill Command

kill *pid*

Replace *pid* with the process id of the process to be killed. No signal number has been specified with this command. Therefore, by default, the TERM (SIGTERM) signal, which is signal number 15, is sent.

kill -1 *pid* or kill -HUP *pid*

This can be used to kill some processes and cause the process to be restarted. When the process is started, it will read the configuration file for itself (if one exists).

kill -9 [*pid* | *ppid*]

Replace *pid* with the process id of the process to be killed. This sends signal 9 to forcibly kill the process. If this does not work, you may want to use the *ppid* rather than the *pid*. Be sure that you do not kill a parent process that you require and do not use the *ppid* of 1, which is init.

The killall Command

The killall command is used to kill a process by specifying the process name or by specifying the filename of an executable that is kept open (in use) while the process is running. The pid or ppid of a process is not used with this command.

Examples of the killall Command

For the following commands, replace *name* with the name of a process or the filename of an executable that is kept open (in use) while the process is running.

killall *name*

Kills the process with the *name* (process name or executable filename) that is specified.

The following command will kill the slocate executable (binary):

> killall slocate

Some services, such as nfs (for the NFS File Server) and http (the Apache Web server) run several processes that have the same name. This command allows you to quickly kill all of these processes with one command.

When the nfs service is started, eight processes (**d**aemons) named nfs**d** are started as well as one named rpc.mountd and another named rpc.rquotad.

When the http service service is started, several processes (**d**aemons) named httpd are started.

The command: killall -9 nfsd kills all eight of the nfsd processes, but does not kill the other two processes (rpc.mountd and rpc.rquotad) that are started when the service named nfs is started.

If you want to kill all of the processes started by a service, and if a script for the service is in the init.d directory, the following command is an easy method of killing all of the processes:

> service *servicename* stop

For example, the following command will kill the ten processes that are started when then nfs service is started:

> service nfs stop

killall -1 *name* or kill -HUP *name*

With some processes, this can be used to kill the process and also cause the process to be restarted. When the process is started, it will read the configuration file for itself (if one exists).

killall -9 *name*

This sends signal 9 to forcibly kill the process.

The nice and renice Commands

The nice command is used to start a program (process) with a specific high or low priority. The highest priority is -20 and the lowest priority is 19. This allows you to increase or decrease the speed with which the process will be completed and how the process runs in relation to other processes.

The renice command is used to change the priority of an existing process (program). The pid of the program is used with this command.

Examples of the nice Command

nice -20 *programname programoptions*

This starts the *programname* with the highest priority. The *programoptions* of the program can be specified at the right of the *programname*.

nice 19 *programname programoptions*

This starts the *programname* with the lowest priority.

Example of the renice Command

renice -15 1277

This changes the priority of the program that has the pid number of 1277 to -15.

The free Command

The free command, without any options, displays memory statistics in kilobytes. This includes swap space statistics. This information is also shown at the top of the top command.

The **-m** option shows the statistics in **megabytes** and the **-t** option adds a line that shows totals. The -t option can be used with the -m options to show totals.

All of the commands discussed in this chapter can be run from any directory.

Hands-On Exercises

 ### Logging In to See the Files Used in the Boot Process

Log in as cwest ; open a terminal emulation window ; maximize it ; su to root.

A printer needs to be created for these exercises so that whenever the lpd process is started, it will start *and stay running*.

]# printconf

Click on the New button ; Forward ; below Queue Name:, type in: abc ;

Local Printer is selected ; Forward ; the /dev/lp0 device is selected ; Forward ;

Postscript Printer is selected ; Forward ; Apply ; File ; Quit ; Yes ; OK.

]# service lpd status

The status should be "running..." and the pid number appears.

 ### Viewing the Files Used in the Boot Process

]# cd /etc

]# cat inittab | nl | less

Lines 2 through 7 describe the file.

Lines 8 through 16 describe the runlevels.

Line 17 contains the following statement, which specifies the default (**initdefault**) runlevel:

> id:**5**:**initdefault**:

The statement above indicates runlevel **5**. If this file is edited and the 5 is changed to a 3, then the system will boot to runlevel 3.

Line 19 contains the following statement, which causes the script named rc.sysinit in /etc/rc.d to be run:

> si::sysinit:/etc/rc.d/rc.sysinit

This script does many tasks, such as set the hostname, display the "Welcome to Red Hat Linux" banner, mount the proc filesystem, configure certain kernel parameters, set the system font and initialize USB devices.

Lines 20 through 26 cause the rc script to be run with an argument that is the same number as the default runlevel. This causes the "S" symlinks in the appropriate rc?.d directory to process the scripts in /etc/rc.d/init.d. These scripts start the services that should be started for the runlevel specified in the **initdefault** statement described above.

For example, the default runlevel (**initdefault**) in the statement above is 5. The statement below (on line 25 in inittab) causes script named rc in /etc/rc.d to execute for runlevel 5.

> l5:5:wait:/etc/rc.d/rc **5**

The first 5 in the above statement is treated as a comment. The second 5 causes the above statement to be processed if **initdefault** is runlevel 5. The "rc 5" at the right of the above statement causes the script named rc in /etc/rc.d to be run with the argument of 5. This causes the symlinks that begin with "S" in /etc/rc.d/rc5.d to be processed. The "S" symlinks point to corresponding scripts in init.d and cause these scripts to be processed so that they start the services. These scripts start the services that have been configured to be started for runlevel 5. These same scripts in init.d are also used to kill services, such as if a symlink in a rc?.d directory begins with a "K".

For example, the rc5.d directory contains an "S" symlink named S60**lpd**. This symlink points to a corresponding script in init.d named **lpd**. The "**S**" in the symlink causes the lpd script to be processed so that the service starts. If this symlink began with "K", as in K60**lpd**, then the process(es) for the service would not be started.

The "K" symlinks in an rc?.d directory are not processed when a system boots, because there are no processes that have been started that need to be killed. A "K" symlink is processed when a system changes from one runlevel to another and a service that was running in one runlevel is not required in the new runlevel.

If the 5s in the above (indented) statement were 3s, then the script named rc would be run with the parameter of 3. In this case, the "S" symlinks in rc3.d would be processed and these would cause the corresponding scripts in init.d to be processed so that they start the services required for runlevel 3.

Line 28 causes the binary named update in /sbin/ to be run.

Line 30 causes /sbin/shutdown -t3 -r now to be run when the Ctrl+Alt+Delete keys are pressed. The -t3 option causes the system to wait 3 seconds and the -r now options cause the system to reboot.

Line 35 causes /sbin/shutdown -f -h +2 to be run when the power goes off and a UPS is connected to the system (see the comments on lines 33 and 34). The -f option causes the system to skip the fsck (filesystem **check**) when it reboots and the -h and +2 options cause the system to wait two minutes before halting.

If the above command has been run and then the power is restored, line 37 causes /sbin/shutdown -c to be run to cancel the shutdown. The **-c** option **c**ancels the shutdown.

Lines 39 through 44 create the six virtual terminals that are accessed with Ctrl+Alt+F**x**, where **x** is a number from 1 through 6. The following statement creates the first virtual terminal.

```
1:2345:respawn:/sbin/mingetty tty1
```

The "1" at the far left is for virtual terminal 1. The "2345" cause the virtual terminals to be created in runlevels 2 through 5 (and not in runlevels 0 or 6). The word "respawn" causes the process to be restarted (respawned) when the process has ended. Therefore, when the process for a virtual terminal is ended, it is automatically restarted. The "tty1" is the device name (/dev/tty1) used for virtual terminal 1.

When in runlevel 5, line 47 causes a script called prefdm in /etc/X11 to be run with the -nodaemon option. This script runs the preferred display manager (X Window Display Manager), such as gdm for GNOME or kdm for KDE. The word "respawn" in this statement causes the display manager to be restarted whenever it has been terminated, such as when Ctrl+Alt+Backspace has been pressed.

③ Viewing the rc.sysinit Script

```
]# cd rc.d          # this is the parent directory for the init scripts

]# clear ; ls -l
```

There are three scripts in this directory named rc, rc.local and rc.sysinit. There are seven rc?.d directories that contain symlinks (**only**) and almost all of these symlinks point to scripts in init.d. The few symlinks that do not point to scripts in init.d point to rc.local (in the current directory).

Now have a look at *some* of the statements in rc.sysinit. This script is over six hundred lines long and is run from inittab. It performs many **system initialization** tasks, such as setting the hostname and displaying the "Welcome to Red Hat Linux" banner. It causes many messages to appear on the screen when the system boots.

```
]#cat  rc.sysinit  |  nl  |  less
```

Lines 13 through 21 assign a value to the HOSTNAME variable.

Line 22 runs the functions script so that the functions in this script are available to the rc.sysinit script.

Lines 24 through 39 cause the "Welcome to Red Hat Linux" banner to appear as the system is booting and also allows a system to go into interactive mode if the letter "I" is pressed. When "I" is pressed, you are prompted (with Yes, No or Continue) and given the chance to stop the script from doing many of its tasks. Therefore, if you need to boot a system without having one or more of the steps in the script executed, you can select No.

Line 43 mounts the /proc filesystem.

Lines 118 through 132 load the system font. Lines 120 to 122 show a for . . . in . . . do control structure and lines 123 to 130 use a case . . . in . . . pattern control structure.

Lines 136 through 146 initialize the USB controller and HID devices.

Spend a few more minutes looking through the file. Look for comments that describe the statements below the comments.

 Viewing the rc Script

Now have a look at *some* of the statements in the rc script. This script is over eighty lines long and is run from inittab when a system boots, and is also run when the runlevel changes. It is used to process the symlinks in an rc?.d directory (where the ? in rc?.d is the runlevel number). The symlinks cause the corresponding script in init.d to start or stop a service (the process(es) that need to be started or stopped for the service).

For example, let's say that a symlink named **K60lpd** exists in the rc?.d directory for the runlevel that the system is changing to (not booting to). This symlink points to the script named **lpd** in init.d. When the rc script processes the K60lpd symlink, this causes the lpd script to be run to kill the lpd process.

To continue the example, let's say that a symlink named **S60lpd** exists in the rc?.d directory for the runlevel that the system is booting into or changing into. This symlink points to the script named **lpd** in init.d. When the rc script processes the S60lpd symlink, this causes the lpd script to be run to start the lpd process (if it is not already running).

```
]#cat  rc  |  nl  |  less
```

Read the comment on lines 3 and 4.

Lines 10 through 21 create a function named check_runlevel.

Read the comment on line 22.

Line 28 runs the functions script.

Lines 46 through 58 process the symlinks that begin with "K" in the rc?.d directory (where the ? in rc?.d is the runlevel number). These symlinks point to corresponding scripts in init.d and these scripts are run to kill the processes that need to be killed (stopped). Line 47 uses the function named check_runlevel that was created in lines 10 through 21.

Lines 60 through 88 process the symlinks that begin with "S" in the rc?.d directory (where the ? in rc?.d is the runlevel number). These symlinks point to corresponding scripts in init.d and these scripts are run to start the processes for the runlevel. Line 61 uses the function named check_runlevel that was created in lines 10 through 21.

Viewing the Contents of the Init Scripts Directory Structure

Now have a look at the contents of the init scripts directory structure. Your current directory path should be /etc/rc.d.

```
]# ls  -lR  |  less
```

Look for "./init.d:". The contents of the init.d directory are shown below this. Each of these files is a script that represents a service. These scripts are used to start and stop services. They are also used to do a few other tasks, such as restart (stop and then start) a service and display the status of a service.

A single script in init.d is used to control the service, such as starting and stopping the service. The same script is used to start a service and stop a service.

For example, the lpd script is used to start a service and is also used to stop a service, based on whether the symlink in rc?.d begins with a "K" or an "S".

Scroll through the listing until you can see "./rc0.d". This is the directory for runlevel 0, which is used to halt the system.

Scroll through the list of files in rc0.d. Each file is a symlink that points to a corresponding file in init.d. All of these symlinks, except two, begin with "K". The "K" files are used to kill all of the services that are running. The two "S" files (at the bottom of the list for rc0.d) run the killall and halt scripts in init.d. These symlinks "start" the killall and halt scripts.

Scroll through the listing until you can see "./rc1.d". This is the directory for runlevel 1, which is **single** used maintenance mode.

Scroll through the list of files. Each file is a symlink that points to a corresponding file in init.d. All of these symlinks, except two, begin with "K". The "K" files are used to kill all of the services that are running. The two "S" files (at the bottom of the list for rc1.d) run the **single** (for **single** mode) and keytable scripts in init.d.

Scroll through the list of files below "./rc2.d". This is the directory for runlevel 2, which is multi-user mode. Some of these symlinks begin with "K" so that the service will be killed and others begin with "S" so that the service will be started.

Scroll through the listing below "./rc3.d". This is the directory for runlevel 3, which is text mode. Some of the symlinks begin with "K" and others begin with "S".

Scroll through the listings below "./rc4.d" and "./rc5.d". These are the directories for runlevels 4 and 5. Some of the symlinks begin with "K" and others begin with "S".

Scroll through the listing below "./rc6.d". This is the directory for runlevel 6, which is used to stop all processes and **reboot** the system. All of these symlinks, except two, begin with "K". The "K" files are used to kill all of the services that are running. The two "S" files run the killall and halt scripts in init.d. Notice that the symlink named S01**reboot** points to the script named halt. It runs the halt script so that the system is rebooted after it is halted.

```
]# cat init.d/halt | nl | less      # look at the halt script
```

Read the comments on lines 3 through 5. Lines 28 through 41 show a case . . . in . . . pattern control structure. The statements below line 29 are processed if the "case" is "halt" and the statements below line 33 are processed if the "case" is "reboot".

6 **Viewing the Files for the Service Named lpd**

```
]# pwd              # you should be in /etc/rc.d
```

```
]# clear ; find /etc/rc.d -name '*lpd'
```

By putting the path to the current directory (/etc/rc.d) as part of the find command, the full path to the directories and files will appear in the output (rather than in the relative path). In this case, only files will appear because there are no directories below the current path that end in lpd.

The script named lpd in init.d appears and then the corresponding symlinks in each of the rc?.d directories appear. If you have not changed the defaults, then the symlinks in rc0.d, rc1.d and rc6.d should begin with "K" and the symlinks in rc2.d through rc5.d begin with "S". Therefore, the lpd service will be started whenever the system boots into, or changes into, runlevels 2 through 5.

Notice that all of the "K" and "S" symlinks have the number 60.

7 **Viewing the Script Named functions**

```
]# cat init.d/functions | nl | less      # view the contents of functions
```

Read the comments on lines 3 and 4.

Lines 65 through 71 create a function named checkpid.

Lines 74 through 112 create a function named daemon.

Lines 140 through 206 create a function named **killproc** (for **kill proc**ess). Notice the word "signal" on line 144 and that the -9 signal is assigned to the killlevel variable on 153. Read line 170. Lines 176, 181 and 192 run the kill command. The variable named $pid contains the **pid** (**p**rocess **id**) number.

```
]# clear ; cat init.d/functions | grep '()' | nl
```

The names of the functions in the script named functions appear. There are seventeen functions that are created in this script. Whenever the script named functions is run from within another script, the functions in functions become available to the script.

```
]# grep functions init.d/* | less
```

This shows the statements in all of the scripts in init.d that contain the word "functions". Notice the filenames at the right of "init.d/". Virtually all script files in init.d run the script named functions from within them. Most of these statements run the script named functions from within a script in init.d and some of these statements are comments.

Notice that some of these scripts contain the following statement (notice the full path):

. /etc/**rc.d**/init.d/functions

and others contain the following statement (notice the full path):

. /etc/init.d/functions

The script named functions is in /etc/rc.d/init.d and a symlink to the init.d directory is in /etc, so that script statements that refer to /etc/init.d (rather than /etc/rc.d/init.d) will work. More on this further below.

 Viewing the lpd Script File in init.d

```
]#  cat  init.d/lpd  |  grep '()'
```

The functions named stop, start and restart are created in lpd.

```
]#  cat  init.d/lpd  |  nl  |  less       # view the contents of the lpd script
```

Line 6 shows: # chkconfig 2345 60 60

The "2345" indicates that the lpd service can be used in runlevels 2 through 5. The two "60"s are the numbers used for the "K" and "S" symlinks in rc2.d through rc5.d.

Line 12 runs the script named functions from within the script named lpd. Notice that the path to the script file is /etc/**rc.d**/init.d.

Line 42 uses the function named daemon that was created by the script named functions and lines 51 and 84 use the function named killproc, that was created by the script named functions. Other statements in the lpd script also use functions created by the script named functions.

Lines 64 through 91 show a case ... in ... pattern control structure. These "cases" do tasks such as start and stop the lpd service and display the status of the service. Notice the "-HUP" in line 84. This is an option (signal) used to kill a process and cause it to be started again.

Viewing the gpm Script File in init.d

```
]# cat init.d/gpm | grep '()'
```

The functions named start and stop are created in gpm.

```
]# cat init.d/gpm | nl | less     # view the contents of the lpd script
```

Line 3 shows: # chkconfig 2345 85 15

The "2345" indicate that the gpm service can be used in runlevels 2 through 5. The "85" is the number used for an "S" symlink in rc2.d through rc5.d and "15" is used for a "K" symlink in the rc?.d directories.

Lines 4 through 7 provide a description of the gpm service. Midnight Commander is a text-based GUI utility that is used to manage files and do tasks, such as copy and move files.

Line 12 runs the script named functions from within the script named gpm. Notice that the path to the script file is /etc/init.d (without an **rc.d** directory between the etc and init.d directories - as seen earlier in the lpd script file).

Scroll to the bottom of the script. This script is very similar to the lpd script.

 The Order Services are Turned On and Turned Off

```
]# ls -l rc3.d | less
```

The "K" symlinks are processed in numerical order, from the lowest to highest. The same is true for the "S" symlinks. The number in the name of the symlink specifies the order in which a service is started in relation to other services.

```
]# clear ; find /etc/rc.d -name '*lpd'
```

For the lpd service, the number 60 is used for both the "K" and "S" symlinks.

```
]# find /etc/rc.d -name '*gpm'
```

Run this command without the clear command.

For the gpm service, the number 15 is used for the "K" symlinks and 85 is used for the "S" symlinks.

(11) Using the service and chkconfig Commands

]# service gpm status   # the service should be running

]# chkconfig --list | less

This lists all of the services and the status (on or off) of each service for the runlevels 0 through 6.

]# clear ; chkconfig --list gpm

This shows the same information as above, but only for the gpm service. Wherever the word "off" appears, there is a "K" script in the rc?.d directory and wherever the word "on" appears, there is an "S" script in rc?.d.

]# find /etc/rc.d -name '*gpm'

The "K" symlinks in rc0.d, rc1.d and rc6.d correspond to the "off" settings that appear beside the gpm service (at the top) for 0, 1 and 6. The "S" symlinks in rc2.d through rc5.d correspond to the "on" settings beside the gpm service for 2 through 5.

]# chkconfig gpm off

The –level option of chkconfig is used to specify runlevels. This option was not used and the off option was used. When off or on (rather than –level) is used, the default setting for the service is set to off or on for runlevels 2 through 5. After running this command, the symlinks for the service in rc2.d through rc5.d for gpm will begin with "K".

]# clear ; chkconfig --list gpm

]# find /etc/rc.d -name '*gpm'

Notice the 15 in the symlinks named K15gpm.

The default setting for the service is off for all runlevels and all symlinks begin with "K".

]# service gpm status

You are currently in runlevel 5. The gpm service is still running, even though the command above turned it off for runlevels 2 through 5 (and it is also turned off for the other runlevels). Turning it off with chkconfig did not stop the process that is currently running for the current runlevel. It specified the default setting for it, for the next time the system changes into any runlevel (by running a command such as init) and stopped it from being started the next time the system starts.

```
]# chkconfig  gpm  on
```

This sets the default setting for the service to on for runlevels 2 through 5. After running this command, the symlinks for the service in rc2.d through rc5.d for gpm will begin with "S".

```
]# clear ; chkconfig --list gpm
```

```
]# find /etc/rc.d -name '*gpm'
```

Notice the **85** in the symlink name of S**85**gpm.

```
]# chkconfig --level 3 gpm off
```

This command uses the –level option and sets the default to off for gpm for runlevel 3 (only). Other runlevels could have been specified, such as using "35" or "5" in place of "3".

```
]# clear ; chkconfig --list gpm      # the default for runlevel 3 is now off
```

```
]# find /etc/rc.d -name '*gpm'
```

Notice the **15** in the symlink name of K**15**gpm.

The symlink file in rc3.d is now named K15gpm.

```
]# service  gpm  status        # the service is still running
```

The chkconfig command was used above to change the default settings of a service for various runlevels. The ntsysv and serviceconf utilities can also be used to do these tasks, but chkconfig is much faster.

Remember that changing the default settings for a service with chkconfig, ntsysv and serviceconf only take effect when the system is started again, or when you change from one runlevel to another. When using these utilities you are changing the default settings for services, you are not turning the service on or off for the runlevel in which you are *currently* working. However, the serviceconf utility does have Start, Stop and Restart buttons that can be used to start, stop and restart services, in addition to the capability of changing the default setting of a service. The ntsysv utility does not have this feature.

(12) **Using the init Command to Change to a Different Runlevel**

```
]# runlevel
```

The "N" is for None and indicates that there has not been a previous runlevel. The 5 is the current runlevel.

```
Press Ctrl+Alt+F1 to go to virtual terminal 1  ;  log in as cwest  ;  su to root  ;
```

```
]# runlevel
```

The runlevel has not changed, just your "location".

```
]# service  gpm  status      #  the gpm service is running
```

```
]# head  /etc/rc.d/init.d/gpm
```

Read the description of the gpm service. A virtual terminal is a "console".

```
move your mouse in a circle on the screen  ;  you should see a square
cursor  ;  this indicates that the gpm (console mouse) service is running.
```

You are about to change from runlevel 5 to 3. There are no applications running at the desktop or anywhere else. Be sure to always save data and close any applications that may be affected by changing from one runlevel to another, prior to changing runlevels.

For example, when you change from runlevel 5 (X GUI mode) to 3 (text mode), X will no longer be running. Therefore, if you have a document in a GUI word processor that was launched from the desktop, save it and close the application prior to changing runlevels.

Watch the screen carefully after running the next command.

```
]# init  3                    #  change to runlevel 3 (from runlevel 5)
```

Notice that "Shutting down console mouse service appeared" because the default setting for gpm for runlevel 3 was set to off. Also notice that some services were started.

```
Press Enter to have the prompt appear again  ;  move your mouse  ;  a
cursor does not appear.
```

```
]# service  gpm  status      #  the service is not running
```

```
]# chkconfig  --list  gpm     #  the service is off for runlevel 3
```

You turned the service off for runlevel 3 and then changed into runlevel 3.

Move your mouse ; the cursor should not appear.

]# service gpm start   # this command allows you to start the service

Move your mouse ; its cursor should appear ; press Alt+F7 ; the desktop does not appear because X is not running (in runlevel 3) ;

press Ctrl+Alt+F1.

]# runlevel

The 5 is the previous runlevel and the 3 is the current runlevel. The current runlevel appears at the right.

]# init 5

Change to runlevel 5 (from runlevel 3), the GUI login prompt appears.

(13) Logging in and Turning on the gpm Service

Log in as cwest ; open a terminal emulation window ; su to root ;

]# runlevel   # current is 5 and previous is 3

change to virtual terminal 1 ; press Enter ; run the exit command and then the logout command ; change to the desktop ;

run the command that will change the current default setting for the gpm service, for runlevel 3, from off to on ;

run the command that has the --list option and look at the settings for the gpm service (only) to verify that you have changed the default setting for runlevel 3 from off to on.

(14) Viewing the killall and halt Script Files in init.d

Unlike most of the script files in the init.d directory, the killall and halt scripts are not used start a specific service. They are used to kill processes.

Change into the **rc.d** directory below /etc.

]# cat init.d/killall | nl | less   # view the contents of the killall script

Read the comment lines at the top of this script.

]# cat init.d/halt | nl | less   # view the contents of the halt script again

Read the comment lines at the top of this script and briefly scan through the comment lines in this script.

How the rc.local Script is Run

The script file named single in init.d does not start a specific service. It is used to run the rc.local script in the rc.d directory.

Let's say you have a service that you have installed and need to start, but you do not have a script file for it in init.d and you do not have the symlink files for it in the rc?.d directories. Rather than putting a script to start the service in the init.d directory and creating symlinks for the service in the rc?.d directories, you can use the rc.local script to start a service.

By default, the /etc/rc.d/rc.local script is processed for runlevels 2, 3, 4 and 5. Symbolic links to execute the rc.local script are in the rc2.d, rc3.d, rc4.d and rc5.d directories. The symlink named S99local is in each of these directories and it causes the rc.local script to be processed (last - due to the 99 in the symlink filename).

```
]# clear ; cat rc.local          # read the description in this script

]# find /etc/rc.d -name '*local*'
```

The S99local symlinks in rc2.d, rc3.d, rc4.d and rc5.d appear, as well as the rc.local script.

 The init Directory Structure Symlinks

There are eleven symlinks in /etc that point to the files and directories in the init script directory structure. This allows compatibility between various UNIX variants and Linux distributions.

For example, the script named rc.sysinit has a comment at the top of it that shows the path to itself of: /etc/**rc.d**/rc.sysinit. This is the correct path to the "real" script file and not a symlink. However, the script named rc contains a statement that runs the script named functions with the following statement:

```
. /etc/init.d/functions
```

The "real" script named functions (and not a symlink) is located in /etc/**rc.d**/init.d and not in /etc/init.d! There is a symlink in /etc named init.d (/etc/init.d). This symlink points to the "real" directory of the same name in /etc/rc.d (/etc/**rc.d**/init.d). This allows the statement in the rc script that runs the script named functions to work. Several script files in init.d also refer to the script named functions in /etc/init.d rather than in /etc/rc.d/init.d.

```
]# cd .. ; clear ; pwd          # your current directory should be /etc

]# ls -l /etc/init.d
```

The init.d symlink in /etc (/etc/init.d) points to the init.d directory in rc.d (/etc/**rc.d**/init.d).

```
]# ls -l /etc/rc* | nl
```

Notice the "l" (for symlink) at the right of the numbers in the first ten lines of output. All of these files are symlinks that exist in /etc and point to the "real" files and directories that are located below /etc/rc.d.

Line 1 shows a symlink named rc that points to the script named rc in /etc/rc.d. The symlink in the path of /etc/rc points to the script in the path of /etc/rc.d/rc.

Line 2 shows a symlink named rc0.d that points to the rc0.d directory below /etc/rc.d. The symlink in the path of /etc/rc0.d points to the directory in the path of /etc/rc.d/rc0.d, and so on.

The output below "/etc/rc.d:" (lines 13 through 23) shows the "real" directories and files that make up the init directory structure. These items have "**d**" (for directory) and "-" (for file) at the left of them and not "**l**" (for symlink).

```
]# ls -l /etc/rc             # this is a symlink

]# ls -l /etc/rc.d/rc         # this is the "real" script file

]# ls -l /etc/rc0.d           # this is a symlink

]# ls -ld /etc/rc.d/rc0.d      # this is the "real" rc0.d directory
```

⑰ Using the ps Command with the -aux Options

```
]# ps -aux | less
```

This shows a "snapshot" of all of the processes running in memory. Notice the information below the USER, PID (process id), %CPU, %MEM, TTY (terminal), STAT (status) and COMMAND headings.

Look for the mingetty items below COMMAND ; scroll to the bottom.

```
]# clear ; ps -aux | grep mingetty
```

Notice the tty? items in column seven and that /sbin/mingetty appears in the COMMAND (far right) column. These are the processes for the virtual terminals 1 through 6. The last line of output is caused by the grep command that you just ran.

```
]# grep mingetty /etc/inittab
```

These are the statements in inittab that created the virtual terminals (seen with the ps command above).

(18) Viewing the Process Status of the slocate Command

Open another terminal emulation window ; su to root ;

]# slocate /*   # run the slocate command for a long time

Alt+Tab to the other terminal emulation window ;

]# ps -aux | grep slocate

The first item that is output is the process status of the slocate process. The first column in the first line of output shows that root is the owner of the process. The second column in the first line of output is the pid of the slocate process.

Write the pid number of the slocate process here: _____

The second item that is output is the process status of the grep command that you just ran.

Alt+Tab to the other (slocate) terminal emulation window ; slocate should still be running ; if not, run the slocate command shown above again ;

Alt+Tab to the other terminal emulation window.

Replace *pid* in the command below with the number that you wrote down above.

]# kill *pid*   # the kill command is used with a pid number

Alt+Tab to the other (slocate) terminal emulation window ; slocate should be stopped and the word "Terminated" should appear on the last line above the prompt ;

run the same slocate command again ;

Alt+Tab to the other terminal emulation window.

Replace *name* in the command below with: slocate.

]# killall *name*   # killall is used with a process name or filename

Alt+Tab to the other (slocate) terminal emulation window and slocate should be terminated.

Alt+Tab to the other terminal emulation window.

Using the ps Command with the -axl Options

]# service lpd status

The lpd service should be running. If not, run the same command as above, but replace the word "status" with the word "start".

]# ps -axl | less

Notice the UID (user id), PID (process id), **PPID** (parent process id), TTY (terminal) and CMD (command) headings. The UID number is shown here rather than the user name. The UID of root is 0 and the UID of cwest is 500.

Scroll through the listing and notice the UID numbers in the UID column ;

look for the UID of 4 and the command at the far right of this number (lpd Waiting) ;

look for the UID of 43 and the command at the far right of this number (xfs -droppr).

]# grep lp /etc/passwd

The third field is the UID field and this contains the number 4. The UID of 4 is the user named lp. Notice the "comment" (which is usually used for the full name of a user) in the fifth field is "lp". The sixth field is usually the path to a user's home directory. In this case, it is the path to the directory that is used for the "spool" directory for printers (described later). The lpd process is run with the "system" user name of lp (represented by the number 4). This user is the owner of the process.

]# grep xfs /etc/passwd

The number in the third field is 43. The UID of 43 is the user named xfs. Notice the "comment" of "X Font Server" in the fifth field and the path to the "home directory" of this "system" user in the sixth field (**/etc/X11/fs**). The xfs process is run with the user name of xfs as the owner (user).

]# ls -l **/etc/X11/fs**

Look at the contents of the path in the sixth field. A file named config appears

]# less /etc/X11/fs/config   # read the comment at the top of this file

Using ps to View and kill to Stop the Clock

```
]# clear ; echo $PATH    # some directories for X are in the PATH
]# whereis xclock        # xclock is an X GUI utility
```

The directory path(s) to xclock are in the PATH.

Minimize the terminal emulation window ; press Ctrl+l to clear the screen ; move and size this window so that it fills the bottom two thirds of the screen.

```
]# xclock
```

This runs the xclock command in the foreground and the shell prompt does not appear.

Press Ctrl+c to stop the process (the xclock program) ; the clock disappears.

```
]# xclock &
```

This runs the command in the background and the shell prompt appears. Above the current prompt, the number in [ ] is the job number and the number at the right is the pid (process id) number.

Write the pid number of the xclock process here: _____

```
]# ps -axl | grep xclock
```

The first line of output is for the xclock process and the second line is the command that you just ran. The number in the third column of the first line is the pid number and the number in the fourth column is the ppid (parent process id) number.

Write the ppid number of the xclock process here: _____

Replace *ppid* in the following command with the ppid number of xclock.

```
]# ps -axl | grep ppid
```

The first line of output has the above *ppid* in the second column, which is the pid number column. Therefore, this is the parent process of the xclock process. If you have run xclock in the first terminal emulation window, then pts/0 is in the third last column of the first line of output and "-bash" appears in the far right (COMMAND) column. The pts/0 represents the first terminal emulation window, which is running the process named "-bash" (the bash shell).

```
]# ps -eH | less
```

This displays all processes (-e) in a hierarchy (-H) with the parent process flush left and the "child" processes indented below parent processes. The PID, TTY (terminal), TIME and CMD (command) headings appear. The PID number of 1 is the CMD of init. All of the items below init are indented below init.

Scroll down until you can see pts/0 several times in the second column.

Look for "gnome-terminal" above the first item that has pts/0. This is the parent process of the pts/0 processes, which are all running in the pts/0 terminal emulation window. The pid number of each item appears in the first column.

All of the pts/0 items are indented below "gnome-terminal". The first pts/0 item is bash. This is the bash shell running in the terminal (emulation window). The next item is the su command that was used to "su to root". The next item is the bash shell (subshell) that was started when you ran the su command. The next three items, xclock, ps and less are all indented the same amount. They are all running in the bash subshell (which appears in the terminal emulation window that you are looking at now). The xclock is the command that you ran a few commands above. The ps and less are the commands you ran above to view the hierarchy of processes.

The pid of the bash item above less, ps and xclock is the ppid number of the less, ps and xclock processes. The pid of the su item is the ppid of the bash item below it. The pid of the bash item below gnome-terminal is the ppid of the su command. The pid of gnome-terminal is the ppid of the bash item below it.

Write the pid of the bash item that has xclock below it here: _____

Replace *pid* in the following command with the pid number that you wrote down above.

```
]# ps -axl | grep pid
```

In the first line of output, the number that you used appears in the third column. This is the pid number of the bash shell in pts/0. In the second line of output, the *ppid* appears in the fourth column for the xclock item. This number also appears in the fourth column for the ps and grep commands that you just ran. The pid number of xclock appears in the third column of the second line of output.

The xclock utility should be visible on the screen. Replace *pid* in the following command with the pid number of xclock.

```
]# kill pid          # the xclock utility disappears
```

The kill command removed the process of the xclock utility from memory!

If a program has "hung", or is not running properly, such as running slowly, you can often use the kill command to remove it from memory *without having to reboot the system*.

If the above command does not kill a process, you can use signal 9 with the kill command, as in:

```
kill -9 pid          # this is an example
```

(21) Using the free Command

The free command can be used to quickly see memory statistics. This information is also available at the top of the top utility.

```
]# clear ; free      # shows memory statistics, including swap space stats

]# free -t           # shows memory stats with totals

]# free -mt          # shows memory stats in megabytes with totals
```

(22) Running the top Command

Minimize the existing window (if necessary) and move it so that it fills the bottom **third** of the screen ;

move and size the other terminal emulation window so that it fills the top half ;

you should be working as root in both windows ; run the next command in the top window ;

```
]# top
```

This utility shows the top processes in memory by CPU usage. Notice the statistics in the top three lines of the top utility. Look at the statistics in the top line and the breakdown of the processes in the second line. The fourth and fifth lines show memory statistics, including swap space statistics (similar to the free command).

```
h                    # type "h" and do not press Enter to get help information
```

If necessary, use the scroll bar at the right of the window to see the top of the help output. Read the descriptions of i, k, P and M.

```
q                    # type "q" and do not press Enter to quit out of help
```

Below the PID, USER and other headings, look for the top command, X and init below the COMMAND heading.

Alt+Tab to the bottom window ; press Ctrl+l ;

run the following command and watch for ls to appear below COMMAND in top ;

watch the %CPU and %MEM statistics change for slocate.

```
]# ls -lR /
```

Alt+Tab to the top window.

i   # type "i" to toggle off the display of idle processes

i   # type "i" to toggle on the display of idle processes

N   # type "N" to sort by process id - see the PID column

M   # type "M" to sort by memory usage - see the %MEM column

P   # type "P" to sort by CPU usage - see the %CPU column

The ls command should still be running in the bottom window. If not, start it again and then make the top window active.

Look for the pid number of the ls command (below PID).

k   # type "k" to kill a process

type in the pid number of the ls command ; press Enter ;

notice the default signal of 15 in the [ ] brackets ;

you could type in a different signal number now, but this should not be necessary ;

press Enter to kill the ls process ; after a short time, ls should no longer appear below COMMAND.

q   # type "q" to quit out of top

(23) Deleting the Printer You Created Earlier

The printer that you created earlier is no longer needed. Do the following steps to remove it.

]# printconf

The queue named abc is selected ; click on the Delete button ;

File ; Quit ; Yes ; OK.

]# service lpd status

]# service lpd start

Notice that "No printers defined appears".

]# service lpd status

Even though it was started (above), the lpd process is not running because no printers have been defined.

Section Review

1. Select two correct statements regarding runlevels.

   ☐ A. runlevel 3 is GUI mode
   ☐ B. runlevel 0 causes the system to halt
   ☐ C. runlevel 6 causes the system to reboot
   ☐ D. runlevel 5 is text mode

2. Which two commands can be used to start or stop a service immediately?

   ☐ A. service
   ☐ B. serviceconf
   ☐ C. ntsysv
   ☐ D. chkconfig

3. Select the item that runs the binary named init during the boot process.

   ○ A. sysinit
   ○ B. the kernel
   ○ C. inittab
   ○ D. rc.sysinit

4. You know the pid number of a process that you need to stop. Which two commands can you use (with the pid number) to stop the process?

   ☐ A. top
   ☐ B. kill
   ☐ C. killall
   ☐ D. ps

5. Which file creates the virtual terminals numbered 1 through 6?

   ○ A. rc.sysinit
   ○ B. rc.local
   ○ C. rc
   ○ D. inittab

6. Select the directory path that contains the scripts that are used to start services, stop services and view the status of services.

    ○ A. /etc
    ○ B. /etc/rc.d
    ○ C. /etc/rc.d/init.d
    ○ D. /root

7. When the word init appears in directory and filenames that are related to system startup, this word usually stands for system initialization. T F

8. Select the two runlevels that should not be set as the default runlevel.

    ☐ A. 0
    ☐ B. 1
    ☐ C. 3
    ☐ D. 6

9. Which script performs many system initialization tasks, such as setting the hostname, mounting filesystems, and configuring ISA PnP devices?

    ○ A. init
    ○ B. init.rc
    ○ C. rc.sysinit
    ○ D. sysinit

10. All services only require one daemon to be started. T F

11. Select two correct statements regarding the symlinks in the rc?.d directories.

    ☐ A. the "K" in a symlink filename indicates that the service will be stopped
    ☐ B. the symlinks point to corresponding script files in the init.d directory
    ☐ C. the "R" in a symlink filename indicates that the service will be restarted
    ☐ D. the symlinks point to the binary file that is run to start the service

12. Select three commands that are used to specify the default settings for services for each runlevel.

    ☐ A. serviceconf
    ☐ B. sysvconf
    ☐ C. ntsysv
    ☐ D. chkconfig

13. What is the pid number of the process named init?

   ○ A. 1
   ○ B. 3
   ○ C. 5
   ○ D. 6

14. Select two sets of options that are commonly used with the ps command.

   ☐ A. -aux
   ☐ B. -level -init
   ☐ C. -HUP
   ☐ D. -axl

15. The rc?.d directories only contain symlinks. T F

16. For the non-GUI command that is used to start a service, select the option of the command that is used so that the modified configuration file of a service is read when the service is stopped and then started.

   ○ A. restart
   ○ B. status
   ○ C. reboot
   ○ D. config

17. Select the number of the default signal that is used to stop a process, when you are viewing the process in the utility that updates the status of processes frequently.

   ○ A. 1
   ○ B. 4
   ○ C. 9
   ○ D. 15

18. Which command can be used to immediately change from one runlevel to another?

   ○ A. service
   ○ B. init
   ○ C. rc.sysinit
   ○ D. runlevel

19. Which two scripts are run directly from inittab?

   ☐ A. init
   ☐ B. rc.sysinit
   ☐ C. init.local
   ☐ D. rc

20. Your system has slowed down considerably and you know that the process named slug is causing the problem. You need to get the pid of this process so that you can use it with a command that will kill the process. Which command will provide this information?

    ○ A. ps -aux | pid
    ○ B. whereis slug
    ○ C. ps -aux | grep slug
    ○ D. memlevel slug

21. Select the command that displays the current "mode" and the previous "mode".

    ○ A. runlevel
    ○ B. runmode
    ○ C. status
    ○ D. servicelevel

22. The current default runlevel is 5 and you need to change this to the runlevel that is used for "text mode". Select the statement in inittab that needs to be edited.

    ○ A. runlevel:5:defstart:
    ○ B. rc:5:sysinit:
    ○ C. init:5:start:
    ○ D. id:5:initdefault:

23. The pid number of a service has the same number as the symlink that was used to start the service. T F

24. The following statement is in a script in the init.d directory. Select two correct statements regarding this statement.

               # chkconfig 345 14 86

    ☐ A. the service cannot be run in runlevels 3, 4 and 5
    ☐ B. the "K" symlink in the rc?.d directories will have the number 345
    ☐ C. the "S" symlink in the rc?.d directories will have the number 14
    ☐ D. by default, the service will start in runlevels 3, 4 and 5

25. Which utility can also be used to start, stop and restart services immediately, by selecting the Start, Stop and Restart buttons?

    ○ A. ntsysconfig
    ○ B. chkconfig
    ○ C. initsysv
    ○ D. serviceconf

26. Which script is used to start services when a system boots?

- A. rc
- B. rcdefault
- C. init.rc
- D. rc.startup

27. When the following command is run, what happens?

    chkconfig apmd on

- A. the apmd service is started in the current runlevel and the default runlevel
- B. the default setting for the apmd service is set to on for runlevels 2 through 5
- C. the apmd binary in the rc?.d directories is executed
- D. the apmd binary causes the symlinks in the rc?.d directories to be created

28. Which file is used to set the default runlevel?

- A. inittab
- B. rc.sysinit
- C. init
- D. rc.local

29. Select the utility that can be used to immediately stop a process.

- A. pstop
- B. ps
- C. service
- D. ntsysv

30. Which option of the chkconfig command is used to specify one or more runlevels?

- A. --level
- B. -r
- C. -rlevel
- D. -on

Chapter 17: Scheduling Tasks and Working with Log Files

In this chapter, you will learn how to schedule unattended tasks with at, cron and anacron. You will see how these programs work, the differences between them, and the benefits of using each of them. The fields used in the configuration files for cron, anacron and user crontab files are also covered. This will show you how to set up these programs to run unattended tasks.

Linux uses many log files that contain messages which are written to these files by programs that are running on the system. We will cover the locations and uses of several common log files, and how this information can be used to get support via a mailing list, newsgroup or search engine.

Over time, log files are written to frequently and increase in size. Therefore, they are "rotated" and then removed so that their size is kept at a manageable level. The methods used to rotate log files are discussed in this chapter.

The Linux email system is used by various programs to send messages regarding "system events" to one or more users. The root user is often notified by email when an "event" has occurred and other users may also be notified. When some events occur, a description of the event is written to one or more log files and notification of the event is also emailed to one or more users. You will learn how to use the mail system to view email messages.

The following commands are described in this chapter and are also used in the Hands-On Exercises:

at	schedule a task to be run once
atq	list the tasks scheduled with at
atrm	remove tasks scheduled with at
crontab	work with user crontab files
mail	work with email
dmesg	displays kernel boot messages
tail	view changes to multiple log files

During the Hands-On Exercises you will schedule tasks with at, cron and anacron and find out about the "inner workings" of these programs. You will also see how log files are affected by the operation of various programs.

You will open one terminal emulation window in the top half of the screen and another in the bottom half. In the bottom window, you will run the tail command to view two log files. In the top window you will run the top utility. While anacron is running, you will see the programs that are run daily (by cron or anacron) in the "top" window and the messages that are written to log files by these programs in the bottom window.

Scheduling Tasks and Working with Log Files

Scheduling Tasks with at, cron and anacron

The at program is used to schedule tasks (a.k.a. jobs) so that they are run *after a period of time or at a specific time*. cron is used to schedule tasks so that they are run *at a specific time*. anacron is used to schedule tasks so that they are run *after a period of time has passed*.

There are many tasks, such as creating a backup or compiling a program, that can be run unattended by a system *at a specific time*. These unattended tasks are often run during off-peak hours when there are few users on the system or no users on the system. The at and cron programs are used to schedule these tasks so that they run unattended.

An at or cron task can be used to diagnose a system problem by automatically running a program (binary or script) that provides information that can help detect a problem.

For example, let's say one of your systems is slowing down every day at some time between 2:15 and 2:45 a.m. You could write a script that sends the output of the ps command to a file (with a unique filename each time) every minute during the slow time and then have the script run as an at or cron task between 2:15 and 2:45 a.m. You could then look at the files to try and detect any processes that are not running properly.

The anacron program is used to schedule tasks so that they are run *after a period of time* has passed. The period of time is measured in days (only). This program can be set up to run *any task* after a period of days have passed. It is commonly used to run tasks that should have been run by cron, but were not run (because the system was not turned on at the time that the task was supposed to run).

Scheduling Tasks with the at Command

The at command is run to schedule a task "at" some time in the future or after a period of time has passed. It provides a quick method of running a task (command or program) once, rather than repeatedly. Tasks created with the at command exist as files in the path of /var/spool/at.

atd is run by executing the atd daemon. This daemon is run as a service via the scripts and symlinks in the init scripts directory structure. By default, the service named atd runs the daemon named atd when a system boots in runlevels 3, 4 or 5. If this service is not already running, the atd daemon will be run when a system changes from the current runlevel (such as runlevel 1) into runlevel 3, 4 or 5.

By default, an *empty* file named at.deny exists in /etc. This empty file allows all users to run the at command and schedule tasks. This file can be modified to deny one or more users from using the at command.

Also by default, a file named at.allow does *not* exist in /etc. This file can be created in /etc and edited to allow one or more users to use the at command. Once this file has been created, only the users in the file and the root user can run the at command.

If the at.deny and at.allow files do not exist in /etc, then only the root user can run the at command.

The Syntax of the at Command

at *time*

After running the at command an "at>" prompt appears. Commands, script names and program names are typed at this prompt, one item per line. Press Enter to get to the next "at>" prompt. These items are typed in until Ctrl+d is pressed to stop the at command.

In the above syntax of the at command, replace *time* with the time when the task should be run. Some examples of the at command and how *time* can be specified are shown below.

Table 17-1 shows several examples of specifying the *time* for the at command.

Table 17-1 - Specifying the *time* for the at Command

Example	Description
at now + 2 minutes	run the task in two minutes from now
at now + 6 hours	run the task in six hours from now
at now + 3 days	run the task in three days - same time as now
at now + 5 weeks	run the task in five weeks - same time as now
at 22:15 today	run the task at 10:15 p.m. today
at 11 pm Wednesday	run the task at 11 p.m. next Wednesday (only)
at 9:30 pm September 5	run the task at 9:30 p.m. on September 5th

The atq and atrm Commands

The **atq** (**at** queue) command, without any options, shows a list of tasks that have been scheduled with the at command, along with the dates and times that the tasks will be run. A number appears at the left of each scheduled item. If an = (equal sign) appears beside a task, the task is currently running.

The **atrm** (**at rem**ove) command is used to remove a scheduled task so that it will not run. The following command will remove a scheduled task by replacing *n* with the number that appears at the left of the task when the atq command is run.

        atrm *n*

Additional task numbers that you want to remove can be specified at the right of the *n*, with a space in between them.

Scheduling Tasks with cron

cron allows you to schedule tasks and then runs these tasks at specific times. It runs a task *at a scheduled time*, rather than *after a period of time*, which is the way anacron works. The tasks that it runs are scheduled by statements in: a file named crontab in /etc, files in /etc/cron.d , and user crontab files in /var/spool/cron.

The /etc/crontab file is the "system" crontab file and can only be edited by the root user.

Additional files for cron tasks can be created in /etc/cron.d. These files have the same format as the /etc/crontab file. Only the root user can create the files in /etc/cron.d.

The /etc/crontab file and files in /etc/cron.d can be edited "directly" with a text editor. This is the opposite of user crontab files, which cannot be edited "directly".

By default, all users can create user crontab files in /var/spool/cron. User crontab files must be edited by running the crontab command with the -e option. These files cannot be edited "directly" with a text editor.

cron is run with the service named crond, which executes the crond daemon. This service is run via the scripts and symlinks in the init scripts directory structure. By default, the service named crond runs the daemon named crond when a system boots in runlevels 2, 3, 4 or 5. If the crond service is not already running, it will be run when a system changes from the current runlevel (such as runlevel 1) into runlevel 2, 3, 4 or 5.

Every minute, the cron daemon (named crond) checks the /etc/crontab file, files in /etc/cron.d, and user crontab files in /var/spool/cron. If any of these files contain a statement to run a cron task at the current minute, the task is run.

The /etc/crontab File

The /etc/crontab (**cron tab**le) file contains settings for tasks that are performed for a system at regular times. This is the "system" **cron tab**le file, as opposed to a "user **cron tab**le file" (in /var/spool/cron). The root user is the only user that can modify this file and unlike user crontab files, this file can be edited directly.

By default, the crontab file in /etc contains the following statements. Line numbers have been added at the left of each statement for the purpose of the discussion below.

```
1       SHELL=/bin/bash
2       PATH=/sbin:/bin:/usr/sbin:/usr/bin
3       MAILTO=root
4       HOME=/

5       # run-parts
6       01 * * * * root  run-parts  /etc/cron.hourly
7       02 4 * * * root  run-parts  /etc/cron.daily
8       22 4 * * 0 root  run-parts  /etc/cron.weekly
9       42 4 1 * * root  run-parts  /etc/cron.monthly
```

Line 1 specifies the shell to be used. Line 2 sets up the directory paths in the PATH that can be used when the file is processed. Line 3 specifies the user name that will be emailed information regarding tasks that have been run. Line 5 is a comment.

Many programs (including some daemons) are set up to email information, such as the completion of a task or the output of a program, to a user and this user is often the root user. The root user receives mail frequently.

When an error has occurred with some programs, a description of the error is emailed to a user, as well as an error message being written to a log file. In addition to looking at log files for information, such as error messages, be sure to read the mail that has been sent to the root user. See the heading "Reading Mail Messages" later in this chapter.

Lines 6 through 9 cause the script named run-parts to be run for each of the directories named cron.hourly, cron.daily, cron.weekly and cron.monthly below the path of /etc. We will refer to these four directories as the cron.* directories. The run-parts script causes each of the items (scripts, symlinks to executable files, and programs) in a cron.* directory to be executed.

For example, line 7 contains the following:

   run-parts /etc/cron.daily

Line 7 in /etc/crontab is processed every day at 4:02 a.m. (if the system is turned on at this time). Line 7 causes the run-parts script to be run "on" each of the items in /etc/cron.daily. The run-parts script causes all items (scripts, symlinks to executable files, and programs) in /etc/cron.daily to be executed.

By default (after doing the Linux installation that you did earlier), there are: no files in cron.hourly, eight files in cron.daily, two files in cron.weekly and one file in cron.monthly.

Each of lines 6 through 9 in /etc/crontab represents a single task. By default, there are four tasks (jobs) and you can add more tasks. Each of these four tasks runs the run-parts script "on" the each of the items in one of the four cron.* directories.

For example, there is script named logrotate in /etc/cron.daily. It contains the following statement, which causes the logrotate binary in /usr/sbin to be executed using the settings in the logrotate.conf file in /etc.

        /usr/sbin/logrotate /etc/logrotate.conf

When the task on line 7 is run by cron, the run-parts script is run "on" the /etc/cron.daily directory and the script named logrotate in this directory is executed.

The Fields in /etc/crontab

Lines 6 through 9 each contain seven "fields". In line 6, the first field contains 01 and fields two through 5 contain an * (asterisk).

Field six contains the user name of root. This causes the scripts in the directory at the end of line 6 to be run with the username of root. Lines 6 through 9 have the same user name.

Field seven contains the name of the run-parts script. This script executes the items (scripts, symlinks and programs) in the directory at the end of line 6. Lines 6 through 9 all use the script named run-parts.

Field eight contains the path to the directory (/etc/cron.hourly) to be processed by the script named run-parts. Lines 6 through 9 cause the items in the cron.* directories to be executed.

Fields one through five indicate the time that the tasks in the directory path at the end, the *.cron directories, will be run. These fields are described in Table 17-2.

Table 17-2 - The Time Fields in /etc/crontab or in a User crontab File

Field	Description
1	the minute (0-59)
2	the hour (0-23)
3	the day of month (1-31)
4	the month of year (1-12) - the number 1 is January
5	the day of week (0-6) - the number 0 is Sunday

Ranges of numbers can be used in fields. For example, using "1-5" (without the quotes) in field 5 (the day of week field) represents Monday through Friday (all weekdays).

Multiple numbers can also be used in fields. For example, using "10, 14, 18" in field 2 (the hour field) represents 10 a.m., 2 p.m. and 6 p.m.

When an * (asterisk) is used in any field, it represents "every" or "all". An asterisk in field 3 represents every month.

Fields are separated by one or more spaces and comments are preceded by the # symbol (as usual).

Line 6 in the /etc/crontab file (above) contains the indented statement below. The 01 in field 1 (the minute field) and the asterisks in fields 2 through 5 cause the run-parts script to execute all items (scripts, symlinks and programs) in the /etc/cron.hourly directory, with the user name of root, one minute after every hour (of every day of month, month of year and day of week - due to the asterisks in fields 2 through 5). By default, the cron.hourly directory is empty and no items are executed one minute after every hour.

```
01 * * * * root run-parts /etc/cron.hourly
```

Line 7 in the crontab file (above) contains the indented statement below. The 02 in field 1 (the minute field), the 4 in field 2 (the hour field) and the asterisks in fields 3 through 5 cause the items in /etc/cron.daily to be run two minutes after the fourth hour (4:02 a.m.) every day. By default, the cron.daily directory contains eight items that are run every day at 4:02 a.m.

```
02 4 * * * root run-parts /etc/cron.daily
```

Line 8 in crontab contains the following statement. The 22 in field 1 (the minute field), the 4 in field 2 (the hour field), the asterisks in fields 3 and 4, and the 0 in field 5 (the day of week field) cause the items in /etc/cron.weekly to be run twenty-two minutes after the fourth hour (4:22 a.m.) every Sunday (due to the 0 in field 5). By default, the cron.weekly directory contains two items that are run every Sunday at 4:22 a.m.

```
22 4 * * 0 root run-parts /etc/cron.weekly
```

Line 9 in crontab contains the following statement. The 42 in field 1 (the minute field), the 4 in field 2 (the hour field), the 1 in field 3 (the day of month field) and the asterisks in fields 4 and 5 cause the run-parts script to be run "on" the files in /etc/cron.monthly, with the user name of root, forty-two minutes after the fourth hour (4:42 a.m.) on the first day of the month (due to the 1 in field 3). By default, the cron.monthly directory contains one item that is run by the run-parts script on the first day of the month at 4:42 a.m.

```
42 4 1 * * root run-parts /etc/cron.monthly
```

You can easily have an item, such as a script or program, processed hourly, daily, weekly or monthly without modifying /etc/crontab (or creating a crontab file in /etc/cron.d or creating a user crontab file). Simply put the item in the appropriate cron.* directory. The item will be executed at the time specified by lines 7 through 9 in /etc/crontab.

For example, to run a script every day named checkit, put the script in the /etc/cron.daily directory. If the system is on at 4:02 a.m., then the checkit script will be run. cron will process line 7 in /etc/crontab, which will run the run-parts script "on" /etc/cron.daily and this will execute your script. If the system is not on at 4:02 a.m., then your script will be run by anacron 65 minutes after the next time the system boots (described further below).

The items in a cron.* directory are processed by the run-parts script in the same order in which they appear in a directory listing with the ls command.

User crontab Files

A user can use the crontab binary to create a "user crontab (**cron tab**le) file" that is used to schedule tasks that will be run by cron. User crontab files are named with user names, one name per user. The user crontab file for the root user is named root. The user crontab file for the cwest user is named cwest. These files are located in the path of /var/spool/cron.

If files named cron.allow and cron.deny do not exist in /etc, then all users can create a user crontab file. By default, these two files do not exist.

A file named cron.allow can be created in /etc and modified to allow specific users to submit user cron tasks. A file named cron.deny can also be created in /etc and modified to deny specific users from submitting user cron tasks.

User crontab files are not edited "directly" with a text editor. You do not run an editor and create a file with your username in /var/spool/cron, or run an editor and edit the file with your username in /var/spool/cron.

User crontab files are edited by running the crontab command (binary) with the -e option. When this is done, the user crontab file, in the path of /var/spool/cron is created (if it does already not exist). If the -u option of crontab is not used, then the user crontab file will have the same name as the user that created the file (i.e. the user name that you were logged in as when you ran the crontab command). Once you have created or edited a user crontab file and saved it, the crontab binary "installs" it as a cron task (a.k.a. cron job) - this is why you cannot simply edit the file "directly" with a text editor. When you create or modify a user crontab file, a message similar to the following appears:

```
crontab: installing new crontab
```

Remember to put comments in crontab files for the same reasons that you put comments in script files. This will allow you or someone else to understand what the task is and why it is being run.

By default, when the crontab command is run with the -e option, the vi editor is used to edit the file. The default editor can be changed by changing the EDITOR variable.

For example, the following command, when run from the command line (rather than from within a script), will change the editor from vi to an editor named emacs:

```
EDITOR=emacs
```

If the above statement is used in a script, put the following statement after it to export the variable:

```
export EDITOR
```

By default, there are no user crontab files. To create a crontab file, a user runs the crontab binary with the -e (edit) option, as shown below.

```
crontab -e
```

If a crontab file does not exist for the user, it is created in /var/spool/cron and the file has the same name as the user that ran the above command. If the file already exists, then the above command allows you to edit the file.

For example, if you are logged in as root, then the user crontab file named root is created in /var/spool/cron. If you are logged in as cwest, then the user crontab file named cwest is created in this same path. If a user crontab file already exists, then the above command allows you to edit the existing file.

The root user can create or modify the crontab file of another user by using the -u *username* option and replacing *username* with the name of the user.

For example, to create or edit the user crontab file for the bford user, run the following command:

```
crontab -e -u bford
```

Any user can use the -l (lower case "l") option of crontab to view the contents of his or her user crontab file, as shown below:

```
crontab -l
```

If the cwest user runs the above command, then the contents of file named cwest in /var/spool/cron are displayed. The following is the output of a user crontab file for the cwest user. Notice the comment on the first line. User crontab files are not edited "directly", they are edited by using the -e option of the crontab command.

```
# DO NOT EDIT THIS FILE - edit the master and reinstall.
# (/tmp/crontab.1772 installed on Wed Jul 16 11:02:00 2003)
# (Cron version -- $Id: crontab.c,v 2.13 1994/01/17 03:20:37 vixie Exp $)

# run the compileprog script to compile a program
# at 10:30 p.m. each weekday

30  22  *  *  1-5  /home/cwest/bin/compileprog
```

The cwest user has created a script named compileprog that runs the commands to compile a software program. The script is located in the bin directory, below the user's home directory. The last line of the above output causes the script to be executed at 10:30 p.m. (30 22) each weekday (1-5).

The root user can use the -u option with the -l option to view the contents of the user crontab file of another user, as shown below:

```
crontab -l -u  cwest
```

The -r option is used to remove a user crontab file from /var/spool/cron. The following command will remove the user crontab file for the current user. For example, if you are logged in as cwest and run the following command, the file named cwest in /var/spool/cron will be removed.

```
crontab -r
```

The root user can use the -u option with the -r option to remove the user crontab file of another user, as shown below:

```
crontab -r -u  cwest
```

By default, anacron is set up (via /etc/anacrontab) to run the cron tasks that are specified in /etc/crontab, if a system was not running when the cron task should have been run (as describe below). However, by default, anacron does not run the tasks that are specified in user crontab files (in /var/spool/cron).

The Difference Between /etc/crontab and User crontab Files

The format of the statements in /etc/crontab are similar to the format required in a user crontab file, but they are not the same.

The statement below is from /etc/crontab. The time fields (one through five) indicate the time that the scripts in /etc/cron.hourly will be executed. Field six is the user name that will run the scripts. Field seven is the name of the script (run-parts) that is used to execute the items in the directory at the end of the path shown in field eight.

```
01 * * * * root run-parts /etc/cron.hourly
```

The statement below is from the user crontab file named cwest (described above). The time fields (one through five) have the same format for both types of files (the system crontab file and a user crontab file). Field six in the statement below is the program (binary or script) that is executed at the time specified. The path to the program is also in field six.

```
30 22 * * 1-5 /home/cwest/bin/compileprog
```

Field six in the /etc/crontab file has a user name, such as root, to indicate the user that is running the task. A user crontab file has the same name as a user and this is used as the name to run the tasks in the file. A user crontab file is not (typically) used to run all items in a directory. Therefore, it does not require the run-parts script in field seven and the directory path in field eight.

Scheduling Tasks with anacron

anacron is a program (that is not a daemon), that runs the tasks specified (scheduled) by statements in /etc/anacrontab. It is scheduled to run tasks *after a period of time has passed*, rather than *at a scheduled time* (which is the way cron works). This can be any task, including tasks that should have been run by cron, but were not run because a system was not turned on when a task was scheduled to run.

If a task should have been run by cron, but did not run because the system was off at the time, it can also be scheduled in anacron to run after a period of time has passed. By default, anacron is set up to run the daily, weekly and monthly tasks in /etc/crontab that were not run by cron because a system was off.

For example, cron is scheduled to run the items (scripts, symlinks and programs) in the /etc/cron.daily directory every day at 4:02 a.m. However, if the system is not running, at 4:02 a.m., then the items are not run.

To run the items that should have been run, a statement in /etc/anacrontab causes the items in /etc/cron.daily to be run after 1 day has passed (since the last time the tasks were run).

To continue the example, if the items in /etc/cron.weekly were not run because the system was not turned on, then there is another statement in anacrontab that causes the items in /etc/cron.weekly to be run after 7 days have passed (since the last time the items were run).

Also, if the items in /etc/cron.monthly were not run, then another statement in anacrontab causes the items in this directory to be run after 30 days have passed (since the last time the items were run).

A comment at the top of the script named anacron in /etc/rc.d/init.d shows "Run cron jobs that were left out due to downtime". By default, anacron is run once when a system boots. It is not a daemon and therefore, it does not stay running in the background. It is run as a service via the scripts and symlinks in the init scripts directory structure. It is also run when a system changes from the current runlevel into runlevels 2 through 5.

By default, the anacrontab file in /etc contains the following statements. Line numbers have been added at the left of each statement for the purpose of the discussion below.

```
1   # /etc/anacrontab: configuration file for anacron
2   # See anacron(8) and anacrontab(5) for details.
3   SHELL=/bin/sh
4   PATH=/usr/local/sbin:/usr/local/bin:/sbin:/bin:/usr/sbin:/usr/bin
5   1    65    cron.daily      run-parts    /etc/cron.daily
6   7    70    cron.weekly     run-parts    /etc/cron.weekly
7   30   75    cron.monthly    run-parts    /etc/cron.monthly
```

Lines 1 and 2 are comments. The man pages for anacron and anacrontab are shown in line 2.

Line 3 specifies the shell to be used and line 4 sets up the directory paths that are used when the file is processed.

Lines 5, 6 and 7 cause the script named run-parts to be run for the directories named cron.daily, cron.weekly and cron.monthly below the path of /etc. This script is run based on the settings in fields 1 and 2. This causes the script files in these cron.* directories to be executed.

Lines 5, 6 and 7 contain four fields which are separated by a tab or a space. The line numbers at the left are for the purpose of discussion and are not being counted as a field. The two columns at the right contain "run-parts" and a directory path to a /etc/cron.* directory. These are counted as one field, referred to as the **command** field. These two columns represent the command to be run. The command consists of the script named run-parts with the argument of a directory path. The fields in anacrontab are described in Table 17-3.

Table 17-3 - The Fields in /etc/anacrontab

Field	Description
1	the **period** of time in days
2	the **delay** in minutes
3	the **job-identifier**
4	the **command** to be run

The delay field is used so that tasks are not all run at once as soon as anacron is run. By default, anacron is run when a system starts in runlevels 2 through 5 or when a system changes into one of these runlevels. The delay stops anacron from running all of the tasks at once after the system boots.

The name in the job-identifier field is assigned to the task (job). It is used when email messages are sent (usually to the root user) regarding the task and is used when messages are written (by anacron) to the log file named cron in /var/log. *It is also used for the name of a file when anacron is run with the -u option.*

By default, a script named 0anacron exists in each of the cron.daily, cron.monthly and cron.weekly directories. These three scripts have the same name, but slightly different contents. They all run the anacron command with the -u option.

When anacron is run with the -u option, the job-identifier name is used for the name of a file that contains a date (only). This file is used by anacron to determine if the command in field 4 should be run.

The 0anacron script in the cron.daily directory is run every day at 4:02 a.m. by cron (if the system is turned on). If the system is not turned on, then this script is run by anacron as described below. The 0anacron script in cron.daily contains the following statement:

```
anacron -u cron.daily
```

The -u option causes the current date, in the form of yyyymmdd to be written to a file named cron.daily in /var/spool/anacron. The statement in line 5 of anacrontab checks the date in the cron.daily file; if it has been 1 day since the date in the cron.daily file, then the task named cron.daily on line 5 is run. This causes all of the items in cron.daily to be executed, including the 0anacron script, which updates the date in the cron.daily file.

The 0anacron script in cron.weekly runs the following command:

anacron -u cron.weekly

The 0anacron script in cron.monthly runs the following command:

anacron -u cron.monthly

The date in the cron.daily file in /var/spool/anacron is used to determine if the job (task) name of cron.daily (in the job-identifier field on line 5 in anacrontab) should be run. The date in the cron.weekly file is used to determine if the job named cron.weekly should be run and the date in cron.monthly is used to determine if the job named cron.monthly should be run. You will see how all of this works during the Hands-On Exercises.

In the default anacrontab file, field 4 consists of the command run-parts with the argument of a directory path at the right.

Line 5 in anacrontab has a period of 1 day, a delay of 65 minutes, and a job-identifier of cron.daily. Therefore, if it has been 1 day since the command in field 4 has been run (based on the date in the cron.daily file), the command is run after a 65 minute delay. This causes the run-parts script to execute all of the items (scripts, symlinks and programs) in the /etc/cron.daily directory.

The items in /etc/cron.daily are normally run by cron every day at 4:02 a.m. If the tasks were not run (because the system was not on, or the crond service (the crond daemon) was not running), then anacron will run them if the current date is one or more days later than the date in the cron.daily file in /var/spool/anacron.

In other words, if the system was not on at 4:02 a.m., the items in cron.daily will be run the next time the system boots, after a delay of 65 minutes. If a system was turned off at the end of the day, then the items in cron.daily are run the next time the system is booted, after a 65 minute delay.

Line 6 in anacrontab has a period of 7 days, a delay of 70 minutes, and a job-identifier of cron.weekly. The items in /etc/cron.weekly are normally run by cron every Sunday at 4:22 a.m. If these items were not run, then anacron will run them if it has been 7 days since the date in the cron.weekly file, after a delay of 70 minutes.

Line 7 in anacrontab has a period of 30 days, a delay of 75 minutes, and a job-identifier of cron.monthly. The items in /etc/cron.monthly are normally run by cron on the first day of the month at 4:42 a.m. If these items were not run, then anacron will run them if it has been 30 days since the date in the cron.monthly file, after a delay of 75 minutes.

Working with Log Files

Log files contain messages that were written to them by the kernel and many different programs, including daemons. Linux uses log files extensively and they are an excellent method of seeing what is going on with a system, particularly if something isn't working properly.

Many log files, such as the files that are written to by the kernel, and by the init scripts that are run during the boot process, are located in the path of /var/log. However, log files are also located in other directories.

For example, the main log file for the CUPS printing system (described a few chapters from now) is named error_log and is located in a subdirectory of /var/log named cups.

Additional log files are often created on a system when a new package is added to the system.

For example, installing the package that provides the Apache Web server causes new log files to be created on a system and these logs are written to by the web server.

Getting Help with Error Messages in Log Files

Log files contain a lot of different kinds of messages, including error messages. If something isn't working properly on a system, check the appropriate log file(s) and see if you can find some type of error message. If you find an error message and need more help to solve the problem, you can get support using all of the various methods described earlier, such as by contacting the creators of your distribution or a software support company. In addition to this, some of the common methods used to get solutions for error messages are described below.

An excellent and fast method of getting help is to type a description of a problem, or the text of an error message (if you have one), into a search engine, such as Google.

If you have the output of an error message, such as the output from a log file, you can paste all or part of the message in the search engine and do a search. If the results of the search are too "broad", reduce the amount of text in the error message and run the search again.

You may get results from a search that are not actually relevant to your problem. The search may present results that match a problem that is similar to yours, but not the same. Try doing searches with different (but similar) strings of text and seeing various results before dedicating time to a specific solution. The solution you have found may not be the solution to your problem!

Another good method of getting support is to see if there is a mailing list or newsgroup that exists for the system component you are having difficulty with. If so, post a message describing your problem and any relevant information from a log file.

For example, if you are having problems with the CUPS printing system software, you can get support at the newsgroup named "cups.general". You can post a description of your problem, along with the relevant output from the error_log file in /var/log/cups. You will likely see a response to your problem posted within twenty-four hours.

The Rotation of Log Files

Many log files are written to frequently and can become quite large in a relatively short period of time, depending on the log file and the usage of the system. Therefore, after a period of time, or after a certain file size has been reached, a log file is "rotated" from its original filename to a similar filename and eventually no longer exists. Some log files are rotated by scripts, such as the system initialization scripts, and many are rotated by the logrotate binary.

For example, there is a log file in /var/log named boot.log. This is written to during the boot process with messages that are generated when the rc.sysinit script is processed to start system components, and also when the rc script is processed to start services. It may also be written to after a system has booted.

After Linux has been installed, this log file begins as an empty file named boot.log and after a period of time it is rotated by the logrotate binary (in /usr/sbin), based on settings in /etc/logrotate.conf. The script named logrotate in /etc/cron.daily runs the logrotate binary. This script is run by either cron or anacron each day and it causes several log files to be rotated, *if they have been configured to be rotated on that day*.

When the boot.log file is rotated, this file is moved to the name of boot.log.1 and a new empty boot.log file is created. The next time the system boots, a log of the boot process is written to the empty file named boot.log.

The next time the logs are rotated, boot.log.1 is moved (rotated) to boot.log.2; boot.log is moved to boot.log.1 and an empty boot.log file is created again. Each time this log is rotated, an empty boot.log file is created.

The next time the logs are rotated, boot.log.2 is moved to boot.log.3 and the .2 file is moved to the .3 file and so on. The next time, the .3 file is moved to .4, the .2 is moved to .3, and so on. The next time the logs are rotated, the same process continues, except that boot.log.4 is not moved to boot.log.5.

The highest number of a boot.log.x file is boot.log.4. Therefore, the text that was in boot.log.4 ceases to exist because the contents of boot.log.4 are replaced with the contents of boot.log.3. This is important, because it signifies the end of the file that was originally named boot.log. If boot.log.5 and additional (higher numbered) log files were created, they would eventually fill the entire system!

Many of the files in /var/log are rotated in the same way that boot.log is rotated. If your system has been in use for a long enough period of time, the log files will have .1, .2, and so on, at the right of the log file name. Some log files, such as the ones that are rotated by a system initialization script, start at .0 and go up to a higher number, such as .6.

Reading Mail Messages

As mentioned earlier, many programs email information, such as the completion of a task or the output of a program, to a user and this user is often the root user.

When an error has occurred with some programs, a description of the error is emailed to a user, in addition to an error message being written to a log file. In addition to looking at log files for information, such as error messages, be sure to read the mail that has been sent to the root user or other applicable user.

To read mail as any user, type: mail and press Enter. The mail for the current user will be displayed. To read the mail for the root user, su to root and run the mail command.

Once you have run the mail command, a "&" prompt appears at the bottom of the screen. A "U" for "**u**nread" appears at the left of unread messages and a ">" symbol at the left indicates your location in the list of messages.

> To read all messages, press Enter. The first message will appear. If "--More--" appears, press the Spacebar to see more of the message or type: q to quit out of the message.
>
> To read the next message, press Enter.
>
> To get a list of active messages, type: h and press Enter.
>
> To read a specific mail message, type: t *number* and replace *number* with the number that appears at the left of the message.
>
> To get help with mail, type: ? and press Enter or run: man mail at a shell prompt to see the man page.
>
> To quit out of mail, type: q and press Enter.
>
> To end a message that you are creating, or one that you are replying to, press Ctrl+d. At the "**Cc**:" prompt, type in the name(s) of users that you want to "**c**arbon **c**opy" and press Enter, or simply press Enter if you do not want to "cc" anyone.

The dmesg Command

The dmesg command displays messages that were generated by the kernel during the boot process. It does not display messages generated from other initialization scripts (such as rc.sysinit and rc) that are run during the boot process, or after the boot process. Therefore, this command does not show messages that are generated when you start a service during the boot process or when you start, stop or restart a service after the boot process (see /var/log/messages for this information).

The dmesg command is commonly used to view error messages and the hardware components of a system. If you see an error message (scrolling quickly off of the screen) during the boot process and need to see it again, this command will allow you to view the error message (hardware error messages can also be seen in /var/log/messages).

Running the dmesg command without any options displays:

kernel information (such as the version of the kernel) and other system information (such as protocols being used)

kernel messages that were generated during bootup - this includes error messages that were generated as a result of errors during bootup, including hardware errors

hardware that the kernel detected during bootup - if a hardware component has been added to a system, it will appear when dmesg is run after the system has been rebooted - if a hardware component has been removed, the component will no longer appear when dmesg is run after the system has been rebooted

kernel messages generated after bootup, such as an error message that has occurred due to the malfunction of a hardware component - therefore, the output of dmesg may change after a system has booted

messages that are generated when a driver is loaded or unloaded during or after the boot process - this occurs when all drivers are loaded, but does not always occur when all drivers are unloaded after the boot process

 The output of the dmesg command will vary from one system to another based on the hardware and software components in the system, but it is typically over one hundred lines long and may be over two hundred lines long. Therefore, the grep command is often used to restrict the output of the dmesg command so that only the information regarding one or more specific hardware components appears.

Some of the messages seen when dmesg is run and some of the messages that are put in /var/log/messages are generated during the boot process. Running dmesg is *similar* to running: cat /var/log/messages.

The command: dmesg > *filename*.txt   will put the output of the dmesg command in *filename*.txt.

For example, you could replace *filename.txt* with a file named 012503.txt (where 01 represents the month, 25 represents the day of the month and 03 is the year).

 As Linux is booting, many messages appear on the screen, and this can include error messages. If you cannot read a message because it scrolled by too fast, *and you have booted to a text-based login prompt,* you can press Shift+PgUp to scroll upwards through the messages and Shift+PgDn to scroll downwards (after scrolling up). This will allow you to read the messages. If you are not at a text-based login prompt, you can do other steps described in this chapter to see the error messages that occurred during the boot process.

The Shift+PgUp and Shift+PgDn key combinations can also be used in a terminal emulation window to scroll up and down, rather than using the scroll bar in the right border of the terminal emulation window to scroll.

The syslogd Daemon and the /etc/syslog.conf File

The daemon named **syslogd** (**sys**tem logging **d**aemon) manages many of the logs on a system. It receives messages from various programs and writes them to the log files used by the programs.

The configuration file named /etc/syslog.conf contains configuration settings for the syslogd daemon. It specifies settings for some of the main system log files, such as /var/log/messages and /var/log/boot.log. If you are using a different distribution, you may be able to see the location of the log files for the distribution in syslog.conf.

Common Linux Log Files

The /var/log/messages Log File

The /var/log/messages file is a general log file that logs many important system messages, such as:

kernel messages that are generated during bootup, such as when filesystems are mounted, drivers are loaded (such as a driver for a network card) and daemons are run (such as when the httpd daemon is run for the Apache web server)

kernel messages generated during bootup include error messages that are generated as a result of errors during bootup

kernel messages that are generated as a result of a hardware malfunction after bootup

messages that are generated when a daemon is run during or after bootup, such as when you run the chkconfig command to start, stop or restart a service that runs a daemon

loading and unloading a driver (such as a driver for a sound card) after bootup - this does not occur when all drivers are loaded and does not occur when all drivers are unloaded

The /var/log/boot.log Log File

Some of the messages that are generated during the boot process are put in this file. This includes messages that are generated when the rc.sysinit script is processed to start system components, and also when the rc script is processed to start services. Some messages are also put in this file after a system has booted, such as a message that indicates that a service has stopped or started.

The /var/log/cron Log File

Among other things, this file shows when cron jobs (tasks) and anacron jobs *will be* started, when they *have* started, when they have terminated (completed), and if they have terminated successfully (by showing "Normal exit" rather than an error message).

The /var/log/maillog Log File

This log file shows activity of the sendmail (mail transport agent) service that is used to "transport" email on a system. It shows when the service was started and stopped and other information regarding this service.

The /var/log/rpmpkgs Log File

A "package" can be any software component that can be installed on a system, such as an application software program, some type of server, a command, a text-based utility or GUI utility. Many "packages" are available as **rpm** (**R**ed Hat **P**ackage **M**anager) packages and others are available in other "package" formats and also as source code. When you installed Linux earlier, you installed over six hundred rpm packages.

The **rpmpkgs (rpm packages)** log contains a listing of all of the packages that are currently installed on a system. It is updated daily by cron or anacron. This causes the log file to be current after packages have been added or removed.

The rpm packages that have been installed on a system can also be seen with: rpm -qa. This command is often output to less or grep.

Keep in mind that many other packages install log files and the programs in these packages write to these log files when they are being used.

The /var/log/secure Log File

This log file is used for security messages related to network activity.

The /var/log/XFree86.x.log Log File

The *x* in XFree86.*x*.log represents a number. This log file is used for messages from the XFree86 server (X).

Using the System Logs GUI Utility

The System Logs utility can be seen by selecting: Menu ; System Tools ; System Logs or by running the command: redhat-logviewer. Several system logs can be seen in this utility. These logs can be selected and scrolled through for system information and error messages.

Figure 17-1 shows the System Logs utility with the "Boot Log" heading selected at the left. A description of the log file appears at the right of the log book icon. The log files at the left can be selected to see a description of them at the right of the book icon.

The "Boot Log" heading shows the contents of the file named /var/log/boot.log. Notice the output on the right side of the graphic.

At the top of the output, a message generated by the rc.sysinit script appears. After this there are two messages from kudzu and then one from the rc script, showing information on iptables. Notice the (small) exclamation mark beside the third last item. There was a failure in loading the NFS filesystem at this workstation. This happened because the workstation tried to mount a "share" (shared directory) that is located on an NFS file server and the server was not running when the workstation booted.

The "Filter for:" field at the bottom of the screen can be used to look for specific information, in the same way as text can be "grepped" for information at the command line. Type text in at the right of "Filter for:", such as "rc.sysinit" (without the quotes) and click Filter. This will show all of the statements in the log file that contain the text "rc.sysinit". To have all of the text in the file appear again, click on Reset.

Figure 17-1 - The System Logs utility with the "Boot Log" heading selected

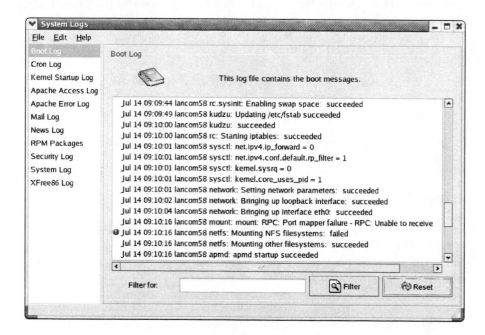

This utility does not allow you to select previous log files (log files that have been rotated). For example, you can see the contents of boot.log, but not the contents of boot.log.1, which is was previously the boot.log file before it was rotated to the name of boot.log.1. If a set of log files, such as boot.log.x has just been rotated, then selecting the log file will not show any contents because the log file, such as boot.log, is empty (and its contents have been moved to boot.log.1).

The tail Command (Revisited)

This command is used to display the (tail) end of a file or the tail of the output of a command. By default, this command causes the last ten lines of a file to be displayed, or the last ten lines of the output of a command.

The -f option is used to continuously display the output of the tail command. The output will change when the tail (end) of the file changes. This option is commonly used to view the changes that occur to log files as the system is running. Press Ctrl+c to stop the (continuous) output when the -f option is used.

The last -n*x* lines (where *x* is a number of lines) option allows you to see *x* lines rather than the default of 10. The "n" in "-n*x*" is required when the -f option is used.

Example of the tail Command

tail -f -n5 maillog cron

The files named maillog and cron are in /var/log and your current directory is /var/log. The -f option causes the end of the files to be displayed continuously and the -n5 option causes only five lines to be displayed, rather than the default of 10. To stop the output, press Ctrl+c.

The tail end of both of these files will appear, with "==> maillog <==" above the output of the maillog file and "==> cron <==" above the output of the cron file.

In the command above, the maillog file appears before the cron file and so the output of maillog will appear above cron. However, *additional* messages that are written to a file will appear below the original output in the order in which they occur.

For example, if the system writes to the maillog file, the output will appear *below* the output of the cron file, and so on.

Hands-On Exercises

 Viewing Boot Messages after Booting to a Text-Based Login Prompt

Boot to the GUI login prompt ; press Ctrl+Alt+F1 to go to virtual terminal 1 ;

log in as cwest ; su to root ;

use the vi editor to edit /etc/inittab ; change the 5 in the initdefault statement (below the description of the runlevels) to a 3.

This will change the default runlevel from 5 to 3.

Also edit /var/spool/anacron/cron.daily and change the date to today's date (if it is not already today's date).

If the 0anacron script in /etc/cron.daily has been run today (via cron or anacron), then the date will be today's date. The 0anacron script will have run if the system was on at 4:02 a.m. last night or if anacron ran it after the system was booted today.

By changing the date in cron.daily to today's date, anacron will not be set up to run the items in /etc/cron.daily (after a 65 minute delay) the next time the system starts. This will stop the cron.daily job from being "busy" in the process of waiting to run the items in /etc/cron.daily. Therefore, the next time the system starts, anacron will not have a job waiting to start in 65 minutes. This will allow you (further below) to change the date in cron.daily to yesterday's date, change the setting for the cron.daily job in anacrontab from 65 (minutes) to 1 (minute) and then run anacron at the command line so that you can see the items in the /etc/cron.daily directory being run (after a 1 minute delay).

>]# shutdown -r now

> when the text-based login prompt appears, do not log in ; press Shift+PgUp until you get to the top ; look through the boot messages as you go and then use Shift+PgDn to scroll downwards.

If you need to see the messages that were displayed when a "server system" (that is not running X) was booted, you can use the Shift+PgUp and then Shift+PgDn keys to scroll through the text. These key combinations can also be used to scroll through output that has scrolled out of sight in a terminal emulation window. This can be very useful.

> At the text-based login prompt, log in as cwest ; su to root ;

> use the vi editor to change the 3 in the initdefault statement to a 5 ;

>]# shutdown -r now

 Logging In to Look at Log Files and Work with Scheduling Tasks

> Log in as cwest ; open a terminal emulation window ; su to root ;

> move and size the window so that it fills the top half of the screen ;

> open another terminal emulation window ; su to root ;

> move and size the window so that it fills the bottom half of the screen ;

> maximize the top window ; you will "unmaximize" (rather than minimize) it later ;

>]# dmesg | nl

Depending on the system, the output from dmesg is usually over 100 lines and is often "grepped" for information.

The dmesg command displays messages that were generated by the kernel during the boot process, but not messages generated from other initialization scripts.

The dmesg command is commonly used to view error messages and the hardware components of a system. If you see an error message (scrolling quickly off of the screen) during the boot process and need to see it again, this command will allow you to view the error message (hardware error messages can also be seen in /var/log/messages).

Press Shift+PgUp several times to scroll to the top ;

press Shift+PgDn to scroll to the bottom.

]# dmesg | grep ^hd   # shows disk information

③ Viewing syslogd and /etc/syslogd.conf

]# ps -aux | grep syslogd   # this daemon manages log files

]# clear ; cat /etc/syslog.conf

This file configures the syslogd daemon and specifies settings for some of the main system log files. Notice the names of the log files at the right of the output.

④ Viewing Log Files in /var/log

]# cd /var/log ; less .   # this dir. contains many system log files

Notice the filenames and extensions of the log files in this directory. The files ending in .0, .1, .2, and so on, are the log files that have been rotated.

]# less boot.log   # if this file is empty, look at boot.log.1

Scroll down until you can see the top of the output for today's date. This file contains a log of events that occurred when the system booted. Notice the word "succeeded" at the right of many of the lines of text. If something did not work correctly, you would see "failed".

At the right of your hostname, such as "lancom57", look for "rc" and "rc.sysinit". These are messages that were output by these two scripts. Also look at the right of "fsck". This is output from the **fsck** (**f**ilesystem **c**heck) binary.

/sendmail   # search for "sendmail"

press "n" until you see "startup succeeded" for this service.

This service should have been started and should have "succeeded" (for today's date).

/cron   # search for "cron" - "anacron" will also appear

press "n" until you see "startup succeeded" for this service.

The crond service, which starts the crond daemon should appear and should have "succeeded". You should also see that anacron "succeeded". anacron was "run", but is not a daemon.

/atd   # search for "atd" - this daemon also started

---

⑤ Continuously Viewing the End of the messages File

Unmaximize the current window ; press Ctrl+l ;

there should now be one window in the top half and another in the bottom half ;

Alt+Tab to the bottom window ; change into the path of /var/log ;

]# clear ; tail -f messages   # the prompt does not appear

open another (third) terminal emulation window ;

move the bottom of the new window up so that you can see all of the output in the window that is in the bottom half of the screen.

Notice the date and time of the last message at the bottom of the screen.

In the "new" (third) window, su to root.

A new entry appeared in the bottom window because an "event" had occurred.

]# exit   # another entry appeared below

]# exit

⑥ Viewing Multiple Log Files

Alt+Tab to the bottom window (if it is not active) ; press Ctrl+c to stop the tail command ;

]# tail -f -n3 messages boot.log   # run in bottom window

Notice "==> messages <==" above the output of the messages log file and "==> boot.log <==" above the boot.log log file. The number of lines being displayed (3) is low because we are looking at two files in a small window. This number can be increased if you are looking at a window that is maximized.

Alt+Tab to the top window ;

sendmail is the name of a "service" that is loaded when you boot your system. It provides the system (programs running on the system), and the users on the system, with the capability of sending email. This service is being used below to show that when a service is stopped or started, these actions are logged in the messages file.

Run the commands below in the top window and watch the bottom window after pressing Enter below.

]# date   # notice the current **time**

]# service sendmail stop

Look at the time of the output in the bottom window. This "event" was logged in both log files.

    ]# date

    ]# service sendmail start   # check the bottom window

The starting and stopping of other services, such as a web server, are also put in these log files. The messages file can also be "tailed" to debug changes that you are making to a system (that aren't working) and to check for the system's response to something that you are doing, such as attempting to load a driver for a network card. The file can also be checked for "authentication failure" messages if you think that your system is being accessed by someone that should not be accessing it.

    Alt+Tab to the bottom window ; press Ctrl+c ; leave it open ;

    Alt+Tab to the top window ;   maximize it and clear it.

(7) Viewing Information About "at"

    ]# whereis atd   # this is where it's at

    ]# ps -aux | grep atd   # /usr/sbin/atd is the atd daemon

    ]# find /etc/rc.d -name '*atd'

The atd script in the init.d directory appears, along with the symlinks in the rc?.d directories. The "S" symlinks indicate that by default, this service is set to on for runlevels 3, 4 and 5.

    ]# ls -l /etc/at.*   # only the at.deny file exists - not at.allow

    ]# cat /etc/at.deny   # this empty file allows users to run the at command

    ]# ls -l /var/spool/at   # no *files* appear

(8) Scheduling a Task with the at Command

    ]# at now + 4 minutes # the prompt changes to "at>".

The "task" that you are about to type runs the ls command "at" in four minutes. Tasks can also be run at much later times, such as during off-peak hours.

    Type the ls command below that appears *at the right of the "at>" prompt.*

    at> ls -lR /home/cwest > /home/cwest/cwestlist.txt

Additional items, such as commands and names of scripts could be typed at the next prompt.

    Press Ctrl+d to end the at command and notice the output.

    ]# atq   # the task (job) appears in the queue

Notice the number that appears at the left of the task. This number can be used with the atrm command to remove the task from the at queue.

If you run the command below within four minutes of running the at command, a file owned by root appears in the at directory. Once the task has been run, the file is deleted.

```
]# ls -l /var/spool/at
```

run atq again to see if the job still exists ; also look in the output for the time that the job should be run ;

run the atq command after the job should have run ; when the job no longer appears in the "at queue", run command below ;

```
]# ls -l ~cwest/cwest*          # notice the date and time of the file
```

Cat out the contents of the text file that was created and pipe the output to less.

```
]# ls -l /var/spool/at          # the file for the job is gone
```

 Viewing Information About cron

```
]# ps -aux | grep cron          # the crond daemon appears
]# find /etc/rc.d -name '*crond'
```

The files in the init scripts directory structure for crond appear. By default, this service is started in runlevels 2 through 5.

(10) Viewing the /etc/crontab File

```
]# cd /etc ; clear ; cat crontab | nl
```

Line 3 shows that mail will be sent to root.

Lines 6 through 9 are cron tasks that run the script named run-parts (as the root user), "on" the directories at the right. The run-parts script runs all of the executable items (scripts, symlinks and programs) in these directories.

The cron task on line 6 is run hourly, at one minute (01) after the hour. The task on line 7 is run at 4:02 a.m. (02 4) each day. The task on line 8 is run at 4:22 a.m. (22 4) each week on Sunday (0). The task on line 9 is run at 4:42 a.m. (42 4) on the first day of each month (1).

The cron jobs in crontab are only run if the system is on at the time the job is scheduled to run.

By default (with this distribution), anacron is set up to run the jobs that were not run by cron (because the system was turned off). However, cron does not require anacron and vice versa. Some distributions may use one and not the other. They are being used by this distribution to complement one another.

The cron.* Directories and the Files in Them

Your current directory should be /etc. Now you will see the cron.* directories. By default, the cron.d directory is empty. The other cron.* directories contain items (scripts, symlinks and programs) that are run by cron (when cron runs the script named run-parts). If you need a task to be run hourly, daily, weekly or monthly, put it in the appropriate cron.* directory below /etc.

>]# clear ; ls -l cron.*

The contents of the cron.* directories appear, along with the files in them. The files in these directories (excluding cron.d) are run by run-parts, when a cron job runs this script. All of the items in the cron.* directories are scripts, except for the 00-logwatch symlink file.

The cron.daily directory contains a symlink named **00-logwatch**. This symlink causes the logwatch utility to be run. This is a utility that monitors system logs, analyzes them, and generates a report. The 00-logwatch symlink points to a perl script that is about five hundred lines long and this symlink causes the logwatch utility to be executed.

 The 0anacron Scripts

The cron.daily, cron.weekly and cron.monthly directories all contain a file named **0anacron**.

>]# clear ; cat cron.daily/0anacron

Read the comments in this script. It runs anacron with the -u option for the job named cron.daily (as seen at the right of the anacron command at the bottom). This job name matches the job name in the job-identifier column in /etc/anacrontab.

>]# clear ; cat /etc/anacrontab | nl

The job-identifier names in column 3 (excluding the line numbers column) of lines 5, 6 and 7 are cron.daily, cron.weekly and cron.monthly.

>]# slocate cron.daily   # /var/spool/anacron/cron.daily appears

>]# cat /var/spool/anacron/cron.daily

A date appears. This is the file that you put today's date in when you edited it earlier. The date in this file is updated when the 0anacron script in /etc/cron.daily is run.

>]# clear ; cat cron.daily/0anacron   # use Up Arrow to get to this

This script runs anacron with the -u option to update the timestamp (current date) in the cron.daily file in /var/spool/anacron. This date is used by anacron (not cron) to determine if the job named cron.daily on line 5 in /etc/anacrontab should be run.

```
]# cat /etc/anacrontab | nl          # use Up Arrow again
```

cron jobs are run at the time they are scheduled to run. anacron runs the jobs in anacrontab based on the number of days since the last time the job was run, based on the date in the file that has the same name as the job, in /var/spool/anacron.

```
]# ls -l /var/spool/anacron
```

The cron.daily, cron.weekly and cron.monthly files appear. These files contain the timestamp created by the -u option of anacron, when the 0anacron script in each of the cron.daily, cron.weekly and cron.monthly directories is run. These files are used to determine if the jobs on lines 5, 6 and 7 in anacrontab should be run.

```
]# clear ; cat /var/spool/anacron/cron.daily
```

The date that you put in this file earlier appears. If you had not edited this file, then the date of the last time that the 0anacron script in /etc/cron.daily was run would appear. The date is written to this file by anacron in yyyymmdd format.

```
]# clear ; cat anacrontab | nl
```

The cron.daily job (on line 5) in anacrontab runs the run-parts script "on" the path of /etc/cron.daily. This script runs all of the items (scripts, symlinks and programs) in the path of /etc/cron.daily.

Notice the "1" in column 1 on line 5 (excluding the line numbers). This number is in the number of days column. The anacron program runs the run-parts script, which runs the items in the cron.daily directory, if it has been 1 day since the last time the tasks were run - based on the timestamp in the cron.daily file above.

When the run-parts script is run "on" the items in /etc/cron.daily, the 0anacron script is run (because it is in the cron.daily directory). The 0anacron script updates the timestamp in the cron.daily file shown above. The updated timestamp stops the cron.daily job in anacrontab from running until 1 day has passed from the date that the timestamp was updated.

In other words, if a system is *on* at 4:02 a.m., then *cron* runs the run-parts script "on" the items in /etc/cron.daily, *including the 0anacron script*. Therefore, the 0anacron script updates the timestamp (date) in the file named cron.daily so that *anacron* will *not* run the items in cron.daily, if anacron is run and it has not been 1 day since the date in the cron.daily file.

If a system is *not on* at 4:02 a.m., then the tasks in cron.daily are not run, and the 0anacron script is not run and the timestamp in the cron.daily file is not updated. The next time the system is turned on (in runlevel 2 through 5), anacron will run. It will "look at" the anacrontab file and see the cron.daily job on line 5, with the setting of "1" in the "period of days" column. It will then check the date in the cron.daily file and then run the cron.daily job because 1 day has passed since the date in the cron.daily file. The cron.daily job will run the run-parts script "on" /etc/cron.daily and all of the items in this path, including the 0anacron script after a delay of 65 minutes.

>]# cat cron.weekly/0anacron

This script runs anacron with the -u option to update the timestamp file named cron.weekly in /var/spool/anacron for the job named cron.weekly on line 6 in /etc/anacrontab.

>]# cat cron.monthly/0anacron

This script updates the timestamp file named cron.monthly in /var/spool/anacron, for the job named cron.monthly on line 7 in /etc/anacrontab.

⑬ Looking at Other Scripts in /etc/cron.daily

>]# clear ; ls -l cron.*   # a file named logrotate is in cron.daily

>]# cat cron.daily/**logrotate**

This script runs the logrotate binary, using the settings in the logrotate.conf file.

>]# whereis logrotate # the binary is in /usr/sbin and the config file is in /etc

>]# clear ; cat /etc/logrotate.conf

This file contains settings that are used for log file rotation. Read the comments in this file.

>]# clear ; ls -l cron.*   # use Up Arrow to get this

A file named **makewhatis.cron** is in cron.daily and also in cron.weekly.

>]# cat cron.daily/makewhatis.cron   # see the second last line

>]# man whatis   # read the description of this command

> /makewhatis   # this command creates the whatis database

>]# whatis whatis   # describes the whatis command

>]# whatis anacron   # describes the anacron command

The makewhatis command creates the "whatis database", which is used to provide descriptions for the whatis command, the apropos command, and the -k option of the man command. The makewhatis.cron file in cron.daily runs the makewhatis command with the -u and -w options. The -u option causes the database to be updated, rather than created from scratch. The makewhatis.cron file in cron.weekly runs the makewhatis command without the -u option. This causes the whatis database to be created from scratch. Therefore, the database is updated daily and also created from scratch weekly.

```
]# clear ; ls -l cron.*
```

```
]# cat cron.daily/rpm
```

This script runs the rpm command with the -qa (query all) and -qf (queryformat) options and uses the sort command to sort the output. The output of these commands (through the use of the > symbol) is put into the log file named /var/log/rpmpkgs.

Use less to view /var/log/rpmpkgs.

This log file contains a list of all currently installed rpm packages (software components).

```
]# cat cron.daily/slocate.cron
```

This script runs the renice command and then the updatedb command. The renice command causes the updatedb command below it to run with a low priority (+19). You will run top in a few minutes to see the updatedb program running, due to the slocate.cron script. There is an NI column in top that shows the "nice" value (priority) of a process. The renice command in slocate.cron sets the priority to 19 (lowest) and this appears below the NI column in the top utility, at the left of the updatedb command.

The updatedb command is used to update the slocate database. This database is used to provide the location of directories and files when the slocate command is run. Notice that the -f and -e options of updatedb are used in this script.

```
]# man updatedb
```

Look for the descriptions of the -f and -e options. The -f and -e options are used to exclude filesystem types and exclude directories, respectively.

```
]# clear ; ls -l cron.*
```

```
]# cat cron.daily/tmpwatch | nl
```

This script is used to run the tmpwatch binary. This binary is used to remove old **temp**orary files in "**tmp**" directories and in other directories that contain temporary files. Lines 1 and 2 cause it to be run "on" the **/tmp** and /var/**tmp** directories, respectively. Lines 3 through 7 cause the tmpwatch binary to also be run "on" several subdirectories of /var (see the text at the right of: for d in /var/).

 Viewing Information About anacron

```
]# ps -aux | grep anacron     # anacron is not run as a daemon

]# find /etc/rc.d -name '*anacron'
```

The anacron script in the init.d directory appears, along with the symlinks in the rc?.d directories. By default, this service is set to on for runlevels 2 through 5. It is run *once* (and then exits) when a system boots in runlevel 2, 3, 4, or 5, or when a system changes into runlevel 2, 3, 4, or 5.

```
]# less /etc/rc.d/init.d/anacron
```

Read the comment regarding "downtime" at the top of the script.

```
]# clear ; cat /etc/anacrontab | nl
```

Lines 5, 6, and 7 run the cron.daily, cron.weekly and cron.monthly jobs (shown in column 3 - excluding the line number column). These jobs run the command at the right of the job name. The command is run-parts and the argument of the command is the directory path at the right. The run-parts script runs all of the items in the directory.

 Clearing Out Old Mail

The steps further below will cause mail to be sent to root. To easily read this mail, do the following steps to review old mail.

```
]# mail       # see the mail of the root user
```

The "**U**" at the left stands for "**u**nread". A "&" prompt appears at the bottom of the screen.

You will likely see "– more –" appear at the bottom of your screen when reading mail. This will indicate some kind of output. Press the Spacebar until "– more –" no longer appears and then press Enter to see the next message.

Press Enter to read the first message ; continue to do this until all mail has been read.

Type: q to quit out of mail.

(16) Preparing to Run anacron

The steps below are not done in normal "day-to-day" operation. They are being done to demonstrate the way that anacron works when jobs are not run by cron because a system was not turned on.

Unmaximize the current terminal emulation window ; press Ctrl+l.

You should have a window in the top half of the screen and another in the bottom half, and you should be working as root in both.

Alt+Tab to the top window (if it is not already active) ;

]# clear ; cat /etc/anacrontab | nl

The steps below will run the cron.daily job on line 5. This will run the run-parts script on the items in /etc/cron.daily. Notice the "65" on line 5. This is the number of minutes of delay before anacron runs cron.daily, if the date in the cron.daily file in /var/spool/anacron is not the current date.

Get a listing of the files in /etc/cron.daily.

The steps below will cause all of the items in the cron.daily directory to be run.

]# slocate cron.daily

Without changing into the directory path, edit the cron.daily file in /var/spool/anacron ;

change the date to yesterday's date ; save and exit.

This will cause anacron to run the cron.daily job in anacrontab because it will appear to anacron that it has been 1 day since the cron.daily job (in anacrontab) has been run.

Edit the anacrontab file in /etc and change the "65" to a "1" (without the quotes) ;

save and exit.

This will cause anacron to run the cron.daily job after a delay of 1 minute, instead of 65.

Setting Up Your bucommon Script to Run Daily

A few chapters ago, you created a script named bucommon in /root/bin.

Copy (not move) the bucommon script from /root/bin to /etc/cron.daily ;

make sure the script is still in /root/bin ;

"cat out" the contents of this script to see what it does ;

get a listing of /misc/archives ; a "bu-*" file with today's date should not appear (if one does, delete it).

By putting the bucommon script in /etc/cron.daily, the script will now run whenever the run-parts script is run "on" the cron.daily directory (by the cron task at 4:02 a.m. (in crontab) or by anacron (via anacrontab) when a system boots or changes into runlevels 2 through 5).

 Running anacron - "Just Like It Was The Day After Yesterday"

Alt+Tab to the bottom window (if it is not active) ;

change into /var/log (if necessary) ;

]# tail -f -n3 maillog cron

watch for messages in the bottom window while the top utility is running in the top window ;

Alt+Tab to the top window ;

]# anacron

]# top

The cron log file (in the bottom window) shows "Anacron x.x started on *date*" and "Will run job 'cron.daily' in 1 min."

At the start of the next minute, you will see "Job 'cron.daily' started" (in the bottom window). You will also see items such as 00logwatch, sed, makewhatis, rpmq, sort and updatedb near the top of the top utility.

After 0anacron has run, the cron log file shows "Updated timestamp for job 'cron.daily' to *date*". This indicates that the file named cron.daily in /var/spool/anacron was updated with the current date.

When you see updatedb, notice the number (priority) of the process, below the NI heading.

Once the job has completed, the cron log file shows "Job 'cron.daily' terminated (mailing output)". The maillog then shows the result of mailing the output of the bucommon script to the root user. These mail messages are very long and are truncated at the right margin. This is why -n3 was used with the tail command instead of a higher number. The cron log also shows "Normal exit (1 jobs run)". The job was cron.daily, which ran run-parts on the items in /etc/cron.daily!

The mail messages in maillog were caused when the root user was mailed the output of the bucommon script. These messages are very long and are truncated at the right margin.

> Alt+Tab to the top window (if necessary) ; type: q to quit out of top ;
>
> "cat out" the cron.daily file in /var/spool/anacron.

The cron.daily file should have today's date. When anacron was run, the 0anacron script in the cron.daily directory was run (by run-parts). This script ran anacron with the -u option "on" the file named cron.daily and updated the date in the cron.daily file to today's date.

> Alt+Tab to the bottom window ; press Shift+PgUp twice to see more information ;
>
> press Shift+PgUp again ; press Shift+PgDn until you get to the bottom ;
>
> press Ctrl+c to stop the tail command ; maximize the bottom window ;
>
>]# mail

Notice the text in quotes at the right of the new mail message.

> Press Enter to look at the message ; press Spacebar if necessary.

The output of the bucommon script appears showing the files that were backed up!

> q   # quit out of mail
>
> Get a listing of files in /misc/archives ; a "bu-" file with today's date should appear!
>
> remove the "bu-" file that has today's date from /misc/archives ;
>
> remove the bucommon file from /etc/cron.daily (only) ;
>
> edit /etc/anacrontab and change the "1" (above the "70") back to "65" ; save the file.

(19) Creating a User crontab File

Unmaximize the open window ;

In the top window, get a listing of the files in the cron directory below /var/spool (not to be confused with the anacron directory below /var/spool) ; the directory should be empty.

You are currently working as root and have not yet created a user crontab file.

Alt+Tab to the bottom window ;

change into /var/log.

]# tail -f -n3 maillog cron

Alt+Tab to the top window.

Now you will create a user crontab file that runs the bucommon script that is in /root/bin (not the script that was in /etc/cron.daily). Watch for messages in the log files in the bottom window.

]# date   # shows the current date and **time**

]# crontab -e

A "(root) BEGIN EDIT (root)" message was written in the cron log file.

You are using the vi editor to create a user crontab file for the root user. Therefore, use vi commands to edit the file. This file will be named root in /var/spool/cron when you exit out of vi.

Type in the following indented three lines of text (flush left) ; replace the 45 and 3 in the last line with values that represent the time, five minutes from now (remember that each field should be separated by a space) ; be sure to add 12 to any time after 12 o'clock (if it is 1 p.m., then it's 13 o'clock!) ; replace the 1-5 in the last line with the single number that represents the current day of week ;

    # run the bucommon script each weekday
    # to back up the /home/common directory structure

    45 3 * * 1-5 /root/bin/bucommon

Do the steps that you would normally use to save a file and exit.

no crontab for root - using an empty one   # output after exiting
crontab: installing new crontab   # output after exiting

The cron log file was written to (twice) again. At the start of the next minute, "RELOAD" will appear in the cron log file. Keep working through the steps below.

```
]# date                 # your job will start in 5 min.
```

Get a listing of the files in the cron directory below /var/spool.

A file named root should appear. This is the user crontab file for the root user.

```
]# clear  ;  crontab -l# the contents of the file name root appear
```

A message was written to the cron log file.

```
]# date
```

When the job starts, messages will be written to maillog and the cron log files.

Once enough time has passed for the script to be started, a message similar to "(root) CMD (/root/bin/common)" will appear in the cron log. Messages will also be written to the maillog log. Do not do any more steps below until the cron job has run.

Get a listing of the files in the /misc/archives and your backup file should appear!

Notice the date and time of the backup file and compare this with the time that you specified (in the user crontab file) for the backup to begin.

Run the tar command with the -tjvf options "on" the backup file that was with created the cron task and pipe the output to the less command ; scroll through the list of items that were backed up.

Get a listing of the cron directory below /var/spool to see that the user crontab file still exists.

```
]# crontab -r       # remove the user crontab file
                    # a message was put in the cron log file
```

Get another listing of the cron directory below /var/spool to see that the file named root no longer exists.

Alt+Tab to the bottom window and use Shift+PgUp/PgDn to look through the log files.

Press Ctrl+c to stop the tail command ; maximize the bottom window.

```
]# mail                 # notice the text at the right of the message
```

Press Enter ; press Spacebar ; type: q to quit out of mail.

Whew!!! Do the steps to shut your system down.

Section Review

1. You are currently logged in as root. Which command should be used to edit the user crontab file for the bford user?

   - ○ A. vi /var/log/anacrontab/bford
   - ○ B. crontab -vi -u bford
   - ○ C. crontab -e -u bford
   - ○ D. crontab -e

2. Select two correct statements regarding the default settings of anacron.

   - ☐ A. it is run when the system boots and every hour afterwards
   - ☐ B. it is run when the system boots and when the system changes into some runlevels
   - ☐ C. it has a delay field so that all scheduled tasks are not run at once
   - ☐ D. it runs the tasks in the /var/log/cron file

3. What unit of measure is used in the "period of time" field in anacron?

   - ○ A. minutes
   - ○ B. hours
   - ○ C. days
   - ○ D. weeks

4. Which statements below are correct?

   - ☐ A. the atlist command is used to list the at tasks in the queue
   - ☐ B. the atq command is used to list the at tasks in the queue
   - ☐ C. the atdel command is used to remove at tasks in the queue
   - ☐ D. the atrm command is used to remove at tasks in the queue

5. Select the "system" crontab file.

   - ○ A. /var/spool/cron/root
   - ○ B. /root/root
   - ○ C. /etc/crontab
   - ○ D. /etc/cron.d/root

6. Which keys are pressed to end the creation of a task with the at command and are also used to end the creation of an email message in the mail program?

   - ○ A. Ctrl+d
   - ○ B. Ctrl+Alt+d
   - ○ C. Alt+q
   - ○ D. Ctrl+:

7. Select the script that is located in three cron.* directories and is used to update the timestamp file used by anacron.

    ○ A.   timestamp
    ○ B.   0anacron
    ○ C.   cronstamp
    ○ D.   00-logwatch

8. Which two programs are daemons?

    ☐ A.   atd
    ☐ B.   anad
    ☐ C.   anacron
    ☐ D.   crond

9. Select the editor that is used to edit user crontab files directly.

    ○ A.   vi
    ○ B.   ed
    ○ C.   croned
    ○ D.   none of the above

10. How often does crond check to see if there are new cron tasks?

    ○ A.   every minute
    ○ B.   every day at 4:02 a.m.
    ○ C.   every week on Sunday
    ○ D.   every month on the first day of the month

11. Select the log file that will indicate if a service was started during the boot process.

    ○ A.   bootloader.0.log
    ○ B.   rpmpkgs
    ○ C.   boot.log
    ○ D.   start.log

12. You are working as the showe user and want to read your existing mail messages. Select the command that will allow you to do this.

    ○ A.   mail
    ○ B.   mail -U
    ○ C.   mail -r showe
    ○ D.   maillist -u showe

13. Which command displays the messages that were generated by the kernel during the boot process?

    ○ A. cat /var/dmesg
    ○ B. cat /var/log/kernellog
    ○ C. dmesg
    ○ D. uname -m

14. Select the daemon that manages many of the logs on a system.

    ○ A. analogd
    ○ B. syslogd
    ○ C. anacron
    ○ D. logd

15. A user crontab file does not have a field for the user name because user crontab files are the same name as the user. T F

16. Select the log file that allows you to see all of the software components installed on a system.

    ○ A. compile.log
    ○ B. binlist.log
    ○ C. instpkgs
    ○ D. rpmpkgs

17. Which binary is used to rotate log files?

    ○ A. cronlogd
    ○ B. logrotate
    ○ C. boot.log
    ○ D. rotated

18. cron is used to schedule tasks so that they are run at a specific time. T F

19. What is the name of the empty file in /etc that allows all users to run the at command and schedule tasks?

    ○ A. at.allow
    ○ B. at.deny
    ○ C. allow.at
    ○ D. allow.all

20. You are working as the root user. You need to quickly look at the contents of the user crontab file of the jbeck user, without editing the file. Which command will allow you to do this?

   O A. cron -e jbeck
   O B. crontab -l -u jbeck
   O C. anacron -e jbeck
   O D. crontab -r -u jbeck

21. Which script is used by cron and anacron to run the files located in some of the cron.* directories below /etc?

   O A. run-parts
   O B. cron-run
   O C. run-scripts
   O D. none of the above

22. By default, the files named cron.allow and cron.deny do not exist in /etc and all users can create a user crontab file. T F

23. Below is a statement that was put in /etc/crontab. When will the cron task be run?

   05 10 * * 2 root /root/bin/compileprog

   O A. at 3 a.m. on May 10th
   O B. at 2 a.m. on October 5th
   O C. at 5:10 p.m. on the second day of every month
   O D. at 10:05 a.m. every Tuesday

24. Which log file will show the activity of the anacron binary?

   O A. chronolog
   O B. anacrond
   O C. cron
   O D. none of the above

25. Select two statements that are correct regarding user crontab files.

   ☐ A. they are created by running crontab with one or more options
   ☐ B. by default, their tasks are automatically run by anacron if the system was not on when they were scheduled to run
   ☐ C. the default editor can be changed by changing the EDITOR variable
   ☐ D. they exist as files, with the same name as the user name in /var/log

Chapter 18: Linux Networking and Setting Up an NFS Server

Linux is extremely popular as a server operating system and is used for many different types of servers, such as NFS, Web, Samba, CUPS, FTP, DNS, SQL and DHCP. These servers, and the hosts that access them, can all communicate via the TCP/IP protocol and use IP addresses. This chapter describes the components of TCP/IP and the IP address numbering scheme used for the different classes of networks.

IP addresses consists of a network address, host address and subnet mask. You will learn to differentiate between the network address portion of an IP address and the host address portion of an IP address. You will also see several methods of specifying an IP address in a configuration file, such as a configuration file used by some type of server.

This chapter will also provide you with an overview of: the purpose of a DNS server, accessing hosts with domain names, the benefits of using DHCP, and the commonly used network interface devices.

This chapter also details each of the files used to configure networking on a system.

The following commands are described in this chapter and are also used in the Hands-On Exercises:

ping	send a request to a host to see if it is available
ifconfig	view the status and settings of network interfaces
ifdown	shut down a network interface
ifup	start up a network interface and make it active
users	see a list of currently logged in users

During the Hands-On Exercises you will look at several network configuration files and also do the steps to required to set up, configure and test an NFS file server.

Linux Networking and Setting Up an NFS Server

Topics Covered in this Chapter

Discuss the TCP/IP protocol and its components
Describe IP address numbering for the different classes of networks
Differentiate between network address, host address and the netmask
Detail various methods of specifying an IP address in a configuration file
Provide an overview of DNS, domain names, DHCP and network interface devices
Describe each of the files used to configure networking on a system
Do the steps required to set up, configure and test an NFS file server

The TCP/IP Protocol

Transmission Control Protocol/Internet Protocol (**TCP/IP**) is the protocol used on the Internet and a protocol that is very commonly used on local area networks. This protocol is a suite of three protocols that consists of the **Transmission Control Protocol (TCP)**, Internet Protocol (**IP**), and User Datagram Protocol (**UDP**).

TCP/IP is a "packet-based" protocol on which data travels in IP packets from one IP address to another IP address. A packet is a portion or "chunk" of data.

TCP and UDP are protocols that package data for transmission by a lower level protocol known as IP.

TCP ensures successful data transmission and reception by creating a session (connection) that must remain open so that TCP can verify data reception and retransmit information if necessary. TCP also ensures that the data arrives in the order in which it was sent (even if there is a retransmission), by keeping track packets by number.

UDP, on the other hand, is a light-weight, connectionless protocol. No session is required, so UDP cannot verify that a packet was received at the destination, nor can it know the order in which packets were sent. UDP is useful for reducing network traffic because it uses a smaller packet size. It is commonly used for applications that do not require a session, such as during most web browsing or when using a program such as ping. The order and reliability of transmission is not as important for these applications as is the speed of transmission. Conversely, TCP is used when a session is required, such as secure web browsing, ftp transfers, or remote login sessions.

IP Addressing

A host is a device connected to a network and can be a server, workstation, printer, router or other device. A unique IP address is assigned to a host so that the host can communicate via the TCP/IP protocol. Each network interface in a system is assigned a unique IP address. Therefore, if a host has more than one interface, such as more than one network interface card, it can have more than one IP address. However, in the following examples we will be using one IP address per host.

An IP address consists of four sets of binary numbers that are separated from each other by three dots. Each number uses eight bits (binary digits), which is one byte. Each set of numbers is referred to as an "octet" because it consists of eight (octa) bits. There are four octets in an IP address and each octet is separated by a dot. An IP address is sometimes referred to as a "dotted quad" because there are four (quad) sets of numbers.

Humans can't read binary IP addresses quite as well as computers, so they are usually shown as decimal numbers. The decimal IP address of 192.168.100.0 has the binary address shown below:

    11000000.10101000.01100100.00000000

Each of the four octets above is separated by a dot. We will refer to each octet as a "position" in the IP address. The first (left) octet has the position of x, the second position is y, the third position is z and the fourth position is a. Therefore, the four positions appear together as "x.y.z.a". Some Linux documentation shows these four positions as a.b.c.d and some other documentation uses different notation. The table below shows the four positions, the decimal number and the binary number for the decimal IP address of 192.168.100.0.

Position	Decimal Number	Binary Number
x	192	11000000
y	168	10101000
z	100	01100100
a	0	00000000

Each binary number in an IP address has eight bits. The highest *decimal* number that can be created with eight bits is 255. Therefore, each of the four sets of numbers in an IP address can be in the decimal number range of 0 to 255. The first number is 0 and the highest number is 255. Therefore, there are 256 possible numbers in each octet.

The number 0.0.0.0 is reserved for the default route used in routing tables and the number 255.255.255.255 is used to broadcast to all hosts.

Network Classes and Subnet Masks

There are "classes" of networks and these are A, B, C, D and E. Class D and E networks are not used for host addresses. Class D networks use the range of numbers from 224 to 239 in the first (left) octet and are reserved for multicast addresses. Class E networks use the range of numbers from 240 to 255 in the first octet and are experimental. Therefore, the discussion below will be focusing on class A, B and C networks.

Class A networks use the range of numbers from 1 through 127 in the first octet. In this range, the number 10 (in the first octet) is reserved for the network number of 10.0.0.0 and is used for local network use (i.e. for use by local area networks - LANs). Also in this range, the number 127 (in the first octet) is reserved for the loopback address of 127.0.0.1. The loopback address (a.k.a. local loopback, loopback interface) is used by a host to access itself and test its internal networking setup.

For example, the ping command can be used to ping the address of 127.0.0.1 to see if the software components that are required for networking are installed in a system and are "up" and running.

Class B networks use the range of numbers from 128 through 191 in the first octet. In this range, the number 128 (in the first octet) is reserved for local network use.

Class C networks use the range of numbers from 192 through 223 in the first octet. In this range, the number 192 (in the first octet) is reserved for use by local networks. The network number of 192.168.0.0 is reserved for private internal networks.

The Network Address, Host Address and the Netmask

An IP address consists of a network address and a host address. The netmask (a.k.a. subnet mask, mask) of the host determines the portion of the IP address that is the network address and the portion that is the host address.

A class A network has a netmask of 255.0.0.0. There is a value of 255 is in the first octet, which we are referring to as the x position. Each octet is 8 bits and there are four octets, for a total of 32 bits. Therefore, the network portion (x) is 8 bits and the host address portion (y.z.a) is 24 bits.

A class B network has a netmask of 255.255.0.0. There is a value of 255 in the first and second octets, which we are referring to as the x and y positions. The network portion (x.y) is 16 bits and the host address portion (z.a) is 16 bits.

A class C network has a netmask of 255.255.255.0. There is a value of 255 in the first, second and third octets, which we are referring to as the x, y and z positions. The network portion (x.y.z) is 24 bits and the host address portion (a) is 8 bits.

The three netmasks described above are *common* netmasks and will be used in our examples. *In addition to this, there are many other netmasks that can be used to create subnets, which further subdivide networks.*

A netmask is used to "mask" a portion of an IP address and indicate the octets that are used for the network number and those that are used for the host number. The netmask of a class C network "masks" the first, second and third octets (x.y.z) and causes these octets to be the network number portion of the IP address. The fourth octet (a) is the host number.

For example, with the IP address of 199.202.234.101 and a netmask of 255.255.255.0, the network number is "199.202.234." and the host number is "101".

In configuration files, there will be times when you need to specify a single host and other times when you need to specify all of the hosts that are on a network (number). The way that you specify a host or network number is dependant on the configuration file. Configuration files often have comments that show examples of how host IP addresses and network numbers are specified.

For example, the CUPS printing system uses a configuration file named **cupsd.conf** (**cups d**aemon **conf**iguration). This file has many lines of comments and some of these comments show examples of how host IP addresses and network numbers are specified.

In a configuration file, the network number of "192." can be shown as:

```
192        # the number without a dot at the right

192.       # the number with a dot at the right

192.*      # an * represents "all" other numbers at the right
```

The following is an example (from a comment the cupsd.conf configuration file) of specifying an IP address and netmask. Each "nnn" represents an octet in the IP address and each "mmm" represents an octet in the netmask.

```
nnn.nnn.nnn.nnn/mmm.mmm.mmm.mmm
```

Using the format shown above, an IP address of 192.168.100.58 and a netmask of 255.255.255.0 results in the statement below.

```
192.168.100.58/255.255.255.0  # a slash separates the two items
```

A netmask of 255.0.0.0 has an 8 bit network address portion (x) and a 24 bit host address portion (y.z.a). A netmask of 255.255.0.0 has a 16 bit network address portion (x.y) and a 16 bit host address portion (z.a). A netmask of 255.255.255.0 has a 24 bit network address portion (x.y.z) and an 8 bit host address portion (a).

The following is another example (from a comment in cupsd.conf) of specifying an IP address and netmask. Each "nnn" represents an octet in the IP address and the "mm" at the right represents the number of bits in the network number (or netmask - they are both the same as the number of bits). The /mm is **CIDR** (Classless Inter-Domain Routing) notation for specifying the number of bits in the network portion (and netmask) of the IP address.

    nnn.nnn.nnn.nnn/mm

Using the format shown above, an IP address of 192.168.100.58 and a netmask of 255.255.255.0 (a 24 bit netmask) results in the statement below.

    192.168.100.58/24

The "24" in "/24" above represents the number of bits in the network portion (and netmask).

The Full Network Number of a Network

In all classes of networks (A, B, C, D and E), the number 0 is reserved for the network address. This means that the number 0 is used in any octets that are not part of the "network number portion" of an IP address.

For example, the IP address for network number "10." is "10.**0.0.0**". The "10." is the "network portion" in position x and the three octets in positions y, z and a (of x.y.z.a), which are not part of the network number, have 0s in each of them.

To continue the example, the IP address for network number "192.168.100." is "192.168.100.**0**". This network number consists of positions x, y and z (of x.y.z.a). The octet in position a, which is not part of the network number has a 0 in it.

The Broadcast Address of a Network (Number)

Network components broadcast messages to hosts (on the same network) over a broadcast address and each host monitors ("watches") the broadcast address . This address is used to broadcast messages to hosts, such as a print server broadcasting its availability, and other information regarding itself.

For example, the CUPS print server is configured by the cupsd.conf file and this file can have a "BrowseAddress" statement. This statement specifies a broadcast address that is used to send "browsing" information to hosts. This address is used by the print server to notify hosts that the print server is available and it also provides other information to hosts regarding the print server.

In cupsd.conf, the statement below causes information regarding the print server to be broadcast from the print server to all hosts on network number "192.168.100.". The network number uses the first three octets of the IP address. The "browse" (broadcast) address consists of the network number (in the first three octets) and 255 in the last octet.

> BrowseAddress 192.168.100.255

In all classes of networks (A, B, C, D and E), the number 255 is reserved for the broadcast address. This means that the number 255 is used in any octets that are not part of the network number. Therefore, the IP address of a host does not have 255s in the octets that are not part of the network number.

For example, the IP address that is the broadcast address for network number "10." is "10.**255.255.255**". The "10." is in position x and the three octets in positions y, z and a (of x.y.z.a), which are not part of the network number, have 255s in each of them.

To continue the example, the broadcast address for network number "132.157." is "132.157.**255.255**". The x and y octets are used for the network number and the z and a octets each have the number 255.

To complete the example, the broadcast address for network number "192.168.100." is "192.168.100.**255**". The x, y and z octets are used for the network number and the remaining octet, which is a, has the number 255.

The following are examples (from comments in cupsd.conf) of specifying the number for a "BrowseAddress" statement in this file.

Example Shown in cupsd.conf	Example Network Number	Example Netmask	Resulting Browse Address
x.y.z.**255**	192.168.100.0	255.255.255.0	192.168.100.**255**
x.y.**255.255**	132.157.0.0	255.255.0.0	132.157.**255.255**
x.**255.255.255**	10.0.0.0	255.0.0.0	10.**255.255.255**

Gateway Addresses

Local area networks often have a host that is referred to as a gateway. This host is configured as a "gateway" to the Internet and it contains, or is attached to, hardware that provides access to the Internet. Each system that is connected to the LAN and needs access to the Internet must be provided with the IP address of the (default) gateway system.

The number 1 is commonly used as the number of a gateway. For example, on network number "192.168.100.", the number of the gateway would likely be "192.168.100.**1**".

The IP address of the default gateway can be specified during the Linux installation. It can also be specified after the installation with the following statement in the ifcfg-eth0 file in /etc/sysconfig/network-scripts.

GATEWAY=x.y.z.a

Replace x.y.z.a with the IP address of the default gateway.

DNS and Domain Names

As described earlier, a DNS server provides the service of converting a domain name, such a gnu.org, into an IP address, such as 199.232.76.164. If you type a domain name into the URL field of a browser and press Enter, a DNS server provides the IP address of the domain name to your system. This allows your system to access the host that matches the domain name.

If you are working on a LAN and accessing the Internet, then your system needs the IP address of a DNS server that is attached to the LAN, or the address of a DNS server on the Internet. If you are accessing the Internet via modem (dial-up), then your system needs the IP address of the DNS server being used by your ISP.

The IP addresses of two different DNS servers (primary and secondary) are usually provided to a system. One server is the backup for the other. If one server cannot be contacted, the other is usually available.

DHCP and BOOTP

As described earlier, a **DHCP** stands for **Dynamic Host Configuration Protocol**. When DHCP is being used, a DHCP server provides a host with an IP address (for itself).

BOOTP (**BOOT**strap Protocol) is an Internet protocol that is used by a diskless workstation to acquire an IP address (and other network configuration information) from a BOOTP server and also load the OS from a server so that the system can boot.

In our examples, we are using "static" IP addressing rather than DHCP or BOOTP.

Network Interface Device Names

A **Network Interface Device** (**NID**) is any piece of hardware that provides the electrical connection between a host and a network. This can be a network interface card, modem, parallel port, wireless device, or any other device that connects a host to a network.

Ethernet network interface cards are very commonly used in servers and workstations on LANs. This type of interface is also commonly used to connect a system to other devices that connect to the Internet.

For example, an Ethernet card can also be used to connect to a high-speed device (such as a cable modem) that connects to a cable T.V. line, that connects to the Internet. If this system is also connected to a LAN, then the system will have two Ethernet cards. One card that connects to the cabling system of the LAN and the other card that connects to the high-speed device.

The device name of the first Ethernet interface card in a system is eth0, the second is eth1, and so on.

If you are using a Token Ring interface card (rare), the first interface is tr0, the second is tr1, and so on.

PPP (Point-to-Point Protocol) is used for TCP/IP dial-up network access via modem. If you are using a modem for a dial-up connection to the Internet, then the first device name is **ppp**0, the second is ppp1, and so on.

Network Configuration Information Provided During Installation

When you installed Linux earlier, you specified network configuration information. Unless you were provided with other information from your instructor, you specified the settings described below (during the installation).

You deselected "Configure using DHCP" and specified a "static" IP address and a netmask number. The static IP address was 192.168.100.**n**, where **n** is your student number plus 50. The netmask number used was 255.255.255.0.

Also during the installation you specified a hostname of lancom**n**.lancom.com, where **n** is your student number, plus 50. The hostname includes the domain name. In the hostname of lancom**n**.lancom.com, the domain name is lancom.com.

Your instructor may have provided you with an IP address for a gateway, a Primary DNS server and Secondary DNS server.

Files Used to Configure Networking

The hosts File in /etc

By default, this file contains:

> the loopback interface IP address of 127.0.0.1
> the fully qualified domain name (**FQDN**) of the host, such as lancom58.lancom.com
> the alias name of the host, such as lancom58
> the domain name of the loopback address, which is localhost.localdomain
> the alias of the loopback address, which is localhost

> A **FQDN** (fully qualified domain name) begins with a host name and ends with a top-level domain, such as .gov, .edu, .org and .com. The FQDN of lancom58.lancom.com begins with the host name of lancom58 and includes the domain name of lancom.com, which ends in the .com top-level domain.

For student 8, with the host IP number of 58 (50 + 8), this file contains the following statement:

        127.0.0.1 lancom**58**.lancom.com lancom**58** localhost.localdomain localhost

All of the above items can be used to refer to this host.

For example, the ping command can be used with each of 127.0.0.1, lancom58 and localhost and each of these three items refers to the same host. The ping command can also be used with lancom58.lancom.com and localhost.localdomain, but these names are longer.

Hosts on small networks can refer to other hosts by FQDN or alias, without using a DHCP server. This can be done by specifying the hostnames and IP addresses of other hosts manually in the hosts file. On large networks this is not practical.

For example, a hosts file (at a host with an IP address other than 192.168.100.57) contains the following statement (in addition to the indented statement shown above):

        192.168.100.57 lancom57.lancom.com lancom57

This allows the host to "refer to" (with commands and via other methods) the host that has the IP address of 192.168.100.57, by using the FQDN of lancom57.lancom.com or by using the alias name of lancom57. When the names of lancom57.lancom.com or lancom57 are used at the host, the hosts file is used for host name resolution. It "resolves" either of these names to the IP address of 192.168.100.57 (which is the number at the far left of the indented statement above).

For example, after putting the above statement in the hosts file (at a host other than 192.168.100.57), the following command can be run at the host to ping the host with the IP address of 192.168.100.57.

        ping lancom57

The ifcfg-lo File in /etc/sysconfig/network-scripts

The configuration settings for lo (local loopback) are in the file named ifcfg-lo in /etc/sysconfig/network-scripts and are shown below. The statements in this file may appear in a different order than shown below.

```
DEVICE=lo
IPADDR=127.0.0.1
NETMASK=255.0.0.0
NETWORK=127.0.0.0
BROADCAST=127.255.255.255
ONBOOT=yes
NAME=loopback
```

The device name is lo, the IP address (IPADDR=) is 127.0.0.1 and the netmask is 255.0.0.0. This netmask causes the network number (NETWORK=) to be "127." (127.0.0.0). The broadcast address (BROADCAST=) of 127.255.255.255 is the combination of the network number of "127." in the x position, and 255 in the other three positions (y, z and a). The ONBOOT= setting is yes, which will cause the network interface to be activated when the system boots.

The ifcfg-eth0 File in /etc/sysconfig/network-scripts

The device name of the first Ethernet interface card is eth0. The configuration settings for this device are in the file named ifcfg-eth0 in /etc/sysconfig/network-scripts and are shown below. The statements in this file may appear in a different order than shown below.

```
DEVICE=eth0
BOOTPROTO=static
IPADDR=192.168.100.58
NETMASK=255.255.255.0
NETWORK=192.168.100.0
BROADCAST=192.168.100.255
ONBOOT=yes
GATEWAY=192.168.100.1
```

When you installed Linux earlier, you specified an IP address for your host of 192.168.100.**n**, where **n** is your student number, plus 50. Therefore, if you have the student number of 8, then you specified an IP address of 192.168.100.58.

In the above indented text, the device name is eth0, the IP address is 192.168.100.58 and the netmask is 255.255.255.0. This netmask causes the network number to be "192.168.100." (192.168.100.0). The broadcast address of 192.168.100.255 is the combination of the network number of "192.168.100." in the x, y and z positions, and 255 in the a position.

In this above indented text, the boot protocol (BOOTPROTO=) is static, as opposed to dhcp or bootp. The ONBOOT= setting is yes, which will cause the network interface to be activated when the system boots. The IP address of the default gateway (GATEWAY=) is 192.168.100.1.

The network File in /etc/sysconfig

The file named network is used to indicate if TCP/IP networking is enabled (NETWORKING=yes) and to specify the name of the host (HOSTNAME= lancom58.lancom.com). It may also contain other settings.

Below is an example of the contents of the network file:

```
NETWORKING=yes
HOSTNAME=lancom58.lancom.com
```

The HOSTNAME File in /etc

This file is no longer used in Red Hat Linux, but is used in some other distributions to contain the name of the host. Notice that the file named network (described above) has a HOSTNAME= statement in it. This statement is used to specify the name of a host, rather than using a file named HOSTNAME.

The host.conf File in /etc

The host.conf file is used to specify the order in which a system will search to resolve domain names (i.e. to convert domain names to IP addresses).

By default, the host.conf file contains the following:

    order hosts,bind

This means that the order in which the system will search to resolve a domain name is hosts (the /etc/hosts file) and then **bind** (**b**erkely internet **n**ame **d**omain - which indicates that a DNS server will be used). Therefore, the system will try to resolve an IP address using the hosts file first. If the host name is not in the hosts file, then the system will attempt to resolve the domain name using a DNS server.

The resolv.conf File in /etc

If you are using DNS servers for domain name resolution, the resolv.conf file is used to specify the search domain name and the IP addresses of the DNS servers that will do the resolution. Notice that there is no "e" after "resolv" in the filename of resolv.conf.

Below is an example of the contents of a resolv.conf file:

    search lancom.com
    nameserver 24.153.23.66
    nameserver 24.153.22.195

The primary (DNS) nameserver has the IP address of 24.153.23.66 and is above the secondary (DNS) nameserver, which has the IP address of 24.153.22.195.

The hosts.allow and hosts.deny Files in /etc

The hosts.allow and hosts.deny files are used to restrict a system from unauthorized access.

The hosts.allow file is used to specify hosts that should be able to access a system. This file can have multiple entries.

For example, the following two statements in the hosts.allow file will allow the IP address of 127.0.0.1 (localhost) and all hosts on network number 192.168.100.0 to access the host (on which the hosts.allow file exists) via all protocols. The comments at the right of the statements below are not required.

```
ALL: 127.0.0.1          # allow ALL hosts access to ALL protocols for localhost
ALL: 192.168.100.0      # allow ALL hosts access to ALL protocols for 192.168.100.0
```

The hosts.deny file is used to specify hosts that should not be able to access a system. Once a statement has been made in the hosts.deny file, you must expressly state the hosts that are allowed in the hosts.allow file. The following statement is commonly used in hosts.deny to restrict all users from accessing a system (except those that have been "allowed" in the hosts.allow file).

```
ALL: ALL                # deny access to ALL protocols for ALL hosts
```

In the hosts.allow example above, "ALL" on network number 192.168.100.0 are allowed. The ALL represents access to all available services at the host. In addition to this "ALL" are denied in hosts.deny. This is better than having no entries in these files, but is not as secure as restricting access on a service-by-service basis.

For example, to allow access to the portmap service only, replace:

> ALL: 192.168.100.0

with:

> portmap: 192.168.100.0

This will only allow the portmap service, rather than ALL available services, to be accessed by hosts on network number 192.168.100.0.

If you allow access (in hosts.allow) on a service-by-service basis, you must specify the services and addresses that are allowed *for each service that should be allowed* in hosts.allow. The "ALL: ALL" statement in the hosts.deny file does not need to be changed.

Commonly Used Networking Commands

The ping Command

This command is used to "ping" an IP address or the name of a host to see if the host is "up" (active) and if so, shows packet transmission time information. It sends a request (packet) to a host to see if the host is "up" (active).

This command is used to determine if a host can be accessed on the network (LAN or Internet). It is extremely useful and is often used to determine if a host can be reached. The ping command will continue to display output until you press Ctrl+c to stop the command.

Below is the output of: ping gnu.org and Ctrl+c was pressed after three packets were transmitted.

```
PING gnu.org (199.232.76.164) from 192.168.100.58 : 56(84) bytes of data.
64 bytes from fencepost.gnu.org (199.232.76.164): icmp_seq=1 ttl=45 time=42.5 ms
64 bytes from fencepost.gnu.org (199.232.76.164): icmp_seq=2 ttl=45 time=41.8 ms
64 bytes from fencepost.gnu.org (199.232.76.164): icmp_seq=3 ttl=45 time=41.8 ms

--- gnu.org ping statistics ---
3 packets transmitted, 3 received, 0% loss, time 2005ms
rtt min/avg/max/mdev = 41.806/42.045/42.519/0.335 ms
```

Examples of the ping Command

ping 127.0.0.1   or ping localhost

This "pings" the address of the local host (local loopback) or the host named "localhost" to see that "networking" is available on the system. If there is a response, then the network interface driver is loaded and the necessary networking software components are loaded.

ping 192.168.100.58

This "pings" the host with the IP address of 192.168.100.58. If there is a response, then the host is "up".

ping 192.168.100.1

The IP address of 192.168.100.1 is the address of a gateway. If there is a response, then the gateway is "up".

ping gnu.org

This "pings" the host with the name of gnu.org. If there is a response, this indicates that you have access to the Internet.

If you ping a host and there is no response, then the network or host is not necessarily "down". If you ping a host name, such as gnu.org, instead of an IP address, then the host name must be resolved. If the name is listed in the /etc/hosts file, then the host name is easily resolved. If not, the name must be resolved by a DNS server. If the DNS server(s) being used by a system is down, the network connection may be fine, but you will not get an answer because the host name cannot be resolved. If a DNS server is available (to resolve the host name), but the host name is not valid, ping will respond with "invalid host".

The ifconfig Command

The **ifconfig** (interface **config**uration) command is used to view the status of a network interface (up or down) and is also used to view the settings of the network interfaces in a system. It also shows the settings of local loopback (a.k.a. lo, localhost, 127.0.0.1).

When ifconfig is run, the names of the network interfaces that are in a system, such as eth0, appear at the left and the local loopback (127.0.0.1) also appears at the left as the device named "lo".

If the driver for a network interface is loaded at a host, then the interface is active and is "up" and the host can access the network via the interface. If not, the interface is "down" and the host cannot access the network.

When the ifconfig command is used to view the status of an interface and the interface is "up", then the words "UP" and "RUNNING" appear in the third line of the output of the command.

The ifconfig command can also be used to temporarily modify the network settings (such as the IP address and netmask) for a network interface that is "up" and active.

For example, the ifconfig command can be used to experiment and test various IP address and netmask settings for an interface. Once the required settings have been determined, they can be put in the appropriate network configuration files.

Examples of the ifconfig Command

ifconfig

Running ifconfig without any options shows the status and settings of all of the network interfaces that are "up" (i.e. "on" and currently active).

ifconfig -a

This shows the status and settings of all network interfaces, including those that are "down" (inactive).

ifconfig eth0

This shows the status and settings of the interface with the device name of eth0 (only).

ifconfig eth0 down

This command is used to "bring down" (turn "off") the network interface with the device name of eth0. See "The ifdown and ifup Commands" heading below for more details.

ifconfig eth0 up

This command is used to "bring up" (turn "on") the network interface with the device name of eth0. See "The ifdown and ifup Commands" heading below for more details.

The ifdown and ifup Commands

The **ifdown** (interface **down**) and **ifup** (interface **up**) commands are scripts in /sbin. When the ifconfig command is used with the down parameter (as shown above), then the route to the IP address of the host and the route to the default gateway are lost. Therefore, after using the ifconfig command with the up parameter, you also must run the route command once for each of these items to specify the IP address of the host and then the IP address of the default gateway.

Alternatively, you can use the ifdown and ifup commands (rather than the ifconfig command with the down and up parameters) to bring down and then bring up a network interface, respectively. When ifup is used, then the route to the IP address of the host and the route to the default gateway are re-established (due to the scripting logic in the ifup script) without having to run the route command for each of these items.

Examples of the ifdown and ifup Commands

ifdown eth0

This command is used to "bring down" (turn "off") the network interface with the device name of eth0. This can be used if there is an IP address conflict; if you do not want anyone to access your system; or if you know that a system is under "attack" from another system.

ifup eth0

This command is used to "bring up" (turn "on") the network interface with the device name of eth0. The route to the IP address of the host and the route to the IP address of the default gateway are automatically re-established (without having to run the route command once for each of these).

The users Command

The users command is used to see a list of currently logged in users at the current host. To run this command, simply type in: users   and press Enter.

The Network Configuration GUI Utility

The Network Configuration GUI utility can be used to view, modify and add network interfaces, and specify networking settings. Settings made with this utility are written to some of the network configuration files described above. This utility provides an easy and convenient way of modifying networking settings.

The following steps provide access to the Network Configuration GUI utility:

    Menu ; System Settings ; Network

The Network Configuration GUI Utility can also be seen by running: neat

Figure 18-1shows the Network Configuration dialog box with the Devices tab selected. The Device named eth0 has been selected and the Type is Ethernet. Another device appears below eth0. The Device is ppp0 and the Type is Modem.

Figure 18-2 shows the Ethernet Device dialog box for the device named eth0. This dialog box appears when eth0 is selected and then the Edit... button is selected on the Network Configuration dialog box. Changes made on this dialog box are written to ifcfg-eth0 in /etc/sysconfig/network-scripts.

Figure 18-1 - The Network Configuration GUI Utility with eth0 selected (left)

Figure 18-2 - The Ethernet Device dialog box for the device named eth0 (right)

The Network Configuration dialog box has four tabs.

The Device tab is used to view, modify and add interfaces. It can also be used to activate and deactivate them.

The Hardware tab is used to add, edit and delete interfaces (from a hardware component perspective). It can also be used to specify settings for a card, such as IRQ and memory. This tab shows the names of interfaces below the Description heading.

For example, the make and model of your Ethernet card will appear below this heading. The make and model will likely be similar to the name of the driver that is loaded to support the card.

To continue the example, the Description of "**VIA** VT86c100A **Rhine**-II PCI" is the make and model of a PCI Ethernet card. The driver (module) for this card is named **via-rhine**.o and is located in the path of:

/lib/**modules**/*kernelversion*/kernel/**drivers**/**net**

You will learn more about drivers (modules) a few chapters from now.

The Hosts tab shows the contents of the /etc/hosts file and can be used to modify this file.

The DNS tab is used to specify the hostname, domain name and the IP addresses of DNS servers that are used to resolve domain names and aliases to IP addresses. Domain name and DNS settings that are modified on this tab are written to resolv.conf in /etc.

The RMG Inc. Case Study Continued

The purpose, benefits and use of an NFS file server, and the way it is used in this Case Study, were detailed in Chapter 12, below the heading "Accessing the Filesystem of an NFS File Server". The description below this heading also provides an overview of part of Hands-On Exercises that you will do in this chapter. Take a moment now to read the information below the "Accessing the Filesystem of an NFS File Server" heading in Chapter 12.

The details required to set up and configure an NFS file server are provided below.

Setting Up and Configuring an NFS File Server

An overview of the steps required to set up and configure an NFS file server are provided below and you will do these steps during the Hands-On Exercises of this chapter.

The packages required by an NFS file server and a client of an NFS file server were installed when you installed Linux earlier. These packages are:

nfs-utils and portmap

At the server, you create an entry in the /etc/exports file for each "share" (shared directory) that will be available at the server. The entry has the following format:

directorypath   machinename(options)   machinename(options)   . . .

The *directorypath* ends in the name of the directory that will be shared. Notice that there can be more than one *machinename*(*options*) setting for a *directorypath*. This indicates that more than one *machinename* (as described below) can be specified per "share".

The *machinename* can specified in several ways, including:

a single IP address, such as 192.168.100.58

an IP address with a wildcard character, such as 192.168.100.*, which specifies all hosts on network number 192.168.100.

a host name, such as lancom57

a domain name with a wildcard character (* or ?), such as: *.lancom.com, which specifies all hosts on lancom.com, or such as: lancom?.lancom.com, which specifies all hosts with a host name that has one character after lancom in the lancom.com domain

an IP network, by specifying the IP address and netmask in the form of: address/netmask, such as 192.168.100.0/255.255.255.0 or 192.168.100.0/24

There are several *options* that can be used in the ( ) brackets at the right of *machinename*, including:

ro, which is the default setting and makes the shared directory "read-only" - if they have permission (through u (user), g (group) or o (other)) users can read the contents of the directory, but they cannot write to the files in the directory or create a file in the directory

rw, which makes the shared directory "read-write" - if they have permission (through u, g or o) users can read from and write to the directory

no_root_squash, which allows root users on remote systems to work as root on the server

noaccess, which prohibits access to a subdirectory of a share (for the *machinename*(s) specified), such as the prod directory below the shared directory named common, below /home

Do not put any "whitespace" (Tabs or spaces) between *machinename* and (*options*). If this is done, then the (*options*) are ignored and the default setting of (ro) is used for (*options*).

In our example, the NFS file server IP address is 192.168.100.57 and the client workstation address is 192.168.100.58. Both have a netmask of 255.255.255.0. The directory that is being exported is the directory named common below /home. The common directory contains the prod and sales directory structures for the Production and Sales Departments of RMG Inc. You created these directory structures earlier.

The following statement will be put in /etc/exports at the server, so that the host with the IP address of 192.168.100.58 will have access to the common directory below /home. Additional *machinename*(*options*) settings could also be specified for this "share".

        /home/common   192.168.100.58(rw)

At the client, a mount point (directory) is created for the "share". This is the directory (at the client) on which the common directory (located on the server) will be mounted (at the client). At the client, once the "share" has been mounted, the prod and sales directory structures will appear below this mount point directory (common).

In our example, you will be working in pairs so that you have a Client system and a Server system. From Hands-On Exercises that you did earlier, each Client and Server system already has a directory named common (that contains the prod and sales directory structures) below /home. Therefore, at the Client system, you will remove the statement from fstab that causes the partition for the common directory to be mounted. The common directory still exists, but the "local" partition will no longer be mounted on it. The (empty) common directory will be used as the mount point for the common directory on the Server system. It will be used as the mount point for the "share" rather than the "local" partition.

When the NFS file server is running and a client boots and has been granted access to a share on the server (via /etc/exports at the Server system and also via u, g and o permissions at the Server system), then the mount command can be used at the command line to mount the share.

For example, the following command is run at the client (with the host name of lancom58). It is used to mount the common directory (share) located on the NFS file server (with the host name of lancom57) on the common directory (mount point) on the client (lancom58). The -t (type) option is used to specify the type of nfs.

        mount -t nfs lancom57:/home/common /home/common

To have the share mounted automatically, you can put a statement for it in /etc/fstab. The /etc/fstab file was described in detail in Chapter 10 - Adding a Disk and Partition to a Linux System.

At the client (a.k.a. remote host, workstation), you will add a statement to /etc/fstab for the "share" directory at the NFS file server. This will cause the share to be automatically mounted when the client system boots (if the NFS file server is already running). The entry has the following format:

        lancom57:/home/common   /home/common   nfs   defaults   0 0

The above statement is very similar to a statement used in /etc/fstab to mount a directory on a local partition. The "lancom57" part of the above statement could be replaced with the IP address of the NFS file server.

The daemons that need to be running at the NFS file server are:

        nfsd (provided by rpc.nfsd), rpc.mountd and rpc.rquotad

To start the service named nfs at the server, which starts the daemons required by nfs, run:

        service nfs start

When the script named nfs in /etc/rc.d/init.d is run (with the above command) to start the service named nfs, the exportfs command is run, and the nfsd (provided by rpc.nfsd), rpc.mountd and rquotad daemons are loaded. When the rpc.nfsd binary is run, the daemon named nfsd is loaded into memory.

Start the nfs service at the server with: service nfs start

Configure the nfs service to automatically start when a system boots in one or more runlevels.

For example, to have the nfs service start in runlevels 3 and 5, the command is:

    chkconfig --level 35 nfs on

If the /etc/exports file has been modified, stop and then start the nfs service with the following command:

    service nfs restart

When you installed Linux earlier, the nfs-utils and portmap packages were installed, and the portmap service was set to on by default (in runlevels 3, 4 and 5). Unlike at the NFS file server, the nfs service does not need to be started at the client and no other software needs to be installed or started at the client. The client software that is required for clients to access some other types of servers does not need to be installed and run at the client of an NFS file server.

Summary of the Steps to Set Up and Configure an NFS File Server

Ensure that the nfs-utils and portmap packages are installed at the server and that portmap is installed at the client. The portmap service must be running at the client and server. With the Linux installation that you did earlier, the nfs-utils and portmap packages were installed and the portmap service is on by default in runlevels 3, 4 and 5 at both the client and server.

At the server, edit /etc/exports and add a statement to allow one or more hosts to access the "share".

In our example, the statement required in /etc/exports is:

    /home/common   192.168.100.58(rw)

Start the nfs service at the server with: service nfs start

Configure the nfs service to automatically start when a system boots in one or more runlevels.

For example, to have the nfs service start in runlevels 3 and 5, the command is:

```
chkconfig --level 35 nfs on
```

Create a mount point directory for the share at the client.

In our example, the command is:

```
mkdir /home/common     # you created this directory earlier
```

Run the mount command at the client to test that the "share" can be mounted, prior to adding a statement for it in /etc/fstab.

In our example, the command is:

```
mount -t nfs lancom57:/home/common /home/common
```

Get a listing of files in the "share" to ensure that it can be accessed.

Edit /etc/fstab at the client and add a statement for the "share".

In our example, the statement is:

```
lancom57:/home/common    /home/common    nfs    defaults    0 0
```

Leave the NFS file server running and restart the client to test the statement in /etc/fstab and get a listing of files in the "share" to ensure that it can be accessed.

Using the NFS Server Configuration GUI Utility

The NFS Server Configuration GUI Utility can be used to view, modify and add NFS "shares". Settings made with this utility are written to the /etc/exports file. The following steps provide access to this utility (the NFS Server Configuration dialog box):

```
Menu ; Server Settings ; NFS Server
```

This dialog box shows three headings, Directory, Hosts and Permissions. In our example, the Directory heading shows /home/common, the Hosts heading shows 192.168.100.58, and the Permissions heading shows Read/Write.

The NFS Server Configuration GUI Utility can also be seen by running:

```
redhat-config-nfs
```

Figure 18-3 shows the NFS Server Configuration dialog box with the Edit NFS Share dialog box inside of it. The path of /home/common has been selected and then the Properties button has been selected. This button causes the Edit NFS

Share dialog box to appear. Notice the settings on the Basic tab in this dialog box. There are also two other tabs, the General Options and User Access tabs.

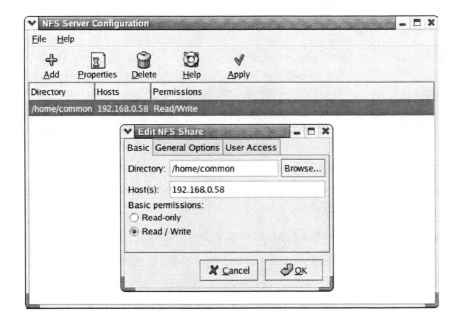

Figure 18-3 - The NFS Server Configuration GUI Utility with the Edit NFS Share dialog box

Hands-On Exercises

① Logging In to do Networking Tasks

Log in as cwest ; open a terminal emulation window ; su to root.

② Viewing Network Configuration Files

]# cd /etc/sysconfig/network-scripts

Get a long listing of the files in this directory.

]# clear ; cat ifcfg-**lo**

The configuration settings for the device named **lo** (local loopback) are in this file. The IP address is 127.0.0.1 and the netmask is 255.0.0.0. This netmask causes the network number to be "127." (the full network number is 127.0.0.0). The broadcast address of 127.255.255.255 is the combination of the network number of "127." in the x position, and 255 in the other three positions (y, z and a). The ONBOOT= setting is yes, which will cause the lo device to be activated when the system boots.

]# cat ifcfg-**eth0**

The device name of the first Ethernet interface card in a system is **eth0**. The IP address of the device is 192.168.100.**n** (where **n** is your student number plus 50) and the netmask is 255.255.255.0. This netmask causes the network number to be "192.168.100." (192.168.100.0). The broadcast address of 192.168.100.255 is the combination of the network number of "192.168.100." in the x, y and z positions, and 255 in the a position.

The boot protocol (BOOTPROTO=) is "static" (or may be "none"), as opposed to dhcp or bootp. If a gateway exists, the IP address of the default gateway will appear beside GATEWAY=.

If there is an IP address for a gateway, write it here: _____

Change up one directory level to the sysconfig directory, below /etc ;

"cat out" the contents of the file named network.

This file is used to indicate if TCP/IP networking is enabled (NETWORKING=yes) and to specify the name of the host (HOSTNAME=lancom**n**.lancom.com). It may also contain other settings.

Change up one directory level to the etc directory, below / ;

"cat out" the contents of the file named host.conf.

The host.conf file is used to specify the order in which a system will search to resolve domain names and aliases (i.e. to convert domain names and aliases to IP addresses). By default, the order is: hosts, bind. The system will search to resolve a domain name in the /etc/hosts file and then use **bind** (a DNS server). The system will try to resolve an IP address using /etc/hosts. If that does not produce a result, then the system will attempt to resolve the domain name using a DNS server (if specified in resolv.conf).

"Cat out" the contents of the file named resolv.conf.

If you are using DNS servers for domain name resolution, the resolv.conf file is used to specify the search domain name and the IP addresses of the DNS servers that will do the resolution.

③ Using the ping Command

]# ping 127.0.0.1

Press Ctrl+c to stop the ping command about five seconds after running it ;

always do this after running the ping command below.

The ping command is used to "ping" an IP address, domain name or alias name of a host to see if the host is "up" (active) and if so, it shows packet transmission time information. This command is often used to determine if a host can be reached.

If there is a response when you ping 127.0.0.1, then "networking" is available on the system. The network interface driver is loaded and the necessary networking software components are loaded.

"Cat out" the contents of the file named hosts.

The hosts file is used to resolve host names and aliases to IP addresses. The statement that begins with "127.0.0.1" in this file shows the fully qualified domain name (in column 2), host alias name (column 3), localhost.localdomain (column 4) and localhost (column 5). Notice the alias names of lancom**n** (where **n** is your student number, plus 50) in column 3 and localhost in column 5.

]# ping localhost

The alias name of "localhost" in /etc/hosts "resolves" to the IP address of 127.0.0.1. Pinging "localhost" is the same as pinging 127.0.0.1.

Replace the **n** in the following command with your student number, plus 50, such as lancom**58**. This should be the same name as shown in column 3 in the hosts file.

]# ping lancom**n**

The alias name of "lancom**n**" in the hosts file "resolves" to the IP address of 127.0.0.1. Pinging "lancom**n**" is the same as pinging 127.0.0.1 and "localhost".

]# ifconfig

Notice the three settings on line 2 for eth0. This line shows the host IP address, broadcast address and netmask address of eth0. This is the IP address of your host. Line 3 should show the words "UP" and "RUNNING". Also notice the settings for "lo". The settings for eth0 and lo are the same as the settings in the files named ifcfg-eth0 and ifcfg-lo, respectively. You looked at these files a few minutes ago.

Replace the **a** in the following command with the number of your host.

```
]#  ping  192.168.100.a      #  ping your host
```

Replace the **a** in the following command with the number of another host in the classroom.

```
]#  ping  192.168.100.a      #  ping another host
```

If there is a response, then you can communicate with that host (and likely every other host on network number 192.168.100.0).

Replace the *gatewayipaddress* in the following command with the IP address of the gateway that you wrote down above (if any).

```
]#  ping  gatewayipaddress
```

If there is a response, then the gateway is "up".

```
]#  ping  gnu.org
```

This "pings" the host (on the Internet) with the name of gnu.org. If there is a response, this indicates that the gateway is providing you with access to the Internet and that a DNS server has resolved the host name of gnu.org to an IP address.

④ Bringing Down and Bringing Up a Network Interface

```
]#  ifdown  eth0        #  take down interface eth0
```

A network interface can be brought "down" if there is an IP address conflict (that needs to be rectified); if you do not want anyone to access your system; or if you know that a system is under "attack" from another system.

```
]#  ifconfig
```

Only lo appears. The device named eth0 does not appear because it is not "up".

```
]#  ifconfig -a        #  show all network interfaces
```

The eth0 device appears, but the IP address, broadcast address and netmask (that were in line 2 of the output earlier) do not appear. The current line 2 does not show the words "UP" and "RUNNING".

Replace the **a** in the following command with the number of another host in the classroom.

```
]#  ping  192.168.100.a
```

The eth0 device is not up and so the network is not available. Packets cannot go out of the system and also cannot come in to the system.

```
]#  ifup  eth0              #  bring up interface eth0

]#  ping  192.168.100.a     #  ping the same address as above
```

The network is now available to your host (and vice versa).

```
]#  users                   #  lists the currently logged in users
```

⑤ Using the Network Configuration GUI Utility

Menu ; System Settings ; Network ; provide the password of root ; OK ;

the eth0 device should be selected on the Devices tab ; Edit . . . ;

the Ethernet Device dialog box should appear ;

"Statically set IP address:" should be selected and your network address settings should appear below "Manual IP Address Settings:

select "Automatically obtain IP address settings with:" ;

click on the pull-down menu at the right of this heading.

Notice that dhcp, bootp and dialup are available. If you were not using a "static" (manually entered) IP address, then you would be using one of these three options.

Select "Statically set IP address:" again ; Cancel ;

select the Hardware tab ; your network card make and model should appear below the Description heading ;

select the Hosts tab ; the contents of the /etc/hosts file appears ;

select the DNS tab ; if you are using DNS, the settings appear here ;

the domain name and DNS IP addresses are from /etc/resolv.conf ;

select the Devices tab ; Add . . . ; the devices that can be added appear ;

Cancel ; Close.

Setting Up an NFS File Server

While setting up the NFS file server, you will work in pairs with a partner. One system will be the **Server system** and the other will be the **Client system**.

Select a partner and exchange IP addresses. Designate one of your systems as the **Server system** and the other as the **Client system**. We will use the names **Server system** and **Client system** in the steps below. Do not confuse the two systems. You may want to write these two system names on pieces of paper along with the IP address of each and put them in front of each system.

Run ifconfig and write the IP addresses below.

Client system IP Address is: _____

Server system IP Address is: _____

If you are not in /etc, change into this directory.

 Editing the /etc/hosts File

In the step below, type in the IP address of your partner. Do this step at the Client and at the Server.

Edit the hosts file in /etc and add the following statement (flush left). Replace the **57** in the IP address, domain name and alias shown below with the number of the host of your partner.

192.168.100.**57**   lancom**57**.lancom.com   lancom**57**

Save the file and exit.

 Testing the /etc/hosts File

The above step allows your host to "refer to" (with commands and via other methods) the host that has the IP address of 192.168.100.57, by using the FQDN of lancom57.lancom.com or by using the alias name of lancom57. When the names of lancom57.lancom.com or lancom57 are used, the hosts file is used for name resolution. It "resolves" either of these names to the IP address of 192.168.100.57.

Replace the **57** in the host name (alias) below with the number of your partner.

]# ping lancom**57**

If you get a response, then the host name (alias) that you used above was "resolved" to an IP address by the /etc/hosts file. If you had not made the above entry in /etc/hosts, then you would not have gotten a response with the above ping command.

 Modifying /etc/fstab and Unmounting the common Directory

At the Client (**only**), run the following commands:

```
]# cd /home ; ls -lR common
```

The prod and sales directory structures at the Client system appear. These are no longer needed at this system.

```
]# mount
```

Notice the device name of the partition that common has been mounted on.

```
]# ls -lR common
```

```
]# umount /home/common        # unmount the existing mount point
```

```
]# mount
```

```
]# ls -lR common
```

```
]# cd /etc
```

The partition that was mounted on common is no longer mounted. The directory structures on the partition still exist (on the "local" partition), but now you will use the "local" (and empty) common directory as the mount point for the common directory on the Server system. This directory is the parent directory for the prod and sales directory structures that are on the Server system.

The Client system has a statement in /etc/fstab that causes the common directory to be mounted on a local partition. This is no longer needed at the client.

Edit /etc/fstab and "comment out" the statement that is used to automatically mount the local partition on the common directory, by putting a # symbol and a space at the left of the statement that begins with:

LABEL=/home/common

The (currently empty) common directory below /home will be used as the mount point for the common directory below /home that is at the Server system. If this mount point (directory) did not already exist (at the Client system), you would create it now.

Checking for the nfs-utils and portmap Packages

Run the following commands at the Client system and at the Server system to check that the required packages are installed. The rpm command is described in detail in an upcoming chapter.

```
]# rpm -qa | grep nfs          # nfs-utils-version should appear
                               # same as:  rpm -qa *nfs*
```

The redhat-config-nfs package provides the Network Configuration GUI utility that you used above.

```
]# rpm -qa | grep portmap      # portmap-version should appear
```

If the packages that are required are not installed, see Chapter 20 for the information required to install them and do the steps to install them.

 Modifying the hosts.allow and hosts.deny Files at the Server System

The hosts.allow file is used to specify hosts that should be able to access a system.

At the Server (**only**), do the following:

Edit the hosts.allow file in /etc and add the following two statements at the bottom (flush left). Replace the **58** in the second statement below with the number of the Client system.

```
ALL: 127.0.0.1
ALL: 192.168.100.58
```

The hosts.deny file is used to specify hosts that should not be able to access a system (other than those specified in the hosts.allow file).

Edit the hosts.deny file in /etc and add the following two statements at the bottom (flush left).

```
ALL: ALL
```

⑫ **Backing Up the /etc/exports and /etc/fstab Files**

At the Server, your current directory should be /etc. Run the following commands:

```
]# cp exports exports.1.bak
```

At the Client, run the following commands:

```
]# cd /etc
```

```
]# cp fstab fstab.1.bak
```

Adding the "Share" to the /etc/exports File and Starting the NFS Server

At the Server, do the following:

Edit /etc/exports and add the following statement (flush left) to allow the Client to access the "share" at the Server. Replace the **58** in the IP address below with the number of the Client system. Do not put a space between **58** and (rw).

/home/common   192.168.100.**58**(rw)

Also at the Server, start the service named nfs with the following command:

]# service nfs start

]# service nfs status

The three daemon names used by the NFS server should appear.

 Configuring the nfs Service to Start in Runlevels 3 and 5

]# chkconfig --list nfs

]# find /etc/rc.d -name '*nfs'

The nfs service is not currently set up to start in any runlevel.

Also at the Server, run the following command so that the nfs service is automatically started each time the Server system boots in runlevels 3 and 5.

]# chkconfig --level 35 nfs on

]# chkconfig --list nfs   # notice runlevels 3 and 5

]# find /etc/rc.d -name '*nfs'

Notice the symlink names in rc3.d and rc5.d

Testing That the "Share" Can Be Mounted

At the Client, run the following commands.

]# ls -l /home/common   # the directory should be empty

The mount command below is used to test that the "share" can be mounted, prior to adding a statement for it in /etc/fstab. Replace the **57** in lancom**57** with the host number of the Server.

]# mount -t nfs lancom**57**:/home/common /home/common

]# ls -lR /home/common

The prod and sales directory structures on the NFS file server should appear. The root user at the Client system does *not* have all permissions to these directory structures on the Server system.

Open another terminal emulation window ; do not su to root.

]# ls -l /home/common

The cwest user is the u (owner) of the prod and sales directories and therefore, has all permissions to the prod and sales directory structures. The g of prod is the prod group and the g of sales is the sales group.

]# ls -lR /home/common | less

]# cd ../common/prod

As cwest, you should be able to create and delete files in the prod directory.

]# touch test.txt ; ls -l   # the test.txt file should appear

]# rm test.txt

Repeat the above two commands in the sales directory below /home/common.

 Adding the "Share" to the /etc/fstab File

At the Client, do the following:

Alt+Tab to the root user window ;

edit /etc/fstab and add the following statement, flush left at the bottom. This statement will cause the Client to automatically mount the "share" that is located at the Server (the next time the Client boots). Press Tab between items, except put a space between the two 0s at the end of the line. Replace the **57** in lancom**57** with the alias name of the NFS file server.

lancom**57**:/home/common   /home/common   nfs   defaults   0 0

(17) **Testing the Client and Server**

Shut down the Client ; once the Client has shut down, shut down the Server ;

start the Server ; log in as cwest ; open a terminal emulation window ; su to root ;

once you have logged in to the Server, start the Client ;

log in to the Client as cwest ; open a terminal emulation window ; su to root.

At the Server, run the following:

```
]# runlevel              # you are in runlevel 5

]# service nfs status
```

The names of the three daemons used by the NFS server should appear because you set the server up to start the nfs service when it boots in runlevel 5 (and also runlevel 3).

At the Client, run the following:

```
]# mount
```

An entry for the "share" on the lancom**n** host (with the type of nfs) should appear because you added a statement for it to /etc/fstab.

```
]# ls -lR /home/common
```

You are currently working as root. The prod and sales directory structures on the NFS file server should appear.

```
]# exit
```

You should now be working in the terminal emulation window as cwest.

```
]# ls -lR /home/common
```

 Testing the Permissions that Users have at the Server

At the Client:

Minimize all windows and look for the "cwest's Home" icon on the desktop ;

you are currently logged in as cwest ; cwest's Home (icon) x 2 (double-click).

This runs the Nautilus file manager. Your current path appears near the top, a the right of "Location:".

Below the Bookmarks menu heading, select "Up" ; common folder x 2.

The prod and sales folders appear. You are at the Client and these folders are on the Server system; not on the Client system.

prod x r ; Properties ; Permissions ; cwest is the owner and prod is the group ;

cwest has rwx, prod has rx and other has none (you may have changed this) ;
Close ;

sales x r ; Properties ; Permissions ; cwest is the owner and sales is
the group ;

cwest has rwx, sales has rx and other has rx (you may have changed this) ;
Close.

In Chapter 12, you logged in as several users and ran the Writer, Impress and
Calc programs at least once. Having done this, you will be able to double-click
on files and automatically run these programs now. You will do this to test the
NFS file server and also test the permissions of users in the prod and sales
directory structures on the server.

prod x 2 ; current-orders x 2 ; dsb-costing.sxc x 2 ; the Calc
program runs.

After you double-click on a file in a folder below /home/common, the program
that is associated with the file, such as Calc, runs automatically. The Calc program
runs locally, *but the file is loaded from the Server system to the Client system.*
The user at the Client system can work on the file and then save it back onto the
Server system (or save it "locally" on the Client system).

Alt+Tab to Nautilus ; dsb-order.sxw x 2 ; the Writer program runs.

Up ; Up ; sales x 2 ; current-quotes x 2 ;

jcjc-card.sxi x 2 ; the Impress program runs.

Alt+Tab to the terminal emulation window ;

]# grep prod /etc/group   # users in the prod group appear

]# grep sales /etc/group   # users in the sales group appear

Due to the Hands-On Exercises that you did in Chapter 12, all of the users
and groups that exist at the Server system also exist at the Client system. In
the steps below, you will log in as a user in the prod group and then as a
user in the sales group.

Close all programs, including the file manager.

Testing Some Other Users

At the Client:

> To experiment and see the permissions of a different user accessing the NFS file server, log in as a user in the prod group ;
>
> run Nautilus ; navigate to the prod directory ;
>
> double-click on some files in subdirectories of prod ;
>
> also navigate to the sales directory ; double-click on some files in subdirectories of sales.

This will show that the user has permissions to access the files on the Server system and that the user can load a file from the Server system to the Client system.

> Repeat the steps above as a user in the sales group.
>
> Close all programs and windows and shut the system down.

 Section Review

1. Select the command that is used to see if a remote host can be accessed.

    ○ A. ifup
    ○ B. ifconfig
    ○ C. hostup
    ○ D. ping

2. Which protocol ensures successful data transmission and reception by creating a session (connection) that must remain open so that it can verify data reception and retransmit information if necessary?

    ○ A. UDP
    ○ B. TCP
    ○ C. IP
    ○ D. PCI

3. With an IP address of 203.231.144.101 and a netmask of 255.255.255.0, what is the network number?

   - A. 203.
   - B. 203.231.
   - C. 203.231.144.
   - D. 101

4. By default, the host.conf file will try to resolve an IP address in the order of:

   - A. hosts,dhcp
   - B. hosts.allow
   - C. bind,hosts
   - D. hosts,bind

5. Select the IP address that is reserved for the loopback address.

   - A. 10.0.0.0
   - B. 127.0.0.1
   - C. 192.168.0.57
   - D. 255.255.0.0

6. PPP is the protocol used for TCP/IP dial-up network access via modem.   T   F

7. Select the type of server that provides the service of converting a domain name into an IP address.

   - A. DNS
   - B. NFS
   - C. DHCP
   - D. NID

8. A host has an IP address of 138.106.57.107 and a netmask of 255.255.0.0. Which of the following will refer to the host when using CIDR notation?

   - A. 138.106.57.107/8
   - B. 138.106.57.107/16
   - C. 138.106.57.107/24
   - D. 138.106.57/8

9. Select the command the will bring "up" a network interface and also cause the route to the IP address of the host and the route to the default gateway to be re-established.

   - ○ A. ifup
   - ○ B. ifconfig
   - ○ C. eth0up
   - ○ D. ethup

10. At an NFS file server, which file in /etc is used to specify the directory path to a share, the machine names that can access a share and options for access to a share?

    - ○ A. hosts.allow
    - ○ B. fstab
    - ○ C. exports
    - ○ D. nfs.allow

11. Which option can be used in /etc/exports at an NFS file server to allow root users on remote systems to work as root on the server?

    - ○ A. root.allow
    - ○ B. no_root_squash
    - ○ C. hosts.root
    - ○ D. nfs_root

12. Select three characteristics of an IP address.

    - ☐ A. it consists of four octets
    - ☐ B. it is connectionless
    - ☐ C. each octet is comprised of eight bits
    - ☐ D. it is sometimes referred to as a dotted quad

13. If you have restricted access with the hosts.allow file, you must also expressly state the hosts that are allowed in the hosts.allow file. T F

14. What is the highest number that can be in an octet in an IP address?

    - ○ A. 16
    - ○ B. 64
    - ○ C. 128
    - ○ D. 255

15. Select the file that is used to specify the IP addresses of primary and secondary DNS servers.

   - ○ A. resolve.conf
   - ○ B. resolv.conf
   - ○ C. dns.conf
   - ○ D. hosts.conf

16. With a network number of 194.145.64.0 and a netmask of 255.255.255.0, select the broadcast address of the network.

   - ○ A. 194.145.64.255
   - ○ B. 255
   - ○ C. 255.255.255.
   - ○ D. 0

17. Which command will show the status and settings of the network interfaces in a system?

   - ○ A. ping
   - ○ B. ifup
   - ○ C. ifconfig
   - ○ D. pstat

18. Which file is used to resolve host names locally?

   - ○ A. hosts
   - ○ B. resolv.conf
   - ○ C. hosts.allow
   - ○ D. ifcfg-eth0

Chapter 19: Printing and Setting Up a Print Server

During this chapter, you will learn about general printing terms and concepts, and the benefits and differences between the two common Linux printing systems named LPRng and CUPS.

The utilities and commands for each printing system are described in detail as well as the main directories, configuration files and log files that are used by each printing system.

The following commands are described in this chapter and are also used in the Hands-On Exercises:

lp	send print jobs to a print queue and specify print job options
lpr	send print jobs to a print queue
lpq	display the status of print jobs currently in a print queue
lprm	remove print jobs from a print queue
lpc	control print queues
lpstat	view the status of print queues and print jobs in print queues
cancel	remove print jobs from a print queue
disable	stop print jobs from being sent from a print queue to a printer
enable	allow print jobs to be sent from a print queue to a printer
reject	stop print jobs from being added to a print queue
accept	allow print jobs to be added to a print queue
lpadmin	do all administration tasks from the command line

During the Hands-On Exercises you will use the commands for each printing system to create printers (print queues), send print jobs to print queues, view jobs in queues, remove jobs from queues, and move jobs up in queues.

You will also do the steps to switch from the LPRng Printing System to the CUPS Printing System and configure a CUPS Print Server system and a Client system. You will then use the web-browser-based CUPS Printer Configuration utility to create printers and test the Print Server.

Printing and Setting Up a Print Server

> ### Topics Covered in this Section
>
> Learn general printing terms and concepts
>
> Discuss the benefits and differences between the two common Linux printing systems named LPRng and CUPS
>
> Describe the main directories, configuration files and log files that are used by each printing system
>
> Detail the steps to create printers in the two printing systems
>
> See many examples of printing commands for each printing system
>
> Use printing commands to create and delete printers, and submit, view, move and remove print jobs
>
> Do the steps to configure a CUPS Print Server system and a Client system

In this chapter, you will learn about general printing terms and concepts, and the benefits and differences between LPRng and CUPS. You will use the utilities and commands for each printing system and discover the main directories, configuration files and log files that are used by each printing system.

The LPRng and CUPS Printing Systems

The two most commonly used printing systems for Linux are the **LPRng** (LPR New Generation) Printing System and the **CUPS** (Common UNIX Printing System).

 The LPRng printing system is currently the default printing system for Red Hat Linux version 8.0. However, the RELEASE-NOTES file in the root directory of CD 1 states that LPRng will be removed from a future release. However, keep in mind that many existing systems will still be using LPRng and so will other distributions. CUPS will likely become the default printing system when LPRng is removed.

The LPRng printing system is a newer implementation of the Berkeley LPR printing system that was created in the 70s. In addition to other features, it allows multiple printers to print to a single queue, has detailed diagnostics, provides enhanced security, and supports the commonly used printing commands that begin with letters "lp".

For more information on the LPRng printing system, go to: http://lprng.com.

The CUPS printing system is designed to provide a standard printing solution for UNIX-based operating systems. In addition to other features, it can be configured and managed via a web browser interface, uses the **IPP** (Internet

Printing Protocol) for managing printing over a network (LAN or Internet), supports **PPD** (**P**ostscript **P**rinter **D**escription) files, and supports the commonly used printing commands that begin with letters "lp".

For more information on the CUPS printing system, go to: http://www.cups.org.

Getting More Information on Printing

For printer drivers and additional printing information, go to: http://www.linuxprinting.org. This site has a several HOWTOs, including a Printing HOWTO, and files that provide support for over 1,000 printers. It also has a compatibility database that allows you to see if an existing printer, or one that you are considering purchasing, will work with Linux.

General Printing Terms and Concepts

A **print job** is anything that has been sent to print. It is a "job" for the printer to do. A ten page word processed letter, a three page spreadsheet and a thirty-three page database are all examples of print jobs. Print jobs can be sent to print from applications, scripts, or from printing commands that are run at the shell prompt.

A queue is a line up and a **print queue** is a line up of print jobs that are waiting to print. It exists in a directory on a hard disk. The directory is used to hold print jobs (as files) until the printer is available to print them. By default, the files are sent to the printer from the hard disk in the order in which they are received.

Let's say you send three documents (print jobs) to print, one after the other. All of these jobs will go into the print queue (directory). The first print job will start printing right away and the other two jobs will stay on the hard disk until the printer is ready to print them.

A print queue is also referred to as a "print spool" and a print queue directory is also referred to as a "spool directory". Print jobs are "spooled" (like thread onto a wooden spool of thread) into a print queue and exist as files until they are printed.

Print jobs in a queue can be removed from the queue, put on hold and moved "up" the queue.

A print job may need to be removed from a queue (prior to being printed) if it was sent to print by accident or if it is no longer needed for some reason.

A print job may be put on hold if it is not needed until a later time. For example, a large print job may be put on hold until the end of the day so that it can print over night.

A print job that is needed in a rush may be moved up to the top of the queue so that it prints before the other jobs that were ahead of it.

When you add a printer to Linux, you specify several items, such as: a print queue name, print queue type, printer device name, such as /dev/lp0, and a printer driver. After adding the printer, a print queue directory is created on the hard disk to hold print jobs that are waiting to print.

Printing for LPRng is handled in the background by the **lpd** (line **p**rinter **d**aemon) process and printing for CUPS is handled by cupsd (**cups d**aemon).

These daemons (processes) accept print jobs and route them to print queues and then to printers.

 A **daemon** is a background process that provides a basic system service. A process is a program that is being run by the kernel. A background process is a program that does not appear on the screen while it is running. A foreground process is one that appears on the screen while it is running. When the printconf utility is running, you can see it on the screen and it is running as a foreground process.

The words "**printer**" and "**print queue**" are often used interchangeably when discussing printing and will be used interchangeably in this chapter. When you create a *printer* in LPRng or CUPS, you are actually creating the necessary components for a *print queue* (such as the print queue directory and its support files) and specifying the settings of the printer that accepts jobs from the print queue.

When you use a utility to create a printer, you must provide a name for it. The printer name will be the print queue name. This name is used at the command line when using several printing commands. Therefore, keep it relatively short and "code" it with letters and numbers that will easily allow you to identify it. For example, you can use the name of hp2200 for an HP LaserJet model 2200.

Prior to running a utility to create a printer, attach the printer to the system and turn it on so that the utility has the possibility of automatically detecting it. The utility may be able to detect the printer port and printer make and model. If this happens, then the port and printer automatically appear in the utility and can be selected.

When creating a printer and selecting a printer driver for your printer, you select the make (manufacturer or brand) and model of the printer. If the model of your printer does not appear below the make, see if your printer manual suggests a compatible model. If not, contact the manufacturer and ask if there is a Linux driver for the printer or the name of a compatible model. If you select a compatible model, you may not be able to access all of the features of the printer.

Using the LPRng Printing System

When using the LPRng Printing System, there are several commands that can be used to administer printing. These commands are described further below. See the "LPRng and CUPS Printing Commands" heading.

A printer is added to the LPRng printing system by running the printconf (printer configuration) utility as the root user.

The **printconf** (**print**er **config**uration) utility can be run from the desktop by selecting: Menu ; System Settings ; Printing. This utility can also be run from the command line with the printconf command.

If the printconf command is run in a terminal emulation window, then printconf-**gui** runs to provide the X GUI version of this utility. If this command is run in at a virtual terminal, then printconf-**tui** runs to provide the text-based GUI version of this utility. The "-**gui**" in the name "printconf-**gui**" indicates the X GUI version of printconf and the "-**tui**" in "printconf-**tui**" indicates the text-based GUI version.

If you are not working as the root user, you must provide the password of the root user when you run the printconf utility.

Providing Information to the Printconf Utility

You need to provide information for the items described below when you run the printconf utility.

Specifying a Queue Name

Print queue names can use the characters a-z, A-Z, 0-9, - (dash) and _ (underscore). They must begin with a letter.

Selecting a Queue Type

Local Printer - select this when installing a printer that is attached to the system at which you are working.

The following options are selected when the system you are working at will be accessing a printer that is attached to another system on a network, or a printer that is attached directly to the network cabling system.

Unix Printer - select this when the system will be accessing a printer that is attached to another Unix/Linux system.

Windows Printer - select this when the system will be accessing a printer that is attached to a Windows network.

Novell Printer - select this when the system will be accessing a printer that is attached to a Novell NetWare network.

JetDirect Printer - select this when the system will be accessing a printer that is attached directly to the network cabling system and the printer is using an HP JetDirect interface (that is built into the printer or is on an HP JetDirect card inserted in the printer).

Specifying a Device Name

The printconf utility will attempt to detect the port to which your printer is attached. If a port is not detected, you can select Custom Device and specify the name of the device.

If the port for your printer is not automatically detected and it is the first (parallel, serial or USB) port, use one of the following device names. If it is the second port, replace the "0" in the device name with a "1" and so on.

/dev/lp0	the first parallel port
/dev/ttys0	the first serial port
/dev/usb/lp0	the first USB printer

If you are using the printconf-gui utility and your printer is not automatically detected, you can select the Rescan Devices button to have the utility try to detect the printer again. This can also be done if you have attached the printer after starting the printconf-gui utility.

Selecting a Printer Driver

If there is no compatible model for your printer or if the make of your printer does not appear in the list of printers, you can select one of the following items from the top of the list:

Postscript Printer - select this if your printer is a postscript printer
Text Only Printer - select this if your printer can only print text
Raw Print Queue - select this if you will be sending preformatted print jobs

PostScript is a page description language that was developed by Adobe Corporation for printing documents. It is used to provide a printer with a description of the formatting of text and graphics on a page. This language describes text, graphics, black and white and color.

When a document is created in a word processor that is using a PostScript printer driver and the document is sent to print as a file, rather than being sent directly to a printer, the file will be a PostScript file. If the file is viewed with a text editor, the contents of the file appears as a series of text statements. The file basically consists of source code that describes how the print job should be printed. The statements (code) in the file are commands that are processed by the PostScript page description language and specify how to print the document.

Among other types of files, PostScript files are considered to be "preformatted" and commonly have the filename suffix of .ps. Preformatted files can be sent to a printer from the command line to a print queue.

Raw Print Queue is the third item in the three items above. If you send a .ps file to a raw print queue that is serviced by a PostScript printer, then the printer will print the file with the PostScript formatting contained in the file.

LPRng Configuration and Log Files

The LPRng configuration files named printcap, lpd.conf and lpd.perms are located in the /etc directory and are described below.

The **printcap** file is located in /etc. It is not edited to configure printing, it is dynamically (immediately and automatically) created when the service named lpd is restarted.

When printconf is used to create a print queue and the settings are saved, the service named lpd is restarted (it is stopped and then started). Whenever this service is started, the printcap file in /etc is created and it contains the settings of the print queues that have been created for the system.

Whenever the printcap file is recreated (when lpd is started), the previous version of it is automatically saved as printcap.old.

After running printconf and creating a printer named hp2200, the printcap file contains the following text. The text that is bold was added to the file after creating the printer. The printcap file contains statements that are similar to the text shown in bold for each print queue that has been created with printconf. The first (top) print queue in printcap is the default print queue. Whenever lpd is started, the top print queue becomes the default print queue.

```
# /etc/printcap
#
# DO NOT EDIT! MANUAL CHANGES WILL BE LOST!
# This file is autogenerated by printconf-backend during lpd init.
#
# Hand edited changes can be put in /etc/printcap.local, and will be included.

hp2200:\
        :sh:\
        :ml=0:\
        :mx=0:\
        :sd=/var/spool/lpd/hp2200:\
        :af=/var/spool/lpd/hp2200/hp2200.acct:\
        :lp=/dev/lp0:\
        :lpd_bounce=true:\
        :if=/usr/share/printconf/util/mf_wrapper:

#########################################################
## Everything below here is included verbatim from /etc/printcap.local    ##
#########################################################
# printcap.local
#
# This file is included by printconf's generated printcap,
# and can be used to specify custom hand edited printers.
```

In the bold text above, the first line (hp2200:\) ends with a \ (backslash). All of the other lines in bold also end with a \, except the last line. The backslashes at the end of these lines simply indicate that the settings for the print queue named hp2200 are continued on the next line. The backslashes do not indicate the / (root) directory or a directory path.

After creating a print queue, the name of the queue appears on the hard disk as a directory named hp2200, below /var/spool/lpd. The word **spool** in the path of /var/**spool**/lpd indicates that the path is pointing to a directory in which print jobs are "spooled". They are "spooled" onto the hard disk into the hp2200 queue directory (like thread onto a wooden spool of thread) until the printer is ready to print them. When a print queue directory is created for a print queue, the files that are required by the system for printing to the queue are automatically installed in the directory.

Notice the setting beside :**sd**= in the printcap file above. The **sd** in :**sd**= stands for **s**pool **d**irectory and this directory (path) for the hp2200 printer is: /var/spool/lpd/hp2200.

Also notice the :**lp**= setting. This setting stands for **l**ine **p**rinter and is used to specify the device name to be used for the queue (printer). In our example, the device is /dev/lp0.

You can manually add a printer to your system without using printconf, by editing the printcap.local file in /etc. The printconf utility does not display settings that have been put in printcap.local.

By default, printcap.local contains the following text:

```
# printcap.local
#
# This file is included by printconf's generated printcap,
# and can be used to specify custom hand edited printers.
```

Printer information that has been manually added to printcap.local is automatically added to the printcap file when lpd is started.

The **lpd.conf** (**lpd conf**iguration) file contains statements that are used to specify "global" printing settings. These are settings that affect all printers installed at a system. By default, all of the statements in this file are all "commented out". To "uncomment" a statement and allow it to have an effect, remove the # at the left of a statement that specifies a setting.

The **lpd.perms** (**lpd perm**issions) file is the permissions control file for LPRng.

There are several LPRng log files that exist for each printer and these files are located in the spool directory of each printer, such as the hp2200 directory below /var/spool/lpd.

Using printconf-tui to Create and Configure Printers

The printconf command can be run at a virtual terminal. When this is done, the printconf-tui utility is used. This is the text-based GUI version of printconf.

Figure 19-1 shows the opening screen of the printconf-tui utility. A + (plus sign) appears at the left of the default printer.

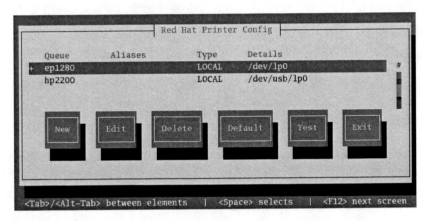

Figure 19-1 - The opening screen of the printconf-tui utility

At the opening screen of the printconf-tui utility ; select New ; the "Create a New Queue: Name and Type" dialog box appears ;

beside Queue Name:, type in a descriptive name to identify the printer ; press Enter ;

below Queue Type, select a print queue type.

The steps below describe the dialog boxes that appear after selecting "Local Printer Device".

Select Next ; the "Setting Up Local Printer Device" dialog box appears ;

select the device name for the printer (if available) or

    select Custom ; type in the device name of your printer ; OK ; Next ;

at the "Queue Driver" dialog box, select the make, model and other setting for your printer or select one of the three general printer types at the top of the list ; Next ;

at the "Create a New Queue: Name and Type" dialog box, check your settings ;

    select Back if you need to modify your settings ;

    select Finish if the settings are correct ;

    select Cancel to go back to the opening dialog box ;

at the opening screen, select Test ; at the prompt to save changes, select Yes ;

> if you are using a postscript printer, select a postscript test page and select Test ; OK ;

> if you are not using a postscript printer, select a text test page and select Test ; OK ;

if the new printer should be the default printer, highlight it and select Default ;

if you need to modify the settings of a printer, highlight it and select Edit ;

if you need to delete a printer, highlight it and select Delete ;

select Exit to leave the printconf-tui utility.

Using printconf-gui to Create and Configure Printers

The printconf utility can be run from the desktop by selecting: Menu ; System Settings ; Printing or by running the printconf command in a terminal emulation window. When either of these steps are done, the printconf-gui utility is used. This is the X GUI version of printconf.

Figure 19-2 shows the opening screen of the printconf-gui utility. A check mark appears at the left of the default printer.

Figure 19-2 - The opening dialog box of the printconf-gui utility

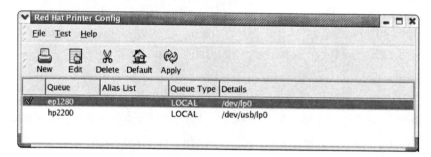

At the opening dialog box of the printconf-gui utility, select New ;

at the "Add A New Print Queue" dialog box, select Forward ;

at the "Set the Print Queue Name and Type" dialog box:

> below Queue Name:, type in a descriptive name to identify the printer ;

> below Queue Type, select a print queue type ; Forward.

The steps below describe the dialog boxes that appear after selecting "Local Printer".

at the "Configure Local Printer" dialog box:

select the device name for the printer (if available) or

select Custom Device ; type in the device name that your printer is using ; OK ;

Forward ;

at the "Select a Printer Driver" dialog box, select the make, model and the other setting for your printer (click on the triangle at the left of an item to expand it) or select one of the three general printer types at the top of the list ;

Forward ;

at the "Finish, and Create the New Print Queue" dialog box, check your settings ;

select Cancel to return to the opening dialog box ;

select Back if you need to modify your settings ;

select Apply to create the print queue ;

at the opening dialog box, select Test ; select an appropriate test page ; OK ;

if the new printer should be the default printer, highlight it and select Default ;

if you need to modify the settings of a printer, highlight it and select Edit ;

if you need to delete a printer, highlight it and select Delete ;

select File ; Save Changes ; File ; Quit ; OK.

Using the CUPS Printing System

CUPS can be administered through the web-browser-based CUPS Printer Configuration utility and also by running commands at the command line. The printing commands that can be used with CUPS are described further below. See the "LPRng and CUPS Printing Commands" heading below.

The Packages Used by CUPS

The packages used by CUPS are:

cups-libs-*version*, cups-*version*, cups-drivers-*version*, cups-drivers-hpijs-*version*, cups-drivers-pnm2ppa-*version*

Detecting and Installing CUPS

When you installed Linux earlier, you selected CUPS and the packages for the CUPS Printing System were installed.

To see if the above CUPS packages are installed:

```
]# rpm -qa | grep cups
```

If these are packages are not installed:

put CD 1 in the CD-ROM drive (and mount it if it is not mounted automatically) ;

```
]# cd /mnt/cdrom/RedHat/RPMS
```

```
]# rpm -ivvh packagename          # installs a .rpm package
```

For each package that is not installed, replace *packagename* with the name of a package and install them in the order shown above. Be sure to include the *version* and the filename suffix of .rpm in *packagename* (use the Tab key to complete the package name). Installing .rpm packages is covered in detail in an upcoming chapter.

Switching Printing Systems

When you switch from LPRng to CUPS and vise versa, several symlinks for the "lp" printing commands, such as lpr, lpq and lprm, are modified so that the binaries for these commands match the printing system being used.

For example, when using LPRng, the lpr symlink in /usr/bin for the lpr command points (through a series of symlinks) to a binary in /usr/bin named lpr.**LPRng**. When you run the lpr command, you are actually running the lpr.LPRng binary. When you switch to CUPS, the lpr symlink in /usr/bin is modified so that it points (through a series of symlinks) to lpr.**cups** in /usr/bin. When you run the lpr command after switching to CUPS, you are actually running the lpr.cups binary.

Also, when you switch from one printing system to another, the printing system that is selected becomes the default printing system that is automatically started the next time the system boots (i.e. the service for the printing system is automatically started). However, the service is not automatically started after switching from one printing system to another. After switching, and prior to rebooting a system, you must run a command to start the printing service, as described below.

Switching from LPRng to CUPS

To see if the lpd service is running, use: service lpd status

If the lpd service is running, stop it with: service lpd stop

To switch from LPRng to CUPS:

from a desktop: Menu ; Extras ; System Settings ; Printer System Switcher ; CUPS ; OK.

from the command line: redhat-switch-printer-nox ; CUPS ; OK.

 After switching from LPRng to CUPS a dialog box appears with: "Your Printing System has successfully been switched, but you must **restart** /etc/init.d/[lpd|cups] for the changes to take effect."

The **restart** option of the service command stops a service and then starts it. The CUPS service has not been started, so it does not need to be stopped. If you used **restart** rather than **start** in the command below, you would see "[FAILED]" at the right of "Stopping cups:" and then "[OK]" at the right of "Starting cupsd:".

Now start the cupsd daemon with: service cups **start**

To check that cups is running, use: service cups status

Configuring a CUPS Print Server

CUPS Configuration Files

CUPS configuration files are located in /etc/cups and some of these files are described below. You will edit CUPS configuration files in the Hands-On Exercises further below to configure a Print Server system and a Client system. The modifications that you make to these files will be described in detail as you edit them.

The **cupsd.conf** (**cups d**aemon **conf**iguration) file configures the **cupsd** print server daemon. This file is over six hundred lines and is "heavily commented" to provide descriptions of the settings that can be made in it. It is used to specify many configuration items, such as hosts that can access the server, hosts that can "browse" (view) the printers at the server, and users and groups that can administer the server.

The **client.conf** (**client conf**iguration) file is about sixty lines and is also "heavily commented". It is used to configure the settings for client systems that are accessing a CUPS server, such as the default print server to be used by the client and whether or not encryption should be used.

The **printers.conf** (**printers configuration**) file contains settings for printers that have been created, such as the printer name, default printer, location and device. This file is automatically updated when printers are added to a print server, removed from a print server, or when the default printer is changed.

Once a printer has been created, the **PPD** (**Postscript Printer Description**) file for it is put in /etc/cups/ppd. This file contains settings that can be configured for a printer, such as print resolution, printer tray to use and paper size.

To configure a printer in the CUPS Printer Configuration utility, select Configure Printer (not Modify Printer) from the Printers menu.

Each ppd file is named *printername*.ppd, where *printername* is the name that you assigned to a printer (print queue) when you created it.

For example, the full path to the PPD file for a printer named hp2200 is: /etc/cups/ppd/hp2200.ppd.

When using CUPS, the /etc/**printcap** file still exists to maintain backwards compatibility with applications that access it. When no printers have been created at a host, the contents of /etc/printcap appear as shown below.

```
# This file was automatically generated by cupsd(1m) from the
# /etc/cups/printers.conf file.  All changes to this file
# will be lost.
```

When printers are created, their names are put below the text shown above.

For example, if a printer named hp2200 is created, then: hp2200: is added to the bottom of the printcap file.

The CUPS Error Log File

The CUPS error log file is named error_log and is located in /var/log/cups.

The LogLevel directive (setting) in cupsd.conf is used to specify the level of detail of the errors that are logged in the error_log file. By default this setting is "info". A setting of "debug" causes almost all information to be written to the error log and a setting of "debug2" causes all information to be written to the error log.

You can get help with a CUPS printing problem from a newsgroup, such as the "cups.general" newsgroup. Prior to posting a message requesting support, you may want to change LogLevel from "info" to "debug" and then do the steps that are not working. This will cause the results of the problem to be written into the /var/log/cups/error_log file. After this, post the relevant output of the log file at the newsgroup along with a description of your problem.

It is worth a visit to this newsgroup to see the problems that others are encountering and to see the descriptions of the types of environments that CUPS is being used in.

CUPS Print Job Files

The print job files that are in print queues for all CUPS printers are maintained in the cups directory below /var/spool. Therefore, the path to the "spool directory" for CUPS is /var/spool/cups.

Using the CUPS Printer Configuration Utility

The CUPS Printer Configuration utility is used to administer a CUPS print server and do tasks such as create, delete and modify printers, and manage print jobs.

This utility is also used by clients (that have sufficient permission) to view printers to see their settings and to see the status of printers, such as whether a printer has been stopped or is rejecting print jobs.

Clients (that have sufficient permission) can also view the print jobs of the printers and can manage print jobs by putting them on hold and canceling them. Clients are typically given permission to manage their own print jobs and not the print jobs of others.

Depending on whether you are working at the Print Server system or the Client system, and depending on the task that you are doing, you may need to select the Reload button at the top of the browser to cause current information to appear. *Remember to click on Reload if a change of information should have occurred and did not.*

Figure 19-3 shows the opening screen of the CUPS Printer Configuration utility.

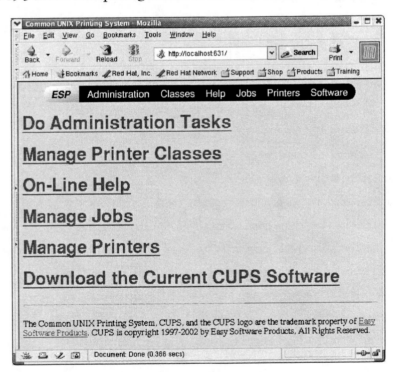

Figure 19-3 - The opening screen of the CUPS Printer Configuration utility

Accessing the CUPS Printer Configuration Utility

To access the CUPS Printer Configuration utility at the **Print Server system** as an administrator or as a client:

> Run a web browser ; type in the following URL: http://localhost:631 ; press Enter.

The equivalent of the above steps can also be accomplished with:

> Menu ; Extras ; System Tools ; CUPS Printer Configuration.

To access the CUPS Printer Configuration utility from a **Client system** as a client, do either of the two sets of steps above. The printers that are available to the Client system (only) will appear and the print jobs that have been sent from the Client system (only) will appear.

To access the CUPS Printer Configuration utility from a **Client system** as an administrator (in order to do remote administration):

> Run a web browser ; type in the following URL: http://*printservername*:631 ; press Enter.

Replace *printservername* with the server name or host IP address of the print server. All printers at the Print Server and all print jobs at the print server will appear.

Getting Help

> To get Help, select Help ; beside Software Administrators Manual, select HTML.

Adding a Printer to CUPS

CUPS printer names are not case sensitive, must start with a letter, and can be up to 127 characters in length.

The Add Printer button appears below the printers that have been created. Once you have created a few printers, you will need to scroll down to the bottom of the list of printers to be able to select this button.

To add a printer to CUPS:

> select Manage Printers from the opening screen ; Add Printer ;
>
> if necessary, log in as an administrative user ;
>
> fill in the Name:, Location: and Description: fields ; Continue ;
>
> beside Device:, select the printer device type from the pull-down menu ; Continue ;
>
> beside Make:, select the printer manufacturer's name from the menu ; Continue ;
>
> beside Model:, select the printer model from the menu ; Continue ;
>
> at this point, "Printer <u>printername</u> has been added successfully" appears ;
>
> click on <u>printername</u> ; the specifications of the printer appear ;
>
> select the Print Test Page button to test your new printer.

The screen that appears at this point has the same buttons as when "Printers" is selected from the Main Menu at the top of the screen. When "Printers" is selected, the Printer screen appears.

The Printer Screen

Selecting Printers from the Main Menu displays the available printers and the default printer is shown beside "Default Destination:" at the top of this screen. The first printer that is created becomes the default printer. The default printer can be changed from the command line with the lpadmin command (see "The lpadmin Command" heading below).

This page has several buttons that can be selected for each printer and these buttons are described below.

Print Test Page - send a test page to a printer to test that it is working correctly.

Stop Printer - used to stop print jobs from being sent from a print queue to a printer. This is typically used if a printer needs to be stopped for "temporary" maintenance. Jobs can still be sent to the queue of the printer and once the printer is started, it will print the jobs in the queue.

When the Stop Printer button is selected it changes to Start Printer. A printer can also be stopped and started from the command line with the disable and enable commands, respectively.

Reject Jobs - used to stop jobs from being added to a print queue. This is typically used to stop jobs from building up in a print queue if a printer requires maintenance and will not be available for more than a day or two. The queue can still send jobs to the printer.

When the Reject Jobs button is selected it changes to Accept Jobs. Print jobs can also be rejected and accepted and from the command line with the reject and accept commands, respectively.

Modify Printer - used to modify the same settings that were specified when the printer was added (created), such as the Location: or Device:. For example, you would use this if you moved the printer to a new location or attached it to a different port.

Configure Printer - used to specify printer settings, such as the print resolution, printer tray to use and paper size. This allows you to easily control the use of the features of the printer. The settings for the features of the printer that can be selected are in the **PPD** (Postscript Printer Description) file for the printer in /etc/cups/ppd/*printername*.ppd file.

This button also allows you to select a Starting Banner and Ending Banner for a print job. A "banner" is a page that can be printed at the start and/or end of a print job to identify the beginning and end of the print job. This can be useful to identify print jobs that have printed at a networked printer that is printing a large volume of print jobs for several people.

Delete Printer - used to remove a printer that is no longer available.

The Jobs Screen

This screen displays the print jobs that have been sent to a printer. If a job is in the queue waiting to print, then the Hold Job and Cancel Job buttons appear at the right of the job.

The Hold Job button will stop a job from printing until you select Release Job and the Cancel Job button is used to remove a job from the queue.

LPRng and CUPS Printing Commands

The "lp" (line printer) printing commands are prefixed with the letters "lp". These commands are lp, lpr, lpq, lprm, lpc and lpstat. These commands have existed for many years and are available for both LPRng and CUPS.

The lpadmin command is specific to the CUPS printing system.

The commands that are used with both LPRng and CUPS are described below. Some options of some commands are only available in one printing system and not another. This is noted for each example of a command. The syntax and options of the commands in this chapter are shown through the examples of the commands.

The lp Command

The **lp** (line printer) command is used to submit print jobs to print queues and specify options for print jobs. This command is available in both LPRng and CUPS. The lpr command is also commonly used for tasks that can be done with the lp command (described below).

The lpr Command

The **lpr** (line printer request) command is used to send a print job to print from the command line.

Examples of the lpr Command

All of the examples below are applicable for both LPRng and CUPS.

lpr list-cwest.txt

Sends the file named list-cwest.txt to the default printer.

lpr -P qms1060 report.ps

This command uses the -P option to send the report.ps file to a PostScript printer named qms1060, which is not the default printer. The printer will interpret the PostScript formatting in the document and print the file.

The report.ps file is a PostScript file that contains the text of the report as well as the description of the formatting of the document. The formatting is done in the PostScript printer language.

cat dog.txt | lpr

"Cats out" the contents of the dog.txt file and pipes the output to lpr, which causes the contents of dog.txt to print on the default printer.

The lpq Command

The **lpq (line printer query)** command is used with LPRng and CUPS to display the status of print jobs currently in a print queue.

Table 19-1 describes the column headings that appear at the top of the output of the lpq command. The headings in this table are the ones that are common to both LPRng and CUPS.

Table 19-1 - Headings Output with the lpq Command

Heading	Description
Rank	the number of the print job in the queue
Owner	the name of the user that sent the job to print
Job	print job number
Files	name of the file(s) being printed
Size	size of the print job in bytes

When using lpq to view print jobs in the queue, do not confuse the Rank and the Job headings.

For example, when you use the lprm command to remove a job from a queue, you must specify a job number, not a rank. Therefore, specify the print job number as seen below the Job heading and not the number below the Rank heading.

Examples of the lpq Command

All of the examples below are applicable for both LPRng and CUPS.

lpq

Display the print jobs in the default print queue.

lpq -P hp2200

Display the print jobs in the print queue named hp2200. The -P option is only required when you need to see print queues other than the default print queue.

lpq cwest

Display only the print jobs for the cwest user. The -P option can also be used to see print jobs for the cwest user in a different print queue.

lpq -a

Display the print jobs in all print queues.

The lprm Command

The **lprm** (line **printer rem**ove) command is used to remove print jobs from a print queue. When a print job has been removed, it has been cancelled (a.k.a. dequeued). Use the lpq command to see the number of a print job that you need to remove.

By default, a user can remove his or her print jobs, but not the print jobs of other users; and the root user can remove all print jobs.

Examples of the lprm Command

The examples below are applicable when a user has permission to do the task.

For example, running: lprm 53 will remove print job 53 from the default print queue, *as long as the user has permission to remove the print job.* By default, the root user can remove all print jobs and a non-root user can only remove his or her own print jobs.

lprm

Removes the top print job from the queue (LPRng and CUPS).

lprm -

When using LPRng, this only removes the top job from the default print queue. When using CUPS, this removes all jobs from the default print queue.

---

lprm -P hp4000 -

The -P option is used to specify the print queue name of hp4000. When using LPRng, this only removes the top job from the print queue. When using CUPS, this removes all jobs from the hp4000 print queue.

lprm -P hp4000 all

When using LPRng, this removes all print jobs (**all**) from the print queue named hp4000.

lprm -a all

When using LPRng, this removes all print jobs (**all**) from all print queues (**-a**).

lprm 53

Removes job 53 from the default print queue (LPRng and CUPS).

lprm -P ep1280 27

Removes print job number 27 from the print queue named ep1280 (LPRng and CUPS).

lprm -P qms1060 44 67

Removes print job numbers 44 and 67 from the print queue named qms1060 (LPRng and CUPS).

lprm cwest

When a user sends (a.k.a. submits) a print job to a queue, the user is the owner of the print job. When using LPRng, this removes all jobs owned by cwest from the default queue.

lprm -P hp4000 cwest

When using LPRng, this removes all print jobs submitted by the cwest user to the print queue named hp4000.

The lpc Command

The **lpc** (**l**ine **p**rinter **c**ontrol) command is used to control printers by doing tasks such as: viewing the status of a printer, stopping print jobs from being added to a queue, allowing jobs to be added to a queue, and changing the order of print jobs in a queue.

This command is typically used with LPRng, but the status option of this command (without any other options) works with CUPS. Use the CUPS lpadmin command to do tasks equivalent to the lpc command.

The Syntax of the lpc Command

The following is the syntax of the lpc command:

lpc [options] [path][pattern]

Options of the lpc Command

Table 19-2 shows the commonly used options of the lpc command. The status, enable and disable options shown below can be used with either "**name**" or "**all**" (replace and **name** with the name of a print queue). Whenever the description of the option shows "one or all print queues", this is an option that will work with "**name**" or "**all**".

For example, to disable a print queue named ep1280: lpc disable ep1280

To disable all print queues: lpc disable all

Table 19-2 - Common Options of the lpc Command

Option	Description
status	display the status of one or all print queues
disable	stop print jobs from entering one or all print queues
enable	allow print jobs to enter one or all print queues
topq	move a job to the top of the queue

Examples of the lpc Command

The examples below are applicable for LPRng. For equivalent CUPS commands, see the "CUPS Printing Commands" heading below.

lpc status all

Displays the status of all print queues.

lpc disable ep1280

Stops print jobs from entering the print queue named ep1280.

lpc enable ep1280

Allows print jobs to be submitted to the print queue named ep1280.

lpc topq hp4000 531

Moves print job number 531 to the top of the print queue named hp4000.

The lpstat Command

The **lpstat** (line **p**rinter **status**) command is used to see the status of print queues and print jobs in print queues.

Examples of the lpstat Command

lpstat

Shows the status of the default print queue and the print jobs in the queue (LPRng).

Shows the status of all print jobs in all print queues for your current user name (CUPS).

lpstat -d

Shows the name of the default print queue (LPRng and CUPS).

lpstat -p

Shows the status of all printers in the printer list (-**p**) (LPRng and CUPS).

lpstat -t

Shows the name of the default print queue, the **status** of all print queues, and the jobs in all queues (LPRng and CUPS).

The cancel Command

The cancel command is used to remove one or all print jobs from a print queue.

Examples of the cancel Command

cancel 33 41

Remove print jobs 33 and 41 from the default print queue (LPRng and CUPS).

cancel -P ok600 54 57

Remove print jobs 54 and 57 from the print queue named ok600 (LPRng). The "-**P**" is not required when using CUPS.

cancel -a ok600

Remove all print jobs from the queue named ok600 (CUPS). A print queue name is required with the -a option. Use lprm to remove all print jobs from one or all print queues when using LPRng.

CUPS Printing Commands

The tasks that can be done in the (web-browser-based) CUPS Printer Configuration utility can also be done at the command line. This includes: adding printers, deleting printers, starting and stopping printers, and accepting and rejecting print jobs that have been sent to a printer. The following commands are specific to the CUPS printing system and by default can only be run by the root user.

The disable and enable Commands

The disable command is used to stop print jobs from being sent from a print queue to a printer. This command is typically used if a printer needs to be stopped for "temporary" maintenance. Jobs can still be added to the print queue of the printer and once the printer is enabled, it will print the jobs in the queue. The enable command does the opposite of the disable command.

Examples of the disable and enable Commands

disable ap2500

Stops print jobs in the queue named ap2500 from being sent to the printer that services the queue. This queue can still accept print jobs. Run this command prior to removing a printer from the system. Once the current job has finished being printed, you can remove the printer.

enable ap2500

This reverses the effect of the above example.

The reject and accept Commands

The reject command is used to stop jobs from being added to a print queue. This is typically used to stop jobs from building up in a queue if a printer requires maintenance and will not be available for more than a day or two. The queue can still send jobs to the printer. The accept command does the opposite of the reject command.

Examples of the reject and accept Commands

reject br700

Stops print jobs from being added to the queue named br700. This queue can still send jobs to the printer.

accept br700

This reverses the effect of the above example.

The lpadmin Command

The lpadmin command can be used to do all CUPS administration tasks from the command line, such as create, configure and delete a printer (print queue). It can also be used to specify the default print queue, restrict user access to a print queue, limit the number of pages a user can send to a queue, and limit the size of print jobs that a user can send to a queue.

Examples of the lpadmin Command

lpadmin -d qms1060

Sets the default print queue for any system (print server or client) to qms1060. This will remain the default printer until the lpadmin command is used again to change the default printer. Therefore, if a user logs out and then logs in, the default printer will still be the same. Also, the default printer at a print server can be different from the default printer at a client, and the default printer can be different from one client to another.

lpadmin -p hp2200 -E -v parallel:/dev/lp0 -m laserjet.ppd

This command is used to create a printer named hp2200, with a device name of /dev/lp0, that uses a .ppd file named laserjet.ppd. Other printer settings, such as the printer description and location can also be included.

lpadmin -x ap600

Deletes the printer (print queue) named ap600.

Hands-On Exercises

If you have classroom printers, you may want to test printing to them *after* doing the exercises below.

A printer is not required for these exercises and we need to be able to see jobs in the queue and do tasks, such as put them on hold and cancel them, rather than having the jobs print before we can complete the exercises! Therefore, turn all local printers off.

These exercises are designed to demonstrate: creating and deleting printers, sending jobs to multiple queues, viewing jobs in queues, putting jobs on hold, deleting jobs from queues, and moving jobs up in queues.

Do not open any applications from the desktop, such as Writer or Calc, until you need them later in these exercises. If you have applications open prior to creating the CUPS printers, then the CUPS printers that you create may not be automatically available to applications that are opened after the printers have been created. Closing all applications and then restarting the cups service at the client will solve this problem.

1 Viewing the printcap File

Log in as cwest ; open a terminal emulation window ; maximize it ; su to root ; clear the screen ;

]# cat /etc/printcap   # you will look at this file again after creating printers

2 Running the X GUI Version of the printconf Utility

]# printconf   # the X GUI version of this utility starts

New ; Forward ; Queue Name: *ep1280* ;

leave Local Printer selected below Queue Type ; Forward ;

/dev/lp0 should be selected ; Forward ; click on the triangle icon at the left of Epson ;

click on the triangle icon at the left of Stylus Photo 1280 ; gimp-print (*) ;

Forward ; Apply ; File ; Quit ; Yes ;

there may be a pause for a minute until the prompt appears again ; OK.

Saving your changes in printconf after creating a printer restarts the lpd service.

]# cat /etc/printcap   # the new printer should appear

Running the Text-Based GUI Version of the Printer Configuration Utility

Press Ctrl+Alt+F1 to go to virtual terminal 1 ; log in as cwest ; su to root ;

]# printconf   # the text-based GUI version of this utility starts

New ; below Queue Name:, type in: qms810 ;

leave Local Printer Device selected below Queue Type ; Next ;

Custom ; Device File: /dev/usb/lp0 ; OK ; QMS ; ps-810 ; Postscript (*) ; Next ;

Finish ; the default printer (ep2200) has a + sign at the left of it ; Exit ; Yes ;

there may be a pause for a minute until the prompt appears again ;

exit ; logout ; Alt+F7.

Looking at the /etc/printcap File and the "Spool" Directories

Get a long listing of the printcap file in /etc and notice the date and time of the file ;

use the less command to view the printcap file.

The settings of the two new printers appear. Notice the settings for sd= for each printer and the name of the directory at the end of the path. Also notice the device names beside lp= for each printer.

]# service lpd status   # the lpd service should be running

Get a long listing of the lpd directory below /var/spool.

Each directory below lpd has the same name as a printer. These are the "spool" directories for each printer. Print jobs are "spooled" into these directories prior to going to print. These directories hold the print jobs as files for each printer. These jobs appear when a listing is done of the queue, such as when the lpq command is used to view the jobs in a queue.

Get a long listing of the ep2200 directory below lpd.

The printer support files and log files for the ep2200 printer appear.

Get a long listing of the qms810 directory below lpd.

The printer support files and log files for the qms810 printer appear.

⑤ Creating Some Text Files and Sending Them to Print (to the Default Queue)

We will create two text files to send to print. Your current directory should be /root and the files that are created below will be created in /root.

]# ls -lR ~mwong > mwong-list.txt

]# ls -lR ~jbeck > jbeck-list.txt

Use less to briefly view the two files that you created.

]# lpstat -d   # the name of the default printer (print queue) appears

]# lpstat -t   # the default printer name and all print queues appear

]# lpr mwong-list .txt   # send the mwong-list.txt file to print
                           # (to the default queue)

repeat the above command two more times.

If a printer was connected to /dev/lp0 (the first parallel printer port) and was turned on, then the above job would start to print.

]# clear ; lpq

The print jobs in the default queue appear. Notice the rank, owner and job numbers of these jobs.

Open another terminal emulation window ; do *not* su to root.

You should now be working as cwest and you should be in the home directory of cwest.

]# ls -lR gr-data > gr-list.txt

"cat out" the contents of gr-list.txt ;

]# ls -lR wp-data > wp-list.txt

"cat out" the contents of wp-list.txt ;

]# lpr gr-list.txt   # send gr-list.txt to print (to the default queue)

repeat the above command two more times.

]# clear ; lpq

The new jobs appear "below" the root user jobs. Notice the owner of the new jobs.

Alt+Tab to the "root user" terminal emulation window ;

]# clear ; lpq   # the print jobs of both users appear

]# lpr jbeck-list.txt   # send the jbeck-list.txt file to print repeat the above command two more times ;

Alt+Tab to the "cwest user" terminal emulation window ;

]# lpr wp-list.txt   # send the wp-list.txt file to print

repeat the above command two more times ;

]# clear ; lpq   # the new jobs appear

⑥ Sending Jobs to the qms810 Queue

You should be in the "cwest user" terminal emulation window.

]# lpstat -t   # shows the name of the other print queue

]# lpq -P qms810   # shows the contents of the qms810 queue

]# lpr -P qms810 wp-list.txt   # the job is sent to the qms810 queue

repeat the above command two more times ;

]# lpq -P qms810   # the new jobs are in the qms810 queue

You may see an error message because a printer is not connected to the USB port. This will not affect the exercises.

Alt+Tab to the "root user" terminal emulation window ;

]# lpr -P qms810 jbeck-list.txt   # the job is sent to the qms810 queue

repeat the above command two more times.

⑦ Removing Jobs from the qms810 Queue

]# clear ; lpq -P qms810

Below the Job column (and *not* the Rank column), look for the job number of the last (bottom) print job. Replace *x* with this number in the command below.

]# lprm -P qms810 *x*

]# lpq -P qms810   # the last job should no longer appear

repeat the above lprm command and remove the second job owned by cwest ;

]# clear ; lpq -P qms810   # the job that you deleted no longer appears

Alt+Tab to the "cwest user" terminal emulation window ;

get a list of jobs in the qms810 print queue ;

try to use the lprm command to remove a job in the qms810 queue that is owned by the root user ; remember the job number ; notice "no permissions" on the second line of output ;

get a list of jobs in the qms810 print queue again.

The job still exists because the cwest user does not have permission to remove jobs owned by root. The root user can remove jobs that are owned by anyone.

Alt+Tab to the "root user" terminal emulation window ;

]# lpstat -t   # printer information and the jobs in both queues appear

]# lprm -P qms810 all

If you were using the CUPS printing system, then you would replace the word "all" in the command above with a - (dash).

Get a list of jobs in the qms810 print queue again ; there should be no jobs in the queue.

 Moving a Job to the Top of the Queue

You should be in the "root user" terminal emulation window.

Get a list of jobs in the default queue.

If you need to move a rush job to the top of the queue, the lpc command below will allow you to do this. The job that you move will start printing after the current job has completed.

Look for the print job number of the third last job in the queue. Replace the x in the command below with this job number.

]# lpc topq ep1280 x # moves job x to the top

Get a list of jobs in the default queue again ; the job is now at the top of the queue.

 Removing Multiple Jobs

If you need to remove more than one print job from a queue, you can do this with the lprm command.

Replace x, y and z with any three job numbers in the queue that are not located one after the other. The command below will remove all three jobs.

]# lprm x y z

Get a list of jobs in the default queue again and check that the three that you deleted are gone.

If you need to remove all of the jobs that have been submitted by a user, you can specify the user's name with the lprm command.

    ]# lpq cwest   # display all jobs owned by cwest

    ]# lprm cwest

Get a list of jobs in the default queue again and check that all of the print jobs that were owned by the cwest user are gone.

Now run the lprm command and remove all of the jobs owned by the root user.

    ]# lpstat -t   # all of the print jobs should be gone

(10) Disabling and Enabling a Print Queue

If you need to stop a print queue from accepting jobs, then use the lpc command as shown below.

    ]# lpc disable ep1280

    ]# lpr jbeck-list.txt   # the bottom line shows spooling has been disabled

get a listing of jobs in the default queue ; the job is not in the list.

    ]# lpc enable ep1280

    ]# lpr jbeck-list.txt

get a listing of jobs in the default queue ; the job should appear ; delete the job.

Except for the "all" option of the lprm command (that you ran above), all of the lpq, lpr, lprm and lpstat commands that you have used above work exactly the same way when using the CUPS printing system. Therefore, we will not repeat these commands after changing to the CUPS printing system below.

(11) Removing LPRng Printers

We will remove the two LPRng printers prior to switching to the CUPS printing system.

    ]# printconf

Select each printer ; select Delete ; File ; Quit ; Yes ; OK.

"cat out" the contents of /etc/printcap ; no printers should appear in this file.

(12) **Viewing the Current "lp" Commands and man Pages Setup**

After installing this version of Linux, the LPRng Printing System is in use by default. The binaries for the "lp" commands, such as lpr and lpq are set up for LPRng, and the man pages for the LPRng versions of these commands, and other LPRng components, are available.

]# whereis lpr   # lpr and most of the "lp" command binaries are in /usr/bin
                        # the lpc binary is in /usr/sbin

change into the bin directory below /usr ; remember your current path ;

]# ls -l lpr   # this is a symlink that points to /etc/alternatives/print

]# ls -l /etc/alternatives/print

If LPRng is being used, the symlink named print in /etc/alternatives points to /usr/bin/lpr.LPRng. If CUPS is being used, the symlink named print in /etc/alternatives points to /usr/bin/lpr.cups. Therefore, if LPRng is being used and you run the lpr command, you are using the lpr.LPRng binary. If CUPS is being used and you run lpr, you use the lpr.cups binary.

]# file lpr.*

The lpr.LPRng binary provides the lpr command for LPRng and the lpr.cups binary provides the lpr command for CUPS.

]# ls -l *.LPRng   # the binaries for the "lp" commands of LPRng appear

]# ls -l *.cups   # the binaries for the "lp" commands of CUPS appear

]# ls -l /etc/alternatives/print-lprman

The print-lprman file is a symlink to the lpr-**LPRng**.1.gz man page file. When you switch to CUPS, the print-lprman file will point to the lpr-**cups**.1.gz man page file.

]# man lpr

This currently shows the man page for the LPRng Printing System. LPR(1) appears at the top left and right of the man page and nothing appears at the top middle of the man page.

]# ls -l /etc/alternatives/print*

The files prefixed with "print" currently point to binaries and man pages for the LPRng Printing System.

⑬ Changing the Printing System from LPRng to CUPS

The steps to switch from LPRng to CUPS are done at all systems that will be using CUPS. Only one of these printing systems should be used at a time.

The lpd service is currently set up to start automatically when you start your system. It is not needed when you are using CUPS and needs to be stopped. If you have deleted all printers, then lpd is not likely running.

```
]# service lpd status    # see if lpd is currently running

]# service lpd stop      # stop the lpd service if it is running
```

The steps below change from LPRng to CUPS. After doing this and restarting your system, the lpd service will not be started automatically when the system starts and the cups service will be started automatically.

Do the following steps to switch from LPRng to CUPS:

```
Menu ; Extras ; System Settings ; Printer System Switcher ;

provide the password for the root user ; OK ; CUPS ; OK ; OK.
```

⑭ Viewing the New "lp" Commands and the man Pages Setup

After switching to CUPS, the binaries for the "lp" commands, such as lpr and lpq, are set up for CUPS. The man pages for these commands and other CUPS printing system components are also available. As you will see below, the symlinks described above that pointed to LPRng binaries and man pages now point to CUPS binaries and man pages.

Your current path should still be /usr/bin.

```
]# ls -l lpr              # this symlink still points to /etc/alternatives/print

]# ls -l /etc/alternatives/print
```

This symlink used to point to /usr/bin/lpr.LPRng and now points to /usr/bin/lpr.cups! Therefore, when you run the lpr command, the lpr.cups binary is run.

Switching printing systems modified the symlink file named print and many other symlink files so that they now point to CUPS binaries and man pages. Therefore, after switching to CUPS, you can still use the "lp" commands at the command line. This also allows existing scripts (that were created during the use of LPRng) that run "lp" commands to be used.

```
]#  file  lpr.cups          #  this is the binary for the lpr command for CUPS
]#  ls  -l  /etc/alternatives/print-lprman
```

The print-lprman file is now a symlink to the lpr-**cups**.1.gz man page file.

```
]#  man  lpr
```

This is not the same man page that you saw earlier for the lpr command. This is the man page for the CUPS version of the lpr command. "Easy Software Products" now appears at the top middle of the man page.

```
/COMPATIBILITY      #  search for "COMPATIBILITY"
```

A description of the options of the lpr command that are not supported appears. Notice that "Common UNIX Printing System" (for CUPS) appears at the bottom middle of the page.

```
]#  ls  -l  /etc/alternatives/print*
```

The files prefixed with "print" now point to binaries and man pages for the CUPS Printing System.

(15) Backing Up cupsd.conf and client.conf

You will be modifying the cupsd.conf and client.conf configuration files in /etc/cups. Therefore, do the steps below to back them up.

```
Change into the cups directory below /etc  ;  get a long listing  ;
]#  cp  -p  cupsd.conf  cupsd.conf.original.bak
]#  cp  -p  client.conf  client.conf.original.bak
```

(16) Getting the IP Addresses of the Client and Print Server Systems

For the following exercises you will work in pairs. Choose a partner and designate one of your systems as the **Print Server system** and the other as the **Client system**. Do not confuse the two systems. You may want to write these two system names on pieces of paper and put them in front of each system.

You will work at the Print Server system as the cwest user. You should currently be logged in to this system as the cwest user. This user will become the administrator of the Print Server.

You will log in and work at the Client system as the bford user. You will create a Terminal Emulation Window icon for this user so that you can easily "su to root" and configure the Client system. This icon can be removed after doing these exercises.

At the **Print Server system**, you should be logged in as cwest and working as root in a terminal emulation window in the /etc/cups directory.

Run ifconfig and look for "inet addr::" to see the IP address of this system ;

write this address here: _____

At the **Client system**, do the following steps:

Log in to the desktop as the bford user ; right-click on a blank area of the panel ;

Add to Panel ; Launcher from menu ; System Tools ; Terminal ;

open a terminal emulation window ; maximize the window ; su to root ;

run ifconfig and look for "inet addr::" to see the IP address of this system ;

write this address here: _____

(17) **Editing cupsd.conf to Configure the Print Server**

At the **Print Server system**, do the following steps:

]# vi cupsd.conf

/BrowseAddress   # search for "BrowseAddress"

Press "n" (for **n**ext) about six times, until you see "#BrowseAddress @IF(name)" at the bottom of the screen.

Add the following statement (flush left) below the existing "#BrowseAddress @IF(name)" statement:

BrowseAddress 192.168.100.**255**

Insert a blank line above and below this statement ; press Esc.

The BrowseAddress directive is used to specify a broadcast address for the Print Server. The above statement causes the Print Server to broadcast its existence to all hosts on network number 192.168.100. (only).

(18) **Allowing Access to the Print Server**

```
/127.0.0.1                    # search for "127.0.0.1"
```

The above search should allow you to see the following statements. A # should *not* be at the left of any of these statements:

```
<Location />
Order  Deny,Allow
Deny  From  All
Allow  From  127.0.0.1
</Location>
```

Add the following statement (flush left) below "Allow From 127.0.0.1" and above "</Location>".   Replace the *a* with the number of the Client system, such as 58.

```
Allow  From  192.168.100.a
```

If you wanted to allow all users on network number "192.168.100." to be "allowed", you would use "Allow From 192.168.100.*" rather than "Allow From 192.168.100.*a*" (as shown above). In these exercises, we only want a single system to access the Print Server.

If the Client system is 192.168.0.58, then the results of your edits should be:

```
<Location />
Order  Deny,Allow
Deny  From  All
Allow  From  127.0.0.1
Allow  From  192.168.100.58
</Location>
```

The statement that you added above explicitly allows the Client system to access the Print Server. This allows the client to see the CUPS Opening screen, the Printers screen (which shows the printers that exist) and the Jobs screen (which shows the jobs in the queues of the printers that have been created at the Print Server). Some additional steps must now be done to allow a user to select the Hold Job or Cancel Job buttons to hold or cancel (remove) a print job (to which they are the owner).

Allowing Users Working at the Print Server to Hold and Cancel Jobs

The statements that you add below will allow a user *that is working at the Print Server* to see his or her print jobs without authenticating (logging in) and will also allow a user to hold or cancel his or her own print jobs (after authenticating). A user is prompted to log in (authenticate) when the Hold Job or Cancel Job button is selected for a print job.

You will put the statements below between <Location /jobs/> (notice the **/** at the right of /jobs) and </Location>, and *not* between the existing <Location /jobs> (that does not have a **/** at the right of /jobs) and </Location>. If you added the statements below in between the existing <Location /jobs> and </Location> statements, then users would need to log in to see their print jobs. By doing the steps below, users can see their print jobs without logging in and only need to log in if they select Hold Job or Cancel Job.

Scroll down until you can see "#<Location /jobs>" and then scroll down until you are on the blank line below the "#</Location>" statement (that is below "<Location /jobs>") ;

press i to go into Insert mode ; press Enter twice to put two blank lines below the "#</Location>" statement ; move up one line ;

add the following text (flush left) on the second blank line below "</Location>" and above the "#<Location /printers>" statement ; replace the *a* in the "Allow From 192.168.100.*a*" statement below with the number of the Client system ;

```
<Location /jobs/>
AuthType  Basic
AuthClass  User
Order  Deny,Allow
Deny  From  All
Allow  From  127.0.0.1
Allow  From  192.168.100.a
</Location>
```

The "AuthType Basic" statement causes the system to use "Basic" authentication rather than "None" (no authentication) or "Digest" authentication.

The "AuthClass **User**" statement allows **users** to access the Print Server to hold and cancel jobs after authenticating (logging in with a user name and password that exists *at the Client system*). If this setting was "System" rather than "User" then only members of the group named sys would be able to hold and cancel jobs after authenticating. If this setting was "Group" then only members of the group name specified with the AuthGroupName directive would be able to hold and cancel jobs after authenticating. If this setting was "Anonymous", then any user could and cancel jobs without having to authenticate.

For example, if the statement was "AuthClass System" rather than "AuthClass User", then only users that are members of the group named sys would be able to log in to hold and cancel print jobs. The group name of sys is the default name for the SystemGroup directive and this name can be changed if necessary.

The "Order Deny,Allow" statement specifies the order in which the Deny and Allow statements (that are put below the "Order Deny,Allow" statement) should appear. The "Deny From All" statement denies access from all locations and the "Allow From 127.0.0.1" allows access from "localhost", which is the Print Server system itself.

The "Allow From 192.168.100.*a*" statement allows a user at the Client system to access the Print Server system, as described below. If you wanted to allow all users on network number "192.168.100." to be "allowed" access to print jobs, you would use "Allow From 192.168.100.*" rather than "Allow From 192.168.100.*a*" (as shown above). In these exercises, we only want a single system to access the jobs on the Print Server.

Users should access the Print Server with the URL (in a browser) of: **localhost**:631. Notice that **localhost** is being used here rather than the name of the Print Server system. Using localhost allows users to see the Printers screen and the Jobs screen (in the CUPS web browser utility). With this URL, users will only be able to see their own print jobs; if they select Hold Job or Cancel Job, they are prompted to log in to CUPS at the Client system (with the user name and password that they normally use to log in at the Client system). However, remote administrative users need to access the server (by *printservername* rather than by localhost) to be able to hold or cancel the print jobs of any user or do other tasks, such as create and delete printers.

A Print Server could be a system at which one or more users work, or it could be a system at which no users work. Therefore, the system may need to be accessed remotely for administration. The bottom "Allow From" statement above allows a remote administrative user, such as cwest, to access the Print Server system from the Client system. If this number was changed from 192.160.100.*a* (where *a* is a single number of a system) to "192.168.100.*", then an administrative user could access the Print Server from any system on network number "192.168.100.".

Remote administrative users use the URL of *printservername*:631 to access the Print Server. If the Print Server name is lancom57, then the URL of lancom57:631 is used. When the Print Server is accessed remotely (with *printservername*:631 rather than localhost:631), then the administrative user authenticates with a user name and password that exists *at the Print Server system*. Any non-root administrative user of the Print Server, such as cwest, needs to be created at the Print Server system and also needs to be added to the group named sys on the Print Server system. The clients that are using the Print Server do not need to be created at the Print Server.

scroll down to the end of the file and look for the "<Location /admin>" statement.

The settings between <Location /admin> and </Location> control access to administrative tasks, such as adding and removing printers. The "AuthClass **System**" statement means that only users in the group specified by the SystemGroup directive can do administration functions. The default group name for SystemGroup is sys.

Add the following statement (flush left) below the "Allow From 127.0.0.1" statement ; replace the *a* with the number of the Client system.

Allow From 192.168.100.*a*

add a blank line below the above statement.

The "Allow From 192.168.100.*a*" statement allows an administrative user, such as cwest, to do administrative tasks, such as adding and deleting printers, from the Client system. If you wanted to "allow" the Print Server to be accessed remotely for administration from all systems on network number "192.168.100.", you would use "Allow From 192.168.100.*" rather than "Allow From 192.168.100.*a*" (as shown above). In these exercises, we only want a single system to be able to remotely administer the Print Server.

/SystemGroup   # search for "SystemGroup"

By default, the SystemGroup directive has the group name of sys. You will add the cwest user to this group so that this user can do administrative tasks.

The "#SystemGroup sys" statement is "commented out". This "commented" statement exists to show the default setting for SystemGroup and also so that you can see an example of the syntax of the SystemGroup directive. If you needed to change the SystemGroup, you could remove the # at the left of the statement and change sys to a different group name.

:wq   # write the file and quit out of vi

Accessing the Print Server System from the Client System

At the **Client system**, do the following steps:

]# vi /etc/hosts

Add the following statement (flush left) at the bottom of the /etc/hosts file. Replace the *a* with the number of the Print Server system. Use a Tab between the first and second "chunks" of text and a space between the second and third "chunks".

192.168.100.*a*   lancom*a*.lancom.com   lancom*a*

For example, if the Print Server system is 192.168.100.57, then add the following statement:

192.168.100.57   lancom57.lancom.com   **lancom57**

:wq   # write the file and quit out of vi

Now run the ping command to confirm that the Print Server system is available. Replace the *a* in the command below with the number for the Print Server host, such as 57 (for lancom57).

]# ping **lancom*a***

Press Ctrl+c to stop the "pinging".

21 **Editing cupsd.conf at the Client to Configure the Client**

At the **Client system**, change into /etc/cups ;

]# vi cupsd.conf

/BrowsePoll   # search for "BrowsePoll"

Add the following statement (flush left) below the existing "#BrowsePoll address:port" statement. Replace the *a* in the statement below with the number for the Print Server system.

BrowsePoll 192.168.100.*a*:631

If the Print Server is 192.168.100.**57**, then the statement will be:
BrowsePoll 192.168.100.**57**:631

The BrowsePoll directive above causes the client to "poll" (check) the Print Server for information regarding its available printers. By default, this is done every 30 seconds. Multiple BrowsePoll statements can be used to cause a client to poll multiple Print Servers. In our example, each pair of students is only polling one server. If a client needed to print to printers at additional Print Servers, then statements for these servers would be added.

Allowing Users Working at a Client to Hold and Cancel Jobs

The statements that you add below will allow a user *that is working at a client system* to see his or her print jobs without logging in and will also allow a user to hold or cancel his or her own print jobs (after logging in). A user is prompted to log in when the Hold Job or Cancel Job button is selected for a print job.

As with the cupsd.conf file at the Print Server system, you will put these statements between <Location /jobs**/**> and </Location>, and *not* between the existing <Location /jobs> and </Location>.

/127.0.0.1   # search for "127.0.0.1"

scroll down until you can see "#<Location /jobs>" and then scroll down until you are on the blank line below the "#</Location>" statement (that is below "<Location /jobs>") ;

put two blank lines below the "#</Location>" statement (above the "#<Location /printers>" statement) ;

add the following text (flush left) on the second blank line below "</Location>" and above the "#<Location /printers>" statement ;

```
            <Location /jobs/>
            AuthType  Basic
            AuthClass  User
            Order  Deny,Allow
            Deny  From  All
            Allow  From  127.0.0.1
            </Location>
```

:wq   # write the file and quit out of vi

Unlike at the Print Server, the "Allow From 192.168.100.*a*" statement was not put in above. Other systems do not need to access the Client system.

 Starting the CUPS Service

Now that you have switched to CUPS, you need to turn on the service named cups (until the next time you start your system). It will be started automatically the next time a system is started after switching to CUPS. The lpd service will not be started.

At the **Print Server system** *and* at the **Client system**, do the following steps:

]# service cups status   # cups is not currently running

]# service cups start   # start the cups service

Adding a User to the sys Group at the Print Server

You must log in to the (web-browser-based) CUPS Printer Configuration utility to do administrative tasks, such as adding a printer to CUPS. You can log in as root, but as usual, this is not recommended.

Linux has several "system" groups, such as mail, news and ftp, that were briefly described earlier. By default, there is a "system" group named "sys". This is the default group name that is used for CUPS administration tasks. By adding a user to the group named "sys", the user acquires the permissions of the group. The user can then log in with the user name and password of the administrative user that was created at the Print Server, such as cwest, to do CUPS administration tasks like creating and deleting printers and putting *any* job on hold or canceling *any* job.

At the **Print Server system**, do the following steps:

```
]# less /etc/group
```

Look for the group named "sys". The statement for this group will be similar to:

```
sys:x:3:root,bin,adm
```

```
]# grep sys /etc/group          # display lines of text in the group file
                                # that contain "sys"

]# usermod -G sys cwest         # add the cwest user to the sys group

]# grep sys /etc/group          # display statements with "sys" again
```

Now the statement for "sys" will have: **,cwest** at the end and be similar to:

```
sys:x:3:root,bin,adm,cwest
```

Rather than running the usermod command above to add the user to the sys group, you could have used a text editor to add: **,cwest** to the end of the statement for the sys group (as shown above).

 Specifying Some Browser Settings

At the **Print Server system** *and* at the **Client system**, do the following steps to ensure that the browser provides current information while you are configuring CUPS. These settings can be reversed once the server has been configured.

Click on the "world" icon in the panel to run the Mozilla browser ;

Edit ; Preferences ; expand the "Advanced" heading ; Cache ;

Memory Cache: _____ ; Disk Cache: _____ ;

set Memory Cache: to 0 ; set Disk Cache: to 0 ;

Clear Memory Cache button ; Clear Disk Cache button ;

select "Every time I view the page" rather than "When the page is out of date" ; OK.

Depending on whether you are working at the Print Server system or the Client system, and depending on the task that you are doing, you may need to select the Reload button at the top of the screen to cause current information to appear. *Remember to click on Reload if a change of information should have occurred and did not.*

Installing Two CUPS Printers

Now you will use the (web-browser-based) CUPS Printer Configuration utility to create two printers at the Print Server system (only).

At the **Print Server system**, do the following steps:

In the URL field of the browser, type in: *http://localhost:631* ; press Enter ;

the opening screen of the CUPS Printer Configuration utility should appear ;

Manage Printers ; Add Printer.

When you select a button for an administrative task, such as adding or deleting a printer, you are prompted a user name and password. You must then provide the name and password of an administrative user. The user name must exist at the Print Server and be in the sys group.

If you are a user at a client and select the Hold Job or Cancel Job buttons, you are also prompted for a user name and password. In this case, you must provide the name and password of the user that was used to log in to the desktop at the client. The user name will exist at the client and does not need to exist at the Print Server.

Once you have logged in as any user, you can do the tasks that are "allowed" by that user without logging in again. For example, if you have logged in as cwest, you can continue to create and delete printers and do other administrative tasks until you close the browser.

If you need to switch user names, such as to change from a non-administrative user to an administrative user, close the browser and then run it again and click on a task that requires a password. The system will then prompt you for a user name and password.

Notice that the top of the dialog box shows "for "CUPS" at localhost:631". The user that you are logging in with must exist at the Print Server and be in the sys group.

Log in with the cwest user name and password.

With the current setup, only a member of the sys group is able to log in to add a printer. The root and cwest users are members of the sys group.

Notice that the URL: field now shows: http://localhost:631**/admin/**?op=add-printer. You are now using the **/admin** directory below the DocumentRoot directory path of /usr/share/doc/cups-*version*. The printers, jobs, classes and images directories are parallel to the admin directory and are below the DocumentRoot directory. The settings that you saw earlier at the end of the cupsd.conf file, between "<Location /admin>" and "</Location>", control access to the /admin directory.

Beside Name:, type in: *hp2200* ; press Tab ; Location: *Production Dept.* ;

Description: *HP LaserJet 2200* ; Continue ; Device: *Parallel Port #1* ; Continue ;

Make: *HP* ; Continue ; Model: *HP LaserJet 2200, Foomatic + Postscript (en)* ; Continue ;

"Printer hp2200 has been added successfully" appears ;

click on hp2200 ; the specifications of the printer appear.

Notice the "Printer State:" and "Device URI:" settings. The "Add Printer" button appears below the new printer. This button moves down the "page" as more printers are added.

select Add Printer ;

beside Name:, type in: pan5400 ; press Tab ; Location: *Sales Dept.* ;

Description: Panasonic KX-P5400 ; Continue ; Device: *Serial Port #1* ; Continue ;

at the Serial Port Settings screen, select Continue ; Make: *Panasonic* ; Continue ;

Model: *Panasonic KX-P5400, Foomatic + Postscript (en)* ; Continue ;

"Printer pan5400 has been added successfully" appears ;

click on "pan5400" ; the specifications of the printer appear.

Notice the "Printer State:" and "Device URI:" settings.

Select Printers from the Main Menu at the top of the screen.

The two new printers appear. The first printer that you created is the default printer and its name appears beside "Default Destination:" (at the top left). Notice the buttons, such as "Print Test Page" and "Stop Printer" that appear for each printer. All of the buttons at the right of "Print Test Page" are for "administrative tasks".

 Viewing CUPS Printer Configuration Files at the Print Server

Alt+Tab to the "root user" terminal emulation window ;

change to the cups directory below /etc ;

use the less command to view the printers.conf file.

This file contains settings for the two printers that you created.

Change into the ppd directory below the current directory ;

get a long listing to see a .ppd file named after each of the two printers ;

Each ppd file is named *printername*.ppd, where *printername* is the name that you assigned to a printer (print queue) when you created it. These files contain settings that can be configured for a printer, such as print resolution, printer tray to use and paper size. These files can be configured from with the CUPS browser utility or by editing them.

use the less command to view the hp2200.ppd file ;

/Double   # search for "Double"

notice the "*DefaultDuplex: On" statement (on the second line) ; quit out of less ;

Alt+Tab to Mozilla ; for the hp2200 printer, select Configure Printer ;

Double-Sided Printing should be On ; select Off for this item ; Continue (any button) ;

select Printers (from the Main Menu at the top of the screen) ;

Alt+Tab to the "root user" terminal emulation window ;

use the less command to view the hp2200.ppd file again ;

/Double   # search for "Double" again

now "*DefaultDuplex: **Off**" appears (on the second line), rather than "**On**" ;

quit out of less.

Changing a printer configuration setting in the browser changes the setting in the text file.

㉘ Creating Some Print Jobs at the Print Server

Click on the icon in the panel for the Writer program ;

open a .sxw file in the wp-data directory below the cwest home directory ;

press Ctrl+p ; beside Name, use the pull-down menu and select hp2200 ; OK.

CUPS printers that are available to a client system are automatically available from within many desktop applications. These applications will "see" CUPS printers and allow you to select them when sending a file to print, but other applications will not.

For example, you can select a CUPS printer when sending a job to print with an OpenOffice.org application, such as Writer or Calc, but some other applications will only allow you to send a job to the default printer.

Alt+Tab to Mozilla ; select Jobs from the Main Menu at the top of the screen.

The print job should appear. Below Name, "(stdin)" (for standard input) appears rather than the name of the file. When you send files to print from the command line with the lpr command, the name of the file appears. Below User, the cwest user name appears.

Alt+Tab to the Writer program ; Ctrl+p ; Enter ;

Ctrl+p ; beside Name, select pan5400 ; OK ; Ctrl+p ; OK ;

Alt+Tab to Mozilla ; the Jobs screen should still be visible ; Jobs (or Reload).

The four print jobs appear. The Jobs screen shows print jobs for all printers.

Alt+Tab to the Writer program ;

open a different .sxw file in the wp-data directory ;

Ctrl+p ; select the hp2200 printer ; OK ; Ctrl+p ; OK ;

Ctrl+p ; select the pan5400 printer ; OK ; Ctrl+p ; OK ;

Alt+Tab to Mozilla ; the Jobs screen should still be visible ; Jobs.

Holding and Canceling Print Jobs at the Print Server

Notice that the ID column shows the name of a printer and then the number of the job.

> For the second job in the list, select the Hold Job button ;
>
> select Jobs from the Main Menu or select the Back button (at the top left) ;
>
> select Cancel Job button for the job with the ID of "-6" ; Jobs.

You are still logged in to the Print Server (through the browser) as the cwest user. Therefore, you were not asked for a user name and password when you selected Hold Job and Cancel Job.

> Select Printers from the Main Menu ;
>
> beside Default Destination or below Default Destination, select hp2200 ;
>
> the hp2200 printer and the jobs for this printer (only) appear (see the ID column) ;
>
> select Printers ; select pan5400 (at the left of the screen) ;
>
> the pan5400 printer and the jobs for this printer (only) appear ;
>
> select Printers.

Both printers should show the "Stop Printer" button rather than the "Start Printer" button. Select "Start Printer" if this button appears at any time during the exercises below.

 Viewing Printers at the Client

With the configuration settings we are using, the printers that have been created at the Print Server should be available to users as though they are "local" printers.

At the **Client system**, the current user should be bford and Mozilla should be running and visible. Do the following:

> In the URL field of the browser, type in: *http://localhost:631* ; press Enter ;
>
> the opening screen of the CUPS Printer Configuration utility should appear ;
>
> Printers (from the Main Menu at the top) and the two printers should appear ;
>
> for the hp2200 printer, select Modify Printer ;
>
> type in the user name and password of the bford user ;
>
> the dialog box asking for the name and password should appear again ;
>
> Cancel ; Back.

The bford user is at the Client system and the Client system is localhost. This user does not have permission to do administration tasks at localhost. The way that the cupsd.conf file is configured, no users have permission to do administration tasks at localhost (the client). An administrative user can do administrative tasks from the client by using *servername*:631, but not localhost:631.

When you are at the Client system, the printers do not exist at localhost, they exist at lancom*a* (where **a is the number of the Print Server**). When you are at the Print Server, the printers exist at localhost. The only tasks that a non-administrator user can do on this screen is select "Print Test Page" or select a printer name (do not do this from this screen as yet).

Jobs (from the Main Menu at the top) ;

make sure that your current URL is: http://localhost:631/jobs.

Although there are jobs in the two print queues at the Print Server (have a look), no jobs appear here (when using the URL of: localhost:631/jobs) because bford at localhost (the Client system) has not sent any jobs to print.

 Creating Some Print Jobs at the Client

Run the Calc program from the panel ;

open a .sxc file in the ss-data directory below the bford home directory ;

press Ctrl+p ; beside Name, select hp2200 ; OK ;

send this file to the same printer two more times ;

now send this file to the pan5400 printer three times ;

Alt+Tab to Mozilla ; select Jobs from the Main Menu.

The print jobs of the bford user (only) should appear. There are other jobs in the queues for these printers, but they do not appear for this user.

 Holding and Canceling Print Jobs at the Client

For the third print job, select the Hold Job button.

You are working at the Client system. Notice that you are being prompted for a user name and password for localhost:631, which is the Client system and not the Print Server system. The user name and password that you used to log in to the Client system is all that is required.

Type in the bford user name and password ;

select Jobs from the Main Menu or select the Back button (at the top left) ;

for the second last print job, select the Cancel Job button ; Jobs.

Any user at a client can log in with his or her password to hold or cancel his or her print jobs. Notice that there are more than two print jobs in the queues for the bford user.

 Accessing the Print Server as a Non-Administrative User with the URL of *servername*:631

At the **Print Server system**, do the following:

Jobs.

Notice that there are only two bford jobs in the queue (at the Print Server system). The others are actually at the Client system and have not yet been sent to the Print Server. There is only one job for bford for each of the two queues.

Close Mozilla at the Print Server system.

At the **Client system**, do the following (replace the *a* in lancom*a* with the number of the Print Server system):

In Mozilla, type in the following URL: http://lancom*a*:631 ; press Enter ;

Jobs (from the Main Menu).

The cwest jobs at the Print Server appear, but only one or two bford jobs appear, even though there are more bford jobs in the queues. When working as a user (that is not working at the Print Server) and using the URL of: http://lancom57:631 rather than: http://localhost:631 then only one or two jobs for the user appear (usually only one job per queue).

Select the Cancel Job button for a job owned by the bford user ;

type in the user name and password for the **bford** user ; OK.

With the current configuration, this user cannot delete her own job when using the URL of: lancom*a*:631.

Cancel ; Back ;

type in the following URL: http://localhost:631 ; press Enter ;

Jobs ; select Cancel Job for the second last print job.

You logged in as bford earlier and can delete jobs owned by this user when using the above URL. You may want to suggest to your users that they only access print jobs with the URL of: localhost:631.

Accessing the Print Server as an Administrative User with the URL of *servername*:631

At the **Client system**, do the following:

Type in the following URL: http://lancom*a*:631 ; press Enter ;

Jobs ; select the Cancel Job button for a job owned by the bford user ;

type in the user name and password for the **cwest** user ; Jobs.

The cwest user can cancel any job remotely (from any system that has been "allowed") by using the URL of: lancom57:631.

(35) Deleting the CUPS Printers

At the **Client system**, do the following:

You are still logged in to "CUPS" at the Client as cwest and are using the URL of: http://lancom*a*:631.

Printers ; beside pan5400, select Delete Printer ; Continue ; Printers.

The pan5400 printer should no longer appear.

Run the browser at the Print Server and check to see the printers that exist.

A user that is created at the Print Server and added to the sys group becomes and administrative user. An administrative user can do any administrative tasks remotely.

After running the browser and logging in to CUPS remotely as an administrative user, remember to close the browser once you have finished doing printing tasks. This will stop anyone from doing administrative tasks in the browser.

Close all programs and terminal emulation windows at both systems and shut the systems down.

Section Review

The questions below are for both the LPRng and CUPS Printing Systems, unless otherwise specified.

1. Which command will send the file named fstab to the print queue named can3500?

    ○ A. lprm -P fstab can3500
    ○ B. lpr -P fstab can3500
    ○ C. lprint -P can3500 fstab
    ○ D. lpr -P can3500 fstab

2. A CUPS print server has just been installed and there were no non-root users created during the installation. A user with the name of bbest will be the administrative user at the print server. Which two steps are required at the print server so that the user can administer it?

    ☐ A. add the user named bbest to the servadmin user
    ☐ B. create a user named bbest
    ☐ C. add the servadmin user to the group named root
    ☐ D. add the bbest user to the group named sys

3. Which two commands can be used to remove print jobs from queues?

    ☐ A. lprm
    ☐ B. lpdel
    ☐ C. rmqueue
    ☐ D. cancel

4. With the default settings in the cupsd.conf file, if an "AuthClass System" statement in this file is below <Location /admin>, then:

    ○ A. only the user named admin can do administrative tasks
    ○ B. only members of the group named sys can do administrative tasks
    ○ C. only members of the group named System can do administrative tasks
    ○ D. only the user named System can do administrative tasks

5. You need to see the name of the default print queue and the print jobs in all queues. Which command will show you this information?

    ○ A. lpstat -t
    ○ B. lps -t
    ○ C. lpqr -t
    ○ D. status -p

6. When using the CUPS Printing System, which directory contains printing configuration files, such as cupsd.conf?

    ○ A. /etc
    ○ B. /var/cups
    ○ C. /etc/cups
    ○ D. /root/cups

7. A print queue directory is also referred to as a "spool directory". T F

8. Which command will remove job number 7 in the print queue named hp2200?

    ○ A. lprq hp2200 7
    ○ B. lprm -P hp2200 7
    ○ C. lprm -P 2200 7
    ○ D. lpq -P hp2200 7

9. You are having a CUPS printing problem and you want to post the output of the error messages in the error_log file at the cups.general newsgroup, so that you can get some help with the problem. What is the name of the directive in cupsd.conf that you can change from "info" to "debug" so that detailed error messages are written to the /var/log/cups/error_log file?

    ○ A. CupsLog
    ○ B. error_level
    ○ C. LogLevel
    ○ D. tail_log

10. When using the LPRng Printing System, which of the following tasks cannot be done with the lpc command?

    ○ A. view the status of a queue
    ○ B. move a jobs to the top of a queue
    ○ C. disable a queue to stop jobs from entering it
    ○ D. create a print job

11. Which CUPS command can be used to create printers, delete printers and specify the name of the default print queue?

 ○ A. cupsadmin
 ○ B. lpadmin
 ○ C. lpcups
 ○ D. admincups

12. Which directive is used in cupsd.conf to specify a broadcast address for a Print Server?

 ○ A. BrowseAddress
 ○ B. BrowseAllow
 ○ C. BrowsePoll
 ○ D. BrowseDeny

13. What is the device name of the first USB printer?

 ○ A. /dev/usb0
 ○ B. /dev/lp1
 ○ C. /dev/usb/lp0
 ○ D. /dev/lp0

14. Select the command that will show the print jobs owned by the jbeck user in the default print queue.

 ○ A. lpq -P jbeck
 ○ B. lpq jbeck
 ○ C. qlist jbeck
 ○ D. lpr jbeck

15. A non-administrative user working at a client of the Print Server should use the URL of _____ to view his or her print jobs after they have been sent to printers at the Print Server.

 ○ A. http://printservername:631
 ○ B. http://cups.server:631
 ○ C. http://www.cups:631
 ○ D. http://localhost:631

16. Which two of the following statements regarding CUPS printing commands are true?

   ☐ A. the reject command is used to stop jobs from being added to a print queue
   ☐ B. the enable command is used to allow users to access other Print Servers
   ☐ C. the accept command is used to send jobs to the default print queue
   ☐ D. the disable command is used to stop jobs in a queue from being sent to a printer

17. When using the LPRng Printing System, which text file is updated after a printer has been created with printconf and the printer's settings have been saved?

   ○ A. /etc/printqueues
   ○ B. /etc/printcap
   ○ C. /etc/cups/printers
   ○ D. /etc/printconfig

18. Select the command that will show the jobs in the queue named ep1280.

   ○ A. lpq -P ep1280
   ○ B. lplist -P ep1280
   ○ C. lpqlist -P ep1280
   ○ D. lprm -P ep1280

19. Select three benefits of the CUPS Printing System.

   ☐ A. it supports Postscript Printer Description files
   ☐ B. it can convert multiple router protocols to single printers
   ☐ C. it uses the Internet Printing Protocol for managing printing over a network
   ☐ D. it can be configured and managed via a web browser interface

20. What is the name of the CUPS daemon configuration file?

   ○ A. lpcups.cf
   ○ B. cups.cfg
   ○ C. cupsd.conf
   ○ D. cupsdp.conf

Chapter 20: Installing Software On A Linux System

This chapter of the course includes three sections. During this chapter you will learn and work with the following:

Installing Red Hat Package Manager Files

In this section, you will learn to differentiate between "installation format files" and tarballs and how to search the Internet for software packages.

You will also get an overview of the benefits of RPM package management software and learn to use many options of the rpm command to install, erase and query .rpm package files.

The following command is described in this chapter and is also used in the Hands-On Exercises:

    rpm   install, upgrade, erase and query .rpm package files

During the Hands-On Exercises of this section you will use many options of the rpm command, erase some software packages, and then install the SSH software components that will allow you to "ssh into a server".

Installing the Apache Web Server

In this section, we will provide an overview of http, html and the Apache Web server. You will also learn about some of the directives (settings) in the main Apache configuration file.

In the Hands-On Exercises for this section you will install the software packages for the Apache Web server and view the main software components and directory structure used by the Apache Web server.

Downloading, Compiling and Installing Software

This section describes downloading binary and source code packages that exist as tarballs. It provides an overview of installing binaries that have been extracted from a tarball. It also details the steps required to install source code that has been extracted from a tarball

The following commands are described in this chapter and are also used in the Hands-On Exercises:

    configure   check that a package can be installed and create a Makefile
    make   build a package from source code and create binary files
    make install   install a package, including binaries, configuration files and libraries

While doing the Hands-On Exercises, you will do the steps to untar, compile and install the source code in a tarball for a package named Anjuta. You will then use the Anjuta program to modify the source code of a small program, compile the program, tar it, untar it and then install it.

Installing Red Hat Package Manager Files

Topics Covered in this Section

Differentiate between "installation format files" and tarballs
Learn to search the Internet for software packages
Provide an overview of RPM package management software
Describe how the dependencies of a package are resolved
Discuss many options and benefits of the rpm command
Detail the steps required to repair the RPM database
Use the rpm command to install, erase and query .rpm package files

In this section you will learn about Red Hat Package Manager (.rpm) files and how to use the rpm command to install, upgrade and erase (uninstall) RPMs. You will also learn how to use the rpm command to "query" (find out) information regarding .rpm files.

During the Hands-On Exercises of this section you will use various query options of the rpm command to do commonly needed tasks, such as find out about the software components that are installed on your system, get detailed descriptions of .rpm files, and also see the files that are installed when a .rpm file is installed. You will also install and uninstall software packages and use SSH software components to "ssh into a server".

During the Hands-On Exercises of the next section, you will use the rpm command to install the Apache web server on your system.

Installing Software Packages from "Installation Format Files" and Tarballs

A software "package" can be any one of many different types of software components, such as an application (the Gimp graphics program), a utility (the Xine media player), a server (the Apache web server), a client (the **ssh secure sh**ell client), a library (the zlib library) and a programming language (the GNU C++ compiler).

A package may also contain a collection of related software components, such as the package named util-linux. This package is comprised of several binaries that are Linux utilities (commands) and includes: cal, fdisk, kill, login, mkfs, renice and whereis. This package also contains the man page (*.x*.gz) files for these binaries.

Red Hat and some other distributions use "installation format files" named RPMs (.rpm files) and these files are installed with the rpm command. Debian is a distribution that uses "installation format files" that end in .deb and these files are installed with the dpkg command. Both of these "installation format files" are similar in concept and functionality. These files can be downloaded and then the software components in them can be easily installed with a single command!

Packages that are not in an "installation file format" (such as .rpm or .deb), and that are in a single compressed file are referred to as "tarballs". These are files that have been "tarred" (compressed) with the tar command and have the filename extensions of .tar.gz, .tgz and tar.bz2. Packages are also available in other compressed formats, such as .z, .gz (without .tar in front of .gz) and .zip.

Tarballs may include compiled binaries or may consist of source code that needs to be compiled prior to being installed. They also usually include documentation files. Installing a tarball requires more steps than installing an "installation format file" and is typically more difficult (particularly if you have never done it before)!

This section and the next describe using .rpm files and the rpm command. The section after that describes installing packages that exist as source code in tarballs. In that section, you will "untar" the source code of an application that exists in a tarball, compile the source code and then install the application.

Searching the Internet for Software

There are web sites all over the world that offer thousands of packages of all different types. These packages are available as "installation file format" files (such as .rpm files), as tarballs and also in other compressed file formats, such as .z and .zip.

The first place to look for a Linux software package is at the web site of the distribution that you are using. These packages are created to work with your distribution.

For example, if you are using the Red Hat distribution, go to Red Hat's web site at http://www.redhat.com for a .rpm package.

However, the package that you require may not exist (at any web site) as a .rpm (or other "installation file format") file. In this case, you will need to install the package from a tarball. The tarball may contain compiled binaries, or you may only be able to find the package as source code. *If it is source code, then you can usually compile it and install it on your system regardless of the name and version number of the distribution that you are using.*

Imagine if the web site of a hardware manufacturer only had to provide drivers for five distributions and only made them available for the last two versions (software releases) of each distribution. Even with these low numbers, the manufacturer would need to keep ten files available for just one hardware component! Now imagine that the hardware manufacturer makes thirty different models of printers. That's a lot of drivers!

By working with source code, you don't need to download a compiled (binary) version of the package that has been precompiled specifically for your distribution name and version number. You can download the most current version of the package that you require and compile it yourself, according to the specifications of your system (such as your kernel version, installed libraries, library locations and library versions).

The source code is the common denominator. It will usually work for all distribution names and versions, provided that the necessary libraries and utilities that are needed to build a package are installed. It is usually more difficult to compile and install a package from source, but the source code for thousands of packages is readily available and the process can be much more rewarding!

If you are looking for a package that provides a driver for a hardware component, then the next place to look (after the web site of the distribution) is the web site of the hardware manufacturer. After that, go to the appropriate project (if one exists), such as www.linuxprinting.org for a printer driver. Next, you can use Google or another search engine to do a search for the package that you need.

When searching for a software package or when searching for information regarding Linux, you may want to include the word "linux" in the search.

For example, to search for a driver for an ABC model of printer, search for "ABC drivers linux".

The following are a few other sites from which software packages in various file formats can be downloaded.

http://sourceforge.net

This site states that it is the largest Open Source software development site and that it has the largest repository of Open Source code and applications on the Internet. There are over seventy thousand projects listed at this site!

http://freshmeat.net

This site states that it has the largest index of Unix (and therefore usually Linux) cross-platform software and provides access to thousands of packages, many of which are Open Source. The site is updated daily and has news and technical content regarding software projects that are under way.

http://rpmfind.net

This site provides the capability of searching a database of RPMs by various categories and by strings of text. In addition to this, you can do an Internet search for "linux rpm" and see what other sites have to offer. There are many sites from which RPMs can be downloaded.

RPM Package Management Software

Red Hat created and released RPM (Red Hat Package Manager) software under the GNU license agreement. Therefore, in addition to Red Hat, some other distributions are using the RPM "format" for the software packages that comprise the distribution. They are also using this format for the packages that are installed "on" the distribution (after it has initially been installed).

RPM is used to deliver all of the files required by a software program in a compressed "package" file with the suffix of .rpm. A .rpm file can contain binaries, libraries, configuration files, documentation and other components of a package.

 All of the software components (packages) included with the Red Hat Linux distribution are provided as .rpm files. The version of Red Hat Linux included with this book consists of over 1,200 RPMs on CD 1 and CD 2. These .rpm files are on these CDs (and on downloaded and purchased Red Hat Linux CDs) in the path of:

/mnt/cdrom/RedHat/**RPMS**

The RPM format allows you to run an easy-to-use GUI utility, or a command at the shell prompt, to install a program and put the files in the .rpm file into the various directories where they are needed. The RPM format allows you to easily install, upgrade, uninstall, and keep track of your packages.

You can get more information on RPM at http://www.rpm.org.

Red Hat Package Manager (.rpm) Files

An RPM is a package that contains software components and has a *packagename*. RPMs are in files that have the filename extension of .rpm. The name of an RPM file has the following format:

packagename-version-release.architecture.rpm

Notice the location of the two - (dashes) and the two . (dots) above.

The *version* and *release* parts of the filename are the version number and release number of the package.

The *packagename* part of the .rpm filename is the name of the package that is installed when the .rpm file is installed. The *packagename* is **not** a file name. It is the name of a package that is contained in a .rpm file. This distinction is necessary in order to understand how to use certain options of the rpm command.

For example, the command in the format of: rpm -qi *packagename* shows information on the *packagename* specified.

Therefore, the command: rpm -qi **openssh** shows information on the *packagename* of: openssh , but openssh is **not** the name of a .rpm file. The openssh package is installed from the .rpm file named: **openssh**-3.1p1-3.i386.rpm.

To continue the example, the command in the format of: rpm -ivh *packagefilename* is used to install a package (the software components in a .rpm file). Whenever you see *packagefilename*, this represents a file that has a .rpm filename extension.

Therefore, the command: rpm -ivh openssh-3.1p1-3.i386.rpm is used to install the **package** named openssh from the **file** with the *packagefilename* of: openssh-3.1p1-3.i386.rpm. A *packagefilename* ends in .rpm, such as openssh-3.1p1-3.i386.rpm.

To continue further, the command in the format of: rpm -qfi *nonpackagefilename* uses the **-q** (query) **-f** (file) **-i** (information) options to get **file** information on a *nonpackagefilename* that has been installed on a system. A *nonpackagefilename* is a file that is not a .rpm file, but one that has that been installed *from* a .rpm file, such as the hosts.allow configuration file in the /etc directory.

Therefore, the command: rpm -qfi hosts.allow shows **file** information on the hosts.allow file. To run this command, you must either be in the /etc directory or specify the full path to the file, such as running the command: rpm -qfi /etc/hosts.allow when you are not "in" the /etc directory.

To continue even further, the command in the format of: rpm -qpi *packagefilename* uses the **-q** (query) **-p** (package) **-i** (information) options to get **package** information on a *packagefilename* file (a file that is a .rpm file) that has **not** been installed on a system.

Therefore, the command: rpm -qpi openssh-3.1p1-3.i386.rpm shows **package** information on the openssh-3.1p1-3.i386.rpm file. To run this command, you must either be in the directory containing the .rpm file or specify the full path to the file.

When getting information on, or installing a .rpm file, you may want to change into the directory containing the .rpm file and then run the command. The reason for this is that the full path to the file (including the .rpm file name) may be very long. The following command shows the default path to the RPMS directory (on a CD) and includes the name of a .rpm file. This is a time when the Tab key becomes extremely useful for completing the path to a file!

    rpm -qpi /mnt/cdrom/RedHat/**RPMS**/openssh-3.1p1.i386.rpm

Notice that when you use the -qpi options, the **-p** stands for **p**ackage. This **-p** does not represent the name of the package, such as openssh, it stands for the *packagefilename* of the .rpm file that contains the package.

Summary of *packagefilename*, *packagename* and *nonpackagefilename*

In summary, *packagefilename* is used to represent a package file name that ends in .rpm and is used to install a *packagename*.

A *packagename* is the name of the package that is installed *from* a *packagefilename* (i.e. from a .rpm file). A *packagename* is not a file name. A *packagename* may contain a - (dash), such as the package named openssh-clients.

When using some options of the rpm command and specifying a *packagename*, you *can* include *-version* and *-release* in the *packagename*, but *do* not include *.architecture* and .rpm. However, when specifying *packagename*, you do not usually need to include *-version* and *-release*.

For example, the .rpm file named **ftp**-0.17-15.i386.rpm is used to install the package named **ftp**. When specifying the *packagename* of this package name, you can use **ftp**, or **ftp-0.17-15** (which includes the *-version number and -release number*), but you do not use the full .rpm file name of ftp-0.17-15.i386.rpm (which also includes the *architecture* and the .rpm suffix).

A *nonpackagefilename* represents the name of a file that has been installed on the system from a .rpm file, but is not the name of a .rpm file.

The *packagefilename* of **openssh**-3.1p1.i386.rpm is used to install the *packagename* of **openssh**.

A *nonpackagefilename* can be the name of almost any file (other than a .rpm file) that has been installed from a .rpm file, such as a binary file (fdisk), a configuration file (cupsd.conf), a script file (rc.sysinit), a man page file (cal.1.gz), or other file.

The following is the full .rpm filename for the package that contains the client files for the **ssh** (secure **sh**ell) utility:

openssh-clients-*version-release.architecture*.rpm

The OpenSSH project at http://www.openssh.com creates the SSH software components that allow a client at a remote site to access a server via a **secure sh**ell. The **ssh** (secure **sh**ell) client is run with the **ssh** command at a workstation to access a remote server that is running the ssh server software.

The **rlogin** (remote **log**in), **rsh** (remote **sh**ell), **ftp** (file transfer protocol) and **telnet** programs are all used to allow a client at a remote site to access a server. All of these programs use unencrypted (clear text) passwords to access the server. These programs are not secure because the passwords used to access systems with them can be seen and read as "clear text" by anyone on the Internet that is running software that is readily available for this purpose.

The **rcp** (remote **c**o**p**y) command is used to copy a file from a remote location and is similar to the four commands above. The rcp command is used to copy a file from a remote location. However, the rsh command is used to access the remote location (with a "clear text" password) and then rcp is used to copy files from the remote location. Therefore, this method of copying files is not secure.

The SSH software components replace the rlogin, rsh, rcp, ftp and telnet commands described above and allow a remote client to *securely* access a server by using an encrypted password. However, many people still used the rlogin, rsh, rcp, ftp and telnet commands even though they are not secure. Some old habits die hard.

The other packages that are a part of SSH (on CD 1 and CD 2) are:

openssh-*version-release.architecture*.rpm
openssh-server-*version-release.architecture*.rpm
openssh-clients-*version-release.architecture*.rpm
openssh-askpass-*version-release.architecture*.rpm
openssh-askpass-gnome-*version-release.architecture*.rpm
kdessh-*version-release.architecture*.rpm

By reading the Description: heading for the above packages (as seen by using the -qi, -qpi or -qfi options of the rpm command) you can determine that the package named openssh needs to be installed at both the client and the server, the package named openssh-server needs to be installed at the server (only), and the package named openssh-clients needs to be installed at the client (only). The other packages (the last three in the list) are not required when using SSH in a terminal emulation window or in a virtual terminal.

If a distribution uses RPMs and is shipped on more than one CD (which is very likely), then all of the above packages may not be on the same CD. Packages that are required by a client system may be on one CD and those required by a server may be on another.

If you are installing some kind of software functionality, such as SSH or a type of server, then you may need to install more than one package at a client and more than one package and at a server. Remember to check all of the CDs of a distribution for the packages that you may require.

When looking for a package in a .rpm file so that you can install it, use the ls command with some of the text that will likely be a part of the .rpm file name. The name of the file may not start with the text that you specify, so use an * (asterisk) at the start and end of the text.

For example, as seen above, there are several packages that provide components of SSH. Most of these packages are in .rpm files that begin with "open**ssh**", *not* *"**ssh**"*. The SSH client is run at a client to log in to a remote host and you need to install the SSH client at a workstation to do this. However, the package that provides the SSH client is not called ssh-client, it is called openssh-client. Therefore, to locate the .rpm file that provides this package, put in a CD that may contain the .rpm file, mount it, change to the RPMS directory and then run the following command: ls -l *ssh* with an * at the beginning and end of "ssh". If you looked for the file with: ls -l ssh* (without an asterisk at the start of the text) you would not find the file because is does not start with "ssh", it starts with 'openssh'.

The RPM that provides the client for SSH is actually called openssh-clients-*version-release.architecture*.rpm, where *version* is the software version, such as 2.9p2, the *release* is the release number, such as 7 and *architecture* is the minimum hardware architecture (platform) required by the package, such as .i386 (for a system with a 386 processor). The full .rpm file name will be similar to openssh-clients-2.9p2-7.i386.rpm.

In other words, if you are installing SSH (at a client or server), then run: ls -l *ssh* in the directory containing the .rpm files on all CDs. The full path to the directory that contains .rpm files on Red Hat CDs is:

    /mnt/cdrom/RedHat/RPMS

In the above directory path, the cdrom directory is the mount point for the CD, below the mnt directory.

When you locate a package that you may need to install, run: rpm -qpi *packagefilename* and check the Description: heading to see if you need to install the package and if so, where to install the package (at the client, at the server or both).

For example, to use SSH, some of the packages listed above need to be installed on the client system, some at the server, and some at both. The location at which a package should be installed (client, server or both) may be indicated in the text of the description (below the Description: heading) that is included in the .rpm package file.

Package Dependencies

Some packages require one or more other packages to be installed before they can be installed. If you run the rpm command with the -i option and attempt to install a package, and it requires one or more other packages, then the package has a "dependency" on one or more other packages.

When you attempt to install a package that has one or more dependencies (on packages that have not been installed), you will see an "error: Failed dependencies:" message. This message will include the name(s) of the package(s) that must be installed first.

For example, a package named "a" may require package "b" to be installed prior to installing it. Package "a" has a dependency on package "b".

To continue the example, package "b" may require packages "c" and "d" to be installed before it can be installed. In this case, you must install packages "c" and "d", and then install package "b", and then install package "a".

The –force option and other options of the rpm command can be used to force a package to be installed if its dependencies are not met.

 When you installed Linux earlier, you selected packages by "package group", such as Editors, Development Tools, and Graphics. This caused several packages to be selected when each package group was selected. You also selected individual packages. After doing this, an "Install packages to satisfy dependencies" option was automatically selected. This caused the installation routine to automatically install the dependencies of all of the packages that you selected. When installing packages with the rpm command, you must install package dependencies manually.

The rpm Command

The rpm command is used to install, upgrade and erase (uninstall) the software components that are in .rpm files. It is also used to "query" information regarding .rpm files.

The following is a general description of what the rpm does when it installs a package:

> it checks that the dependencies required by the package have been installed

> it checks that the correct version (or range of versions) of a dependency have been installed

> it creates directories for the files that are being installed, if necessary

> it copies files, such as binaries, scripts and configuration files, from inside the .rpm file onto the hard disk

it does software configuration tasks, such as modify configuration files and creating symbolic links to files

it may stop a service, modify a configuration file used by the service and then start the service so that the new settings in the configuration file are read and used by the service

it modifies the RPM database to add the package to the database

Some of the above steps will be done in reverse if the package is being erased (uninstalled).

In addition to the above steps, the rpm command may do some of the following steps when a package is upgraded:

it may remove or overwrite the files that were installed when the previous version of the package was installed

it may rename existing files, such as configuration files, so that they will still exist and can be referred to (with the new name rather than be deleted)

Some .rpm files (packages) contain scripts and some of the above steps may be done by the scripts in a package.

An * (asterisk) can be used with the rpm command to fill in the name of a single package or install multiple packages.

Options of the rpm Command - Excluding Query Options

Table 20-1 shows common options used with the rpm command when installing, upgrading or erasing (uninstalling) .rpm packages. The -q (query) options of the rpm command are described further below.

Table 20-1 - Common Options of the rpm Command

Option	Description
-i	install the software components in a .rpm file
-e	erase (uninstall) a package
-U	upgrade an existing package - or install one, if not already installed
-v	show "verbose" (detailed) output
-vv	show "very verbose" (very detailed) output
-h	show "hash marks" (the # symbol) to indicate activity during installation
--test	test that the -i or -e options will work
--verify	verify the files that were installed from a package
--nodeps	install a package if its dependencies are not installed
--force	force the installation of a package
--noscripts	stop any scripts (scriptlets) in the package from running
--import	import the "signature" file
--checksig	check the signature in a .rpm file
--help	displays help information on the rpm command

The -i (install), -v (verbose) and -h (hash mark) Options

Use the **-i** (install) option with the **-v** (verbose) and **-h** (hash mark) options to install a packagefilename (a .rpm file). This is a very common set of options used to install a package.

The -v option causes some "verbose" output, such as a description of failed dependencies and the -h option causes 50 "hash marks" (# symbols) to be displayed across the screen as the package is being installed. This indicates the progress of the installation and that the command has not "hung".

Below is an example of installing a package file named openssh-3.4p1-2.i386.rpm:

    rpm -ivh   openssh-3.4p1-2.i386.rpm

If the dependencies of the package are not installed, an error similar to below will appear:

    error: Failed dependencies:
        packagename = 2.3.3 is needed by openssh-3.4p1-2

In this case, you must install the package(s) shown below "error: Failed dependencies:".

An additional "v" can be used with the -ivh options, so that the -ivvh options are used. This provides "very verbose" (and very long) output that can be very useful for debugging installation problems.

Use the Shift+PgUp and Shift+PgDn keys to scroll through the output provided when two "v"s are used. Near the top, for each statement that shows "Requires:", make sure that "Yes" appears (at the right of the output). If "NO" appears (at the right of the output), then the package was *not* installed. If there are failed dependencies, an error similar to above ("error: Failed dependencies:") will appear near the bottom of the output.

The -U (Upgrade) Option

Use the **-U** (Upgrade) option with the **-v** (verbose) and **-h** (hash mark) options to upgrade an existing package with a more current *packagefilename*. The -Uvh options are commonly used to upgrade an existing package to a newer version. The -U option will not install the configuration files in the *packagefilename*. The configuration files in an installed package can be seen by using the -qc options and the configuration files in a *packagefilename* can be seen by using the -qpc options (of the rpm command).

The -v option and -h options work the same as when used with the -i option and an additional "v" can be used to provide additional debugging information.

Below is an example of upgrading a package file named openssh-4.5p1-1.i386.rpm:

```
rpm -Uvh  openssh-4.5p1-1.i386.rpm
```

The -U option can be used to install a package even if an earlier version of the package has *not* been installed. Some people use the -U option to install as well as upgrade a package.

The -e (erase) Option

Use the **-e** (erase) option to uninstall a *packagename*, such as openssh. A *packagefilename is not used with this command*. The *version* and *release* are not required as part of the *packagename*.

Below is an example of uninstalling the package named openssh:

```
rpm -evv  openssh
```

If you do not use the -v or -vv options and the package was successfully uninstalled, there will be no output from the command. The -v option shows some additional information and the -vv options show a lot of information, including the names of the files that are erased (removed from the system).

If there are other packages that depend on the package that you are uninstalling, an error similar to below will appear:

```
error: Failed dependencies:
        packagename = 4.3p1-5 is needed by packagename-version-release
```

In this case, the package is not uninstalled.

The --test Option

The --test option is used with other options, such as -i or -e option. When used with the -i option, it tests that a package will install properly and that all of the dependencies of the package have been installed. The names of dependencies that are required (and are not installed) are displayed.

When used with the -e option, it tests that a package will be uninstalled properly. If there are other packages that are dependant on the package (that the -e option is being used on), the names of these packages will be displayed.

When the --test option is used with the -i option, the package is not installed. When –test is used with the -e option, the package is not uninstalled. The --test option is used to test that an option will work and provide output.

Below is an example of using the --test option to see if a package will install properly:

```
rpm -ivvh --test packagefilename
```

The --verify Option

Use the --verify option on the name of an installed *packagename*. This command will verify the existence and integrity of files that were installed when the package was installed. If a file has been removed or modified, such as by an intruder, this option will let you know. The -V option is the same as the --verify option.

Below is an example of using the –verify option on the package named XFree86:

    rpm --verify XFree86

If all of the files that were installed from package exist and have not been modified, there will be no output. If a file has been modified, such as a configuration file, then it will appear in the output and this is not a problem.

If an executable has been modified unexpectedly (i.e. not through an upgrade), this will also show up in the output and an intruder may have modified a file on your system. To replace a single file, see the "Extracting a Single File from a .rpm File" heading below.

The --nodeps Option

Software components can be compiled and installed on a system from tarballs and via methods other than the rpm command. In this situation, the components required by an RPM may exist on a system, but will not exist in the RPM database. In this case a dependency of a package may exist on the system, but may not exist in the RPM database. When you attempt to install or upgrade an RPM that requires one or more packages (dependencies) and they are not in the RPM database, the RPM command will "complain" (i.e. display some kind of error message). This is the time to use the --nodeps option.

The **--nodeps (no dep**endencie**s)** option is used to install or upgrade a package when one or more of the dependencies of a package have not been installed from an RPM. This option is typically used if you know that the software components of the dependencies have been installed by some other means.

For example, you install software components from tarballs (.tar.gz, .tgz or .tar.bz2) that provide the items required by the package that you are trying to install or upgrade. The components installed from tarballs provide the equivalent of the dependency package.

To continue the example, you manually compile and install a library that was not previously installed on your system. You then run the rpm command and it complains that a package on which it depends is not installed. You know that the library that you manually installed provides the software component that the dependency package would install, which is the library that you manually installed. Therefore, you use the --nodeps option to install or upgrade the rpm.

In addition to using the --nodeps option when installing and upgrading a package, it can also be used with the -e option when uninstalling a package. This will allow you to uninstall a package on which other packages depend.

Below is an example of using the --nodeps option to install a package:

> rpm -ivvh --nodeps *packagefilename*

Below is an example of using the --nodeps option to uninstall a package:

> rpm -evv --nodeps *packagename*

The --force Option

The --force option is used to install a package that is already installed. This option is usually used when the installed package does not work properly. It is also used to install a package if the rpm command "complains" that the currently installed package is a more current version than the version that you are trying to install.

For example, you have installed the most current version of a program and it does not work correctly (or there is some other reason that you need the older version of the program). The --force option is used to force the rpm command to install the older package. This option can be used when installing, upgrading or erasing (uninstalling) a package.

Below is an example of using the --force option to install a package:

> rpm -ivvh --force *packagefilename*

The --noscripts Option

Some packages files contain one or more scripts that are run when a package is installed, upgraded or uninstalled. These scripts are run to do additional installation, upgrade or uninstallation tasks that are required by the package.

For example, a script, such as a *preinstall* scriptlet, may run the useradd command to create a "system" user that the package requires, prior to installing a package.

As another example, a *preuninstall* scriptlet may run the service command to stop a service prior to uninstalling the package that provides the service.

The --noscripts option is used to stop any scripts in a package from running when a package is installed, upgraded or uninstalled.

The contents of the scripts in a *packagefilename* or *packagename* (if there are any) can be seen by using the --scripts option when querying a *packagefilename* or *packagename*.

Below is an example of using the --noscripts option to install a package:

rpm -ivvh --noscripts *packagefilename*

The scripts (scriptlets) in a package can be seen with the --scripts option, as described below the **-q** (query) options of the rpm command.

The --help Option

Displays help information on the rpm command. The man page for rpm also provides help information.

The --import and --checksig options of the rpm command are described further below.

Query Options of the rpm Command

The **-q** option of the rpm command can be used without any other options and it can also be used with several other options. It is used to "query" (find out about) installed packages, .rpm files and other files.

When you use the -qa options, you do not specify anything else and you get a listing of all packages that are installed on a system. The -qa options can be run from any directory because you are not running the command "on" a file. You are not querying a .rpm file or any other file; you are querying the RPM database.

When you use options that start with -q and use only one other letter, such as -qi and -ql, you specify a *packagename*, such as openssh (and not a *packagefilename* file, such as openssh-3.1p1.i386.rpm). These options can be run from any directory.

When you use options and start with -qf, such as -qfi and -qfl, you specify a *nonpackagefilename* that has been installed *(from an .rpm file)*, such as a binary file or a configuration file. The **-f** option in -qfi and -qfl is for file (a *nonpackagefilename* file - a file that is not a .rpm file). If the file is not in the current directory, the full path to the file must be specified.

The **-i** in -qfi is for information, and shows information on *nonpackagefilename* as text beside headings, such as Name:, Version:, Release:, Build Date:, Description and URL:. The URL: heading shows the address of a web site where you can get more information on a package. This heading does not appear for all packages.

The name of the daemon for the Apache Web server is httpd and this file is installed in /etc. Below is the output of: rpm -qfi /etc/httpd

```
Name      : httpd                Relocations: (not relocateable)
Version   : 2.0.40               Vendor: Red Hat, Inc.
Release   : 8                    Build Date: Wed 04 Sep 2002 05:23:55 PM EDT
Install date: Monday 4 August 2003 06:15:23 AM EST    Build Host: daffy.perf.redhat.com
Group     : System Environment/Daemons    Source RPM: httpd-2.0.40-8.src.rpm
Size      : 2702244              License: Apache Software License
Signature : DSA/SHA1, Wed 04 Sep 2002 06:51:41 PM EDT, Key ID 219180cddb42a60e
Packager  : Red Hat, Inc. <http://bugzilla.redhat.com/bugzilla>
URL       : http://httpd.apache.org/
Summary   : Apache HTTP Server
Description :
Apache is a powerful, full-featured, efficient, and freely-available Web server.
Apache is also the most popular Web server on the Internet.
```

The Name: heading shows the name of the package, not the full .rpm filename that was used to install the package. The Summary: heading provides a short description of the package and the Description: heading gives you a more detailed description. Notice the last sentence in the Description: heading above!

The -l in -qfl is for list, and shows a list of the files that were installed with the *nonpackagefilename*. This is the list of files that were installed when the package (that installed the *nonpackagefilename*) was installed.

For example, when you run the rpm command with the -qfl options "on" the mv binary file, you see a list of files that were installed when the mv binary was installed.

When you use options that start with -qp, such as -qpi and -qpl, you specify a *packagefilename* (the full filename of a .rpm package file). The -p option in -qpi and -qpl is for package (a *packagefilename* file).

The -i in -qfi is for information and the -l in -qfl is for list. The letters i and l represent the same thing (as described above) when using the -qpi and -qpl options. When using -qpi, the information is regarding the *packagefilename* and when using -qpl, the list is also regarding the *packagefilename*.

The -qa, -ql and -qi options are used "on" a *packagename* (i.e. used on packages that have been installed on a system). These options are *not* used "on" files and can be run from any directory.

The -qfi, -qfl, -qpi and -qpl options are used "on" a file name that has been installed from a .rpm file (and not "on" a .rpm file). The file must be in the current directory or the full path to the file must be specified.

The -qpi and -qpl options work "on" a .rpm file that has not been installed. The file must be in the current directory or the full path to the file must be specified.

The same concepts as above are applicable to other options that are used with -q, such as -qc and -qpc, -qd and -qpd.

Table 20-2 details a summary of using the **-q** (query) option of the rpm command.

Table 20-2 - Summary of Using the -q (query) Option of the rpm Command

Options	Output
-qa	**all** *packagenames* that have been installed on a system displays the full *packagename*, including *version* and *release*
-q *packagename*	displays the full *packagename* of a package, including *version* and *release*
-qi *packagename*	information on the installed *packagename* (not filename)
-ql *packagename*	lists all files installed by the *packagename* (not filename)
-qfi *nonpackagefilename*	information on the installed *nonpackagefilename* (non-.rpm filename)
-qfl *nonpackagefilename*	lists all files installed with the *nonpackagefilename* (non-.rpm filename)
-qpi *packagefilename*	information on the *packagefilename* (.rpm filename)
-qpl *packagefilename*	lists all files installed by the *packagefilename* (.rpm filename)
-qc *packagename*	lists the configuration files in the *packagename*
-qpc *packagefilename*	lists the configuration files in the *packagefilename*
-qd *packagename*	lists the documentation files in the *packagename*
-qpd *packagefilename*	lists the documentation files in the *packagefilename*
-qR *packagename*	lists the software components on which the *packagename* depends
-qpR *packagefilename*	lists the software components on which the *packagefilename* depends
-q --whatrequires	lists the packages that require the *packagename* specified
-q --provides	lists the main software components installed with the *packagename*
-qp --provides	lists the main software components installed with the *packagefilename*
-q --scripts	displays the contents of the scripts in the *packagename*
-qp -- scripts	displays the contents of the scripts in the *packagefilename*

Examples of Using -q (query) Options of the rpm Command

Using the -qa Options

The **-q** (query) **-a** (all) options of the rpm command are used to see a listing of all packages installed on a system and can be run from any directory.

rpm -qa

The output of the above command is usually several hundred lines of text. Each line shows the name of a package, including the version number, revision number and platform. The output is commonly piped to other commands, such as less and grep. An alpha sorted list of packages also exists in /var/log/rpmpkgs.

Using the -q Option

This option is used on a package name to display the full name of a package, including version and release.

rpm -q nfs-utils

This displays the output of: nfs-utils-1.0.1-2

Using the -qi Options

The **-q** (query) **-i** (information) options are used to see information on a specific package that has been installed on a system and can be run from any directory (i.e. it is not run "on" a file). The -qa options (described above) will give you the names of the packages that have been installed and the -qi options will give you a description of a particular package.

rpm -qi *packagename*

The output provides several headings, such as: Name:, Version:, Release:, Build Date:, Install date:, Summary:, Description: and URL:. An example of this output, for the file named httpd in /etc is shown above.

The package named httpd is used to install the Apache Web Server. When the httpd package is installed, the daemon named httpd is installed in /etc.

The following command is run "on" the httpd file in /etc:

    rpm -qfi /etc/**httpd**

The following command is run "on" the file named httpd-2.0.40-8.i386.rpm in the RPMS directory:

    rpm -qpi /mnt/cdrom/RedHat/RPMS/**httpd-2.0.40-8.i386.rpm**

The following command is run "on" the installed package named httpd:

    rpm -qi httpd

The above command is not run "on" a file. The system acquires its output from the RPM database. Notice that a path was not used with this command. This command can be run from any directory.

All three of the above commands produce exactly the same output.
The first command is run on a file that was installed from the package named httpd. The second command is run on the .rpm file that is used to install the package named httpd. The third command is run on the installed package named httpd. If the package named httpd was not installed, the output of the third command would be "package httpd is not installed".

Using the -ql Options

The **-q** (query) **-l** (list) options are used to see a list of files (including the full path to the file) that were installed when a package was installed and can be run from any directory. It is used to see the files (binary, configuration, script and others) that were installed when the *packagename* specified was installed. These options are used when you know the name of a package (that has been installed) and want to know the names of the files that were installed when the package was installed.

rpm -ql *packagename*

For example, the package named tar is used to install the tar binary file (and some other files) so that the tar command is available on a system. The full name of the .rpm file that contains the package named tar is:

tar-*version-release.architecture*.rpm

This package may have been installed when the OS was installed on the system, or afterwards by running the following command:

rpm -ivh tar-*version-release.architecture*.rpm

The full .rpm filename (tar-*version-release.architecture*.rpm) was required in the above command. You cannot simply run: rpm -ivh tar to install the package named tar. You must also either be in the directory that contains the .rpm file or specify the path to it (when running the rpm command), in order to install it.

If the package has been installed, you can run: rpm -ql tar and the following output appears:

```
/bin/gtar
/bin/tar
/usr/share/info/tar.info.gz
/usr/share/man/man1/tar.1.gz
```

Four files were installed when the tar package was installed. The second line in the output above shows that the tar binary file was installed in the /bin directory. The third line shows the name and location of the info file (tar.info.gz) that was installed so that you can run: info tar to see info on the tar command. The last line shows the name and location of the file that is used when you run: man tar to see the man page of the tar command.

When you install most packages, they install many more files than the four files that are installed with the tar command.

For example, the packaged named fileutils is used to install many commonly used binaries, such as those that allow you to run the ls, cp, mv and rm commands. When you install the fileutils package, it installs over seventy files, including twenty binaries (such as the ls binary for the ls command), several documentation files and several man page files.

The text for the Summary: heading, that appears when you run: rpm -qi fileutils shows that these files are "The GNU versions of the common file management utilities."

Using the -qfi Options

The **-q** (query) **-f (file)** **-i** (information) options are used to see file information "on" a file (that was installed from a .rpm file) by specifying the name of a file with the command (such as the name of a binary, ASCII text, script, man page file or other file) that has been installed on a system. You must either be in the directory in which the file is located or specify the full path to the file.

rpm -qfi /sbin/fdisk

In this example, the command has been run on the fdisk binary in the path of /sbin. The name of the package from which the file was installed appears beside Name: and other information, such as Version, Release and Description appear.

The -q and –whatprovides options of the rpm command can be used to display the name of the packages that is provided by a file, but these options do not show the large amount of information provided with the -qfi options.

Using the -qfl Options

The **-q** (query) **-f** (file) **-l** (list) options are used "on" a file that has been installed from a .rpm file. You must either be in the directory that contains the file or specify the path to the file with the command. This command is used to see the files that were installed when the file (that you are using the command "on") was installed.

rpm -qfl /bin/umount

After running the above command on the umount (binary file) in /bin, the following output appears:

```
/bin/mount
/bin/umount
/usr/share/man/man5/fstab.5.gz
/usr/share/man/man5/nfs.5.gz
/usr/share/man/man8/mount.8.gz
/usr/share/man/man8/swapoff.8.gz
/usr/share/man/man8/swapon.8.gz
/usr/share/man/man8/umount.8.gz
```

The benefit of using the -qfl options is that the output actually indicates the files that are "related" to the umount file (command). This is useful if you see a file (that was installed from a .rpm file) and want to know more about it.

In the above output, the mount binary appears in line one. Lines three through eight are man page files for the mount and umount binaries, and other files that are related to mount and umount, such as the fstab (text file) that is used by the mount and umount commands.

Using rpm with the -qfl options "on" *most* files (system files, not user data files) on a system (that is using a distribution that was installed using .rpm files) usually shows the files that are related to the file that you used the command "on". However, it does not work "on" all files that exist on a system, such as some text configuration files.

For example, the third line in the above output indicates that the man page file (fstab.5.gz) that describes the fstab text configuration file was installed when umount was installed. Using the -qfl options on the man page file (fstab.5.gz as shown in line three) will display the same output as above. The umount file and fstab.5.gz file were both installed by the same package and therefore, both display the same output.

However, if you use the -qfl options on the fstab text file (i.e. not the fstab.5.gz man page file), the output of the command will state: "file fstab is not owned by any package". This indicates that the file is not "tracked" in the RPM database.

Using the -qpi Options

The **-q** (query) **-p** (package) **-i** (information) options are used to get package information "on" a *packagefilename* file (a file that is a .rpm file).

rpm -qpi /mnt/cdrom/RedHat/RPMS/httpd-2.0.40-8.i386.rpm

In this example, the command has been run on the .rpm package file name that provides the Apache web server and it shows package information on the .rpm file.

The -p option is used with the -q option (and other options) to extract information from a .rpm file. This is done when a package has *not* been installed on a system. If the package has been installed, use the -q option (and other options) on the name of the package rather than on the name of a .rpm file. This is easier because the package name is shorter and you do not need to either: be in the directory that contains the file, or specify the path to the file.

Using the -qpl Options

The -q (query) -p (package) -l (list) options are used "on" a .rpm file to get a list of files that are in a .rpm file.

rpm -qpl /mnt/cdrom/RedHat/RPMS/httpd-2.0.40-8.i386.rpm

In this example, the command has been run on the .rpm package file name that provides the Apache web server and it shows a list of files that are installed from the .rpm file.

Using the -qc and -qpc Options

The -q (query) -c (configfiles) options are used "on" an installed *packagename* to get a list of the configuration files that were installed when the package was installed.

rpm -qc cups

In this example, the command has been run on the installed package named cups and it shows the configuration files that were installed when the package was installed. This is a quick way of seeing all of the configuration files of a package.

Use -qpc and specify a .rpm file name to see the same information as above for a .rpm file.

Using the -qd and -qpd Options

The -q (query) -d (documentation) options are used "on" an installed *packagename* to get a list of the documentation files that were installed when the package was installed. This is a quick way of locating documentation for a package when you need more information on one.

rpm -qd anacron

In this example, the command has been run on the installed package named anacron and it shows the documentation files that were installed when the package was installed.

Use -qpd and specify a .rpm file name to see the same information as above for a .rpm file.

Using the -qR and -qpR Options

The **-q** (query) **-R** (Requires) options show a list of software components on which the installed package depends. In this example, the package named nfs-utils is specified. This package requires over twenty other packages. Many of these packages are installed during a "basic" Linux installation. The -R option is the same as the --requires option.

rpm -qR nfs-utils

Use -qpR and specify a .rpm file name to see the same information as above for a .rpm file.

The -q and --whatrequires Options

These two options are used on a package name to display the full package name(s), including version and release, of packages that require the *packagename* specified.

rpm -q --whatrequires cups

This displays the output of: cups-**drivers**-1.9-1.20020617.6. The cups-drivers package requires the cups package.

The -q, -qp and --provides Options

These options are used on a package name to display the "capabilities" (main software components) that are installed with the package, such as the binaries and libraries that are installed.

rpm -q --provides   bind-utils

Lists the main software components installed with the bind-utils package.

Use -q**p** and --provides and specify a .rpm file name to see the same information as above for a .rpm file.

The -q, -qp and --scripts Options

These options are used on a package name to display the *contents* of the scripts (scriptlets) that are run when the package is installed. These are *not* scripts that are installed *from* a .rpm file (to a directory on the system), they are scripts in a package that are run when a package is installed, upgraded or uninstalled. Some packages do not have these scripts.

rpm -q --scripts openssh-server

Displays the contents of the scripts in the openssh-server package.

Use -q**p** and --scripts and specify a .rpm file name to see the same information as above for a .rpm file.

Extracting a Single File from a .rpm File

A file that was installed from a .rpm file may have been accidentally deleted or may have been deleted because it was corrupted. The steps below will allow you to extract a file from a .rpm file and then put it in the correct directory.

The rpm2cpio and cpio commands are used below to extract a file from a .rpm file.

The cal binary in the path of /usr/bin provides the cal command. In the example below, the cal binary will be extracted from the util-linux-*version-revision*.i386.rpm file and will be put in /usr/bin.

The following command must be run from the / directory. Replace *packagefilename* with the name of the .rpm file that contains the file that you need to extract, such as util-linux-*version-revision*.i386.rpm.

The path to the file that is being is extracted in the example below is /usr/bin/cal. Notice that there is a . (dot) that precedes this path. This . (dot) is required.

```
]# rpm2cpio /mnt/cdrom/RedHat/RPMS/packagefilename | cpio -ivd ./usr/bin/cal
```

Importing the Public Key Into the RPM Database

Prior to installing a package with the rpm command, import the "public key" (signature file) into the rpm database. This is used to verify the "signature" (integrity) of a package.

To import the public key, do the following steps:

```
]# ls -ld /usr/share/doc/rpm-*
```

This will show a version number at the right of "rpm-". Replace **version** in the command below with the version number that appears. The version number for Red Hat Linux 8.0 is 4.1.

```
]# rpm --import /usr/share/doc/rpm-version/RPM-GPG-KEY
```

This command can be run from any directory and does not display any output.

To list the keys that have been imported, run: rpm -qa gpg-pubkey*

To see the loaded key, run: rpm -qi *pubkey* where *pubkey* is one of the names listed when the command above is run.

To remove the key, run: rpm -e *pubkey*

Here is an example of above: rpm -e gpg-pubkey-db42a60e-37ea5438

If you have imported the key more than once, attempting to remove it will result in an error "specifies multiple packages".

To remove all matches, run: rpm -e –allmatches *pubkey*

Checking the "Signature" of a .rpm File

The --checksig option of the rpm command is used to check that the "signature" in a .rpm file matches a signature "key" that has been installed with the --import option. The -K option is the same as the --checksig option.

The .rpm files that are provided with a distribution can usually be "trusted" and may not need to be checked. However, you should use the --checksig command to check a downloaded .rpm file to test the integrity of the file. In addition to the "public key" described above, a signature file for a downloaded .rpm file can be downloaded from a site that provides the .rpm file.

Do the steps (similar to above) to import the public key (in addition to any existing keys) from the site at which you obtained the .rpm file and then do the following:

```
]# rpm --checksig packagefilename
```

The output should show the name of the .rpm file and the word "OK" at the far right if the signature of the "checks out". If not, then the .rpm file may have been tampered with and should not be installed. Download the file from a different location or contact the site at which you obtained the file.

Repairing the RPM Database

The RPM database and support files are located in /var/lib/rpm. If you run the rpm command and the command hangs, then you may need to "manually" repair the RPM database by doing the steps described below. The RPM database may need to be repaired after you have installed, upgraded or uninstalled several packages. A software "patch" or "bug fix" is not currently available for this problem.

For example, if you run: rpm -qa and the command hangs after only displaying a partial list of packages, you will likely need to repair the RPM database. You will also likely need to repair the RPM database if the rpm command hangs when you are installing, upgrading or uninstalling a package.

However, if you make a mistake with the rpm command and the system hangs, then you do not need to repair the RPM database.

For example, if you run: rpm -qa grep ssh and forget to put a | (vertical bar) between "-qa" and "grep", then the command will hang and Ctrl+c or Ctrl+z may not stop the command (and cause the prompt to return). In this case, close the terminal emulation window, open another one and run the command again.

Do the following steps to repair the RPM database:

If you cannot stop the "hung" rpm command with Ctrl+c, do the following two steps to kill the processes that relate to "rpm".

```
]# ps -aux | grep rpm
```

Use the kill command with the -9 option to kill all process id numbers that relate to "rpm", as shown below.

```
]# kill -9 processidnumber
```

```
]# cd /var/lib/rpm ; ls -l
```

There are two "_" (underscore) characters in the "__db.*" pattern below.

```
]# rm -f __db.*          # remove the __db.* files
```

```
]# rpm --initdb          # use the --initdb option
```

The prompt should appear almost immediately after running the above command.

```
]# rpm --rebuilddb       # use the --rebuilddb option
```

The above command takes about 3 minutes when there are about 650 packages installed on a Pentium II 350 Mhz system. You can run the top command in a different terminal emulation window to see the activity of "rpmd". Notice the output below the STAT and %CPU headings.

You may need to do the steps above to manually repair the RPM database at some point during the Hands-On Exercises below.

Hands-On Exercises

During the Hands-On Exercises of this section you will use various query options of the rpm command to do commonly needed tasks. You will also install packages and uninstall packages.

During the Hands-On Exercises of the next section, you will use the rpm command to install an Apache web server on your system.

 Logging In to Use the rpm Command

Log in as cwest ; open a terminal emulation window ; su to root.

 Viewing the RPM Database Files

]# cd /var/lib/rpm ; clear ; ls -l

This changes into the directory that contains the RPM database files and lists the database files.

These files contain information regarding the .rpm packages that have been installed on your system.

Various options of the rpm command are used to access these files for information.

]# cd /root

This changes into a directory other than the one above. You do not need to be in the above directory to view information on the rpm packages that have been installed (with the rpm command).

 Viewing Your Installed Packages

]# rpm -qa   # query all of the packages installed on your system

All of the packages that have been installed on your system appear with the version number of the package at the right of the filename.

Run the same command as above and pipe the output through the nl command to see the number of packages on your system.

The total number of packages installed appears beside the last package.

> Run the same command and pipe the output to grep for the packages that contain the name "cups".

Several packages should appear. These packages provide the software components for the cups printing system. If there were no packages that contained "cups", then no output would have appeared. This is a commonly used method of determining if a package has been installed on a system.

If you know the name of a package, such as XFree86, but do not know the version number and release number, you can run the following command.

>]# rpm -q XFree86   # shows the "full" package name

 ④ Using Other Query Options on an Installed Package

In the steps below, you will be using a *packagename* rather than a *packagefilename*. The -q option will be used with other options, but the **-p** (package) option will not be used because you are not running these commands on a *packagefilename* (a .rpm file).

>]# rpm -qi cups   # shows detailed information on an installed package

>]# rpm -ql cups   # shows a list of files installed from the package

>]# rpm -qR cups

This shows a list of software components on which the installed package depends.

>]# rpm -q --whatrequires cups

The cups-drivers package requires the cups package.

>]# rpm -q --provides cups

This lists the main software components installed with the cups package. In this case, several binaries that are installed from the .rpm file that provides the cups package appear.

The **-p** (package) option of the rpm command can be combined with most of the examples above and used "on" a *packagefilename* (a .rpm) file to provide exactly the same output as when they are run on an installed *packagename*.

Locating the Package that Includes fdisk

In the steps below, we are going to find out the name of the .rpm file that the fdisk binary was installed from. These steps are used if you know the name of the file that you want to find out information on, but not the name of the package that provided the file. If you are working in a system and need the same command (binary) on another system, but it does not exist, these steps will show you the name of the .rpm file to install on the other system.

The concept and steps described below can be used on any file (such as a binary file, configuration file, script file, man page file or other file) that was installed from a .rpm file.

```
]#  whereis  fdisk        #  the fdisk binary is in /sbin

]#  whatis  fdisk         #  notice the (8) in the description
```

Further below, you will see that the same package that provides the fdisk binary also provides the fdisk.8.gz man page file for fdisk and puts this file in the path of /usr/share/man/man**8**.

When you ran: rpm -qa above, you did not need to be in the directory that contained the RPM database files. However, to use the -qfi options of the rpm command, you need to either be in the directory that contains the fdisk program file or specify the path to it when running the command.

```
]#  rpm -qfi  /sbin/fdisk      #  uses query to show file information fdisk
```

Read all of the output of the above command. The Build Date: heading is the date that the programs in the package were compiled from source (code) and packaged into a .rpm file. If you are having a problem with a program, this date will give you an idea as to whether a more current version of the program is available.

Also notice the text below the Description: heading. This indicates that other utilities are a part of the package that the fdisk binary came from.

The Version: heading shows the version number of the package and the Release: heading shows the release number. These two numbers appear in the .rpm filename of the package. Write these two numbers below:

Version: _____   Release: _____

Beside the Name: heading, **util-linux** appears. When the package named util-linux was installed, the fdisk binary and other files in the package were installed. If you were working on one system that had a command that you wanted on another system, you now know the steps to find the name of the package that you want to install!

Now you know the name of the package, but not the full name of the .rpm file from which the fdisk program was installed. You also do not know if you have the .rpm file that provides the package. The name of the package is **util-linux**, but the .rpm filename is actually **util-linux**-*version-release.architecture*.rpm. Notice that this .rpm filename contains the **util-linux** package name.

In the exercises below, you will be working with CD 1 and CD 2. Remember to mount a CD if it is not automatically mounted and to change out of a directory on the CD prior to ejecting a CD. You cannot eject a CD if you are "in" a directory on the CD. Use the eject command to eject a CD when necessary.

To get the full name of the .rpm file that contains the util-linux package and see if you have it on one of your CDs, do the following:

Put in CD 1 and mount it (if it does not mount automatically) ;

change into the path of: /mnt/cdrom/RedHat/RPMS ;

run the ls command with the -l option and put an * (asterisk) at the *beginning* and end of "linux" (without the quotes) ;

if the package is on the CD, the full name of the .rpm filename for the package will appear ;

if the package does not appear, repeat the above steps with CD 2.

After doing the above steps, the *packagefilename* for the util-linux package should appear. Notice that the *version* number and *release* number in the filename match the *version* and *release* numbers that you wrote down above. The *packagename*, *version* number and *release* number were seen earlier when you used the -qfi options on the fdisk binary.

The *packagefilename* of package consists of the *packagename,* the *version* number, the *release* number, the *architecture,* such as .i386, and the .rpm filename suffix. The full filename of a .rpm file will be dependant upon the version number, release number and architecture of the file.

The name of the package that contains fdisk is util-linux, but you will not always know the name of a package, such as when trying to find the package that provides SSH (Secure SHell). Most of the packages that relate to SSH begin with the word "open", as in "openssh".

When using the ls command to locate a package, the asterisk at the *beginning* of the package name is actually only required if you do not know the full name of the package, such as when you are looking for the package that provides SSH and the package is actually called: openssh-*version-release-architecture*.rpm. The indented steps above are used when you are looking for a package and are using some of the text that you think will be a part of the package name.

(6) **Viewing the Files in a .rpm File**

Now that we have found out the *packagefilename* of package that provides the fdisk program (**util-linux**), we can run the rpm command to see the names of the other files that are included with the package. The **-p** (package) option is used below because you are specifying the *packagefilename* of the package.

    ]# rpm -qpl util-linux   # press Tab to complete the .rpm file name

This shows a list of over 160 files in the package named util-linux.

> Run the command again and pipe the output to the less command ;
>
> scroll to the bottom of the list of files.

Notice that the path is shown for each file name. This is the path in which each file is installed when the rpm command is used to install the package.

> Scroll back up to the top of the list of files ;
>
> /fdisk   # search for fdisk

Now fdisk (beside the path of /sbin) is appears highlighted and fdisk also appears beside another utility named sfdisk.

> n   # go to the next occurrence of fdisk (sfdisk)
>
> Continue to press: n to see other occurrences of fdisk

Notice that there is a README.fdisk file that the package installs in the path of:

> /usr/share/doc/*packagename-version*

Also notice that a man page file for fdisk named fdisk.8.gz is installed in the path of:

> /usr/share/man/man8
>
>]# rpm -ql util-linux

When the -ql options are run on the *packagename*, you get the same output when you used the -qpl options on the .rpm file name (above).

>]# rpm -qfl /sbin/fdisk

This provides the same output as above. The -qpl options are used on a .rpm file, the -ql options are used on a package name and the -qfl options are used on a file that came from the package. Each of these three sets of options displays exactly the same output. The -p option (with -ql) is used on a *packagefilename* and the -f option (with -ql) is used on a file (that was installed from the package). The -ql options are all that is required when specifying a package name.

Importing the Public Key Into the RPM Database

Prior to installing a package with the rpm command, you can import the "public key" into the rpm database. This allows you to use the –checksig (or the -K) option of the rpm command to check the "signature" of a package.

```
]# ls -ld /usr/share/doc/rpm-*
```

Notice the *version* number at the right of the - (dash) in the directory name of "rpm-*version*", below the doc directory. Replace the **version** in rpm-**version** in the command below with the version number that appears. The version number is 4.1 for Red Hat version 8.0.

```
]# rpm --import /usr/share/doc/rpm-version/RPM-GPG-KEY
```

This command can be run from any directory and does not display any output.

 Viewing and Removing the SSH Packages

Your system should currently have several packages that contain "openssh" in the package name and will likely contain a package named kdessh.

```
]# rpm -qa | grep ssh

]# rpm -e --test openssh        # try to uninstall the openssh package
```

The name of an installed package (a *packagename*) is used with the -e (erase) option, rather than a *packagefilenme*. The --test option will stop the package from being uninstalled and will show problems that may occur. In this case, the openssh package has dependencies and these packages must be removed prior to removing the openssh package. This output would also appear if the --test option was not used.

Use the commands below to remove several packages, if they are installed on your system. In other words, remove all of the dependencies of the openssh package.

```
]# rpm -e openssh-askpass

]# rpm -e openssh-askpass-gnome

]# rpm -e openssh-clients
```

If kdessh is installed, you will need to remove this prior to removing openssh-clients.

```
]# rpm -e kdessh

]# rpm -e openssh-clients

]# rpm -e openssh-server
```

Now you should be able to remove the openssh package. The -vv options are used below to provide "very verbose" output regarding the "uninstallation" of the package.

```
]# rpm -evv openssh     # all packages related to SSH are now removed
```

Press Ctrl+PgUp to scroll to the top of the output and then Ctrl+PgDn to down scroll though the output ;

look for "D: fini" at the left side of the screen to see the names of the files were erased at the right of "D: fini" ;

look a few lines above the list of erased files to see "erase: *packagename* has *nn* files".

⑨ Viewing Information on the SSH Packages on CD 1 and CD 2

Do the steps to change into the RPMS directory on CD 1.

```
]# ls -l *ssh*       # several .rpm files appear
```

Remove CD 1 and do the steps to change into the RPMS directory on CD 2.

```
]# ls -l *ssh*       # the .rpm file for kdessh appears
```

Unless you know that the package(s) that you require are all on one CD, it is a good idea to check both CDs for a package that you may require.

⑩ Viewing the Description: Heading for Some openssh Packages

Work in pairs again and designate one system as the Client system and another as the Server system.

Do the following exercises at the Server system and at the Client system.

For our purposes, we only need openssh and openssh-server on the Server system and we only need openssh and openssh-client on the Client system.

Do the steps to change into the RPMS directory on CD 1.

```
]# ls -l *ssh*
]# rpm -qpi openssh-version-release.i386.rpm
```

Read the text below the "Description:" heading.

```
]# rpm -qpi openssh-server-version-release.i386.rpm
```

Read the text below the "Description:" heading. The Server system needs the openssh and openssh-server packages.

```
]# rpm -qpi openssh-clients-version-release.i386.rpm
```

Read the text below the "Description:" heading. The Client system needs the openssh and openssh-client packages.

Viewing the Files that are Installed from Some of the openssh Packages

]# rpm -qpl openssh-*version-release*.i386.rpm

Notice the files that will be installed *from* this .rpm file. Among other files, the **scp** (**s**ecure **c**opy) command is installed from the above .rpm file into /usr/bin.

Repeat the above command for the "-server" .rpm file (for openssh).

Among other files, the sshd "init script" is installed in /etc/rc.d/init.d and the sshd daemon file for the SSH server is installed in /usr/sbin.

Repeat the above command for the "-clients" .rpm file (for openssh).

Among other files, the ssh binary that is used at a client to run the ssh command, to "ssh into a system", is installed in /usr/bin. You will run the ssh command in a few minutes.

12 **Viewing the Scripts (Scriptlets) in the .rpm File for the openssh-server Package**

]# rpm -qp --scripts openssh-server-*version-release*.i386.rpm

Look for "preinstall", "postinstall", "preuninstall" and "postuninstall". These words appear at the start of each of these "scriptlets".

The postinstall scriptlet is run after a package has been installed. Notice that this one runs the chkconfig command with --add option to add the sshd service to a system.

Run the man command for the chkconfig command and read the description of the --add option.

13 **Viewing the Configuration and Documentation Files of a Package**

]# rpm -qpc openssh-server-*version-release*.i386.rpm

The configuration files in the openssh-server package appear. This includes the sshd script file that is installed in /etc/rc.d/init.d.

]# rpm -qpd openssh-server-*version-release*.i386.rpm

The documentation files in the openssh-server package appear.

Installing the openssh and openssh-server Packages at the Server

]# rpm -qa | grep ssh

At the Server system (**only**), do the following steps to install the openssh and openssh-server packages:

Try to install openssh-server prior to installing openssh.

]# rpm -ivvh openssh-server-*version-release*.i386.rpm

The two "v"s provide "very verbose" output.

Press Ctrl+PgUp to scroll to the top of the output ;

press Ctrl+PgDn to scroll through the output.

look for "Requires:" and beside this, the word "YES" should always appear (at the right).

In this case, you should see "NO" beside "Requires: openssh" because this package is required and is not installed. This is one indication that the above command did not install the package.

Look for error messages and you should see an "error: Failed dependencies:" message (near the end of the output) and then the name of the openssh package (on the next line).

]# rpm -qa | grep ssh   # no packages should appear

This is another method of checking to see if a package was installed.

Now install openssh and *then* install openssh-server.

]# rpm -ivvh openssh-*version-release*.i386.rpm

Check the output for "NO" and "error: Failed dependencies:" as described above. These items should not appear. The files that were installed appear at the right of lines that begin with "D: fini".

]# rpm -qa | grep ssh   # the openssh package should appear

]# rpm -ivvh openssh-server-*version-release*.i386.rpm

Check the output for "NO" and "error: Failed dependencies:" as described above. These items should not appear. Notice the files that were installed (at the right of lines that begin with "D: fini").

]# rpm -qa | grep ssh   # openssh and openssh-server should appear

Congratulations, you just installed two software packages!

Installing the openssh and openssh-clients Packages at the Client

At the Client system (**only**):

Do all of the steps to install the openssh and openssh-clients packages.

Check that the packages were installed.

Remove the CD from the drive.

 Starting the sshd Service at the Server System

At the Server system:

```
]# service  sshd  status          # the service is not running
```

In this case, the name of the service (sshd) matches the name of the daemon that provides the service (sshd). This is not always the case.

```
]# ps -aux | grep  sshd           # the daemon is not in memory

]# chkconfig --list  sshd
```

The service is set to "on" for runlevels 2 through 5, but the system has not been restarted since the openssh-server package was installed. Therefore, the service is not currently running.

```
]# service  sshd  start

]# service  sshd  status          # the service is now running

]# ps -aux | grep  sshd           # the daemon is now in memory
```

 Using the ssh Command to Access a Host

At the Client system:

```
]# service  sshd  status
```

The service is not running (and is not installed) at the Client system. It does not need to be running on the Client system.

Check to see that the alias for the host name of the Server system (lancomn), that you will use below, can be resolved via the hosts file in /etc.

Replace the **n** in lancomn below with the number of the Server system.

```
]# ssh  lancomn                   # notice the text in the password prompt
```

An IP address or host name can be used in place of the lancomn alias name.

Type in the password for the root user (*on the Server system*).

]# service sshd status   # the service is running

The service is running at the Server system and you are now "on" the Server system (from the Client system)! You can now administer this system remotely (and securely) just as though you are typing at the keyboard of the server system.

After removing all SSH software components from the Client and Server systems, you installed the required SSH software components for each system (and not the same components at both systems). You then logged in to test that they worked.

]# logout   # end the "ssh session" for the Client

]# ssh -l cwest lancom57   # provide the cwest password at lancom57

Get a long listing of the cwest home directory.

You are now working as the cwest user at the lancom57 host.

]# logout

We hope you found that interesting!

 ## Section Review

1. Which command will install the package named xpdf (version number 1.0.1 and release number 8)?

    O A.   rpm -vvh xpdf
    O B.   rpm -ivvh xpdf-1.0.1-8.i386.rpm
    O C.   rpm -ivh xpdf-1.0.1.i386.rpm
    O D.   rpm -evh xpdf-1.0.1.i386.rpm

2. With the -q option, which option can be used to see the documentation files in a package?

    O A.   -doc
    O B.   -d
    O C.   -readme
    O D.   -list

3. A *packagename* can include (choose two):

    ☐ A. the architecture
    ☐ B. the version number
    ☐ C. the release number
    ☐ D. the .rpm filename suffix

4. When using the ls command to search a disk or CD for a .rpm file that contains a package, use some text that may be in the package name and (choose two):

    ☐ A. an asterisk at the end of the text
    ☐ B. an exclamation mark at the end of the text
    ☐ C. an asterisk at the start of the text
    ☐ D. a slash at the end of the text

5. A *packagename* can include a - (dash). T F

6. The term commonly used when one software program requires another software program is:

    ○ A. inter-link
    ○ B. dependency
    ○ C. reliance
    ○ D. necessity

7. A *packagename* is the same as a .rpm file name . T F

8. Which option of the rpm command can be used to cause a package to be installed if its dependencies are not met?

    ○ A. -qpd
    ○ B. --nodeps
    ○ C. --installd
    ○ D. --importregardless

9. With the -q option of the rpm command, the -p option is used (with other options) to query:

    ○ A. a *packagefilename* (that ends in .rpm)
    ○ B. a *packagename* (that does not end in .rpm)
    ○ C. a file name that was installed from a .rpm file
    ○ D. none of the above

10. What is the directory path to the .rpm files on Red Hat Linux CDs?

      ○ A.   /mnt/cdrom/RedHat
      ○ B.   /mnt/cdrom/RPMS
      ○ C.   /mnt/cdrom/RedHat/RPMS
      ○ D.   /mnt/RHL/RPMS

11. If package "a" requires package "b" and package "b" requires package "c", what is the order in which these packages need to be installed?

      ○ A.   a, b, c
      ○ B.   b, c, a
      ○ C.   c, b, a
      ○ D.   any order will work

12. In the *packagefilename* of modules-devel-2.14.18-2.i386.rpm, what is the package name?

      ○ A.   modules
      ○ B.   modules-devel
      ○ C.   modules-devel-2.18
      ○ D.   modules-devel-2.14-2

13. Only the Red Hat Linux distribution uses RPMs. T F

14. Which option of the rpm command can be used to install a package when the package is already installed, but is not working properly?

      ○ A.   --pushinst
      ○ B.   --instforce
      ○ C.   --inspkg
      ○ D.   --force

15. The -qfi options of the rpm command are used to query:

      ○ A.   a *packagefilename* (that ends in .rpm)
      ○ B.   a file name that was installed from a .rpm file
      ○ C.   a *packagename* (that does not end in .rpm)
      ○ D.   none of the above

16. Which command can be used to see if a package named XFree86 has been installed?

      ○ A.   rpm -qa | grep XFree86
      ○ B.   rpm --installed XFree86
      ○ C.   rpm -qpN XFree86
      ○ D.   rpm --list XFree86

17. If you are installing packages from a CD, then all of the packages required by a software component, such as a server, will be on one CD. T F

18. The --scripts option of the rpm command can be used to see:

    ○ A. the script files that are installed when a package is installed

    ○ B. the scriptlets that are run when a package is installed, upgraded or erased

    ○ C. only the init scripts that are installed when a package is installed

    ○ D. the scripts that were used to compile the package

19. A *packagefilename* includes (choose three):

    ☐ A. the package name

    ☐ B. the version and release numbers

    ☐ C. the architecture and a .rpm filename suffix

    ☐ D. the source file used to create the package

20. Which option of the rpm command (along with other options) can be used to see the URL: heading of a package (if there is one), so that you can get more information on a package?

    ○ A. -l

    ○ B. -i

    ○ C. -c

    ○ D. -p

21. In the *packagefilename* of openssh-3.1p1-3.i386.rpm, what is the version number?

    ○ A. 3.1p1

    ○ B. 3

    ○ C. i386

    ○ D. .rpm

22. Which option of the rpm command is used to stop the scripts (scriptlets) in a package from running when the package is installed, upgraded or uninstalled?

    ○ A. --noscripts

    ○ B. --scriptstop

    ○ C. --scripts

    ○ D. --norun

23. The minimum packages that are required at a server to allow a client to "ssh into a server" are:

    ○ A.   openssh and openssh-clients
    ○ B.   openssh, openssh-clients and openssh-server
    ○ C.   openssh and openssh-server
    ○ D.   openssh and server-ssh

24. A *nonpackagefilename* can be:

    ○ A.   a .rpm file
    ○ B.   a package name
    ○ C.   a package file name
    ○ D.   a file installed from a .rpm file

25. Select the option of the rpm command that is used to check that a .rpm file has the correct "key"?

    ○ A.   --check
    ○ B.   --verify
    ○ C.   --keyverify
    ○ D.   --checksig

Installing the Apache Web Server

Topics Covered in this Section

Provide an overview of http, html and the Apache Web server
Describe some of the directives in the httpd.conf configuration file
Install the software packages for the Apache Web server
View the main software components and directory structure used by the Apache Web server

The Apache Web Server

As stated in the description of the httpd package, which provides the Apache Web server:

"Apache is a powerful, full-featured, efficient, and freely-available Web server. Apache is also the most popular Web server on the Internet".

A Web server is commonly accessed using the **http** (**h**ypertext **t**ransfer **p**rotocol). When accessing a Web server with this protocol, http is used in the URL, such as **http**://www.lancom-tech.com.

For the Apache Web server, the package that is used to install this server is named **httpd**. When this package is installed http**d** (hypertext transfer protocol **d**aemon) is installed (and the other software components that are required by the server). The manual (in html format) for this server is installed from the package named httpd-manual.

A Web server uses **html** (**h**ypertext **m**arkup **l**anguage) to provide web content. A web site created with html consists of pages of text that have been "marked up" and contains "tags" or "codes" that point to other pages. Clicking on a link on a web page causes whatever the link points to, such as the text of another web page, to appear. The link might point to another html document on the hard disk of the Web server or an html document on the hard disk in a Web server on the other side of the world! Other software components (in addition to html) are also used to deliver web content.

In earlier versions of this distribution, the httpd package was named "apache" and the httpd-manual package was named "apache-manual".

The httpd.conf File

The main configuration file for the Apache Web server is /etc/httpd/conf/httpd.conf. The format of the cupsd.conf file that you worked with earlier was based on the format of the Apache configuration file named httpd.conf. The httpd.conf file is "heavily commented" and is over nine hundred lines long.

Some of the *many* "directives" (settings) in the httpd.conf file are described below. These are describe in the order that they appear in this file. All of the directives that can be used in httpd.conf are detailed in the Apache manual, which is installed when the httpd-manual package is installed.

ServerRoot

This directive specifies the **top** of the directory tree, under which configuration, error and log files are kept. By default this directive is set to "/etc/httpd".

The following directories are below /etc/httpd (parent directory):

conf - this directory contains the httpd.conf file
logs - this directory is a symlink that points to /var/log/httpd
modules - this directory is a symlink that points to /usr/lib/httpd/modules
run - this directory is a symlink that points to /var/run

Listen

This specifies the IP address and port to be used by the server. By default, an IP address is not specified and the port number (for the http protocol) is 80.

User and Group

The User specified with this directive is the "system" username under which the server runs and Group is the "system" group name under which the server runs. By default both User and Group are set to "apache".

ServerAdmin

This directive specifies the email address of the administrator of the server. By default this directive is set to "root@localhost".

DocumentRoot

This setting specifies the top of directory tree (a.k.a. top level directory) for "documents", such as html files, that are "served" by the server. By default this directive is set to "/var/www/html".

UserDir

This directive is used to specify the name of a directory for user web site content. This is a subdirectory of the home directory of a user, such as a directory named public_html. The default permissions must be modified to allow users to access this content. By default this directive is set to "disable" so that existing user names cannot be detected.

For example, if UserDir is set to "public_html", then web site content for the cwest user can be seen with the URL of: http://localhost/~cwest. The actual content will exist in the path of: ~cwest/public_html.

Hands-On Exercises

In the steps below, you will use the rpm command to install the package named httpd (the Apache Web server) and the package named httpd-manual (the manual for the Apache Web server).

① **Logging In to Install An Apache Web Server**

Log in cwest ; open a terminal emulation window ; su to root.

② **Checking to See If Any of the Packages Named httpd are Installed**

]# rpm -qa | grep httpd

If the package named redhat-config-httpd is installed, you will need to uninstall it below.

The packages that are required for these exercises are: **httpd** and **httpd-manual** and **redhat-config-httpd**.

If these packages are installed, do the steps to **uninstall** them now.

Check to see that they have been uninstalled.

③ **Installing the Packages for the Apache Web Server**

Use the -vv options (in addition to any other required option(s)) when installing the packages below.

Do the steps to check the RPMS directory on CD 1 and CD 2 for any packages that contain the text of "httpd" ;

install the httpd and httpd-manual packages ;

also install the redhat-config-httpd package ;

check that all of the packages were installed successfully ;

remove the CD from the drive.

Querying the httpd Package

Use the -qi options of the rpm command to get information on the httpd and httpd-manual packages and read the "Description:" heading for these packages.

Use the -qc and -qd options of the rpm command to see the configuration and documentation files in these packages. The httpd-manual package does not include configuration and documentation files, it *is* documentation.

Use the -ql options of the rpm command to get information on the httpd package and pipe the output to less.

Near the top, you will see the Apache Web server configuration file named /etc/httpd/**conf**/httpd.conf. The ServerRoot directive of "/etc/httpd" specifies as the top of the directory tree. The **conf** directory, below the ServerRoot is used for configuration files.

Notice the path of /etc/rc.d/init.d near the top of the listing. This path points to a file named **httpd**. This file is the script that is run to start and stop the httpd service (the Apache Web server). It runs the httpd daemon. You will use this script when you run: service httpd start in one of the steps below.

Further down you can see files that are put in the path of /usr/bin. These are commands related to the use of the Web server.

The .so files in the path of /usr/lib/httpd/modules are modules that are shared libraries. These modules are similar in concept to hardware driver modules and they provide various software features to the Web server.

Files in the path of /usr/sbin are programs for the Web server. The **httpd** file (in /usr/sbin) is the binary that is run to load the Apache Web server.

Apache Web server documentation files (not the documentation in the httpd-manual package) are in the path of: /usr/share/doc/httpd-*versionnumber*.

Scroll down to see the remaining files.

Home	# go to the top of the file
/.gz	# these are the man pages installed with the package
Home	
/noindex.html	# search for the file named noindex.html

The above file provides an opening screen (web page) for the server, if a file named index.html does not exist in the "DocumentRoot" directory (in the path of /var/www/html). You will work with this file in a few minutes. Notice that the path to this file is /var/www/error.

The parent directory for web site content is the html directory (/var/www/html). Subdirectories of the html directory are also used for web site content. That is, html (text) files, graphic files (that appear on web pages), and other files that comprise the web site, are put in /var/www/html and its subdirectories.

In addition to graphic files that you create yourself and use in web pages, graphic files that are used by the Apache Web server as icons, when you access the Apache Web server are located in: /var/www/icons.

 Querying the httpd-manual Package

Use the -ql options of the rpm command to get information on the httpd-manual package and pipe the output to less.

The **.html** files that you see contain the text of the Apache Web server manual in **h**ypertext **m**arkup language format.

Home

/index.html.en # notice the path of: /var/www/manual

The above file is used by the web site to deliver the opening page of the Apache Web server documentation files. You will see this web page in a few minutes.

 Looking at the Contents of the httpd Script

As seen by querying the list of files installed with the httpd package, a script file named httpd was installed in the path of /etc/rc.d/init.d. This is the script that is run to start and stop the httpd service (the Apache Web server).

When you run: service httpd start further below, you are running this script to start the Apache Web server.

]# less /etc/rc.d/init.d/httpd   # view the httpd script with the less command

The following comment appears near the top of the script file:

chkconfig: - 85 15

This number shows an S (start) number of 85 for the service and the K (kill) number of 15 for the service. These numbers indicate the order in which a service is started and stopped, in relation to the other services.

⑥ Listing the httpd Scripts Below /etc/rc.d

```
]# find /etc/rc.d -name '*httpd'
```

You saw the **15** that is being used in K15httpd when you looked at the contents of the httpd script in the init.d directory (above). Currently, the httpd service is set to off (Kill) whenever you boot or go into any runlevel.

⑦ Viewing and Modifying the runlevel Settings for the Apache Web Server

After installing the Apache Web server, you need to specify the runlevels in which it should be run.

```
]# chkconfig --list  httpd     # view the runlevel settings for the httpd service
```

By default, after installing the Apache Web server with the rpm command (rather than during the installation of the operating system) the httpd service is off for all runlevels. This was indicated above, by the K15 prefix to each of the K15httpd files in the rc**x**.d directories.

```
]# chkconfig --level 35 httpd  on  # set httpd to start in runlevels 3 and 5

]# chkconfig --list  httpd         # see the new runlevel settings

]# find /etc/rc.d -name '*httpd'
```

Now **S85**httpd appears in rc3.d and rc5.d. The next time that the system boots into runlevel 3 or 5, or changes into runlevel 3 or 5, the Apache Web server will be started.

Now start the Apache Web server for the current "session".

```
]# service  httpd  start
```

⑧ Viewing the httpd.conf Configuration File

Use less to look at the httpd.conf file in the conf directory, below **/etc/httpd**.

The cupsd.conf file was "patterned after" this configuration file and this file was "patterned after" another configuration file!

```
/ServerRoot
```

Look for ServerRoot at the left margin and "/etc/httpd" appears at the right. This is the path to the parent directory of configuration, error and log files.

/Listen   # by default, this is set to port 80

/User   # User and Group are set to apache

/ServerAdmin   # root will be emailed error messages

/DocumentRoot   # the path is "/var/www/html"

By default, the DocumentRoot, which is the html directory is empty. This is the "root" directory for this server. You will copy a file into /var/www/html in a minute.

/UserDir   # by default this is set to disable

]# ps -aux | grep httpd | nl   # apache appears at the left

The above ps command shows that there are nine processes running with "apache". The first process is owned by root and the remaining eight processes are owned by apache, due to the User directive in httpd.conf.

Starting the Apache Web server starts the first httpd (parent) process and then this process starts another eight processes. The Apache Web server creates additional processes, as needed, to respond to requests for the content of web pages.

 Copying the noindex.html File to the DocumentRoot

Get a long listing of /var/www/html.

This directory is the default "DocumentRoot" directory and it should be empty.

A file named noindex.html was installed in /var/www/error, from the httpd package. This file is typically used to display a web page for the Web server, if an index.html file does not exist in the "DocumentRoot" (/var/www/html) directory. We will copy this file to the "DocumentRoot" directory and assign it the name of index.html, to test the Web server.

]# cd /var/www/error

The command below will copy the **no**index.html file from **/**var/www/error to a file named index.html in **/**var/www/html (the DocumentRoot directory).

]# cp noindex.html /var/www/html/**index.html**

(10) Testing the Apache Web Server

Run the Mozilla web browser (use the "world" icon in the panel).

In the URL field, type in: http://localhost

You should see the Test Page of the Apache Web server. This is the index.html file that you just copied to the html directory.

Read all of the text of this Test Page.

Near the bottom of the screen, look for the sentence that says "The Apache **documentation** has been included with this distribution".

Click on the word: **documentation**

This shows a page that allows you access to the files that were installed when you installed the httpd-manual package. It will also provide access to http://apache.org (if you have an Internet connection).

Click on the FAQ link at the top left of the web page.

Below Categories, click on Support ;

In the paragraph below "1. Check the errorlog!", click on ErrorLog.

Have a look at some of the "directives" and then look around the documentation for a while.

Close your browser.

Congratulations! Now you have the most popular Web server in the world installed on your system!

(11) Modifying the index.html File in /var/www/html

Change into /var/www/html.

Do the following steps to copy the index.html file to a backup copy (a .bak file) and then modify the index.html file. After modifying the file, you will run your web browser and view the modified web page.

```
]# cp index.html index.html.bak     # make a back up copy of the
                                     # index.html file

]# vi index.html                    # edit the index.html file
```

This html document contains plain text that is formatted with "codes" that begin with a < (left angle bracket) and end with a > (right angle bracket).

/TITLE   # search for the word: TITLE

The text that appears between <TITLE>, which is the beginning "code" and </TITLE>, which is the ending code, will appear in the "title bar" of the web browser screen. This is the top border of the Web browser window.

Without removing the <TITLE> or </TITLE> codes, change the following text, which appears between the two codes from:

Test Page for the Apache Web Server on Red Hat Linux

to:

Test Page for *yourname*'s Web Site!

Replace *yourname* with your name.

Be sure to press the Esc key prior to doing the searches shown below.

/H1   # search for: H1

Without removing the any "codes", change the following text at the right of <H1 ALIGN="CENTER">, from:

Test Page

to:

Hello! Welcome to *yourname*'s Web Site!

Replace *yourname* with your name.

Save the file and exit out of vi.

 ### Testing the Revised index.html File

Look at the contents of /etc/hosts.

Beside 127.0.0.1, the alias name for your system appears, such as lancom**n** (where **n** is your host number). You should also see an alias name for another host.

Now run your web browser to test the changes that you made above. Type in the alias name of your system in place of *aliasname* below.

In the URL field, type in: http://*aliasname*

Now you should see your name in the title bar (border) at the top of the browser window and also at the top of the web page!

From an earlier exercise, your /etc/hosts file should have an *aliasname* in it for a host, other than your host. Replace *aliasname* below with the alias name of a different host (that can be resolved through /etc/hosts).

In the URL field, type in: http://*aliasname*

You should see opening web page of the *aliasname* host! You are now accessing the Apache Web server on a different host.

Close all programs, terminal emulation windows and shut down your system.

 Section Review

1. For the Apache Web server, the default setting for the User and Group directives is:

    ○ A. apache
    ○ B. httpd
    ○ C. html
    ○ D. webserver

2. Which package provides the html manual for the Apache Web server?

    ○ A. http
    ○ B. httpd-html
    ○ C. web-manual
    ○ D. httpd-manual

3. You have installed the packages named httpd and httpd-manual and then uploaded the content (text, graphic and other files) of your web site to the server (into the correct location). You run a browser and try to view the content of the web site and it does not appear. What may be the problem?

    ○ A. you did not install one of the required packages, named httpd-browse
    ○ B. you did not start the Web server
    ○ C. you need to install the httpd-client package at the workstation
    ○ D. you must compile the html web site content before it can be viewed

4. What is the full path, including filename, of the binary that is executed when a script is run to start the Apache Web server?

    ○ A. /sbin/usr/http
    ○ B. /usr/sbin/httpd
    ○ C. /etc/init/httpd
    ○ D. /rc.d/service

5. You have run the ps command to see the processes named httpd. Most of the processes are "owned" by:

    ○ A. apache
    ○ B. httpd
    ○ C. html
    ○ D. webserver

6. Which directive is used to specify the "top level" directory for web site content of the Apache Web server?

    ○ A. ServerRoot
    ○ B. SiteRoot
    ○ C. DocumentRoot
    ○ D. UserDir

7. After installing the httpd package, all of the scripts in the rcx.d (rc0.d through rc6.d) directories have the same name and are prefixed with: K15 (as in K15httpd). What does this indicate?

    ○ A. that the httpd service is configured to be off for all runlevels by default
    ○ B. that the httpd service will kill other processes if they try to use process 15
    ○ C. that the httpd-manual package has not been installed and is required to start the service
    ○ D. that the httpd service is using the K15httpd.conf configuration file in /etc/ by default

8. What is the full path, including filename, of the script used to load (run) the Apache Web server?

    ○ A. /sbin/http
    ○ B. /usr/sbin/httpd
    ○ C. /etc/rc.d/service
    ○ D. /etc/rc.d/init.d/httpd

9. You want to see which runlevels the Apache Web server is configured to start in. Which of the following commands will display this information?

    ○ A. chkservice --list httpd
    ○ B. cd /www ; ls -lR | grep httpd
    ○ C. server --status show
    ○ D. chkconfig --list httpd

10. Select the name of the main configuration file for the Apache Web server.

    ○ A. html.config
    ○ B. apache.cfg
    ○ C. httpd.conf
    ○ D. sitemap.cf

11. Which of the following is the "top level" directory for web site content of the Apache Web server?

    ○ A. /www
    ○ B. /var/www/html
    ○ C. /etc/rc.d
    ○ D. /usr/sbin

12. Select the default name of the Web server administrative user that will be sent email.

    ○ A. webmin
    ○ B. root
    ○ C. admin
    ○ D. webroot

13. You have installed the packages named httpd and httpd-manual and then uploaded the content (text, graphic and other files) of your web site to the server. You use the service command to start the Web server; then you run a browser and test the Web server and it works. You start your system the next day in runlevel 5 and run a browser and try to view your web site content again and it does not appear! What may be the problem?

    ○ A. you must install the TCP/IPC stack after configuring you harmonic site-converter
    ○ B. you can not run the Apache Web server in runlevel 5, only in runlevel 3
    ○ C. you need to reconfigure the main Web server configuration file so that it will operate in runlevel 5
    ○ D. you did not configure the Web server service to start for the runlevel that you are using

14. By default, what is the port number used by the Apache Web server for the http protocol?

    ○ A. 60
    ○ B. 80
    ○ C. 100
    ○ D. 180

Downloading, Compiling and Installing Software

Topics Covered in this Section

Discuss downloading binary and source code packages in tarballs
Provide an overview of installing binaries extracted from a tarball
Detail the steps required to install source code extracted from a tarball
Do the steps to untar, compile and install the source code in a tarball

As describe earlier, you can often get a software package as an "installation format file", such as a .rpm, .deb or other file. This type of software package can be installed with a single command.

However, you may need to work with the source code of a package because it is not currently available as an "installation format file"; or you may need a more current version of a package, that is not yet available as a .rpm file.

By working with source code of a package, you can also modify a package to suite your needs. If you download a tarball and then untar, compile and install it, the package in the tarball will not be "tracked" in the RPM database.

 Technically speaking, a tarball is a file that contains one or more files and has a .tar extension. A tarball can contain any type of file. However, when discussing software packages, we will use the term tarball to refer to a file that contains software components. The file may also include other components, such as text files that provide documentation.

A tarball may or may not be compressed. A tarball that has not been compressed simply has a .tar extension. A tarball that has been compressed has a .tar.gz, .tgz or .tar.bz2 extension.

Virtually all packages that are available as tarballs are compressed so that they take less space when they are provided to you on disk (floppy, CD, or other) and also so that they can be downloaded faster. Therefore, whenever we use the term tarball in relation to software packages, rather than archived data files, we are referring to compressed tarballs that contain binaries or source code.

A tarball will commonly contain one or more binary files, or it will contain the source code files required to compile and create a package. A single tarball can contain both binary files and source code files, but this is less common. Therefore, we will discuss tarballs that contain binary files and then discuss tarballs that contain source code files.

If a tarball contains binary files, then the package does not need to be compiled prior to being installed.

If a tarball contains source code files, then the source code in the tarball must be compiled before the package can be installed.

Unlike files that are in an installation file format, tarballs are not installed by running a single command. The general steps for installing tarballs that contain binary files are described below. The general steps for installing tarballs that contain source code files are described further below.

Overview of Downloading and Installing Binaries

Copy or download the tarball into a directory.

Use the tar command to extract the files from the tarball. This may create a subdirectory in the directory in which the tarball is located. The binaries and other support files, such as documentation files, that are extracted from the tarball will either be in the same directory as the tarball or in the subdirectory that was created.

It is always a good idea to check the contents of a tarball to see the destination directories of the files in it. This will ensure that the tarball does not overwrite an existing file that is required, such as a configuration file in the /etc directory.

Run the command: tar -tvf *tarballname.suffix* | less

If the *.suffix* of the tarball indicates that the file is compressed (and it likely will be), add the -z or -j options to the above command.

Look for and read the documentation files that describe installing the binaries. The installation may be as simple as using the cp command to copy a binary to a directory, or may involve running a script that does the installation steps for you (such as create directories and copy files).

The Anjuta IDE Program

Anjuta is an Integrated Development Environment (IDE) for C and C++ on GNU/Linux. It has been written for GTK/GNOME and among its many features, it provides an easy-to-use graphical editing environment for writing, organizing and compiling source code.

The Anjuta program is Open Source software and is available under the GNU General Public License. For more information on Anjuta, go to http://anjuta.sourceforge.net.

The source code for Anjuta is available as a tarball that ends in .tar.gz. During this section, we will be using the Anjuta IDE program as an example of downloading a tarball, untarring it to extract the source code from it, compiling the source code and then installing the program.

We have downloaded a tarball containing the source code of the Anjuta program from the above web site for you, and it has been put in the path of /downloads/anjuta on CD 3. You will copy this tarball into a directory on your system and do the steps to install Anjuta during the Hands-On Exercises of this section. You will then use Anjuta to create a small program, compile it into a binary, install it, and then run it to test it!

Overview of Downloading, Compiling and Installing Source Code

The general steps for downloading, compiling and installing the source code of a package in a tarball are outlined below. These steps include an example of installing a tarball and the example program used is the Anjuta IDE program.

The source code of the Anjuta program is on CD 3 in a tarball named anjuta-1.0.0.tar.gz. In the description below, the parent directory on your system that is being used *for subdirectories* that contain tarballs is named downloads, and you will create this directory below your home directory.

To install a tarball other than the anjuta tarball, replace *anjuta* in the steps below with the name of the tarball that you are installing.

Put the Tarball in a Directory

Create a directory named downloads below your home directory.

Create a directory named anjuta below the downloads directory.

When a tarball is "untarred", it *typically* (but not always) creates a subdirectory in the directory in which it is located. The subdirectory name *often* (but not always) has the same name as the tarball, excluding the suffix of the tarball.

For example, when the tarball named **anjuta-1.0.0**.tar.gz is untarred, the **anjuta-1.0.0** subdirectory is created in the directory that contains the anjuta-1.0.0.tar.gz file (the anjuta tarball file). The subdirectory name is the same as the tarball name, excluding the .tar.gz suffix.

All of the contents of the tarball are *usually* put in the subdirectory that is created when the tarball is untarred (and also in subdirectories of this subdirectory) and *no files are put in the directory that contains the tarball file.*

However, this is not always the case. There will be times when a tarball puts files in the directory in which it is located. Therefore, if you put the file in downloads, instead of in a subdirectory of downloads, then files from some tarballs could be put in the downloads directory. If you later untarred a different tarball in downloads, it could do the same thing, and one tarball could end up overwriting files that were previous installed from another tarball.

By putting a tarball in a subdirectory of downloads and then untarring it, the tarball cannot put any files in downloads and therefore cannot overwrite any existing files in downloads.

Download or copy the anjuta tarball into the anjuta directory, below the downloads directory.

Change into the anjuta directory in the path of /home/cwest/downloads/anjuta.

When the anjuta tarball is untarred (from the anjuta directory), it creates a subdirectory named anjuta-1.0.0 below the anjuta directory and it does not put any files in the anjuta directory.

The full path to the top level directory of the Anjuta source code tree is:

/home/cwest/downloads/anjuta/anjuta-1.0.0

The anjuta-1.0.0 directory is the "top of the source tree". It is the top directory of the directory structure (tree) that contains the source code of the program.

Extract the Source Code from the Tarball

Run the tar command to extract the source code files from the tarball.

For example, if the package is named anjuta-1.0.0.tar.gz, the following options of the tar command **extract**, **gunzip** and **verbosely** display all of the files in the tarball.

tar **-xzvf** anjuta-1.0.0.tar.gz

The .tar.gz extension of the tarball indicates that it was "tarred" with the -z option of the tar command. Therefore, the file was compressed with the gzip program (as opposed to a .tar.bz2 file that was tarred with the -j option, using bzip2). Therefore, the -z option of the tar command, rather than the -j option, is used to decompress the tarball. After a tarball has been "untarred", it still exists in the directory in which it was put.

As described above, untarring a tarball will usually create a subdirectory in the directory that contains the tarball. This subdirectory will usually have the same name as the tarball, excluding the suffix, such as .tar.gz. All of the source code files (and other support files) in the tarball are usually extracted into this subdirectory (and subdirectories of the directory).

For example, the anjuta-1.0.0.**tar.gz** tarball has been put in the anjuta directory, below downloads. When this tarball is untarred, a subdirectory named anjuta-1.0.0 (without the **.tar.gz** suffix) is created below the anjuta directory. This subdirectory is the **top level of the source code tree** of the anjuta-1.0.0 program.

The path to the anjuta-1.0.0.tar.gz file is: /home/cwest/downloads/anjuta and there are no other files in this directory.

The path to the source code is: /home/cwest/downloads/anjuta/anjuta-1.0.0 and several files that we will be discussing below are in the anjuta-1.0.0 directory, which is the parent directory of the source code. The anjuta-1.0.0 directory is the top of the source code (directory) "tree".

Change into the directory that was created when the tarball was untarred, such as the anjuta-1.0.0 directory.

Read the Documentation Extracted from the Tarball

When a tarball is untarred, the source code in the tarball is extracted into the top level directory of the source code, such as anjuta-1.0.0. In addition to this, other support files for the package are also usually extracted into this directory.

These files can include script files, configuration files and usually some form of documentation that describes the installation of the software. The documentation may be in a "readme" file, such as README or README.TXT and may also be in a subdirectory named docs (or in a similar subdirectory name).

Locate and read the documentation file(s) that were extracted from the tarball. These will provide installation information that is specific to the package.

The commands described below are run from the parent directory of the source code.

Run the Script Named configure

The parent directory of the source code, such as anjuta-1.0.0 will likely contain a script file named configure. If there are any options that need to be specified when running the configure script, these are usually described in the documentation file(s) that were extracted from the tarball.

If the configure script exists, use the following to run it:

```
./configure
```

This script performs several tasks, including checking for the existence of a compiler, the existence of the libraries that are required to compile the program (dependencies) and the utilities that are required to compile the program. It then creates a custom file named Makefile. If configure does not find the software components that it requires, it fails and produces an error message (that usually describes the missing components).

The dependencies required by a source code package need to be installed prior to compiling the source code, in the same way as the dependencies required by a .rpm package need to be installed prior to installing a .rpm package (as described in the first section of this chapter). The dependencies of a source code package will likely be described in the documentation file(s) that were extracted from the tarball with the source code. The dependencies can either be installed from a .rpm package or a from tarball.

Run the make Command

The make command compiles (a.k.a. builds) the source code of a package and creates one or more binaries. It is used to run statements that exist in a text file. These statements cause the make command to do tasks that are related to the compilation of a program, such as prepare a system to compile a program, and then compile the program. If the name of a text file is not specified with the make command, a text file named Makefile (or makefile) in the current directory is used.

The contents of a text file that is used with the make command look like a script. However, the text file is not executable. It is a file that contains instructions (statements) that are used by the make command to build and install a program from source code. The binary file named make is in /usr/bin.

If you have already compiled a program and try to compile it again, you may see a message similar to "nothing to be done". In this case, you may need to run: make clean in the top level directory of the source tree to remove some existing files from the source tree, such as object and binary files.

The amount of time required to compile a package varies greatly, from a few seconds to several hours.

Run the make install Command

This command will install the package, including its compiled binaries, configuration files, and any libraries that are required. You must be working as root when you run this command.

The Makefile supplied with some tarballs includes an uninstall: target (heading) that allows you to run: make uninstall to remove the program from a system.

Post-Installation Steps

After installing a tarball, the contents of the tarball directory are no longer required.

You can run the indented command below in the directory that contains the tarball directory, such as the anjuta directory, to remove the anjuta-1.0.0 directory (that is in the anjuta directory). As you are using the -f option of the rm command, do not run the command below when logged in as root.

For the anjuta program, you would run the following command while "in" the anjuta directory, to recursively remove the anjuta-1.0.0 subdirectory and all of the files and directories below it:

    rm -rf anjuta-1.0.0

If you remove the tarball directory, you remove the Makefile of the program (from the tarball directory). If you need to uninstall the program later, you will need to untar the tarball, run configure to create the Makefile and then run: make uninstall to uninstall the program (if there is an uninstall: target in the Makefile).

When you install a .rpm file, the RPM database keeps track of the files that are installed. A file named Makefile is not required to uninstall a .rpm file. When you uninstall a .rpm some or all of the steps done during the installation of the .rpm file are reversed.

We recommend that you keep all tarballs (on your system or on a backup) so that you can use them in the future, if necessary. A tarball, and in particular, a specific version of a tarball, may not always be available for download in the future.

Overview of the Hands-On Exercises

During the Hands-On Exercises of this section you will:

    create a directory named downloads, for downloaded software
    create a directory named anjuta below downloads, for the anjuta tarball
    copy the Anjuta tarball from CD 3 into the anjuta directory
    untar the Anjuta tarball to extract the source code and other files in it
    compile the source code that was extracted from the tarball
    install the Anjuta IDE program

In addition to the steps above, you will use the Anjuta program to:

    modify the source code of a small program to create a program
    named *yourname*
    compile the *yourname* program with Anjuta to create the *yourname* binary
    install the *yourname* binary and test it
    uninstall the *yourname* binary

You will also do the steps below to make the *yourname* program a downloadable tarball:

    create a *yourname* tarball, that includes the source code of the
    yourname program
    copy the *yourname* tarball into the downloads directory
    untar the *yourname* tarball to extract the source code and other files in it
    compile the source code that was extracted from the tarball
    install the *yourname* program

Hands-On Execises

 Logging In to Compile and Install the Anjuta IDE Program

Log in as cwest ; open a terminal emulation window ; do not su to root ;

move and size the window to fill the top half of the screen ;

open another terminal emulation window ; su to root ;

move and size the window to fill the bottom half of the screen.

You will work as cwest (a non-root user) in the top window and work as the root user in the bottom window.

With a multiple window setup, you can run a command to view documentation regarding the software installation (or a man page or some other source of information) in one window and do the steps required for the installation in another window.

Alt+Tab to the top (cwest) window ; maximize the cwest window.

]# whereis anjuta   # the program is not yet installed

 Creating a Directory for Anjuta

Your current directory should be your home directory.

Create a directory below your home directory named downloads ;

change into the downloads directory ;

below downloads, create a directory named anjuta ;

change into the anjuta directory ;

]# pwd

Tthe path should be: /home/cwest/downloads/anjuta

 Copying the Anjuta Tarball into the anjuta Directory

Locate the anjuta tarball on CD 3 ;

copy the anjuta tarball from CD 3 into the anjuta directory below downloads ;

if necessary, change into the anjuta directory ; get a long listing.

There are currently no subdirectories of the anjuta directory.

Untarring the anjuta Tarball

>]# tar -xzvf anjuta-*version*.tar.gz

This creates a directory named anjuta-*version* below the anjuta directory. This directory has the same name as the anjuta tarball, excluding the .tar.gz suffix. The anjuta tarball is still in the anjuta directory. Tarballs do not always create a directory for their contents, but usually do.

>]# ls -lR | less   # scroll to the bottom

When you untarred the anjuta tarball, the anjuta-*version* directory was created and the source code files and other support files in the tarball were put in this directory (and subdirectories of this directory).

 Viewing the Contents of the anjuta-*version* Directory

> Change into the anjuta-*version* directory.

>]# less README

> /REQUIREMENTS   # search for REQUIREMENTS

The text below "From Tarball:" lists the packages (dependencies) that are required to compile Anjuta. You installed these packages during the Linux installation.

> /INSTALLATION   # search for INSTALLATION

Read the text below "From Tarball:". This shows the general steps for installing the program. Steps 3 and 4 can be combined by using the -z option of the tar command.

6   **Running the configure Script**

>]# ls -l Make*

A file named Makefile (without an extension) does not yet exist.

On a 1 GHz system, the following command will take about one minute.

>]# ./configure   # this creates Makefile (without a suffix)

>]# ls -l Make*

The Makefile file is used by the make command when compiling the program.

⑦ **Running the make Command to Compile the Source Code for Anjuta**

```
]#  whereis  make        #  in /usr/bin
```

The following command will compile the anjuta source code. On a 1 GHz system, the compile time is less than 10 minutes.

```
]#  make
```

The make command will use the Makefile file (that you created above with the configure script) when compiling the source code for the Anjuta program.

Run the following command when make has finished compiling.

```
]#  ls  -l  src/anjuta
```

The anjuta binary was created in the src directory below the anjuta-*version* directory. It should be about 16 MB.

```
]#  whereis anjuta        #  the binary is not yet installed
```

 Installing the Anjuta Program

The command below will install the Anjuta program and put the anjuta binary file in /usr/local/bin. The cwest user does not have permission to put files in the path of /usr/local/bin. Therefore, you need to be working as root to run: make install.

Alt+Tab to the bottom window where you are working as root ;

change into the anjuta-*version* directory.

On a 1 GHz system, the following command will take less than two minutes.

```
]#  make  install        #  install the anjuta program
```

Alt+Tab to the cwest window.

When you compiled anjuta, you created a binary file named anjuta, which is used to launch the program, and library files that are used by the anjuta program.

```
]#  whereis  anjuta       #  the program is now in /usr/local/bin
```

The anjuta **bin**ary file is in /usr/local/**bin** and the library files are in /usr/local/**lib**/anjuta.

```
]#  echo  $PATH
```

The directory path of /usr/local/bin is in the PATH variable (for all users, including root) and the anjuta binary is in this directory path. This allow any user to run the anjuta program from any directory.

    ]# file /usr/local/bin/anjuta

    ]# ls -l /usr/local/lib   # the anjuta directory appears

The anjuta directory in the path of /usr/local/lib/anjuta did not exist prior to running: make install.

    ]# ls -l /usr/local/lib/anjuta   # anjuta library files are listed

You should be working as the cwest user.

    Change to the cwest home directory ;

    ]# anjuta   # run the Anjuta IDE program

    read the information in the "Welcome" dialog box ; click OK ;

    maximize the Anjuta program window.

    File ; New Project ... ; Next ; maximize the "New Project" window.

Notice the *many* different project types that are shown.

In the steps below, replace *firstname* with your first name, in lower case letters. Do not use *username* (such as cwest) for *firstname*. In the steps below, do not confuse *username* with *firstname* ;

    Generic/Terminal project ; Next ;

    Project Name: *firstname* ; type in your first name in lower case letters ;

    Leave Programming language as C and Target type as Executable target ; Next ;

    Type in: *Test Project* ; Next ; leave the Additional Options settings as is ; Next ;

    read the Summary screen ; Finish.

Notice that the "l.e.d." light under the File menu is "flashing". Watch the text at the bottom of the screen for about two minutes.

Among other things, the system is creating a directory below the cwest home directory named Projects and a subdirectory of Projects named *yourname*. In the *yourname* directory, a file named **configure** file and a file named **Makefile** is created for your project.

The configure file is a script that is run with: ./configure. If someone downloads the tarball of the source code of your project, they will run this configure script as part of the process of installing your program. The Makefile that is created is used when someone runs the make command to compile the source code of your program.

In the window at the left, main.c x 2 (double-click on main.c) ;

A very small sample C program appears on the main.c tab at the right. This program is edited to create your own program.

Read all of the text of this small program.

Now you can edit this program in the window at the right.

On the line with the "printf" statement, remove the word: **world** and type the following word in its place: **Linux!** ;

File ; Save ; save the changes to your program/project ;

Build ; Build ; this compiles the source code of the program ;

Build ; Execute ; this runs the program ;

Hello Linux! appears in a terminal emulation window ;

notice the path near the top of the window.

The full path to the *firstname* binary (including the binary named *firstname*) is:

/home/cwest/Projects/*firstname*/src/*firstname*

Press Enter to close the terminal (emulation window) ;

close Anjuta.

]# cd ~   # you should be the cwest home directory

]# cd Projects/*firstname*/src   # this path is below your home directory

get a long listing ; run the file command on the new binary ;

When you ran: make install above for the anjuta program, the binary named anjuta was installed in the path of: /usr/local/bin so that this program could be run from any directory. This has not been done for the binary named *firstname*.

If you ran: make install or if you copied the *firstname* binary to a directory in the PATH, such as /usr/local/bin, then you would be able to run the *yourname* binary from any directory. The ./ would not be required in front of the name of the binary below. Do not run: make install yet.

]# ./*firstname*   # "Hello Linux!" should appear

Congratulations! You have done all of the steps to untar, decompress, compile and install a program!

In addition to this, you ran your new program and used it to create a program, and then ran the new program as well!

 Compiling the *yourname* Binary from the Command Line

In the steps above, you selected: Build ; Build from within Anjuta to create the binary named *firstname*. This created the binary in the ~/Projects/*firstname*/src directory. Now you will do the steps to compile the program as though you had downloaded the source code as a tarball and untarred it (so that it created a directory named *firstname* below ~/Projects.

In the same way as all of the steps (commands) to compile and install a tarball are run from the directory that is created when the tarball is untarred, you will run all of the steps to compile and install your program from the *firstname* directory.

You should be in the cwest window ;

change into ~/Projects/*yourname* ;

]# ls -l configure   # this file should exist in the current directory

]# file configure   # configure is a script file

]# ls -l Makefile   # this file should exist in the current directory

]# make # try to compile the program

Notice that "nothing to be done" appears several times. The program has already been compiled. You need to run: make clean prior to doing any steps to compile and install the program.

]# ls -l src   # the *firstname* binary is in the src directory

]# file src/*   # notice the output for the *firstname* and main.o files

The file named *firstname* is "executable" and the file named main.o is "relocatable". The main.o file is an object file.

]# make clean   # remove existing files, such as object and binary files

Notice the output immediately after running the above command. Read the text between "Making clean in src" and "Making clean in po". Files and directories that are no longer needed are "cleaned up" (removed) so that you can compile the program again.

]# ls -l src   # the *firstname* and main.o files no longer exist

]# ls -l Make*   # notice the time of the file named Makefile

Now we're going to "take it from the top" and install the program as though it had just been untarred, and as though the act of untarring it created the directory named *firstname*, and that you have changed into the *firstname* directory.

```
]#  ./configure            # a new Makefile will be created

]#  ls -l Make*            # the time of the file named Makefile has changed

]#  make                   # compile the firstname binary

]#  ls -l src              # the firstname and main.o files were created

]#  whereis firstname      # the firstname binary is not installed

]#  make install           # try to install the firstname binary
```

Look for the long line in the output (about six lines from the bottom) that shows "Permission denied". You must be logged in as root to install a program.

At the left of "Permission denied", the path of /usr/local/bin/*firstname* appears. This path includes the binary file named *firstname*. The problem is that you do not have enough permission in the bin directory, below /usr/local, to install the *firstname* binary in this directory.

```
]#  cd /usr/local          # change to the parent directory of the bin directory

]#  ls -ld bin
```

The root user is the "user owner" and "group owner" of the bin directory and you are not currently logged in as this user.

The permissions for the bin directory are: rwxr-xr-x. The user owner (root) has the rwx permissions and the group owner (root) has r-x permissions. The "others" (other users or groups) have r-x permissions. Therefore, the cwest user is "other" and has r-x permissions, which does not include the w permission, which is required to install the *firstname* binary in the bin directory.

Alt+Tab to the root user window.

```
]#  cd ~cwest/Projects/firstname

]#  whereis firstname      # the firstname binary is not installed

]#  make install           # install the firstname binary

]#  whereis firstname      # the binary was installed in /usr/local/bin

]#  echo $PATH             # /usr/local/bin is in the PATH
```

The *firstname* binary can now be run from any directory and "./" does not need to be used in front of the binary for you to be able to execute it.

```
]#  firstname                # run the binary
```

Get a long listing the src directory, below the current directory.

The *firstname* binary and main.o object files still exist in the src directory after running make install.

```
]#  make  uninstall
```

Notice the output of this command. The *firstname* binary is removed

```
]#  whereis  firstname        # the program is no longer installed
```

Alt+Tab to the cwest user window ;

change into the cwest home directory.

 ## Preparing the Source Code for Download by Others

Now you will do the steps to prepare the source code for download by others. You will create a tarball (a .tar.gz file) so that it can be downloaded onto another system, compiled and installed. You could create a .tar.bz2 file for download, but you are going to create a .tar.gz file.

```
]#  cd  Projects/yourmane     # change into the firstname directory
```

```
]#  make  clean
```

This removes the files that do not need to be in the tarball, except for the file named Makefile.

```
]#  find  -name  Makefile
```

A file named Makefile exists in the *firstname* directory and also in the po, src and intl subdirectories.

You do not want to have any files named Makefile in the .tar.gz file that you are about to create. The Makefile file should be created on the system where the downloaded tarball will be compiled. The following command removes all of the files named Makefile in four directories.

```
]#  rm  Makefile  po/Makefile  src/Makefile  intl/Makefile
```

```
]#  find  -name  Makefile      # no files named Makefile should appear
```

```
]#  cd  ..                     # change to the parent directory of the
                               # firstname directory
```

```
]#  ls  -lR  |  less
```

This shows a listing of the files that will be "tarred" when the command below creates a tarball of the source code for the *yourname* binary. It "tars" the *yourmane* directory and everything below it. The *firstname* at the far right of the command below is the directory name that is the parent directory of the source code files.

```
]# tar -czvf firstname.tar.gz firstname

]# ls -l                    # the firstname.tar.gz tarball was created in
                            # ~/Projects
```

(11) Testing the "Downloaded" Source Code

If you are unsure as to whether or not a subdirectory is created by a tarball that you have downloaded (when you untar the tarball), then you may want to create a directory for it below the downloads directory, rather than just putting it in the downloads directory and untarring it. However, we know that this tarball will create a *firstname* directory below downloads, so this step is not needed.

```
]# mv firstname.tar.gz ~/downloads
```

The above step is the equivalent of downloading the tarball into the downloads directory.

```
]# cd ../downloads          # same as running: cd ~/downloads

]# ls -l                    # a firstname directory does not exist below
                            # downloads yet
```

Run the command to untar the *yourname*.tar.gz tarball.

```
]# ls -l                    # now the firstname directory exists
```

Change into the *firstname* directory.

```
]# find -name Makefile      # a file named Makefile (without an
                            # extension) does not exist

]# ./configure              # create the files named Makefile

]# find -name Makefile      # the files named Makefile now exists

]# make                     # compile the program

]# find -name firstname
```

The binary exists in the src directory, below the current directory.

]# whereis *firstname*   # the program is not yet installed

Alt+Tab to the root user window so that you have permission to install the program ;

change into the *firstname* directory, below the downloads directory, below the home directory of cwest ;

]# make install   # install the program

]# whereis *firstname*   # the program is now installed

]# *firstname*   # the *firstname* binary runs!

close all terminal emulation windows, programs and shut down your system

Congratulations again! You created a downloadable tarball, did the equivalent of downloading it into a directory (by moving it), and then you compiled it and installed it to test it.

 ## Section Review

1. You have downloaded a tarball named hello-1.1.tar.tgz into a directory named hello, below downloads, below your home directory. When you untar the hello-1.1.tar.tgz file, what will most likely happen?

    ○ A. a directory named hello will be created in your home directory
    ○ B. a directory named hello-1.1 will be created in the hello directory
    ○ C. a directory named hello-1.1.tar.gz will be created in the hello directory
    ○ D. a directory named hello-1.1 will be created in the downloads directory

2. In addition to the -xvf options of the tar command, which option is used to decompress the files in a .tar.bz2 file?

    ○ A. -j
    ○ B. -z
    ○ C. -b
    ○ D. -t

3. When a tarball is untarred, it always creates a subdirectory below the directory in which it is located and extracts its files into this subdirectory. T F

4. Select the command that is used to install a package that has been compiled from source code.

   ○ A. install compiled
   ○ B. install -comp
   ○ C. make install
   ○ D. make it go

5. Which file creates the file named Makefile?

   ○ A. configure
   ○ B. make
   ○ C. makeinst
   ○ D. compile

6. The dependencies of the source code in a tarball are always resolved by compiling the source code of the tarball. T F

7. You have already compiled a program and attempt to compile it again. You see an error message that says "nothing to be done". Which command do you need to run so that you can compile again?

   ○ A. compile new
   ○ B. make new
   ○ C. configure
   ○ D. make clean

Chapter 21: Configuring, Compiling and Installing a New Kernel

The Linux kernel kernel is highly configurable. It consists of hundreds of software components that exist as source code. When configuring the kernel for a system, you can specify what to do with the source code components of it. Some components, such as commonly used hardware components, are compiled into the kernel. Other components can either be compiled into the kernel, compiled as modules, or excluded altogether.

In this chapter, you will learn about the kernel source code, the methods of configuring the kernel components, the benefits of compiling your own kernel and the documentation provided with the source code.

The following commands are described in this chapter and are also used in the Hands-On Exercises:

make config	a text-based kernel configuration utility
make menuconfig	a graphical kernel configuration utility
make xconfig	an X Windows kernel configuration utility
make dep	create module dependencies
make clean	do a cleanup of the kernel source tree
make bzImage	compile the kernel
make modules	compile the modules used by the kernel
make modules_install	install the modules used by the kernel
make install	install the kernel and modify the grub config file
make mrproper	do a comprehensive cleanup of the kernel source tree
make oldconfig	migrate a kernel .config file to the current kernel version

During the Hands-On Exercises, you will do all of the steps to configure and compile your own kernel and the modules for the kernel. You will also modify the Grub boot loader configuration file so that you can select your new kernel when the system boots to test these components.

Configuring, Compiling and Installing a New Kernel

Topics Covered in this Chapter

Describe the Linux kernel, its features and functionality
Compare the differences between monolithic and modular kernels
Discover the different options that can be used for configuring the kernel
Explain why some software components are compiled into the kernel and others are compiled as modules
Introduce the utilities that can be used to configure the kernel
Discuss the different methods of installing the kernel source code
Detail the steps to configure, compile and install a new kernel
Do all of the steps to install the kernel source code and configure, compile and install a new kernel

The Linux Kernel

The Linux operating system *is* the Linux kernel; the kernel executable program file. All of the functions that are required of an operating system are provided by the kernel.

To work on a system and maintain it, additional programs are installed that provide commands and utilities that are used to work "on" the system. As describe earlier, these programs, such as ls, cp, grep and tar are open source software components that are distributed under the GNU General Public License.

The kernel is constantly being updated and enhanced to fix bugs and to provide additional functionality. Some of these enhancements are to accommodate new software features, such as additional network protocols, and some are for new hardware components, such as when the capability of using USB devices was added to the kernel.

The kernel includes hundreds of features, which are provided through software components in the form of source code. These software components enable a system to have some kind of functionality, such as: access to a network protocol (IP, IPX, Appletalk and others), access to a type of filesystem (ext3, vfat, Macintosh and others), or access to a certain type of hardware (such as SCSI hard disk support). Many of these features can either be compiled into the kernel, compiled as modules that the kernel can load when needed, or not included at all! This makes the kernel highly customizable.

Customizing the Kernel

A software utility is run to configure the kernel and specify which kernel functions are to be built in to the kernel, which can be loaded as modules and which ones are not required.

For example, when creating a customized kernel for a system, you run a Linux Kernel Configuration utility and specify the features (source code components) that will be included in the kernel. You also specify which features should be compiled as (loadable) modules and which features to leave out. Therefore, if you do not require the Appletalk networking protocol and do not require the Macintosh filesystem you can select "n" (no) for these items and they will not be compiled into the kernel. They will also not be compiled as modules that can be loaded by the kernel.

By selecting "n" for items, you are specifying which parts of the kernel source code should not be included in the kernel.

For some items, rather than not compiling a software component into the kernel, you may choose to compile the source code of the component as a (loadable) module. This will make the component available to the system (as a .o module file in a directory) so that the kernel can load the module (the .o file) when it is needed.

You specify that a component should be a module if you do not need a feature to be available to your system at all times. This may happen if you are only occasionally accessing a certain type of network filesystem on a server. The module that provides support for the filesystem on the server can be loaded as needed.

A component may also be set up as a module if you expect that it (the source code of it) will need to be updated, such as when you expect that new source code will be released for a hardware component. The new source code will allow you to compile a new module (a new .o driver file) and replace the existing .o file with the new file, rather than having to recompile the entire kernel and all modules to add the new driver.

You also typically set up a software component as a module if it is a hardware component in a system that may change, such as a network card or sound card.

For example, an interface card, such as a sound card or network card, may become defective and need to be replaced with a different card; or you may need to get an updated card due to new features that are required, such as a faster network card. By compiling the drivers for these components as modules, rather than compiling them into the kernel, you can easily replace the old driver with the new driver that the card requires.

Monolithic vs. Modular Kernels

There are two "types" of kernels - monolithic and modular.

A monolithic kernel contains built-in (compiled-in) support for a wide variety of hardware components. It has a large file size and uses a lot of system resources, such as memory and processing time.

Chapter 21: Configuring, Compiling and Installing a New Kernel

A modular kernel is compact and optimized for the system on which it runs. Rather than having many software components (in the form of source code that provides some kind of functionality) compiled into the kernel, components that are not required are not compiled into the kernel.

In addition to this, some components, such as modules that provide for support of network protocols and various filesystems, and drivers for hardware, are compiled as modules. Some of these components are dynamically loaded by the kernel and some can also be loaded by using the modprobe or insmod commands.

By using a modular kernel that loads modules separately, you can update modules by replacing older ones with newer ones without having to recompile the kernel

The kernel that is installed with many distributions is monolithic. This makes it easy to install the OS and automatically provides support for many different common hardware components.

To make a system more efficient and therefore faster, you can modify the kernel and remove unneeded software components from it, and change some items that do not need to be compiled into the kernel into modules. This reduces the size of the kernel and the resources that it requires.

 For information on downloading, configuring, compiling and installing a kernel that is more current than your current kernel, go to: http://kernel.org. In addition to the information at this site, there is a link to "The Linux Kernel HOWTO", which is at the http://www.tldp.org (The Linux Documentation Project) web site.

The most recent version of the Linux kernel is available as a tarball at:

> http://www.kernel.org or ftp://ftp.kernel.org/pub/linux/kernel

The finger command can be used to query the kernel.org server for information on the kernel. If you have established an Internet connection (via dial-up or high-speed) you can query the kernel information at http://kernel.org and see descriptions of kernel versions, by running the following command at the shell prompt: finger @kernel.org. Below is sample output from running this command.

The latest stable version of the Linux kernel is:	2.4.22
The latest prepatch for the stable Linux kernel tree is:	2.4.23-pre4
The latest snapshot for the stable Linux kernel tree is:	2.4.22-bk22
The latest beta version of the Linux kernel is:	2.6.0-test5
The latest snapshot for the beta Linux kernel tree is:	2.6.0-test5-bk5
The latest 2.2 version of the Linux kernel is:	2.2.25
The latest 2.0 version of the Linux kernel is:	2.0.39
The latest prepatch for the 2.0 Linux kernel tree is:	2.0.40-rc6
The latest -ac patch to the stable Linux kernels is:	2.4.22-ac1
The latest -ac patch to the beta Linux kernels is:	2.6.0-test1-ac3

The Steps to Install the Kernel Source Code

With this distribution, the kernel source code is provided as a .rpm package named kernel-source-*version-release*.rpm on CD 2. This version of the kernel will not be as current as one that is available for download at kernel.org. If you are using the source code provided with this distribution, use the rpm command to install the package named kernel-source. After installing the package, a directory named linux-*kernelversion* will be created in the /usr/src directory.

When the kernel-source package is installed, over 8,000 source code, documentation and other files are installed. Included in these files are over 500 documentation files regarding the kernel, the kernel source code, and other software and hardware components. These documentation files are installed in /usr/src/linux-*kernelversion*/Documentation and its subdirectories.

Summary of the Steps to Configure, Compile and Install a New Kernel

A summary of the steps to configure, compile and install a new kernel are shown below. These steps are described in more detail further below.

Change into the path of /usr/src/linux-*kernelversion*.

Put a .config file in the path of /usr/src/linux-*kernelversion*.

Run a kernel configuration utility and specify configuration settings for the kernel.

Make a backup of the .config file.

]# make dep

]# make clean

]# make bzImage

]# make modules

]# make modules_install

]# make install

Reboot your system and test your new kernel!

The steps above are described in more detail further below.

The command: make install will copy the kernel to /boot and make an entry in the grub boot loader configuration file.

An alternative to running: make install is to do the following two steps:

> Copy the kernel (bootable Linux executable) file named bzImage from the path of:
>
> > /usr/src/linux-*kernelversion*/arch/i386/boot
>
> to the path of: /boot.
>
> Edit your grub or lilo boot loader configuration file to make the new kernel available.

You will do the above two steps rather than running: make install during the Hands-On Exercises to learn how to edit the grub boot loader configuration file.

The make mrproper Command

The steps above show that you should back up your .config file after specifying settings in it. They also show running the command: make clean.

After downloading and installing a more current version of the kernel, and prior to doing the steps (above) to compile and install a new kernel, you should run: make mrproper to clean up your system and remove configuration files, including the .config file. This provides a more comprehensive cleanup of your system than running the command: make clean (shown above). If you have run: make mrproper then you do not need to run: make clean the *first time* you do the steps above (but this will not cause a problem either way).

The command: make mrproper prepares your system for the compiling of a new version of kernel source code and this includes removing configuration files. This command will remove any files that begin with ".config" (.config*) from the linux-*kernelversion* directory. Therefore, make sure you have a backup of this file (that does not begin with ".config") prior to running: make mrproper. Also, do not use ".bak" for the suffix of the backup file.

The command: make mrpoper runs the command: make clean and also removes the following: configuration files (autoconf.h, version.h .version .config* config.in config.old), generated sound driver files, generated network driver files, generated scripts for xconfig, log files from menuconfig, the hardware specific assembler directory, kernel specification file (kernel.spec), third party generated files, generated include files and generated documentation files.

The make oldconfig Command

When a new kernel is released, old source code components are removed (deprecated) and new source code components are added to provide new features. Therefore, if you install a more current version of the kernel, you cannot use a .config file (that you may have spent hours configuring) for the more current kernel version. However, you can run: make oldconfig to migrate a kernel .config file from one kernel version to the current version.

The command: make oldconfig can also be used in place of running a kernel configuration utility, such as during "The Steps Required Prior to Compiling and Installing a Module" described below. Running the command: make oldconfig is faster than running a kernel configuration utility and then selecting save and exit.

The Steps Required Prior to Compiling and Installing a Module

In the next chapter you will compile and install a module that has been downloaded as a tarball. If you have not configured, compiled and installed a kernel, you need to do the following steps prior to compiling and installing a module.

Change into the path of /usr/src/linux-*kernelversion*.

Put a .config file in the path of /usr/src/linux-*kernelversion*.

Run a kernel configuration utility and specify configuration settings for the kernel and save and exit out of the configuration utility.

or

Run: make oldconfig

Run: make dep

The Steps to Configure, Compile and Install a New Kernel - Expanded

1. **Change into the path of /usr/src/linux-*kernelversion* directory.**

2. **Put a .config file in the path of /usr/src/linux-*kernelversion*.**

Prior to compiling the kernel, or compiling modules for the kernel, a file named **.config** is put in the kernel source code directory named linux-*kernelversion*, below /usr/src.

The .config file provides configuration information that is used when you compile the kernel and when you compile modules for the kernel. This file is put in the linux-*kernelversion* directory by copying an appropriate *filename*.config file from the configs directory, below the linux-*kernelversion* directory, up to the linux-*kernelversion* directory, and renaming the file to .config. These steps are described in detail below and are done in the Hands-On Exercises.

The linux-*kernelversion* directory, below /usr/src is the parent directory of the configs directory. The configs directory contains configuration files for various architectures (such as i386, i586 and i686) and for other configuration situations (that are described further below).

The files in the configs directory are basically templates that are used to provide configuration information for compiling the kernel and for compiling modules. Only one of these files is used at a time. A template file in the configs directory that is required for compiling the kernel and modules is copied up one directory level to the linux-*kernelversion* directory and is then renamed to .config (or copied and renamed with a single command).

The filenames of the configuration files in the configs directory begin with "kernel-*kernelversion*" and have the suffix of ".config". Between the "kernel-*kernelversion*" beginning and the ".config" ending, these files have other letters and numbers that identify the type of configuration information that they provide.

Examples of .config file names are: kernel-*kernelversion*-**i386**.config, kernel-*kernelversion*-**i586**.config, kernel-*kernelversion*-**i586-smp**.config, kernel-*kernelversion*-**i686-bigmem**.config, kernel-*kernelversion*-**i586**.config.

The **-i386** in a .config filename, such as kernel-*kernelversion*-**i386**.config, represents a configuration file for a 386 (80386) or greater processor. This .config file will also work for systems with processors that are *compatible* with the 80386 processor. The -586 in a .config filename represents a configuration file for a Pentium (or greater, or compatible) processor. The -686 in a .config filename represents a configuration file for a Pentium Pro or Pentium II (or compatible, or greater) processor. The -athlon in a .config filename represents a configuration file for a AMD Athlon processor.

The .config filenames that include: -smp, -BOOT, -bigmem, -debug, and -uml are for use with kernels that need to be configured and installed with additional functionality, such as **smp** (**s**ymmetric **m**ulti-**p**rocessor, multiple processor) support, **bigmem** (**big mem**ory support) or **debug** support (to locate kernel errors).

The process of copying a template configuration file up one directory and changing the name from kernel-*kernelversion*-i386.config (or other configuration file name) to .config only needs to be done on a system once (for the .config file that you require). If you need to compile with a different .config file, then the process of copying the file up and renaming it to .config needs to be repeated for the processor type and configuration situation that you require.

Your current path should be /usr/src/linux-*kernelversion*. A file named Makefile is in the linux-*kernelversion* directory. This file is used by the make command to do kernel installation tasks.

3. Run a kernel configuration utility and specify configuration settings for the kernel.

The three kernel configuration utilities are described below. Use one of these to configure the kernel. The remaining steps to configure, compile and install a new kernel are continued after the description of these utilities.

The Kernel Configuration Utilities

The config, menuconfig or xconfig utilities can be used to configure the settings of kernel source code components. These utilities are used to specify which components are compiled into the kernel (by specify **y** for **yes**), which ones will be compiled as modules (by specifying **m** for **module**) and which ones will not be compiled at all (by specifying **n** for **no**).

The config Utility

The command: make config is used to run the config utility. This is a text-based utility that asks you questions and you respond to them, one line at a time. A script can be run with this utility to automatically respond to each question and specify settings for the kernel.

The opening output of running: make config is shown below.

```
[root@lancom58 linux-2.4.18-14]# make config
rm -f include/asm
(cd include ; ln -sf asm-i386 asm)
/bin/sh scripts/Configure arch/i386/config.in
#
# Using defaults found in .config
#
*
* Code maturity level options
*
Prompt for development and/or incomplete code/drivers (CONFIG_EXPERIMENTAL) [Y/n/?]
```

Chapter 21: Configuring, Compiling and Installing a New Kernel

The menuconfig Utility

The command: make menuconfig is used to run the menuconfig utility. This utility does not require X Windows and is often used on systems on which X Windows is not installed. The text at the top of the Main Menu of this utility describes how to use it.

Figure 21-1 shows the opening screen of the menuconfig utility.

Figure 21-1 - The menuconfig Utility

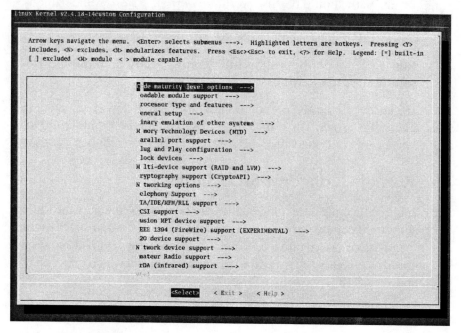

The xconfig Utility

The command: make xconfig is used to run the xconfig utility. This is a GUI utility that requires X Windows. This utility has a clear, easy-to-use interface. You can use this utility if X Windows is installed on a system.

Figure 21-2 shows the opening screen of the xconfig utility.

Figure 21-2 - The xconfig Utility

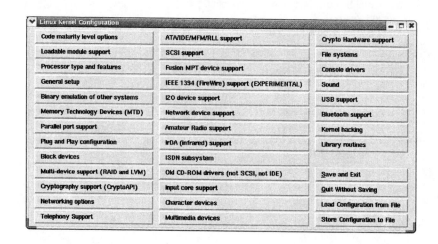

Run one of the above three utilities to configure the kernel. Use it to remove components from the kernel that are not required and add any new items that you need. For some of the items that you are adding, you can specify whether the item will be compiled into the kernel, or compiled as a module and loaded as necessary. Some items can be compiled as modules and some can not.

After using a utility to configure the kernel, save your configuration and Exit.

4. Make a backup of the .config file.

]# cp .config *backupfilename*

Do not start the name of the *backupfilename* with ".config" or it will be removed when the command: make mrproper is run. Use a descriptive name, such as test-config.1. You may want to call the next backup file test-config.2.

5.]# make dep

This command is run to set up module dependencies.

6.]# make clean

If you have previously compiled a kernel on a system, you need to run the following command to "clean up " and remove old files so that you can compile a "clean" kernel.

7.]# make bzImage

This command: compiles the kernel source code based on your configuration settings, creates a kernel program file named bzImage, and puts the file in the /usr/src/linux-*kernelversion*/arch/i386/boot directory.

8.]# make modules

The .o (module) files that can be used by the kernel are not compiled when the kernel is compiled. They are compiled as a separate step with this command. This command compiles the software components (source code) that you configured as modules (using one of the three utilities described above). The compiled modules are put in directories below /usr/src/linux-*kernelversion*.

9.]# make modules_install

This command creates a directory named *kernelversion***custom** below /lib/ modules and installs (copies) the compiled module files from the directories in which they were created when they were compiled (directories below /usr/src/ linux-*kernelversion*) to the directories in which they need to be located for the new kernel (directories below /lib/modules/*kernelversion***custom**/kernel).

10.]# make install

This command copies the kernel executable file named bzImage to the /boot directory. It will also put an **initrd.img** (initial ram disk image) file in /boot. The initrd.img file provides support for the ext3 filesystem at bootup.

The above command also edits the grub configuration file and adds the new kernel to it so that the new kernel can be selected when the system boots. (You will still be able to select the original kernel.) If you are using the lilo boot loader, you must manually edit its configuration file to add the new kernel to it.

 As an alternative to step 10 you can copy the bzImage file to /boot and manually edit the Grub boot loader configuration file. You will do these two steps during the Hands-On Exercises.

11. Reboot your system and test your new kernel!

 Hands-On Exercises

① Logging In to Configure, Compile and Install a New Kernel

Log in as cwest ; open a terminal emulation window ;

maximize the terminal emulation window ; su to root.

② Installing the Package Named kernel-source

For this exercise, we will be using the .rpm file that contains the kernel source code, as opposed to a downloaded tarball. Therefore, you need the kernel-source package to be installed on your system so that you can configure and compile this source code to create a new kernel.

]# rpm -qa *kernel*

Shows the names of the packages that include the word: kernel and is the same as running: rpm -qa | grep kernel.

If the package named kernel-source does not appear, then it is not installed. Do the steps to install it now.

③ Querying the Package Named kernel-source

```
]# uname -r           # displays the kernelversion

]# rpm -qi kernel-source  # get information on kernel-source
```

Notice the numbers beside the Version: and Release: headings. The *kernelversion* is the combination of the version number and release number, with a dash between the two.

Read the text below the Description: heading.

Now run the following command to see the files that are installed when the kernel-source package is installed. Press and hold down the Page Down key to scroll to the bottom. Notice the number of files that are installed.

```
]# rpm -ql kernel-source | nl | less
```

Run the following command to view the list of documentation files that are installed when the kernel-source package is installed. Hundreds of files are installed in the Documentation directory and its subdirectories. Scroll through the listing and notice the various directory names below the Documentation directory, such as cdrom, filesystems, networking, sound and usb. These directories basically represent and contain "categories" of information for documentation files on various kernel source code components.

```
]# rpm -ql kernel-source | grep Documentation | nl | less
```

④ Listing and Viewing Kernel Documentation Files

```
]# uname -r       # displays the kernelversion again
```

The "short" kernel version that is referred to in the next few paragraphs is 2.4 and the "long" or **full** version is 2.4.18-14. Replace these version numbers with the version numbers that exist on your system. Do the following command to see these version numbers as directories (prefixed with "linux-").

```
]# ls -l /usr/src     # the "short" directory name is a symlink to the long one
```

In the following command, replace *kernelversion* (in the directory named linux-*kernelversion*) with the current **full** version number of your kernel, such as 2.4.18-14. In other words, change into the directory named linux-2.4.18-14 and do not change into the directory named linux-2.4. Use the Tab key and press Tab (one or two more times) until the directories below /usr/src appear so that you can see the directory with the full version number.

The directory named linux-2.4 is a symlink to linux-2.4.18-14. If you change into the directory that is the symlink (in the command below), *some commands (such as find and ls) that you will use in the exercises below may not work correctly*, to display information in *subdirectories* of the symlink directory. These commands will work correctly, however, if you are in the directory to which the symlink points. (They will work in the linux-2.4.18-14 directory and not in the linux-2.4 directory).

```
]#  cd  /usr/src/linux-kernelversion/Documentation
```

This changes into the top level directory of the kernel documentation files.

```
]#  ls  -l  |  less
```

This displays directories and files in the Documentation directory. There are still several hundred files in subdirectories of the Documentation directory. Notice the files named Changes and Configure.help.

```
]#  less  Changes
```

Read the first paragraph and then scroll through it to see the headings in the file.

```
]#  less  Configure.help      #  view the Configure.help text file
```

The Configure.help file provides the text that appears when you select "Help" in a kernel configuration utility.

```
Home

/Information                    #  search for the word "Information"
```

Read the description of how to get more information on the how to work with the kernel.

```
/CONFIG_EISA
```

The text below this heading is the text that appears when you select "Help" for "EISA support" in a kernel configuration utility. This text will be seen again when you select Help for this item below. The Configure.help file can be searched quickly (without having to run a kernel configuration utility) for information on a configuration setting that can be made in the .config file.

The steps to configure, compile and install a new kernel begin below.

 ## Putting a .config File in the configs Directory

Prior to compiling the kernel below, you need to put a file named .config in the linux-*kernelversion* directory. This file is used for configuration settings when you compile the kernel. You will use a kernel configuration utility to modify *many* settings in this .config file further below.

Your current path should be: /usr/src/linux-*kernelversion*/Documentation

Change into the path of /usr/src/linux-*kernelversion*.

]# ls -l configs   # full path is: /usr/src/linux-*kernelversion*/configs

The files that begin with "kernel-*kernelversion*" and end in ".config" are template configuration files that are used for settings when the kernel is compiled and when a module is compiled.

You need to copy one of the template configuration files in the configs directory up to the linux-*kernelversion* directory and rename it to .config. The file you need to copy is dependant on your processor.

]# uname -p   # you processor type appears

The filename that you need to copy up one directory is listed below.

kernel-*kernelversion*-i386.config - for a i386 or greater processor
kernel-*kernelversion*-i586.config - for a i586 or greater processor
kernel-*kernelversion*-i686.config - for a i686 or greater processor

In the copy command below, replace *filename*.config with the name of the file for your processor type (from the list above).

For example, if the output of: uname -p was "i686", then copy the following file:

kernel-*kernelversion*-i686.config

to the linux-*kernelversion* directory.

Your current path should be: /usr/src/linux-*kernelversion*

We will use the file named kernel-*kernelversion*-i686.config in the copy command below (and in the exercises to configure the kernel below). Replace this file name with the name of the file that you need to copy to the linux-*kernelversion* directory. The command below copies the kernel-*kernelversion*-i686.config file to your current directory.

]# cp configs/kernel-*kernelversion*-i686.config .config

This copies a file from the configs directory up to the current directory *and renames it to .config*.

 If you do *not* put the .config file in the kernel-*kernelversion* directory, and run: make xconfig (or one of the other two utilities that are used to configure the kernel) and save the settings that you have made, then a .config file is automatically created in /usr/src/linux-*kernelversion*. This file uses "generic" default settings and *many* of the items that you can configure are set to "n" and must be set to "y" or "m" so that the kernel will function.

]# ls -la .con*

The .config file should appear in the linux-*kernelversion* directory and should have the current date.

Viewing the Contents of the File Named Makefile

>]# less Makefile   # Makefile is in /usr/src/linux-*kernelversion*

Notice the VERSION, PATCHLEVEL, SUBLEVEL and EXTRAVERSION variables (headings). The *kernelversion* that will be assigned to the kernel that you will create in the following steps will be the combination of the four values of these four variables.

The *kerenelversion* of the kernel that you are about to create will be:

> VERSION.PATCHLEVEL.SUBLEVELEXTRAVERSION

A period will be put between VERSION, PATCHLEVEL and SUBLEVEL. Nothing will be put between SUBLEVEL and EXTRAVERSION, as the value for EXTRAVERSION has a - (dash) at the start of it. The resulting version number of the kernel will be:

> 2.4.18-14custom

> /xconfig   # search for "xconfig"

The text below "xconfig", up to "menuconfig" is the text for the "target" named "xconfig" and is processed when the command: make xconfig is run.

Each time you run the make command and specify a word at the right of this command, such as: make xconfig the "target" text in Makefile is run.

 Running the xconfig (GUI) Kernel Configuration Utility

The command below will run the kernel configuration utility named xconfig so that you can modify the existing kernel configuration settings.

>]# make xconfig

(8) Modifying the Kernel Configuration Settings in the .config File

In doing the following exercise, for the current version of the kernel, you will get a sense of the main categories of items that can be selected. You will also see, for each category, the default items that are built into the kernel (set to "y"), the default items that are modules (set to "m") and the items that are not included by default (set to "n"). These "defaults" are coming from the file that you copied up from the configs directory. If you did not copy the file up from configs (and therefore did not have a .config file in linux-*kernelversion*) then you would be using a different set of defaults and *many* items would be set to "n" for "no".

In the steps below, you will set several items to "n". Some of the items that you set to "n" will be for a "main category" of item, such as Token Ring devices. Setting a main item to "n" will "turn off" many other items that would be compiled into the kernel or compiled as modules. There are *many* additional items that you could deselect to make the kernel more efficient (and reduce the compile time of the kernel, reduce the compile time of modules, and the size of the kernel). However, for these exercises you will select and deselect the items described below to get a "feel" for the process.

> Code maturity level options ; this is set to "y" for Prompt for development ... ; select Help at the right of this item ; OK ; Main Menu.

When the above item is set to "y", several items that show "(EXPERIMENTAL)" at the right of them can be selected. If the above item was set to "n", then these items would be "shaded" and you would not be able to select them.

> Select Processor type and features ;

Scroll down and notice that some items are set to "y" (include in the kernel), some are set to "n" (exclude from the kernel) and some are set to "m" (compile as a module).

Notice that there are Help buttons at the right of each item. If you are unsure of the functionality of an item, use the Help button to get more information on the item.

> If you are not using a laptop, scroll down and select "n" for Toshiba Laptop support and also for Dell Laptop support ; Main Menu.

For all of the items that you are selecting and modifying below, select either: Main Menu to get back to the main dialog box or select: OK at a "sub-dialog box" (when the Main Menu button is not available) so that you can "get back" and continue with selecting the next item.

> General Setup ; beside EISA support, select Help ; if you are not using any EISA cards, select "n" for EISA support ; "n" should be selected for MCA support ;

> in General Setup, select PCMCIA/CardBus support ; this is set to "m" ; Help ; OK ; notice the items that are "black" as opposed to "shaded" below PCMCIA/CardBus support ;

> if you are not using PCMCIA or PC cards, select "n" and notice that the items below the PCMCIA/CardBus support heading are now "shaded" ; OK ; Main Menu ;

> select Block Devices.

Notice the items where "m" is selected. These items will be compiled as modules and each module takes time to compile. The fewer items with "m" selected, the shorter the time to compile the modules. In addition to the item below, there may be other items that you can set to "n" here, but continue.

Set XT hard disk support to "n" ; Main Menu ;

Multi-device support (RAID and LVM) and notice that several items are set to "m" ; select "n" for Multiple devices driver support (RAID and LVM) ; Main Menu ;

Cryptography support (CryptoAPI) ; set Crypto API support to "n" ; Main Menu ;

Networking options ; scroll down and notice the networking items that have "y" selected ;

select "n" for The IPX protocol, Appletalk protocol support, DECnet Support and 802.1d Ethernet Bridging ; Main Menu ;

Telephony ; set Linux telephony support to "n" ; Main Menu ;

Fusion MPT device support ; set Fusion MPT (base+SCSIHost) drivers to "n" ; Main Menu ;

IEEE 1394 (Firewire) support (EXPERIMENTAL) ; set IEEE 1394 (Firewire) support (EXPERIMENTAL) to "n" ; Main Menu ;

I2O device support ; set I2O support to "n" ; Main Menu ;

Network device support ; Network device support should be set to "y" ;

if you are not using a Wireless LAN (non-hamradio) device, select this item and then set it (the top item) to "n" ; OK ;

if you are not using a Token Ring device (such as a Token Ring network card), select this item and then set Token Ring driver support to "n" ; OK ;

if you are not using Wan interfaces, select this item and then set Wan interfaces support to "n" ; OK ; Main Menu ;

ISDN Subsystem ; set ISDN support to "n" ; Main Menu ;

Multimedia devices ; set Video for Linux to "n" ; Main Menu ;

File systems ; set Ext3 journalling file system support to "y" ;

if you are accessing an NTFS partition, such as a NTFS Windows partition on a dual-boot system, select "m" for NTFS file system support (read only) ; Main Menu ;

Bluetooth support ; set Bluetooth subsystem support to "n".

That's it - finally!

Select Save and Exit ; read the text in the dialog box.

This text states that you must run: make dep (which you will do further below).

Select OK.

⑨ Backing Up the .config File in the linux-*kernelversion* Directory

If you run one of the following commands:

```
make  mrproper      #  do not run now
make  distclean     #  do not run now
```

the .config file in the linux-*kernelversion* directory will be erased. Therefore, after specifying the settings in a .config file, back it up (to a different file name). This will allow you to copy the backup file to .config if your .config file is erased. You may want to copy this file to a name that represents the "version" of the .config file.

```
]#  cp  .config  test-config.1
```

Do not use .config at the beginning of the backup file name and do not use the suffix of .bak.

⑩ Checking Your Directory Location and Running make dep

```
]#  pwd             #  the path should be: /usr/src/linux-kernelversion
```

The following command is run to set up module dependencies. On a 1 GHz system, this will take less than 10 minutes.

```
]#  make  dep       #  make dependencies
```

⑪ Running make clean

If you have previously compiled a kernel on a system, you need to run the following command to remove old files so that you can compile a "clean" kernel. On a 1 GHz system, this will take less than one minute.

```
]#  make clean
```

Compiling the Kernel

The next command compiles the Linux kernel, creates the bootable Linux executable file named bzImage and puts this file in the path of: /usr/src/ *kernelversion*/arch/i386/boot. With the settings specified above, the command below will take approximately 10 minutes on a 1 GHz system.

 ]# make bzImage

If you get an error message at the end of the output (and the kernel does not compile), do the following:

 ]# make mrproper # takes less than one minute

 copy the backup of the .config file to .config ;

 # make oldconfig # faster than: make xconfig (or other utility)

 # make dep

 ]# make bzImage

 Viewing the Contents of the Modules Directory

The modules directory below /lib contains a directory for the module files for each version of the kernel that is on a system.

 ]# ls -l /lib/modules # a *kernelversion* directory is below modules

If you have *not* previously compiled and installed modules on this system, then the modules directory (below /lib) only contains one directory and this directory is the same name as the version number of the kernel that you are currently using. After compiling the modules (with the command: make modules) and installing the modules into the directories in which they are required (with the command: make modules_install), then a new directory will exist below /lib/modules. You will see this directory after doing the steps see below.

 Compiling the Modules

The modules (.o files) that can be used by the kernel are not compiled when the kernel is compiled. They are compiled as a separate step (command). Once the system has finished compiling the kernel, run the following command to compile the modules. Compiling the modules with the settings specified above will take approximately one hour on a 1 GHz system.

 ]# make modules

Installing the Modules

Now run the command below to install the individually compiled module files into the directories in which they need to be located for the new kernel. Installing the modules with the settings specified above will take less than 2 minutes on a 1 GHz system.

    ]# make modules_install

 Viewing the Contents of the Modules Directory Again

    ]# ls -l /lib/modules

The command: make modules created a *kernelversion***custom** directory below modules. The compiled module files were installed (copied) below this parent directory.

    ]# ls -lR /lib/modules/*kernelversion***custom** | less

These directories contain the modules that were individually compiled with the command: make modules above.

 Installing the New Kernel

Now you need to copy the kernel binary file that you compiled to the /boot directory. This program file is named bzImage and is put in the following path once the kernel has been compiled:

> /usr/src/linux-*kernelversion*/arch/i386/boot

Change into the directory containing bzImage.

    ]# ls -lh   # the bzImage file is the newly compiled kernel

    ]# cp bzImage /boot

This copies the kernel (bootable Linux executable) file from /usr/src/ *kernelversion*/arch/i386/boot to /boot

    ]# cd /boot ; ls -l   # check that bzImage is in /boot

(18) **Configuring Grub to Make the New Kernel Available**

```
]# cd grub ; ls -l
```

Above changes into the directory containing grub configuration files (such as the grub.conf configuration file) and the "splash screen" (splash.xpm.gz) for the grub boot loader.

```
]# cp grub.conf grub.conf.bak   # make a backup of the grub.conf file
```

```
]# mount
```

Write the device name of the / (root) partition here: /dev/_____.

You will replace LABEL=/ in the grub.conf file with /dev/*devicename* below.

```
]# vi grub.conf        # open the grub configuration file in the vi editor
```

press: i to go from Normal mode into Insert mode ;

above the line: title Red Hat Linux (*kernelversion*)   add the following line of text (flush left):

title Test Kernel (*kernelversion*)

press Esc to go into Normal mode ;

move to the first line below: title Red Hat Linux (*kernelversion*) ;

type: 2dd to remove the two lines below the statement: title Red Hat Linux (*kernelversion*) ;

type: u to undo the deletion ;

move your cursor *on top of* the line: title Test Kernel (*kernelversion*) ;

type: p to put the two deleted lines below the line: title Test Kernel ;

on the line below "Test Kernel" that shows:

kernel **/vmlinuz-*kernelversion*** ro root=LABEL=/ ;

change: **vmlinuz-*kernelversion*** to: bzImage

and change: root=LABEL=/ to: root=/dev/*devicename*

The "title Test Kernel" heading that you added for the new kernel, and the "title Red Hat Linux" heading below it should be *similar* to the indented text below.

On your system, the two lines of text below "title Test Kernel" should be the *same* as the indented text below "title Red Hat Linux (*kernelversion*)", except that below "title Test Kernel", "bzImage" appears rather than "vmlinuz-*kernelversion*".

Your grub.conf file should now look like the following:

```
title Test Kernel
      root  (hdx,x)
      kernel  /bzImage  ro  root=/dev/devicename
title Red Hat Linux (kernelversion)
      root  (hdx,x)
      kernel  /vmlinuz-kernelversion  ro  root=LABEL=/
      initrd  /initrd-kernelversion.img
```

In both occurrences of "root (hdx,x)" above, you will have numbers in place of **x**.

Press Esc to go into Normal mode ;

type: ZZ   to save the grub.conf file and exit out of vi ;

close all programs and terminal emulation windows.

⑲ Rebooting to Select the New Kernel

Menu ; Log out ; Restart the computer ; OK ;

select "Test Kernel" (your new kernel) from the splash screen ;

log in as cwest ; open a terminal emulation window ; su to root ;

]# uname -r

This shows the kernel version, which has the word **custom** at the right of the number.

⑳ Renaming Your New Kernel and Editing grub.conf to Reflect the Change

Now that you know the new kernel works, you will rename the bzImage file and modify grub.conf.

]# cd /boot   # change into the directory containing bzImage

In the step below, rename the bzImage file to vmlinuz-*kernelversion*custom. Replace *kernelversion* in vmlinuz-*kernelversion*custom with the version number of your kernel, such as: 2.4.18-14.

]# mv bzImage vmlinuz-*kernelversion*custom

run vi so that it loads /boot/grub/grub.conf ;

change the text: Test Kernel to: Red Hat Linux (Lite)

also change the text: bzImage to: vmlinuz-*kernelversion*custom

The file that you created with the mv command above must be the same as the file that is referenced in grub.conf.

Restart your system ; select "Red Hat Linux (Lite)" to test the above changes.

You will select "Red Hat Linux (Lite)" when working through the exercises of the next chapter.

Congratulations! You just configured, compiled and installed a new kernel!

 ## Section Review

1. Select the command that is used to copy the compiled kernel modules to the directories in which they need to be located for the kernel?

    ○ A.   make modules
    ○ B.   copy modules
    ○ C.   copy install_modules
    ○ D.   make modules_install

2. What step would you typically do prior to editing the configuration file of your boot loader?

    ○ A.   copy the vmlinuz file to the /root directory
    ○ B.   copy the boot loader configuration file to the /usr/src/linux-kernelversion directory
    ○ C.   copy the bzImage file to the /boot directory
    ○ D.   copy the bzImage file to the / directory

3. In which of the following situations are you likely to compile a software component of the kernel source code as a module rather than compile the component into the kernel (choose three).

    ☐ A.   the software component is used for a hardware component in a system that may change
    ☐ B.   you do not need the software component to be available to your system at all times
    ☐ C.   the software component represents an item that will be accessed almost constantly
    ☐ D.   you expect that the source code of the software component will need to be updated

4. Select the two "types" of kernels.

☐ A. bipolar
☐ B. modular
☐ C. monolithic
☐ D. megalithic

5. Select the suffix that is used for a kernel component that is a driver for a network card and has been compiled as a module.

○ A. .h
○ B. .c
○ C. .o
○ D. .exe

6. Components of the kernel can be: (choose three)

☐ A. compiled as modules rather than being compiled into the kernel
☐ B. compiled as GUI utilities rather than being compiled into the kernel
☐ C. compiled into the kernel
☐ D. not compiled into the kernel

7. In which directory should you be located in order to run the "make" commands to configure and compile the kernel?

○ A. /usr/src
○ B. /usr/lib
○ C. /usr/src/linux-*kernelversion*
○ D. /lib/modules

8. What is the name of the bootable kernel file that is created when you compile the kernel?

○ A. bzlboot
○ B. bzlmage
○ C. vmlinuz-kernelversion
○ D. vmlinuz

9. Which of the following will likely be a components of the kernel that can be set up as items that can be: compiled into the kernel, compiled as a module or not compiled (choose three)?

☐ A. a sound card
☐ B. a new type of hard disk
☐ C. a file manager utility
☐ D. a revised network protocol

10. To get more information on a component that you are configuring in the xconfig utility, what can you do from within the utility?

    - ○ A. press the F1 function key
    - ○ B. click on the URL that is show to run a browser and access the web site
    - ○ C. click on the Help button
    - ○ D. read the information on the pull-down menu at the left

11. Which command can be used to migrate a .config file so that it can be used with a more current version of the kernel?

    - ○ A. make confignew
    - ○ B. make oldconfig
    - ○ C. make migrateconfig
    - ○ D. make install_config

12. You are working on a server and do not have X Windows installed. You need to run a utility to configure the kernel, but do not want to use the one that is text-based and does not have a menu. In other words, you do not want to use the one that prompts you with questions and can be used with scripts. Select the utility that can be used.

    - ○ A. xconfig
    - ○ B. menuconfig
    - ○ C. config
    - ○ D. configit

13. Which of the following commands is used to compile the kernel modules?

    - ○ A. make modules
    - ○ B. make modules_install
    - ○ C. install_modules
    - ○ D. modules

14. Which of the following commands is built into the kernel?

    - ○ A. xconfig
    - ○ B. modprobe
    - ○ C. make
    - ○ D. none of the above

Chapter 22: Working with Modules and the Kudzu Utility

During this chapter you will get an overview of how modules are configured, compiled and loaded into memory to provide software support for system components. You will also learn about module dependencies and how to unload modules that are in memory and are no longer needed.

You will see the contents of the configuration files that specify the hardware components in a system and that specify the alias names of modules. Some of the commonly used modules will also be discussed.

Over time, a driver for a hardware component may need to be updated and installed on a system. You will learn how to compile the source code for a driver and install it.

This chapter also covers the Kudzu utility, which checks for hardware that has been added to a system and also for hardware that has been removed from a system. This utility allows you to easily add the software configuration required for a new hardware component or remove the software configuration of a component that has been removed.

The following commands are described in this chapter and are also used in the Hands-On Exercises:

lsmod	list currently loaded modules and dependencies
depmod	create and maintain a module dependency file
modprobe	load modules into memory and remove modules from memory
insmod	load modules into memory
rmmod	remove modules from memory
modinfo	display information on a module

During the Hands-On Exercises, you will view module configuration files, do the steps to compile and install a hardware driver, and use various commands to work with modules. You will also see the steps used by the Kudzu utility to determine the module required for a hardware component and add the module to the system.

Working with Modules and the Kudzu Utility

Topics Covered in this Chapter

Discuss the benefits and usage of modules and drivers
Detail the configuration files associated with modules
Describe the purpose of various commonly used modules
Explain the need to update a driver for a hardware component
Detail the steps to compile and install a driver file
Discuss the purpose and benefits of the Kudzu utility
Do the steps to compile and install a hardware driver and use various commands to work with modules

Working with Modules

Modules (a.k.a. loadable modules) are software components that are loaded to provide some kind of functionality to a system. They provide a system with software support for various system components, such as support for a type of filesystem and support for hardware components.

For example, the ext3.o driver file is loaded to put the ext3 module into memory and this provides a system with software support for the ext3 filesystem. The emu10k1.o driver is loaded for the emu10k1 module and this provides support for the EMU10K1 chip, commonly found on SoundBlaster sound cards. The emu10k1.o driver file also provides support for some EMU10K1 compatible models of sound card.

Modules have the same name as the driver file that is loaded to provide the module, but without the .o (filename suffix).

For example, a driver file named emu10k1.o is loaded to provide the emu10k1 module.

There are several commands that are used to work with modules. These commands do various tasks, such as probe for the existence of a module, insert a module into memory, and remove a module from memory. When using these commands, sometimes the module name, such as emu10k1, is used with the command rather than the driver file name, such as emu10k1.o.

In the same way that one software package can have a dependency on another package, one module can have a dependency on another.

For example, if a module called one.o has a dependency on a module called two.o, and two.o has a dependency on three.o, then three.o must be loaded before two.o, and two.o must be loaded before one.o. If you use the modprobe command to load one.o, the command will use a file named modules.dep to determine the dependencies of one.o and the dependencies of any modules required by one.o, such as the dependencies of two.o. It will then load the modules in the following order: three.o, then two.o and then one.o.

When you configure (customize) the kernel, you specify which software components of the kernel are to be built into the kernel, which components are to be loaded as modules, and which ones are not required. Therefore, when you configure the kernel, there are some software components of the kernel that can either be built into the kernel (and become part of the kernel) or they can be compiled as separate modules, which are files that are loaded by the kernel when needed.

For example, when creating a customized kernel, you run a Linux Kernel Configuration utility and specify the features (source code components) that will be included in the kernel. You also specify which features should be compiled as (loadable) modules and which features to leave out. Therefore, if you do not require the Appletalk networking protocol, and you do not require the Macintosh filesystem, and the system will not be using a SCSI hard disk, you can select "**n**" (for "**no**") for these items and they will not be compiled into the kernel (and they will also not be compiled as modules that can be loaded by the kernel).

By selecting "**n**" for items (in the kernel configuration utility), you are specifying which parts of the kernel source code should not be included in the kernel.

For some items, rather than not compiling (the source code of) a software component into the kernel, you may choose to compile the source code of the component as a (loadable) module. You select "**m**" (for "**module**") to have the source code of a software component compiled as a module. This will make the component available to the system (as a .o module file in a directory) so that the kernel can load the module (the .o file) when it is needed.

In short, for many of the software components of the kernel, you can select "y" to have the component compiled as part of the kernel, "n" to exclude the component from the kernel, and "m" to have the component compiled as a separate module (.o) file. Some of the software components of the kernel cannot be compiled as modules. You can only select "y" or "n" for these items.

You may need to remove a module from a system because it is no longer required, does not work correctly, or needs to be changed from an older version to a newer version (or vice versa, if a newer version does not work correctly). If a module is currently loaded in memory and you need to load a replacement for the module, you must remove the current module from memory before loading the replacement. You cannot remove the dependency of a module prior to removing the module.

For example, if one.o is dependent on two.o and both of these modules are loaded, you cannot remove two.o without removing one.o first.

The /etc/modules.conf Configuration File

Some modules that the kernel uses are loaded by the kernel during startup and others are loaded as needed by various services and applications. The /etc/modules.conf configuration file is used to modify the manor in which depmod and modprobe search for, resolve, load, and configure modules. This file is also used to specify alias names for modules.

An alias statement in modules.conf allows an application or server to request a module by a generic name, such as eth0, without the software having to know the name of the driver file that will be used, such as via-rhine.

In the indented statements below, eth0 represents the module named via-rhine, usb-controller represents the module named usb-uhci and sound-slot-0 represents the module named emu10k1.

The indented text below shows an example of **the contents of a modules.conf file**. *The text below will be referred to several times further below as **the contents of modules.conf***.

```
alias  eth0  via-rhine
alias  usb-controller  usb-uhci
alias  sound-slot-0  emu10k1
post-install  sound-slot-0  /bin/aumix-minimal  -f  /etc/.aumixrc  -L  >/dev/null 2>&1  || :
pre-remove  sound-slot-0  /bin/aumix-minimal  -f  /etc/.aumixrc  -S  >/dev/null 2>&1  || :
```

We will discuss the first three indented statements below. The last two statements load support for the sound card for audio mixing. The contents of modules.conf on your system will likely be different from above. If you are using a different brand of network card, then the driver for the network card will be different (i.e. not **via-rhine**) and the same is true for the sound card (i.e. not **emu10k1**). You may also have other module names in this file and the order of the items may also be different.

The alias eth0 via-rhine Statement

The following statement appears in /etc/modules.conf:

```
alias  eth0  via-rhine
```

This statement causes the via-rhine.o driver file to be loaded for the **Ethernet** network card, with the alias name of **eth0**. Notice the text of: via-rhine in this statement. This is the name of the module for the network card installed in the system. The module name is the same as the driver file name, excluding the .o suffix. The driver file is loaded into memory and becomes the module.

The above statement allows a service such as "network" to request the eth0 module from the kernel without having to know which driver file name to use. The module is requested by executing: modprobe eth0 which in turn replaces the eth0 with via-rhine and loads the via-rhine.o module, which is located at:

/lib/modules/*kernelversion*/kernel/**drivers**/**net**/via-rhine.o

Notice each of the directory names in the above path.

Drivers are kept in the directory named drivers below /lib/**modules/** *kernelversion*/kernel. The **drivers** directory is the parent directory for drivers and the **net** directory is the parent directory for network card drivers, and also for drivers required by other network devices.

The *kernelversion* directory in the above statement has the same name as the version number of the kernel that is being used on the system, such as 2.4.18-14.

The alias sound-slot-0 emu10k1 Statement

The following statement also appears in the above modules.conf file:

alias sound-slot-0 emu10k1

This statement causes the emu10k1.o driver file to be loaded to provide the emu10k1 module when sound-slot-0 is requested by the service named sound. This module is for the EMU10K1 chip on a sound card.

It uses the alias name of sound-slot-0. The text of: emu10k1 in the above statement is the name of the module, which is also the name of the driver file, excluding the .o suffix. The suffix of .o does not appear in the statement in modules.conf.

The emu10k1.o file is located on the hard disk in the path of:

/lib/**modules**/*kernelversion*//kernel/**drivers**/**sound**/emu10k1/emu10k1.o

Notice each of the directory names in the above path. The **drivers** directory is the parent directory for drivers and the **sound** directory is the parent directory for sound card drivers, and also for drivers required by other sound devices.

Compare the above path (to emu10k1.o) to the path (to via-rhine.o) below:

/lib/**modules**/*kernelversion*/kernel/**drivers**/**net**/via-rhine.o

The path to emu10k1.o is the same as to via-rhine.o (reading from left to right), up to the drivers directory. The emu10k1.o file is a sound card driver and is in a subdirectory below the sound directory. The via-rhine.o file is a network card driver and is below the net directory.

The alias usb-controller usb-uhci Statement

The following statement also appears in modules.conf:

```
alias usb-controller usb-uhci
```

If the rc.sysinit script finds a usb entry in /proc/devices, this script will cause depmod to load the usb-uhci.o driver for the usb-controller, due to the above statement in modules.conf. This driver provides a system with support for the chip on the usb controller that controls the usb port(s)). It supports devices that may become attached to the usb port(s). The usb-uhci.o driver file is in the path of:

/lib/**modules**/*kernelversion*/kernel/**drivers**/**usb**/usb-uhci.o

The lsmod Command

The **lsmod** (**list modules**) command shows the modules that are currently loaded and their dependencies. The "stack" of currently loaded modules is maintained in the modules file in /proc and the lsmod command displays the information in this file.

The text below is an example of **the output of the lsmod command**. The lsmod command shows the "stack" of modules that are currently loaded. *The text below will be referred to several times below and will be compared to the indented contents of the modules.conf file, as shown further above.*

```
Module            Size   Used by    Not tainted
emu10k1          68744   0  (autoclean)
ac97_codec       13384   0  (autoclean) [emu10k1]
soundcore         6532   7  (autoclean) [emu10k1]
autofs           13348   0  (autoclean) (unused)
via-rhine        15628   1
mii               2156   0  [via-rhine]
ide-cd           33608   0  (autoclean)
cdrom            33696   0  (autoclean) [ide-cd]
usb-uhci         26188   0  (unused)
usbcore          77024   1  [usb-uhci]
ext3             70368   6
jbd              52212   6  [ext3]
```

Modules that Appear In the Output of lsmod, that are Also In modules.conf

Below the Module heading in the above output of the lsmod command, the following modules appear. These modules are for hardware components and are loaded due to startup scripts or requests by services.

```
emu10k1
via-rhine
usb-uhci
```

The dependencies of the above modules are described below, for each of the above modules.

Modules that Appear In the Output of lsmod, that are Not In modules.conf

To continue the kernel discussion above, the kernel is highly configurable. It consists of hundreds of software components that exist as source code. When configuring the kernel for a system and specifying what to do with the source code components of it, some components, such as commonly used hardware components, are compiled into the kernel. Other components, such as the three modules (emu10k1, via-rhine and usb-uhci) shown above, can either be compiled into the kernel or compiled as modules. The above three components were configured and compiled as modules.

The Linux kernel is configured and then compiled. When specifying configuration settings for the kernel, you can specify whether or not a software component (its source code) is: compiled into the kernel, not compiled into the kernel (i.e. not used), or separately compiled as a module.

The above three indented modules are drivers for hardware components and they were configured as modules and then compiled as modules.

Some modules load other modules that they depend on (their dependencies) when they are loaded. In addition to this, some modules are loaded during the boot process and are then unloaded (because they are no longer needed). Other modules are loaded during the operation of the system and then unloaded.

The lsmod command shows the modules that are currently loaded (and not those that were loaded and then unloaded). The three modules indented below (autofs, ide-cd and ext3) were loaded into memory by the kernel when the system booted and they were still in memory when lsmod was run. Statements for these modules do not exist in modules.conf.

In our example, the modules that appear in **the output of the lsmod command** (shown above) that are not in the example of **the contents of a modules.conf file** (shown further above) are:

```
autofs
ide-cd
ext3
```

We will now discuss the emu10k1 module and its dependencies and then discuss the via-rhine and usb-uhci modules and their dependencies. Statements for these modules exist in modules.conf.

After describing the modules that appear in modules.conf, we will discuss the other modules (autofs, ide-cd and ext3) that appeared when lsmod was run.

Modules that Appear In Statements in modules.conf

The modules.conf file contains statements for the following modules.

The emu10k1 Module and Its Dependencies

In **the output of the lsmod command** (above), below the Module heading, the module (driver) named emu10k1 appears at the top of the list of modules. Below this, the modules named ac97_codec and soundcore appear.

At the right of both of the ac97_codec and soundcore modules, you can see [emu10k1]. The [ ] square brackets around the module name of emu10k1 (at the right of the ac97_codec and soundcore) indicate that the emu10k1 module is dependant on the ac97_codec and soundcore modules.

The output of the lsmod command (above) shows a list of modules in a "stack". When modules are put in memory, they are added to the stack.

Looking at the "stack" of modules from top to bottom, the emu10k1 module appears above the ac97_codec module and the ac97_codec module appears above the soundcore module. The [emu10k1] at the right of ac97_codec and soundcore indicates that these modules are dependencies of the emu10k1 module. Therefore, the soundcore and a97_codec modules module must be loaded before the emu10k1 module.

As described above, the emu10k1 module and its dependencies provide support for the sound card in a system.

The via-rhine Module and Its Dependency

In the output of the lsmod command (above), the fifth module (driver) from the top has the name of via-rhine. Below this, the module named mii appears.

At the right of mii you can see [via-rhine]. The [ ] square brackets around via-rhine indicate that the via-rhine module is dependant on the mii module. No other modules have [via-rhine] at the right of them. Therefore, via-rhine only has one dependency and the mii module must be loaded (added to the stack) before the via-rhine module.

As described above, the via-rhine module and its dependency provide support for the network card in the system.

The usb-uhci Module and Its Dependency

In the output of the lsmod command (above), the module name of usb-uhci appears. Below this, the module named usbcore appears with [usb-uhci] at the right of it. The usb-uhci module is dependent on the usbcore module.

As described above, the usb-uhci module and its dependency provide support for the usb controller (the chip that controls the usb port(s)). This provides support for devices that may become attached to the usb port(s).

Modules that Do Not Appear in modules.conf

The modules.conf file does *not* contain statements for the following modules.

The autofs Module

The autofs (automount filesystem) module is used by the system to automount a filesystem, such as a filesystem that exists on a removable device, such as a CD-ROM. When you put a CD in your CD-ROM drive, the autofs module is used to automatically mount the filesystem on the CD. This module does not have a dependency.

The ide-cd Module and Its Dependency

The ide-cd module provides support for IDE hard disks and ATAPI CD-ROM drives. In the above output of lsmod, you can see that ide-cd has the module dependency named cdrom. The [ide-cd] at the right of the cdrom module indicates that the ide-cd module is dependent on the cdrom module.

The ext3 Module and Its Dependency

The ext3 module provides the kernel with the software support required to read and write to an ext3 filesystem. In the above output of lsmod, you can see that ext3 has the module dependency named jbd.

The ext3 module appears in the above output of the lsmod command because it is a module. However, if you ran a kernel configuration utility and chose "**y**" (for "**yes**", compile this into the kernel), rather than "**m**" (for compile this as a "**module**"), then ext3 it would be compiled into the kernel, rather than be loaded as a module. If this item was not compiled as a module, it will not appear in the output of lsmod.

Let's say you are using a utility to configure a new kernel for a system and at the "Ext3 journalling file system support" dialog box, you select "**y**" (for "**yes**", build this item into the kernel). This specifies that the ext3 module be built into the kernel, rather than being compiled as a module. (If you selected "**m**" for **module**, then the this item would be compiled as a module.) After selecting "**y**" and compiling the kernel, you boot the system with the new kernel. At this point, ext3 will not appear as a module when you run lsmod! It was not configured and compiled as a module. It is now a part of the kernel (and is built into the kernel).

Other Commands Used to Work with Modules

In addition to the lsmod command (described above), the following commands are used to work with modules.

The depmod Command

The depmod command is used to create and maintain a module dependency file and do other tasks related to modules. Modules and their dependencies are maintained in the modules.dep file in the *kernelversion* directory, below /lib/modules.

Each module name that can be used by the OS, *including the full path to the module*, is located in modules.dep. If a module has one or more dependencies, these are listed at the right of the module name (and may continue onto the next line - as described below).

For example, if module one.o has a dependency on both modules two.o and three.o, the following statement will appear in modules.dep (the *path* is the full path to the module file name):

```
path/one.o:  path/two.o  \
        path/three.o
```

Notice the \ (backslash) at the right of "two.o" above in the first indented line. This indicates that the statement is continued on the next line. The *path* to a module file name can be very long and therefore, the \ is used to continue the statement on the next line (rather than having it continue out of sight at the right side of the screen). When the \ is used to continue a line, the system "sees" the line as one long continuous line.

The above two indented lines would be interpreted by the system as:

    path/one.o: *path*/two.o *path*/three.o

The depmod command is commonly run via scripting logic in a text file when a module is being added to a system or removed from a system.

For example, the command: make install may cause the scripting logic in a file named Makefile to run the depmod command to add a module and its dependencies to the modules.dep file.

The modprobe command accesses the modules.dep file to determine the dependencies of a module.

Linux documentation will sometimes show a \ (backslash) at the far right of a line to indicate that a line continues on the next line. This is often needed to show an example of a long command or an example of a long line of text from a file, such as a configuration file. There will be one or more spaces before the \ and there will not be any other text at the right of the backslash.

The modprobe Command

The **modprobe** (**mod**ule **probe**) command is used to load a module (and any dependencies that are required by the module) into memory, as well as remove a module (and its dependencies) from memory. The dependencies of a module are determined from the modules.dep file. This command is also used for other tasks related to modules.

modprobe *modulename*

This command loads the *modulename*.o file for the *modulename* and also loads the dependencies of the *modulename* (as listed in modules.dep).

modprobe -r *modulename*

This command removes the *modulename* and its dependencies (as listed in modules.dep).

The insmod Command

The **insmod** (**ins**ert **mod**ule) command is used to "insert" one or more modules into the module stack in memory. This command is also used for other tasks related to modules. The syntax of the modprobe command allows you to insert modules that have dependencies more easily than by using the insmod command.

insmod *modulename*

This command inserts the *modulename* into the module stack in memory. If *modulename* has a dependency, the above command will not load *modulename*.

The rmmod Command

The **rmmod** (**rem**ove **mod**ule) command is used to remove one or more modules from the module stack in memory. This command is also used for other tasks related to modules. The -r option of modprobe command can be used to remove modules that have dependencies more easily than by using the rmmod command.

rmmod *modulename*

This command removes the *modulename* from the module stack in memory. If another module is dependent on *modulename*, the above command will not remove *modulename*.

The modinfo Command

The **modinfo** (**mod**ule **info**rmation) command is used to display information, such as author, description, license and version for a *modulename*.o file. An email address or URL at which you can get more information on a module may also be included in the information.

modinfo *modulename*.o

This command displays information on the *modulename*.o file.

Example of Installing An Updated Driver for a Sound Card

The discussion below describes the need to update a driver, methods of locating a current driver, and the steps to compile the source code for a driver and install it.

As described earlier, a driver for a hardware component is a software component that provides access to a hardware device. Other software components of a system that need to access the device, use the driver (software) to access it.

For example, a media player that is used to play a CD through a sound card to the speakers attached to the sound card, uses the driver (software) for the sound card to access the sound card (hardware).

The Need To Update A Driver

You may need to update a driver for one of your hardware components because: it does not work with the current driver, does not work correctly with the current driver, or a more current driver allows you to use a feature of the hardware device that an earlier driver did not provide access to.

For example, you may have an older driver for a sound card that does not allow you to use a feature of the sound card. An updated driver has become available and now you want to use it to get the benefit(s) of this additional feature.

Locating A Current Driver

When you purchase a hardware component, it may include a Linux driver on a diskette or CD, or it may not. If you get a driver with the hardware component and it does not provide the access to the device that you require, or if you did not get a driver for Linux, search the Internet (as described earlier) to locate a driver.

If you locate a driver for your hardware component on the Internet, but cannot get an exact match for the component, you may want to try a driver for a hardware component that may be compatible with your component.

For example, if you need a driver for a device that uses a chip with the model number of: ABC1002-3, you may want to try a driver for the chip with the model number of: ABC1002-4.

Driver Software Components

When you download a driver file to install it on your system, you usually get more than just a single file. The driver may (not often) be in an installation file format of the distribution that you are using (such as a .rpm file for Red Hat) or may (most likely) be in a tarball (.tar.gz, .tgz or .tar.bz2 file) with other files that are used to install the driver and are used to provide information about it. Therefore, driver files and support files, such as documentation, exist in either an installation file format or as a tarball.

For example a driver file may be in a .rpm file that contains all of the information (commands and settings) required to install the driver and may also include some documentation regarding the driver. To install a driver provided as a .rpm file (or in another installation file format), you simply run the rpm command (or other command) to install the driver.

To continue the example, if the driver is in a tarball, the tarball may contain one or more binaries (and other support files) or it may contain the source code for the driver.

If the tarball contains one or more binaries (rather than source code), then support files may be included with the driver that will provide a (relatively) simple method of installing the driver (manually or via one or more scripts). The tarball will likely also include some type of documentation regarding the driver and a description of the steps to install it.

The files that you get when you download a driver (in an installation file format or as a tarball) will usually include one or more "readme" (text) files, such as readme.txt or README.TXT or some other form of documentation.

To see the names and locations of the documentation files in a .rpm file (if any exist), run: rpm -qpd *rpmfilename*.rpm.

The names and locations of documentation files that are extracted when a tarball is untarred are not standard. If documentation is included in a tarball, it may be in a file named README, INSTALL (or similar name), in the directory that is created when the tarball is untarred. The documentation may also be in a subdirectory, named doc, docs (or a similar name) that is created when the tarball has been untarred.

Compiling A Driver From Source Code

If the driver that you require is provided as source code in a tarball, then you need to do the steps to untar, compile and install the driver. You will do all of these steps during the Hands-On Exercises below.

In the Hands-On Exercises of this section, you will compile and install the emu10k1.o driver file for a SoundBlaster or compatible sound card that contains the EMU10K1 chip. This is a very popular sound card chip and there are compatible sound cards that use a compatible chip.

A chip, such as EMU10K1, or a chipset may be used on multiple cards by multiple manufacturers. Therefore, the driver for the chip or chipset will often work on many different cards that have been manufactured by several different manufacturers.

The site for Open Source drivers for Creative Labs products is:

> http://opensource.creative.com

This site has an "EMU10K1 Project (code for Audigy and Live Cards)" link that points to:

> http://sourceforge.net/projects/emu10k1

The driver for EMU10K1 can be downloaded at the above site.

The Kudzu Utility

When Linux is installed, the Kudzu utility is used to detect the hardware components inside a system, or attached to a system, and add software support for the hardware components.

After the installation, Kudzu can also detect that a hardware component has been added to a system or removed from a system, and it can be used to add or remove the software support for the hardware.

When you are installing Linux on a system, or when you boot Linux (in runlevels 3, 4 and 5), or when you manually run the kudzu command, the Kudzu utility is run. This utility attempts to detect the hardware components in a system, or attached to a system.

 When Kudzu is installed and a system boots in runlevels 3, 4 or 5, you will see a "Checking for new hardware" message. This indicates that the Kudzu utility is currently running and checking for new hardware. When the "Checking for new hardware" message appears, Kudzu is also checking to see if any hardware has been removed.

If Kudzu detects that a hardware component has been added to a system, it will prompt you to ask if you want to add software support for the component. If a hardware component has been removed, Kudzu will ask if you want to remove software support for the component.

Kudzu does not currently detect all types of hardware components. Kudzu will likely detect the removal or addition of a PnP card, but may not detect the removal or addition of certain other devices, such as PCMCIA cards and USB devices.

When Kudzu detects that hardware components have been added to a system, and you agree to add software support for the component, Kudzu puts settings for the component in the hwconf file in /etc/sysconfig, and if necessary, puts a statement for the hardware component in modules.conf in /etc. The opposite of this occurs if a hardware component is removed from a system.

The text below was put in the hwconf file by Kudzu for a Creative Labs Sound Blaster Live! sound card:

```
class: AUDIO
bus: PCI
detached: 0
driver: emu10k1
desc: "Creative Labs|SB Live! EMU10k1"
vendorId: 1102
deviceId: 0002l
subVendorId: 1102
subDeviceId: 8061
pciType: 1
```

The class: of the hardware device shown above is AUDIO and the desc: (description) is "Creative Labs|SB Live! EMU10k1". Notice that the setting for **driver:** as shown in the above text is **emu10k1**. This represents the driver file named emu10k1.o in the path of: /lib/modules/*kernelversion*/kernel/drivers/ sound/emu10k1. The emu10k1.o (driver file) is in the emu10k1 directory.

If the above sound card is removed from a system, the next time Kudzu is run, it will prompt you to ask if you wanted to remove software support for the card from the system. If you select "Remove Configuration", then the above indented text will be removed from hwconf and the statement for the module used by the card will be removed from modules.conf.

If a new and different sound card is added to the system, then a new set of statements for the card (very similar to the indented text above) will be put in hwconf and a new statement will also be added to modules.conf.

 ## Hands-On Exercises

You need to do all of the Hands-On Exercises in the previous chapter prior to doing the exercises below. The exercises in the last chapter create a *kernelversion***custom** directory that is referred to in the steps below and also prepare the system so that modules can be compiled on it. You created a "Red Hat Linux (Lite)" heading on the boot loader screen for the kernel that you configured and compiled in the last chapter. *You need to select this version of the kernel in the steps below.*

 ### 1 Logging In to Work with Modules

Boot to the Grub splash screen ; select "Red Hat Linux (Lite)" ;

log in as cwest ; open a terminal emulation window ; do su to root ;

move and size the window so that it fills the top half of the screen ;

open another terminal emulation ; su to root ;

move and size the window so that it fills the bottom half of the screen ;

maximize the root user (bottom) window.

Using lsmod and Viewing modules.conf

Do the steps below in the root user window.

```
]#  lsmod              #  the currently loaded modules appear
```

The dependencies of a module appear with [ ] at the right. The name of the module in the [ ] has a dependency on the module at the left.

If the emu10k1 module appears in the list, then this is the module for your sound card. The emu10k1.o driver file has been loaded into memory to provide this module. The modules upon which this module is dependent appear with [emu10k1] at the right.

```
]#  clear  ;  cat /etc/modules.conf
```

Statements for the configuration of modules, such as specifying the alias name of a module, are in modules.conf. If you are using the emu10k1 module, a statement for it will appear in this file. If your system is using a network card, a statement for eth0 will also appear in this file.

 Creating a Directory for the emu10k1 Tarball and Copying the Tarball Into It

Some of the steps below are very similar to the steps done when you copied the anjuta tarball onto your system, untarred, compiled and then installed the program. The steps below are provided with less detail than when you worked on the anjuta program. If you need some more detail in order to do the steps below, see the last section of Chapter 20.

```
Alt+Tab to the cwest window  ;
```

You should be in the cwest home directory. If you did not create a downloads directory below your home directory in an earlier exercise, create it now.

```
Change into the downloads directory (below your home directory)  ;

below downloads, create a directory named emu10k1 and change into it  ;

put CD 3 in your CD-ROM drive and mount it if it does not automount.
```

There is a file named emu10k1-*version*.tar.bz2 on CD 3. This tarball contains the source code for the emu10k1.o driver. This is a relatively small file that was downloaded from: http://sourceforge.net/projects/emu10k1. You will compile this source code in the steps below.

Do the following steps without "changing" out of the emu10k1 directory, below downloads, below cwest.

Locate the tarball file named emu10k1-*version*.tar.bz2 on CD 3 ;

copy this tarball from CD 3 into the emu10k1 directory (on your system) ;

get a directory listing to see that the above command worked.

Your current directory should still be the emu10k1 directory, below downloads, below cwest.

 Untarring the emu10k1 Tarball

From the emu10k1 directory on your system, untar the emu10k1 tarball ;

get a long directory listing.

Untarring the emu10k1-*version*.tar.bz2 (tarball) file created a directory named emu10k1-*version* in the same directory as the tarball.

Change ("down") into the directory that was created when you untarred the tarball.

 Looking at the Documentation Extracted from the Tarball

Get a long recursive directory listing and pipe it to the less command.

Notice the file named INSTALL in the current directory and that the directory named docs contains a file named README.

"Cat out" the contents of the file named INSTALL ;

maximize the cwest terminal emulation window ;

without changing directory, use the less command to view the contents of README in docs ;

Read the text below the Requirements heading.

The .config file (that you put in linux-*kernelversion* in the last chapter) needs the following settings. This is explained in more detail below:

```
CONFIG_MODULES = y
CONFIG_SOUND = y/m (this can be set to y or m)
CONFIG_SOUND_EMU10K1 = m/n (this can be set to m or n)
```

Read the text below the Configuring heading.

Step 1 is not required. Step 2 is describing the steps to copy the *filename*.config file from the configs directory to the build directory. Step 3 is not required.

Read the text below the Compilation heading.

Read the text below the Installation heading.

For step 1, running: make install   does the commands and scripting logic beside and below the "install:" heading in the Makefile. You will run: make install   in the steps below (even if you do not require the emu10k1 driver), so that you can see where the driver file is installed.

Step 2 describes adding the statement for the module to modules.conf. If you are already using the emu10k1 driver, then this statement is already in modules.conf.

Step 3 tests the driver. *Notice that this steps says that the module should be autoloaded when you play a sound.* In other words, you do not need to run a command to load the new driver file into memory (as a module). As soon as you play a sound, the module will automatically be loaded.

 6   Viewing the install: Heading in the Makefile File

]# cat Makefile | nl | less

/install:

When you run: make install   to install the driver, the statements between "install:" and "clean:" in this Makefile file are processed. Notice that the mkdir, install, depmod (line 76) and modprobe (line 77) commands are used for the target (heading) named "install:" in this Makefile file.

 7   Viewing the Settings in the .config File in the build Directory

Alt+Tab to the root user window ;

change into the path of /lib/modules/*kernelversion***custom**/build.

You put the .config file in the /usr/src/linux-*kernelversion* directory prior to compiling the kernel in the previous chapter. The build directory below /lib/modules/*kernelversion***custom** is a symlink to the linux-*kernelversion* directory below /usr/src. Therefore, when you put the .config file in the linux-*kernelversion* directory in the last chapter, it is also available in the build directory.

Change into /lib/modules/*kernelversion***custom**/build ;

use less to view the file named .config ;

/CONFIG_MODULES

Search for the CONFIG_MODULES setting. It should be set to "**y**" (for "**yes**").

/CONFIG_SOUND	# the **top** item is set to "**m**" (for "**module**")
/CONFIG_SOUND_EMU10K1	# this is set to "**m**" (for "**module**")

The .config file in the build directory has the settings that we require (as seen in the README file above) for compiling the emu10k1.o driver file (which becomes the emu10k1 module when it is loaded into memory).

    ]# cd .. ; cd ..   # move up two directory levels

Your current directory path should be: /lib/modules.

    ]# uname -r

Replace *kernelversion* below with the version number of your kernel. This is the name of a directory below your current directory.

    ]# ls -l *kernelversion*   # the original directory structure

    ]# ls -l *kernelversion***custom**   # the directory structure created
                                  # last chapter

Notice that the build directory appears below both of these directories. The build directory points to a "real" directory in the path of /usr/src/linux-*kernelversion*. This is the directory that contains the .config file.

In the command below, replace *kernelversion* in linux-*kernelversion*, with the full version number of the kernel. In other words, if the kernel version is 2.4.18-14, do not use just 2.4. (The directory named *kernelversion*-2.4 (below /usr/src) is a symlink to *kernelversion*-2.4.18-14). Whenever you see *kernelversion* in any of the directory paths below, use the full kernel version.

    ]# ls -la /usr/src/linux-*kernelversion*/.config

Notice the date and time on the .config file. This is the file that you put in the linux-*kernelversion* directory in the last chapter.

 Getting a Listing of Driver Files

    ]# ls -l /lib/modules/*kernelversion*/kernel/drivers

This gives you a listing of the drivers directory for your "original" kernel. Notice the directory names in this directory, such as cdrom, net, pcmcia, scsi, sound and usb. These directories are basically categories of drivers for various hardware components. There is a sound directory below the drivers directory.

   ]# ls -l /lib/modules/*kernelversion***custom**/kernel/drivers

This gives you a listing of the drivers directory for the drivers (modules) that you configured with the command: make xconfig and then compiled individually with the command: make modules in the last chapter.

   ]# ls -l /lib/modules/*kernelversion***custom**/kernel/drivers/sound

Many sound driver files (ending in .o) appear. If you are already using the emu10k1 driver, a **directory** named emu10k1 will exist below sound. If so, get a listing of this directory and notice the date and size of the emu10k1.o driver file.

If a emu10k1.o driver file exists in the emu10k1 directory, write the size, date and time of the file on the line below:

   _____

If the emu10k1.o file exists on your system, run the modinfo command on the emu10k1.o file in the path of:

   /lib/modules/*kernelversion*/kernel/drivers/sound/emu10k1

Beside "description:", notice the version number, such as v0.19. Also notice the date of copyright. Also notice that the authors of the source code for the driver and the email address for information on the driver are shown.

If an emu10k1.o driver file exists in the emu10k1 directory, write the version number of the file on the line below:

   _____

⑨ Compiling the emu10k1.o Driver File

Alt+Tab to the cwest user window.

Your current path should be: ~cwest/downloads/emu10k1/emu10k1-*version*.

On a 1 GHz system, the following step will take less than one minute.

   ]# make   # configure kernel information for your *kernelversion*

After running make, the last three lines show: "Compilation configured for KERNEL_VERSION := *kernelversion***custom**, now compile it with: make"

Now run make again to compile the driver from source code. On a 1 GHz system, the compile time will be less than two minutes.

   ]# make

Notice the message on the last three lines. You will run: make install further below.

```
]#  ls  -lh  emu10k1.o
```

The driver file was created in the current directory. Notice the date and time of the file.

```
]#  modinfo  emu10k1.o
```

The cwest user does not have the path to the modinfo command in the PATH.

```
]#  whereis  modinfo        #  modinfo is in /sbin
]#  echo  $PATH             #  cwest does not have /sbin in the PATH
]#  /sbin/modinfo  emu10k1.o
```

By putting the path of /sbin in front of modinfo, the command can be run. In this case, *the cwest user has sufficient permission to /sbin to run the command!*

Write the version number of the driver file on the line below:

_____

The above number will be the same as the version number in the current shell prompt (for cwest). Compare this number with the version number of the existing driver (that you wrote down earlier).

⑩ Backing Up Your Existing Driver

When you install a program, you need to be working as the root user so that you have permission to install files where they are needed. Prior to installing the driver, we will back it up.

If an earlier version of the emu10k1.o driver file exists, do the following steps to back it up prior to installing the driver file that you just compiled.

```
Alt+Tab to the root user window  ;
]#  find  /lib  -name  'emu10k1.o'
]#  cd  /lib/modules/kernelversioncustom/kernel/drivers/sound/emu10k1
]#  cp  emu10k1.o  emu10k1.o.bak
```

When you compiled emu10k1.o above, you also compiled a driver file named ac97_codec.o. This drive file will also be installed when the emu10k1.o file is installed below.

Use the find command to find the ac97_codec.o file (below /lib) ;

```
]#  cd  /lib/modules/kernelversioncustom/kernel/drivers/sound
```

make a backup copy of the ac97_codec.o file (as shown above).

Always back up an existing driver file before installing a new driver file.

Copying from One Window to Another

You need to be in the root user window and in the emu10k1-*version* directory to run make install.

The steps below copy the path from one window to another so that you can easily change into the emu10k1-*version* directory.

> Alt+Tab to the cwest window.
>
>]# pwd   # display the path to the current directory

Now you will copy some text from one terminal emulation window to another.

> Use your mouse and select (highlight) the full path that was displayed with the pwd command ;   keep this text selected ;
>
> right-click anywhere on the current terminal emulation window ; select Copy ;
>
> Alt+Tab to the root user window.
>
>]# cd   # type in: cd   and press the Spacebar once

The following steps use the mouse to paste the path into the current window.

> Point to any location in the root user window ;
>
> right-click and select Paste.

The path that you selected in the cwest window should now appear in the root user window.

> Press Enter to run the cd command with the path that you pasted.

Alternatively, you could paste the text using your mouse buttons (and without selecting Copy and Paste from a menu). If you are using a two button mouse, you can select text in one window (*and keep it selected - and do not press Ctrl+c*), Alt+Tab to the other window and type in: cd (or whatever command is required) and then press both buttons together at the same time to paste the selected text. If you are using a three button mouse, you can press the middle mouse button to paste the selected text.

In the root user window, you should be in the directory that was created when you untarred the emu10k1 source code file above.

(12) Installing the emu10k1 Driver

Now run the following command to install the emu10k1.o driver file. The ac97_codec.o file will also be installed in the sound directory. The scripting logic in Makefile that you saw earlier, between "install:" and "clean:" will be processed by running the command below.

```
]# make install      # install the driver file in the emu10k1 directory
```

In the last few lines of output, a message regarding "make tools" appears. You do not need to do this.

Also at the end of the output, notice that the mkdir, install, depmod and modprobe commands were run.

The mkdir command was run to create a directory for the driver file, if necessary.

The install command was used to install the emu10k1.o driver file in the emu10k1 directory and also install the ac97_codec.o driver file in the sound directory. The permissions on these files were set (by the install command) to 664.

The depmod command was run to add the emu10k1.o driver and a list of its dependencies to the modules.dep file.

The modprobe (last) command was run to remove the older versions of the emu10k1.o and ac97_codec.o driver files (for the emu10k1 and ac97_codec modules) from memory. Therefore, the next time you play a sound or restart the system, the new modules will be loaded from the new driver files.

```
]# less /lib/modules/kernelversioncustom/modules.dep

/emu10k1.o
```

The emu10k1.o driver file should appear and the dependencies of the driver should appear at the right of this driver file (and on the line below). The dependencies are a97_codec.o and soundcore.o. The full path appears for all of these driver files.

Notice the \ at the far right of the line that contains "emu10k1.o". This \ is used to indicate that the first line continues on the next line and that the two lines will be treated as though they are one line.

```
]# lsmod
```

The emu10k1, ac97_codec and soundcore modules are not currently loaded. When you play a sound below, these modules will automatically be loaded and will appear when the lsmod command is run.

If you are using the emu10k1 driver and do not have a statement for this driver in modules.conf, do step 2 below the Installation heading in docs/README (that you saw above) to add the statement below:

alias sound-slot-0 emu10k1

to modules.conf (use "sound-slot-0" rather than "sound" - the docs/README file shows "sound" (only)).

 The alias statement allows an application or server to request a module by a generic name, such as sound-slot-0, without the software having to know the name of the driver file that will be used, such as emu10k1.o. The same is done for eth0, parport_lowlevel, and the usb-controller.

(13) Testing the New Module

If you are *not* using an EMU10K1 compatible sound card, read the text below, but do not do the steps; continue working through the Hands-On Exercises at the "Viewing the Date of the emu10k1.o File" heading.

Menu (at the bottom left) ; Sound & Video ; Audio Player ;

at the bottom of the Audio Player, click on the far right button and the Load file(s) dialog box should appear ;

type in the following path (with a / at the far right):

/usr/lib/openoffice/share/gallery/sounds/

press Enter ; applause.wav (below Files) ; OK.

You should hear sound! The emu10k1 and ac97_codec modules were autoloaded to play the sound.

Close the Audio Player ; Alt+Tab to the root user window.

]# lsmod

The emu10k1, ac97_codec and soundcore modules should now appear.

]# modprobe -r emu10k1.o

This removes the emu10k1.o module and the modules upon which this module is dependent (a97_code and soundcore).

]# lsmod   # emu10k1, ac97_codec and soundcore were removed

]# modprobe emu10k1   # the .o suffix is not used

The dependencies of a module are loaded when the modprobe command is used.

]# lsmod   # emu10k1, ac97_codec and soundcore were loaded!

Viewing the Date of the emu10k1.o File

When you run the command below, you should see a file named emu10k1.o that has the current date! This file was autoloaded (with two other driver files) when you played .wav file above.

]# ls -l /lib/modules/*kernelversion***custom**/kernel/drivers/sound/emu10k1

Congratulations! You have just copied a source code tarball for a driver onto your system, untarred it, compiled it and installed the driver!

 Looking at the Way that Kudzu Works

The exercises below demonstrate the way that Kudzu works. You will manually "trace back" the steps done by Kudzu to determine the driver for a hardware component (in this case, a PCI card) and add it to a system.

Do all of the steps below in the maximized root user window.

Change to the /etc directory ; "cat out" modules.conf in /etc.

Look for "alias eth0". At the right of this is the name of the module for your network card. The driver for the card has the same name, plus the .o suffix.

Write the name of your network card driver below (without the .o suffix):

_____

If you have a sound card in your system, look for "alias sound-slot-0" and write the name of the driver for your sound card below.

Write the name of your sound card driver below (without the .o suffix):

_____

16 **Viewing the hwconf File**

The **hwconf** (hardware **configuration**) file in /etc/sysconfig contains settings for hardware components installed in a system.

]# less sysconfig/hwconf

In the following search, replace *networkcarddrivername* with the name of the network card driver that you wrote down above. If there are extra characters on the end of the driver name that is found, press: n to search for the next occurrence of the driver (until the driver name, without extra characters appears).

/*networkcarddrivername*

Press the Up Arrow key until you can see: class: NETWORK

For your network card driver,

write the number beside the vendorId: heading below:

_____

and also write the number beside the deviceId: heading below:

_____

Press Home so that the following search starts at the top of the file

Now, using the name of the sound card driver that you wrote down above, use the / (slash) key and search for your sound card driver. If there are extra characters on the end of the driver name that is found, press: n to search for the next occurrence of the driver (until the driver name, without extra characters appears).

Press the Up Arrow key until you can see: class: AUDIO

For your sound card driver,

write the number beside the vendorId: heading below:

_____

and write the number beside the deviceId: heading below:

_____

 ## Viewing the pcitable File

]# cd /usr/share/**hwdata**

This changes into the directory that contains **hard**w**are data**.

]# less pcitable

The **pcitable** (**PCI** interface card **table**) file is a database of vendor ids, device ids, module names and card descriptions for over 2,300 PCI interface cards. When you are installing the OS, when you boot the OS (and the service named kudzu is run), or when you manually run the kudzu command, the Kudzu utility autoprobes the cards in your system.

When Kudzu finds the vendorId: and deviceId: numbers on a chip on a card, it looks in the pcitable file for the driver name to be used for the card. It basically cross-references vendorId: and deviceId: numbers to get the name of the driver (moduleName) to be used. The moduleName (driver name) and cardDescription (vendor name and card description) is then added below a heading, such as: class: Network in hwconf and a statement to load the module is added to modules.conf (if necessary)!

/cardDescription   # search for the cardDescription heading

Read the comment line near the top that shows the first occurrence of "cardDescription". This line describes the format of the pcitable file. The format of this file (mostly) consists of four columns.

The first column is vendid, which is the same as vendorId: (as seen hwconf). The second column is for the devid, which is the same as deviceId: (as seen hwconf). The third column is moduleName, which is the name of the module/driver (file) that provides support for the card. cardDescription is the name of the far right column that appears in the file. This column contains the name of the vendor, a | (vertical bar) and then a descriptive name of the card. We will refer to the far right (fourth) column as cardDescription.

In the steps below, you will search the pcitable file for the driver name that matches the numbers that you wrote down above.

Press Home.

For below, replace *networkcardvendorid* with the network card vendorId: number that you wrote down above. If the first number that is highlighted is in the second column, press: n   until the number is highlighted in the first column.

/networkcardvendorid

Notice the cardDescription in the far right column (of the first number that is highlighted). This description contains the name of the vendor of the card and then a description of the card. A | (vertical bar) separates these two items. If more than one item is highlighted, then there is more than one driver in the database for the vendid.

Press Home.

For below, replace *networkcarddeviceid* with the network card deviceId: number that you wrote down above. If the first item found does not have the correct vendorId: number at the left, press: n   until you get to the item that does. You may need to do this many times until the correct vendorId: number appears at the left.

/networkcarddeviceid

This deviceId: number (*when matched on the same line as the vendorId: number*) is the number that specifically points to the driver name for your network card. The name of the driver is in the third column, which is the moduleName column, at the right of the deviceId: number. This is the same driver name that you saw in modules.conf and hwconf!

You just did a process very similar to the process done when Kudzu autoprobes a card, but in reverse!

Kudzu autoprobes a PCI card for the vendor id and device id. It then "looks" in the pcitable file, at the right of these numbers, for the module name to use for the card. The moduleName (driver name) and cardDescription (vendor name and card description) is then added below a heading, such as: class: Network in the hwconf file and a statement to load the module is added to modules.conf (if necessary)!

 ## Repeating the Above Steps for the Sound Card

Press Home.

Now we'll check for the vendor name that matches the *soundcardvendorid* with the sound card vendorId: number that you wrote down above. If the first number that is highlighted is in the second column, press: n until the number is highlighted in the first column.

Notice the cardDescription in the far right column, for the first number that is highlighted. This description contains the name of the vendor of the card and the description of the card.

/*soundcardvendorid*

Press Home.

For below, replace *soundcarddeviceid* with the sound card deviceId: number that you wrote down above. If the fist item found does not have the correct vendorId: number at the left (the vendorId: number of your sound card), press: n until you get to the item that does. You may need to do this many times (possibly twenty or more times) until the correct vendorId: number appears at the left.

/*soundcarddeviceid*

When the vendorId: number and the deviceId: number are both the same as those that you wrote down above, the driver for your sound card appears in the moduleName (third) column (at the right of the deviceId: number). This is the same driver name that you saw in modules.conf and hwconf!

 ## Viewing the Network Card and Sound Card Settings in modules.conf and hwconf

Without changing directory, "cat out" the contents of modules.conf in /etc again.

The driver names for your network card and sound card appear.

Use the less command to look at the hwconf file in /etc/sysconfig.

/NETWORK

Notice the driver: heading and other settings below this heading.

Press Home ;

now search for "AUDIO" and look at the driver: heading and other settings below this heading.

⟨20⟩ Grepping for Driver Names in the pcitable File

You should still be in the path of: /usr/share/hwdata.

Run the command to check your current path.

In the next command, replace *networkcarddriver* with your network card driver name.

]# cat pcitable | grep *networkcarddriver*

Do the same command as above, but now "grep" for the *soundcarddriver* name.

Close all windows and programs and shut down your system.

Section Review

1. A module named three has a dependency on a module named four. Which command will unload both of these modules?

   ○ A. modprobe -r three
   ○ B. depmod one.o
   ○ C. insmod one.o
   ○ D. modprobe four

2. When Kudzu adds a new hardware component to a system, which file is updated with information regarding the hardware component?

   ○ A. .config
   ○ B. hwconf
   ○ C. hw.conf
   ○ D. mod.conf

3. Select the two commands that will display the list of modules that are currently loaded.

   ☐ A. listmod
   ☐ B. lsmod
   ☐ C. cat /proc/modules
   ☐ D. cat /lib/modules/*kernelversion*/modules.dep

---

4. Which file is used to specify the module names to use in place of generic names, such as eth0, usb-controller or sound-slot-0?

    ○ A. modules.dep
    ○ B. modprobe.conf
    ○ C. modules.conf
    ○ D. modules.drv

5. Kudzu can detect all types of hardware components. T F

6. Which two commands can be used to add a module to the "stack" of modules in memory?

    ☐ A. insmod
    ☐ B. lsmod
    ☐ C. depmod
    ☐ D. modprobe

7. If the file that is used to specify the alias names of modules contains the following statement for eth0, what is the name of the driver file for the network card?

    alias eth0 3c503

    ○ A. 3c503.eth0
    ○ B. 3c503.drv
    ○ C. eth0.o
    ○ D. 3c503.o

8. Select the command that may display an email address or the URL of a web site that could provide more information on a module.

    ○ A. depprobe
    ○ B. infoprobe
    ○ C. modinfo
    ○ D. none of the above

9. Which file is used to provide configuration information when you compile the kernel and when you compile modules for the kernel?

    ○ A. kernmod.config
    ○ B. kernel.conf
    ○ C. settings.cfg
    ○ D. .config

10. In a listing of modules, the abc module has [def] at the right of it. This indicates that:

   ○ A. the def module needs to be loaded
   ○ B. the def module has a dependency on the abc module
   ○ C. the def module is defective
   ○ D. the def module is independent of the abc module

11. Which utility is run to detect added or removed hardware components?

   ○ A. kudzu
   ○ B. probehard
   ○ C. hwprobe
   ○ D. kudprobe

12. A module file named one.o has a dependency on a module named two.o. Select the command will load both of these modules.

   ○ A. insmod one.o
   ○ B. modprobe one
   ○ C. modprobe two.o
   ○ D. depmod one

13. Which two commands can be used to remove a module from memory?

   ☐ A. modprobe
   ☐ B. depmod
   ☐ C. rmmod
   ☐ D. remmod

14. All modules must be compiled into the kernel prior to being loaded. T F

15. Select the file name that is used to load support for the ext3 filesystem.

   ○ A. ext3.o
   ○ B. ext3.drv
   ○ C. filsystem3.o
   ○ D. ext3.mod

Well ...THAT'S IT!

We hope you enjoyed working through this course and that this experience will help to further your career.

Appendix A - Answers To Section Review Questions

Chapter 1: The Linux Operating System

Section 1 - Hello Linux Course Overview

There are no section review questions for this section.

Section 2 - UNIX, Linus and Linux

1. A.C.D. 2. A.B.C. 3. F 4. A.C.D. 5. A.D. 6. F 7. B.D. 8. F 9. A.B.C. 10. A.B.D.

11. C.D. 12. T 13. A.B.C. 14. B.

Section 3 - Understanding the Linux Distributions

1. A. 2. A.B.D. 3. F 4. A.B.C. 5. F 6. A.C.D. 7. T 8. B.

Chapter 2: Understanding x86 Hardware Components

Section 1 - Linux Hardware Requirements and Documenting Your Hardware Setup

1. B.C. 2. F 3. B. 4. T 5. B. 6. T 7. A.C. 8. F 9. B.C. 10. T 11. A. 12. F

Section 2 - Interface Card Types and Methods of Hardware Communication

1. A.D. 2. C. 3. F 4. C.D. 5. A.B. 6. T 7. A.D. 8. A.C. 9. T 10. D. 11. B.C. 12. A.C.

Section 3 - Partitions, Filesystems and Device Names

1. B.C. 2. D. 3. A.B. 4. C. 5. A. 6. C. 7. A.D. 8. B.C. 9. C. 10. B.D. 11. D. 12. B.C.

Chapter 3: Installing Linux On An x86 System

Section 1 - Linux Installation Methods and Boot Disks

1. B.D. 2. A.B. 3. D. 4. B. 5. B.C. 6. A. 7. C. 8. B.

Section 2 - Creating Space for Linux

1. B. 2. T 3. C.D. 4. F 5. B.D. 6. C. 7. C. 8. F 9. D.

Section 3 - Installing Linux

1. B.C. 2. B. 3. D. 4. A.B. 5. F 6. A.C. 7. B.C. 8. B. 9. B. 10. F 11. A.C.D.

12. C. 13. B.

Section 4 - Post-Installation Configuration of Linux

1. A.B.D. 2. C. 3. B.D. 4. T 5. A. 6. B. 7. T 8. B.C.D. 9. B. 10. F 11. C.

12. A.C. 13. B. 14. A.D.

Appendix A - Answers To Section Review Questions

Chapter 4: Working with Desktops and Terminals

1. C.D. 2. B. 3. F 4. B.C. 5. B. 6. A. 7. F 8. B. 9. D. 10. A. 11. F 12. A. 13. C. 14. F 15. B.C.D. 16. B. 17. C. 18. C. 19. A. 20. A.D. 21. T 22. D. 23. A.

Chapter 5: The Linux Filesystem and the Shell Environment

1. cd / ; ls -la 2. cd /var/log ; ls -l 3. less rpmpkgs 4. cd .. ; ls -l ; pwd
5. cd mail ; less root 6. cd ../run 7. cd /usr/share/doc 8. less . 9. cd grub-x.xx ; ls -l
10. less README 11. cd /proc ; less meminfo 12. A.B. 13. A.D. 14. C.D. 15. B.
16. C. 17. A. 18. B.C. 19. A.C. 20. C. 21. A. 22. B. 23. D. 24. D. 25. C.D. 26. B.C.
27. B.D. 28. A.C. 29. B.D. 30. B.C. 31. B. 32. A.C. 33. B.D. 34. D.

Chapter 6: Using Linux Commands

1. ls -lS /etc/*.conf | less 2. ls -lF /lib | less 3. find -name 'FAQ' 4. find -name '*FAQ*'
5. find /var -name '*log*' 6. grep www. * 7. grep -r 'networking configuration' /etc/sysconfig
8. cat fstab 9. head /etc/lpd.conf 10. ls -l /etc/*.conf | head 11. tail -f /var/log/messages
12. history | tail 13. history 25 14. history | grep grep 15. C. 16. A.D. 17. F 18. C.
19. C. 20. F 21. D. 22. A. 23. D. 24. F 25. A. 26. B. 27. C. 28. T 29. C. 30. B.C.
31. C. 32. B. 33. C. 34. D. 35. C. 36. A.C. 37. B. 38. B.C. 39. A.

Chapter 7: Getting Help with Linux

1. A.B. 2. F 3. D. 4. D. 5. A. 6. C. 7. A. 8. A.C. 9. C. 10. B. 11. C. 12. B.
13. D. 14. A. 15. T 16. C. 17. B. 18. D.

Chapter 8: The VIM (Vi IMproved) Editor

1. D. 2. C. 3. A. 4. A.B.C. 5. A. 6. B. 7. D. 8. A. 9. B.

Chapter 9: Understanding the PATH and Shell Configuration Files

1. unalias ls 2. alias lslh='ls -lh --color=tty' 3. which mv 4. ls -l .bash* 5. B. 6. C.
7. A.C. 8. D. 9. C. 10. F 11. B.D. 12. A.C.D. 13. F 14. C. 15. C. 16. A. 17. C.
18. B. 19. D. 20. D. 21. A.C. 22. T 23. B. 24. A.

Chapter 10: Adding a Disk and Partition to a Linux System

1. A. 2. T 3. C. 4. C. 5. A. 6. B. 7. F 8. C. 9. T 10. C. 11. D. 12. F
13. A. 14. C.

Chapter 11: Using Filesystem Commands

1. B. 2. B. 3. A. 4. D. 5. C. 6. A.C. 7. D. 8. A. 9. D. 10. A. 11. B. 12. D.

Chapter 12: Users, Groups, Permissions and Attributes

1. B. 2. C. 3. A. 4. B. 5. B.C.D. 6. F 7. A.C.D. 8. A. 9. T 10. A. 11. D. 12. B.
13. D. 14. F 15. C. 16. T 17. A.C. 18. A. 19. F 20. B.C. 21. C. 22. C. 23. B.D.
24. D. 25. A.D. 26. C. 27. A. 28. T 29. C. 30. F 31. D. 32. A. 33. C. 34. A. 35. F
36. C. 37. B. 38. A. 39. B. 40. T 41. A. 42. B. 43. T 44. C. 45. F 46. A. 47. B.
48. T 49. B.C. 50. B. 51. D. 52. T 53. C. 54. T 55. B.D. 56. C. 57. F 58. B. 59. A.
60. B. 61. C. 62. D. 63. T 64. D. 65. F 66. B. 67. C. 68. A. 69. T

Chapter 13: Backing Up Your System

1. B. 2. A.C. 3. A. 4. T 5. B. 6. C.D. 7. F 8. A. 9. B.D. 10. F 11. C. 12. D.
13. C. 14. B.D.

Chapter 14: The X Window System

1. B. 2. A.B.D. 3. B. 4. A. 5. B. 6. D. 7. F 8. C. 9. A. 10. B. 11. F 12. C. 13. B.
14. D. 15. T 16. C. 17. B. 18. A. 19. C. 20. D. 21. A.C.D.

Chapter 15: Creating and Running Linux Scripts

1. A.D. 2. D. 3. B. 4. B.C. 5. A. 6. D. 7. B.D. 8. A.C.D. 9. A.C. 10. A. 11. F
12. C. 13. B. 14. C. 15. A.B. 16. A. 17. T 18. C.D. 19. F 20. C.D. 21. B.D.

Chapter 16: Runlevels, The Boot Process, Services and Processes

1. B.C. 2. A.B. 3. B. 4. A.B. 5. D. 6. C. 7. T 8. A.D. 9. C. 10. F 11. A.B.
12. A.C.D. 13. A. 14. A.D. 15. T 16. A. 17. D. 18. B. 19. B.D. 20. C. 21. A.
22. D. 23. F 24. C.D. 25. D. 26. A. 27. B. 28. A. 29. C. 30. A.

Chapter 17: Scheduling Tasks and Working with Log Files

1. C. 2. B.C. 3. C. 4. B.D. 5. C. 6. A. 7. B. 8. A.D. 9. D. 10. A. 11. C.
12. A. 13. C. 14. B. 15. T 16. D. 17. B. 18. T 19. B. 20. B. 21. A. 22. T
23. D. 24. C. 25. A.C.

Chapter 18: Linux Networking and Setting Up an NFS Server

1. D. 2. B. 3. C. 4. D. 5. B. 6. T 7. A. 8. B. 9. A. 10. C. 11. B. 12. A.C.D.
13. F 14. D. 15. B. 16. A. 17. C. 18. A.

Chapter 19: Printing and Setting Up a Print Server

1. D. 2. B.D. 3. A.D. 4. B. 5. A. 6. C. 7. T 8. B. 9. C. 10. D. 11. B. 12. A.
13. C. 14. B. 15. D. 16. A.D. 17. B. 18. A. 19. A.C.D. 20. C.

Appendix A - Answers To Section Review Questions

Chapter 20: Installing Software On A Linux System

Section 1 - Installing Red Hat Package Manager Files

1. B. 2. B. 3. B,C. 4. A,C. 5. T 6. B. 7. F 8. B. 9. A. 10. C. 11. C. 12. B.
13. F 14. D. 15. C. 16. A. 17. F 18. B. 19. A,B,C. 20. B. 21. A.
22. A. 23. C. 24. D. 25. D.

Section 2 - Installing the Apache Web Server

1. A. 2. D. 3. B. 4. B. 5. A. 6. C. 7. A. 8. D. 9. D. 10. C. 11. B. 12. B.
13. D. 14. B.

Section 3 - Downloading, Compiling and Installing Software

1. B. 2. A. 3. F 4. C. 5. A. 6. F 7. D.

Chapter 21: Configuring, Compiling and Installing a New Kernel

1. D. 2. C. 3. A,B,D. 4. B,C. 5. C. 6. A,C,D. 7. C. 8. B. 9. A,B,D. 10. C. 11. B.
12. B. 13. A. 14. D.

Chapter 22: Working with Modules and the Kudzu Utility

1. A. 2. B. 3. B,C. 4. C. 5. F 6. A,D. 7. D. 8. C. 9. D. 10. B. 11. A. 12. B.
13. A,C. 14. F 15. A.

0

0anacron scripts – see anacron
& – see Ampersand (&)
^ (caret) – see Caret (^)
- (dash) option – see Dash option
. (dot) and/or .. (2 dots) – see Directory
(number) sign 5-23
+ (plus) sign – see Plus sign (+)
" ' – see Quotation marks (" ')
~ – see Tilde (~)

A

a (all) option 5-6, 5-33
Absolute path 5-7, 5-26, 5-27
    tar files with 13-7, 13-8, 13-9, 13-16
accept command **19-24**
Account configuration 3-48
AGP card 2-35
Aliases 9-22, 9-23, 9-24, 9-25, 9-30
    lsld 9-28, 9-29
alias command **9-14**, 9-15, 9-16
AMANDA 13-2
Ampersand (&) 3-61, 4-24, 4-25
Anaconda 3-4, 3-5, 3-20, 3-22, 3-33, 3-34, 5-13
anacron 17-4, see also Task(s)
    0anacron scripts 17-29, 17-30, 17-31
    running 17-34, 17-35, 17-36
    view info about 17-33
Anjuta IDE Program 20-56, 20-57
Answers to Section Review
    Questions A-1, A-2, A-3, A-4
Apache Web Server 20-43, see also Server(s)
apropos command **7-13**
Archive – see Backup
at command **17-3**, 17-27, 17-28, see
    also Task(s)
atq (at queue) command **17-4**
atrm (at remove) command **17-4**
Attributes 12-2, 12-64, 12-65, 12-66
Authentication
    failure 6-57
Automount 4-16, see also Mount floppy
    disk/CD
Autorun file 4-14

B

Backup – see also tarball, tar (tape archive)
command
    common directory 13-19
    data archive 13-7, 13-9, 13-10, 13-11,
        13-12, 13-13, 13-20
    system 2-4, 2-7, 13-2, 13-3
        with tar command – see tar (tape
            archive) command
bash shell – see Shell
bin directory 5-10, 5-15, 5-48, 9-5, 9-6
Binaries 4-12, 5-10, 5-43, 9-3, 9-4, 9-19
    installing 20-56
BIOS 2-9

boot directory 2-58, 5-10, 5-46, 5-47
Boot disk(s) 3-2, 3-5
    CD installation 3-6
        testing 3-8
    creation 3-8, 3-52
        at Windows workstation 3-12
    hard disk installation 3-6
    Rescue Boot Disk – see Rescue Boot Disk
Boot loader 3-19, 3-20
    configuration 3-43
        password 3-44
    GRUB – see GRUB
    LILO – see LILO
    MBR – see MBR
    setup 3-66, 3-67, 3-68
    Windows 3-68
Boot messages, viewing 17-23, 17-24
Boot partition 2-57, 2-58
    creation of 3-41
Boot process 16-2, 16-4
    rc script file 16-6, 16-28, 16-29
    rc.sysinit script file 16-5, 16-27, 16-28
    view files used in 16-25, 16-26, 16-27
Boot sequence
    setting in CMOS 2-12
boot.img 3-6, see also Installation
BOOTP – see Network(ing)
bootnet.img 3-7, see also Installation
Bourne Again Shell (bash) – see Shell
Builtin commands 7-14, 7-15, 9-8
bunzip2 command **13-14**
Bus 2-31
bzcat command **6-25**
bzgrep command **6-24**
bzip2 command **13-14**
bzip2 program 13-6, 13-7, 13-22, 13-23
bzless command **5-35**
bzmore command **5-35**

C

cal (calendar) command **6-32**, 6-60
Calc program 12-78, 12-79
cancel command **19-23**
Card
    AGP – see AGP card
    EISA – see EISA card
    interface – see Interface card
    ISA – see ISA card
    MCA – see MCA card
    PCI – see PCI card
    PCMCIA – see PCMCIA card
    SCSI – see SCSI card
    video graphics – see Video card
    VL-Bus – see VL-Bus card
Caret (^) 10-4
Case Study 11-11, 11-12, 11-13, 11-14
cat command **6-24**, 6-25, 6-39
    with nl command 6-52
    with grep 6-58
CD
    eject with exit command 4-36
    installation – see Installation

Index

Index

Index

Index

Index

Index

Index

Hello Linux! Course CDs

CD 1 and CD 2 - Red Hat® Linux® 8.0 Publisher's Edition

This book includes a copy of the Publisher's Edition of Red Hat® Linux® from Red Hat, Inc., which you may use in accordance with the license agreement found at www.redhat.com/licenses. Official Red Hat® Linux®, which you may purchase from Red Hat, includes the complete Red Hat Linux distribution, Red Hat's documentation, and may include technical support for Red Hat® Linux®. You may also purchase technical support from Red Hat. You may purchase Red Hat® Linux® and technical support from Red Hat through the company's web site (www.redhat.com) or its toll-free number 1-888-REDHAT1.

CD 3 - Lab Data and Source Code Files

The third CD includes student lab data files and source code files that are used during the Hands-On Exercises.